Financial
Theory and
Corporate Policy

Financial Theory and Corporate Policy

Thomas E. Copeland
J. Fred Weston
University of California at Los Angeles

Addison-Wesley Publishing Company   Reading, Massachusetts
Menlo Park, California · London · Amsterdam · Don Mills, Ontario · Sydney

Library of Congress Cataloging in Publication Data

Copeland, Thomas E   1946-
    Financial theory and corporate policy.

    1. Corporations--Finance. 2. Finance. I. Weston,
Fred J., joint author. II. Title.
HG4011.C833   658.1'5   78-73366
ISBN 0-201-00971-4

ISBN 0-201-00971-4
ABCDEFGHIJ-MA-89876543210

This book is dedicated to the pioneers in the development of the modern theory of finance: Hirshleifer, Arrow, Debreu, Miller, Modigliani, Markowitz, Sharpe, Lintner, Jensen, Fama, Roll, Black, Scholes, Merton, Ross, and others cited in the pages that follow.

"Even the novice student can view powerful new vistas when employing the ideas of the scholars who have made giant contributions." A paraphrase from an ancient proverb.

Preface

A. PURPOSE AND ORGANIZATION

Over the past twenty years a branch of applied microeconomics has been developed and specialized into what is known as the modern finance theory. The historical demarkation point was roughly 1958, when Markowitz and Tobin were working on the theory of portfolio selection and Modigliani and Miller were working on capital structure and valuation. Prior to 1958, finance was largely a descriptive field of endeavor. Since then major theoretical thrusts have transformed the field into a positive science. As evidence of the changes which have taken place we need only look at the types of people who teach in the schools of business. Forty years ago the faculty were drawn from the ranks of business and government. They were the respected and experienced statesmen within their fields. Today, finance faculty are predominantly academicians in the traditional sense of the word. The majority of them have no business experience whatsoever except for consulting. Their interest and training is in developing theories of economic behavior, then testing them with the tools provided by statistics and econometrics. Anecdotal evidence and individual business experience have been superseded by the analytic approach of modern finance theory.

The rapid changes in the field of finance have profound implications for management education. As usual, the best students (and the best managers) possess rare intuition, initiative, common sense, strong reading and writing skills, and the ability to work well with others. But those with the greatest competitive advantage also have strong technical training in the analytical and quantitative skills of management. Modern finance theory emphasizes these skills. It is to the students and faculty who seek to employ them that this textbook is addressed.

The five seminal and internally consistent theories upon which modern finance is founded are: (1) utility theory, (2) state-preference theory, (3) mean-variance theory and the capital asset pricing model, (4) the Modigliani-Miller theorems, and (5) option pricing theory. They are discussed in Chapters 4, 5, 6 and 7, 11, and 15 and 16 respectively. Their common theme is, "How do individuals and society allocate scarce resources through a price system based on the valuation of risky assets?" Utility theory establishes the basis of rational decision-making in the face of risky alternatives. It focuses on the question "How do people make choices?" On the other hand, the objects of choice are described by state-preference theory, mean-variance portfolio theory, and option-pricing theory. When we combine the theory of choice with the objects of choice, we are able to determine how risky alternatives are valued in equilibrium. When correctly assigned, the asset prices provide useful signals to the economy for the necessary task of resource allocation. Finally, the Modigliani-Miller theory asks the question: "Does the method of financing have any effect on the value of assets (the firm in particular)?" The answer to this question has important implications for the firm's choice of capital structure (debt to equity mix) and dividend policy.

It is important to keep in mind that what counts for a positive science is the development of theories which yield valid and meaningful predictions about observed phenomena. The critical first test is whether or not the hypothesis is consistent with the evidence at hand. Further testing involves deducing new facts capable of being observed but not previously known, then checking those deduced facts against additional empirical evidence. As students of finance, we must not only understand the theory, but also review the empirical evidence in order to determine which hypotheses have been validated. Consequently, every effort has been made to summarize the empirical evidence related to the theory of finance. Chapter 7 discusses empirical evidence on the capital asset pricing model. Chapter 9 covers evidence on the efficient markets hypothesis. Chapter 12 reviews evidence on capital structure; Chapter 14 on dividend policy; Chapter 16 on the option pricing model; Chapter 18 on mergers and acquisitions; and Chapter 20 on international finance.

Finally, in addition to the theory and empirical evidence there is always the practical question of how to apply the concepts to difficult and complex real world problems. Toward this end Chapters 2 and 3 are devoted to capital budgeting, Chapter 12 shows how to estimate the cost of capital for a large, publicly held corporation, and Chapter 14 determines the value of the same company. Throughout the text we attempt, wherever practical, to give examples of how to apply the theory. Among other things we show how the reader can: estimate his or her own utility function, calculate portfolio means and variances, value a call option, determine the terms of a merger or acquisition, and use international exchange rate relationships.

In sum, we believe that a sound foundation in finance theory requires not only a complete presentation of the theoretical concepts, but also a review of the empirical evidence which either supports or refutes the theory as well as enough examples to allow the practitioner to apply the validated theory.

B. SUGGESTED USE IN CURRICULUM

The basic building blocks which will lead to the most advantageous use of this text include algebra and elementary calculus; basic finance skills such as discounting, cash flows, and pro-forma income statements and balance sheets; elementary statistics; and an intermediate level microeconomics course. Consequently, the book would be applicable as a second semester (or quarter) in finance. This could occur at the junior or senior undergraduate year, for MBA's during the end of their first year or beginning of their second year, or as an introductory course for Ph.D. students.

At UCLA we used earlier (manuscript) versions of the text as a second course in finance for MBA students and as the first finance course for doctoral students. We found that requiring all finance majors to take a theory-of-finance course before proceeding on to upper-level courses eliminated a great deal of redundancy. For example, a portfolio theory course which uses the theory of finance as a prerequisite does not have to waste time with the fundamentals. Instead, after a brief review, most of the course can be devoted to more recent developments and applications.

Because finance theory has developed into a cohesive body of knowledge, it underlies almost all of what had formerly been thought of as disparate topics. The theory of finance, as presented in this text, is prerequisite to security analysis, portfolio theory, money and capital markets, commercial banking, speculative markets, investment banking, international finance, insurance, case courses in corporation finance, and quantitative methods of finance. The theory of finance can, and is, applied in all of these courses. That is why, at UCLA at least, we have made it a prerequisite to all the aforementioned course offerings.

C. USE OF THE SOLUTIONS MANUAL

The end-of-chapter problems and questions ask the students not only to feed back what they have just learned, but also to take the concepts and extend them beyond the material covered directly in the body of the text. Consequently, we hope that the solutions manual will be employed almost as if it were a supplementary text. It should not be locked up in the faculty member's office, as so many instructor's manuals are. It is not an instructor's manual in a narrow sense. Rather, it is a solutions manual, intended for use by the students. (We place multiple copies on reserve in the library.)

Understanding of the theory is increased by efforts to apply it. Consequently, most of the end-of-chapter problems are oriented toward applications of the theory. They require analytical thinking as well as a thorough understanding of the theory. If the solutions manual is used as we hope it will be, then students who learn how to apply their understanding of the theory to the end-of-chapter problems will at the same time be learning how to apply the theory to real world tasks.

D. ACKNOWLEDGEMENTS

In preparation, the book has been worked on and critically reviewed by numerous individuals. All this help has helped improve the quality of the book. We especially benefitted from the insightful corrections, clarifications and suggestions of Eugene Fama. We are also indebted to the following individuals: William Carleton, Halimah Clark, S. Kerry Cooper, Harry DeAngelo, David Eiteman, M. Chapman Findlay, Joseph Finnerty, Robert Geske, Glenn Graves, Charles W. Haley, Ronald Hanoian, Chi Cheng Hsia, William C. Hunter, Clement Krouse, Steven Lippman, Stephen Magee, Charles Martin, Ronald Masulis, Timothy J. Nantell, R. Richardson Pettit, Richard Roll, Keith Smith, Dennis Soter, Joel Stern, and Richard West. Naifu Chen and Ronald Bibb wrote Appendixes B and D, respectively. For their patient help in preparation of the text we thank Mary Blackburn, Margaret Eaton, Lynn Hickman, Kathy Masulis, Marilyn McElroy, and Barbara Tennison. Finally, we are indebted to the Addison-Wesley staff: Bill Hamilton, Herb Merritt, and Beth Watson.

There are undoubtedly errors in the final product, both typographical and conceptual as well as differences of opinion. We invite readers to send suggestions, comments, criticisms, and corrections to the authors at the Graduate School of Management, University of California, Los Angeles, CA 90024. Any form of communication will be welcome.

Los Angeles, California   T. E. C.
March 1979   J. F. W.

Contents

Part I

The Theory of Finance

Part I of this text covers what has come to be the accepted theory of financial decision-making. Its theme is an understanding of how individuals and their agents make choices among alternatives which have uncertain payoffs over multiple time periods. The theory which explains how and why these decisions are made has many applications in the various topic areas which traditionally make up the study of finance. The topics include security analysis, portfolio management, financial accounting, corporate financial policy, public finance, commercial banking, and international finance.

Chapter 1 shows why the existence of financial marketplaces is so important for economic development. Chapters 2 and 3 describe the appropriate investment criterion in the simplest of all possible worlds—a world where all outcomes are known with certainty. For many readers they will represent a summary and extension of material covered in traditional texts on corporate finance. Chapter 4 covers utility theory. It provides a model of how individuals make choices among risky alternatives. An understanding of individual behavior in the face of uncertainty is fundamental to understanding how financial markets operate. Chapter 5 introduces the objects of investor choice under uncertainty in the most general theoretical framework—state preference theory. Chapter 6 describes the objects of choice in a mean-variance partial equilibrium framework. In a world of uncertainty each combination of assets provides risky outcomes which are assumed to be described in terms of two parameters: mean and variance. Once the opportunity set of all possible choices has been described, we are able to combine Chapter 4, "The Theory of Choice," with Chapter 6, "The Objects of Choice," in order to predict exactly what combination of assets an individual will choose. Chapter 7 extends the study of choice into a market equilibrium framework, thereby closing the cycle of logic which we begin here. Chapter 1 shows why capital markets exist and assumes that all outcomes are known with certainty.

1

Chapter 7 extends the theory of capital markets to include equilibrium with uncertain outcomes and, even more important, describes the appropriate concept of risk and shows how it will be priced in equilibrium.* Therefore, it provides a framework for decision-making under uncertainty which can be applied by financial managers throughout the economy. Chapter 8, the last chapter in Part I, discusses the concept of efficient capital markets. It serves as a bridge between theory and reality. Most of the theory assumes that markets are perfectly frictionless, that is, free of transactions costs and other "market imperfections" which cannot be easily modeled. The questions arise: What assumptions are needed to have efficient (but not necessarily frictionless) capital markets? How well does the theory fit reality?

The empirical evidence on these and other questions is left to Part II of the text. It focuses on applications of financial theory to corporate policy issues such as capital budgeting, the cost of capital, capital structure, dividend policy, mergers and acquisitions, and international finance. For almost every topic there is material which covers the implications of theory for policy, the empirical evidence relevant to the theory, and provides detailed examples of applications.

---

* Readers who are interested in the equilibrium prices of assets which cannot be completely described by their mean and variance are referred to Chapter 16, "The Option Pricing Model."

Chapter 1

Introduction:
Capital Markets,
Consumption, and Investment

Through the alterations in the income streams provided by loans or sales, the
marginal degrees of impatience for all individuals in the market are
brought into equality with each other and with the market rate of interest.

Irving Fisher *The Theory of Interest*
Macmillan, New York, 1930, p. 122

A. CONSUMPTION AND INVESTMENT WITHOUT CAPITAL MARKETS

The answer to the question How do capital markets benefit society? requires that we
compare a world without capital markets to one with them and show that no one is
worse off and at least one individual is better off in a world with capital markets. In
order to make things as simple as possible, we assume that all outcomes from
investment are known with certainty, that there are no transactions costs or taxes,
and that decisions are made in a one-period context. Individuals are endowed with
income (manna from heaven) at the beginning of the period, y_0, and at the end of the
period, y_1. They must decide how much to actually consume now, C_0, and how to
invest in productive opportunities in order to provide end-of-period consumption,
C_1. Every individual is assumed to prefer more consumption to less. In other words,
the marginal utility of consumption is always positive. Also, we assume that the
marginal utility of consumption is decreasing. The total utility curve (Fig. 1.1) shows
the utility of consumption at the beginning of the period. Changes in consumption
have been marked off in equal increments along the horizontal axis. Note that each
increase in consumption causes total utility to increase (marginal utility is positive)
but that the increments in utility become smaller and smaller (marginal utility is
decreasing). We can easily construct a similar graph to represent the utility of end-of-
period consumption, $U(C_1)$. When combined with Fig. 1.1, the result (shown in Fig.
1.2) provides a description of trade-offs between consumption at the beginning of the

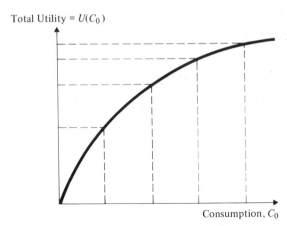

Fig. 1.1 Total utility of consumption

period, C_0, and consumption at the end of the period, C_1. The dashed lines represent contours along the utility surface where various combinations of C_0 and C_1 provide the same total utility (measured along the vertical axis). Since all points along the same contour (for example, points A and B) have equal total utility, the individual will be indifferent with respect to them. Therefore, the contours are called *indifference curves*. Looking at Fig. 1.2 from above, we can project the indifference curves onto the consumption argument plane (Fig. 1.3). To reiterate, all combinations of consumption today and consumption tomorrow which lie on the same indifference curve

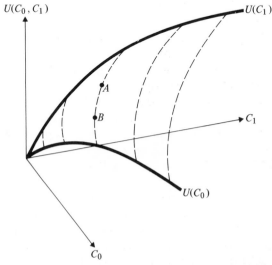

Fig. 1.2 Trade-offs between beginning and end-of-period consumption

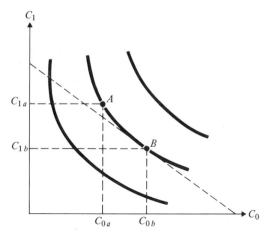

Fig. 1.3 Indifference curves representing the time preference of consumption

have the same total utility. The decision maker whose indifference curves are depicted in Fig. 1.3 would be indifferent as to point A with consumption (C_{0a}, C_{1a}) and point B with consumption (C_{0b}, C_{1b}). Point A has more consumption at the end of the period but less consumption at the beginning than point B does.

The slope of the straight line just tangent to the indifference curve at point B measures the rate of trade-off between C_1 and C_0 at point B. This trade-off is called the marginal rate of substitution, MRS, between consumption today and tomorrow. It also reveals the decision maker's subjective rate of time preference, r_i, at point B. We can think of the subjective rate of time preference as an interest rate because it measures the rate of substitution between consumption bundles over time. Mathematically, it is expressed as[1]

$$\text{MRS}_{C_1}^{C_0} = -\left.\frac{\delta C_1}{\delta C_0}\right|_{U=\text{const.}} = -(1 + r_i). \qquad (1.1)$$

Note that the subjective rate of time preference is greater at point A than at point B. The individual has less consumption today at point A and will therefore demand relatively more future consumption in order to have the same total utility.

Thus far we have described individuals' preference functions which tell us how they will make choices among consumption bundles over time. What happens if we introduce productive opportunities which allow a unit of current savings/investment to be turned into more than one unit of future consumption? We assume that each

---

[1] Equation (1.1) can be read as follows. The marginal rate of substitution between consumption today and end-of-period consumption, $\text{MRS}_{C_1}^{C_0}$, is equal to the slope of a line tangent to an indifference curve given constant total utility $-[\delta C_1/\delta C_0]|_{U=\text{const.}}$. This in turn is equal to the individual's subjective rate of time preference, $-(1 + r_i)$.

individual in the economy has a schedule of investment opportunities which can be arranged from the highest rate of return down to the lowest (Fig. 1.4). Although we have chosen to graph the investment opportunities schedule as a straight line, any decreasing function would do. This implies diminishing marginal returns to investment because the more an individual invests, the lower the rate of return on the marginal investment. Also, all investments are independent of one another and perfectly divisible.

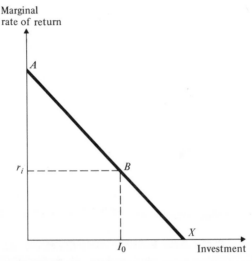

Fig. 1.4 An individual's schedule of productive investment opportunities

An individual will make all investments which have rates of return higher than his subjective rate of time preference, r_i. This can be demonstrated if we transform the schedule of investment opportunities into the consumption argument plane (Fig. 1.5). The slope of a line tangent to curve ABX in Fig. 1.5 is the rate at which a dollar of consumption foregone today is transformed into a dollar of consumption tomorrow. It is the marginal rate of transformation offered by the investment opportunity set. The line tangent to point A has the highest slope in Fig. 1.5 and represents the highest rate of return at point A in Fig. 1.4. If an individual is endowed with a resource bundle (y_0, y_1) which has utility U_1, he can move along his investment opportunity set to point B, where his indifference curve is tangent to it and he receives the maximum attainable utility, U_2. Because his current consumption, C_0, is less than his beginning-of-period endowment, y_0, he has chosen to invest. The amount of investment is $y_0 - C_0$. Of course, if $C_0 > y_0$, he will disinvest.

Note that the marginal rate of return on the last investment made (the slope of a line tangent to the investment opportunity set at point B) is exactly equal to the investor's subjective time preference (the slope of a line tangent to his indifference curve at point B). This will always be true in a world where there are no capital

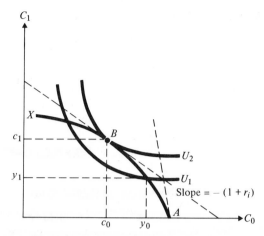

Fig. 1.5 The investment opportunity set

markets. The individual decision maker starts with his initial endowment (y_0, y_1) and compares the marginal rate of return on a dollar of investment (or disinvestment) with his subjective time preference. If the rate on investment is greater (as it is in Fig. 1.5), he will gain utility by making the investment. This process continues until the rate of return on the last dollar of investment just equals his rate of subjective time preference (at point B).

Without the existence of capital markets individuals with the same endowment and the same investment opportunity set may choose completely different investments because they have different indifference curves. This is shown in Fig. 1.6. Individual 2, who has a lower rate of time preference (why?), will choose to invest more than individual 1.

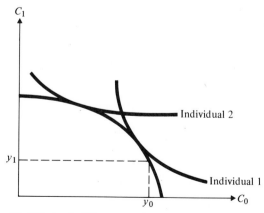

Fig. 1.6 Individuals with different indifference curves choose different investment/consumption patterns.

B. CONSUMPTION AND INVESTMENT WITH CAPITAL MARKETS

Financial markets facilitate the transfer of funds between lenders and borrowers. Assuming that interest rates are positive, any amount of funds lent today will return interest plus principal at the end of the period. Ignoring production for the time being, we can graph borrowing and lending opportunities along the capital market line in Fig. 1.7 (line $W_1 BAW_0$). An individual with an initial endowment of (y_0, y_1) with utility U_1 can reach any point along the market line by borrowing or lending at the market interest rate, r. If X_0 dollars are lent, their end-of-period value is rX_0 dollars of interest plus repayment of principal, X_0. If we designate the future value as X_1, we can write

$$X_1 = X_0 + rX_0, \qquad X_1 = (1 + r)X_0.$$

Similarly, the present value of an individual's initial endowment, W_0, is the sum of his current income, y_0, and the present value of his end-of-period income, $y_1(1 + r)^{-1}$.

$$W_0 = y_0 + \frac{y_1}{(1 + r)}. \tag{1.2}$$

Referring to Fig. 1.7, we see that an individual with endowment (y_0, y_1) will maximize his utility by moving along the market line to the point where his subjective time preference equals the market interest rate (at point B). At his initial endowment (point A) his subjective time preference, represented by the slope of a line tangent to his indifference curve at point A, is less than the market rate of return. Therefore, he will desire to lend. Ultimately he reaches a consumption decision (C_0^*, C_1^*) where he maximizes his utility. The present value of this consumption is also equal to his

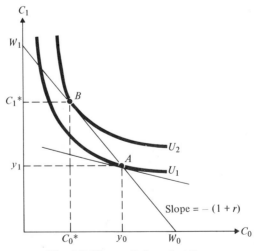

Fig. 1.7 The capital market line

wealth, W_0:

$$W_0 = C_0^* + \frac{C_1^*}{1 + r}. \tag{1.3}$$

This can be rearranged to give the equation for the capital market line;

$$C_1^* = W_0(1 + r) - (1 + r)C_0^*, \tag{1.4}$$

and since $W_0(1 + r) = W_1$, we have

$$C_1^* = W_1 - (1 + r)C_0^*. \tag{1.5}$$

Therefore, the market line in Fig. 1.7 has an intercept at W_1 and a slope of $-(1 + r)$. Also note that by equating (1.2) and (1.3) we see that the present value of the individual's endowment equals the present value of his consumption, and both are equal to his wealth, W_0.

What happens if the consumption/investment decision takes place in a world where capital markets facilitate the exchange of funds at the market rate of interest? Figure 1.8 combines production possibilities with market exchange possibilities. What actions will an individual with the family of indifference curves $U_1, U_2,$ and U_3 and endowment (y_0, y_1) at point A take in order to maximize his utility? Starting at point A, he can move either along the production opportunity set or along the capital market line. Both alternatives offer a higher rate of return than his subjective time preference, but production offers the higher return, therefore he chooses to invest and move along the production opportunity frontier. Without the opportunity to borrow or lend along the market line he would stop investing at point D, where the marginal

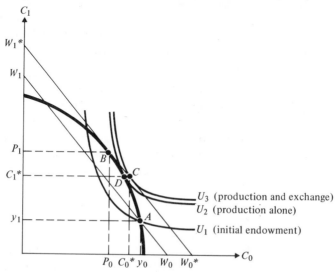

Fig. 1.8 Consumption and investment with capital markets

return on investment equals his subjective time preference. This was the result shown for consumption and investment without capital markets in Fig. 1.5. At this point, his level of utility has increased from U_1 to U_2. However, with the opportunity to borrow, he can actually do better. Note that at point D the borrowing rate, represented by the slope of the market line, is less than the rate of return on the marginal investment, which is the slope of the investment opportunity set at point D. Since further investment returns more than the cost of borrowed funds, he will continue to invest until the marginal return on investment is equal to the borrowing rate at point B. At point B he receives the output from production (P_0, P_1) and the present value of his wealth is W_0^* instead of W_0. Furthermore, he can now reach any point on the market line. Since his time preference at point B is greater than the market rate of return, he will consume more than P_0, which is the current payoff from production. By borrowing, he can reach point C on the market line. His optimal consumption is found, as before, where his subjective preference just equals the market rate of return. His utility has increased from U_1 at point A, to U_2 at point D, to U_3 at point C. He is clearly better off when capital markets exist since $U_3 > U_2$.

The decision process which takes place with production opportunities and capital market exchange opportunities occurs in two separate and distinct steps: (1) First choose the optimal production decision by taking on projects until the marginal rate of return on investment equals the objective market rate, and (2) choose the optimal consumption pattern by borrowing or lending along the market line to equate your subjective time preference with the market rate of return. The separation of the investment and consumption decisions is known as the Fisher separation theorem.

Fisher Separation Theorem Given perfect and complete capital markets, the production decision is governed solely by an objective market criterion (represented by attained wealth) without regard to the individuals' subjective preferences which enter into their consumption decisions.

An important implication for corporate policy is that the investment decision can be delegated to managers. Given the same opportunity set, every investor will make the same production decision (P_0, P_1) regardless of the shape of his indifference curves. This is shown in Fig. 1.9. Investor 1 and investor 2 both will direct the manager of their firm to choose production combination (P_0, P_1). They can then take the output of the firm and adapt it to their own subjective time preferences by trading in the capital market. They are both better off as a result. Without capital market opportunities, investor 1 would choose to produce at point Y, which has lower utility. Similarly, investor 2 would be worse off at point X.

The importance of capital markets cannot be overstated. They allow the efficient transfer of funds between borrowers and lenders. Individuals who have insufficient wealth to take advantage of all their investment opportunities which yield rates of return higher than the market rate are able to borrow funds and invest more than they would without capital markets. In this way, funds can be efficiently allocated

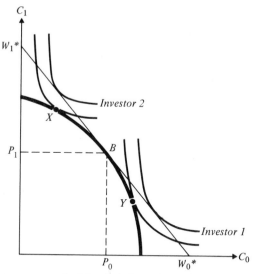

Fig. 1.9 The investment decision is independent of individual preferences

from individuals with few productive opportunities and great wealth to individuals with many opportunities and insufficient wealth. As a result, everyone (borrower and lender) is better off than he would have been without capital markets.

C. MARKETPLACES AND TRANSACTIONS COSTS

The foregoing discussion has demonstrated the advantages of capital markets for funds allocation in a world without transactions costs. In such a world there is no need for a central location for exchange; that is, there is no need for a marketplace *per se*. But let us assume that we have a primitive economy with N producers, each making a single product and consuming a bundle of all N consumption goods. Given no marketplace, bilateral exchange is necessary. During a given time period each visits the other in order to exchange goods. The cost of each leg of a trip is T dollars. Individual 1 makes four trips, one to each of the other four producers. Individual 2 makes three trips, and so on. Altogether there are $[N(N-1)]/2 = 10$ trips, at a total cost of $10T$ dollars. If a middleman establishes a central marketplace and carries an inventory of each of the N products, as shown in Fig. 1.11, the total number of trips can be reduced to five with a total cost of $5T$ dollars. Therefore, if the middleman has a total cost (including the cost of his living) of less than $10T - 5T$ dollars, he can profitably establish a marketplace and everyone will be better off.[2]

---

[2] In general, for N individuals making two-way exchanges there are $\binom{N}{2} = N(N-1)/2$ trips. With a marketplace the number of trips is reduced to N. Therefore the savings is $[N(N-1)/2 - N]T$.

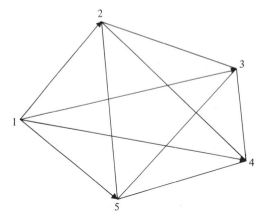

Fig. 1.10 A primitive exchange economy with no central marketplace

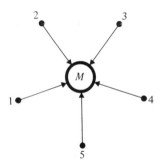

Fig. 1.11 The productivity of a central marketplace

This example provides a simple explanation for the productivity of marketplaces. Among other things, they serve to efficiently reduce transactions costs. Later on, we shall refer to this fact as the *operational efficiency* of capital markets. The lower the transactions costs are, the more operationally efficient a market will be said to be.

D. TRANSACTIONS COSTS AND THE BREAKDOWN OF SEPARATION

To the extent that transactions costs are nontrivial, financial intermediaries and marketplaces will provide a useful service. In such a world, the borrowing rate will be greater than the lending rate. This will have the effect of invalidating the Fisher separation principle. As shown in Fig. 1.12 individuals with different indifference curves will now choose different levels of investment. Without a single market rate they will not be able to delegate the investment decision to the manager of their firm. Individual 1 would direct the manager to use the lending rate and invest at point *B*.

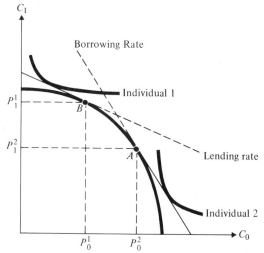

Fig. 1.12 Markets with different borrowing and lending rates

Individual 2 would use the borrowing rate and choose point A. A third individual might choose investments between points A and B, where his indifference curve is directly tangent to the production opportunity set.

The theory of finance is greatly simplified if we assume that capital markets are perfect. Obviously they are not. The relevant question then is whether the theories which assume frictionless markets fit reality well enough to be useful, or whether they need to be refined in order to provide greater insights into reality.

Through most of this text we shall adopt the convenient and simplifying assumption that capital markets are perfect. The only major imperfection to be considered in detail is the impact of corporate and personal taxes. The effects of taxes are certainly nontrivial and, as we shall see, they do change the predictions of many models of financial policy.

E. SUMMARY

The rest of the text follows almost exactly the same logic as this chapter, except that from Chapter 4 onward it focuses on decision-making under uncertainty. The first step is to develop indifference curves to model individual decision-making in a world with uncertainty (Chapter 4 is analogous to Fig. 1.3). Next, the opportunity set, which represents choices among combinations of risky assets, is developed. Chapters 5 and 6 are similar to Fig. 1.5. The tangency between the indifference curves of a risk-averse investor and his opportunity set provides a theory of individual choice in a world without capital markets (this is discussed in Chapter 6). Finally in Chapter 7, we introduce the opportunity to borrow and lend at a riskless rate and develop a model of capital market equilibrium. Chapter 7 follows logic similar to Fig. 1.8. In fact, we show that a type of separation principle (two-fund separation) obtains, given uncertainty and perfect capital markets. Chapters 8 and 9 take a careful look at the meaning of efficient capital markets and at empirical evidence which relates to the question of how well the perfect capital market assumption fits reality.

PROBLEM SET

1.1 Graphically demonstrate the Fisher separation theorem for the case where an individual ends up lending in financial markets. Label the following points on the graph: initial endowment, W_0; optimal production investment (P_0, P_1); optimal consumption (C_0^*, C_1^*); present value of final wealth, W_0^*.

1.2 Graphically analyze the effect of an exogenous decrease in the interest rate on (a) the utility of borrowers and lenders, (b) the present wealth of borrowers and lenders, and (c) the investment in real assets.

1.3 The interest rate cannot fall below the net rate of return from storage. True or false. Why?

1.4 Graphically illustrate the decision-making process faced by an individual in a Robinson Crusoe economy where (a) storage is the only investment opportunity and (b) there are no capital markets.

1.5 Suppose that the investment opportunity set has N projects all of which have the same rate of return, R^*. Graph the investment set.

REFERENCES

ALDERSON, W., "Factors Governing the Development of Marketing Channels," reprinted in Richard M. Clewett, *Marketing Channels for Manufactured Products.* Irwin, Homewood, Ill., 1954.

FAMA, E. F., and M. H. MILLER, *The Theory of Finance.* Holt, Rinehart and Winston, New York, 1972.

FISHER, I., *The Theory of Interest.* Macmillan, New York, 1930.

HIRSHLEIFER, J., *Investment, Interest, and Capital.* Prentice-Hall, Englewood Cliffs, N.J., 1970.

Chapter 2

Investment Decisions: The Certainty Case

When the first primitive man decided to use a bone for a club instead of eating its marrow, that was investment.

Anonymous

A. INTRODUCTION

The investment decision is essentially how much not to consume in the present in order that more can be consumed in the future. The optimal investment decision maximizes the expected satisfaction (expected utility) gained from consumption over the planning horizon of the decision maker. We assume that all economic decisions ultimately reduce to questions about consumption. Even more fundamentally, consumption is related to survival.

The consumption-investment decision is important to all sectors of the economy. An individual who saves does so because the benefit of future consumption provided by an extra dollar of saving exceeds the benefit of using it for consumption today. Managers of corporations, who act as agents for the owners (shareholders) of the firm, must decide between paying out earnings in the form of dividends, which may be used for present consumption, and retaining the earnings to invest in productive opportunities which are expected to yield future consumption. Managers of not-for-profit organizations try to maximize the expected utility of contributors—those individuals who provide external funds. And public sector managers attempt to maximize the expected utility of their constituencies.

The examples of investment decisions in this chapter are taken from the corporate sector of the economy, but the decision criterion, which is to maximize the present value of lifetime consumption, can be applied to any sector of the economy. For the time being, we assume that intertemporal decisions are based on knowledge of the market-determined time value of money—the interest rate. Furthermore, the interest

15

rate is assumed to be known with certainty in all time periods. It is nonstochastic. In addition, all future payoffs from current investment decisions are known with certainty. And finally, there are no imperfections in capital markets. These assumptions are obviously an oversimplification, but they are a good place to start. Most of the remainder of the text after this chapter is devoted to decision-making under uncertainty. But for the time being it is useful to establish the fundamental criterion of economic decision-making—the maximization of the net present value of wealth, assuming perfect certainty.

The most important theme of this chapter is that the objective of the firm is to maximize the wealth of its shareholders. This is seen to be the same as maximizing the present value of shareholders' lifetime consumption and no different than maximizing the price per share of stock. Alternative issues such as agency costs are also discussed. Then the maximization of shareholder wealth is more carefully defined as the discounted value of future expected cash flows. Finally, techniques for project selection are reviewed and the net present value criterion is shown to be consistent with shareholder wealth maximization.

B. FISHER SEPARATION. THE SEPARATION OF INDIVIDUAL UTILITY PREFERENCES FROM THE INVESTMENT DECISION

To say that the goal of the firm is the maximization of its shareholders' wealth is one thing, but the problem of how to do it is another. We know that interpersonal comparison of individuals' utility functions is not possible. For example, if we give individuals A and B one hundred dollars each, they will both be happy. However, no one, not even the two individuals, will be able to discern which person is happier. How then can a manager maximize shareholders' utility when individual utility functions cannot be compared or combined?

The answer to the question is provided if we turn to our understanding of the role of capital markets. If capital markets are perfect in the sense that they have no frictions which cause the borrowing rate to be different from the lending rate, then (as we saw in Chapter 1) Fisher separation obtains. This means that individuals can delegate investment decisions to the manager of the firm in which they are owners. Regardless of the shape of the shareholders' individual utility functions, the managers maximize the owners' individual (and collective) wealth positions by choosing to invest until the rate of return on the least favorable project is exactly equal to the market-determined rate of return. This result is shown in Fig. 2.1. The optimal production/investment decision, (P_0, P_1), is the one which maximizes the present value of the shareholders' wealth, W_0. The appropriate decision rule is the same, independent of the shareholders' time preferences for consumption. The manager will be directed, by all shareholders, to undertake all projects which earn more than the market rate of return.

If the marginal return on investment equals the market-determined opportunity cost of capital, then the shareholders' wealth, W_0, is maximized. Individual share-

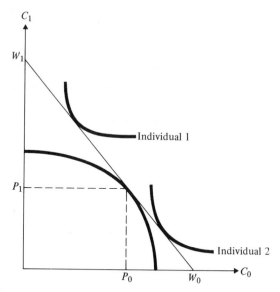

Fig. 2.1 Separation of shareholder preferences from the production/investment decision

holders can then borrow or lend along the market line in order to satisfy their time pattern for consumption. In other words, they can take the cash payouts from the firm and use them for current consumption or save them for future consumption according to their individual desires.

The separation principle implies that the maximization of the shareholders' wealth is identical to maximizing the present value of their lifetime consumption. Mathematically, this was demonstrated in Eq. (1.3),

$$W_0 = C_0 + \frac{C_1}{1 + r}.$$

Even though the two individuals in Fig. 2.1 choose different levels of current and future consumption, they have the same current wealth, W_0. This follows from the fact that they receive the same income from productive investments (P_0, P_1).

Because exchange opportunities permit borrowing and lending at the same rate of interest, an individual's productive optimum is independent of his resources and tastes. Therefore, if asked to vote on their preferred production decisions at a shareholders' meeting, different shareholders of the same firm will be unanimous in their preference. This is known as the unanimity principle. It implies that the managers of the firm, in their capacity as agents of the shareholders, need not worry about making decisions which reconcile differences of opinion among shareholders. All shareholders will have identical interests. In effect, the price system by which profit is measured conveys the shareholders' unanimously preferred productive decisions to the firm.

C. THE AGENCY PROBLEM. DO MANAGERS HAVE THE CORRECT INCENTIVE TO MAXIMIZE SHAREHOLDERS' WEALTH?

So far, we have shown that in perfect markets all shareholders will agree that managers should follow a simple investment decision rule: take projects until the marginal rate of return equals the market-determined discount rate. Therefore, the shareholders' wealth is seen to be the present value of cash flows discounted at the opportunity cost of capital (the market-determined rate).

Shareholders can agree on the decision rule which they should give to managers. But they must be able to costlessly monitor management decisions if they are to be sure that management really does make every decision in a way which maximizes their wealth. There is obviously a difference between ownership and control, and there is no reason to believe that the manager, who serves as an agent for the owners, will always act in the best interest of the shareholders. In most agency relationships the owner will incur nontrivial monitoring costs in order to keep the agent in line. Consequently, the owner faces a trade-off between monitoring costs and forms of compensation which will cause the agent to always act in the owner's interest. At one extreme, if the agent were to receive all of his compensation in the form of shares in the firm, then monitoring costs would be zero. Unfortunately, this type of scheme is practically impossible because the agent will always be able to receive part of his compensation in the form of nonpecuniary benefits such as larger office space, expensive lunches, an executive jet, etc. At the opposite extreme, the owner would have to incur inordinate monitoring costs in order to guarantee that the agent always makes the decision the owner would prefer. Somewhere between these two extremes lies an optimal solution. The reader who wishes to explore this classic problem in greater depth is referred to books by Williamson [1964], Marschak and Radner [1972], or Cyert and March [1963], and to articles by Jensen and Meckling [1976] or Machlup [1967] as good references to an immense literature in this area.

We shall assume that managers always make decisions which maximize the wealth of the firm's shareholders. In order to do so, they must find and select the best set of investment projects to accomplish their objective.

D. MAXIMIZATION OF SHAREHOLDERS' WEALTH

1. Dividends vs. Capital Gains

Assuming that managers behave as though they were maximizing the wealth of the shareholders, we need to establish a usable definition of what is meant by shareholders' wealth. We can say that shareholders' wealth is the discounted value of after-tax cash flows paid out by the firm.[1] After-tax cash flows available for consumption can be shown to be the same as the stream of dividends, D_t, paid to shareholders.

---

[1] Since much of the rest of this chapter assumes familiarity with discounting, the reader is referred to Appendix A for a review.

The discounted value of the stream of dividends is

$$S_0 = \sum_{t=0}^{\infty} \frac{D_t}{(1+k)^t},$$

(2.1)

where S_0 is the present value of shareholders' wealth (in Fig. 2.1 it is W_0) and k is the market-determined rate of interest.

Equation (2.1) is a multiperiod formula which assumes that future cash flows paid to shareholders are known with certainty and that the market-determined discount rate is nonstochastic and constant over all time periods. These assumptions are maintained throughout this chapter because our main objective is to understand how the investment decision, shown graphically in Fig. 2.1 in a one-period context, can be extended to the more practical setting of many time periods in a manner consistent with the maximization of the shareholders' wealth. For the time being, we shall ignore the effect of personal taxes on dividends, and we shall assume that the discount rate, k, is the market-determined opportunity cost of capital for equivalent income streams. It is the slope of the market line in Fig. 2.1.

One question that often arises is: What about capital gains? Surely shareholders receive both capital gains and dividends; why then do capital gains not appear in Eq. (2.1)? The answer to this question is that capital gains *do* appear in Eq. (2.1). This can be shown by use of a simple example. Suppose a firm pays a dividend, D_1, of $1.00 at the end of this year and $1.00 $(1+g)^{t-1}$ at the end of each year thereafter, where g is the growth rate of the dividend stream. If the growth rate in dividends, g, is 5% and the opportunity cost of investment, k, is 10%, how much will an investor pay today for the stock? Using the formula for the present value of a growing annuity stream, we get[2]

$$S_0 = \frac{D_1}{k-g} = \frac{\$1.00}{.10 - .05} = \$20.00.$$

Next, suppose that an investor bought the stock today for $20 and held it for five years. What would it be worth at the end of the fifth year?

$$S_5 = \frac{D_6}{k-g}.$$

The dividend, D_6, at the end of the sixth year is

$$D_6 = \$1.00(1+g)^5, \qquad D_6 = \$1.00(1.05)^5 = \$1.2763.$$

Therefore, the value of the stock at the end of the fifth year would be

$$S_5 = \frac{\$1.2763}{.10 - .05} = \$25.5256.$$

---

[2] The formula used here, sometimes called the Gordon growth model, is derived in Appendix A. It assumes that the dividend grows forever at a constant rate, g, which is less than the discount rate, $g < k$.

The value of the stock at the end of the fifth year is the discounted value of all dividends from that time on. Now we can compute the present value of the stream of income of an investor who holds the stock only five years. He gets five dividend payments plus the market price of the stock in the fifth year. The discounted value of these payments is S_0.

$$S_0 = \frac{D_1}{1+k} + \frac{D_1(1+g)}{(1+k)^2} + \frac{D_1(1+g)^2}{(1+k)^3} + \frac{D_1(1+g)^3}{(1+k)^4} + \frac{D_1(1+g)^4}{(1+k)^5} + \frac{S_5}{(1+k)^5}$$

$$= \frac{1.00}{1.1} + \frac{1.05}{1.21} + \frac{1.10}{1.33} + \frac{1.16}{1.46} + \frac{1.22}{1.61} + \frac{25.52}{1.61}$$

$$= .91 + .87 + .83 + .79 + .76 + 15.85$$

$$= 20.01.$$

Except for a one-cent rounding difference, the present value of the stock is the same if an investor holds it forever, or if he only holds it for, say five years. Since the value of the stock in the fifth year is equal to the future dividends from that time on, the value of dividends for five years plus a capital gain is exactly the same as the value of an infinite stream of dividends.

Equation (2.1) is the discounted value of the stream of cash payments to shareholders and is equivalent to the shareholders' wealth. Because we are ignoring the different tax rates between dividends and capital gains (this will be discussed in Chapter 14, "Dividend Policy") we can say that Eq. (2.1) incorporates all cash payments, both dividends and capital gains.

2. The Economic Definition of Profit

Frequently there is a great deal of confusion over what is meant by profits. When an economist says profits, he means cash flow. Therefore, the appropriate profits for managers to use when making decisions are the discounted stream of cash flows to shareholders; in other words, dividends.

We can use a very simple model to show the difference between the economic definition of profit and the accounting definition. Assume that we have an all-equity firm and that there are no taxes.[3] Then sources of funds are revenues, R, and sale of new equity (on M shares at P dollars per share). Uses of funds are wages, salaries, materials, and services, W&S; investment, I; and dividends, D. For each time period, t, we can write the *equality between sources and uses of funds* as

$$R_t + M_t P_t = D_t + (\text{W\&S})_t + I_t. \tag{2.2}$$

To simplify things even further, assume that the firm issues no new equity, that is, $M_t P_t = 0$. Now we can write dividends as

$$D_t = R_t - (\text{W\&S})_t - I_t, \tag{2.3}$$

---

[3] The conclusions to be drawn from the model do not change if we add debt and taxes, but the arithmetic becomes more complex.

which is the *simple cash flow definition of profit*. Dividends are the cash flow left over after costs of operations and new investment are deducted from revenues. Using Eq. (2.3) and the definition of shareholders' wealth (Eq. (2.1)), we can rewrite shareholders' wealth as

$$S = \sum_{t=0}^{\infty} \frac{R_t - (W\&S)_t - I_t}{(1+k)^t}.$$

(2.4)

The accounting definition of profit does not deduct gross investment, I_t, as investment outlays are made. Instead the book value of new investment is capitalized on the balance sheet and written off at some depreciation rate, Z_t. The *accounting definition of profit* is

$$A_t = R_t - (W\&S)_t - Z_t.$$

(2.5)

Let N_t be the net change in the book value of assets during a year. The net change will equal gross new investment during the year, I_t, less accumulated depreciation during the year, Z_t,

$$N_t = I_t - Z_t.$$

(2.6)

We already know that the accounting definition of profit, A_t, is different from the economic definition, D_t. However, it can be adjusted by subtracting net investment. This is done in Eq. (2.7):

$$S = \sum_{t=0}^{\infty} \frac{R_t - (W\&S)_t - Z_t - (I_t - Z_t)}{(1+k)^t}$$

$$= \sum_{t=0}^{\infty} \frac{A_t - N_t}{(1+k)^t}.$$

(2.7)

The main difference between the accounting definition and the economic definition of profit is that the former does not focus on cash flows when they occur, while the latter does. The economic definition of profit, for example, correctly deducts the entire expenditure for investment in plant and equipment at the time the cash outflow occurs.

Financial managers are frequently misled when they focus on the accounting definition of profit, or earnings per share. The objective of the firm is *not* to maximize earnings per share. The correct objective is to maximize shareholders' wealth which is the price per share which in turn is equivalent to the discounted cash flows of the firm. There are two good examples which point out the difference between maximizing earnings per share and maximizing discounted cash flow. The first example is the difference between FIFO and LIFO inventory accounting during a time period of inflation. Earnings per share are higher if the firm adopts first-in/first-out, FIFO, inventory accounting. The reason is that the cost of manufacturing the oldest items in inventory is less than the cost of producing the newest items. Consequently, if the cost of the oldest inventory (the inventory which was first in) is written off as an expense against revenue, earnings per share will be higher than if the cost of the newest items (the inventory which was in last) is written off. A numerical example is given in Table 2.1. It's easy to see how managers might be tempted to use FIFO accounting techniques. Earnings per share are higher. However, FIFO is the wrong technique to use in an inflationary period because it minimizes cash flow by maximizing taxes. In our example, production has taken place during some previous time period, and we are trying to make the correct choice of inventory accounting in the present. The sale of an item from inventory in Table 2.1 provides $100 of cash inflow (revenue) regardless of which accounting system we are using. Cost of goods sold involves no current cash flow, but taxes do. Therefore, with FIFO, earnings per share are 45¢ but cash flow per share is ($100 − $30) ÷ 100 shares, which equals 70¢ per share. On the other hand, with LIFO, earnings per share are only 6¢ but cash flow is ($100 − $4) ÷ 100 shares, which equals 96¢ per share. Since shareholders care only about discounted cash flow, they will assign a higher value to the shares of the company using LIFO accounting. The reason is that LIFO provides higher cash flow because it pays lower taxes to the government. This is a good example of the difference between maximizing earnings per share and maximizing shareholders' wealth.[4]

Table 2.1 LIFO vs. FIFO

	LIFO	FIFO	Inventory at cost
Revenue	100	100	4th item in 90 → LIFO
Cost of goods sold	−90	−25	3rd item in 60
Operating income	10	75	2nd item in 40
Taxes at 40%	−4	−30	1st item in 25 → FIFO
Net income	6	45	
Earnings per share (100 shs)	.06	.45	

A second example is the accounting treatment of goodwill in mergers. Since the accounting practices for merger are discussed in detail in Chapter 17, only the salient features will be mentioned here. There are two types of accounting treatment for merger: pooling and purchase. Pooling means that the income statements and balance sheets of the merging companies are simply added together. With purchase, the acquiring company adds two items to its balance sheet: (1) the book value of the assets of the acquired company and (2) the difference between the purchase price and the book value. This difference is an item called *goodwill*. Opinion 17 of the Accounting Principles Board (APB No. 17, effective October 31, 1970) of The American Institute of Certified Public Accountants requires that goodwill be written off as an expense against earnings *after* taxes over a period not to exceed 40 years. Obviously earnings per share will be lower if the same merger takes place by purchase rather

---

[4] See Chapter 9 for a discussion of empirical research on this issue.

than pooling. There is empirical evidence, collected in a paper by Jean-Marie Gagnon [1971], which indicates that managers choose to use pooling rather than purchase if the write-off of goodwill is substantial. Managers seem to behave as if they were trying to maximize earnings per share. The sad thing is that some mergers which are advantageous to the shareholders of acquiring firms may be rejected by management if substantial goodwill write-offs are required. This would be unfortunate because *there is no difference in the effect on cash flows between pooling and purchase*. The reason is that goodwill expense is not a cash flow and it has no effect on taxes because it is written off *after* taxes.[5]

It is often argued that maximization of earnings per share is appropriate if investors use earnings per share to value the stock. There is good empirical evidence to indicate that this is not the case. Shareholders do, in fact, value securities according to the present value of discounted cash flows. Evidence which substantiates this is presented in detail in Chapter 9.

E. TECHNIQUES FOR CAPITAL BUDGETING

Having argued that maximizing shareholders' wealth is equivalent to maximizing the discounted cash flows provided by investment projects, we now turn our attention to a discussion of investment decision rules. We assume, for the time being, that the stream of cash flows provided by a project can be estimated without error, and that the opportunity cost of funds provided to the firm (this is usually referred to as *the cost of capital*) is also known. We also assume that capital markets are frictionless so that financial managers can separate investment decisions from individual shareholder preferences, and that monitoring costs are zero so that managers will maximize shareholders' wealth. All that they need to know is cash flows and the required market rate of return for projects of equivalent risk.

Three major problems face managers when they make investment decisions. First they have to search out new opportunities in the marketplace or new technologies. These are the basis of growth. Unfortunately, the Theory of Finance cannot help with this problem. Second, the expected cash flows from the projects have to be estimated, and finally the projects have to be evaluated according to sound decision rules. These latter two problems are central topics of this text. In the remainder of this chapter we look at project evaluation techniques assuming that cash flows are known with certainty, and in Chapter 10 we'll assume that cash flows are uncertain.

Investment decision rules are usually referred to as *capital budgeting techniques*. The best technique will possess the following essential property: it will maximize shareholders' wealth. This essential property can be broken down into separate criteria:

- All cash flows should be considered.
- The cash flows should be discounted at the opportunity cost of funds.

---

[5] See Chapter 9 for a discussion of empirical evidence relating to this issue.

- The technique should select from a set of mutually exclusive projects the one which maximizes shareholders' wealth.
- Managers should be able to consider one project independently from all others (this is known as the value-additivity principle).

The last two criteria need some explanation. *Mutually exclusive projects* are a set from which only one project can be chosen. In other words, if a manager chooses to go ahead with one project from the set, he cannot choose to take on any of the others. For example, there may be three or four different types of bridges which could be constructed to cross a river at a given site. Choosing a wooden bridge excludes other types, e.g., steel. Projects are also categorized in other ways. *Independent projects* are those which permit the manager to choose to undertake any or all, and *contingent projects* are those which have to be carried out together or not at all. For example, if building a tunnel also requires a ventilation system, then the tunnel and ventilation system should be considered as a single, contingent project.

The fourth criterion, *the value-additivity principle*, implies that if we know the value of separate projects accepted by management, then simply adding their values, V_j, will give us the value of the firm, V. In mathematical terms,

$$V = \sum_{j=1}^{N} V_j. \tag{2.8}$$

This is a particularly important point because it means that projects can be considered on their own merit without the necessity of our looking at them in an infinite variety of combinations with other projects.

There are four widely used capital budgeting techniques: (1) the payback method, (2) the accounting rate of return, (3) the net present value, and (4) the internal rate of return. Our task is to choose the technique which best satisfies the four desirable properties discussed above. It will be demonstrated that only one technique—the net present value method—is correct. It is the only technique which is always consistent with shareholder wealth maximization.

In order to provide an example for discussion, Table 2.2 lists the estimates of cash flow for four projects, each of which has a five-year life. Since they are mutually

Table 2.2 Four mutually exclusive projects

	Cash flows				
Year	A	B	C	D	PV factor at 10%
0	− 1000	− 1000	− 1000	− 1000	1.000
1	100	0	100	200	.909
2	900	0	200	300	.826
3	100	300	300	500	.751
4	− 100	700	400	500	.683
5	− 400	1300	1250	600	.621

exclusive, there is only one which will maximize the price of the firm's stock; in other words, there is only one which will maximize shareholders' wealth. We would normally assume at this point that all four projects are equally "risky." However, according to the assumption used throughout this chapter, their cash flows are known with certainty; therefore, their "risk" is zero.

1. The Payback Method

The payback period for a project is simply the number of years it takes to recover the initial cash outlay on a project. The payback periods for the four projects in Table 2.2 are:

Project A,   2 years;
Project B,   4 years;
Project C,   4 years;
Project D,   3 years.

If management were adhering strictly to the payback method, it would choose project A which has the shortest payback period. A casual inspection of the cash flows shows that this is clearly wrong. The difficulty with the payback method is that it does not consider all cash flows and it fails to discount them. Failure to consider all cash flows results in ignoring the large negative cash flows which occur in the last two years of project A. Failure to discount them means that management would be indifferent in its choice between project A and a second project which paid $900 in the first year and $100 in the second. Both projects would have the same payback period. We reject the payback method because it violates (at least) the first two of the four properties which are desirable in capital budgeting techniques.

2. The Accounting Rate of Return (ARR)

The *accounting rate of return* is the average after-tax profit divided by the initial cash outlay. For example, assuming, for the sake of convenience, that the numbers in Table 2.2 are accounting profits, the average after-tax profit for project A is

$$\frac{-1000 + 100 + 900 + 100 - 100 - 400}{5} = -80,$$

and the ARR is

$$ARR = \frac{\text{Average after-tax profit}}{\text{Initial outlay}} = \frac{-80}{1000} = -8\%. \tag{2.9}$$

The ARR's for the four projects are:

Project A, $ARR = -8\%$;
Project B, $ARR = 26\%$;
Project C, $ARR = 25\%$;
Project D, $ARR = 22\%$.

If we were using the ARR, we would choose project B as the best. The problem with the ARR is that it uses accounting profits instead of cash flows and it does not consider the time value of money. The difference between accounting profits and cash flows has been discussed at length, and it is therefore unnecessary to repeat here that it is incorrect to use the accounting definition of profits. Failure to use the time value of money (i.e., failure to discount) means that managers would be indifferent in their choice between project B and a project with after-tax profits which occur in the opposite chronological order because both projects would have the same accounting rate of return.

3. Net Present Value (NPV)

The *net present value* criterion will accept projects which have an NPV greater than zero. The NPV is computed by discounting the cash flows at the firm's opportunity cost of capital. For the projects in Table 2.2 we assume that the cost of capital is 10%. Therefore, the present value of project A is[6]

(Cash flow)	×	(PV factor)	=	PV
− 1000		1.000		− 1000.00
100		.909		90.90
900		.826		743.40
100		.751		75.10
− 100		.683		− 68.30
− 400		.621		− 248.40
			NPV =	− 407.30

We have discounted each of the cash flows back to the present and summed them. Mathematically this can be written as

$$NPV = \sum_{t=1}^{N} \frac{NCF_t}{(1 + k)^t} - I_0, \qquad (2.10)$$

where NCF_t is the net cash flow in time period t, I_0 is the initial cash outlay, k is the firm's cost of capital, and N is the number of years in the project. The net present values of the four projects are:

Project A, NPV = − 407.30;
Project B, NPV =   510.70;
Project C, NPV =   530.75;
Project D, NPV =   519.20.

If these projects were independent instead of mutually exclusive, we would reject A and accept B, C, and D. (Why?) Since they are mutually exclusive, we select the project with greatest NPV, project C. The NPV of a project is exactly the same as the increase in shareholders' wealth. This fact makes it the correct decision rule for

---

[6] The reader who wishes to brush up on the algebra of discounting is referred to Appendix A.

capital budgeting purposes. More will be said about this when we compare the NPV rule with the internal rate of return.

4. Internal Rate of Return (IRR)

The *internal rate of return* on a project is defined as that rate which equates the present value of the cash outflows and inflows. In other words, it is the rate which makes the computed NPV exactly zero. Hence this is the rate of return on invested capital which the project is returning to the firm. Mathematically, we solve for the rate of return where the NPV equals zero:

$$\text{NPV} = 0 = \sum_{t=1}^{N} \frac{\text{NCF}_t}{(1 + \text{IRR})^t} - I_0. \tag{2.11}$$

We can solve for the IRR on project C by trial and error. (Most firms have computer programs which can quickly solve for the IRR by using similar iterative techniques.) This is done in Table 2.3, and graphed in Fig. 2.2.

Table 2.3 IRR for Project C

Year	Cash flow	PV at 10%		PV at 20%		PV at 25%		PV at 22.8%	
0	− 1000	1.000	− 1000.00	1.000	− 1000.00	1.000	− 1000.00	1.000	− 1000.00
1	100	.909	90.90	.833	83.33	.800	80.00	.814	81.40
2	200	.826	165.20	.694	138.80	.640	128.00	.663	132.60
3	300	.751	225.30	.579	173.70	.512	153.60	.540	162.00
4	400	.683	273.20	.482	192.80	.410	163.84	.440	176.00
5	1250	.621	776.15	.402	502.50	.328	410.00	.358	447.50
	1250		530.75		91.13		− 64.56		− .50

Figure 2.2 shows that the NPV of the given set of cash flows decreases as the discount rate is increased. If the discount rate is zero, there is no time value of money and the NPV of a project is simply the sum of its cash flows. For project C, the NPV equals $1250 when the discount rate is zero. At the opposite extreme, if the discount rate is infinite, then future cash flows are valueless and the NPV of project C is its

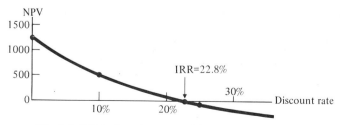

Fig. 2.2 NPV of project C at different discount rates

current cash flow, $-\$1000$. Somewhere between these two extremes is a discount rate which makes the present value equal to zero. Called the IRR on the project, this rate, as said before, equates the present value of cash inflows with the present value of cash outflows. The IRR's for the four projects are:

Project A,   IRR does not exist;
Project B,   IRR = 20.9%;
Project C,   IRR = 22.8%;
Project D,   IRR = 25.4%.

If we use the IRR criterion and the projects are independent, we accept any project which has an IRR greater than the opportunity cost of capital, which is 10%. Therefore, we would accept projects B, C, and D. However, since these projects are mutually exclusive, the IRR rule leads us to accept project D as the best one.

F. COMPARISON OF NET PRESENT VALUE WITH INTERNAL RATE OF RETURN

As the example shows, the net present value and the internal rate of return can favor conflicting project choices. The net present value favors project C while IRR favors project D. Both techniques consider all cash flows and both use the concept of the time value of money in order to discount cash flows. However, we must choose from among the four mutually exclusive projects the one project which maximizes shareholders' wealth. Consequently, only one of the two techniques can be correct. We shall see that the NPV criterion is the only one which is necessarily consistent with maximizing shareholders' wealth.

Figure 2.3 compares projects B, C, and D. For very low discount rates project B

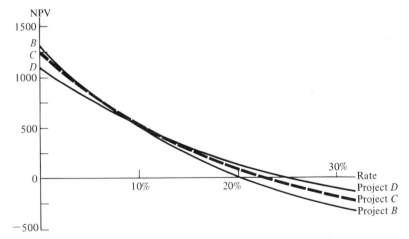

Fig. 2.3 Comparison of three mutually exclusive projects

has the highest net present value, for intermediate discount rates project C is best, and for high discount rates project D is best. The NPV rule compares the three projects at the same discount rate. Ten percent was not arbitrarily chosen. It is the market-determined opportunity cost of capital. We saw earlier in the chapter that this market-determined discount rate is the one managers should use if they desire to maximize the wealth of all shareholders. Consequently, no other discount rate is appropriate. Project C is the best project because it gives the greatest NPV when the opportunity cost of funds invested is 10%.

The IRR rule does not discount at the opportunity cost of capital. Instead, it implicitly assumes that the time value of money is the IRR, since all cash flows are discounted at that rate. This implicit assumption has come to be called the reinvestment rate assumption.

1. The Reinvestment Rate Assumption

The reinvestment rate is really the same thing as the opportunity cost of capital. Both the NPV rule and the IRR rule make implicit assumptions about the reinvestment rate. The NPV rule assumes that shareholders can reinvest their money at the opportunity cost of capital which in our example was 10%. Because 10% is the market-determined opportunity cost of funds, the NPV rule is making the correct reinvestment rate assumption. On the other hand, the IRR rule assumes that investors can reinvest their money at the IRR for each project. Therefore, in our example, it assumes that shareholders can reinvest funds in project C at 22.8% and in project D at 25.4%. But we have been told that both projects have the same risk (namely, cash flows are known with certainty). Why should investors be able to reinvest at one rate for project C and at another rate for project D? Obviously, the implicit reinvestment rate assumption in the IRR rule defies logic. Although the IRR does discount cash flows, it does not discount them at the opportunity cost of capital. Therefore, it violates the second of the four properties mentioned earlier.

2. The Value Additivity Principle

The fourth of the desirable properties of capital budgeting rules demands that managers be able to consider one project independently of all others. This is known as the value additivity principle and it implies that the value of the firm is equal to the sum of the values of each of its projects (Eq. 2.8). In order to demonstrate that the IRR rule can violate the value additivity principle, consider the three projects whose cash flows are given in Table 2.4. Projects 1 and 2 are mutually exclusive and project 3 is independent of them. If the value additivity principle holds, we should be able to choose the better of the two mutually exclusive projects without having to consider the independent project. The NPV's of the three projects as well as their IRR's are also given in Table 2.4. If we use the IRR rule to choose between projects 1 and 2, we would select project 1. But if we consider combinations of projects, then the IRR rule would prefer projects 2 and 3 to projects 1 and 3. In this example, the IRR rule does not obey the value additivity principle. The implication for management is that it

Table 2.4 Example of value additivity

Year	Project 1	Project 2	Project 3	PV factor at 10%	1 + 3	2 + 3
0	− 100	− 100	− 100	1.000	− 200	− 200
1	0	225	450	.909	450	675
2	550	0	0	.826	550	0

Project	NPV at 10%	IRR
1	354.30	134.5%
2	104.53	125.0%
3	309.05	350.0%
1 + 3	663.35	212.8%
2 + 3	413.58	237.5%

would have to consider all possible combinations of projects and choose the combination which has the greatest internal rate of return. If, for example, a firm had only five projects, it would need to consider 32 different combinations.[7]

The NPV rule always obeys the value additivity principle. Given that the opportunity cost of capital is 10%, we would choose project 1 as being the best either by itself or in combination with project 3. Note that the combinations of 1 and 3 or 2 and 3 are simply the sums of the NPV's of the projects considered separately. Consequently, if we adopt the NPV rule, the value of the firm is the sum of the values of the separate projects. Later (in Chapter 7) we shall see that this result holds even in a world with uncertainty where the firm may be considered as a portfolio of projects.

3. Multiple Rates of Return

Still another difficulty with the IRR rule is that it can result in multiple rates of return if the stream of estimated cash flows changes sign more than once. A classic example of this situation has come to be known as the oil well pump problem. An oil company is trying to decide whether or not to install a high-speed pump on a well which is already in operation. The estimated incremental cash flows are given in Table 2.5.

Table 2.5 Oil well pump incremental cash flows

Year	Estimated cash flow
0	− 1,600
1	10,000
2	− 10,000

[7] The number of combinations is

$$\binom{5}{0} + \binom{5}{1} + \binom{5}{2} + \binom{5}{3} + \binom{5}{4} + \binom{5}{5} = 32.$$

The pump will cost $1600 to install. During its first year of operation it will produce $10,000 more oil than the pump which is currently in place. But during the second year, the high-speed pump produces $10,000 less oil because the well has been depleted. The question is whether or not to accept the rapid pumping technique, which speeds up cash flows in the near term at the expense of cash flows in the long term. Figure 2.4 shows the NPV of the project for different discount rates. If the opportunity cost of capital is 10% the NPV rule would reject the project because it has negative NPV at that rate. If we are using the IRR rule, the project has two IRR's, 25% and 400%. Since both exceed the opportunity cost of capital, the project would probably be accepted.

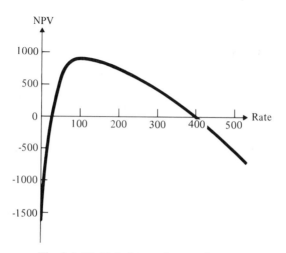

Fig. 2.4 Multiple internal rates of return

Mathematically, the multiple IRR's are a result of Descartes' rule of signs, which implies that every time the cash flows change signs there will be a new root to the problem solution. For the above example, the signs of cash flows change twice. The IRR is the rate which causes the discounted value of the cash flows to equal zero. Hence we solve the following equation for IRR.

$$NPV = 0 = \frac{-1600}{(1 + IRR)^0} + \frac{10,000}{(1 + IRR)^1} + \frac{-10,000}{(1 + IRR)^2}$$

$$0 = \frac{-1600(1 + IRR)^2 + 10,000(1 + IRR) - 10,000}{(1 + IRR)^2},$$

$$1600(1 + IRR)^2 - 10,000(1 + IRR) + 10,000 = 0.$$

This is clearly a quadratic equation and has two roots. It has the general form

$$ax^2 + bx + c = 0,$$

and can be solved using the quadratic formula

$$x = \frac{-b \pm \sqrt{b^2 - 4ac}}{2a}.$$

Therefore, for our example, the roots are

$$(1 + IRR) = x = \frac{10,000 \pm \sqrt{10,000^2 - 4(1600)10,000}}{2(1600)},$$

$$(1 + IRR) = \frac{10,000 \pm 6,000}{3200},$$

$$IRR = 25\% \quad \text{or} \quad 400\%.$$

An economic interpretation to the multiple root problem has been provided by Teichroew [1964]. We can think of the project as an investment, with the firm putting money into it twice: first, at the time of the initial investment, and again in the second time period. Also the project can be thought of as lending money to the firm in the first time period. Let us assume that the positive cash flows provided by the project to the firm are lent at 10%, the opportunity cost of capital. The cash flows provided by the firm to the project earn the IRR. Therefore, the firm invests $1600 and expects to earn the IRR at the end of the first time period. Mathematically,

$$1600(1 + IRR).$$

The difference between this result and the amount of money the project gives to the firm in the second period is the amount borrowed at rate, k, equal to the opportunity cost of capital, that is,

$$[10,000 - 1600(1 + IRR)](1 + k).$$

The firm then repays 10,000 at the end of the second period:

$$10,000 = [10,000 - 1600(1 + IRR)](1 + k).$$

Recalling that $k = 10\%$, we can solve for the rate of return on investment:

$$\frac{10,000 - 11,000}{-1760} = 1 + IRR,$$

$$-43.18\% = IRR.$$

This way of looking at the cash flows of the project solves the multiple root problem because positive cash flows provided by the project are assumed to be lent at a known rate of return equal to the opportunity cost of capital. This makes it possible to isolate the rate of return on money invested in the project. This rate can be thought of as the IRR. For the example of the oil well pump we see that when it is viewed properly, the IRR gives the same answer as the NPV. We should reject the project because the rate of return on investment is less than the opportunity cost of capital.

4. Summary of Comparison of IRR and NPV

The IRR rule errs in several ways. First it does not obey the value additivity principle, and consequently managers who use the IRR cannot consider projects independently of each other. Second, the IRR rule assumes that funds invested in projects have opportunity costs equal to the IRR for the project. This implicit reinvestment rate assumption violates the requirement that cash flows be discounted at the market-determined opportunity cost of capital. Finally, the IRR rule can lead to multiple rates of return whenever the sign of cash flows changes more than once. However, we saw that this problem can be avoided by the simple expedient of assuming that all positive cash flows are loaned to the firm by the project at the market opportunity cost and that the rate of return on negative cash flows invested in the project is the IRR.

The NPV rule avoids all the problems which the IRR is heir to. It obeys the value additivity principle, it correctly discounts at the opportunity cost of funds, and most important, it is precisely the same thing as maximizing the shareholders' wealth.

G. CASH FLOWS FOR CAPITAL BUDGETING PURPOSES

Up to this point we have made the implicit assumptions that the firm has no debt and that there are no corporate taxes. This section adds a note of realism by providing a definition of cash flows for capital budgeting purposes given debt and taxes. In particular, we shall see that some cash flows, such as interest paid on debt and repayment of principal on debt, should not be considered cash flows for capital budgeting purposes. At the same time, we shall demonstrate, by using an example, that there is only one definition of cash flows which is consistent with shareholder wealth maximization.

In order to understand discounted cash flows it is also necessary to have a rudimentary understanding of the opportunity cost of capital of the firm. Chapter 11 discusses the cost of capital in great depth; however, the basics will be given here. The firm receives its investment funds from two classes of investors: creditors and shareholders. They provide debt and equity capital respectively. Both groups expect to receive a rate of return which compensates them for the level of risk which they take.[8] Debt holders receive a stream of fixed payments and can force the firm into receivership or bankruptcy if they do not receive payment. On the other hand, shareholders receive the firm's residual cash flows which remain after all other payments are made. Consequently, the interest rate paid to debt holders is less than the required rate of return on equity because it is less risky. In a world without taxes the cost of capital would simply be a weighted average of the cost of debt and equity. However, in the real world the government allows corporations to deduct the interest paid on debt as an expense before paying taxes. This tax shield on debt payments makes the after-tax

---

[8] The assumption that future cash flows are known with certainty must be relaxed at this point, in order to allow risk-free debt and risky equity. The reader who is interested in the related theoretical problems is referred to Chapters 11 and 12.

cost of debt even less expensive from the firm's point of view. The after-tax weighted average cost of capital, k_0, is

$$k_0 = k_d(1 - \tau_c) \frac{B}{B + S} + k_e \frac{S}{B + S}, \qquad (2.12)$$

where

k_d = the before-tax cost of debt capital,
τ_c = the marginal corporate tax rate,
B = the market value of debt,
S = the market value of equity,
k_e = the cost of equity capital.

The weighted average cost of capital is the same as the market-determined opportunity cost of funds provided to the firm.

It is important to understand that projects undertaken by the firm must earn enough cash flow to provide the required rate of return to creditors, repayment of the face amount of debt, and payment of dividends to shareholders. Only when cash flows exceed these amounts will there be any gain in shareholders' wealth. When we discount cash flows at the weighted average cost of capital this is exactly what we are saying. A positive NPV is achieved only after creditors and shareholders receive their expected risk-adjusted rates of return.

In order to provide an example of this very important concept, consider the following (somewhat artificial) situation. We have a firm with 50% debt in its capital structure, a corporate tax rate of 50%, and equity holders who expect a 20% rate of return on equity. The firm is considering a five-year project which costs $1000 and will yield $400 per year for the life of the project. Furthermore, the firm uses straight-line depreciation, and the project will have zero salvage value at the end of its life. In order to maintain its current capital structure, the firm will finance the project with $500 of equity and a five-year bond which pays a coupon of $50 per year and returns the face value at the end of five years.

For their $500 investment shareholders require an annual dividend payment of $100, that is, 20% per year assuming no growth in dividends. If S_0 is their initial investment, its value is[9]

$$S_0 = \frac{D_1}{k_e}, \qquad \$500 = \frac{\$100}{.20}.$$

Bondholders require an annual coupon of $50 and the face value repaid at the end of five years. The present value of this stream of payments when discounted at their opportunity cost of capital is the market value of the bonds, B.

---

[9] Again, this is the Gordon growth model. However, since dividends do not grow, the growth rate is zero, $g = 0$.

$$B = \sum_{t=1}^{5} \frac{\text{coupon}}{(1 + k_d)^t} + \frac{\text{face value}_5}{(1 + k_d)^5},$$

$$\$500 = \frac{50}{1 + k_d} + \frac{50}{(1 + k_d)^2} + \frac{50}{(1 + k_d)^3} + \frac{50}{(1 + k_d)^4} + \frac{50}{(1 + k_d)^5} + \frac{500}{(1 + k_d)^5}.$$

Solving for k_d, we see that the cost of debt capital before taxes is

$$k_d = 10\%.$$

Therefore, the weighted average cost of capital after taxes is calculated by substituting k_d and k_e into Eq. (2.12):

$$k_0 = (.10)(1 - .50)\left(\frac{500}{500 + 500}\right) + .20\left(\frac{500}{500 + 500}\right)$$

$$= .05(.5) + .20(.5) = 12.5\%.$$

Now that we know the weighted average cost of capital, we need to discount the cash flows from the project in order to determine its net present value. But which cash flows do we use? Interest payments of $50 per year are definitely a cash outflow, but as we shall see, they should not be discounted if the project's NPV is to be consistent with shareholders' wealth.

In order to provide a definition of cash flow for capital budgeting purposes which can be discounted at the weighted average cost of capital, we turn to Table 2.6, which shows the project cash flows in each of the five years. The column of interest is residual cash flows which accrue to shareholders. We want to determine their value at the end of five years, then allow shareholders to remove their original investment. The result is the residual value of shareholders' wealth at the end of five years.

Table 2.6 Cash flows

Year	Inflow	Outflow	Depreciation	Interest	Tax	Net Cash	Dividends	Residual cash flows
0	1000	− 1000						
1	400		200	50	75	275	100	175
2	400		200	50	75	275	100	175
3	400		200	50	75	275	100	175
4	400		200	50	75	275	100	175
5	400	− 500	200	50	75	275	100	− 325

Referring to Table 2.6, the current cash flows are inflows of $500 in debt provided by creditors and $500 of equity provided by equity holders; outflows are $1000, which is the cost of the project. In years 1 through 4 the project returns $400 in cash after the cash costs of production are deducted from revenues. Then depreciation, a noncash cost, is deducted, leaving $200 in earnings before interest and taxes. The deduction of interest expenses leaves taxable income of $150. After taxes there is $75 in net income left over. However, the depreciation expense was not a cash charge, therefore $200 must be added back to get net cash flow after taxes. Shareholders withdraw their required $100 dividend, and what is left over, $175, becomes an addition to the shareholders' wealth. In the fifth year, cash flows provided by the project are the same, but bondholders must be repaid the face value of debt, $500. Therefore, the excess available for shareholders is -325. If we compound the residual cash flows to shareholders at the weighted average cost of capital and deduct the shareholders' initial investment, we will know exactly how much the project will increase the shareholders' wealth at the end of the fifth year. This is shown in Table 2.7. When shareholders take back the current value of their initial investment of $500 the increase in their wealth at the end of the fifth year is $122.85.[10] This represents the positive increment in wealth above their required rate of return of 20%. The present value of this wealth change is

$$PV = \$122.85(1.125)^{-5} = \$68.17.$$

Because the NPV of their wealth has increased, shareholders will be willing to undertake the project.

Table 2.7

Year	Residual cash flows	Future value factor at 12.5%	Future value
0	0	1.802	0
1	175	1.602	280.32
2	175	1.424	249.17
3	175	1.266	221.48
4	175	1.125	196.88
5	-325	1.000	-325.00
			622.85

The purpose of the above example was to emphasize the meaning of increase in shareholders' wealth. Their wealth increases only after creditors are repaid and after shareholders receive their expected return. Now let's look at the same problem in a different way. This time our purpose is to find a definition of cash flow for use in standard capital budgeting procedures which is consistent with maximizing shareholders' wealth. The appropriate definition of cash flow for capital budgeting purposes is after-tax cash flows from operations. Operating cash flows are revenues, R,

---

[10] We have assumed that common stock is a perpetual investment paying $100 per year forever. Therefore, if the cost of equity capital is 20%, the value of the stock at the end of the fifth year is $100 \div 20\% = \$500$.

minus direct cash costs or variable costs of operations, VC:

$$\text{Operating cash flows} = \Delta R - \Delta VC.$$

Taxes on operating cash flows are the tax rate, τ_c, times revenues less direct cash costs and depreciation (dep).

$$\text{Taxes on operating cash flows} = \tau_c(\Delta R - \Delta VC - \Delta\text{dep}).$$

Therefore, the correct definition of cash flows for capital budgeting purposes is[11]

$$\text{Cash flow for capital budgeting} = (\Delta R - \Delta VC) - \tau_c(\Delta R - \Delta VC - \Delta\text{dep})$$
$$= (\Delta R - \Delta VC)(1 - \tau_c) + \tau_c(\Delta\text{dep}). \qquad (2.13)$$

This definition is very different from the accounting definition of net income. For example, interest expenses and their tax shield are not included. The reason is that when we discount at the weighted average cost of capital we are implicitly assuming that the project will return the expected interest payments to creditors and the expected dividends to shareholders. Hence inclusion of interest payments (or dividends) as a cash flow to be discounted would be double counting. Furthermore, the tax shield provided by depreciation, $\tau_c(\Delta\text{dep})$, is treated as if it were a cash inflow. Table 2.8 shows the appropriate cash flows for capital budgeting. To demonstrate that these are the correct cash flows, we can discount them at the weighted average cost of capital. The resulting number should exactly equal the increment to the shareholders' wealth, that is, $68.17 (see Table 2.9). It is no coincidence that this works out correctly. We are discounting the after-tax cash flows from operations at

Table 2.8 Cash flows for capital budgeting

Year	Operating cash flow	Depreciation	Tax*	Cash flow
0	− 1000			− 1000
1	400	200	100	300
2	400	200	100	300
3	400	200	100	300
4	400	200	100	300
5	400	200	100	300

* The tax is the tax on operating income.

[11] An equivalent definition is

$$\text{Cash flow for capital budgeting} = \Delta\text{NI} + \Delta\text{dep} + (1 - \tau_c)\,\Delta rD \qquad (2.13a)$$

where NI stands for net income, the accounting definition of profit, and rD is the coupon rate on debt times the face value of debt. Although easier to use, it obscures the difference between cash flows for capital budgeting purposes and the accounting definition of profit.

Table 2.9

Year	Cash flow	PV factor at 12.5%	PV
0	− 1000	1.000	− 1000.00
1	300	.889	266.67
2	300	.790	237.04
3	300	.702	210.70
4	300	.624	187.29
5	300	.555	166.48
			68.18

the weighted average cost of capital. The result is exactly the same thing as the increase in shareholders' wealth. No other definition will work.

H. SUMMARY AND CONCLUSION

The objective of the firm is assumed to be the maximization of shareholders' wealth. Toward this end managers should take projects with positive NPV's down to the point where the NPV of the last acceptable project is zero. When cash flows are properly defined for capital budgeting purposes and are discounted at the weighted average cost of capital, the NPV of a project is exactly the same as the increase in shareholders' wealth. Given perfect capital markets, the owners of the firm will unanimously support the acceptance of all projects with positive NPV. Other decision criteria, such as the payback method, the accounting rate of return, and the IRR, do not necessarily guarantee the acceptance of projects which maximize shareholders' wealth.

PROBLEM SET

2.1 *Basic capital budgeting problem with straight-line depreciation.* The Roberts Company has cash inflows of $140,000 per year on project A and cash outflows of $100,000 per year. The investment outlay on the project is $100,000; its life is 10 years; the tax rate τ_c is 40%. The applicable cost of capital is 12%.

a) Present two alternative formulations of the net cash flows adjusted for the depreciation tax shelter.

b) Calculate the net present value for project A, using straight-line depreciation for tax purposes.

2.2 *Basic capital budgeting problem with accelerated depreciation.* Assume the same facts as in Problem 2.1 except that the earnings before depreciation, interest, and taxes are $22,000 per year.

a) Calculate the net present value, using straight-line depreciation, for tax purposes.

b) Calculate the net present value, using the sum-of-the-years digits method of accelerated depreciation, for tax purposes.

2.3 *Basic replacement problem.* The Virginia Company is considering replacing a riveting machine with a new design that will increase the earnings before depreciation from $20,000 per year to $51,000 per year. The new machine will cost $100,000 and have an estimated life of 8 years with no salvage value. The applicable corporate tax rate is 40% and the firm's cost of capital is 12%. The old machine has been fully depreciated and has no salvage value. Should it be replaced by the new machine?

2.4 *Replacement problem when old machine has a positive book value.* Assume the same facts as in Problem 2.3 except that the Virginia Company will be able to realize an investment tax credit of 7% on the purchase of the new machine which will have a salvage value of $12,000. Assume further that the old machine has a book value of $40,000 with a remaining life of eight years. If replaced, the old machine can, at present, be sold for $15,000. Should the machine replacement be made?

2.5 *Cash flows.* The Cary Company is considering a new investment which costs $10,000. It will last five years and have no salvage value. The project would save $3000 in salaries and wages each year and would be financed with a loan with interest costs of 15% per year and amortization costs (repayment of principal on the loan) of $2000 per year. If the firm's tax rate is 40% and its after-tax cost of capital is 20%, what is the present value of the project? [*Note:* The annuity factor for five years at 20% is 2.991.]

2.6 Calculate the internal rate of return for the following set of cash flows.

t_1:   400
t_2:   400
t_3: -1000

If the opportunity cost of capital is 10%, should the project be accepted?

2.7 The Ambergast Corporation is considering a project which has a three-year life and costs $1200. It would save $360 per year in operating costs and increase revenue by $200 per year. It would be financed with a three-year loan with the following payment schedule (the annual rate of interest is 5%).

Payment	Interest	Repayment of Principal	Balance
440.65	60.00	380.65	819.35
440.65	40.97	399.68	419.67
440.65	20.98	419.67	0
	121.95	1200.00	

If the company has a 10% after-tax cost of capital, a 40% tax rate, and uses straight-line depreciation, what is the net present value of the project?

2.8 The treasurer of United Southern Capital Co. has submitted a proposal to the board of directors which, he argues, will increase profits for the all-equity company by a whopping 55%. It costs $900 and saves $290 in labor costs, providing a 3.1 year payback even though the equipment has an expected five-year life (with no salvage value). If the firm has a 50% tax rate, uses straight-line depreciation, and has a 10% after-tax cost of capital, should the project be accepted? Income statements before and after the project are given in Tables Q2.1 and Q2.2, respectively.

Table Q2.1

Before	Year 1	Year 2	Year 3	Year 4	Year 5
Revenue	1000	1000	1000	1000	1000
Variable cost	500	500	500	500	500
Fixed cost	300	300	300	300	300
Net operating income	200	200 ·	200	200	200
Interest expense	0	0	0	0	0
Earnings before taxes	200	200	200	200	200
Taxes	− 100	− 100	− 100	− 100	− 100
Net income	100	100	100	100	100

Table Q2.2

After	Year 1	Year 2	Year 3	Year 4	Year 5
Revenue	1000	1000	1000	1000	1000
Variable cost	210	210	210	210	210
Fixed cost	480	480	480	480	480
Net operating income	310	310	310	310	310
Interest expense	0	0	0	0	0
Earnings before taxes	310	310	310	310	310
Taxes	− 155	− 155	− 155	− 155	− 155
Net income	155	155	155	155	155

2.9 The cash flow for projects A, B, and C are given below. Calculate the payback period and net present value for each project (assume a 10% discount rate). If A and B are mutually exclusive and C is independent, which project, or combination of projects, is preferred using (a) the payback method or (b) the net present value method? What do the results tell you about the value additivity properties of the payback method?

		Project	
Year	A	B	C
0	− 1	− 1	− 1
1	0	1	0
2	2	0	0
3	− 1	1	3

2.10 Calculate the internal rate of return on the following set of cash flows, according to Teichroew's economic interpretation of internal rate of return. Assume that the opportunity cost of capital is 10%.

Year	Cash flow
0	− 5,000
1	10,000
2	− 3,000

REFERENCES

BIERMAN, H. JR., and S. SMIDT, *The Capital Budgeting Decision*, 4th ed. Macmillan, New York, 1975.

BODENHORN, D., "A Cash-Flow Concept of Profit," *The Journal of Finance*, March 1964, pp. 16–31.

CYERT, R. M., and J. G. MARCH, *A Behavioral Theory of the Firm*. Prentice-Hall, Englewood Cliffs, N.J., 1963.

GAGNON, J.-M., "The Purchase-Pooling Choice: Some Empirical Evidence," *The Journal of Accounting Research*, Spring 1971, 52–72.

HIRSHLEIFER, J., *Investment, Interest and Capital*. Prentice-Hall, Englewood Cliffs, N.J., 1970.

HONG, H., R. S. KAPLAN, and G. MANDELKER, "Pooling vs. Purchase: The Effects of Accounting Mergers on Stock Prices," *The Accounting Review*, January 1978, 31–47.

JENSEN, M., and W. MECKLING, "Theory of the Firm: Managerial Behavior, Agency Costs and Ownership Structure," *Journal of Financial Economics*, October 1976, 305–360.

MACHLUP, F., "Theories of the Firm: Marginalist, Behavioral, Managerial," *The American Economic Review*, March 1967, 1–33.

MARSCHAK, J., and R. RADNER, *Economic Theory of Teams* (Cowles Foundation Monograph 22). Yale University Press, 1972.

STERN, J., "Earnings Per Share Doesn't Count," *Financial Analysis Journal*, July/August, 1974, 39–43.

SUNDER, S., "Stock Price and Risk Related to Accounting Changes in Inventory Valuation," *Accounting Review*, April 1975, 305–315.

———, "Relationship between Accounting Changes and Stock Prices: Problems of Measurement and Some Empirical Evidence," *Empirical Research in Accounting: Selected Studies*, 1973, 1–45.

TEICHROEW, D., *An Introduction to Management Science: Deterministic Models*. Wiley, New York, 1964, 78–82.

WILLIAMSON, O. E., *The Economics of Discretionary Behavior: Managerial Objectives in a Theory of the Firm*. Prentice-Hall, Englewood Cliffs, N.J., 1964.

Chapter 3

More Advanced
Capital Budgeting Topics

*The basic problem of time valuation which Nature sets us is always that of
translating the future into the present, that is, the problem of
ascertaining the capital value of future income.*

Irving Fisher, *The Theory of Interest*,
Macmillan, New York, 1930, p. 14

A. INTRODUCTION

Although Chapter 2 introduced the net present value (NPV) criterion, there were several implied assumptions which require further investigation. For example, all of the illustrations in Chapter 2 assumed that mutually exclusive projects had the same life and scale. What happens when these assumptions are relaxed? This question is dealt with in the first part of this chapter.

Next, we turn the usual capital budgeting problem around and attempt to determine the optimal life for a project with growing cash flows. For example, when should growing trees be harvested or aging wine be bottled? Finally, let us suppose that the firm is operating under a fixed budget. How will this affect the project selection process?

The above topics are not usually covered in introductory finance texts. One reason is that they require more than an introductory level of mathematical sophistication. For example, the optimal harvest problem requires calculus optimization techniques (see Appendix D), and multiperiod constrained capital budgeting requires linear programming. The reader who is not interested in the mathematics need read only the introduction and conclusion to Sections C.2 and D.2 of this chapter.

The last topic covered is capital budgeting under inflation. Needless to say, there has been growing interest over the last decade in this important applied problem. The reader should be cautioned, however, that solution techniques assume that future rates of inflation are known with certainty. Therefore, an important element of realism, namely uncertainty, is lacking. Capital budgeting under uncertainty is covered in Chapter 10.

B. CAPITAL BUDGETING TECHNIQUES IN PRACTICE

Chapter 2 argued that the NPV and the internal rate of return (IRR) techniques of capital budgeting were the most sophisticated of the four commonly used criteria. They both consider cash flows (not earnings per share) and discount them in order to take into account the time value of money. Yet the question often arises: Do corporations actually employ these techniques?

A survey of large corporations conducted by Thomas Klammer [1972] and reported in the *Journal of Business* has provided an estimate of the actual usage of different capital budgeting techniques. His results are duplicated in Table 3.1.

Approximately 180 firms responded in 1970, 150 in 1964, and 145 in 1959. For our purposes the most interesting statistic is the most sophisticated primary evaluation standard. Note the increased usage of discounted cash flow techniques such as

Table 3.1 Project evaluation techniques

Technique	Percentage using in*		
	1970	1964	1959
Profit contribution analysis required:			
For over 75% of projects	53	53	50
For 25%–75% of projects	41	40	34
For less than 25% of projects	6	7	16
Total	100	100	100
Minimum profitability standards required:			
For most projects	77	65	58
For some projects	13	23	20
For few projects	10	12	22
Total	100	100	100
Most sophisticated primary evaluation standard:			
Discounting (rate of return or present worth)	57	38	19
Accounting rate of return	26	30	34
Payback or payback reciprocal	12	24	34
Urgency	5	8	13
Total	100	100	100

* Percentages shown are yes divided by yes + no multiplied by 100.

Klammer, T., "Empirical Evidence of the Adoption of Sophisticated Capital Budgeting Techniques," reprinted from *The Journal of Business*, July 1972, 393.

the IRR or NPV and the simultaneous decrease in payback. With the advent of computer technology it is very easy to use the more sophisticated, and more correct, discounted cash flow techniques. If the trend continues, by 1978 over 80% of large (Fortune 500) corporations will have switched to discounted cash flows as their most sophisticated primary evaluation technique.

C. PROJECTS WITH DIFFERENT LIVES

All the examples used in Chapter 2 compared projects with the same life. Now we turn our attention toward the choice among mutually exclusive projects with different lives. We begin by demonstrating the correct technique. It uses the NPV rule assuming that projects are replicated indefinitely at constant scale. Next, we borrow from Hirshleifer [1970] to show why the NPV criterion (when correctly formulated) is superior to the IRR criterion given that projects have different lives.

1.   An NPV Technique for Evaluating Projects with Different Lives

Consider the cash flows estimated for the two projects in Table 3.2. If the opportunity cost of capital is 10%, the (simple) NPV's of the projects are

$$\text{NPV (project } A) = 41\text{¢}, \qquad \text{NPV (project } B) = 50\text{¢}.$$

However, it makes sense that if the projects can be replicated at constant scale, project A should be superior to project B because it recovers cash flow faster. In order to compare projects with different lives we compute the NPV of an infinite stream of constant scale replications. Let $\text{NPV}(N, \infty)$ be the NPV of an N-year project with $\text{NPV}(N)$, replicated forever. This is exactly the same as an annuity paid at the beginning of the first period and at the end of every N years from that time on. The NPV of the annuity is

$$\text{NPV}(N, \infty) = \text{NPV}(N) + \frac{\text{NPV}(N)}{(1+k)^N} + \frac{\text{NPV}(N)}{(1+k)^{2N}} + \cdots. \tag{3.1}$$

In order to obtain a closed-form formula, let

$$\frac{1}{(1+k)^N} = U.$$

Table 3.2 Projects with different lives

Year	Project A	Project B
0	-10	-10
1	6	4
2	6	4
3		4.75

Then we have

$$NPV(N, \infty) = NPV(N)(1 + U + U^2 + \cdots + U^n). \tag{3.2}$$

Multiplying both sides by U, this becomes

$$U[NPV(N, \infty)] = NPV(N)(U + U^2 + \cdots + U^n + U^{n+1}). \tag{3.3}$$

Subtracting Eq. (3.3) from (3.2) gives

$$NPV(N, \infty) - U\,NPV(N, \infty) = NPV(N)(1 - U^{n+1}),$$

$$NPV(N, \infty) = \frac{NPV(N)(1 - U^{n+1})}{1 - U}.$$

And taking the limit as the number of replications, n, approaches infinity gives

$$\lim_{n \to \infty} NPV(N, \infty) = \frac{NPV(N)}{1 - U} = NPV(N)\left[\frac{1}{1 - [1/(1 + k)^N]}\right],$$

$$NPV(N, \infty) = NPV(N)\left[\frac{(1 + k)^N}{(1 + k)^N - 1}\right]. \tag{3.4}$$

Equation (3.4) is the NPV of an N-year project replicated at constant scale an infinite number of times. We can use it to compare projects with different lives because when their cash flow streams are replicated forever it is as if they had the same (infinite) life.

In our example, the value of the two-year project, A, replicated at constant scale forever, is

$$NPV(2, \infty) = NPV(2)\left[\frac{(1 + .10)^2}{(1 + .10)^2 - 1}\right]$$

$$= (\$.41)\left[\frac{1.21}{.21}\right]$$

$$= \$2.36,$$

and for project B, the three-year project, we have

$$NPV(3, \infty) = NPV(3)\left[\frac{(1.10)^3}{(1.10)^3 - 1}\right]$$

$$= (\$.50)\left(\frac{1.33}{.33}\right)$$

$$= \$2.02.$$

Consequently, we would choose to accept project A over project B, because when the cash flows are adjusted for different project lives, A provides the greater cash flow. We could also multiply the NPV's of the infinitely replicated projects by the opportunity cost of capital to obtain what is called the annual equivalent value which is given in Eq. (3.5).[1]

$$k\text{NPV}(N, \infty) = \text{NPV}(N)\left[\frac{k(1 + k)^N}{(1 + k)^N - 1}\right]. \tag{3.5}$$

This decision rule is equivalent to that provided by Eq. (3.4).

2. The Duration Problem

We have just seen that when projects have different lives the simple NPV rule, when misused, can lead to incorrect decisions. The correct NPV rule compares the NPV of infinite streams of projects, assuming that they are replicated at constant scale. But why is this the correct decision criterion? Why does it maximize the NPV of the shareholders' wealth when a simple comparison of NPV's or use of the IRR rule does not?

An interesting type of problem which highlights the differences between simple NPV, NPV with infinite replication at constant scale, and IRR is the determination of the optimal life, or duration, of a project. For example, when should growing trees be harvested or when should aging wine be bottled?

.*a. Using the Simple NPV Rule to Solve the Duration Problem*   Assume that we own a growing stand of trees. Let the revenue, R_t, which can be obtained from harvesting them at time t be represented by the expression

$$R_t = 10,000\sqrt{1 + t}.$$

Also, let the initial cost, c, be \$15,000 and the opportunity cost of capital be 5% compounded continuously.[2] Figure 3.1 is a graph of the revenues as a function of time. Note that the vertical axis is a logarithmic scale so that geometrically increasing functions, for example continuously compounded interest, appear as straight lines.

First, we shall determine the harvesting time which maximizes the simple NPV of the project. For a project with a life of t years,

$$\text{NPV} = R_t e^{-kt} - c.$$

In order to find the harvesting time, t, which maximizes the NPV, we take the first derivative of NPV with respect to t and set it equal to zero:

$$\frac{d\text{NPV}}{dt} = -kR_t e^{-kt} + \frac{dR_t}{dt} e^{-kt} = 0.$$

---

[1] Note that Eq. (3.5) is equivalent to

$$k\text{NPV}(N, \infty) = \frac{\text{NPV}(N)}{\text{annuity factor}},$$

where annuity factor $= [1 - (1 + k)^{-N}]/k$.

[2] Appendix A contains a complete reference to the mathematics of continuous compounding.

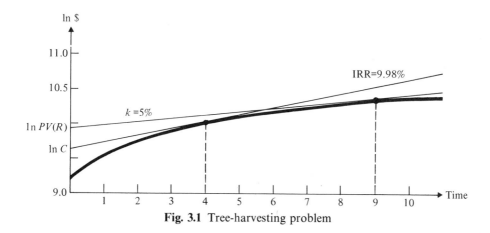

Fig. 3.1 Tree-harvesting problem

Solving for k, we have

$$k = \frac{dR_t/dt}{R_t},$$

which says that the NPV is maximized when the marginal rate of return, $(dR_t/dt)/R_t$, is equal to the opportunity cost of capital, k. Graphically, this is the point of tangency between the straight line whose slope is 5% and the revenue function. As shown in Fig. 3.1, tangency occurs at $t = 9$ years. The same result can be shown mathematically by using the revenue function to solve for marginal revenue and setting the result equal to $k = 5\%$. The revenue function is

$$R_t = 10,000(1 + t)^{1/2}.$$

Its derivative with respect to t is the marginal revenue

$$\frac{dR_t}{dt} = \frac{1}{2}(10,000)(1 + t)^{-1/2},$$

and the marginal rate of return is

$$\frac{dR_t/dt}{R_t} = \frac{5,000(1 + t)^{-1/2}}{10,000(1 + t)^{1/2}} = \frac{1}{2(1 + t)}.$$

Setting this equal to the opportunity cost of capital, k, we get

$$\frac{1}{2(1 + t)} = .05, \qquad t = 9 \text{ years}.$$

b. Using the IRR Rule to Solve the Duration Problem   Next, we would like to compare the simple NPV result with the harvest time which maximizes the IRR on the project. The IRR is the rate which sets the NPV of the project equal to zero.

Mathematically, this is

$$\text{NPV} = 0 = R_t e^{-(\text{IRR})t} - c.$$

Adding c to both sides and taking the natural logarithm, we have

$$\ln R_t - (\text{IRR})t = \ln c,$$

and solving for IRR, we have

$$\text{IRR} = \frac{1}{t} \ln \left(\frac{R_t}{c} \right).$$

Substituting in the revenue function, we obtain

$$\text{IRR} = \frac{1}{t} \ln \left[\frac{10,000(1 + t)^{1/2}}{15,000} \right].$$

If we try different values of t, the project life which maximizes the IRR at a value of 9.98% is four years.

We can find this result graphically in Fig. 3.1 by rotating a line which passes through an intercept of $\ln c$ (at $t = 0$, if the NPV of revenue is equal to $\ln c$, then the NPV of the project is zero) until it is just tangent to the revenue curve. The point of tangency gives the optimal harvest time, four years, and the slope of the line is the maximum IRR, 9.98%.

It is frequently argued that the IRR rule gives the best solution to the simple duration problem. However, this is incorrect because the IRR rule implicitly assumes that the funds provided in the project can continuously be reinvested in projects with proportional expansion of scale. In other words, we started out in our example with an investment of $15,000. After four years we would reinvest

$$\$15,000 e^{\text{IRR}(t)} = \$22,359,$$

and so on, in ever increasing amounts. So long as the IRR is greater than the opportunity cost of capital (5% in our example) the present value of an infinite replication of a proportionately growing stream of projects is infinite. This is patently absurd.

c. Using the NPV Rule with Constant Scale Replication   The correct formulation of the optimal duration problem is to assume that the project can be replicated indefinitely at constant scale. In the tree-harvesting problem this is equivalent to assuming that once the trees are harvested, the same acreage is replanted so that the project begins again at constant scale.

If the project is reformulated with constant scale replication, the NPV of an infinite stream of projects would be

$$\text{NPV} = -c + (R_t - c)e^{-kt} + (R_t - c)e^{-2kt} + \cdots.$$

The second term is the present value of the revenue received at the time of harvest less the cash outlay for replanting at constant scale. The third term is the present value of the cash flows at the time of the second harvest, and so on. The NPV of this stream is

$$\text{NPV} = -c + \frac{R_t - c}{e^{kt} - 1}.$$

In order to maximize, we set the derivative of the NPV with respect to project life, t, equal to zero.[3]

$$\frac{d\text{NPV}}{dt} = \frac{dR_t}{dt} - \frac{(R_t - c)k}{1 - e^{-kt}} = 0, \qquad \frac{dR_t}{dt} = \frac{(R_t - c)k}{1 - e^{-kt}}.$$

Using the numbers from our example, we get

$$\frac{5000}{(1 + t)^{1/2}} = \frac{(10,000(1 + t)^{1/2} - 15,000).05}{1 - e^{-.05t}}.$$

Table 3.3 shows the values at the left- and right-hand sides of the solution for various values of t. The optimal duration is approximately 4.6 years. This answer lies between the solution for simple duration with the NPV rule (nine years) and replication with proportionately increasing scale using the IRR rule (four years).

Table 3.3 Solution to the duration problem with constant scale replication

t	Left-hand side	Right-hand side	Difference
4	2236.07	2033.31	202.76
4.5	2132.20	2097.76	34.44
4.6	2112.89	2108.81	4.08
5	2041.24	2146.38	− 105.14

d. A Comparison of the Three Techniques for Solving the Duration Problem   Table 3.4 compares the three project evaluation techniques (simple NPV, IRR, and NPV with constant scale replication) for projects of different lives. All three projects have the same scale because each requires an outlay of $15,000. However, their lives vary

---

[3]
$$\frac{d\text{NPV}}{dt} = \frac{d}{dt}[-c + (R_t - c)(e^{kt} - 1)^{-1}] = 0,$$

$$= \frac{dR_t}{dt}(e^{kt} - 1)^{-1} + [(R_t - c)](-1)(e^{kt} - 1)^{-2}ke^{kt} = 0.$$

$$= \frac{dR_t}{dt}(e^{kt} - 1) - (R_t - c)ke^{kt} = 0,$$

$$= \frac{dR_t}{dt} = \frac{k(R_t - c)}{1 - e^{-kt}}.$$

Table 3.4 Comparison of three techniques

		A	B	C
Initial outlay		− 15,000	− 15,000	− 15,000
Cash inflow at t years	4.0 years	22,361	0	0
	4.6 years	0	23,664	0
	9.0 years	0	0	31,623
IRR		9.98%	9.91%	8.29%
Simple NPV		3,308	3,802	5,164
NPV with constant scale replication		18,246	18,505	14,249

between four and nine years. An important question is: How much would you pay to purchase the forestry operation assuming that you harvest after t years, then replant, and that the time value of money to you is 5%? The answer is $18,505. It is the current value of the forestry operation because it represents the present value of the cash stream provided by the operation into the indefinite future.

The above example demonstrates that the correct procedure for comparing projects with different lives is the same as the correct solution to the optimal duration problem. Both require that NPV maximization be formulated as the maximization of the NPV of a stream of projects replicated at constant scale.

D. CONSTRAINED CAPITAL BUDGETING PROBLEMS

A capital budgeting constraint implies that the firm can obtain only N dollars of funding at a fixed cost of capital. Implicitly the cost of capital in excess of N dollars is infinite. Therefore the firm is limited to a fixed budget. Most economists would agree that strict capital budgets simply do not exist in the real world. For example, consider a small firm with a "budget" of only a few thousand dollars of capital which suddenly acquires a new patent for economically converting garbage into gasoline. Certainly the firm would not find it very difficult to raise large amounts of money even though its initial budget was quite limited. As long as capital markets are reasonably efficient, it will always be possible for a firm to raise an indefinite amount of money so long as the projects are expected to have a positive net present value.

Weingartner [1977] discusses capital rationing in terms of situations imposed from within the firm and those imposed by the capital market. Self-imposed expenditure limits may arise to preserve corporate control or reflect the view of owners of closely held firms that the sale of the firm as a whole at a future date will provide a greater present value of wealth than the piecemeal sale that may permit faster growth. Externally imposed capital rationing could result from an attitude of the capital markets that providing funds beyond a specific amount would lead to increased risks of high bankruptcy costs—so high that feasible interest rates would not be adequate compensation. An aspect of this is the "Penrose effect" which holds that the organizational problems of obtaining and training additional personnel are large. Hence growth that involves increasing the organization's size by more than some percentage, for example 50%, in one year is fraught with high risks of organizational inefficiencies which increase risks of bankruptcy and give rise to high costs due to the loss of efficiency of a previously effectively functioning organization system or firm.

Although it is hard to justify the assumption of limited capital, nevertheless we shall review various decision-making techniques, assuming that capital constraints do, in fact, exist.

1. Projects with Different Scale. The Present Value Index (PVI)

Suppose we are comparing two projects which have the same life. Project A costs $1,000,000 and has a net present value of $1,000, while project B costs $10 and has a net present value of $500. It is very tempting to argue that project B is better because it returns more net present value per dollar of cost. However, the NPV rule is very clear. If these are mutually exclusive projects, the correct decision is to take the one that has the highest NPV, project A.

But let us assume that there is a meaningful capital constraint imposed on our firm. How should the NPV rule be modified to consider projects of different scale? Table 3.5 shows the present value of the cash inflows and outflows of four independent projects which have identical lives. If there were no capital constraint we would accept all four projects because they all have positive NPV's. Project 1 has the highest NPV, followed by projects 3, then 2, and finally 4. Suppose that there is a capital constraint which limits our spending to $300,000 or less. Now we would accept only projects 2 and 3 because they have the greatest NPV among those combinations of projects which use no more than $300,000. The logic leading to this decision is formalized by what is known as the *present value index* (PVI).

Table 3.5 Present value index

Project	PV of inflows	Current outflows	PVI	NPV
1	230,000	200,000	1.15	30,000
2	141,250	125,000	1.13	16,250
3	194,250	175,000	1.11	19,250
4	162,000	150,000	1.08	12,000

The PVI is defined as the present value of cash inflows divided by the present value of cash outflows:

$$PVI = \frac{\text{Present value of inflows}}{\text{Present value of outflows}}. \qquad (3.6)$$

When used correctly, it is equivalent to maximizing the NPV of a set of projects subject to the constraint that project outlays be less than or equal to the firm's budget. The PVI for each project is given in Table 3.5. The PVI of excess funds, not invested in any of the projects, is always assumed to be equal to 1.0. (Why?)

The objective is to compare all sets of projects which meet the budget and find the one which maximizes the weighted average PVI. For example, if projects 2 and 3 are selected, the weighted average PVI is

$$\text{PVI} = \frac{125,000}{300,000}(1.13) + \frac{175,000}{300,000}(1.11) = 1.1183.$$

It is computed by multiplying the PVI of each project by the percentage of the total budget allocated to it. If project 1 is selected, no additional project can be undertaken; therefore the PVI for project 1 is

$$\text{PVI} = \frac{200,000}{300,000}(1.15) + \frac{100,000}{300,000}(1.00) = 1.1000.$$

Project 1 is not preferred to projects 2 and 3 because $100,000 must be invested in marketable securities which have a PVI of 1.0 (i.e., their cost is always equal to the present value of their cash inflows).

The PVI can be used to solve simple problems where there is a one-period capital constraint. It can also be used to compare mutually exclusive projects of different scale although a simple comparison of NPV's provides the same result. For example, refer to projects A and B (Section D.1). The first project cost $1,000,000 and had an NPV of $1,000 while the second cost only $10 and had an NPV of $500. If these are the only two projects available to the firm and if they are mutually exclusive, we can evaluate them by comparing their PVI's with the assumption that the firm has a $1,000,000 budget.[4]

The PVI of project A is

$$\frac{1,000,000}{1,000,000}\left(\frac{1,001,000}{1,000,000}\right) = 1.001,$$

and the PVI of project B is

$$\frac{10}{1,000,000}\left(\frac{510}{10}\right) + \frac{999,990}{1,000,000}(1.0) = 1.0005.$$

Because project A has a higher PVI it is superior. The PVI solution is exactly the same as the NPV solution; that is, we take the project with the highest NPV. The PVI merely helps to highlight the assumption that if the projects really are mutually

---

[4] We could also assume any budget whatsoever as long as it is greater than $1,000,000 without changing the results. (Why?)

exclusive, then the extra $999,990 which is not invested in project B must be invested in marketable securities with a PVI of 1.0.

Usually, the projects to be compared are not so exaggerated as the above example; however, it does help to illustrate the meaning of a capital constraint. If a strict budget exists, then the PVI should be used. Otherwise the firm should accept all projects with a positive NPV.

2. Multiperiod Capital Constraints. Programming Solutions

The capital constraint problem can be extended to consider budget constraints $(C_0, C_1, \ldots, C_t)$ in many future time periods. If we assume that it is possible to undertake fractions of projects then the problem may be formulated using linear programming. If projects are indivisible, then integer programming may be used. With binding capital constraints it is conceivable that a project with negative NPV may be accepted in the optimal solution if it supplies the funds needed during a later time period to undertake very profitable projects.

A great deal has been written on the topic of constrained capital budgeting.[5] However, because of space limitations, only the simplest model is presented here. Lorie and Savage [1955] posed the two-period problem given in Table 3.6.

Table 3.6 Two-period capital constraint

Project	Period-1 outlay	Period-2 outlay	NPV
1	12	3	14
2	54	7	17
3	6	6	17
4	6	2	15
5	30	35	40
6	6	6	12
7	48	4	14
8	36	3	10
9	18	3	12

Let us assume that cash flows cannot be transferred between time periods, that projects are infinitely divisible, and that the cash budget in period 1 is $50 while in period 2 it is $22. The problem is to find the set of projects which maximizes NPV and satisfies the cash constraints. Weingartner [1963] solved the problem by using linear programming. If we designate b_j as the NPV of each project, X_j as the fraction of each project which is accepted, c_{tj} as the cash outlay used by the jth project in the

---

[5] The interested reader is referred to Lorie and Savage [1955], Weingartner [1963], Baumol and Quandt [1965], Carleton [1969], Bernhard [1969], and Myers [1972] as an excellent set of references.

tth time period, and C_t as the cash budget, the linear programming problem is written as

$$\text{MAX} \quad \sum b_j X_j, \quad \text{(Primal problem)} \qquad (3.7)$$

$$\text{subject to} \quad \sum c_{tj} X_j \leq C_t,$$

$$X_j \leq 1.$$

If S_t and q_j are designated as slack variables, the primal problem can be rewritten as

$$\text{MAX} \quad \sum b_j X_j, \qquad (3.8)$$

$$\text{subject to} \quad \sum c_{tj} X_j + S_t = C_t,$$

$$X_j + q_j = 1.$$

The objective is to choose the set of weights, X_j, which maximize the combined NPV of all projects. The constraints require (1) that the set of projects undertaken use less cash than is budgeted and (2) that no more than 100% of any project be undertaken.

Every linear programming problem has a counterpart called the *dual problem* where the primal constraints appear in the dual objective function and the primal decision variables become dual constraints. The dual for this problem can be written as

$$\text{MIN} \quad \sum \rho_t C_t + \mu_j \cdot 1 \qquad (3.9)$$

$$\text{subject to} \quad \sum \rho_t c_{tj} + \mu_j - \gamma_j = b_j, \quad \text{(Dual problem)}$$

$$\rho_t, \mu_j \geq 0.$$

The dual introduces three new variables, ρ_t, μ_j, and γ_j. The last, γ_j, is a slack variable. We can define μ_j by using the notion of complementary slackness. When one of the projects enters into the primal solution (that is, $X_j > 0$), then the corresponding constraint in the dual is binding and therefore $\gamma_j = 0$. Thus the dual constraint can be written as an equality

$$\sum \rho_t c_{tj} + \mu_j = b_j,$$

or, solving for μ_j, we have

$$\mu_j = b_j - \sum \rho_t c_{tj}. \qquad (3.10)$$

Therefore, μ_j may be thought of as the difference between the NPV of a project's cash flows, b_j, and the imputed value of the outlays needed to undertake the project, $\sum \rho_t c_{tj}$. Conceptually, it is similar to the PVI in the single-period problem because it is a measure of the benefit (NPV) minus the imputed cash cost of a project. Finally, ρ_t may be thought of as the implicit one-period discount rate caused by the cash constraints in the linear programming problem. It is the value of relaxing the cash constraint by one dollar, the shadow price. This can be demonstrated by using (3.10) and noting that for fractionally accepted projects, where the constraint is binding, $\mu_j = 0$. Therefore, (3.10) becomes

$$\sum \rho_t c_{tj} = b_j.$$

This says that the NPV of a project, b_j, equals the discounted value of its cash flows. Consequently ρ_t is the one-period discount rate

$$\rho_t = \frac{1}{1 + {_0}r_{t+1}}. \tag{3.11}$$

Table 3.7 shows the linear programming problem and solution to the Lorie-Savage problem. Projects 1, 3, 4, and 9 are accepted, and projects 6 and 7 are fractionally accepted into the optimal solution which has a NPV of $70.27. Cash constraints in both time periods are binding since the primal slacks, S_1 and S_2, are zero. The project

Table 3.7 Linear programming model and solution

Maximize:

$$14x_1 + 17x_2 + 17x_3 + 15x_4 + 40x_5 + 12x_6 + 14x_7 + 10x_8 + 12x_9$$

Subject to:

$$12x_1 + 54x_2 + 6x_3 + 6x_4 + 30x_5 + 6x_6 + 48x_7 + 36x_8 + 18x_9 + s_1 = 50$$
$$3x_1 + 7x_2 + 6x_3 + 2x_4 + 35x_5 + 6x_6 + 4x_7 + 3x_8 + 3x_9 + s_2 = 20$$

$x_1 + q_1 = 1$	$x_4 + q_4 = 1$	$x_7 + q_7 = 1$
$x_2 + q_2 = 1$	$x_5 + q_5 = 1$	$x_8 + q_8 = 1$
$x_3 + q_3 = 1$	$x_6 + q_6 = 1$	$x_9 + q_9 = 1$

Solution	Primal slack	Dual variable	Dual slacks
$x_1^* = 1.0$	$q_1^* = 0$	$\mu_1^* = 6.77$	$\gamma_1^* = 0$
$x_2^* = 0$	$q_2^* = 1.0$	$\mu_2^* = 0$	$\gamma_2^* = 3.41$
$x_3^* = 1.0$	$q_3^* = 0$	$\mu_3^* = 5.0$	$\gamma_3^* = 0$
$x_4^* = 1.0$	$q_4^* = 0$	$\mu_4^* = 10.45$	$\gamma_4^* = 0$
$x_5^* = 0$	$q_5^* = 1$	$\mu_5^* = 0$	$\gamma_5^* = 29.32$
$x_6^* = 0.970$	$q_6^* = 0.030$	$\mu_6^* = 0$	$\gamma_6^* = 0$
$x_7^* = 0.045$	$q_7^* = 0.955$	$\mu_7^* = 0$	$\gamma_7^* = 0$
$x_8^* = 0$	$q_8^* = 1.0$	$\mu_8^* = 0$	$\gamma_8^* = 0.5$
$x_9^* = 1.0$	$q_9^* = 0$	$\mu_9^* = 3.95$	$\gamma_9^* = 0$

$$s_1^* = 0 \quad \text{—primal slacks—} \quad s_2^* = 0$$
$$\rho_1^* = 0.136 \quad \text{—dual variables—} \quad \rho_2^* = 1.864$$

Total present value: $70.27

Weingartner, H. M., reprinted from *Mathematical Programming and the Analysis of Capital Budgeting Problems*, Prentice-Hall, Englewood Cliffs, N.J., 1963 (reissued by Kershaw Publishing Co., London, 1974).

with the greatest net "benefit" is project 4 with $\mu_4 = 10.45$. Although it has a smaller NPV than several of the other projects, it also uses less cash than the others. Finally, a comparison of the dual variables, ρ_1 and ρ_2, tells us that the value of relaxing the second-period constraint is greater. In other words, providing extra cash in the second period would increase the firm's NPV more than providing extra cash in the first time period. We can also use the values of ρ_t to calculate one-period implicit interest rates:

$$_1 r_2 = \frac{1 - \rho_1}{\rho_1} = 635\%,$$

$$_2 r_3 = \frac{1 - \rho_2}{\rho_2} = -46.4\%.$$

Linear programming solutions to capital budgeting have great versatility and have been applied to many types of problems. However, it is difficult to justify the existence of capital constraints in the first place. Also, once uncertainty is introduced as a major consideration, linear programming models fail to adequately handle it. For these and other reasons, linear programming models have become less popular in recent years.

E. CAPITAL BUDGETING PROCEDURES UNDER INFLATION[6]

The United States has experienced persistent inflation since 1966 at levels exceeding the moderate price level changes of previous peacetime periods. What effects does this have on the results of capital budgeting analysis? We can analyze the impacts of inflation by using an illustrative example to clarify the new influences introduced.

Let us begin with the standard capital budgeting case in which inflation is absent. The expression for calculating the NPV of the investment is shown in Eq. (3.12).

$$\text{NPV} = \sum_{t=1}^{N} \frac{\text{NCF}_t}{(1 + k)^t} - I_0. \tag{3.12}$$

The symbols used have the following meanings and values:

NPV = net present value of the project,
NCF_t = net cash flows per year from the project = \$26,500,
k = cost of capital applicable to the project = 9%,
N = number of years the net cash flows are received = 5,
I_0 = required investment outlay for the project = \$100,000,
τ_c = applicable tax rate of 50%.

---

[6] For articles on this subject see Van Horne [1971] and Cooley, Roenfeldt, and Chew [1975]; also see their exchange with Findlay and Frankle [1976].

With the data provided, we can utilize (3.12) as follows:

$$NPV_0 = \sum_{t=1}^{N} \frac{\$26,500}{(1.09)^t} - \$100,000$$

$$= 26,500(3.8896) - \$100,000$$

$$= 103,074 - 100,000$$

$$= \$3,074.$$

We find that the project has an expected NPV of $3,074 and under the simple conditions assumed, we would accept the project. Now let us consider the effects of inflation. Suppose that inflation at an annual rate of 6% will take place during the five years of the project. Note that we assume that the future inflation rate is known with certainty.

Since investment and security returns are based on expected future returns, the anticipated inflation rate will be reflected in the required rate of return on the project or the applicable cost of capital for the project. This relationship has long been recognized in financial economics and is known as the Fisher effect. In formal terms we have:

$$(1 + k_j)(1 + \eta) = (1 + K_j), \tag{3.13}$$

where K_j is the required rate of return in nominal terms and η is the anticipated annual inflation rate over the life of the project. For our example, Eq. (3.13) would be:

$$(1 + .09)(1 + .06) = (1 + .09 + .06 + .0054).$$

If the cross-product term, .0054, is included in the addition, we would have .1554 as the required rate of return in nominal terms. However, since the cross-product term is generally small and since both k_j, the required rate of return in real terms, and the anticipated inflation rate are estimates, it is customary to make a simple addition of the real rate and the inflation rate. The required nominal rate of return that would be used in the calculation would therefore be 15%. Note, then, that the applicable discount rate reflects the summation of the 6% anticipated inflation rate to the 9% rate of return in real terms to obtain the total of 15%.

The market returns will also include a factor for the uncertainty associated with the future rate of inflation. The nominal returns provided by market data will therefore, in addition to the Fisher effect for anticipated inflation, include an additional uncertainty adjustment factor for the uncertainty of the future inflation rate. However, no analytic solution to the problem of uncertain inflation exists. Therefore, we must ignore it here.

It is at this point that some biases in capital budgeting under inflationary conditions may be introduced. The market data utilized in the estimated current capital costs will include the premium for anticipated inflation. But while the market remembers to include an adjustment for inflation in the capitalization factor, the cash-flow estimates used by the firm in the capital budgeting analysis may fail to include an element to reflect future inflation. Conceptually, the decision maker can correct for inflation either by (a) adding an estimate of inflation to the cash flows in the numerator or (b) expressing the numerator without including an adjustment for inflation and subtracting an inflationary factor from the market rate in the denominator.

It is more natural to utilize market data and to explicitly incorporate estimates of the anticipated inflation rate in the cash flows in the numerator.

Without an adjustment for inflation in the cash flows the analysis would appear as in the following calculations for NPV_1:

$$NPV_1 = \sum_{t=1}^{N} \frac{\$26,500}{(1.09)^t(1.06)^t} - \$100,000 = \sum_{t=1}^{N} \frac{\$26,500}{(1.15)^t} - \$100,000$$

$$\doteq 26,500(3.3522) - 100,000$$

$$\doteq 88,833 - 100,000 = -\$11,167.$$

It now appears that the project will have a negative NPV of over $11,000. With a negative NPV of substantial magnitude, the project would be rejected. However, a sound analysis requires that the anticipated inflation rate also be taken into account in the cash flow estimates. Initially, for simplicity, let us assume that the same inflation rate of 6% is applicable to the net cash flows. We take this step in setting forth the expression for NPV_2 as follows:

$$NPV_2 = \sum_{t=1}^{N} \frac{\$26,500(1.06)^t}{(1.09)^t(1.06)^t} - 100,000 = \sum_{t=1}^{N} \frac{\$26,500}{(1.09)^t} - \$100,000.$$

Since the inflation factors are now in both the numerator and the denominator and are the same, they can be canceled. The result for the calculation of NPV_2 will therefore be the same as for NPV_0, which was a positive $3,074. Thus when anticipated inflation is properly reflected in both the cash flow estimates in the numerator and the required rate of return from market data in the denominator, the resulting NPV calculation will be both in real and nominal terms. This was noted by Findlay [1976] as follows: "Any properly measured, market-determined wealth concept is, simultaneously, *both nominal and real*. ... Hence, NPV, or any other wealth measure, gives the amount for which one can 'cash out' now (nominal) and also the amount of today's goods that can be consumed at today's prices (real)." Thus if inflation is reflected in both the cash flow estimates and in the required rate of return, the resulting NPV estimate will be free of inflation bias.

To this point we have purposely kept the analysis simple to focus on the basic principles since controversy has erupted over the issues involved. We may expect that the effect of the anticipated inflation on the required rate of return will differ from that on the cash flow estimates. Indeed, the components of the net cash flows, the cash outflows and the cash inflows, may themselves be influenced to different degrees by the anticipated inflation. These complications will not, however, change the basic method of analysis, only the specifics of the calculations. The nature of the more complex case is illustrated by Eq. (3.14):

$$NPV_0 = \sum_{t=1}^{N} \frac{[(\text{inflows})_t(1 + \eta_i)^t - (\text{outflows})_t(1 + \eta_0)^t](1 - \tau_c) + (\text{dep.})_t(\tau_c)}{(1 + K)^t} - I_0.$$

(3.14)

The cash inflows may be subject to a rate of inflation η_i that is different from the rate of inflation in the cash outflows η_0. Both may differ from the anticipated rate of inflation reflected in the required rate of return in the denominator. Some illustrative data will demonstrate the application of (3.14).

Table 3.8 sets forth data for expected cash flows without inflation effects. The pattern is a constant $26,500 per year for five years as in the original example. In Table 3.9 the estimates of expected net cash flows include inflation effects. The cash inflows are subject to a 6% inflation rate while the cash outflows are subject to a 7% inflation rate. The resulting expected net cash flows are shown in the bottom line of the table. The required rate of return of 15% is assumed to reflect a 6% inflation rate as before.

Table 3.8 Expected net cash flows without inflation effects

	Year 1	Year 2	Year 3	Year 4	Year 5
Expected cash inflows	$53,000	$53,000	$53,000	$53,000	$53,000
Expected cash outflows	20,000	20,000	20,000	20,000	20,000
Earnings before taxes	$33,000	$33,000	$33,000	$33,000	$33,000
Multiplied by $(1 - \tau_c)$	16,500	16,500	16,500	16,500	16,500
Earnings after taxes	$16,500	$16,500	$16,500	$16,500	$16,500
Depreciation tax shelter	10,000	10,000	10,000	10,000	10,000
Expected net cash flows	$26,500	$26,500	$26,500	$26,500	$26,500

Table 3.9 Expected net cash flows including inflation effects

	1	2	3	4	5
Expected cash inflows $(\eta = 6\%)$	$56,180	$59,551	$63,124	$66,912	$70,927
Expected cash outflows $(\eta = 7\%)$	21,400	22,898	24,501	26,216	28,051
Earnings before taxes	$34,780	$36,653	$38,623	$40,696	$42,876
Multiplied by $(1 - \tau_c)$	17,390	18,327	19,312	20,348	21,438
Earnings after taxes	$17,390	$18,327	$19,312	$20,348	$21,438
Depreciation tax shelter	10,000	10,000	10,000	10,000	10,000
Expected net cash flows	$27,390	$28,327	$29,312	$30,348	$31,438

The calculation of the expected NPV ($\overline{NPV}_3$) is shown in Table 3.10. Taking all the inflation influences into account, we find that $\overline{NPV}_3$ is a negative $2,507. The project would be rejected. In this example, the inflationary forces on the cash outflows were greater than on the cash inflows. Some have suggested that this influence has been sufficiently widespread and that it accounts for the sluggish rate of capital investment in the United States since the early 1970s.

Table 3.10 Calculation of $\overline{NPV}_3$

Year	Cash flow (1)	Discount factor 15% (2)	PV (1 × 2)
1	$27,390	.8696	$23,818
2	28,327	.7561	21,418
3	29,312	.6575	19,273
4	30,348	.5718	17,353
5	31,438	.4972	15,631
			$\overline{NPV}_3 = \$97,493 - \$100,000 = -\$2,507$

The situation we illustrated initially was that failure to take inflation into account in the expected cash flows resulted in an erroneous capital budgeting analysis. A project was rejected which, when measured correctly, produced a return exceeding the required rate of return. The allocation of capital would be unsound if the bias in the analysis due to inflation had not been taken into account. In our second and more complex example, inflation caused the cash outflows to grow at a higher rate than the cash inflows. As a consequence, the expected NPV of the project was negative. Making the inflation adjustment does not always necessarily result in a positive NPV for the project—it simply results in a more accurate estimate of the net benefits from the project, positive or negative.

F. SUMMARY AND CONCLUSIONS

Perhaps the single most important decision faced by management is the selection of investment projects which maximize the present value of shareholders' wealth. Therefore, it is hardly surprising that much of the literature in finance focuses on the capital budgeting problem. Both this chapter and its predecessor have emphasized capital budgeting techniques. However, the story is far from complete. Throughout, we have maintained the assumption that future cash flows are known with certainty and can be estimated without error. In addition, we assumed that the opportunity cost of capital (the discount rate) was given.

Chapters 4 through 7 introduce the reader to a world where decisions must be made under the assumption of uncertainty. It is not until Chapter 10 that we return, for a second time, to the important capital budgeting decision. However, at that time, we will be able to discuss the problem of project selection under uncertainty. Fortunately, the inclusion of uncertainty does not change the material presented in Chapters 2 and 3. However, some important extensions to project selection techniques will be introduced. Finally, the logical cycle is completed in Chapter 11, when we discuss the determination of the appropriate opportunity cost of capital in a world of uncertainty. At that time all the necessary elements will have been covered under the assumption of uncertainty. They include: the correct definition of cash flows for capital budgeting purposes, determination of the appropriate cost of capital, and a proof of why the NPV criterion is consistent with shareholder wealth maximization.

PROBLEM SET

3.1 The Johnson Company is considering the following mutually exclusive projects:

	Project J	Project K	Project L	Project M
Investment	$48,000	$60,000	$60,000	$36,000
NCF	20,000	12,000	16,000	10,000
N	5	15	10	15

The cost of capital used by the Johnson Company is 16%.

a) How should the fact that the projects have differences in scale be taken into consideration?

b) Rank the projects, assuming that they can be repeated in permanent replacement chains, and that differences in scale are invested at the cost of capital.

3.2 If the opportunity cost of capital is 10%, which of the following three projects has the highest PVI? Which will increase shareholders' wealth the most?

Year	Project A	Project B	Project C
0	− 1,000	− 2,000	− 3,000
1	1,000	1,000	4,000
2	1,000	1,000	
3		1,000	

3.3 The Hansen Company is considering four mutually exclusive projects as follows:

	Project A	Project B	Project C	Project D
Investment	$40,000	$25,000	$40,000	$30,000
NCF	12,000	8,000	8,000	6,500
N	5	5	10	10
K	12%	12%	12%	12%

a) Compute the NPV and IRR of each project, and rank the investments from best to worst under each method. What factors are responsible for the differences in rankings between the two approaches?

b) Compute the PVI for each project and rank the alternatives. What are the implicit assumptions of the PVI method with respect to scale and duration of projects? When is it appropriate to use the PVI method?

c) If the projects are mutually exclusive, which should be accepted? Why? Which should be accepted if they are independent? Why?

3.4 The Dandy Candy Company is considering two mutually exclusive projects. They are the only projects available. The risk-free rate is 5%. The cash flows from the projects are known with certainty and are given below.

Year	Project 1	Project 2
0	− 10,000	− 1,000
1	4,000	2,700
2	4,000	2,700
3	4,000	
4	4,000	

a) Which project has the higher net present value?

b) If the firm has no capital constraints, which project would you select?

c) If the firm has a capital constraint of $12,000, which project would you select? Why?

3.5 *Optimal duration.* Plaid Scotch Ltd. has just kegged its latest Scotch whiskey at a cost of $50,000. The whiskey's value will increase over the years according to the following formula:

$$V_t = \$100,000 \ln t.$$

What is the optimal time of bottling for the Scotch if the firm's cost of capital is 15% compounded continuously?

3.6 You are given the following information: The Dorkin Company has made an investment of $40,000 which is expected to yield benefits over a five-year period. Annual cash inflows of $90,000 and annual cash outflows of $75,000 are expected, excluding taxes and the depreciation tax shelter. The tax rate is 40% and the cost of capital is 8%. Dorkin Company uses straight-line depreciation.

a) Compute the NPV of the investment.

b) On investigation, you discover that no adjustments have been made for inflation or price level changes. The data for the first year are correct but after that inflows are expected to increase at 4% per year, outflows at 6% per year, and the annual rate of inflation is expected to be about 6%. Reevaluate the NPV of the project in light of this information.

3.7 The Baldwin Company is considering investing in a machine that produces bowling balls. The cost of the machine is $100,000. Production by year during the five-year life of the machine is expected to be as follows: 5,000 units, 8,000 units, 12,000 units, 10,000 units, and 6,000 units.

The interest in bowling is declining, and hence management believes that the price of bowling balls will increase at only 2% per year, compared to the general rate of inflation of 5%. The price of bowling balls in the first year will be $20.

On the other hand, plastic used to produce bowling balls is rapidly becoming more expensive. Because of this, production cash outflows are expected to grow at 10% per year. First-year production cost will be $10 per unit.

Depreciation of the machine will be straight-line for five years, after which time the salvage value will be zero. The company's tax rate is 40% and its cost of capital is 15%, based on the existing rate of inflation. Should the project be undertaken?

REFERENCES

BAUMOL, W. S., and R. E. QUANDT, "Investment and Discount Rates Under Capital Rationing," *The Economic Journal*, June 1965.

BERNHARD, R. H., "Mathematical Programming Models for Capital Budgeting—A Survey, Generalization and Critique," *Journal of Financial and Quantitative Analysis*, June 1969, 111–158.

BIERMAN, H., JR., and S. SMIDT, *The Capital Budgeting Decision*, 4th ed., Macmillan, New York, 1975.

CARLETON, W., "Linear Programming and Capital Budgeting Models: A New Interpretation," *Journal of Finance*, December 1969, 825–833.

COOLEY, P. L., R. L. ROENFELDT, and I.-K. CHEW, "Capital Budgeting Procedures Under Inflation," *Financial Management*, Winter 1975, 18–27.

FINDLAY, M. C., and A. W. FRANKLE, "Capital Budgeting Procedures under Inflation: Cooley, Roenfeldt and Chew vs. Findlay and Frankle," *Financial Management*, Autumn 1976, 83–90.

HIRSHLEIFER, J., *Investment, Interest and Capital*, Prentice-Hall, Englewood Cliffs, N.J., 1970.

KLAMMER, T., "Empirical Evidence of the Adoption of Sophisticated Capital Budgeting Techniques," *The Journal of Business*, July 1972, 387–397.

LORIE, J. H., and L. J. SAVAGE, "Three Problems in Capital Rationing," *Journal of Business*, October 1955, 229–239.

MYERS, S. C., "A Note on Linear Programming and Capital Budgeting," *Journal of Finance*, March 1972, 89–92.

VAN HORNE, J. C., "A Note on Biases on Capital Budgeting Introduced by Inflation," *Journal of Financial and Quantitative Analysis*, January 1971, 653–658.

WEINGARTNER, H. M., *Mathematical Programming and the Analysis of Capital Budgeting Problems*, Prentice-Hall, Englewood Cliffs, N.J., 1963.

——, "Capital Rationing: *n* Authors in Search of a Plot," *The Journal of Finance*, December 1977, 1403–1432.

Chapter 4

The Theory of Choice: Utility Theory Given Uncertainty

We wish to find the mathematically complete principles which define "rational behavior" for the participants in a social economy, and derive from them the general characteristics of that behavior.

J. Von Neumann and O. Morgenstern,
Theory of Games and Economic Behavior,
Princeton Univ. Press, Princeton, 1944, p. 31

Economics is the study of how people and societies choose to allocate scarce resources and distribute wealth among one another and over time. Therefore, one must understand the objects of choice and the method of choice. The following two chapters are devoted to the objects of choice faced by an investor. Here, we focus on the theory of how people make choices when faced with uncertainty. Later on, once the theory of choice and the objects of choice are understood, we shall combine the two in order to produce a theory of optimal decision-making under uncertainty. In particular, we shall study the allocation of resources in an economic system where prices provide a system of signals for optimal allocation. There are, however, other means of allocation. Instead of using prices, we might allow an individual or committee to make all the allocation decisions, or we might program allocational rules into an algorithm run by machine.

We shall begin with a discussion of the axioms of behavior used by economists. However, before rushing into them, we must recognize that there are other theories of behavior. Social sciences such as anthropology, psychology, political science, sociobiology, and sociology also provide great insight into the theory of choice. And very early in this chapter we shall be forced to recognize that individuals have different tastes for the time preference of consumption and different degrees of risk aversion. Economic theory recognizes these differences but has little to say about why they exist or what causes them. The other social sciences study these problems. However,

64

as we shall see, there is much one can say about the theory of choice under uncertainty without, for example, understanding why a seventy-year-old person is more or less risk averse than the same person at age twenty, or why some people prefer meat while others prefer vegetables.

The theory of investor choice is only one corner of what has come to be known as utility theory. Most students are already familiar with the microeconomic price theory treatment of choices among various bundles of perishable commodities such as apples and oranges at an instant in time. The indifference curves which result are shown in Fig. 4.1(a). Another type of choice available to individuals is whether to consume now or to save (invest) and consume more at a later date. This is the utility theory of choices over time which is fundamental for understanding interest rates. This type of one-period consumption/investment decision was discussed in Chapter 1 and is illustrated in Fig. 4.1(b). Our main concern here is the choice between timeless risky alternatives which we call the theory of investor choice. The theory begins with nothing more than five assumptions about the behavior of individuals when confronted with the task of ranking risky alternatives and the assumption of nonsatiation (i.e., greed). The theory ends by parameterizing the objects of choice as the mean and variance of return and by mapping trade-offs between them which provide equal utility to investors. These mappings are indifference curves for timeless (or one-period) choices under uncertainty. They are shown in Fig. 4.1(c), and are used extensively in Chapters 6 and 7.

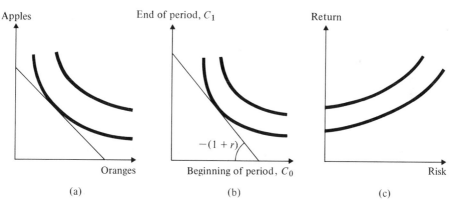

Fig. 4.1 Indifference curves for various types of choices: (a) Choice between consumption goods under certainty (b) Choice between consumption and investment under certainty (c) Choice between risk and return

A. FIVE AXIOMS OF CHOICE UNDER UNCERTAINTY

In order to develop a theory of rational decision-making in the face of uncertainty, it is necessary to make some very precise assumptions about an individual's behavior. Known as the axioms of cardinal utility, these assumptions provide the minimum set

of necessary conditions for consistent and rational behavior. Once they are established, all the remaining theory must follow.[1]

Axiom 1   Comparability (sometimes called completeness). For the entire set, S, of
uncertain alternatives, an individual can say either that outcome x is preferred to
outcome y (we write this $x \succ y$) or y is preferred to x ($y \succ x$) or the individual is
indifferent as to x and y ($x \sim y$).[2]

Axiom 2   Transitivity (sometimes called consistency). If an individual prefers x to
y and y to z, then x is preferred to z. (If $x \succ y$ and $y \succ z$, then $x \succ z$.) If an
individual is indifferent as to x and y and is also indifferent as to y and z, then he
is indifferent as to x and z. (If $x \sim y$ and $y \sim z$, then $x \sim z$.)

Axiom 3   Strong independence. Suppose we construct a gamble where an individual has a probability α of receiving outcome x and a probability $(1 - \alpha)$ of
receiving outcome z. We shall write this gamble as $G(x, z: \alpha)$. Strong independence says that if the individual is indifferent as to x and y, then he will also be
indifferent as to a first gamble, set up between x with probability α and a mutually exclusive outcome z, and a second gamble, set up between y with probability α and the same mutually exclusive outcome, z.

If $x \sim y$, then $G(x, z: \alpha) \sim G(y, z: \alpha)$.

Axiom 4   Measurability. If outcome y is preferred less than x but more than z,
then there is a *unique* α (a probability) such that the individual will be indifferent
between y and a gamble between x with probability α and z with probability
$1 - \alpha$.[3]

If $x \succ y \geq z$ or $x \geq y \succ z$, then there exists a unique α, such that
$y \sim G(x, z: \alpha)$.

Axiom 5   Ranking. If alternatives y and u both lie somewhere between x and z
and we can establish gambles such that an individual is indifferent between y and
a gamble between x (with probability α_1) and z, while he is also indifferent
between u and a second gamble, this time between x (with probability α_2) and z,
then if α_1 is greater than α_2, y is preferred to u.

If $x \geq y \geq z$ and $x \geq u \geq z$, then, if $y \sim G(x, z: \alpha_1)$ and $u \sim G(x, z: \alpha_2)$, it
follows that if $\alpha_1 > \alpha_2$, then $y \succ u$, or if $\alpha_1 = \alpha_2$, then $y \sim u$.

---

[1] The notation and much of the conceptual outline follow the development found in Fama
and Miller [1972].
[2] The symbol used to indicate preference ($\succ$) is not a mathematical inequality. It can rank
only preferences. For example, an individual may prefer one Picasso to two Rembrandts or
vice versa.
[3] The reason for bounding y on only one side or the other is to eliminate the possibility of
$x \sim y \sim z$ in which case any α would satisfy the indifference condition required by the gamble.

These are known as the axioms of cardinal utility. They boil down to the following assumptions about behavior. First, all individuals are assumed to always make completely rational decisions. A statement that "I like Chevrolets more than Fords and Fords more than Toyotas, but Toyotas more than Chevrolets" is not rational. Second, people are assumed to be able to make these rational choices among thousands of alternatives—not a very simple task.

The axiom of strong independence is usually the hardest to accept. In order to illustrate it, consider the following example. Let outcome x be a security with 10% mean return and a standard deviation of 10%, let y be a second security also with 10% return and 10% standard deviation, and finally, let z be a portfolio which is one-half x and one-half y. Suppose that x and y are perfectly negatively correlated. Then portfolio z will have an average return of 10% but no risk at all because variations of return between x and y are completely offsetting in portfolio z. Obviously z would be preferred to either x or y by any risk-averse individual, because it has the same expected return but lower risk. However, this makes no difference when comparing $G(x, z: \alpha)$ with $G(y, z: \alpha)$ in Axiom 3. The reason is that even though z is a portfolio made up of x and y, it is treated as a completely *mutually exclusive* outcome. Both x and y are separate outcomes from z. It is an independent alternative.

Having established the five axioms, we add to them the assumption that individuals always prefer more wealth to less. In other words, people are greedy. The marginal utility of wealth is always positive. This assumption in conjunction with the other five is all that is needed to provide a complete development of utility theory.

Next, we need to answer the question, How do individuals rank various combinations of risky alternatives? We can use the axioms of preference to show how preferences can be mapped into measurable utility. How do we establish a utility function which allows the assignment of a unit of measure (a number) to various alternatives so that we can look at the number and know that if, for example, the utility of x is 35 and the utility of y is 27, then x is preferred to y? In order to do this we need to discuss two properties of utility functions.

B. DEVELOPING UTILITY FUNCTIONS

The utility function will have two properties: (1) It will be order preserving. In other words if we measure the utility of x as greater than the utility of y, $U(x) > U(y)$, it means that x is actually preferred to y, $x \succ y$. (2) Expected utility can be used to rank combinations of risky alternatives. Mathematically, this means that

$$U(G(x, y: \alpha)) = \alpha U(x) + (1 - \alpha)U(y).$$

In order to prove that utility functions are order preserving, consider the set of risky outcomes, S, which is assumed to be bounded above by outcome a and below by outcome b. Next consider two intermediate outcomes x and y such that

$$a \succ x \succeq b \quad \text{or} \quad a \succeq x \succ b$$

and

$$a \succ y \succeq b \quad \text{or} \quad a \succeq y \succ b.$$

By using Axiom 4 we can choose unique probabilities for x and y in order to construct the following gambles:

$$x \sim G(a, b: \alpha(x)), \qquad y \sim G(a, b: \alpha(y)).$$

Then we can use Axiom 5 so that the probabilities $\alpha(x)$ and $\alpha(y)$ can be interpreted as numerical utilities which uniquely rank x and y. By Axiom 5,

$$\text{If} \quad \alpha(x) > \alpha(y) \quad \text{then} \quad x \succ y.$$

$$\text{If} \quad \alpha(x) = \alpha(y) \quad \text{then} \quad x \sim y.$$

$$\text{If} \quad \alpha(x) < \alpha(y) \quad \text{then} \quad x \prec y.$$

In this way we have developed an order-preserving utility function. The maximum and minimum outcomes, a and b, may be assigned any number at all (for example, let $a = 100$ and $b = 0$). Then by forming simple gambles we can assign cardinal utility numbers to the intermediate outcomes x and y.

In order to demonstrate how this might be done, suppose we arbitrarily assign a utility of -10 utiles to a loss of \$1000 and ask the following question: When we are faced with a gamble with probability α of winning \$1000 and probability $(1 - \alpha)$ of losing \$1000, what probability would make us indifferent between the gamble and \$0.0 with certainty? Mathematically, this problem can be expressed as

$$0 \sim G(1000, -1000: \alpha)$$

or

$$U(0) = \alpha U(1000) + (1 - \alpha)U(-1000).$$

Suppose that the probability of winning \$1000 must be .6 in order for us to be indifferent between the gamble and a sure \$0.0. By assuming that the utility of \$0.0 with certainty is zero and substituting $U(-1000) = -10$ and $\alpha = .6$ into the above equation, we can solve for the utility of \$1000:

$$U(1000) = -\frac{(1 - \alpha)U(-1000)}{\alpha},$$

$$= -\frac{(1 - .6)(-10)}{.6} = 6.7 \text{ utiles.}$$

By repeating this procedure for different payoffs it is possible to develop a utility function. Table 4.1 shows various gambles, their probabilities, and the utility of payoffs for a risk-averse investor. The cardinal utility function which obtains for the set of preferences indicated in Table 4.1 is given in Fig. 4.2.[4]

---

[4] This example can be found in Walter [1967].

Table 4.1 Payoffs, probabilities, and utilities

Loss	Gain	Probability of gain	Utility of gain	Utility of loss
− 1000	1000	.60	6.7	− 10.0
− 1000	2000	.55	8.2	− 10.0
− 1000	3000	.50	10.0	− 10.0
− 1000	4000	.45	12.2	− 10.0
− 1000	5000	.40	15.0	− 10.0
− 1000	6000	.35	18.6	− 10.0
− 1000	7000	.30	23.3	− 10.0
− 2000	2000	.75	8.2	− 24.6
− 3000	3000	.80	10.0	− 40.0
− 4000	4000	.85	12.2	− 69.2
− 5000	5000	.90	15.0	− 135.0

From *Dividend Policy and Enterprise Evaluation*, by James E. Walter. © 1967 by Wadsworth Publishing Company, Inc., Belmont, Calif. Reprinted by permission of the publisher.

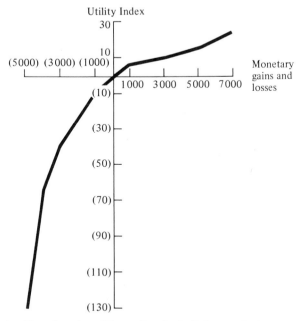

Fig. 4.2 Cardinal utility function (From *Dividend Policy and Enterprise Evaluation*, by James E. Walter. © 1967 by Wadsworth Publishing Company, Inc. Belmont, Calif. Reprinted by permission of the publisher.)

Next it is useful to show that expected utility can be used to rank risky alternatives. This is the second important property of utility functions. Let us begin by establishing the elementary gambles in exactly the same way as before. This is illustrated in Fig. 4.3. Next, consider a third alternative, z. By Axiom 4 there must exist a unique probability, $\beta(z)$, which would make an individual indifferent as to outcome z and a gamble between x and y. (See Fig. 4.4.) Now we can relate z to the elemental prospects a and b. If we can trace out the branches in the decision tree represented by Fig. 4.4, the individual will be indifferent between z and outcome a with probability $\gamma = \beta(z)\alpha(x) + (1 - \beta(z))\alpha(y)$ and outcome b with probability $1 - \gamma$. This is shown in Fig. 4.5. We can write the gamble as follows:

$$z \sim G[a, b: \beta(z)\alpha(x) + (1 - \beta(z))\alpha(y)].$$

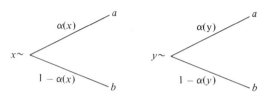

Fig. 4.3 Elementary gambles

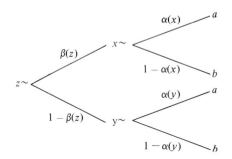

Fig. 4.4 Outcome z compared with a gamble between outcomes x and y

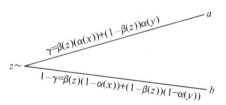

Fig. 4.5 Outcome z related to elementary prospects a and b

Now we have already established, by Axiom 5, that the utilities of x and y can be represented by their probabilities, namely $U(x) = \alpha(x)$ and $U(y) = \alpha(y)$. Therefore, the above gamble can be rewritten as

$$z \sim G[a, b: \beta(z)U(x) + (1 - \beta(z))U(y)].$$

Finally, by using Axiom 5 a second time, it must be true that the unique probability of outcome z can be used as a cardinal measure of its utility relative to the elemental prospects a and b. Therefore, we have

$$U(z) = \beta(z)U(x) + (1 - \beta(z))U(y). \tag{4.1}$$

In this way we have shown that the correct ranking function for risky alternatives is expected utility. Equation (4.1) says that the utility of z is equal to the probability of x times its utility plus the probability of y times its utility. This is an expected utility which represents a linear combination of the utilities of outcomes.

In general, we can write the expected utility of wealth as follows

$$\text{MAX } E[U(W)] = \sum_i p_i U(W_i).$$

Given the five axioms of rational investor behavior and the additional assumption that all investors always prefer more wealth to less, we can say that investors will always seek to maximize their expected utility of wealth. In fact, the above equation is exactly what we mean by the theory of choice. All investors will use it as their objective function. In other words, they will seem to calculate the expected utility of wealth for all possible alternative choices and then choose the outcome which maximizes their expected utility of wealth.

An important thing to keep in mind is that utility functions are specific to individuals. There is no way to compare one individual's utility function to another's. For example, we could perform an experiment by giving two people $1000. We would see that they are both happy, having just experienced an increase in utility. But whose utility increased more? It is impossible to say! Interpersonal comparison of utility functions is impossible. If it were not, we could establish a social welfare function which would combine everyone's utility, and could then use it to solve such problems as the optimal distribution of wealth. Also group utility functions such as the utility function of a firm have no meaning.

Another important property of cardinal utility functions is that we can sensibly talk about increasing or decreasing marginal utility. This can best be illustrated with an example taken from the centigrade and fahrenheit temperature scales. Consider two outcomes: the freezing point of water and its boiling point. Call them x and y, respectively. Each scale may be likened to a function which maps various degrees of heat into numbers. Utility functions do the same thing for risky alternatives. The difference between two outcomes is marginal utility. On the centigrade scale the difference between freezing and boiling is 100°C. On the fahrenheit scale the difference is 180°F. The ratio of the "changes" is

$$\frac{212° - 32°}{100° - 0°} = 1.8.$$

If the two scales really do provide the same ranking for all prospects, then the ratio of changes should be the same for all prospects. Mathematically,

$$\frac{U(x) - U(y)}{\psi(x) - \psi(y)} = \text{constant},$$

where $U(\cdot)$ and $\psi(\cdot)$ are the two utility functions. Compare any two points on the two temperature scales and you will see that the ratio of changes between them is a constant, that is, 1.8. Hence, differences in utility have meaning for the cardinal utility function of an individual.

C. ESTABLISHING A DEFINITION OF RISK AVERSION

Having established a way of converting the axioms of preference into a utility function, we can make use of the concept to establish definitions of risk premia and of precisely what is meant by risk aversion. A useful way to begin is to compare three simple utility functions (Fig. 4.6) which assume that more wealth is preferred to less—in other words, the marginal utility of wealth is positive $(MU(W) > 0)$. Suppose that we establish a gamble between two prospects, a and b. Let the probability of receiving prospect a be α and the probability of b be $(1 - \alpha)$. The gamble can be written as before: $G(a, b: \alpha)$. Now the question is, Will an individual prefer the actuarial value of the gamble (i.e., its expected outcome) with certainty or will he prefer the gamble itself? If he prefers the gamble, he is a risk lover; if he is indifferent, he is risk neutral; and if he prefers the actuarial value with certainty, he is a risk averter. In Fig. 4.7, we have graphed a logarithmic utility function: $U(W) = \ln (W)$. The gamble is an 80% chance of winning $5 or a 20% chance of winning $30. The

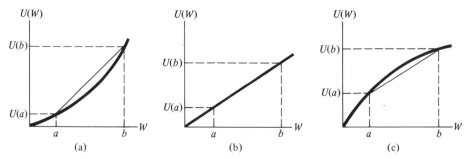

Fig. 4.6 Three utility functions with positive marginal utility: (a) Risk lover (b) Risk neutral (c) Risk averter

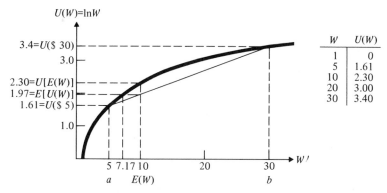

Fig. 4.7 Logarithmic utility function

actuarial value of the gamble is its expected outcome. In other words, the expected wealth is

$$E(W) = .8(\$5) + .2(\$30) = \$10.$$

The utility of the expected wealth can be read directly from the utility function: $U[E(W)] = 2.3$. That is, if an individual with a logarithmic utility function could receive $10 with certainty, it would provide him with 2.3 utiles. The other possibility is the utility of the gamble. We know from Eq. (4.1) that it is equal to the expected utility of wealth provided by the gamble

$$E[U(W)] = .8U(\$5) + .2U(\$30),$$

$$= .8(1.61) + .2(3.40) = 1.97.$$

Because the individual receives more utility from the actuarial value of the gamble obtained with certainty than from taking the gamble itself, he is risk averse. In general, if the utility of expected wealth is greater than the expected utility of wealth, the individual is risk averse. The three definitions are:[5]

If $U[E(W)] > E[U(W)]$, then we have risk aversion.   (4.2a)

If $U[E(W)] = E[U(W)]$, then we have risk neutrality.   (4.2b)

If $U[E(W)] < E[U(W)]$, then we have risk loving.   (4.2c)

Note that if an individual's utility function is strictly concave, he will be risk averse; if it is linear, he will be risk neutral; and if it is convex, he will be a risk lover.

It is even possible to compute the maximum amount of wealth an individual would be willing to give up in order to avoid the gamble. This is called a *risk premium*. Suppose that Mr. Smith is faced with the gamble illustrated in Fig. 4.7 and

---

[5] These definitions can be found in Markowitz [1959].

has a logarithmic utility function. How much will he pay to avoid the gamble? If he does nothing, he has an 80% chance of ending up with $5 (a decline of $5) and a 20% chance of ending up with $30 (an increase of $20). The expected utility of the gamble has already been determined to be 1.97 utiles. From the logarithmic utility function in Fig. 4.7, we see that the level of wealth which provides 1.97 utiles is $7.17. On the other hand, he receives an expected level of wealth of $10 if he accepts the gamble. Therefore, given a logarithmic utility function, he will be willing to pay up to $2.83 in order to avoid the gamble. If he is offered insurance against the gamble which costs less than $2.83, he will buy it. We shall call this the *Markowitz risk premium*.

Throughout the remainder of this text we shall assume that all individuals are risk averse. Their utility functions are assumed to be strictly concave. Mathematically, this implies two things: (1) they always prefer more wealth to less (the marginal utility of wealth is positive, $MU(W) > 0$), and (2) their marginal utility of wealth decreases as they have more and more wealth $(dMU(W)/dW < 0)$.

Now we know how to characterize a risk-averse utility function and how to measure a risk premium for a given gamble, but it is even more interesting to provide a specific definition of risk aversion. This was done by Pratt [1964] and Arrow [1971]. Take an individual, say Ms. Miller, with a current amount of wealth, W, and present her with an actuarially neutral gamble of $\tilde{Z}$ dollars (by actuarially neutral we mean that $E(\tilde{Z}) = 0$). What risk premium, $\pi(W, \tilde{Z})$, must be added to the gamble to make her indifferent between it and the actuarial value of the gamble? In Fig. 4.7, the risk premium is analogous to the difference between $U[E(W)]$ and $E[U(W)]$ if it is measured in utiles, or the difference between $10 and $7.17 if measured in dollars. Presumably, the risk premium will be a function of the level of wealth, W, and the gamble $\tilde{Z}$. Mathematically, the risk premium, π, can be defined as the value which satisfies the following equality:

$$E[U(W + \tilde{Z})] = U[W + E(\tilde{Z}) - \pi(W, \tilde{Z})]. \tag{4.3}$$

The left-hand side is the expected utility of the current level of wealth and the gamble. Its utility must equal the utility of the right-hand side, namely current level of wealth, W, plus the utility of the actuarial value of the gamble, $E(\tilde{Z})$, minus the risk premium, $\pi(W, \tilde{Z})$. We can use a Taylor's series approximation to expand the utility function of wealth (whatever it might be) around both sides of Eq. (4.3).[6] Working with the right-hand side of (4.3), we have

$$U[W + E(\tilde{Z}) - \pi(W, \tilde{Z})] = U[W - \pi(W, \tilde{Z})].$$

Since $E(\tilde{Z}) \equiv 0$, an actuarially neutral risk, the Taylor's series expansion is[7]

$$U(W - \pi) = U(W) - \pi U'(W) + \text{terms of order at most } (\pi^2). \tag{4.4}$$

---

[6] Students not familiar with Taylor's series approximations are referred to Appendix D.
[7] We assume that the third absolute central moment of $\tilde{Z}$ is of smaller order than σ_z^2 (normally it is of order σ_z^3).

The Taylor's series expansion of the left-hand side of (4.3) is

$$E[U(W + \tilde{Z})] = E[U(W) + \tilde{Z}U'(W) + \tfrac{1}{2}\tilde{Z}^2 U''(W)$$

$$+ \text{ terms of order at most } (\tilde{Z}^3)]$$

$$= U(W) + \tfrac{1}{2}\sigma_z^2 U''(W)$$

$$+ \text{ terms of smaller order than } \sigma_z^2. \tag{4.5}$$

The above result may require a little explanation. It is true, because

$$E[U(W)] = U(W), \qquad \text{wealth is not random;}$$

$$E[\tilde{Z}] \equiv 0, \qquad \text{the risk is actuarially neutral;}$$

$$E[\tilde{Z}^2] = \sigma_z^2, \qquad \text{because } \sigma_z^2 \equiv E[\tilde{Z} - E(\tilde{Z})]^2.$$

Next we can equate (4.4) and (4.5),

$$U(W) - \pi U'(W) + \cdots = U(W) + \tfrac{1}{2}\sigma_z^2 U''(W) + \cdots \tag{4.6a}$$

Solving (4.6a) for the risk premium, we obtain

$$\pi = \frac{1}{2}\sigma_z^2 \left(-\frac{U''(W)}{U'(W)} \right). \tag{4.6b}$$

This is the Pratt-Arrow measure of a local risk premium. Since $\tfrac{1}{2}\sigma_z^2$ is always positive, the sign of an individual's risk premium is always determined by the sign of the term in parentheses. We shall define the measure of absolute risk aversion (ARA) as

$$\text{ARA} = -\frac{U''(W)}{U'(W)}. \tag{4.7}$$

It is called *absolute risk aversion* because it measures risk aversion for a given level of wealth. Note that there is a difference between the risk premium, π, and the definition of risk aversion. The Pratt-Arrow definition of risk aversion is useful because it provides much more insight into people's behavior in the face of risk. For example, how does an individual's ARA change with his wealth level? Casual empiricism tells us that ARA will probably decrease as an individual's wealth increases. A $1000 gamble may seem trivial to a billionaire but most people would be very risk averse to it. On the other hand we can multiply the measure of absolute risk aversion by an individual's level of wealth to obtain what is known as *relative risk aversion* (RRA):

$$\text{RRA} = -W \frac{U''(W)}{U'(W)}. \tag{4.8}$$

It might be reasonable to expect RRA to be constant.

We can use these definitions of risk aversion to provide a more detailed examination of various types of utility functions to see whether or not they have decreasing ARA and constant RRA. The quadratic utility function has been used widely in the academic literature. It can be written (for $W \leq a/2b$)

quadratic utility function, $U(W) = aW - bW^2; \quad (4.9)$

first derivative, marginal utility, $U'(W) = a - 2bW;$
second derivative, change in MU with
respect to changes in wealth, $U''(W) = -2b.$

ARA and RRA are:

$$ARA = -\frac{-2b}{a - 2bW}, \qquad \frac{d(ARA)}{dW} > 0;$$

$$RRA = \frac{2b}{(a/W) - 2b}, \qquad \frac{d(RRA)}{dW} > 0.$$

Unfortunately, the quadratic utility function exhibits increasing ARA and increasing RRA. Neither of these properties makes sense intuitively.

Friend and Blume [1975] have used Internal Revenue Service data to replicate, from reported dividends, the portfolios held by individual investors. Sophisticated econometric techniques were used to estimate changes in ARA and RRA as a function of the wealth of investors. The results were consistent with decreasing ARA and constant RRA equal to 2.0. These properties are consistent with a power utility function with $a = -1$. It can be written as:

$$U(W) = -W^{-1}, \qquad U'(W) = W^{-2} > 0, \qquad U''(W) = -2W^{-3} < 0. \quad (4.10)$$

ARA and RRA are:

$$ARA = -\frac{-2W^{-3}}{W^{-2}} = \frac{2}{W}, \qquad \frac{d(ARA)}{dW} < 0.$$

$$RRA = W\frac{2}{W} = 2, \qquad \frac{d(RRA)}{dW} = 0.$$

The power function given by Eq. (4.10) is consistent with the empirical results of Friend and Blume and exhibits all the intuitively plausible properties: the marginal utility of wealth is positive, it decreases with increasing wealth, the measure of ARA decreases with increasing wealth, and RRA is constant.

D. COMPARISON OF RISK AVERSION IN THE SMALL AND IN THE LARGE

The Pratt-Arrow definition of risk aversion provides useful insights into the properties of ARA and RRA, but it assumes that risks are small and actuarially neutral. The Markowitz concept, which simply compares $E[U(W)]$ with $U[E(W)]$, is not limited by these assumptions.

An interesting comparison of the two measures of risk premiums is offered in the following example. An individual with a logarithmic utility function and a level of wealth of $20,000 is exposed to two different risks: (1) a 50/50 chance of gaining or losing $10, and (2) an 80% chance of losing $1000 and a 20% chance of losing $10,000. What is the maximum amount he will pay to avoid each of these risks?

The first risk is a small, actuarially neutral gamble, so the Pratt-Arrow measure of risk premium (Eq. (4.6b)) should yield a result almost identical to the Markowitz measure. The Pratt-Arrow measure is

$$\pi = -\frac{1}{2}\sigma^2 \frac{U''(W)}{U'(W)}.$$

The variance of the first risk is

$$\sigma^2 = \sum p_i(X_i - E(X))^2$$
$$= \tfrac{1}{2}(20{,}010 - 20{,}000)^2 + \tfrac{1}{2}(19{,}990 - 20{,}000)^2$$
$$= 100.$$

The ratio of the second and first derivatives of a logarithmic utility function evaluated at a level of wealth of $20,000 is

$$U'(W) = \frac{1}{W}, \qquad U''(W) = -\frac{1}{W^2}, \qquad \frac{U''(W)}{U'(W)} = -\frac{1}{W} = -\frac{1}{20{,}000}.$$

Combining these results, we obtain an estimate of the Pratt-Arrow risk premium:

$$\pi = -\frac{100}{2}\left(-\frac{1}{20{,}000}\right) = \$.0025.$$

The Markowitz approach requires computation of the expected utility of the gamble as follows:

$$E[U(W)] = \sum p_i U(W_i),$$
$$= \tfrac{1}{2}U(20{,}010) + \tfrac{1}{2}U(19{,}990)$$
$$= \tfrac{1}{2}\ln(20{,}010) + \tfrac{1}{2}\ln(19{,}990) = 9.903487428.$$

The certainty equivalent wealth level which would make the individual indifferent to his current level of wealth plus the gamble and a lower but certain level of wealth is the level of wealth which has a utility of 9.903487428. This is

$$W = e^{\ln(W)} = \$19{,}999.9974998.$$

Therefore the individual would pay a risk premium as large as $.0025002. The difference between the Pratt-Arrow risk premium and that of Markowitz is negligible in this case.

If we repeat similar computations for the second risk in the above example, the Pratt-Arrow assumptions of a small, actuarially neutral risk are not closely approximated. Nevertheless, if we apply the Pratt-Arrow definition, the risk premium is calculated to be \$324. The Markowitz risk premium for the same risk is the difference between his expected wealth, \$17,200, and the certainty equivalent wealth, \$16,711, or \$489. Now the dollar difference between the two risk premia is much larger.

The above example illustrates the difference between risk aversion for small, actuarially neutral risks, where the Pratt-Arrow assumptions are closely approximated, and risk aversion in the large, where the magnitude of the gamble is large or where it is not actuarially neutral. In general, the Markowitz measure of a risk premium is superior for large risks. This does not mean that the Pratt-Arrow definition of risk aversion is not useful. As we have seen, the intuition provided by the definition of risk aversion was useful for distinguishing between various types of concave utility functions.

E. STOCHASTIC DOMINANCE

So far we have discussed the axioms of investor preference, then used them to develop cardinal utility functions, and finally employed the utility functions to measure risk premia and derive measures of risk aversion. Clearly, any investor, whether he is risk averse or not, will seek to maximize the expected utility of his wealth. The expected utility rule can be used to introduce the economics of choice under uncertainty. An asset is said to be stochastically dominant over another if an individual receives greater wealth from it in every (ordered) state of nature. This definition is known as first-order stochastic dominance. Mathematically, asset x, with cumulative probability distribution $F_x(W)$, will be stochastically dominant over asset y, with cumulative probability distribution $G_y(W)$, for the set of all nondecreasing utility functions if

$$F_x(W) \leq G_y(W) \quad \text{for all } W,$$
$$F_x(W_i) < G_y(W_i) \quad \text{for some } W_i. \qquad \textit{First-order stochastic dominance} \qquad (4.11)$$

In words, the cumulative probability distribution (defined on wealth, W) for asset y always lies to the left of the cumulative distribution for x. If true, then x is said to dominate y. Figure 4.8 shows an example of first-order stochastic dominance assuming that the distribution of wealth provided by both assets is a (truncated) normal distribution. It is obvious from the figure that x dominates y because the cumulative distribution of y always lies to the left of x.

First-order stochastic dominance applies to all increasing utility functions. This means that individuals with any of the three utility functions in Fig. 4.6 would prefer asset x to asset y, because first-order stochastic dominance guarantees that the expected utility of wealth offered by x will be greater than that offered by y for all increasing utility functions. This fact can be illustrated by using Fig. 4.9 and the definition of expected utility:

$$E[U(W)] \equiv \int_{-\infty}^{\infty} U(W)f(W)\,dW, \qquad (4.12)$$

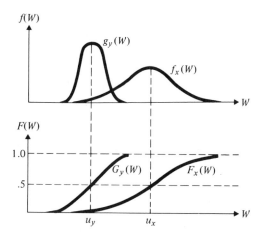

Fig. 4.8 An example of first-order stochastic dominance

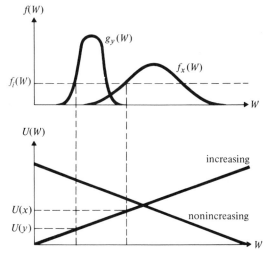

Fig. 4.9 First-order stochastic dominance and expected utility

where

$U(W)$ = the utility function,

W = the level of wealth,

$f(W)$ = the probability distribution of wealth.

The utility functions in Fig. 4.9 are linear, but they could just as easily be any of the set of increasing functions which we are comparing with any set of nonincreasing functions. Expected utility is the sum of the utilities of all possible levels of wealth weighted by their probability. For a given frequency of wealth, $f_i(W)$, in the top half of Fig. 4.9, the increasing utility function assigns higher utility to the level of wealth offered by asset x than by asset y. This is true for every frequency. Consequently, the expected utility of wealth from asset x is greater than that from asset y for the set of increasing utility functions (that is, all utility functions which have a positive marginal utility of wealth). Of course, the opposite would be true for utility functions non-increasing in wealth.

Second-order stochastic dominance not only assumes utility functions where marginal utility of wealth is positive, but also that total utility must increase at a decreasing rate. In other words, utility functions are nondecreasing and strictly concave. Thus individuals are assumed to be risk averse. Asset x will be stochastically dominant over asset y for all risk averse investors if

$$\int_{-\infty}^{W_i} [G_y(W) - F_x(W)]\, dW \geq 0 \quad \text{for all } W,$$

Second-order stochastic dominance

$$G_y(W_i) \neq F_x(W_i) \quad \text{for some } W_i.$$

(4.13)

This means that in order for asset x to dominate asset y for all risk-averse investors, the accumulated area under the cumulative probability distribution of y must be greater than the accumulated area for x, below any given level of wealth. This implies that, unlike first-order stochastic dominance, the cumulative density functions can cross. Figure 4.10 provides a graphic example, again assuming normal distribu-

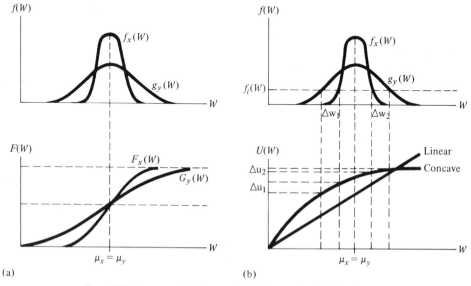

Fig. 4.10 An example of second-order stochastic dominance

tions. Obviously asset x will dominate asset y if an investor is risk averse because they both offer the same expected level of wealth ($\mu_x = \mu_y$), and because y is riskier. It has greater variance. The second-order stochastic dominance criterion requires that the difference in areas under the cumulative density functions be positive below any level of wealth, W_i. Up to the mean, $G_y(W)$ is strictly greater than $F_x(W)$. Beyond the mean, the opposite is true. Figure 4.11 shows that the difference between the two cumulative density functions is always greater than or equal to zero, therefore x dominates y.

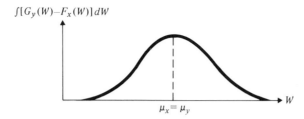

Fig. 4.11 Graphical representation of the sum of the differences in cumulative probabilities

Figure 4.10(b) ties the concept of second-order stochastic dominance back to the notion of maximizing expected utility.[8] The concave utility function has the property that the increase in utility for constant changes in wealth declines as a function of wealth. Therefore, if we select a given frequency of wealth such as $f_i(W)$, it maps out equal changes in wealth ΔW_1 and ΔW_2. The difference in utility between x and y below the mean is much greater than the difference in utility for the same change in wealth above the mean. Asset x is much better than y below the mean and only a little worse above the mean. Consequently, if we take the expected utility by pairing all such differences with equal probability, the expected utility of x is seen to be greater than the expected utility of y. If the individual were risk neutral, with a linear utility function the differences in utility above and below the mean would always be equal. Hence a risk-neutral investor would be indifferent relative to x and y.

Stochastic dominance is an extremely important and powerful result. It is properly founded on the basis of expected utility maximization, and even more important, it applies to any probability distribution whatsoever. This is because it takes into account every point in the probability distribution. Furthermore, we can be sure that if an asset demonstrates second-order stochastic dominance, it will be preferred by all risk-averse investors, regardless of the specific shape of their utility functions. We could use stochastic dominance as the basis of a complete theory of how risk-averse investors choose among various risky alternatives. All an individual

---

[8] The graphical presentation given here is intuitive and not meant to be a proof of the fact that second-order stochastic dominance maximizes expected utility for risk-averse investors. For proof, the reader is referred to Hanoch and Levy [1969].

needs to do is find the set of portfolios which is stochastically dominant and then select his portfolio from among those in the set.[9]

F. USING MEAN AND VARIANCE AS CHOICE CRITERIA

If the distribution of returns offered by assets is jointly normal, then we can maximize expected utility simply by selecting the best combinations of mean and variance. This is computationally much simpler than stochastic dominance, but requires that we restrict ourselves to normal distributions. Every normal distribution can be completely described by two parameters: its mean and variance—return and risk. If we adopt utility functions which maximize expected utility of end-of-period wealth (assuming a single-period model), it is easy to show the relationship between wealth and return:

$$\tilde{R}_j = \frac{\tilde{W}_j - W_0}{W_0}.$$

If the end-of-period wealth from investing in asset j is normally distributed with mean $\bar{W}$ and variance σ_w^2, then the return on asset j will also be normally distributed with mean $E(R_j) = [(E(\tilde{W}_j)/W_0) - 1]$ and variance $\sigma_R^2 = (\sigma_w^2/W_0^2)$.

Assuming that the return on an asset is normally distributed with mean E and variance σ^2, we can write an individual's utility function as[10]

$$U = U(R_j; E, \sigma).$$

His expected utility is

$$E(U) = \int_{-\infty}^{\infty} U(R)f(R; E, \sigma)\, dR. \tag{4.14}$$

We would like to express the indifference curve of a risk-averse investor as a function of the mean and standard deviation of a distribution of returns. The indifference curve is a mapping of all combinations of risk and return (standard deviation or variance) which yield the same expected utility of wealth. Obviously, if the combinations offer identical expected utility, the individual will be indifferent between them. Figure 4.12 shows the end result of the following proofs, i.e., the indifference curves of a risk-averse investor.

We want to show that the marginal rate of substitution between return and risk is positive and that the indifference curves are convex. This can be done, first by

---

[9] There is a growing body of literature which uses this concept. The interested reader is referred to Bawa [1975, 1976], Whitmore [1970], Porter, Wart, and Ferguson [1973], Levy and Kroll [1976], Vickson and Altman [1977], and Jean [1975].
[10] This proof can be found in Tobin [1958]. Also note that the proof applies equally well to any continuous, symmetric two-parameter distribution.

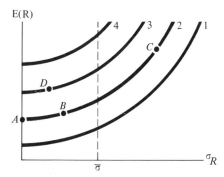

Fig. 4.12 Indifference curves for a risk-averse investor

converting the random return into a unit normal variable, Z, which has a mean of zero and a variance of one.

$$\tilde{Z} = \frac{\tilde{R} - E}{\sigma}. \tag{4.15}$$

From this we see that

$$\tilde{R} = E + \sigma\tilde{Z}, \qquad \frac{dR}{dZ} = \sigma, \qquad dR = \sigma\, dZ,$$

and when $R = -\infty$, then $Z = -\infty$, and when $R = \infty$, then $Z = \infty$. Now, by using the change of variables technique from integral calculus we can rewrite (4.14) as[11]

$$E(U) = \int_{-\infty}^{\infty} U(E + \sigma\tilde{Z}) f(Z; 0, 1)\, dZ. \tag{4.16}$$

Next, we take the derivative of the expected utility with respect to a change in the standard deviation of return:[12]

$$\frac{dE(U)}{d\sigma} = \int_{-\infty}^{\infty} U'(E + \sigma\tilde{Z})\left(\frac{dE}{d\sigma} + \tilde{Z}\right) f(Z; 0, 1)\, dZ = 0. \tag{4.17}$$

An indifference curve is defined as the locus of points where the change in the expected utility is equal to zero. Therefore (4.17) has been set equal to zero and the solution of the equation represents an indifference curve. Separating terms, we have

$$0 = \frac{dE}{d\sigma}\int_{-\infty}^{\infty} U'(E + \sigma Z) f(Z; 0, 1)\, dZ + \int_{-\infty}^{\infty} U'(E + \sigma Z) Z f(Z; 0, 1)\, dZ.$$

---

[11] Since $f(R; E, \sigma) = (1/\sigma)f(z; 0, 1)$, it follows that

$$E(U) = \int_{-\infty}^{\infty} U(E + \sigma\tilde{Z}) f(Z; 0, 1)\, \frac{\sigma}{\sigma}\, dZ.$$

[12] $\delta f(z)/\delta\sigma = 0$.

Therefore, the slope of the indifference curve is

$$\frac{dE}{d\sigma} = -\frac{\int U'(E + \sigma Z)Zf(Z; 0, 1)\, dZ}{\int U'(E + \sigma Z)f(Z; 0, 1)\, dZ} > 0. \tag{4.18}$$

The denominator must be positive because of the assumption that marginal utility, $U'(E + \sigma Z)$, must always be positive. People always prefer more return to less. The numerator will be positive only if we have a risk-averse investor with a strictly concave utility function. The marginal utility of every negative value of Z in Fig. 4.13 is greater than the marginal utility of an equally likely positive value of Z. Because this is true for every pair of outcomes $\pm Z$, the integral in the numerator of (4.18) is negative and the (entire) numerator is positive. Consequently, the slope of a risk averter's indifference curve in Fig. 4.12, that is, his marginal rate of substitution between mean and variance, is everywhere positive, except when $\sigma = 0$ where the slope is also zero.[13]

---

[13] The convexity of the utility function can be shown as follows. Let (E_1, σ_1) and (E_2, σ_2) be two points on the same indifference curve so that they have the same expected utility. If a third point is constructed to be a weighted average of the first two, $(E_1 + E_2)/2$, $(\sigma_1 + \sigma_2)/2$, the indifference curve is convex, if for every Z,

$$\tfrac{1}{2}U(E_1 + \sigma_1 Z) + \tfrac{1}{2}U(E_2 + \sigma_2 Z) < U\left(\frac{E_1 + E_2}{2} + \frac{\sigma_1 + \sigma_2}{2} Z\right).$$

In the case of declining marginal utilities this is obviously true because the utility of the second point will be less than twice the utility of the first. Consequently,

$$E\left[U\left(\frac{E_1 + E_2}{2}, \frac{\sigma_1 + \sigma_2}{2}\right)\right] > E[U(E_1, \sigma_1)] = E[U(E_2, \sigma_2)],$$

and the third point, which is a weighted average of the first two, lies above the indifference curve. This is shown graphically in Fig. 4.A.

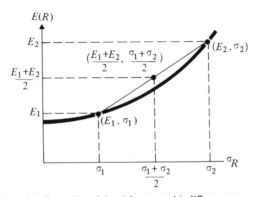

Fig. 4A Convexity of the risk-averters' indifference curve

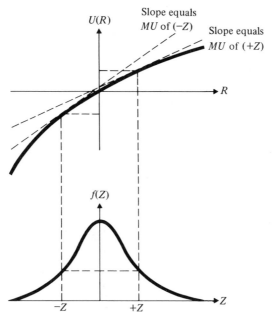

Fig. 4.13 Graphic representation for $\int U'(E + \sigma Z)Zf(Z; 0, 1)\, dZ < 0$

The indifference curves in Fig. 4.12 will be used throughout the remainder of the text to represent the indifference curves of risk-averse investors. Any points along a given indifference curve provide the investor with equal total utility. For example, he would not care whether he was at point A in Fig. 4.12, which has no risk, at point B with higher risk and return, or at point C. They all lie on the same indifference curve. Moving from right to left across the family of indifference curves provides the investor with increasing levels of expected utility. He would prefer point D on indifference curve 3 to point C on indifference curve 2, even though it has a lower return. The reason, of course, is that it has a much lower risk, which more than makes up for the lower return. The easiest way to see that expected utility increases from right to left is to fix the level of risk at $\bar{\sigma}$ and then note that the expected return increases as we move from curve 1 to curve 4.

G. A MEAN-VARIANCE PARADOX

Although it is convenient to characterize return and risk by the mean and variance of distributions of return offered by assets, it is not always correct. In fact, it is correct only when the returns have a normal distribution. Consider the following example. Two companies with equal total assets and exactly the same distribution of net operating income differ only with regard to their financial leverage. Table 4.2 shows their respective income statements in different, equally likely, states of nature.

Table 4.2 Mean variance paradox

	Economic state of nature				
	Horrid	Bad	Average	Good	Great
Net operating income	$1200	$1600	$2000	$2400	$2800
Probability	.2	.2	.2	.2	.2
Firm A					
Interest expense	0	0	0	0	0
Earnings before tax	1200	1600	2000	2400	2800
Tax at 50%	−600	−800	−1000	−1200	−1400
Net income	600	800	1000	1200	1400
Earnings per share (200 shares)	$3.00	$4.00	$5.00	$6.00	$7.00
Firm B					
Interest expense	−600	−600	−600	−600	−600
Earnings before tax	600	1000	1400	1800	2200
Tax at 50%	−300	−500	−700	−900	−1100
Net income	300	500	700	900	1100
Earnings per share (100 shares)	$3.00	$5.00	$7.00	$9.00	$11.00

Firm A				*Firm B*			
Assets		Liabilities		Assets		Liabilities	
		Debt	0			Debt	10,000
		Equity	20,000			Equity	10,000
$20,000			$20,000	$20,000			$20,000

   The mean and standard deviation of earnings per share for firm *A* are $5 and $1.41 respectively. For firm *B*, they are $7 and $2.82. These alternatives are plotted in Fig. 4.14. According to the mean-variance criterion, individual I would be indifferent between the risk-return combinations offered by *A* and *B*. Individual II, who is less risk averse, would prefer alternative *B* which has a greater return. Finally individual

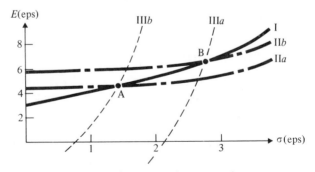

Fig. 4.14 A mean-variance paradox

III would prefer alternative *A*, which has lower risk. The paradox arises when we reexamine the earnings per share offered by the two firms. The earnings per share for firm *B* are equal to or greater than the earnings per share for firm *A* in every state of nature. Obviously, the mean-variance criterion provides misleading results. No investor with positive marginal utility would prefer firm *A*.

The problem with trying to apply the mean-variance criterion to the above problem is that the distribution of outcomes is not normal. Instead it is a rectangular distribution with equal probabilities for each state of nature. However, we can use second-order stochastic dominance regardless of the shape of the probability distribution. This is done in Table 4.3. Because the accumulated area under the distribution of earnings per share offered by firm *B* is always less than or equal to the accumulated distribution for firm *A*, we can say that *B* clearly dominates *A*. The density functions and cumulative density functions are shown in Fig. 4.15.

Table 4.3 Using second-order stochastic dominance

Eps	Prob. (B)	Prob. (A)	F(B)	G(A)	F − G	Σ (F − G)
3.00	.2	.2	.2	.2	0	0
4.00	0	.2	.2	.4	−.2	−.2
5.00	.2	.2	.4	.6	−.2	−.4
6.00	0	.2	.4	.8	−.4	−.8
7.00	.2	.2	.6	1.0	−.4	−1.2
8.00	0	0	.6	1.0	−.4	−1.6
9.00	.2	0	.8	1.0	−.2	−1.8
10.00	0	0	.8	1.0	−.2	−2.0
11.00	.2	0	1.0	1.0	0	−2.0
	1.0	1.0				

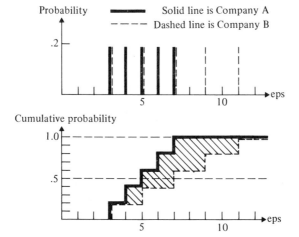

Fig. 4.15 Stochastic dominance applied to the mean-variance paradox

This mean-variance paradox example demonstrates very clearly the shortcomings of a theory of choice which relies on the (somewhat heroic) assumption that returns are normally distributed. Nevertheless, much of the remainder of this text will assume that returns are, in fact, normally distributed.

H. SUMMARY

The logic of the theory of investor choice can best be summarized by listing the series of logical steps and assumptions necessary to derive the indifference curves of Fig. 4.12.

- First we described the five axioms of rational behavior.

- The expected utility rule was derived from the axioms.

- Cardinal utility functions were derived from the axioms.

- We assumed positive marginal utility. This and the expected utility rule were used to argue that individuals will always maximize the expected utility of wealth.

- Risk premia were defined and a Pratt-Arrow measure of local risk aversion was developed.

- Stochastic dominance was shown to be a general theory of choice which maximizes expected utility for various classes of utility functions.

- Mean-variance indifference curves (which exhibit second-order stochastic dominance for normally distributed returns) were developed as a parametric theory of choice.

In Chapter 6 we shall use the mean-variance theory of choice as embodied in the mean-variance indifference curves to describe the manner in which investors actually choose optimal portfolios.

PROBLEM SET

4.1 State in your own words the minimum set of necessary conditions needed to obtain mean-variance indifference curves like those graphed in Fig. Q4.1.

4.2 Figure 4.6 shows the utility curve of a risk lover. What does the indifference curve of a risk lover look like?

4.3 You have a logarithmic utility function, $U(W) = \ln W$, and your current level of wealth is $5000.

a) Suppose you are exposed to a situation which results in a 50/50 chance of winning or losing $1000. If you can buy insurance which completely removes the risk for a fee of $125, will you buy it or take the gamble?

Mean

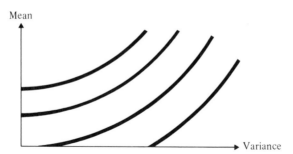

Fig. Q4.1 Mean-variance indifference curves

b) Suppose you accept the gamble outlined in (a) and lose, so that your wealth is reduced to $4000. If you are faced with the same gamble and have the same offer of insurance as before, will you buy the insurance the second time around?

4.4 Assume that you have a logarithmic utility function for wealth $U(W) = \ln(W)$ and that you are faced with a 50/50 chance of winning or losing $1000. How much will you pay to avoid this risk if your current level of wealth is $10,000? How much would you pay if your level of wealth were $1,000,000?

4.5 Given the exponential utility function $U(w) = -e^{-aw}$.

a) Graph the function, assuming $a > 0$.
b) Does the function exhibit positive marginal utility and risk aversion?
c) Does the function have decreasing absolute risk aversion?
d) Does the function have constant relative risk aversion?

4.6 What kind of utility function of wealth might be consistent with an individual gambling and paying insurance at the same time?

4.7 Suppose that $A > B > C > D$ and that the utilities of these alternatives satisfy $U(A) + U(D) = U(B) + U(C)$. Is it true that $U(\frac{1}{2}B + \frac{1}{2}C)$ is greater than $U(\frac{1}{2}A + \frac{1}{2}D)$ because the former has a smaller variance? Why or why not?

4.8 A small businessman faces a 10% chance of having a fire which will reduce his net worth to $1.00, a 10% chance that fire will reduce it to $50,000, and an 80% chance that nothing detrimental will happen, so that his business will retain its worth of $100,000. What is the maximum amount he will pay for insurance if he has a logarithmic utility function (i.e., $U(W) = \ln W$)? [*Note:* The insurance pays $99,999 in the first case, $50,000 in the second, and nothing in the third.]

4.9 If you are exposed to a 50/50 chance of gaining or losing $1000 and insurance which removes the risk costs $500, at what level of wealth will you be indifferent relative to taking the gamble or paying the insurance? Assume your utility function is $U(W) = -W^{-1}$.

4.10 Consider a lottery which pays 2^n if n consecutive heads turn up in $n + 1$ tosses of a fair coin (i.e., the sequence of coin flips ends with the first tail). If you have a logarithmic utility function, $U(W) = \ln W$, what is the utility of the expected payoff? What is the expected utility of the payoff?

4.11 Mr. Casadesus's current wealth consists of his home, which is worth $50,000, and $20,000 in savings which are earning 7% in a savings and loan account. His (one-year) home owner's insurance is up for renewal and he has the following estimates of the potential losses on his house due to fire, storm, etc., during the period covered by the renewal:

Value of loss, $	Probability, %
0	.98
5,000	.01
10,000	.005
50,000	.005

His insurance agent has quoted the following premiums:

Amount of insurance, $	Premium, $
30,000	$30 + \text{AVL}_1$*
40,000	$27 + \text{AVL}_2$
50,000	$24 + \text{AVL}_3$

* Actuarial value of loss = expected value of insurer's loss.

Mr. Casadesus expects neither to save nor dissave during the coming year, and he does not expect his home to change appreciably in value over this period. His utility for wealth at the end of the period covered by the renewal is logarithmic, that is, $U(W) = \ln (W)$.

a) Given that the insurance company agrees with Mr. Casadesus's estimate of his losses, should he renew his policy for the full value of his house, for $40,000, for $30,000, or should he cancel it?

b) Suppose that Mr. Casadesus had $320,000 in a savings account. Would this change his insurance decision?

c) If Mr. Casadesus has $20,000 in savings, and if his utility function is

$$U(W) = -200{,}000W^{-1},$$

should he renew his home insurance, and if so, for what amount of coverage?

[*Note:* Insurance covers the first x dollars of loss. For simplicity, assume all losses occur at the end of the year, and the premium is paid at the beginning of the year.]

4.12 Assume that security returns are normally distributed. Compare portfolios A and B, using both first- and second-order stochastic dominance.

Case 1	Case 2	Case 3
$\sigma_A > \sigma_B$	$\sigma_A = \sigma_B$	$\sigma_A < \sigma_B$
$E_A = E_B$	$E_A > E_B$	$E_A \leq E_B$

4.13 Given the following probability distributions for risky assets X and Y.

Probability X_i	X_i	Probability Y_i	Y_i
.1	−10	.2	2
.4	5	.5	3
.3	10	.2	4
.2	12	.1	30

a) If the only available choice is 100% of your wealth in X or 100% in Y and you choose on the basis of mean and variance, which asset is preferred?

b) According to the second-order stochastic dominance criterion, how would you compare them?

4.14 You have estimated the following probabilities for the earnings per share of companies A and B:

Probability	A	B
.1	0	− .50
.2	.50	− .25
.4	1.00	1.50
.2	2.00	3.00
.1	3.00	4.00

a) Calculate the mean and variance of the earnings per share for each company.

b) Explain how some investors might choose A and others might choose B if preferences are based on mean and variance.

c) Compare A and B using the second-order stochastic dominance criterion.

4.15 Answer the following questions either true or false:

a) T   F   If asset A is stochastically dominant over asset B according to the second-order criterion, it is also dominant according to the first-order criterion.

b) T   F   If asset A has a higher mean and higher variance than asset B, it is stochastically dominant according to the first-order criterion.

c) T   F   A risk-neutral investor will use second-order stochastic dominance as his decision criterion only if the returns of the underlying assets are normally distributed.

d) T   F   The second-order stochastic dominance criterion is consistent with utility functions which have positive marginal utility and risk aversion.

4.16 Consider the following two risky projects:

Project 1		Project 2	
Probability	Cash flow, $	Probability	Cash flow, $
.2	4,000	.4	0
.6	5,000	.2	5,000
.2	6,000	.4	10,000

Given that the firm has fixed debt payments of $8000, which project will shareholders choose and why?

4.17 Two widows, each with $10,000 to invest, have been advised by a trusted friend to put their money into a one-year real estate trust which requires a minimum investment of $10,000. They have been offered a choice of seven trusts with the following estimated yields:

							Probability that yield will be										
Trust	−2	−1	0	1	2	3	4	5	6	7	8	9	10	11	12	13	14
A							.4	.2	.2	.2							
B	.1		.1	.1		.1	.1				.1		.1	.1	.1	.1	
C						.2	.2	.2	.2	.2							
D		.2		.2					.1	.1		.1	.1				.2
E							.4		.6								
F		.2		.2					.1	.1		.1	.1			.1	.1

Before making up their minds, they have called on you for advice.

a) The first widow leaves you unsure as to whether she is risk averse. What advice can you give her?

b) The second widow shows definite risk aversion. What is your advice to her?

4.18

a) Reorder the seven real estate trusts in Problem 4.17, using the mean-variance criterion.

b) Is this ranking and the "efficient set" the same as that achieved by stochastic dominance?

REFERENCES

ARROW, K. J., *Essays in the Theory of Risk-Bearing.* North-Holland, Amsterdam, 1971.

BAWA, V. J., "Optimal Rules for Ordering Uncertain Prospects," *Journal of Financial Economics,* March 1975, 95–121.

FAMA, E. F., and M. H. MILLER, *The Theory of Finance,* Chapter 5. Holt, Rinehart and Winston, New York, 1972.

FRIEDMAN, M., and L. J. SAVAGE, "The Utility Analysis of Choices Involving Risk," *The Journal of Political Economy,* August 1948, 279–304.

FRIEND, I., and M. BLUME, "The Demand for Risky Assets," *The American Economic Review,* December 1975, 900–922.

HANOCH, G., and H. LEVY, "The Efficiency Analysis of Choices Involving Risk," *Review of Economic Studies,* 1969, 335–346.

HERSTEIN, I. N., and J. MILNOR, "An Axiomatic Approach to Expected Utility," *Econometrica,* April 1953, 291–297.

JEAN, W., "Comparison of Moment and Stochastic Dominance Ranking Methods," *Journal of Financial and Quantitative Analysis,* March 1975, 151–162.

LEVY, H., and Y. KROLL, "Stochastic Dominance with Riskless Assets," *Journal of Financial and Quantitative Analysis,* December 1976, 743–778.

MARKOWITZ, H., *Portfolio Selection.* Yale University Press, New Haven, 1959.

PORTER, R. B., J. R. WART, and D. L. FERGUSON, "Efficient Algorithms for Conducting Stochastic Dominance Tests of Large Numbers of Portfolios," *Journal of Financial and Quantitative Analysis,* January 1973, 71–82.

PRATT, J. W., "Risk Aversion in the Small and in the Large," *Econometrica,* January–April, 1964, 122–136.

TOBIN, J., "Liquidity Preference as a Behavior Toward Risk," *The Review of Economic Studies*, February 1958, 65–86.

VICKSON, R. G., "Stochastic Dominance for Decreasing Absolute Risk Aversion," *Journal of Financial and Quantitative Analysis*, December 1975, 799–812.

————, and M. ALTMAN, "On the Relative Effectiveness of Stochastic Dominance Rules: Extension to Decreasingly Risk-Averse Utility Functions," *Journal of Financial and Quantitative Analysis*, March 1977, 73–84.

VON NEUMANN, J., and O. MORGENSTERN, *Theory of Games and Economic Behavior*. Princeton University Press, Princeton, N.J., 1947.

WALTER, J. E., *Dividend Policy and Enterprise Valuation*. Wadsworth, Belmont, CA, 1967.

WHITMORE, G. A., "Third Degree Stochastic Dominance," *American Economic Review*, June 1970, 457–459.

Chapter 5

State-Preference
Theory

*In this formulation the objects of choice are not derivative statistical
measures of the probability distribution of consumption opportunities
but rather the contingent consumption claims themselves set out
in extensive form.*

J. Hirshleifer, "Efficient Allocation of Capital in an Uncertain World,"
The American Economic Review, May, 1964, p. 80

Finance deals with taking security positions by individuals and firms through the intermediation of the marketplace. In state-preference theory, the notion of investing in securities is used to explain many of the decisions of financial managers and investors.

In the modern theory of finance, the assumption is generally made that all the wealth of society is ultimately held by individuals in the form of real resources. Each individual has some initial endowment or wealth which he divides between consumption and saving. The portion of wealth that is saved provides the wherewithal for firms to invest. The individuals supply the funds and the firms invest the funds. Firms use the resources that are saved in the current period to increase future wealth. The increase in future wealth is then available to individuals either for future consumption or for future savings.

Securities present opportunities for intertemporal shifts of both consumption and productive activities. Securities represent positions with regard to the relation between present and future wealth. Firms issue securities in response to the preferences which they judge individuals to have. Thus the decisions of firms must be responsive to the *theory of individual optimization* which states what individuals desire in the form of securities. Firms seek to respond to individual optimization through the mediation of financial markets.

A. UNCERTAINTY AND ALTERNATIVE FUTURE STATES

Securities inherently have a time dimension. The securities investment decisions of individuals are decisions with regard to the timing of consumption over some future time interval or succession of time periods. The passage of time involves uncertainty about the future, and hence about the future value of a security investment. From the standpoint of the issuing firm and from the standpoint of individual investors the uncertain future value of a security can be represented as a vector of probable payoffs at some future date, and an individual's portfolio of investments is a matrix of probable payoffs on the different securities that compose the portfolio.

In the language of state preference, uncertainty takes the form of not knowing what the state of the world will be at some future date. However, given the state, the payoff of the security is assumed certain. Thus, to the investor, a security is a set of certain payoffs, each associated with uncertain states of the world. Once the true state of the world is revealed the payoff on the security is determined exactly.

The basic concepts are portrayed in Fig. 5.1. The payoffs are in the form of different patterns of returns, control, tax shelter, cash flow, and various types of options under alternative future states of the world.[1] Securities are defined by payoffs under alternative states. Securities are issued by different companies j, k, up to the total number of companies indicated by J. In addition, each company may issue different types of securities. For example, company j could issue common stock, straight debt, mortgage bonds, debentures, secured debt, unsecured debt, preferred

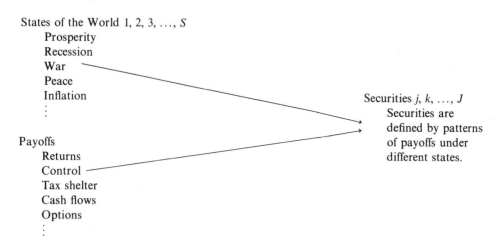

States of the World 1, 2, 3, ..., S
    Prosperity
    Recession
    War
    Peace
    Inflation
    ⋮

Payoffs
    Returns
    Control
    Tax shelter
    Cash flows
    Options
    ⋮

Securities j, k, ..., J
Securities are defined by patterns of payoffs under different states.

Fig. 5.1 Securities are defined by patterns of payoffs under different states

[1] Many of the important results of state-preference theory make the assumption of state independence. In effect this means that it must be possible to express all aspects of the payoff in terms of some standard unit, say money.

stock as well as convertible debt, or preferred stock along with other forms of warrants and options. The different securities from different firms have payoffs of various forms under alternative future states of the world.

Potentially, a multitude of factors will affect alternative future states of the world, so there are infinitely many possible outcomes or states. Table 5.1 lists only a few of the factors which may affect future states. To make meaningful decisions, it is necessary to narrow down the wide range of possibilities and to combine alternative states of the world into "broader" or coarser partitions. An example of this process is set forth in Table 5.2, which illustrates that a firm's sales forecast can be based on a narrower range of alternative variables than those listed in Table 5.1. The wide range of factors analyzed in Fig. 5.1 has been reduced to the three broad influences in Table 5.2. But even these involve a large number of variables. For individual decision makers (in practice, because of the cost of making calculations and because of the "bounded rationality" of individuals) the number of variables actually considered is relatively small. Thus there is a practical limit to the number of factors that a person will ordinarily review in making a decision. Hence alternative future states of the world are likely to be defined in terms of a more limited number of economic and financial characteristics. Individual decision makers will select those variables judged to be most critical for influencing the payoff characteristics of the securities in which a wealth position has been taken.

Table 5.1 Economic and financial factors affecting future states of the world

   I. The Status of International Military Activities
     A. A U.N. international peace force
     B. Suspension of national sovereignty
     C. An outbreak of war in various parts of the world
     D. Attempts at internal subversion and overthrow of government in various countries
     E. Nuclear rearmament or disarmament
     F. Missile fleets

  II. Military Posture of the United States
     A. Armed forces in Europe
     B. Military aid programs to uncommitted nations
     C. Economic aid program to attract allies

 III. U.S. International Policies
     A. Support of export programs
     B. Controls over export of financial capital
     C. International tax policies
     D. International merger policies
     E. Fixed exchange rates
     F. Free exchange rates
     G. Oil price policies of oil exporting nations

 IV. Domestic Economic Policy
     A. Spending programs
     B. Revenue and tax programs

C. Monetary policy
D. Financial management of deficits and surpluses
E. The use of incomes and price policy
F. Guaranteed annual income
G. Types of taxes
H. Capital-gains definitions and rates
I. Inheritance tax definitions and rates

V. The Status of the Individual
A. Healthy or ill
B. Single, married, or divorced
C. Level of education
D. Level of training
E. Shifts in the patterns of consumer standing
F. Aspiration patterns of individuals

VI. Decisions by Individual Firms
A. Rate of growth
B. Composition of assets
C. Financial structure
D. Dividend policy
E. Merger policy
F. Inventions

VII. Policies of Financial Intermediaries
A. Nature of institutional competition
B. Forms of deposits created
C. Forms of investment utilized by the financial intermediary
D. Collection policies of financial intermediaries

Table 5.2 Central factors influencing estimates of future states
of the world for use in forecasting the sales of the firm

A. Economy
1. Real growth rate of gross national product
2. Inflation rate
3. Growth rate of monetary base
4. Interest rate movements

B. Competition
1. Prices of rivals' products
2. New products by rivals
3. Changes in products by rivals
4. New advertising campaigns by rivals
5. Salesmen and other selling efforts by rivals
6. Quality of industry-substitute products

C. Cultural and Political Factors
1. Externalities and their influences on sales of the firm's products
2. Product liabilities

For the practical reasons indicated, alternative future states of the world may be summarized in forecasts of alternative levels or rates of growth in gross national product. There is considerable justification for such a procedure. Ultimately, international economic policy and domestic fiscal and monetary policy will be reflected in the growth rate of the GNP. Furthermore, the rate of growth and the performance of most, if not all, individual industries in the economy are highly correlated with movements in GNP. Thus for many of the examples that will be utilized in this book, alternative future states of the world will be characterized in terms of prospective levels of the GNP. Usually, for convenience of calculation, four alternatives will be considered: a strong rate of growth, a moderate rate of growth, a moderate decline, or a substantial decline.

Most generally, however, the state-preference framework will be used as a *way of looking at problems*. This is one of the great values of the state-preference approach. Most empirical work and empirically oriented illustrations utilize the second approach toward uncertainty that will be used in this book—the mean-variance or parameter-preference approach.

B. THE CONTINGENT CLAIMS ECONOMY

In the timeless market under certainty, choices are made with respect to commodities based on the utility value of their physical properties. In moving to a multiperiod economy under uncertainty, we define a commodity not only by its physical properties, but also by a time period and state of the world upon which the availability of the commodity is contingent. In the initial period before production takes place there is trading in future markets for commodity claims. This is the contingent commodity market economy which yields the same results as the standard model of the microeconomics of a timeless economy under certainty does.

When a securities market is added, the markets for contingent commodity claims are replaced by a market for contingent claims to only one commodity of account, *money*, and the conditional (spot market) exchange of money for other commodities. The efficiency advantage of the securities market is that the need to trade actual commodities and likewise the number of markets in which trading takes place is substantially reduced.

The consumer now allocates his initial endowment over present consumption and future wealth.[2] He maximizes utility over current and future consumption subject to the earning power of his current endowment. In the process his current wealth is optimally allocated between current consumption and savings, and the part of wealth that is saved is optimally invested to yield the highest value of claims on future production. The terminal wealth of the next period, savings plus the payoff on

---

[2] It is being assumed here that an individual gets paid all labor income in the initial period in the form of an endowment. The endowment also includes all income that has been saved from earlier periods.

new production (and also labor services), can then be used to buy a mix of real commodities which will maximize the consumer's utility over future periods.

In the real world, of course, decisions to maximize utility with respect to current and future consumption are subject to uncertainties about the value of claims on commodities in future periods. However, if the total number of unique securities is equal to the total number of alternative future states of the world, the market is said to be complete. Given a *complete securities market*, an individual could theoretically reduce the uncertainty about the value of his future wealth to zero. All that would remain is uncertainty about which state of the world will actually occur. That is, by dividing his wealth among all the available securities the investor could, if he chose, construct a portfolio that would have the same payoff in every state even though the payoffs of individual securities varied over states.

Analytically, the generalization of the standard, timeless, microeconomic analysis under certainty to a multiperiod economy under uncertainty with securities markets is facilitated by the concept of a pure security. A *pure or primitive security* is defined as a security which pays a return of $1 if a given state occurs and nothing if any other state occurs. The concept of pure security allows the logical decomposition of market securities into portfolios of pure securities.[3] Thus every real security may be considered a combination of various pure securities.

If a market portfolio could be constructed to represent the totality of all real securities, it would constitute a claim to the total production output regardless of the state of the world. By holding a proportionate share of the market portfolio an individual could be assured of a proportionate share of the total output of the production process of the state that occurs. And in one sense, the market portfolio can be viewed as the totality of all existing pure securities.

Without going through a complex solution process to attain the general equilibrium results which the concept of a pure security facilitates, we shall convey the role of the concept of a pure security in a more limited setting. We shall demonstrate how the implicit price of a pure security can be derived from the market prices of existing complex securities and how in turn the market prices of other securities can be developed from the implicit prices of pure securities.

C. THE PRICE OF A PURE SECURITY

In terms of state preference, a security represents a position with regard to each possible future state of the world. With reference to Fig. 5.1, market securities are defined with respect to the characteristics of their payoffs under each alternative future state. A market security thus consists of a set of payoff characteristics distributed over states of the world. The complexity of the security may range from numerous payoff characteristics in many states to no payoff at all in most states. In

---

[3] Pure or primitive securities are often called Arrow-Debreu securities, since Arrow and Debreu [1954] set forth their original specification.

contrast, a pure security is one that pays $1 if a specific state occurs and nothing if any other state occurs.

To show how actual securities represent a combination of underlying pure securities let us begin with an analogy. The Mistinback Company sells baskets of fruit, limiting its sales to only two types of baskets. Basket 1 is composed of 10 bananas and 20 apples and sells for $8. Basket 2 is composed of 30 bananas and 10 apples and sells for $9. The situation may be summarized by the payoffs set forth in Table 5.3.

Table 5.3 Payoffs in relation to prices of baskets of fruit

	Bananas	Apples	Prices
Basket 1	10	20	$8
Basket 2	30	10	$9

Using the relationships in Table 5.3, we can solve for the prices of apples and bananas separately. Let us denote the market security price by P, the pure security price by p, quantity by Q, apples by A, bananas by B, and the baskets of fruit by 1 and 2, respectively. Using this notation, we can express the prices of the two baskets as follows:

$$P_1 = p_A Q_{1A} + p_B Q_{1B}, \qquad P_2 = p_A Q_{2A} + p_B Q_{2B}.$$

Only p_A and p_B are unknown. Thus there are two equations and two unknowns, and the system is solvable as follows: Substitute the known values in each equation:

(1) $\$8 = p_A 20 + p_B 10,$ (2) $\$9 = p_A 10 + p_B 30.$

Subtract three times Eq. (1) from Eq. (2) to obtain p_A:

$$
\begin{aligned}
\$9 &= p_A 10 + p_B 30 \\
-\$24 &= -p_A 60 - p_B 30 \\
\hline
-\$15 &= -p_A 50 \\
p_A &= \$.30.
\end{aligned}
$$

Then substituting the value of p_A into Eq. (1), we have

$$\$8 = (.30)20 + p_B 10 = 6 + p_B 10,$$

$$2 = p_B 10,$$

$$p_B = \$.20.$$

We may now apply this same analysis to securities. Consider security j which pays $10 if state 1 occurs and $20 if state 2 occurs. The price of security j is $8. Security k pays $30 if state 1 occurs and $10 if state 2 occurs. Its price is $9. Note that state 1 might be a GNP growth of 8% in real terms during one year while state 2 might represent a GNP of only 1% growth in real terms. This information is summarized in Table 5.4.

Table 5.4 Payoff table for securities j and k

Security	State 1	State 2	
j	$p_{j1} = \$10$	$p_{j2} = \$20$	$P_j = \$8$
k	$p_{k1} = \$30$	$p_{k2} = \$10$	$P_k = \$9$

Any individual security is similar to a mixed basket of goods with regard to alternative future states of the world. Recall that a pure security pays \$1 if a specified state occurs and nothing if any other state occurs. We may proceed to determine the price of a pure security in a manner analogous to that employed for the fruit baskets. The equations for determining the price for two pure securities related to the situation described are

$$p_1 Q_{j1} + p_2 Q_{j2} = P_j, \tag{5.1}$$

$$p_1 Q_{k1} + p_2 Q_{k2} = P_k, \tag{5.2}$$

where Q_{j1} represents the quantity of pure securities paying \$1 in state 1 included in security j. Proceeding analogously to the situation for the fruit baskets, we insert values into the two equations. Substituting the respective payoffs for securities j and k, we obtain \$.20 as the price of pure security 1 and \$.30 as the price of pure security 2:

$$\$8 = p_1 10 + p_2 20,$$

$$\$9 = p_1 30 + p_2 10,$$

$$p_1 = \$.20, \qquad p_2 = \$.30.$$

It should be emphasized that the p_1 of \$.20 and the p_2 of \$.30 are not assigned to securities j and k. Securities j and k represent bundles of returns under alternative future states. Any actual security provides different payoffs for different future states. But under appropriately defined conditions, the prices of actual securities permit us to determine the prices of pure securities. The concept of pure security is useful for analytical purposes as well as for providing a useful point of view in financial analysis. Thus our results indicate that for pure security 1, a \$.20 payment is required for a promise of a payoff of \$1 if state 1 occurs and nothing if any of the other states occur.

We have illustrated in a simple setting how the prices of pure securities may be obtained. We next consider some uses of the concept.

D. EQUILIBRIUM IN A CONTINGENT CLAIMS ECONOMY

The concept of a pure security enables us to solve the utility maximization problem for individuals under uncertainty. This can also be illustrated in a relatively simple setting. We continue with the basic facts of the payoff table for securities j and k in relation to their prices as set forth in Table 5.4. In addition, we assume that initial savings out of wealth is equal to $720. Since we are concerned with the problem of allocating savings between market securities to maximize the individual's expected utility of wealth when the true state s is revealed, we have simplified the problem by not considering the allocation of initial wealth, W_0, among current consumption and savings. We formulate the problem in terms of achieving a terminal wealth which maximizes the individual's expected utility.

If the individual buys only security j or only security k, how many of each can he buy? Also what will his final wealth, W_s, be in both cases under each state? If the individual invests his entire initial savings, S_0 or W_0, of $720 in security j or security k, the results are as follows:

(1) If security j is purchased,

$$n_j = W_0/P_j = \$720/\$8 = 90. \tag{5.3}$$

Under s_1,

$$W_1 = n_j p_{j1} = 90(10) = \$900.$$

Under s_2,

$$W_2 = n_j p_{j2} = 90(20) = \$1800.$$

(2) If security k is purchased,

$$n_k = W_0/P_k = 720/9 = 80.$$

Under s_1,

$$W_1 = n_k p_{k1} = 80(30) = \$2400.$$

Under s_2,

$$W_2 = n_k p_{k2} = 80(10) = \$800.$$

These results are illustrated in Fig. 5.2. Wealth under state 1 is plotted on the horizontal axis and wealth under state 2 is plotted on the vertical axis. The ordinates for the purchase of security j are $900, and $1800 for states 1 and 2, respectively; for security k, the ordinates are $2400 and $800, respectively. Each is shown on the figure. Alternatively, the initial wealth of the individual may be divided equally between security j and security k. The results would be as follows: For security j,

$$n_j = .5W_0/P_j = 360/8 = 45.$$

Under s_1,

$$W_1 = n_j p_{j1} = 45(10) = 450.$$

Under s_2,

$$W_2 = n_j p_{j2} = 45(20) = 900.$$

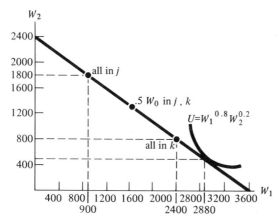

Fig. 5.2 Graph for the analysis of the price of a pure security

For security k,

$$n_k = .5W_0/P_k = 360/9 = 40.$$

Under s_1,

$$W_1 = n_k p_{k1} = 40(30) = 1200.$$

Under s_2,

$$W_2 = n_k p_{k2} = 40(10) = 400.$$

$$W_1 = 450 + 1200 = 1650; \qquad W_2 = 900 + 400 = 1300.$$

From the approach we are taking here, we can determine the prices of the pure securities, implicit in the payoff table. To do so, we need the intercepts of the individual's budget line. We have observed from graphing the points previously calculated that all lie on a straight line.[4] We can therefore determine the slope and the intercept of the straight line using the general linear form $Y = a + bX$, where a represents the W_2-intercept. The equations read as follows:

$$Y = a + bX, \qquad W_2 = a + bW_1.$$

We can use any two of the points we have plotted to determine the value of both a and b. Using the two points where all the initial wealth is invested in either security j or security k, we have the two equations set forth below, and can solve for the two unknowns, a and b.

(1) $1800 = a + 900b.$ (2) $800 = a + 2400b.$

---

[4] Since market prices are expressed as linear functions of pure securities we can extend the budget constraint to a plane in the case of three pure securities, or more generally to an n-dimensional hyperplane where n is the number of pure securities.

Subtracting Eq. (1) from Eq. (2) gives the solution for b:

$$-1000 = 1500b,$$

$$b = -\tfrac{2}{3}.$$

Then by substituting for b in (1) we determine a:

$$1800 = a + 900(-\tfrac{2}{3}),$$

$$= a - 600,$$

$$a = 2400.$$

Using the known values of a and b, we can write the general form of the budget line.

$$W_2 = 2400 - (\tfrac{2}{3})W_1.$$

Setting W_1 to zero and solving, we obtain the value of a (which is the W_2-intercept), namely $2400. We may now proceed to obtain the W_1-intercept. At the W_1-intercept, the W_2-value is zero. Substituting zero for the W_2-value in the equation just used to obtain the W_2-intercept, we obtain the intercept for W_1, which is $3600.

$$W_2 = -(\tfrac{2}{3})W_1 + 2400,$$

$$0 = -(\tfrac{2}{3})W_1 + 2400,$$

$$(\tfrac{2}{3})W_1 = 2400,$$

$$W_1 = 3600.$$

From the intercept values we can determine the prices of the two pure securities.

The intercept value for W_1 is 3600. This represents the maximum amount that can be obtained if state 1 occurs; the result is zero if any other state occurs. We therefore divide the initial endowment of $720 by $3600 to obtain p_1, the price of a pure security that pays $1 if state 1 occurs. Thus p_1 can be obtained by dividing the initial wealth by the maximum amount of wealth if state 1 occurs.

$$\frac{\$720}{\$3600} = \$.20.$$

In words, we divide the total number of dollars of wealth in state 1 into the initial endowment (or the initial savings) to obtain the outlay of initial wealth per dollar of return if state 1 occurs and to obtain nothing if any other state occurs. The result is $.20. We proceed similarly for the price of pure security k: we divide $720 by the W_2-intercept value, which is 2400; the result is $.30. Recall that the same results were obtained by using two linear simultaneous equations in analogy to the fruit basket example.

But an interesting question has come up. We observe that if all the initial wealth is invested in security j the individual is on point j in Fig. 5.2. Similarly, if all the wealth is invested in security k, the individual is at point k. But how is it possible for the individual to be at either of the intercept points?

To reach either of the intercept points requires some short sales, i.e., selling more securities than the seller owns. Indeed, it represents engaging in the maximum degree of short sales possible subject to the investor's budget constraint. The maximum degree of short sales possible would be to have zero wealth (at a minimum) if other states occurred, because in this model no net borrowing at the end of the period is permitted. Then to be at point (3600,0) implies $W_1 = 3600$ and $W_2 = 0$. So, the individual must sell some shares of security j short. The question is how many? We can determine how many by formulating the following two sets of equations:

$$\text{If } s = 1: \quad 30n_k + 10n_j = 3600.$$

$$\text{If } s = 2: \quad 10n_k + 20n_j = 0.$$

The first equation states that if state 1 occurs and only then, the payoff from investing in securities k and j must be \$3600, the state-1 intercept of the budget line. If state 1 occurs, each share of k pays \$30 and each share of j pays \$10. Hence $30n_k + 10n_j = \$3600$. The reasoning for the second equation, which measures the investor's wealth if state 2 occurs, is analogous.

The two equations above can be solved for the two unknowns, n_k and n_j, as follows:

$$\begin{array}{r} 30n_k + 10n_j = 3600 \\ -30n_k - 60n_j = 0 \\ \hline -50n_j = 3600 \\ n_j = -72. \end{array}$$

Thus we find that the individual must sell 72 shares of j short. By selling 72 shares of j at \$8 per share, he receives \$576. The total number of shares of security k at \$9 per share he can then buy is determined as follows:

$$\begin{array}{r} \frac{576}{9} = 64k \\ + W_0/p_k = \frac{720}{9} = 80k \\ \hline \text{Total purchase } k = 144 \end{array}$$

Now we can determine what the wealth position will be under the two alternative states. This is shown below:

$$\begin{array}{r} s = 1: \quad 144 \times 30 = \$4320 \\ -72 \times 10 = -720 \\ \hline \$3600 \end{array}$$

$$\begin{array}{r} s = 2: \quad 144 \times 10 = 1440 \\ -72 \times 20 = 1440 \\ \hline 0 \end{array}$$

Given the portfolio $n_k = 144$ and $n_j = -72$, we can see that if state 1 occurs, the individual is at the W_1-intercept of \$3600. If state 2 occurs, the individual has zero wealth. The point (3600,0) represents the W_1-intercept. This portfolio maximizes the investor's wealth if state 1 occurs.

In a similar fashion, we can determine what the individual must do in order to be at point (0,2400). This represents a situation in which $W_1 = 0$ and $W_2 = \$2400$. In order to achieve this position, he must sell some shares of security k short. Again, we set up two simultaneous equations:

$$s = 1: \quad 10n_j + 30n_k = 0,$$

$$s = 2: \quad 20n_j + 10n_k = 2400.$$

The solution proceeds as follows:

$$
\begin{array}{r}
20n_j + 10n_k = 2400 \\
-20n_j - 60n_k = 0 \\
\hline
-50n_k = 2400 \\
n_k = -48.
\end{array}
$$

Thus the individual will sell 48 shares of k short. By selling 48 shares of k at \$9 he receives \$432. The total number (n) of shares of j he can then buy is determined as follows:

$$
\begin{array}{r}
\frac{432}{8} = 54j \\
+\frac{720}{8} = 90j \\
\hline
n_j = 144
\end{array}
$$

The \$432 obtained by selling 48 shares of k short, plus his initial wealth of \$720, enables him to buy 144 shares of j at \$8. His wealth position under the two alternative states can then be indicated as follows:

$$s = 1: \quad (144 \times 10) - (30 \times 48) = 0 = W_1,$$

$$s = 2: \quad (144 \times 20) - (10 \times 480) = \$2400 = W_2.$$

Given the portfolio $n_j = 144$ and $n_k = -48$ if state 1 occurs, the individual obtains zero wealth. If state 2 occurs, the individual achieves a wealth of \$2400. We thus have the W_2-intercept as shown in Fig. 5.2.

None of the points which we have illustrated thus far necessarily represent the individual's optimum. We need additional information conveyed by the shape of the individual's utility function. The utility function of the individual reflects utility preferences if various states occur. In order to solve for the equilibrium position of the individual we must know his utility function. Therefore, let us assume that the individual has the following utility function:

$$U = W_1^{.8} W_2^{.2}. \tag{5.4}$$

A rationale for the greater utility placed on wealth in period 1 could be that the investor felt his job to be more uncertain under state 1, so he valued W_1 more. Under state 2, the investor is more certain of his job income, so places less emphasis on W_2. Given the individual's utility preferences with regard to wealth in state 1 as compared with wealth in state 2, and the ratio of the prices of the two pure securities under consideration, we can determine the optimal security position for the individual. This is determined by the condition which states that the ratio of the utility preferences must equal the ratio of the pure security prices. Or equivalently, the slope of the budget line must equal the slope of the utility curve at the optimum. In symbols,

$$\frac{\partial U/\partial W_1}{\partial U/\partial W_2} = \frac{\partial W_2}{\partial W_1} = \frac{p_1}{p_2}. \tag{5.5}$$

The equality of the slope of the utility preference curve for the ratio of wealth under state 1 to wealth under state 2 to the ratio of the prices of pure securities is quite logical. It indicates that *the ratio of the marginal utility of wealth under state 1 to the marginal utility of wealth under state 2 is equal to the ratio of the price of pure security 1 to the price of pure security 2.* This is a basic theorem of microeconomics and accords with common sense as well. We already know the slope of the price line from the prices of the two securities. It is $\frac{2}{3}$. From the slope of the utility function we can therefore determine the necessary relationship between W_1 and W_2. This is done by differentiating Eq. (5.4). We proceed as follows: The marginal utility of wealth in state 1 is

$$\frac{\partial U}{\partial W_1} = .8 W_1^{-.2} W_2^{.2},$$

and the marginal utility of wealth in state 2 is

$$\frac{\partial U}{\partial W_2} = .2 W_1^{.8} W_2^{-.8}.$$

The optimal allocation of savings is achieved by investing in securities j and k such that the ratio of the marginal utilities equals the ratio of the pure security prices under states 1 and 2. Thus

$$\frac{\partial U/\partial W_1}{\partial U/\partial W_2} = \frac{\partial W_2}{\partial W_1} = \frac{.8 W_1^{-.2} W_2^{.2}}{.2 W_1^{.8} W_2^{-.8}} = 4\frac{W_2}{W_1}. \tag{5.6}$$

Then setting the above expression equal to the price ratio, we obtain

$$4\frac{W_2}{W_1} = \frac{2}{3}, \qquad W_1 = 6 W_2.$$

This result indicates the relative values of wealth in state 1 compared to state 2,[5] and we find that W_1 is equal to $6W_2$. From this relationship we can determine what the wealth will be under each of the two alternative states and find the optimal portfolio which achieves the wealth positions indicated. We begin by utilizing the budget constraint:

$$W_0 \quad \text{or} \quad S_0 = p_1 W_1 + p_2 W_2,$$
$$720 = .2W_1 + .3W_2. \tag{5.7}$$

Substituting for W_1, we obtain

$$720 = .2(6W_2) + .3W_2,$$
$$1.5W_2 = 720,$$
$$W_2 = \$480,$$
$$W_1 = 6W_2 = 6(480) = \$2880.$$

Recall that the prices of the pure securities reflect the payoffs under alternative states. Thus considering the relative values of wealth under different states, these results indicate the wealth patterns of the desired state, given the initial wealth endowment, the prices of the pure securities, and the state-wealth ratios.

We now have the optimal wealth positions, W_1 and W_2. From these we can obtain the portfolios of securities j and k to achieve these wealth positions by using the following relationships:

$$W_1 = p_{j1} n_j + p_{k1} n_k, \quad 2880 = 10n_j + 30n_k,$$
$$W_2 = p_{j2} n_j + p_{k2} n_k, \quad 480 = 20n_j + 10n_k.$$

$$\begin{array}{rcl} 10n_j + 30n_k &=& 2880 \\ -10n_j - 5n_k &=& -240 \\ \hline 25n_k &=& 2640 \\ n_k &=& 105.6. \end{array}$$

$$480 = 20n_j + 1056$$
$$n_j = -28.8.$$

---

[5] If the exponents of the utility function had each been .5, this ratio would be 1 to 1.5, reflecting the lower price of the pure security 1.

$$U = W_1^{.5} W_2^{.5},$$
$$\frac{\partial U / \partial W_1}{\partial U / \partial W_2} = \frac{.5 W_1^{-.5} W_2^{.5}}{.5 W_1^{.5} W_2^{-.5}},$$
$$\partial W_2 / \partial W_1 = W_1^{-1} W_2.$$

Setting this result equal to the price ratio, we have

$$W_2 / W_1 = \tfrac{2}{3}, \quad 2W_1 = 3W_2, \quad W_1 = 1.5W_2.$$

The optimal portfolio requires that we hold 105.6 shares of security k and sell short 28.8 shares of security j. As a practical matter we could round to the nearest whole share to obtain the approximate results, but for illustrating subsequent tests of the validity of the solutions we will continue to employ fractional shares. We can now demonstrate that the portfolio chosen is consistent with the wealth positions under the two alternative states previously calculated, as we can see from the following check on the results:

$$s = 1: \quad 10(-28.8) + 30(105.6) = W_1$$
$$-288 + 3168 = \$2880 = W_1;$$
$$s = 2: \quad 20(-28.8) + 10(105.6) = W_2,$$
$$-576 + 1056 = \$480 = W_2.$$

The natural question to be raised at this point is, What are the implications of the exercise worked through to this point? Again, we go back to first principles. We observe that every security position represents a bundle or a basket of pure securities. Every security represents a form of diversification albeit an imperfect or inefficient one as we will demonstrate later. Every security represents a combination of positions with regard to alternative future states of the world.

A market security represents a combination of underlying pure securities. By virtue of these underlying relationships, the price of any other security can be determined from the relationship between the prices of pure securities for the two alternative states and the payoffs under the two alternative states from the third security. Suppose we specify that the payoffs in periods 1 and 2, respectively, from security i will be $15 and $40. We can then determine the equilibrium price of security i, using the payoffs under the two alternative states, and the prices of the pure securities. We can use the following relationships:[6]

$$P_i = p_1 n_{i1} + p_2 n_{i2} = (.2)(15) + (.3)(40) = 15. \tag{5.8}$$

This example illustrates that the prices of actual securities reflect the prices of their underlying pure securities. Thus given the payoffs in future states of an actual security and the prices of pure securities, we obtain the price of each security as a weighted average of its payoffs multiplied by the prices of its underlying pure securities.[7]

The foregoing example is a simple illustration of how the individual's choice problem can be solved in a contingent commodity market economy associated with a security market. More formal models in a more general formulation have been

---

[6] The proof of the equation is set forth in Sharpe [1970].
[7] An alternative way to express this is that security i is redundant. Given that the number of states is 2, it is possible to construct a portfolio of securities j and k that has a payoff pattern identical to that of security i. If the price of security i were anything but a linear combination of the prices of j and k, a profitable arbitrage opportunity would exist.

developed to illustrate the same point in a more sophisticated setting. They have broader implications as discussed in the next section.[8]

E.   CONTINGENT CLAIMS, SEPARATION, VALUATION[9]

The state-preference approach has given rise to a stream of literature that provides a useful perspective for our subject. In Chapter 1, the concept of separation was developed. We used Fig. 1.8 to show that when production is added to individual endowments, individuals move to a higher level of satisfaction or utility. When exchange is added to endowments plus production, individuals move to still higher levels of utility. In addition, the property of (Fisher) separation obtains: production or investment decisions can be separated from consumption decisions. The former are delegated to managers who choose the mix or composition of output on the basis of technological conditions given by the production possibility curve. The optimum production decision is given by the tangency between the production possibilities curve and the market price line for the relationship between current and future consumption. In addition, individuals can take the output of the firm and adapt it to their own subjective time preferences between current and future consumption by trading in the financial markets.

Fama and Miller [1972] have expressed the separation principle as applied to the production or operating decisions of the firm in the context of security values. They state that "in making its operating decisions an optimal policy for the firm is to maximize the market value of the holdings of its current owners, irrespective of the details of owners' tastes," and go on to observe that with perfect certainty and perfect capital markets the external interest rates provided by the market represent the appropriate investment hurdle rate or cost of capital for the firm's production/ investment decisions.

These statements of the basic separation principle for a world of perfect certainty and perfect capital markets parallel a similar statement of separation relationships in standard microeconomic theory. In standard microeconomic theory the essential requirements are (1) pure competition and (2) perfect or frictionless markets. With pure competition there are many buyers and sellers of homogeneous products and no economies of scale in production. No buyer or seller influences the prices of factor inputs or product outputs. There are frictionless markets in that there is complete knowledge because information can be obtained without cost. Resources flow without friction and adjustments take place instantaneously. Separation obtains in the

---

[8] See the presentations by Neilson [1976] and Baron [1976] and the stream of literature cited by them.
[9] This section has benefited from the draft of a monograph on the subject by Clement G. Krouse and from extended discussions with him. We also drew heavily on Harry C. DeAngelo's manuscripts and presentations.

model of standard microeconomic theory under certainty: consumers maximize utility, and business firms make output decisions by equating marginal revenue to marginal costs. Under conditions of perfect markets and competition, marginal revenue is always equal to price as well. Under well-known conditions the process develops demand and supply functions whose interactions produce equilibrium for individuals, firms, and for the economy as a whole.

The analysis in Chapter 1 assumed certainty. Now that we have moved to consider explicitly the impact of uncertainty, fundamental questions are raised as to whether separation obtains under uncertainty. The objective here is to find the conditions under which separation and the other properties of an idealized world are satisfied. Then as the highly restrictive assumptions are relaxed, we can progressively analyze the imperfections or frictions which give rise to various institutional arrangements in the real world. By understanding the conditions under which a number of real world phenomena would *not* exist, we have a better understanding of their nature and role. We can then identify the specific departures from the idealized conditions which give rise to various real world institutions whose functions require analysis and explanation.

The timeless economy under certainty has been generalized to a multiperiod economy under uncertainty by the use of the concepts of contingent commodities or contingent claims on commodities (under specified assumptions). These results were achieved in a series of studies by Fisher [1930], Debreu [1959], Arrow [1964], and Hirshleifer [1965, 1966]. The contingent-claim market economy consists of individuals and firms issuing one or more securities. Securities are precisely defined as conditional or unconditional payoffs in terms of alternative future states of the world. Consumers are characterized by their initial endowments (wealth) and by their preferences. Firms are characterized by production functions which define the ability to transform present resources into future consumption goods. *Ex post*, the sum of the payoffs from all securities issued by a firm must be equal to the total output produced by the firm.

The most basic model requires only a single commodity with two time periods. The uncertainty in this world is described by a set of possible states of the world. The state of the world in the second period is unknown in the first period. The total number of possible states is assumed to be finite and mutually exclusive. Consumers do not necessarily agree in their probability assessments of state occurrences. Each consumer is endowed with a specified amount of the commodity and partial ownership in some or all of the firms. Consumers choose between using their endowment for present consumption or supplying part of it to firms against claims on the future output of these firms representing claims on future income or consumption for individuals.

All decisions are made and all trading occurs at the beginning of the first period and all uncertainty is resolved at the beginning of the second period. Consumers maximize their expected utility of present and future consumption. Firms maximize an objective function. Equilibrium is established by a process similar to that of standard microeconomic theory. In the general contingent-claims market economy the numeráire is present consumption, the price of which is equal to one.

The model can be expressed in one of a number of formulations. If there are as many linearly independent securities as there are possible states of the world, the capital market is complete. If there are fewer linearly independent securities than states of the world, the capital market is incomplete. The properties of the models of exchange equilibrium developed have a number of important implications. Particularly, in evaluating many public policy issues with regard to the functioning of firms, the security markets, and the economy, the insights provided by the contingent-claims economy model are valuable. Importantly, the model describes the general financial market framework to which the decisions of individuals and firms must relate.

F. A SECOND FORM OF SEPARATION: PORTFOLIO SEPARATION

We next consider the conditions under which the valuation equation can be expressed in empirically tractable form. This requires the introduction of another concept of separation, termed *portfolio* separation. Portfolio separation requires that the equilibrium price of risk be independent of individuals' utility functions or their risk preferences. This means that there is one market price of risk for all individuals and that the riskiness of any given security is measured by its own characteristics in relation to the market, independent of an individual's risk preferences.

In the earlier literature this result was said to depend upon the form of the utility function of individuals or the form of the distribution of returns. It was said that if utility functions were quadratic or returns were normally distributed, portfolio separation followed and provided sufficient conditions for a valuation equation. The valuation relationship can be expressed in means and variances and is termed the *capital asset pricing model*. The resulting form of the valuation expression is particularly convenient for formulating testable propositions and conducting empirical studies.

However, subsequent literature has established that the necessary and sufficient conditions for portfolio separation are broader than quadratic utility or a normally distributed return. For example, Cass and Stiglitz [1970] established that for arbitrary return distributions, utility functions with the property of linear risk tolerance yielded portfolio separation. The concept of risk tolerance can be briefly set forth utilizing the notation of Brennan and Kraus [1976]. The risk tolerance of the utility function of wealth, $T(W)$, is the reciprocal of the Pratt-Arrow measure of absolute risk aversion discussed in the previous chapter. Thus risk tolerance is defined by Eq. (5.9):

$$T(W) \equiv - U'(W)/U''(W).$$ (5.9)

A linear risk-tolerance utility function can be expressed as a linear function of wealth:

$$T(W) = \mu + \lambda W. \tag{5.10}$$

Utility functions exhibiting linear risk tolerance include the quadratic, logarithmic, power, and exponential functions.

Portfolio separation also obtains for special classes of distribution of returns [Ross, 1976]. The class of return distributions for which portfolio separation obtains include the normal distribution (but not the lognormal distribution), some stable Paretian distributions, and some distributions which are not stable Paretian.[10] Thus the conditions under which portfolio separation obtain are much broader than had been expressed in earlier formulations. This in turn implies broader applicability of mean-variance analysis.

Another line of analysis has been developed which also provides valuation equations. This is the option pricing model. In some respects it is more general than the valuation relationships depending upon portfolio separation. Instead of trading in one period, the option pricing model encompasses trading in more than one period; and in addition to the technological uncertainty of the conventional contingent claims and CAPM models, there is also explicit price uncertainty in the option pricing model. However, the price behavior of securities over time must correspond to a particular process or pattern. Given the price diffusion process, to any option there corresponds a security portfolio (a hedge portfolio) which has to have the same price. Hence the second requirement for option pricing theory is the law of one price.

Thus two important threads of analysis have been developed as illustrated in Fig. 5.3. These concepts will be utilized in the remainder of the book. Both start from the concept of contingent claims contracts. Option pricing theory is concerned with a sequence of trading periods and requires an exogenously given pricing process plus the law of one price. Option pricing theory is an important area of application of the general analysis of contingent claims pricing. It can be utilized in valuing a wide variety of complex contingent claim assets, such as the equity of the levered firm, the value of corporate debt, the effects of mergers and acquisitions or scale expansions and spinoffs on the relative values of the debt and equity claims of the firm, and in valuing commodity options, forward contracts, and future contracts.

Specialization of the conventional contingent claims economy to yield portfolio separation results in an empirically tractable valuation equation expressed in means and covariances. This comes about by requiring risk tolerance for arbitrary security distributions, or alternatively, specialized classes of security distribution returns. As we shall discuss in the following chapters, many of the implications of contingent claims economies exhibiting portfolio separation are consistent with observed behavior and some of its derived statements have been supported by empirical tests. On

---

[10] Paretian distributions have "fat tails," i.e., many extreme values.

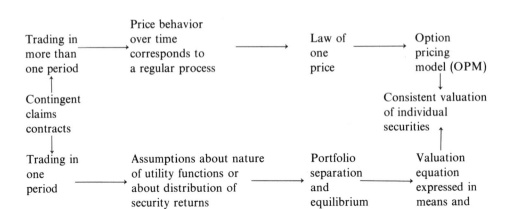

Fig. 5.3 Relationship between contingent claims markets, OPM and CAPM

the other hand, the resulting capital asset pricing model has been found to be inconsistent with some empirical findings and the validity of the empirical procedures themselves have been called into question. Nevertheless, the main threads of analysis and empirical work generated by the basic contingent claims theory have resulted in considerable progress in quantifying and testing the relationships between risk and return.

G. SUMMARY

Wealth is held over periods of time and the different future states of the world will change the value of a person's wealth position over time. Securities represent positions with regard to the relation between present and future wealth. Since securities involve taking a position over time, the passage of time inherently involves risk and uncertainty.

A wide variety of factors may influence alternative future states of the world. The individual decision maker selects those variables judged to be most critical for influencing the payoff characteristics of the securities which he holds. Or alternatively, the form in which a person holds his wealth may be influenced by that person's judgment of the nature of alternative future states of the world.

The individual must formulate some judgments about payoffs under alternative future states of the world. He can then observe prices of securities. From the payoff data and the prices of securities, the prices of the underlying pure securities can be developed. Knowing the wealth of the individual and his utility of wealth function, we can develop a rational basis for the combinations of securities that he will hold in his portfolio. On the basis of the underlying relationships developed, the price of any other security can be determined from the relationship between the prices of pure securities. Conceptually, then, the price of any security represents an equilibrium position reflecting the utility preferences of the individual and the underlying prices of pure securities. The concept of a pure security is also useful to provide an analytical solution to individual choices in a multiperiod model under uncertainty.

The state preference approach is a framework for analysis to provide a solution to the individual's choice decision as well as to achieve equilibrium conditions for the economy as a whole in a multiperiod setting under uncertainty. By extending the concept of a commodity with physical characteristics to a time- and state-dependent set of claims mediated by securities, solution processes are developed. The result is a set of prices or valuation relationships. To make the valuation relationships independent of individual utility preferences, portfolio separation must hold. This second form of portfolio separation requires that the equilibrium price of risk be independent of individuals' utility functions or their risk preferences.

In the earlier literature, portfolio separation was said to require either quadratic utility functions or normally distributed returns. The resulting valuation expression can then be expressed in a mean-variance framework which is termed the *capital asset pricing model*. Later literature broadened the necessary and sufficient conditions for portfolio separation. The class of utility functions with the property of linear risk tolerance yield portfolio separation; these include the quadratic, logarithmic, power, and exponential forms of utility functions. The class of return distributions for which portfolio separation obtains includes the normal distribution and some of the stable Paretian distributions.

The state-preference approach is a useful way of looking at investment decisions under uncertainty. In addition, it provides a conceptual basis for developing analytical models that provide important insights. For example, in models for analyzing capital structure and option pricing, it has been found useful to order the outcomes under alternative states. One can think of the outcomes for future states as arranged in an ordered sequence from an outcome representing the lowest return to outcomes representing the highest returns. Keeping in mind the ordered outcomes for alternative future states, we can specify the conditions under which a security such as corporate debt will be risk free or risky.[11] Also, by combining securities with claims on various portions of the ordered outcomes and by combining long and short positions, portfolios of a variety of types of outcome characteristics can be created. From such portfolios various propositions with regard to option pricing relationships have been developed.[12] Thus, the state-preference approach provides a useful way of thinking about finance problems both for the individual investor and for the analyst seeking to strengthen his conceptual and analytical models.

To date, the state-preference approach has been utilized primarily for the formulation of analytical models of finance problems. It has been used most extensively in formal models for the analysis of capital structure decisions. Since the mean-variance

---

[11] Kraus and Litzenberger [1973].
[12] Breeden and Litzenberger [1977].

approach has been the dominant formulation used in empirical studies in finance, in Chapter 6 we develop the fundamental properties of the mean-variance model. In Chapter 7 the mean-variance framework is used to develop the risk and return market equilibrium relationships that provide a basis for asset pricing.

PROBLEM SET

5.1 Security A pays $30 if state 1 occurs and $10 if state 2 occurs. Security B pays $20 if state 1 occurs and $40 if state 2 occurs. The price of security A is $5 and the price of security B is $10.

a) Set up the payoff table for securities A and B.
b) Determine the prices of the two pure securities.

5.2 You are given the following information:

Security j	$P_{j1} = \$12$	$P_{j2} = \$20$	$P_j = \$22$
Security k	$P_{k1} = \$24$	$P_{k2} = \$10$	$P_k = \$20$

a) What are the prices of pure security 1 and pure security 2?
b) What is the initial price of a third security i, for which the payoff in state 1 is $6 and the payoff in state 2 is $10?

5.3 An interplanetary starship captain has been pondering the investment of his recent pilot's bonus of 1,000 stenglers. His choice is restricted to two securities: Galactic Steel, selling for 20 stenglers per share, and Nova Nutrients, at 10 stenglers per share. The future state of his solar system is uncertain. If there is a war with a nearby group of asteroids, the captain expects Galactic Steel to be worth 36 stenglers per share. However, if peace prevails, Galactic Steel will be worth only 4 stenglers per share. Nova Nutrients should sell at a future price of 6 stenglers per share in either eventuality.

a) Construct the payoff table which summarizes the starship captain's assessment of future security prices, given the two possible future states of the solar system. What are the prices of the pure securities implicit in the payoff table?
b) If the captain buys only Nova Nutrients shares, how many can he buy? If he buys only Galactic Steel, how many shares can he buy? What would be his final wealth in both cases in peace? At war?
c) Suppose the captain can issue (sell short) securities as well as buy them, but he must be able to meet all claims in the future. What is the maximum number of Nova Nutrients shares he could sell short to buy Galactic Steel? How many shares of Galactic Steel could he sell short to buy Nova Nutrients? What would be his final wealth in both cases and in each possible future state?
d) Suppose a third security, Astro Ammo, is available, and should be worth 28 stenglers per share if peace continues, and 36 stenglers per share if war breaks out. What would be the current price of Astro Ammo?
e) Summarize the results of (a) through (d) on a graph with axes W_1 and W_2.
f) Suppose the captain's utility function can be written $U = W_1^8 W_2^2$. If his investment is restricted to Galactic Steel and/or Nova Nutrients, what is his optimal portfolio, i.e., how many shares of each security should he buy or sell?

5.4 An individual has initial wealth $W_0 = \$1200$ and faces an uncertain future which he partitions into two states, $s = 1$ and $s = 2$. He can invest in two securities, j and k, with initial prices of $P_j = \$10$ and $P_k = \$12$, and the following payoff table:

<table>
<tr><th></th><th colspan="2">State</th></tr>
<tr><th>Security</th><th>$s = 1$</th><th>$s = 2$</th></tr>
<tr><td>j</td><td>$p_{j1} = \$10$</td><td>$p_{j2} = \$12$</td></tr>
<tr><td>k</td><td>$p_{k1} = \$20$</td><td>$p_{k2} = \$8$</td></tr>
</table>

a) If he buys only security j, how many shares can he buy? If he buys only security k, how many can he buy? What would the individual's final wealth, W_s, be in both cases and each state?

b) Suppose the individual can issue as well as buy securities; however he must be able to meet all claims under the occurrence of either state. What is the maximum number of shares of security j he could sell to buy security k? What is the maximum number of shares of security k he could sell to buy security j? What would the individual's final wealth be in both cases and in each state?

c) What are the prices of the pure securities implicit in the payoff table?

d) What is the initial price of a third security i for which $p_{i1} = \$5$ and $p_{i2} = \$12$?

e) Summarize the results of (a) through (d) on a graph with axes W_1 and W_2.

f) Suppose the individual has a utility function of the form $U = W_1^{.6} W_2^{.4}$. Find the optimal portfolio, assuming the issuance of securities is possible, if the investor restricts himself to a portfolio consisting only of j and k. How do you interpret your results?

5.5 Two securities have the following payoffs in two equally likely states of nature at the end of one year:

Security	State 1	State 2
j	\$10	\$20
k	\$30	\$10

If security j costs \$8 today while k costs \$9, and if your total wealth is currently \$720, then:

a) If you wanted to buy a completely risk-free portfolio (i.e., one which has the same payoff in both states of nature), how many shares of j and k would you buy? (You may buy fractions of shares.)

b) What is the one-period risk-free rate of interest?

c) If there were two securities and three states of nature, you would not be able to find a completely risk-free portfolio. Why not?

REFERENCES

Arrow, K. J., *Theory of Risk-Bearing*. Markham, Chicago, 1971.

——, "The Role of Securities in the Optimal Allocation of Risk-Bearing," *Review of Economic Studies*, 1964, 91–96.

Baron, D. P., "Default Risk and the Modigliani-Miller Theorem: A Synthesis," *The American Economic Review*, March 1976, 204–212.

BREEDEN, D. T., and R. H. LITZENBERGER, "Prices of State-Contingent Claims Implicit in Option Prices," *Stanford University Research Paper No. 385*, August 1977.

BRENNAN, M. J., and A. KRAUS, "The Geometry of Separation and Myopia," *Journal of Financial and Quantitative Analysis*, June 1976, 171–193.

CASS, D., and J. E. STIGLITZ, "The Structure of Investor Preferences and Asset Returns, and Separability in Portfolio Allocation: A Contribution to the Pure Theory of Mutual Funds," *Journal of Economic Theory*, June 1970, 122–160.

DEANGELO, H. C., "Three Essays in Financial Economics," Unpublished doctoral dissertation, Graduate School of Management, UCLA, 1977.

DEBREU, G., *The Theory of Value*. Wiley, New York, 1959.

FAMA, E. F., and M. H. MILLER, *The Theory of Finance*, New York, Holt, Rinehart and Winston, 1972.

FISHER, IRVING, *The Theory of Interest*, London: Macmillan, 1930.

HAGEN, K. P., "Default Risk, Homemade Leverage, and the Modigliani-Miller Theorem: Note," *The American Economic Review*, March 1976, 199–203.

LELAND, H. E., "Production Theory and the Stock Market," *Bell Journal of Economics and Management Science*, 1974, 125–144.

HIRSHLEIFER, J., "On the Theory of Optimal Investment Decision," *Journal of Political Economy*, August 1958, 329–352.

———, "Efficient Allocation of Capital in an Uncertain World," *The American Economic Review*, May 1964, 77–85.

———, "Investment Decision Under Uncertainty: Choice-Theoretic Approaches," *Quarterly Journal of Economics*, November 1965, 509–536.

———, "Investment Decision Under Uncertainty: Application of the State-Preference Approach," *Quarterly Journal of Economics*, May 1966, 252–277.

KRAUS, A., and R. LITZENBERGER, "A State-Preference Model of Optimal Financial Leverage," *Journal of Finance*, September 1973, 911–922.

MYERS, S. C., "A Time-State-Preference Model of Security Valuation," *Journal of Financial and Quantitative Analysis*, March 1968, 1–33.

NIELSEN, N. C., "The Investment Decision of the Firm under Uncertainty and the Allocative Efficiency of Capital Markets," *The Journal of Finance*, May 1976, 587–602.

ROSS, S. A., "The Arbitrage Theory of Capital Asset Pricing," *Journal of Economic Theory*, December 1976, 341–360.

———, "Return, Risk, and Arbitrage," in *Risk and Return in Finance, Volume I*, I. Friend and J. L. Bicksler, Eds., Ballinger Publishing Company, Cambridge, Mass., 1977, 189–218.

SHARPE, W. F., *Portfolio Theory and Capital Markets*, Chapter 10, "State-Preference Theory," 202–222. McGraw-Hill, New York, 1970.

Chapter 6

Objects of Choice: Mean-Variance Uncertainty

The results of a portfolio analysis are no more than the logical consequence of its information concerning securities.

Harry Markowitz, *Portfolio Selection*,
Yale University Press, New Haven, 1959, p. 205

Chapter 4 introduced the theory of how risk-averse investors make choices in a world with uncertainty. Chapter 5 used a state-preference framework to show that the fundamental objects of choice are payoffs offered in different states of nature. While this is a very general approach, it lacks empirical content. It would be difficult, if not impossible, to list all payoffs offered in different states of nature. In order to provide a framework for analysis where objects of choice are readily measurable, this chapter develops mean-variance objects of choice. Investors' indifference curves are assumed to be defined in terms of the mean and variance of asset returns. While much less general than state-preference theory, the mean-variance portfolio theory introduced here is statistical in nature and therefore lends itself to empirical testing. Some of the empirical tests of a mean-variance equilibrium pricing model are discussed in Chapter 7.

One of the most important developments in finance theory in the last few decades is the ability to talk about risk in a quantifiable fashion. If we know how to correctly measure and price financial risk, we can properly value risky assets. This in turn leads to better allocation of resources in the economy. Investors can do a better job of allocating their savings to various types of risky securities, and managers can better allocate the funds provided by shareholders and creditors among scarce capital resources.

This chapter begins with simple measures of risk and return for a single asset and then complicates the discussion by moving to risk and return for a portfolio of many risky assets. Decision rules are then developed to show how individuals choose optimal portfolios which maximize their expected utility of wealth, first in a world without riskless borrowing and lending, then in a world with such opportunities.

A. MEASURING RISK AND RETURN FOR A SINGLE ASSET

Suppose the task at hand is to describe the relevant features of a common stock to a friend who is an investor. What are the really crucial facts which you should communicate? You could start off by giving the company's name, say Bayside Cigar Co. Then you would discuss the financial ratios of the company: its earnings per share, its inventory turnover, its financial leverage, its interest coverage, and so on. All of this data are merely one way of getting at what is crucial—how will your friend's wealth position be affected if he invests in Bayside Cigar? Consequently, it is wise to talk about measures of the effect on relative wealth at the end of an investment period. The terminology used is end-of-period wealth.

The link between end-of-period wealth and an initial dollar investment is the rate of return. For the time being, we will not specify what calendar interval we are working with except to say that it is a single time period. If the initial investment is I and the final wealth is W, then the investor's rate of return, R is

$$R = \frac{W - I}{I}.$$ (6.1)

The reader will recognize that this is the same expression as that used for the present- or future-value formulas for one time period.

$$W = (1 + R)I, \qquad \text{future-value formulation;}$$ (6.1a)

$$I = (1 + R)^{-1}W, \qquad \text{present-value formulation.}$$ (6.1b)

If end-of-period wealth is known with certainty, then so is the present value of the investment and the rate of return. However, this is seldom the case in the real world. Even short-term default-free bonds such as United States Government Treasury Bills are not completely risk free (although later on we shall use them as a close approximation to a risk-free security).

For risky assets often the best that can be done is to assign probabilities to various possible outcomes. Suppose the current price (P_0) of Bayside Cigar is $25 per share and you tell your friend that after a careful analysis the best estimate of the price per share at the end of the time period is as given in Table 6.1.

1. Measures of Location
It is desirable to develop some statistics which can summarize a wide set of possible outcomes. The most commonly used statistics are measures of location and dispersion. Measures of location are intended to describe the most likely outcome in a set

Table 6.1 Hypothetical prices for Bayside Cigar Co.

p_i = probability	End-of-period price per share	R_i = return
.1	$20.00	-20%
.2	22.50	-10%
.4	25.00	0%
.2	30.00	$+20\%$
.1	40.00	$+60\%$
1.0		

of events. The most often used measure of location is the mean or expectation. It is defined as (the tilde, $\tilde{\ }$, is used to designate randomness):

$$E(\tilde{X}) = \sum_{i=1}^{N} p_i X_i, \tag{6.2}$$

where p_i is the probability of a random event, X_i, and N is the total number of possible events. Hence, the mean weights each event by its probability, then sums all events. For Bayside Cigar, the expected end-of-period price is

$$E(\tilde{P}) = .1(20) + .2(22.5) + .4(25) + .2(30) + 1(40) = \$26.50.$$

The expected or mean return is the expected price less the current price divided by the current price.

$$E(\tilde{R}) = \frac{E(\tilde{P}) - P_0}{P_0} = \frac{26.50 - 25}{25} = .06 \quad \text{or} \quad 6\%. \tag{6.3}$$

This same result could have been reached by using the definition of expected return. However, we have used two probability properties of the expected value operator in Eq. (6.3).

Property 1   The expected value of a random variable $\tilde{X}$ plus a constant a is equal to the expected value of the random variable plus the constant:

$$E(\tilde{X} + a) = E(\tilde{X}) + a. \tag{6.4}$$

Property 1 can be proved by using the definition of expected value. Since the random variable is $\tilde{X} + a$, we take its expectation by substituting $\tilde{X} + a$ for X_i in Eq. (6.2):

$$E(\tilde{X} + a) = \sum_{i=1}^{N} p_i(X_i + a).$$

Writing out all the terms in the sum, we have

$$E(\tilde{X} + a) = [p_1(X_1 + a) + p_2(X_2 + a) + \cdots + p_n(X_n + a)].$$

By simply collecting terms, we get

$$E(\tilde{X} + a) = \sum_{i=1}^{N} p_i X_i + a \sum_{i=1}^{N} p_i.$$

And since we know that the sum of the probabilities of all events must add to 1 ($\sum p_i \equiv 1$), we have proved Property 1:

$$E(\tilde{X} + a) = \sum_{i=1}^{N} p_i(X_i) + a$$

$$E(\tilde{X} + a) = E(\tilde{X}) + a. \quad \text{QED}$$

Property 2   The expected value of a random variable $\tilde{X}$ multiplied by a constant a is equal to the constant multiplied by the expected value of the random variable:

$$E(a\tilde{X}) = aE(\tilde{X}). \tag{6.5}$$

Property 2 can also be proved by using the definition of the expected-value operator. Substituting aX_i for X_i in Eq. (6.2), we get

$$E(a\tilde{X}) = \sum_{i=1}^{N} p_i[aX_i].$$

Then by expanding the sum, we have

$$E(a\tilde{X}) = p_1 aX_1 + p_2 aX_2 + \cdots + p_N aX_n.$$

Next, a can be factored out:

$$E(a\tilde{X}) = a \sum_{i=1}^{N} p_i X_i.$$

And finally, recognizing that $\sum p_i X_i = E(\tilde{X})$, we have

$$E(a\tilde{X}) = aE(\tilde{X}). \quad \text{QED}$$

When we used the definition of return and the expected end-of-period price to derive the expected return, we were using both properties of the expected-value operator described above. In the numerator of (6.3) the price of Bayside Cigar today, P_0, is known and is a constant. The end-of-period price is a random variable. Therefore, the right-hand side of Eq. (6.3) uses Property 1 in the numerator and Property 2 when the numerator is multiplied by $(1/P_0)$, a constant.

The expected outcome, or *the average*, is the most frequently used statistical measure of location, but it is not the only one. Before moving on to measures of dispersion, we should also mention *the median* and *the mode*, which are also measures of location. The median is defined as the outcome in the middle, often referred to as the 50th percentile. Consider the set of numbers (which are equally likely, that is $p_i = 1/N$) given in Table 6.2.

Table 6.2 Set of numbers with equal probability

17	0	7	10	13	3
15	−4	6	−1	17	13
13	25	13	150	−1	6
−8	2	54	32	202	16
13	21	120	24	29	37

Figure 6.1 is a histogram for the set of numbers. Note that most of the probability (in fact 53.3%) lies between −1 and 20. However, the mean, which assigns equal weight to all observations in this case, gives 28.13 as the best measure of location. The median is 13. Clearly, in this case where we have a distribution of outcomes which is skewed to the right, the median is a better measure of location than the mean is. Later on, when we actually look at empirical distributions of security returns, the choice of mean return as the best measure of central tendency will depend a great deal on whether or not the actual distributions are skewed.

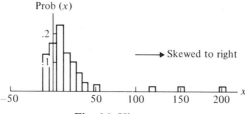

Fig. 6.1 Histogram

The last measure of location to be considered is the mode. It is defined as the most frequent outcome. In the above example it is the number 13, which occurs five times, or the interval between 6 and 13, which contains 23.3% of the probability. The mode is not often used as a measure of location for empirical distributions of security returns because security returns are real numbers (that is, they can take on any decimal value) and consequently do not repeat themselves frequently.

2. Measures of Dispersion

So far we have looked at statistical measures which can be used to best describe the most likely outcome when our friend invests in Bayside Cigar. If he invests $1000, he can expect to have an end-of-period wealth of $1060. (Why?) But the question still remains—what risks is he taking? There are five measures of dispersion which we could use: the range, the semi-interquartile range, the variance, the semivariance, and the absolute mean deviation. Each of these has slightly different implications for risk.

The *range* is the simplest statistic and is defined as the difference between the highest and lowest outcomes. For an investment in one share of Bayside Cigar (see

Table 6.1) the worst outcome is $20 and the best outcome is $40. Therefore, the range is $20. However, the range is a very poor descriptive statistic because it becomes larger as sample size increases. Whenever the underlying probability distribution of investment outcomes is being estimated, for example, by looking at observations of past performance, the estimated range will increase as more observations are included in the sample.

The semi-interquartile range is the difference between the observation of the 75th percentile, $X_{.75}$, and the 25th percentile, $X_{.25}$, divided by 2

$$\text{Semi-interquartile range} = \frac{X_{.75} - X_{.25}}{2}. \tag{6.6}$$

Unlike the range, this statistic does not increase with sample size and is therefore much more reliable than the range.[1] For the set of 30 numbers which we were using earlier (in Table 6.2) the semi-interquartile range is

$$\text{Semi-interquartile range} = \frac{27.0 - 4.5}{2} = 11.25.$$

This statistic is frequently used as a measure of dispersion when the variance of a distribution does not exist.

The variance is the statistic most frequently used to measure the dispersion of a distribution, and later on in this chapter it will be used as a measure of investment risk. It is defined as the expected squared difference from the mean.

$$\text{VAR}(\tilde{X}) = E[(X_i - E(\tilde{X}))^2]. \tag{6.7a}$$

Recalling the definition of the mean as the sum of the probabilities of events times the value of the events, the definition of variance can be rewritten as

$$\text{VAR}(\tilde{X}) = \sum_{i=1}^{N} p_i(X_i - E(\tilde{X}))^2. \tag{6.7b}$$

Therefore, for Bayside Cigar the variance of end-of-period prices is

$$\text{VAR}(\tilde{P}) = .1(20 - 26.5)^2 + .2(22.5 - 26.5)^2 + .4(25 - 26.5)^2$$
$$+ .2(30 - 26.5)^2 + .1(40 - 26.5)^2$$
$$= .1(42.25) + .2(16) + .4(2.25) + .2(12.25) + .1(182.25)$$
$$= 29.00, \text{ which represents dollars squared.}$$

Note that the variance is expressed in dollars squared. Since people do not usually think in these terms, the standard deviation, which is the square root of the variance, is often used to express dispersion:

$$\sigma(\tilde{P}) = \sqrt{\text{VAR}(\tilde{P})} = \$5.39.$$

---

[1] The interested reader is referred to Crámer [1961, pp. 367–370] for proof that sample quantiles converge to consistent estimates as sample sizes increase.

The variance of the return from investing in Bayside Cigar is

$$\text{VAR}(\tilde{R}) = \frac{\text{VAR}(\tilde{P})}{P_0^2} = \frac{29}{(25)^2} = 4.64\%,$$

and the standard deviation is

$$\sigma(\tilde{R}) = \sqrt{\text{VAR}(\tilde{R})} = 21.54\%.$$

This result is derived by using two properties of the variance in much the same way as properties of the mean were used earlier.

Property 3   The variance of a random variable plus a constant is equal to the variance of the random variable.

It makes sense that adding a constant to a random variable would have no effect on the variance because the constant by itself has zero variance. This is demonstrated by using the definition of variance (Eq. (6.7)) and substituting $(\tilde{X} + a)$ for X_i as follows:

$$\text{VAR}(\tilde{X} + a) = E[((\tilde{X} + a) - E(\tilde{X} + a))^2].$$

From Property 1 of the expected-value operator, we know that

$$E(\tilde{X} + a) = E(\tilde{X}) + a;$$

therefore

$$\text{VAR}(\tilde{X} + a) = E[((\tilde{X}) + a - E(\tilde{X}) - a)^2].$$

Because the constant terms cancel out, we have

$$\text{VAR}(\tilde{X} + a) = E[(\tilde{X} - E(\tilde{X}))^2] = \text{VAR}(\tilde{X}). \quad \text{QED} \tag{6.8}$$

Property 4   The variance of a random variable multiplied by a constant is equal to the constant squared times the variance of the random variable.

For proof we again refer to the definition of variance and substitute $a\tilde{X}$ for X_i in Eq. (6.7):

$$\text{VAR}(a\tilde{X}) = E[(a\tilde{X} - aE(\tilde{X}))^2].$$

The constant term can be factored out as follows:

$$\begin{aligned} \text{VAR}(a\tilde{X}) &= E[((a(\tilde{X} - E(\tilde{X}))^2] \\ &= E[a^2(\tilde{X} - E(\tilde{X}))^2] \\ &= a^2 E[(\tilde{X} - E(\tilde{X}))^2] = a^2\, \text{VAR}(\tilde{X}). \quad \text{QED} \end{aligned} \tag{6.9}$$

Going back to the example where we computed the variance of return on Bayside Cigar directly from the variance of its price, we can readily see how Properties 3 and 4 were used. Let us recall that the definition of return is

$$R_i = \frac{P_i - P_0}{P_0},$$

and that the expected return is

$$E(\tilde{R}) = \frac{E(\tilde{P}) - P_0}{P_0}.$$

Therefore the variance of return is

$$VAR(\tilde{R}) = E[(\tilde{R} - E(\tilde{R}))^2]$$

$$= E\left[\left(\frac{P_i - P_0}{P_0} - \frac{E(\tilde{P}) - P_0}{P_0}\right)^2\right].$$

Because P_0 is a constant, we can use Property 4 to write

$$VAR(\tilde{R}) = \frac{1}{P_0^2} E[(P_i - E(\tilde{P}))^2]$$

$$= \frac{VAR(\tilde{P})}{P_0^2}.$$

And, of course, this is exactly the formula used earlier to compute the variance of return from our knowledge of the variance of prices.

The next section of this chapter uses the properties of the mean and variance which we have developed here in order to discuss the mean and variance of a portfolio of assets. At this point we could summarize the investment opportunity offered by Bayside Cigar by saying that the expected price is $26.50 with a standard deviation of $5.39. Or else we could say that the expected return on this investment is 6% with a standard deviation of $\pm 21.54\%$. However, before moving on, it will be useful to contrast the variance as a measure of risk with the *semivariance* and the *mean absolute deviation*.

One problem with the variance is that it gives equal weight to possibilities above as well as below the average. However, suppose that risk-averse investors are more concerned with downside risk. The semivariance is a statistic which does just this. It is defined as the expectation of the mean differences *below* the mean, squared. Mathematically, the definition is as follows. Let

$$X_i^- = \begin{cases} X_i - E(X) & \text{if} \quad X_i < E(X) \\ 0 & \text{if} \quad X_i \geq E(X) \end{cases}$$

then

$$SEMIVAR = E\{(X_i^-)^2\}. \tag{6.10}$$

If the semivariance is used as a measure of risk, an increase in probability of events above the mean will change risk only slightly because the only effect would be to increase the mean slightly. For example, the semivariance of return for Bayside Cigar is

$$SEMIVAR = .1(-.20 - .06)^2 + .2(-.10 - .06)^2 + .4(0 - .06)^2$$

$$= 1.332\%.$$

But if the probability of a 60% return (in Table 6.1) were to increase to .2 while the probability of a 20% return fell to .1, the impact on semivariance would be slight. The new expected return would be 10% and the semivariance would increase to 2.1%. Given the same change in probabilities, the variance would increase from 4.64% to 7.824%.

Both the variance and semivariance are sensitive to observations distant from the mean because the mean differences are squared. Squaring gives them greater weight. A statistic that avoids this difficulty is the absolute mean deviation (AMD), which is defined as the expectation of the absolute value of the differences from the mean:

$$AMD = E[|X_i - E(\tilde{X})|]. \tag{6.11}$$

For the Bayside Cigar example, the absolute mean deviation is

$$AMD = .1|(-.2 - .06)| + .2|(-.1 - .06)| + .4|(0 - .06)|$$
$$+ .2(.2 - .06) + .1(.6 - .06)$$
$$= 16.4\%.$$

Although, for the most part we shall measure risk and return by using the variance (or standard deviation) and the mean return, it is useful to keep in mind that there are other statistics which, in some situations, may be more appropriate. An understanding of these statistics helps to put the mean and variance into proper perspective.

B. MEASURING PORTFOLIO RISK AND RETURN

From this point on we assume that investors measure the expected utility of choices among risky assets by looking at the mean and variance provided by combinations of those assets. For a financial manager, the operating risk of the firm may be measured by estimating the mean and variance of returns provided by the portfolio of assets which the firm holds: its inventory, cash, accounts receivable, marketable securities, and physical plant. For a portfolio manager, the risk and return are the mean and variance of the weighted average of the assets in his portfolio. Therefore, in order to understand how to manage risk it becomes necessary to explore the risk and return provided by combinations of risky assets.

1. The Normal Distribution
By looking only at mean and variance, we are necessarily assuming that no other statistics are necessary to describe the distribution of end-of-period wealth. Unless investors have a special type of utility function (quadratic utility function), it is necessary to assume that returns have a normal distribution, which can be completely described by mean and variance. This is the bell-shaped probability distribution which most natural phenomena obey. For example, measures of IQs follow this distribution. An example is given in Fig. 6.2. The probability of a return is measured along the vertical axis, and the returns are measured along the horizontal axis. The

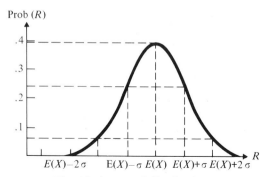

Fig. 6.2 A normal distribution

normal distribution is perfectly symmetric and 50% of the probability lies above the mean, 15.9% above a point one standard deviation above the mean, and 2.3% above a point two standard deviations above the mean. Because of its symmetry, the variance and semivariance are equivalent measures of risk for the normal distribution. Furthermore, if you know the mean and standard deviation (or semivariance) of a normal distribution, you know the likelihood of every point in the distribution. This would not be true if the distribution were not symmetric. If it were skewed to the right, for example, one would also need to know a measure of skewness in addition to the mean and standard deviation, and the variance and semivariance would not be equivalent.

2.   Calculating the Mean and Variance of a Two-Asset Portfolio

Consider a portfolio of two risky assets which are both normally distributed. How can we measure the mean and standard deviation of a portfolio with $a\%$ of our wealth invested in asset X and $b\% = (1 - a\%)$ invested in asset Y? Mathematically, the portfolio return can be expressed as the sum of two random variables.

$$\tilde{R}_p = a\tilde{X} + b\tilde{Y}.$$

By using the properties of mean and variance derived earlier we can derive the mean and variance of the portfolio. The mean return is the expected outcome

$$E(\tilde{R}_p) = E[a\tilde{X} + b\tilde{Y}].$$

Separating terms, we have

$$E(\tilde{R}_p) = E(a\tilde{X}) + E(b\tilde{Y}).$$

Using Property 2 (i.e., that $E(a\tilde{X}) = aE(\tilde{X})$), we have

$$E(\tilde{R}_p) = aE(\tilde{X}) + bE(\tilde{Y}). \tag{6.12}$$

Thus the portfolio mean return is seen to be simply the weighted average of returns on individual securities, where the weights are the percentage invested in those securities.

The variance of a portfolio return is expressed as

$$\text{VAR}(\tilde{R}_p) = E[\tilde{R}_p - E(\tilde{R}_p)]^2$$
$$= E[(a\tilde{X} + b\tilde{Y}) - E(a\tilde{X} + b\tilde{Y})]^2.$$

Again, using Property 2 and rearranging terms, we have

$$\text{VAR}(\tilde{R}_p) = E[(a\tilde{X} - aE(\tilde{X})) + (b\tilde{Y} - bE(\tilde{Y}))]^2.$$

By squaring the term in brackets and using Property 4, we have

$$\text{VAR}(\tilde{R}_p) = E[a^2(\tilde{X} - E(\tilde{X}))^2 + b^2(\tilde{Y} - E(\tilde{Y}))^2 + 2ab(\tilde{X} - E(\tilde{X}))(\tilde{Y} - E(\tilde{Y}))].$$

The reader will recognize that from the definition of variance and by Property 4,

$$\text{VAR}(a\tilde{X}) = a^2 E[(\tilde{X} - E(\tilde{X}))^2] = a^2 \text{ VAR}(\tilde{X}).$$

Also,

$$\text{VAR}(b\tilde{Y}) = b^2 E[(\tilde{Y} - E(\tilde{Y}))^2] = b^2 \text{ VAR}(\tilde{Y}).$$

Therefore the portfolio variance is the sum of the variances of the individual securities multiplied by the square of their weights plus a third term, which is called the *covariance*, $\text{COV}(\tilde{X}, \tilde{Y})$.

$$\text{VAR}(\tilde{R}_p) = a^2 \text{ VAR}(\tilde{X}) + b^2 \text{ VAR}(\tilde{Y}) + 2abE[(\tilde{X} - E(\tilde{X}))(\tilde{Y} - E(\tilde{Y}))],$$
$$\text{COV}(\tilde{X}, \tilde{Y}) \equiv E[(\tilde{X} - E(\tilde{X}))(\tilde{Y} - E(\tilde{Y}))].$$

The covariance is a measure of the way in which the two random variables move in relation to each other. If the covariance is positive, the variables move in the same direction. If it is negative, they move in opposite directions. The covariance is an extremely important concept because it is the appropriate measure of the contribution of a single asset to portfolio risk. The variance of a random variable is really the same thing as its covariance with itself:[2]

$$\text{COV}(aX, aX) = a \cdot aE[(X - E(X))(X - E(X))]$$
$$= a^2 E[(X - E(X))^2] = a^2 \text{ VAR } X.$$

We now see that the definition of variance for a portfolio of two assets is

$$\text{VAR}(R_p) = a^2 \text{ VAR } X + b^2 \text{ VAR } Y + 2ab \text{ COV}(X, Y). \qquad (6.13)$$

In order to provide a better intuitive feel for portfolio variance and for the meaning of covariance, consider the following set of returns for assets X and Y.

---

[2] From this point on, the tilde, ~, will be used to designate a random variable only when it is needed to prevent ambiguity.

Probability	X_i	Y_i
.2	11%	-3%
.2	9%	15%
.2	25%	2%
.2	7%	20%
.2	-2%	6%

In order to simplify matters we have assumed that each pair of returns $[X_i, Y_i]$ has equal probability (Prob $= .2$). The expected value of X is 10%, and the expected value of Y is 8%. The variances are computed below.

$$\text{VAR}(X) = .2(.11 - .10)^2 + .2(.09 - .10)^2 + .2(.25 - .10)^2$$
$$+ .2(.07 - .10)^2 + .2(-.02 - .10)^2$$
$$= .0076.$$

$$\text{VAR}(Y) = .2(-.03 - .08)^2 + .2(.15 - .08)^2 + .2(.02 - .08)^2$$
$$+ .2(.20 - .08)^2 + .2(.06 - .08)^2$$
$$= .00708.$$

The covariance between X and Y is

$$\text{COV}(X, Y) = E[(X - E(X))(Y - E(Y))]$$
$$= .2(.11 - .10)(-.03 - .08) + .2(.09 - .10)(.15 - .08)$$
$$+ .2(.25 - .10)(.02 - .08) + .2(.07 - .10)(.20 - .08)$$
$$+ .2(-.02 - .10)(.06 - .08)$$
$$= -.0024.$$

The negative covariance means that the returns on asset X and asset Y tend to move in opposite directions. If we invest in both securities at once, the result is a portfolio which is less risky than holding either asset separately: while we are losing with asset X we win with asset Y. Therefore our investment position is partially hedged, and risk is reduced.

As an illustration of the effect of diversification, suppose we invest half our assets in X and half in Y. By using Eqs. (6.12) and (6.13) we can compute portfolio return and risk directly.

$$E(R_p) = aE(X) + bE(Y) \tag{6.12}$$
$$= .5(.10) + .5(.08) = 9\%.$$

$$\text{VAR}(R_p) = a^2 \text{ VAR}(X) + b^2 \text{ VAR}(Y) + 2ab \text{ COV}(X, Y)$$
$$= (.5)^2(.0076) + (.5)^2(.00708) + 2(.5)(.5)(-.0024)$$
$$= .00247 \quad \text{or} \quad \sigma(R_p) = 4.97\%. \tag{6.13}$$

The advantage of portfolio diversification becomes clear in this example. With half our assets in X and half in Y, the expected return is halfway between that offered by X and by Y, but the portfolio risk is considerably less than half of either $VAR(X)$ or $VAR(Y)$.

Of course, an investor may choose any combination of X and Y. Table 6.3 gives the mean and standard deviation of returns for some of the possibilities. Figure 6.3 graphs them.

Table 6.3 Mean and standard deviation of returns

Percent in X	Percent in Y	$E(\tilde{R}_p)$	$\sigma(\tilde{R}_p)$
100	0	10.0%	8.72%
75	25	9.5%	6.18%
50	50	9.0%	4.97%
25	75	8.5%	5.96%
0	100	8.0%	8.41%

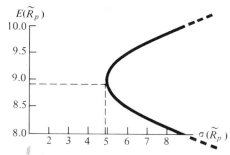

Fig. 6.3 Trade-off between mean and standard deviation

If an investor can sell an asset short without restriction, then the dashed portions of the lines in Fig. 6.3 are also feasible. For example, it might be possible to sell short 50% of one's wealth in asset X and buy 150% of asset Y. If you sell X short, you should receive the proceeds which you can then use to buy an extra 50% of Y. This is not possible in the real world because investors do not receive funds equal to the value of securities which they sell short. Furthermore, they have to post collateral on the value of what they have sold short. Nevertheless, for expositional purposes, we assume that short sales are not constrained. The mean and variance of the above short position are calculated below.

$$E(R_p) = -.5E(X) + 1.5E(Y)$$
$$= -.5(.10) + 1.5(.08) = 7.0\%.$$

$$VAR(R_p) = (-.5)^2 \ VAR(X) + (1.5)^2 \ VAR(Y) + 2(-.5)(1.5) \ COV(X, Y)$$
$$= .25(.0076) + (2.25)(.00708) + 2(-.75)(-.0024) = .02143.$$
$$\sigma(R_p) = \sqrt{VAR(R_p)} = 14.64\%.$$

Now that we have developed ways of measuring the risk (variance) and return (mean) of returns for a portfolio of assets, there are several interesting questions to explore. For example, what happens if the covariance between X and Y is zero, that is, what happens if the two securities are independent? On the other hand, what happens if they are perfectly correlated? How do we find the combination of X and Y which gives minimum variance?

3. The Correlation Coefficient
In order to answer some of these questions, it is useful to explain the concept of correlation, which is similar to covariance. The *correlation, r_{xy}, between two random variables is defined as the covariance divided by the product of the standard deviations*:

$$r_{x,y} \equiv \frac{COV(X, Y)}{\sigma_x \sigma_y}. \tag{6.14}$$

Obviously, if returns on the two assets are independent, that is, if the covariance between them is zero, then the correlation between them will be zero. Such a situation is shown in Fig. 6.4, which is a scatter diagram for two independent returns.

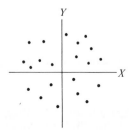

Fig. 6.4 Independent returns

The opposite situation occurs when the returns are perfectly correlated, as in Fig. 6.5, in which the returns all fall on a straight line. Perfect correlation will result in a correlation coefficient which is equal to 1. To see that this is true we can use the fact that Y is a linear function of X. In other words, if we are given the value of X, we know for sure what the corresponding value of Y will be. This is expressed as a linear function:

$$Y = a + bX.$$

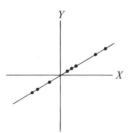

Fig. 6.5 Perfectly correlated returns

We also use the definition of the correlation coefficient. First, we derive the expected value and standard deviation of Y by using Properties 1 through 4:

$$E(Y) = a + bE(X),$$

$$\text{VAR}(Y) = b^2 \text{ VAR}(X),$$

$$\sigma_y = b\sigma_x.$$

The definition of the correlation coefficient is

$$r_{xy} = \frac{\text{COV}(X, Y)}{\sigma_x \sigma_y} = \frac{E[(X - E(X))(Y - E(Y))]}{\sigma_x \sigma_y}.$$

By substituting the mean and variance of Y, we obtain

$$r_{xy} = \frac{E[(X - E(X))(a + bX - a - bE(X))]}{\sigma_x b\sigma_x}$$

$$= \frac{E[(X - E(X))b(X - E(X))]}{b\sigma_x^2} = \frac{b\sigma_x^2}{b\sigma_x^2} = 1.$$

Therefore, the correlation coefficient equals $+1$ if the returns are perfectly correlated, and equals -1 if the returns are perfectly inversely correlated.[3] It is left as an exercise for the student to prove that the latter is true. The correlation coefficient ranges between $+1$ and -1:

$$-1 \le r_{xy} \le 1. \tag{6.15}$$

For the example we have been working with, the correlation between x and y is

$$r_{xy} = \frac{\text{COV}(X, Y)}{\sigma_x \sigma_y} = \frac{-.0024}{(.0872)(.0841)} = -.33.$$

By rearranging the definition of the correlation coefficient (Eq. (6.14)) we get another definition of covariance:

$$\text{COV}(X, Y) = r_{xy}\sigma_x \sigma_y. \tag{6.16}$$

---

[3] The linear relationship between Y and X for perfect inverse correlation is $Y = a - bX$.

This in turn can be substituted into the definition of the variance of a portfolio of two assets. Substituting (6.16) into (6.13), we have

$$VAR(R_p) = a^2 \, VAR(X) + b^2 \, VAR(Y) + 2abr_{xy}\sigma_x\sigma_y. \qquad (6.17)$$

4. The Minimum Variance Portfolio

This reformulation of the variance definition is useful in a number of ways. First, it can be used to find the combination of random variables, X and Y, which provides the portfolio with minimum variance. This portfolio is the one where changes in variance (or standard deviation) with respect to changes in the percentage invested in X are zero.[4] First, recall that since the sum of weights must add to 1, $b = 1 - a$. Therefore the variance can be rewritten:

$$VAR(\tilde{R}_p) = a^2\sigma_x^2 + (1 - a)^2\sigma_y^2 + 2a(1 - a)r_{xy}\sigma_x\sigma_y.$$

We can minimize portfolio variance by setting the first derivative equal to zero:

$$\frac{d \, VAR(\tilde{R}_p)}{da} = 2a\sigma_x^2 - 2\sigma_y^2 + 2a\sigma_y^2 + 2r_{xy}\sigma_x\sigma_y - 4ar_{xy}\sigma_x\sigma_y = 0$$

$$a(\sigma_x^2 + \sigma_y^2 - 2r_{xy}\sigma_x\sigma_y) + r_{xy}\sigma_x\sigma_y - \sigma_y^2 = 0.$$

Solving for the optimal percentage to invest in X in order to obtain the minimum variance portfolio, we get

$$a^\star = \frac{\sigma_y^2 - r_{xy}\sigma_x\sigma_y}{\sigma_x^2 + \sigma_y^2 - 2r_{xy}\sigma_x\sigma_y}. \qquad (6.18)$$

Continuing with the example used throughout this section, we see that the minimum variance portfolio is the one where

$$a^\star = \frac{.00708 - (-.33)(.0872)(.0841)}{.0076 + .00708 - 2(-.33)(.0872)(.0841)} = .487.$$

The portfolio return and variance for the minimum variance portfolio are:

$$E(\tilde{R}_p) = aE(X) + (1 - a)E(Y)$$

$$= .487(.10) + (.513)(.08) = 8.974\%.$$

$$VAR(\tilde{R}_p) = a^2 \, VAR(X) + (1 - a)^2 \, VAR(Y) + 2(a)(1 - a)r_{xy}\sigma_x\sigma_y$$

$$= (.487)^2(.0076) + (.513)^2(.00708) + 2(.487)(.513)(-.33)(.0872)(.0841)$$

$$= .0018024 + .0018632 - .0012042 = .0024565.$$

$$\sigma_p = 4.956\%.$$

---

[4] The student who wishes to review the mathematics of maximization is referred to Appendix D.

The minimum variance portfolio is represented by the intersection of the dashed lines in Fig. 6.3.

5. Perfectly Correlated Assets

Up to this point we have considered an example where the returns of the two risky assets had a negative correlation. What happens if they are perfectly correlated? Suppose $r_{xy} = 1$. Table 6.4 gives an example of security returns where $X = 1.037Y + 1.703$. All combinations of X and Y lie along a straight line and hence are perfectly correlated.

Table 6.4 Perfectly correlated security returns

Probability	X	Y
.2	− 1.408%	−3%
.2	17.258%	15%
.2	3.777%	2%
.2	22.443%	20%
.2	7.929%	6%

$$\sigma_x = 1.037\sigma_y = 8.72\%,$$

$$\sigma_y = 8.41\%,$$

$$\text{COV}(X, Y) = r_{xy}\sigma_x\sigma_y = .007334.$$

Since we have used the same numbers for the returns on asset Y as were used in the previous example, its standard deviation is 8.41%. We can derive the standard deviation of X by using Property 4 and the covariance X and Y by using the definition of covariance (Eq. (6.16)). It is also interesting to look at the graph of mean versus variance (Fig. 6.6). Point A represents the risk and return for a portfolio consisting of 100% of our investment in X and B represents 100% in Y. The dashed line represents the risk and return provided for all combinations of X and Y when they are perfectly correlated. To see that this trade-off is a straight line, in the mean

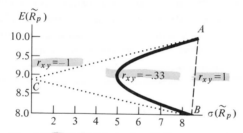

Fig. 6.6 Risk-return trade-offs for two assets

variance argument plane, we take a look at the definitions of mean and variance when $r_{xy} = 1$:

$$E(\tilde{R}_p) = aE(X) + (1 - a)E(Y),$$

$$\text{VAR}(\tilde{R}_p) = a^2\sigma_x^2 + (1 - a)^2\sigma_y^2 + 2a(1 - a)\sigma_x\sigma_y. \tag{6.19}$$

Note that the variance can be factored:

$$\text{VAR}(\tilde{R}_p) = [a\sigma_x + (1 - a)\sigma_y]^2;$$

therefore the standard deviation is

$$\sigma(\tilde{R}_p) = a\sigma_x + (1 - a)\sigma_y. \tag{6.20}$$

The easiest way to prove that the line between A and B is a straight line is to show that its slope does not change as, a, the proportion of the portfolio invested in X changes. The slope of the line will be the derivative of expected value with respect to the weight in X divided by the derivative of standard deviation with respect to the weight in X.

$$\text{Slope} = \frac{dE(\tilde{R}_p)}{d\sigma(\tilde{R}_p)} = \frac{dE(\tilde{R}_p)/da}{d\sigma(\tilde{R}_p)/da}.$$

The derivative of expected portfolio return with respect to a change in a is

$$\frac{dE(\tilde{R}_p)}{da} = E(X) - E(Y),$$

and the derivative of standard deviation with respect to a is

$$\frac{d\sigma(\tilde{R}_p)}{da} = \sigma_x - \sigma_y.$$

Therefore, the slope is

$$\frac{dE(\tilde{R}_p)}{d\sigma(\tilde{R}_p)} = \frac{E(X) - E(Y)}{\sigma_x - \sigma_y} = \frac{.10 - .08}{.0872 - .0841} = .645.$$

This proves that AB is a straight line because no matter what percentage of wealth, a, we choose to invest in X, the trade-off between expected value and standard deviation is constant.

Finally, suppose the returns on X and Y are perfectly inversely correlated; in other words $r_{xy} = -1$. In this case, the graph of the relationship between mean and standard deviation is the dotted line ACB in Fig. 6.6. We should expect that if the assets have perfect inverse correlation it would be possible to construct a perfect hedge. That is, the appropriate choice of a will result in a portfolio with zero variance. The mean and variance for a portfolio with two perfectly inversely correlated assets are

$$E(\tilde{R}_p) = aE(X) + (1 - a)E(Y),$$

$$\text{VAR}(\tilde{R}_p) = a^2\sigma_x^2 + (1 - a)^2\sigma_y^2 - 2a(1 - a)\sigma_x\sigma_y, \quad \text{since} \quad r_{xy} = -1. \tag{6.21}$$

The variance can be factored as follows:

$$\text{VAR}(\tilde{R}_p) = (a\sigma_x - (1-a)\sigma_y)^2,$$

$$\sigma(\tilde{R}_p) = \pm(a\sigma_x - (1-a)\sigma_y). \tag{6.22}$$

Note that Eq. (6.22) has both a positive and a negative root. The dotted line in Fig. 6.6 is really two line segments, one with a positive slope and the other with a negative slope. The following proofs show that the signs of the slopes of the line segments are determined by Eq. (6.22) and that they will always intersect the vertical axis in Fig. 6.6 at a point where the minimum variance portfolio has zero variance.

In order to show this result, we can use Eq. (6.18) to find the minimum variance portfolio:

$$a^* = \frac{\sigma_y^2 - r_{xy}\sigma_x\sigma_y}{\sigma_x^2 + \sigma_y^2 - 2r_{xy}\sigma_x\sigma_y}.$$

Because $r_{xy} = -1$, we have

$$a^* = \frac{\sigma_y^2 + \sigma_x\sigma_y}{\sigma_x^2 + \sigma_y^2 + 2\sigma_x\sigma_y} = \frac{\sigma_y}{\sigma_x + \sigma_y} = \frac{.0841}{.0872 + .0841} = 49.095\%.$$

By substituting this weight into the equations for mean and standard deviation we can demonstrate that the portfolio has zero variance.

$$E(\tilde{R}_p) = .49095(.10) + (1 - .49095)(.08) = 8.834\%,$$

$$\sigma(\tilde{R}_p) = .49095(.0872) - (1 - .49095)(.0841) = 0\%.$$

This result is represented by point C in Fig. 6.6.

Next, let's examine the properties of the line segments AC and CB in Fig. 6.6. In order to do so it is important to realize that the expression for the standard deviation (Eq. (6.22)) for a portfolio with two perfectly inversely correlated assets has both positive and negative roots. In our example, suppose that none of the portfolio is invested in X. Then $a = 0$, and the standard deviation is

$$\sigma(\tilde{R}_p) = -(1-0)\sigma_y < 0.$$

Because standard deviations cannot be negative, the two roots of Eq. (6.22) need to be interpreted as follows. So long as the percentage invested in X is greater than or equal to 49.095% (which is a^*, the minimum variance portfolio), the standard deviation of the portfolio is

$$\sigma(\tilde{R}_p) = a\sigma_x - (1-a)\sigma_y \quad \text{if} \quad a \geq \frac{\sigma_y}{\sigma_x + \sigma_y}. \tag{6.22a}$$

On the other hand, if less than 49.095% of the portfolio is invested in X, the standard deviation is

$$\sigma(\tilde{R}_p) = (1-a)\sigma_y - a\sigma_x \quad \text{if} \quad a < \frac{\sigma_y}{\sigma_x + \sigma_y}. \tag{6.22b}$$

We can use these results to show that the line segments AC and CB are linear. The proof proceeds in precisely the same way that we were able to show that AB is linear if $r_{xy} = 1$. For the positively sloped line segment, AC, using Eq. (6.21), we have

$$\frac{dE(\tilde{R}_p)}{da} = E(X) - E(Y),$$

and using Eq. (6.22a), we have

$$\frac{d\sigma(\tilde{R}_p)}{da} = \sigma_x + \sigma_y \quad \text{if} \quad a \geq \frac{\sigma_y}{\sigma_x + \sigma_y}.$$

Therefore the slope of the line is

$$\frac{dE(\tilde{R}_p)}{d\sigma(\tilde{R}_p)} = \frac{dE(\tilde{R}_p)/da}{d\sigma(\tilde{R}_p)/da}$$

$$= \frac{E(X) - E(Y)}{\sigma_x + \sigma_y} = \frac{.10 - .08}{.0872 + .0841} = .117 > 0.$$

The slope of AC is positive and AC is linear because the slope is invariant to changes in the percentage of an investor's portfolio invested in X.

For the negatively sloped line segment, CB, using Eq. (6.21), we have

$$\frac{dE(\tilde{R}_p)}{da} = E(X) - E(Y),$$

and using Eq. (6.22b), we have

$$\frac{d\sigma(\tilde{R}_p)}{da} = -\sigma_y - \sigma_x \quad \text{if} \quad a < \frac{\sigma_y}{\sigma_x + \sigma_y}.$$

Therefore the slope of the line is

$$\frac{dE(\tilde{R}_p)}{d\sigma(\tilde{R}_p)} = \frac{dE(\tilde{R}_p)/da}{d\sigma(\tilde{R}_p)/da}$$

$$= \frac{E(X) - E(Y)}{-(\sigma_y + \sigma_x)} = \frac{.10 - .08}{-(.0872 + .0841)} = -.117 < 0.$$

The slope of CB is negative and CB is linear.

6. The Minimum Variance Opportunity Set

Line AB in Fig. 6.6 shows the risk-return trade-offs available to the investor if the two assets are perfectly correlated, and line segments AC and CB represent the trade-offs if the assets are perfectly inversely correlated. However, these are the two extreme cases. Usually assets are less than perfectly correlated, that is $-1 < r_{xy} < 1$. The general slope of the mean-variance opportunity set is the solid line in Fig. 6.6. The opportunity set can be defined as follows:

Minimum Variance Opportunity Set   The minimum variance opportunity set is the locus of risk and return combinations offered by portfolios of risky assets which yield the minimum variance for a given rate of return.

In general, the minimum variance opportunity set will be convex (as represented by the solid line in Fig. 6.6). This property is rather obvious because the opportunity set is bounded by the triangle ACB in the figure. Intuitively, any set of portfolio combinations formed by two risky assets which are less than perfectly correlated must lie inside the triangle ACB and will be convex.

The concepts developed in this section can now be used to discuss the way investors are able to select portfolios which maximize their expected utility. The portfolio mean return and variance are the measures of return and risk. The investor chooses the percentages of his wealth which he wants to invest in each security in order to obtain the required risk and return. We have shown the choices which are possible if two risky assets are perfectly correlated, perfectly inversely correlated, and where their correlation lies between -1 and $+1$. We have also seen how the investor can find the minimum variance portfolio. Later in this chapter these results will be extended from the two-asset case to portfolios of many assets.

C. OPTIMAL PORTFOLIO CHOICE: THE EFFICIENT SET WITH TWO RISKY ASSETS (AND NO RISK-FREE ASSET)

In the chapter on utility theory we saw that indifference curves for the risk-averse investor were convex in the mean-variance plane. Figure 6.7 shows a family of indifference curves as well as the convex set of portfolio choices offered by various percentages of investment in two risky assets. An investor who knows his risk-return trade-off and who also knows the possibilities offered by combinations of risky assets will maximize his expected utility at point C in Fig. 6.7. This is where his indifference curve is tangent to the opportunity set offered by combinations of X and Y. Each indifference curve maps out all combinations of risk and return which provide an investor with the same total utility. Moving from right to left in Fig. 6.7, we know (from Chapter 4) that indifference curve I has less total utility than indifference curve II, and

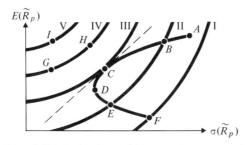

Fig. 6.7 Optimal portfolio choice for a risk-averse investor and two risky assets

so on. The investor could put all of his money in one asset and receive the risk and return at point F, which is on indifference curve I, but of course he can do better at points B and E, and best at point C (on indifference curve III). Points G, H, and I have higher total utility than point C, but they are not feasible because the opportunity set offered by the risky assets does not extend that far.

An important feature of the optimal portfolio chosen by an individual seeking to maximize his utility is that the marginal rate of substitution between his preference for risk and return represented by the indifference curve must equal the marginal rate of substitution offered by the minimum variance opportunity set. The slope of the dashed line drawn tangent to his indifference curve at point C is his marginal rate of substitution between risk and return. This line is also tangent to the opportunity set at point C. Hence its slope also represents the trade-off between risk and return offered by the opportunity set. Therefore, the way an investor can find his utility-maximizing portfolio is to try different portfolios along the opportunity set until he finds the one where the marginal rate of substitution between risk and return just equals the marginal rate of substitution along his indifference curve. The fact that this point is unique is guaranteed by the convexity of his indifference curve and the convexity of the upper half of the minimum variance opportunity set.

Let's take a look at Fig. 6.8. Suppose an investor finds himself endowed with a portfolio which has the mean-variance opportunities at point A. By changing the percentage of his wealth in each of the risky assets, he can reach any point along the minimum variance opportunity set. At point A, the marginal rate of substitution between return and risk along the minimum variance opportunity set is equal to the slope of the line DAF. The low slope indicates that he will get rid of a lot of risk in exchange for giving up only a little return. On the other hand, the slope of his indifference curve, U_1, the slope of line CAB at point A, indicates his subjective

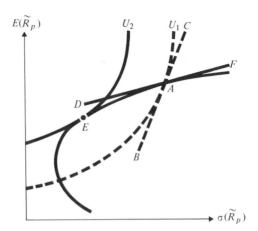

Fig. 6.8 The utility maximizing choice equates the marginal rates of substitution

trade-off between return and risk. At point A, where he already has a relatively high level of risk, he is willing to give up a lot of return in order to get rid of a little risk. If he can, without incurring any cost, move along the opportunity set toward point E, he will clearly do so because the opportunity set at point A allows him to trade off return and risk at a more favorable rate than he requires (according to his indifference curve). He will continue to move along the opportunity set until he reaches point E. At this point he attains the highest possible expected utility on indifference curve U_2. Furthermore, the marginal rate of substitution between return and risk along the opportunity set is exactly equal to the marginal rate of substitution along the indifference curve. Thus we have shown that a necessary condition for expected utility maximization is that the marginal rates of substitution must be equal. This also implies that at the optimum portfolio choice, an individual has a linear trade-off between return, $E(\tilde{R}_p)$, and risk, $\sigma(\tilde{R}_p)$.[5]

Even though different investors may have the same assessment of the return and risk offered by risky assets, they may hold different portfolios. Later we shall discover that when a riskless asset is introduced into the opportunity set, investors will hold identical combinations of risky assets even though they have different attitudes toward risk. However, in the current framework for analysis, we assume that investors have homogeneous beliefs about the opportunity set, that no risk-free asset exists, and that investors have different indifference curves which reflect their differing attitudes toward risk. Figure 6.9 shows three different indifference curves and the investment opportunity set. Investor III is more risk averse than investor II, who, in turn, is more risk averse than investor I. (Why is this true?) Consequently, they each will choose to invest a different percentage of their portfolio in the risky assets which make up the opportunity set.

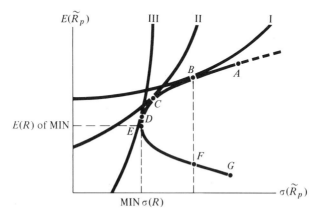

Fig. 6.9 Choices by investors with different indifference curves

---

[5] For an excellent mathematical development of this fact, see Fama and Miller [1972], Chapter 6.

Note that rational investors will never choose a portfolio below the minimum variance point. They can always attain higher expected utility along the positively sloped portion of the opportunity set represented by the line segment *EDCBA*. This concept leads to the definition of the efficient set.

Efficient Set   The efficient set is the set of mean-variance choices from the investment opportunity set where for a given variance (or standard deviation) no other investment opportunity offers a higher mean return.

The notion of an efficient set considerably narrows the number of portfolios from which an investor might choose. In Fig. 6.9, for example, the portfolios at points *B* and *F* offer the same standard deviation, but *B* is on the efficient set because it offers a higher return for the same risk. Hence no rational investor would ever choose point *F* over point *B* and we can ignore point *F*. Point *B* is stochastically dominant over point *F*.

Interesting special cases of the efficient set for two risky assets occur when their returns are perfectly correlated. Figure 6.10 shows perfect correlation, and Fig. 6.11 shows perfect inverse correlation. In both cases, the efficient set is linear. In Fig. 6.10 it is line *XY* and in Fig. 6.11 it is line *XZ*.

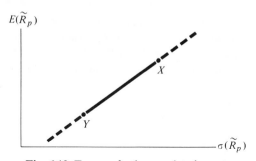

Fig. 6.10 Two perfectly correlated assets

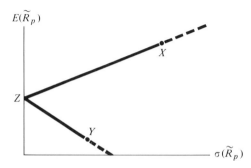

Fig. 6.11 Two assets with perfect inverse correlation

In general, the opportunity set can be found by solving either of the following two mathematical programming problems. Both use the definition of the opportunity set.

Programming Problem 1:

$$\text{Min } \sigma^2(\tilde{R}_p) \qquad \text{subject to} \qquad E(\tilde{R}_p) = K. \qquad (6.23a)$$

Programming Problem 2:

$$\text{Max } E(\tilde{R}_p) \qquad \text{subject to} \qquad \sigma^2(\tilde{R}_p) = K. \qquad (6.23b)$$

The first minimizes variance subject to a constraint that the expected return must equal some constant, K. The second maximizes the expected return subject to a constraint on variance. If we write out the first problem at greater length,

$$\text{Min } \{\sigma^2(\tilde{R}_p) = [a^2\sigma_x^2 + (1-a)^2\sigma_y^2 + 2abr_{xy}\sigma_x\sigma_y]\},$$

subject to

$$E(\tilde{R}_p) = aE(X) + (1-a)E(Y) = K,$$

we see that it is a quadratic programming problem because the objective function contains squared terms in the choice variable, a. The decision variable in either problem, of course, is to choose the percentage, a, to invest in asset X which minimizes variance subject to the expected return constraint. Markowitz [1959] was the first to define the investor's portfolio decision problem in this way and to show that it is equivalent to maximizing the investor's expected utility. The interested student is referred to his book for an excellent exposition. However, it is beyond the scope of the present text to explore the details of a quadratic programming solution to the efficient set. Furthermore, the problem can be simplified greatly by introducing a risk-free asset into the analysis.

D. THE EFFICIENT SET WITH ONE RISKY AND ONE RISK-FREE ASSET

If one of the two assets has zero variance, then the mean and variance of the portfolio become

$$E(\tilde{R}_p) = aE(X) + (1-a)E(Y),$$

$$\text{VAR}(\tilde{R}_p) = a^2 \text{ VAR}(X).$$

We have assumed that the risk-free asset is Y. Its variance is zero. Therefore the second and third terms in the general expression for variance, Eq. (6.17), are equal to zero, and portfolio variance is simply the variance of the risky asset.

Knowledge of the mean and variance of a portfolio with one risk-free and one risky asset allows us to plot the opportunity set in Fig. 6.12. It is linear. Proof of linearity proceeds in the same way as earlier proofs. All we need to do is show that the slope is independent of a, the percentage of the portfolio invested in the risky

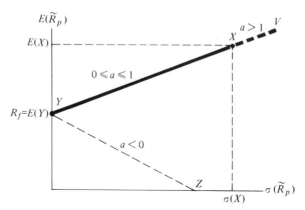

Fig. 6.12 Opportunity set with one risky and one risk-free asset

asset. The change in expected return with respect to the percentage invested in X is

$$\frac{dE(\tilde{R}_p)}{da} = E(X) - E(Y),$$

and the change in standard deviation with respect to a is

$$\frac{d\sigma(\tilde{R}_p)}{da} = \sigma_x.$$

Therefore the slope of the line is

$$\frac{dE(\tilde{R}_p)}{d\sigma(\tilde{R}_p)} = \frac{dE(\tilde{R}_p)/da}{d\sigma(\tilde{R}_p)/da} = \frac{E(\tilde{X}) - E(\tilde{Y})}{\sigma_x}.$$

Consequently, the line VXY must be linear because its slope does not change with the percentage invested in X.

It is usually assumed that the rate of return on the risk-free asset is equal to the borrowing and lending rate in the economy. In the real world, of course, the borrowing and lending rates are not equal. One possible cause is transactions costs, i.e., frictions in the marketplace. However, like physicists who assume that friction does not exist in order to derive the laws of mechanics, economists assume that asset markets are frictionless in order to develop price theory. A frictionless world to an economist is one where all assets are infinitely divisible and where there are no transactions costs. In such a world, the borrowing rate would equal the lending rate for risk-free assets. We shall use this assumption to develop a theory for the price of risk, then provide empirical evidence which indicates that in spite of several unrealistic assumptions, the theory describes reality surprisingly well.

Given the assumption that the borrowing rate equals the lending rate, YXV is a straight line. To reach portfolios along the line segment XV it is necessary to borrow in order to invest more than 100% of the portfolio in the risky asset. Note that borrowing is analogous to selling short the risk-free asset. Therefore, along the line segment XV, the percentage invested in X is greater than 1; in other words $a > 1$. The mean and standard deviation of the portfolio along this portion of the line are

$$E(\tilde{R}_p) = aE(\tilde{X}) + (1 - a)E(\tilde{Y}),$$

$$\sigma(\tilde{R}_p) = a\sigma_x.$$

On the other hand, when the investor decides to invest more than 100% of his portfolio in the risk-free asset, he must sell short the risky asset. Assuming no restrictions on short sales (another assumption necessary for frictionless markets) the mean and variance of the portfolio for $a < 0$ are

$$E(\tilde{R}_p) = (1 - a)E(\tilde{Y}) + aE(\tilde{X}),$$

$$\sigma(\tilde{R}_p) = |a|\sigma_x.$$

Note that because negative standard deviations are impossible, the absolute value of a is used to measure the standard deviation of the portfolio when the risky asset is sold short. The line segment YZ represents portfolio mean and variance in this case.

What about the efficient set for portfolios composed of one risk-free and one risky asset? Clearly no risk-averse investor would prefer line segment YZ in Fig. 6.12 because he can always do better along the positively sloped line segment YXV. Therefore, the efficient set is composed of long positions in the risky asset combined with borrowing or lending. Why then do we observe short sales in the real world? The answer, of course, is that not all people hold the same probability beliefs about the distributions of returns provided by risky assets. Some investors may believe that the expected return on asset X is negative, in which case they would sell short. In equilibrium, however, we know that so long as investors are risk averse, the final price of the risky asset X must be adjusted so that its expected rate of return is greater than the risk-free rate. In equilibrium, assets of higher risk must have higher expected return.

E.   OPTIMAL PORTFOLIO CHOICE: MANY ASSETS

Until now it has been convenient to discuss portfolios of only two assets. By generalizing the argument to many assets we can discuss several important properties such as portfolio diversification, the separation principle, and the capital market line. We begin by developing the mean and variance for portfolios of many assets.

1.   Portfolio Mean, Variance, and Covariance with N Risky Assets

Suppose we wish to talk about the mean and variance of portfolios of three assets instead of just two. Let x_1, x_2, and x_3 be the percentages of an investor's portfolio invested in the three assets; let u_1, u_2, and u_3 be the expected returns; let σ_1^2, σ_2^2, and σ_3^2 be the variances; and let σ_{12}, σ_{23}, and σ_{13} be the covariances. Finally, let $\tilde{X}_1$, $\tilde{X}_2$, and $\tilde{X}_3$ be the random returns. The definition of the portfolio mean is

$$E(\tilde{R}_p) = E[x_1 \tilde{X}_1 + x_2 \tilde{X}_2 + x_3 \tilde{X}_3],$$

and using Property 1, we have

$$E(\tilde{R}_p) = x_1 E(\tilde{X}_1) + x_2 E(\tilde{X}_2) + x_3 E(\tilde{X}_3)$$
$$= x_1 u_1 + x_2 u_2 + x_3 u_3.$$

As was the case for a portfolio with two assets, the expected portfolio return is simply a weighted average of the expected return on individual assets. This can be rewritten as

$$E(\tilde{R}_p) = \sum_{i=1}^{3} x_i u_i. \tag{6.24}$$

The definition of portfolio variance for three assets is the expectation of the sum of the mean differences squared.

$$\begin{aligned} \text{VAR}(\tilde{R}_p) &= E\{[(x_1 X_1 + x_2 X_2 + x_3 X_3) - (x_1 u_1 + x_2 u_2 + x_3 u_3)]^2\} \\ &= E\{[x_1(X_1 - u_1) + x_2(X_2 - u_2) + x_3(X_3 - u_3)]^2\} \\ &= E\{x_1^2(X_1 - u_1)^2 + x_2^2(X_2 - u_2)^2 + x_3^2(X_3 - u_3)^2 \\ &\quad + 2x_1 x_2(X_1 - u_1)(X_2 - u_2) + 2x_1 x_3(X_1 - u_1)(X_3 - u_3) \\ &\quad + 2x_2 x_3(X_2 - u_2)(X_3 - u_3)\} \\ &= x_1^2 \text{ VAR}(X_1) + x_2^2 \text{ VAR}(X_2) + x_3^2 \text{ VAR}(X_3) + 2x_1 x_2 \text{ COV}(X_1, X_2) \\ &\quad + 2x_1 x_3 \text{ COV}(X_1, X_3) + 2x_2 x_3 \text{ COV}(X_2, X_3). \end{aligned}$$

The portfolio variance is a weighted sum of variance and covariance terms. It can be rewritten as

$$\text{VAR}(\tilde{R}_p) = \sum_{i=1}^{3} \sum_{j=1}^{3} x_i x_j \sigma_{ij}, \tag{6.25}$$

where x_i and x_j are the percentages invested in each asset and σ_{ij} is the covariance of asset i with asset j. The reader will recall from the discussion of covariance earlier in the text that the variance is really a special case of covariance. The variance is the covariance of an asset with itself. For example, when $i = 2$ and $j = 2$, then we have $x_2 x_2 \sigma_{22}$, which is the same thing as $x_2^2 \text{ VAR}(X_2)$. Therefore, Eq. (6.25) contains three variance and six covariance terms.

If we replace the three assets with N, Eqs. (6.24) and (6.25) can be used as general representations of the mean and variance of a portfolio of N assets. We can also write Eqs. (6.24) and (6.25) in matrix form,[6] which for two assets looks like this

$$E(\tilde{R}_p) = \begin{bmatrix} u_1 & u_2 \end{bmatrix} \begin{bmatrix} x_1 \\ x_2 \end{bmatrix} = \mathbf{R'W}$$

$$\text{VAR}(\tilde{R}_p) = \begin{bmatrix} x_1 & x_2 \end{bmatrix} \begin{bmatrix} \sigma_{11} & \sigma_{12} \\ \sigma_{21} & \sigma_{22} \end{bmatrix} \begin{bmatrix} x_1 \\ x_2 \end{bmatrix} = \mathbf{W'} \sum \mathbf{W}$$

The expected portfolio return is the $(1XN)$ row vector of expected returns, $[u_1 \ u_2] = \mathbf{R'}$, postmultiplied by the $(NX1)$ column vector of weights held in each asset, $[x_1 \ x_2]' = \mathbf{W}$. The variance is the (NXN) variance-covariance matrix, $\sum$, premultiplied and postmultiplied by the vector of weights, $\mathbf{W}$. To see that the matrix definition of the variance is identical to Eq. (6.25) first postmultiply the variance-covariance matrix by the column vector of weights to get:

$$\text{VAR}(\tilde{R}_p) = \begin{bmatrix} x_1 & x_2 \end{bmatrix} \begin{bmatrix} x_1\sigma_{11} + x_2\sigma_{12} \\ x_1\sigma_{21} + x_2\sigma_{22} \end{bmatrix}.$$

Postmultiplying the second vector times the first, we have

$$\text{VAR}(\tilde{R}_p) = x_1^2\sigma_{11} + x_1 x_2 \sigma_{12} + x_2 x_1 \sigma_{21} + x_2^2\sigma_{22}.$$

Finally, collecting terms, we see that this is equal to

$$\text{VAR}(\tilde{R}_p) = \sum_{i=1}^{N} \sum_{j=1}^{N} x_i x_j \sigma_{ij}, \qquad \text{where } N = 2.$$

This shows that the matrix definition of variance is equivalent to Eq. (6.25).

Suppose we want to express the covariance between two portfolios, A and B, using matrix notation. This will prove to be an extremely powerful and useful tool later on. Let $\mathbf{W'_1}$ be the $(1XN)$ row vector of weights held in portfolio A. For example, we might construct portfolio A by holding 50% of our wealth in asset X and the remaining 50% in asset Y. Next, let $\mathbf{W_2}$ be the $(NX1)$ column vector of weights used to construct portfolio B. For example we might have 25% in X and 75% in Y. If $\sum$ is the (NXN) variance-covariance matrix, then the covariance between the two portfolios is defined as

$$\text{COV}(A, B) \equiv \mathbf{W'_1} \sum \mathbf{W_2} \tag{6.26}$$

$$= \begin{bmatrix} x_{1a} & x_{2a} \end{bmatrix} \begin{bmatrix} \sigma_{11} & \sigma_{12} \\ \sigma_{21} & \sigma_{22} \end{bmatrix} \begin{bmatrix} x_{1b} \\ x_{2b} \end{bmatrix}.$$

Postmultiplying the variance-covariance matrix, $\sum$, by the column vector, $\mathbf{W_2}$, we have

$$\text{COV}(A, B) = \begin{bmatrix} x_{1a} & x_{2a} \end{bmatrix} \begin{bmatrix} x_{1b}\sigma_{11} + x_{2b}\sigma_{12} \\ x_{1b}\sigma_{21} + x_{2b}\sigma_{22} \end{bmatrix},$$

---

[6] The reader is referred to Appendix B for a review of matrix algebra.

and postmultiplying the row vector, $\mathbf{W}_1$, by the column vector above, we obtain

$$\text{COV}(A, B) = x_{1a}x_{1b}\sigma_{11} + x_{1a}x_{2b}\sigma_{12} + x_{2a}x_{1b}\sigma_{21} + x_{2a}x_{2b}\sigma_{22}.$$

In order to show that this matrix result is indeed the same as the traditional definition, we begin with the usual covariance equation

$$\text{COV}(A, B) = E[(A - E(A))(B - E(B))].$$

We know that

$$A = x_{1a}X + x_{2a}Y,$$

$$B = x_{1b}X + x_{2b}Y.$$

Substituting these expressions as well as their expected values into the covariance definition, we have

$$
\begin{aligned}
\text{COV}(A, B) &= E[(x_{1a}X + x_{2a}Y - x_{1a}E(X) - x_{2a}E(Y)) \\
&\quad \times (x_{1b}X + x_{2b}Y - x_{1b}E(X) - x_{2b}E(Y))] \\
&= E\{[x_{1a}(X - E(X)) + x_{2a}(Y - E(Y))] \\
&\quad \times [x_{1b}(X - E(X)) + x_{2b}(Y - E(Y))]\} \\
&= x_{1a}x_{1b}\sigma_{11} + x_{1a}x_{2b}\sigma_{12} + x_{2a}x_{1b}\sigma_{21} + x_{2a}x_{2b}\sigma_{22}.
\end{aligned}
$$

Note that this is exactly the same as the expanded covariance expression obtained from the matrix definition, Eq. (6.26).

The matrix definitions of portfolio mean, variance, and covariance are particularly powerful and useful because the size of the vectors and matrices can easily be expanded to handle any number of assets. The matrix form also lends itself naturally to computer programs.

2.   The Opportunity Set with N Risky Assets

When considering portfolios with many assets, we can discover the opportunity set and efficient set if we know the expected returns and the variances of individual assets as well as the covariances between each pair of assets. This requires a great deal of information. The New York Stock Exchange alone lists at least 2000 securities. In order to determine the opportunity set it would be necessary to estimate 2000 mean returns, 2000 variances, and 1,999,000 covariances.[7] Fortunately, we shall soon see that there are ways around this computational nightmare.

The investment opportunity set has the same shape with many risky assets as it did with two. The only difference is that with many assets to be considered, some may fall in the interior of the opportunity set (Fig. 6.13). The opportunity set will be composed of various portfolios and of some individual assets which are mean-variance efficient by themselves. As long as there is no riskless asset, a risk-averse

---

[7] In general, if N securities are analyzed, the variance-covariance matrix will have $\frac{1}{2}(N - 1)N$ *different* covariance elements and N variance elements.

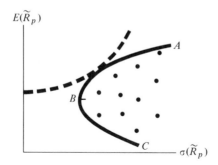

$E(\widetilde{R}_p)$

A

B

C

$\sigma(\widetilde{R}_p)$

Fig. 6.13 The investment opportunity set with many risky assets

investor would maximize his expected utility in the same way as before—by finding the point of tangency between the efficient set and his highest indifference curve. But in order to do so, he would have to estimate all the means, variances, and covariances mentioned earlier.

3. The Efficient Set with N Risky Assets and One Risk-Free Asset

Once the risk-free asset is introduced into the analysis, the problem of portfolio selection is simplified. If, as before, we assume that the borrowing rate equals the lending rate, a straight line can be drawn between any asset and the risk-free asset. Points along the line represent portfolios consisting of combinations of the risk-free and risky assets. Several possibilities are graphed in Fig. 6.14. Portfolios along any of the three lines are possible, but only one line dominates. All investors will prefer combinations of the risk-free asset and portfolio M on the efficient set. (Why?) These combinations lie along the positively sloped portion of line NMR_fO. Therefore, the efficient set (which is represented by line segment $R_f MN$) in the presence of a

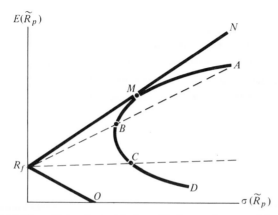

$E(\widetilde{R}_p)$

N

A

M

B

C

R_f

O

D

$\sigma(\widetilde{R}_p)$

Fig. 6.14 The efficient set with one risk-free and many risky assets

risk-free asset is linear. All an investor needs to know is the combination of assets which makes up portfolio M in Fig. 6.14 as well as the risk-free asset. This is true for any investor, regardless of his degree of risk aversion. Figure 6.15 clarifies this point. Investor III is the most risk averse of the three pictured in Fig. 6.15. He will choose to invest nearly all of his portfolio in the risk-free asset. Investor I, who is the least risk averse, will borrow (at the risk-free rate) to invest more than 100% of his portfolio in the risky portfolio M. However, no investor will choose to invest in any other risky portfolio except portfolio M. For example, all three could attain the minimum variance portfolio at point B, but none will choose this alternative because all can do better with some combination of the risk-free asset and portfolio M. Next we shall see that portfolio M can be identified as the market portfolio of all risky assets.

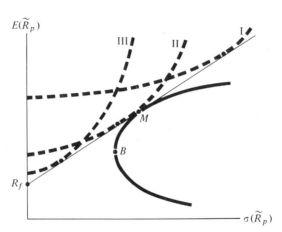

Fig. 6.15 Dominance of the linear efficiency set

4. A Description of Equilibrium

If, in addition to the earlier assumption of equality between the borrowing and lending rate which follows from frictionless capital markets, we add the assumption that all investors have homogeneous (i.e., identical) beliefs about the expected distributions of returns offered by all assets, then all investors will perceive the same efficient set. Therefore, they will all try to hold some combination of the risk-free asset, R_f, and portfolio M.

For the market to be in equilibrium, we require a set of market-clearing prices. All assets must be held so that excess demand for any asset will be zero. The market-clearing condition implies that an equilibrium is not attained until the single-tangency portfolio, M, which all investors (with homogeneous expectations) try to combine with risk-free borrowing or lending, is a portfolio in which all assets are held according to their market value weights. In other words, the percent of wealth held in each asset is equal to the ratio of the market value of the asset to the market value of all assets. Thus market equilibrium is not reached until the tangency portfolio, M, is the market portfolio. Also, the value of the risk-free rate must be such that aggregate borrowing and lending are equal.

The fact that the portfolios of all risk-averse investors will consist of different combinations of only two portfolios is an extremely powerful result. It has come to be known as the two-fund separation principle. Its definition is given below.

> *Two-Fund Separation* Each investor will have a utility-maximizing portfolio which is a combination of the risk-free asset and a portfolio (or fund) of risky assets which is determined by the line drawn from the risk-free rate of return tangent to the investor's efficient set of risky assets.

The straight line in Fig. 6.15 will be the efficient set for all investors. This line has come to be known as the capital market line. It represents a linear relationship between portfolio risk and return.

> *Capital Market Line* (CML) If investors have homogeneous beliefs, then they all have the same linear efficient set called the capital market line.

Figure 6.16 is a graph of the capital market line. The intercept is the risk-free rate, R_f, and its slope is $[E(R_m) - R_f]/\sigma(R_m)$. Therefore, the equation for the capital market line is

$$E(\tilde{R}_p) = R_f + \frac{E(\tilde{R}_m) - R_f}{\sigma_m} \sigma(\tilde{R}_p). \tag{6.27}$$

It provides a simple linear relationship between the risk and return for *portfolios* of assets. Having established the principle of two-fund separation and defined the capital market line, we find it useful to describe the importance of capital market equilibrium from an individual's point of view. We wish to compare expected utility-maximizing choices in a world without capital markets (as depicted in Fig. 6.8) with those in a world with capital markets (seen in Fig. 6.17). As in Chapter 1, a

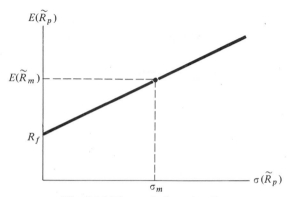

Fig. 6.16 The capital market line

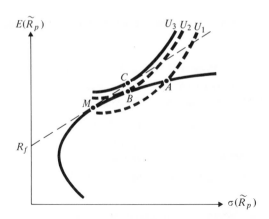

Fig. 6.17 Individual expected utility maximization in a world with capital markets

capital market is nothing more than the opportunity to borrow and lend at the risk-free rate. Chapter 1 emphasized that in a world with certainty, everyone was better off given that capital markets existed and Fisher separation obtained. Now, we have extended this result to a world with mean variance uncertainty. Everyone is better off with capital markets where two-fund separation obtains.

Figure 6.17 shows an individual endowed with the mean-variance combination at point A. With a capital market, he always has two choices available. He can move along the mean-variance opportunity set or he can move along the capital market line. Initially, at point A, the trade-off between return and risk is more favorable along the opportunity set than along the market line. Therefore, he will move along the opportunity set toward point B where the marginal rate of substitution between return and risk on the opportunity set is equal to his subjective marginal rate of substitution along his indifference curve. In the absence of capital markets he would have maximized his expected utility at point B. His level of utility would have increased from U_1 to U_2. However, if he has the opportunity to move along the capital market line, he will be even better off. By moving to point M, then borrowing to reach point C, he can increase his expected utility from U_2 to U_3. Therefore we have three important results. First, nearly everyone is better off in a world with capital markets (and no one is worse off). Second, two-fund separation obtains. This means that everyone, regardless of the shape of his indifference curves, will decide to hold various combinations of two funds: the market portfolio and the risk-free asset. And third, in equilibrium, the marginal rate of substitution (MRS) between return and risk is the same for every individual, regardless of his subjective attitude toward risk.

If the marginal rate of substitution between risk and return is the same for every individual in equilibrium, then the slope of the capital market line is the equilibrium price of risk (EPR):

$$\text{EPR} = \text{MRS}^{E(R_p)}_{\sigma(R_p)} = \frac{E(\tilde{R}_m) - R_f}{\sigma_m}. \tag{6.28}$$

The implication is that decision makers, for example managers of firms, can use the market-determined equilibrium price of risk to evaluate investment projects regardless of the tastes of shareholders. Every shareholder will unanimously agree on the price of risk, even though different shareholders have different degrees of risk aversion.

Next, and in Chapter 7, we turn our attention to the problem of measuring risk. We have already established that variance is an adequate measure of risk for portfolios of assets; however, it is not particularly useful when we wish to evaluate the risk of individual assets which do not lie on the efficient set. Therefore it is necessary to distinguish between portfolio risk and the contribution of a single asset to the riskiness of a well-diversified portfolio (such as the market portfolio).

In order to set the framework for the difference between portfolio risk and individual asset risk, we observe the average return and variance of return calculated for a single asset, Bayside Cigar, and for a 100-stock portfolio of randomly selected common stocks. Return on the assets was defined as total return, i.e., dividends, D_t, plus capital gains, $P_t - P_{t-1}$. The equation for a monthly return is given below:

$$R_t = \frac{P_t - P_{t-1} + D_t}{P_{t-1}}.$$

Data were collected for the 306 months between January 1945 and June 1970.[8] The average monthly return on Bayside Cigar was .45% which is approximately 5.4% per year and the standard deviation of return was 7.26%. By comparison, the 100-stock portfolio had an average return of .91% per month or 10.9% per year. Its standard deviation was 4.45%. Normally, one would expect the standard deviation of a well-diversified portfolio to be lower than for a single asset, and the empirical results bear this out. But we also know that riskier assets should have higher returns. Therefore, if standard deviation is the appropriate measure of risk for an individual asset, then Bayside Cigar should have a higher return. But it doesn't! We shall see in the next chapter that the resolution to this apparent paradox is that although the standard deviation is appropriate for measuring the risk of a portfolio, it is not the appropriate measure of risk for individual assets.

F. PORTFOLIO DIVERSIFICATION AND INDIVIDUAL ASSET RISK

We begin by taking a look at what happens to portfolio variance as we increase the number of assets in a portfolio. Equation (6.25),

$$\text{VAR}(\tilde{R}_p) = \sum_{i=1}^{N} \sum_{j=1}^{N} x_i x_j \sigma_{ij},$$

provided an expression for the variance of a portfolio of many assets. As the number of assets in the portfolio increases, portfolio variance decreases and

---

[7] See Modigliani and Pogue [1974].

approaches the average covariance. There are several ways to prove this. The easiest is simply to note that a two-asset portfolio has two variance and two covariance terms. A three-asset portfolio has three variance but six covariance terms. A four-asset portfolio has four variance terms and 12 covariance terms. In general, the number of variance terms equals the number of assets in the portfolio, N, while the number of covariance terms equals $N^2 - N$ or $N(N - 1)$. Suppose that we have an equally weighted portfolio so that $x_i = x_j = 1/N$. Then the portfolio variance can be written from Eq. (6.25) as

$$\text{VAR}(\tilde{R}_p) = \sum_{i=1}^{N} \sum_{j=1}^{N} \frac{1}{N} \frac{1}{N} \sigma_{ij} = \frac{1}{N^2} \sum_{i=1}^{N} \sum_{j=1}^{N} \sigma_{ij}.$$

This expression can be separated into variance and covariance terms as follows:

$$\text{VAR}(\tilde{R}_p) = \frac{1}{N^2} \sum_{i=1}^{N} \sigma_{ii} + \frac{1}{N^2} \sum_{\substack{i=1 \\ i \neq j}}^{N} \sum_{j=1}^{N} \sigma_{ij}. \tag{6.29}$$

Suppose that the largest individual asset variance is V. Then the first term, the variance term, is always less than or equal to

$$\frac{1}{N^2} \sum_{i=1}^{N} V = \frac{VN}{N^2} = \frac{V}{N},$$

and as the number of assets in the portfolio becomes large, this term approaches zero.

$$\lim_{N \to \infty} \frac{V}{N} = 0.$$

On the other hand, the covariance terms do not vanish. Let $\bar{\sigma}_{ij}$ be the average covariance. Then in the right-hand term in Eq. (6.29), there are $(N^2 - N)$ covariance terms, all equal to $\bar{\sigma}_{ij}$; therefore (6.29) can be rewritten as

$$\frac{1}{N^2} (N^2 - N)\bar{\sigma}_{ij} = \frac{N^2}{N^2} \bar{\sigma}_{ij} - \frac{N}{N^2} \bar{\sigma}_{ij},$$

and the limit as N approaches infinity is

$$\lim_{N \to \infty} \left(\frac{N^2}{N^2} \bar{\sigma}_{ij} - \frac{N}{N^2} \bar{\sigma}_{ij} \right) = \bar{\sigma}_{ij}. \tag{6.30}$$

Consequently, as we form portfolios which have large numbers of assets and which are better diversified, the covariance terms become relatively more important.

Still another way of looking at the risk of a single asset is to evaluate its contribution to total portfolio risk. This can be done by taking the partial derivative of the expression for portfolio variance (Eq. (6.25)) with respect to x_i, the percentage invested in the ith risky asset:

$$\frac{\delta \text{ VAR}(\tilde{R}_p)}{\delta x_i} = 2x_i \sigma_i^2 + 2 \sum_{j=1}^{N} x_j \sigma_{ij}. \tag{6.31}$$

Again, consider a portfolio where an equal percentage is invested in each asset, $x_i = 1/N$. As the number of assets in the portfolio increases, x_i approaches zero and $\sum_{j=1}^{N} x_j$ approaches one. Therefore, for well-diversified portfolios, the appropriate measure of the contribution of an asset to portfolio risk is its covariance with the other assets in the portfolio. In the marketplace for assets (the stock market for example), the number of risky assets is extremely large. We shall see (in Chapter 7) that the contribution of a single asset to market risk is its covariance with the market portfolio. Hence this is the measure appropriate to risk for a single asset, even though individual investors may not, in reality, hold well-diversified portfolios. Relationships (6.30) and (6.31) help provide an intuitive appeal for covariance as the appropriate measure of risk for individual assets, but they are not proofs. For proof, we need to consider market equilibrium. In the next chapter we shall show that the covariance risk of an asset is the only portion of an asset's risk which an investor will pay to avoid. This important idea is embodied in what has come to be known as the *capital asset pricing model*. It is an equilibrium theory which is the main topic of Chapter 7.

But why can't variance be used as a measure of risk? After all, we know that expected utility-maximizing investors choose their optional portfolios on the basis of mean and variance. The answer lies in Fig. 6.18. Asset I is inefficient because it does not lie on the capital market line. Consequently, even though we know the mean and variance of asset I, we cannot be sure what rate of return the market will require to hold the asset because it is not on the efficient frontier. Investors have available to them other opportunities which have the same expected return but lower variance. Therefore, we cannot use our knowledge of the mean and variance of asset I to determine the rate of return which the market will require from asset I in order to hold it in equilibrium. In Chapter 7, given a market equilibrium setting, we shall see that only the portion of total variance which is correlated with the economy is relevant. Any portion of total risk which is not correlated with the economy is irrelevant and can be avoided at zero cost through diversification. Assets I, J, and K have the same expected return, $\bar{R}$, yet they all have different variances. If variance is the correct measure of the riskiness of an individual asset, then the implication is that these three assets, each with different "risk," all have the same expected return. This is

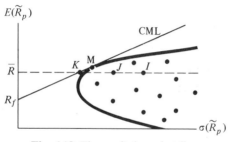

Fig. 6.18 The capital market line

nonsense. It would violate what has come to be known as the single price law of securities.

The Single Price Law of Securities All securities or combinations of securities which have the same joint distributions of return will have the same price in equilibrium.

Since the three securities clearly have different distributions of return, they also have different prices. Even though we know the mean and variance of return offered by assets *I*, *J*, and *K* we cannot be sure what prices they will have in equilibrium. In Chapter 7 we shall see that variance is not the appropriate measure of risk for an individual asset. This was the point of Eqs. (6.30) and (6.31). As the number of assets in a portfolio increases, the risk which an asset contributes to a portfolio reduces to be exclusively the covariance risk. Therefore, that portion of an asset's risk which is uncorrelated with the economy can be avoided at no cost. No rational investor will pay a premium to avoid diversifiable risk. On the other hand, because covariance risk cannot be diversified away, investors will pay a premium to escape it. Therefore covariance is the relevant measure of risk for an asset because it measures the contribution of an individual asset to the variance of a well-diversified portfolio.

G. SUMMARY

This chapter has combined our knowledge of the theory of investor choice (utility theory) with the objects of investor choice (the portfolio opportunity set) to show how risk-averse investors wishing to maximize expected utility will choose their optimal portfolios. We began with simple measures of risk and return, (and simple probability theory) and ended with portfolio theory. Finally, we saw that when a risk-free asset exists, the opportunity set offered by a portfolio of risky assets can be reduced to the simple, linear capital market line. Given frictionless capital markets and homogeneous investor expectations, all individuals will choose to hold some combination of the risk-free asset and the market portfolio.

PROBLEM SET

6.1 Historically, the empirical distributions of stock prices on the NYSE have been skewed right. Why?

6.2 Given the following relationship between x and y,

$$y = a + bx, \quad b < 0,$$

prove that x and y are perfectly negatively correlated.

6.3 Given the following hypothetical end-of-period prices for shares of the Drill-On Corporation,

Probability	.15	.10	.30	.20	.25
End-of-period price per share	35.00	42.00	50.00	55.00	60.00

and assuming a current price of $50/share:

a) Calculate the rate of return for each probability. What is the expected return? the variance of end-of-period returns? the range? the semi-interquartile range?
b) Suppose forecasting is refined such that probabilities of end-of-period prices can be broken down further, resulting in the following distribution:

Probability	.01	.05	.07	.02	.10	.30	.20	.15	.05	.05
End-of-period price per share	0	35.00	38.57	40.00	42.00	50.00	55.00	57.00	60.00	69.00

Calculate and explain the change in
a) the expected return;
b) the range of returns;
c) the semi-interquartile range of returns.
Calculate the semivariance of end-of-period returns. Why might some investors be concerned with semivariance as a measure of risk?

6.4 Derive an expression for the expectation of the product of two random variables:

$$E(\tilde{x}\tilde{y}) = ?$$

6.5 Using the definition of portfolio variance, prove that a perfectly hedged stock portfolio that is 100 shares long and 100 shares short is perfectly risk free.

6.6 Given the variance-covariance matrix

$$\begin{bmatrix} 24 & -10 & 25 \\ -10 & 75 & 32 \\ 25 & 32 & 12 \end{bmatrix}$$

a) Calculate the variance of an equally weighted portfolio.
b) Calculate the covariance of a portfolio which has 10% in asset 1, 80% in asset 2, and 10% in asset 3 with a second portfolio which has 125% in asset 1, -10% in asset 2, and -15% in asset 3.

6.7 Given two random variables, x and y.

Probability of state of nature	State of nature	Variable x	Variable y
.2	I	18	0
.2	II	5	-3
.2	III	12	15
.2	IV	4	12
.2	V	6	1

a) Calculate the mean and variance for each of these variables, and the covariance between them.
b) Suppose x and y represent the returns from two assets. Calculate the mean and variance for the following portfolios:

% in x	125	100	75	50	25	0	-25
% in y	-25	0	25	50	75	100	125

c) Find the portfolio which has the minimum variance.

d) Let portfolio A have 75% in x and portfolio B have 25% in x. Calculate the covariance between the two portfolios.

e) Calculate the covariance between the minimum variance portfolio and portfolio A, and the covariance between the minimum variance portfolio and portfolio B.

f) What is the covariance between the minimum variance portfolio and any other portfolio along the efficient set?

g) What is the relationship between the covariance of the minimum variance portfolio with other efficient portfolios, and the variance of the minimum variance portfolio?

6.8 Prove that for any securities, $\tilde{X}$ and $\tilde{Y}$:

a) $E(a\tilde{X} + b\tilde{Y}) = aE(\tilde{X}) + bE(\tilde{Y})$.

b) $\text{VAR}(a\tilde{X} + b\tilde{Y}) = a^2\,\text{VAR}(\tilde{X}) + b^2\,\text{VAR}(\tilde{Y}) + 2ab\,\text{COV}(\tilde{X},\ \tilde{Y})$.

c) $\text{COV}[(a\tilde{X} + b\tilde{Z}),\ \tilde{Y}] = a\,\text{COV}(\tilde{X},\ \tilde{Y}) + b\,\text{COV}(\tilde{Z},\ \tilde{Y})$.

d) $E(\tilde{X}^2) = (E(\tilde{X}))^2 + \text{VAR}(\tilde{X})$.

e) If $r_{XY} = 1$, then $\sigma(\tilde{X} + \tilde{Y}) = \sigma_X + \sigma_Y$. If $r_{XY} = -1$, then $\sigma(\tilde{X} + \tilde{Y}) = \sigma_X - \sigma_Y$.

6.9 Let R_1 and R_2 be the returns from two securities with $E(R_1) = .03$ and $E(R_2) = .08$, $\text{VAR}(R_1) = .02$, $\text{VAR}(R_2) = .05$, and $\text{COV}(R_1, R_2) = -.01$.

a) Plot the set of feasible mean-variance combinations of return, assuming that the two above securities are the only investment vehicles available.

b) If the investor wants to minimize risk, how much of his portfolio will he invest in security 1?

c) Find the mean and standard deviation of a portfolio which is 50% in security 1.

6.10 Two securities have the following joint distribution of returns, r_1 and r_2:

$$P\{r_1 = -1.0 \text{ and } r_2 = .15\} = .1,$$
$$P\{r_1 = .5 \text{ and } r_2 = .15\} = .8,$$
$$P\{r_1 = .5 \text{ and } r_2 = 1.65\} = .1.$$

a) Compute the means, variances, and covariance of returns for the two securities.

b) Plot the feasible mean-standard deviation (μ, σ) combinations, assuming that the two securities are the only investment vehicles available.

c) Which portfolios belong to the mean-variance efficient set?

d) Show that security 2 is mean-variance dominated by security 1, yet enters all efficient portfolios but one. How do you explain this?

e) Suppose that the possibility of lending, but not borrowing, at 5% (without risk) is added to the previous opportunities. Draw the new set of (μ, σ) combinations. Which portfolios are now efficient?

6.11 Suppose a risk-averse investor can choose a portfolio from among N assets with independently distributed returns, all of which have identical means $(\mu_i = \mu_j)$ and identical variances $(\sigma_i^2 = \sigma_j^2)$. What will be the composition of his optimal portfolio?

6.12 Given decreasing marginal utility, it is possible to prove that in a mean-variance framework no individual will hold 100% of his/her wealth in the risk-free asset. Why? [*Hint:* The answer requires an understanding of the shape of investors' indifference curves as well as of the *ex ante* capital market line.]

REFERENCES

CRÁMER, H., *Mathematical Methods in Statistics*. Princeton University Press, Princeton, N.J., 1961.

FAMA, E., and M. MILLER, *The Theory of Finance*. Holt, Rinehart and Winston, New York, 1972.

MARKOWITZ, H. M., *Portfolio Selection: Efficient Diversification of Investment* (Cowles Foundation Monograph 16). Yale University Press, New Haven, 1959.

MERTON, R., "An Analytic Derivation of the Efficient Set," *Journal of Financial and Quantitative Analysis*, September 1972, 1851–1872.

MODIGLIANI, F., and G. POGUE, "An Introduction to Risk and Return: Concepts and Evidence," *Financial Analysts Journal*, March/April and May/June, 1974, 68–80 and 69–85.

SHARPE, W., "A Simplified Model for Portfolio Analysis," *Management Science*, January, 1963, 277–293.

——, *Portfolio Theory and Capital Markets*. McGraw-Hill, New York, 1970.

TOBIN, J., "Liquidity Preference as Behavior Towards Risk," *Review of Economic Studies*, February 1958, 65–86.

Chapter 7

Market Equilibrium: Mean-Variance Uncertainty and Asset Valuation

Lucy: "I've just come up with the perfect theory. It's my theory that Beethoven would have written even better music if he had been married."
Schroeder: "What's so perfect about that theory?"
Lucy: "It can't be proved one way or the other!"

Charles Schulz, PEANUTS, 1976

A. INTRODUCTION

We now extend the concept of market equilibrium in order to determine the market price for risk and the appropriate measure of risk for a single asset. The economic model used to solve this problem was developed almost simultaneously by Sharpe [1963, 1964], and Treynor [1961], while Mossin [1966], Lintner [1965, 1969], and Black [1972] developed it further. The model which we are about to discuss is usually referred to as the *Capital Asset Pricing Model*, CAPM.

The CAPM is developed in a hypothetical world where the following assumptions are made about investors and the opportunity set:

1. Investors are risk-averse individuals who maximize the expected utility of their end-of-period wealth.

2. Investors are price takers and have homogeneous expectations about asset returns which have a joint normal distribution.

3. There exists a risk-free asset such that investors may borrow or lend unlimited amounts at the risk-free rate.

4. The quantities of assets are fixed. Also, all assets are marketable and perfectly divisible.

5. Asset markets are frictionless and information is costless and simultaneously available to all investors.

6. There are no market imperfections such as taxes, regulations, or restrictions on short selling.

Many of these assumptions have been discussed earlier. However, it is worthwhile to discuss some of their implications. For example, if markets are frictionless, the borrowing rate equals the lending rate, and we are able to develop a linear efficient set called the capital market line (Fig. 6.16 and Eq. (6.27)). If all assets are divisible, we exclude the possibility of human capital as we usually think of it. In other words, slavery is allowed in the model. Everyone is able to sell (not rent for wages) various portions of his human capital (e.g., typing ability, or reading ability) to other investors at market prices. Another important assumption is that investors have homogeneous beliefs. They all make decisions based on an identical efficient set. In other words, no one can be fooled. Also, since all investors maximize the expected utility of their end-of-period wealth, the model is implicitly a one-period model.

Although not all these assumptions conform to reality, they are simplifications which permit the development of the CAPM, which is extremely useful for financial decision-making because it quantifies and prices risk. Many of the more restrictive assumptions will be relaxed later on.

B. THE EFFICIENCY OF THE MARKET PORTFOLIO

Proof of the CAPM requires that in equilibrium, the market portfolio must be an efficient portfolio. It must lie on the upper half of the minimum-variance opportunity set graphed in Fig. 7.1. One way to establish its efficiency is to argue that so long as investors have homogeneous expectations, they will all perceive the same minimum variance opportunity set.[1] Even without a risk-free asset, they will all select efficient portfolios regardless of their individual risk tolerances. As shown in Fig. 7.1, individual I chooses efficient portfolio B while individual II, who is less risk averse, chooses efficient portfolio C. Given that all individuals hold positive proportions of their wealth in efficient portfolios, then the market portfolio must be efficient because (1) the market is simply the sum of all individual holdings and (2) all individual holdings are efficient.

Thus, in theory, when all individuals have homogeneous expectations, the market portfolio must be efficient. Without homogeneous expectations, the market portfolio is not necessarily efficient and the equilibrium model of capital markets which is derived in the next section does not necessarily hold. Thus, the efficiency of the market portfolio and the capital asset pricing model are inseparable, joint

---

[1] For a more rigorous proof of the efficiency of the market portfolio see Fama [1976], Chapter 8.

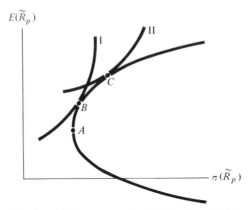

Fig. 7.1 All investors select efficient portfolios

hypotheses. One cannot test one without the other. We shall return to this important point when we discuss Roll's critique later in the chapter.

C. DERIVATION OF THE CAPM

Figure 7.2 shows the expected return and standard deviation of the market portfolio, M, the risk-free asset, R_f, and a risky asset, I. The straight-line connecting the risk-free asset and the market portfolio is the capital market line. We know that if a market equilibrium is to exist, the prices of all assets must adjust until all are held by investors. There can be no excess demand. Consequently, in equilibrium the market portfolio will consist of all marketable assets held in proportion to their value weights. The equilibrium proportion of each asset in the market portfolio must be

$$x_i = \frac{\text{market value of individual asset}}{\text{market value of all assets}}. \tag{7.1}$$

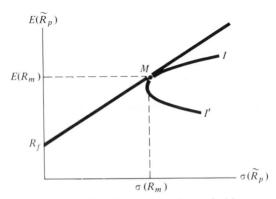

Fig. 7.2 The opportunity set provided by combinations of risky asset I and the market portfolio, M

A portfolio consisting of $a\%$ invested in risky asset I and $(1 - a)\%$ in the market portfolio will have the following mean and standard deviation:

$$E(\tilde{R}_p) = aE(\tilde{R}_i) + (1 - a)E(\tilde{R}_m), \tag{7.2}$$

$$\sigma(\tilde{R}_p) = [a^2\sigma_i^2 + (1 - a)^2\sigma_m^2 + 2a(1 - a)\sigma_{im}]^{1/2}. \tag{7.3}$$

where:

σ_i^2 = the variance of risky asset I.
σ_m^2 = the variance of the market portfolio.
σ_{im} = the covariance between asset I and the market portfolio.

The opportunity set provided by various combinations of the risky asset and the market portfolio is the line IMI' in Fig. 7.2. The change in the mean and standard deviation with respect to the percent of the portfolio, a, invested in asset I is determined as follows:

$$\frac{\delta E(\tilde{R}_p)}{\delta a} = E(\tilde{R}_i) - E(\tilde{R}_m), \tag{7.4}$$

$$\frac{\delta \sigma(\tilde{R}_p)}{\delta a} = \tfrac{1}{2}[a^2\sigma_i^2 + (1 - a)^2\sigma_m^2 + 2a(1 - a)\sigma_{im}]^{-1/2}$$

$$\times [2a\sigma_i^2 - 2\sigma_m^2 + 2a\sigma_m^2 + 2\sigma_{im} - 4a\sigma_{im}]. \tag{7.5}$$

Sharpe and Treynor's insight which allowed them to use the above facts to determine a market equilibrium price for risk was that in equilibrium, the market portfolio already has the market value weight, x_i percent, invested in the risky asset I. Therefore, the percent a in the above equations is the excess demand for an individual risky asset. But we know that in equilibrium the excess demand for any asset must be zero. Prices will adjust until all assets are held. Therefore, if Eqs. (7.4) and (7.5) are evaluated where excess demand, a, equals zero, then we can determine the equilibrium price relationship at point m in Fig. 7.2. This will provide the equilibrium price of risk. Evaluating Eqs. (7.4) and (7.5), where $a = 0$, we obtain

$$\left.\frac{\delta E(\tilde{R}_p)}{\delta a}\right|_{a=0} = E(\tilde{R}_i) - E(\tilde{R}_m), \tag{7.6}$$

$$\left.\frac{\delta \sigma(\tilde{R}_p)}{\delta a}\right|_{a=0} = \tfrac{1}{2}[\sigma_m^2]^{-1/2}[-2\sigma_m^2 + 2\sigma_{im}] = \frac{\sigma_{im} - \sigma_m^2}{\sigma_m}. \tag{7.7}$$

The slope of the risk-return trade-off evaluated at point m, in market equilibrium, is

$$\left.\frac{\delta E(R_p)/\delta a}{\delta \sigma(R_p)/\delta a}\right|_{a=0} = \frac{E(R_i) - E(R_m)}{(\sigma_{im} - \sigma_m^2)/\sigma_m}. \tag{7.8}$$

The final insight is to realize that the slope of the opportunity set IMI' provided by the relationship between the risky asset and the market portfolio at point M must also be equal to the slope of the capital market line, $R_f M$.

As established in Chapter 6, the capital market line is also an equilibrium relationship. Given market efficiency, the tangency portfolio, m, must be the market portfolio where all assets are held according to their market value weights. Recall that the slope of the capital market line in Eq. (6.27) is

$$\frac{E(R_m) - R_f}{\sigma_m}.$$

Equating this with the slope of the opportunity set at point m, we have

$$\frac{E(R_m) - R_f}{\sigma_m} = \frac{E(R_i) - E(R_m)}{(\sigma_{im} - \sigma_m^2)/\sigma_m}.$$

This relationship can be arranged to solve for $E(\tilde{R}_i)$ as follows:

$$E(R_i) = R_f + [E(R_m) - R_f]\frac{\sigma_{im}}{\sigma_m^2}. \tag{7.9}$$

Equation (7.9) is known as the Capital Asset Pricing Model. It is shown graphically in Fig. 7.3, where it is also called the Security Market Line. The required rate of return on *any* asset, $E(R_i)$ in Eq. (7.9), is equal to the risk-free rate of return plus a risk premium. The risk premium is the price of risk multiplied by the quantity of risk. In the terminology of the CAPM, the price of risk is the slope of the line, the difference between the expected rate of return on the market portfolio and the risk-free rate of return.[2] The quantity of risk is often called beta, β_i. It is the covariance

$$\beta_i = \frac{\sigma_{im}}{\sigma_m^2} = \frac{\text{COV}(R_i, R_m)}{\text{VAR}(R_m)} \tag{7.10}$$

between returns on the risky asset, I, and market portfolio, M, divided by the variance of the market portfolio. The risk-free asset has a beta of zero because its covariance with the market portfolio is zero. The market portfolio has a beta of one

---

[2] Note that the CAPM terminology is somewhat different from that used in Chapter 6. Earlier, the price of risk was seen to be the marginal rate of substitution between return and risk and was defined as

$$\frac{E(R_m) - R_f}{\sigma_m}.$$

Using this definition for the price of risk, the quantity of risk is

$$\frac{\text{COV}(R_i, R_m)}{\sigma_m}.$$

Because σ_m, the standard deviation of the market, is assumed to be constant it doesn't make much difference which terminology we adopt. Hereafter, risk will be β and the price of risk will be $[E(R_m) - R_f]$.

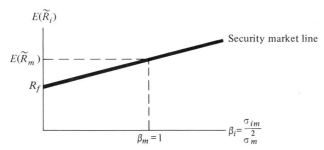

Fig. 7.3 The capital-asset pricing model

because the covariance of the market portfolio with itself is identical to the variance of the market portfolio:

$$\beta_m = \frac{\text{COV}(R_m, R_m)}{\text{VAR}(R_m)} = \frac{\text{VAR}(R_m)}{\text{VAR}(R_m)} = 1.$$

D. PROPERTIES OF THE CAPM

There are several properties of the CAPM which are important. First, in equilibrium, every asset must be priced so that its risk-adjusted required rate of return falls exactly on the straight line in Fig. 7.3, which is called the *security market line*. This means, for example, that assets such as *I* and *J* in Fig. 6.18 which do not lie on the mean-variance efficient set, will lie exactly on the security market line in Fig. 7.3. This is true because not all of the variance of an asset's return is of concern to risk-averse investors. As we saw in the previous chapter, investors can always diversify away all risk except the covariance of an asset with the market portfolio. In other words, they can diversify away all risk except the risk of the economy as a whole, which is inescapable (undiversifiable). Consequently, the only risk which investors will pay a premium to avoid is covariance risk. Therefore the total risk of any individual asset can be partitioned into two parts, systematic risk which is a measure of how the asset covaries with the economy, and unsystematic risk, which is independent of the economy. Mathematical precision,

$$\text{Total risk} = \text{Systematic risk} + \text{unsystematic risk}, \tag{7.11}$$

can be attached to this concept by noting that empirically the return on any asset is a linear function of market return plus a random error term, $\tilde{\epsilon}_j$, which is independent of the market:

$$\tilde{R}_j = a_j + b_j \tilde{R}_m + \tilde{\epsilon}_j.$$

The variance of this relationship is

$$\sigma_j^2 = b_j^2 \sigma_m^2 + \sigma_\epsilon^2. \tag{7.12}$$

The variance is total risk; it can be partitioned into systematic risk, $b_j^2 \sigma_m^2$, and unsystematic risk, σ_ϵ^2. It turns out that b_j in the simple linear relationship between individual asset return and market return is exactly the same as β_j in the CAPM.[3]

If systematic risk is the only type of risk which investors will pay to avoid and if the required rate of return for every asset in equilibrium must fall on the security market line, we should be able to go back to the example of Bayside Cigar Company and resolve the paradox which was introduced in Chapter 6. Table 7.1 summarizes the empirical findings. We know that if investors are risk averse, there should be a positive trade-off between risk and return. When we tried to use the standard deviation as a measure of risk for an individual asset, Bayside Cigar, we were forced to make the inappropriate observation that the asset with higher risk has a lower return. The difficulty was that we were using the wrong measure of risk. The appropriate measure of risk for a single asset is beta, its covariance with the market divided by the variance of the market. This risk is nondiversifiable and is linearly related to the rate of return $[E(R_i)$ in Eq. (7.9)] required by equilibrium. When we look at the appropriate measure of risk, we see that Bayside Cigar is *less risky* than the 100-stock portfolio, and we have the sensible result that lower risk is accompanied by lower return.

Table 7.1 Risk and return for Bayside Cigar and a 100 stock portfolio

	Annual return	Standard deviation	Beta
100-stock portfolio	10.9%	4.45%	1.11
Bayside Cigar	5.4%	7.25%	.71

Table 7.2 shows the realized rates of return and the betas of many different assets between January 1945 and June 1970. The calculations are taken from an article by Modigliani and Pogue [1974] which used monthly observations. In most cases the risk-return relationships make sense. Consumer product companies like Swift and Co., Bayside Cigars, and American Snuff are all less risky than the market portfolio (represented here by the NYSE index). On the other hand, steel, electronics, and automobiles are riskier. Figure 7.4 plots the empirical relationship between risk (measured by beta) and return for the companies listed in Table 7.2. The linearity of the relationship appears to be reasonable, and the trade-off between risk and return is positive. A more thorough discussion of empirical tests of the CAPM will be given later in this chapter.

A second important property of the CAPM is that the measure of risk for individual assets is linearly additive when the assets are combined into portfolios.

---

[3] The interested reader is referred to Appendix C on linear regression for proof that the slope coefficient, b_j, equals

$$b_j = COV(R_j, R_m)/VAR(R_m).$$

Table 7.2 Rates of return and betas for selected companies (1945–1970)

	Average annual return	Standard deviation	Beta
City Investing Co.	17.4%	11.09%	1.67
Radio Corporation of America	11.4%	8.30%	1.35
Chrysler Corporation	7.0%	7.73%	1.21
Continental Steel Co.	11.9%	7.50%	1.12
100-stock portfolio	10.9%	4.45%	1.11
NYSE index	8.3%	3.73%	1.00
Swift and Co.	5.7%	5.89%	.81
Bayside Cigars	5.4%	7.26%	.71
American Snuff	6.5%	4.77%	.54
Homestake Mining Co.	4.0%	6.55%	.24

Modigliani, F., and G. Pogue, "An Introduction to Risk and Return," reprinted from *The Financial Analysts Journal*, March/April 1974, 71.

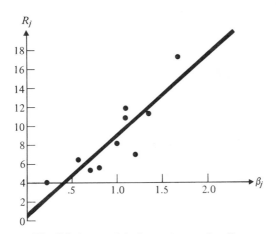

Fig. 7.4 An empirical security market line

For example, if we put $a\%$ of our wealth into asset X, with systematic risk of β_x, and $b\%$ of our wealth into asset Y, with systematic risk of β_y, then the beta of our portfolio, β_p, is simply the weighted average of the betas of the individual securities.

$$\beta_p = a\beta_x + b\beta_y. \tag{7.13}$$

Proof of this follows from the definition of covariance and the properties of the mean and variance. The definition of the portfolio beta is

$$\beta_p = \frac{E\{[aX + bY - aE(X) - bE(Y)][R_m - E(R_m)]\}}{\text{VAR}(R_m)}.$$

Rearranging terms, we have

$$\beta_p = \frac{E\{[a[X - E(X)] + b[Y - E(Y)]][R_m - E(R_m)]\}}{VAR(R_m)}.$$

Next, we factor out a and b:

$$\beta_p = a \frac{E[(X - E(X))(R_m - E(R_m))]}{VAR(R_m)} + b \frac{E[(Y - E(Y))(R_m - E(R_m))]}{VAR(R_m)}.$$

Finally, using the definition of β,

$$\beta_p = a\beta_x + b\beta_y. \quad \text{QED}$$

The fact that portfolio betas are linearly weighted combinations of individual asset betas is an extremely useful tool. All that is needed to measure the systematic risk portfolios is the betas of the individual assets. It is not necessary to solve a quadratic programming problem (see Eqs. (6.23a) and (6.23b)) to find the efficient set.

It is worth reiterating the relationship between individual asset risk and portfolio risk. The correct definition of an individual asset's risk is its contribution to portfolio risk. Referring to Eq. (6.25), we see that the variance of returns for a portfolio of assets is

$$VAR(\tilde{R}_p) = \sigma^2(\tilde{R}_p) = \sum_{i=1}^{N} \sum_{j=1}^{N} x_i x_j \sigma_{ij}, \tag{6.25}$$

which can be rewritten as[4]

$$\sigma^2(\tilde{R}_p) = \sum_{i=1}^{N} x_i \left(\sum_{j=1}^{N} x_j \sigma_{ij} \right) = \sum_{i=1}^{N} x_i \, COV(R_i, R_p). \tag{7.14}$$

---

[4] In order to see that $\sum x_i(\sum x_j \sigma_{ij}) = \sum x_i \, COV(R_i, R_p)$, consider a simple three-asset example. Rewriting the left-hand side, we have

$$\sum x_i(\sum x_j \sigma_{ij}) = x_1(x_1 \sigma_{11} + x_2 \sigma_{12} + x_3 \sigma_{13})$$
$$+ x_2(x_1 \sigma_{21} + x_2 \sigma_{22} + x_3 \sigma_{23})$$
$$+ x_3(x_1 \sigma_{31} + x_2 \sigma_{32} + x_3 \sigma_{33}).$$

From the definition of covariance, we have

$$COV(R_1, R_p) = [1 \quad 0 \quad 0] \begin{bmatrix} \sigma_{11} & \sigma_{12} & \sigma_{13} \\ \sigma_{21} & \sigma_{22} & \sigma_{23} \\ \sigma_{31} & \sigma_{32} & \sigma_{33} \end{bmatrix} \begin{bmatrix} x_1 \\ x_2 \\ x_3 \end{bmatrix}$$

$$= x_1 \sigma_{11} + x_2 \sigma_{12} + x_3 \sigma_{13}.$$

Then multiplying by the weight in the first asset, we obtain

$$x_1 \, COV(R_1, R_p) = x_1(x_1 \sigma_{11} + x_2 \sigma_{12} + x_3 \sigma_{13}).$$

Finally, by repeating this procedure for each of the three assets we can demonstrate the equality in Eq. (7.14).

One could interpret

$$x_i \, \text{COV}(R_i, R_p) \tag{7.15}$$

as the risk of security i in portfolio p. However, at the margin, the change in the contribution of asset i to portfolio risk is simply

$$\text{COV}(R_i, R_p). \tag{7.16}$$

Therefore covariance risk is the appropriate definition of risk since it measures the change in portfolio risk as we change the weighting of an individual asset in the portfolio.

Although the use of systematic risk and undiversifiable risk have arisen in the literature as synonyms for covariance risk, they are somewhat misleading. They rely on the existence of diversification opportunities and on the existence of a large market portfolio. The definition of covariance risk given above does not. It continues to be relevant, even when the market portfolio under consideration has few assets.

E. USE OF THE CAPM FOR VALUATION: SINGLE-PERIOD MODELS, UNCERTAINTY

Because it provides a quantifiable measure of risk for individual assets, the CAPM is an extremely useful tool for valuing risky assets. For the time being, let us assume that we are dealing with a single time period. This assumption was built into the derivation of the CAPM. We want to value an asset which has a risky payoff at the end of the period. Call this $\tilde{P}_e$. It could represent the capital gain on a common stock or the capital gain plus a dividend. If the risky asset is a bond, it is the repayment of the principle plus the interest on the bond. The expected return on an investment in the risky asset is determined by the price we are willing to pay at the beginning of the time period for the right to the risky end-of-period payoff. If P_0 is the price we pay today, our risky return, $\tilde{R}_j$, is

$$\tilde{R}_j = \frac{\tilde{P}_e - P_0}{P_0}. \tag{7.17}$$

The CAPM can be used to determine what the current value of the asset, P_0, should be. The CAPM is

$$E(R_j) = R_f + [E(R_m) - R_f] \frac{\text{COV}(R_j, R_m)}{\text{VAR}(R_m)},$$

which can be rewritten as

$$E(R_j) = R_f + \lambda \, \text{COV}(R_j, R_m), \quad \text{where} \quad \lambda = \frac{E(R_m) - R_f}{\text{VAR}(R_m)}. \tag{7.18}$$

Note that λ can be described as the market price per unit risk. From Eq. (7.17) and the properties of the mean, we can equate the expected return from Eq. (7.17) with the expected return in Eq. (7.18):

$$\frac{E(\tilde{P}_e) - P_0}{P_0} = R_f + \lambda \, COV(R_j, R_m).$$

We can now interpret P_0 as the equilibrium price of the risky asset. Rearranging the above expression, we get

$$P_0 = \frac{E(\tilde{P}_e)}{1 + R_f + \lambda \, COV(\tilde{R}_j, \tilde{R}_m)}, \tag{7.19}$$

which is often referred to as the *risk-adjusted rate of return valuation formula*. The numerator is the expected end-of-period price for the risky asset and the denominator can be thought of as a discount rate. If the asset has no risk, then its covariance with the market will be zero and the appropriate one-period discount rate is $1 + R_f$, that is $1 +$ the risk-free rate. For assets with positive systematic risk, a risk premium, $\lambda \, COV(\tilde{R}_j, \tilde{R}_m)$, is added to the risk-free rate so that the discount rate is risk-adjusted.

An equivalent approach to valuation is to deduct a risk premium from $E(\tilde{P}_e)$ in the numerator, then discount at $1 + R_f$. The covariance between the risky asset and the market can be rewritten as

$$COV(\tilde{R}_j, \tilde{R}_m) = COV\left[\frac{\tilde{P}_e - P_0}{P_0}, \tilde{R}_m\right]$$

$$= E\left[\left(\frac{\tilde{P}_e - P_0}{P_0} - \frac{E(\tilde{P}_e) - P_0}{P_0}\right)(\tilde{R}_m - E(\tilde{R}_m))\right]$$

$$= \frac{1}{P_0} COV(\tilde{P}_e, \tilde{R}_m).$$

By substituting this into the risk-adjusted rate-of-return equation (Eq. (7.19)),

$$P_0 = \frac{E(\tilde{P}_e)}{1 + R_f + \lambda(1/P_0) \, COV(\tilde{P}_e, \tilde{R}_m)},$$

we can derive the *certainty-equivalent valuation formula*:

$$P_0 = \frac{E(\tilde{P}_e) - \lambda \, COV(\tilde{P}_e, \tilde{R}_m)}{1 + R_f}. \tag{7.20}$$

The risk-adjusted rate of return and the certainty-equivalent approaches are equivalent for one-period valuation models. It is important to realize that in both cases value does not depend on the utility preferences of individuals. All one needs to know in order to determine value is the expected end-of-period cash payoff, the quantity of risk provided by the asset, the risk-free rate, and the price of risk (which are market-determined variables). Consequently, individuals who perceive the same distribution of payoffs for a risky asset will price it in exactly the same way regardless of their individual utility functions.

F.   APPLICATIONS OF THE CAPM FOR CORPORATE POLICY

In Chapter 11 these one-period valuation models shall be used to develop decision-making rules for the selection of investment projects by the firm, for measuring the firm's cost of capital, and for capital structure (optimal debt/equity ratios) decisions. However, for the sake of curiosity, we shall take a quick look at the implications of the CAPM for some corporate policy decisions, assuming that our firm has no debt and that there are no corporate taxes. The more complex results in a world with debt and taxes are left to Chapter 11.

The cost of equity capital for a firm is given directly by the CAPM. After all, the company's beta is measured by calculating the covariance between the return on its common stock and the market index. Consequently the beta measures the systematic risk of the common stock and if we know the systematic risk we can use the CAPM to determine the required rate of return on equity. Equation (7.21) is the capital asset pricing model.

$$E(R_j) = R_f + [E(R_m) - R_f]\beta_j. \tag{7.21}$$

If it is possible to estimate the systematic risk of a company's equity as well as the market rate of return, then $E(R_j)$ is the required rate of return on equity, i.e., the cost of equity for the firm. If we designate the cost of equity as k_e, then

$$E(R_j) = k_e.$$

This is shown in Fig. 7.5. As long as all projects have the same risk as the firm, then k_e may also be interpreted as the minimum required rate of return on new capital projects.

But what if the project has a different risk than the firm as a whole? Then all that is necessary is to estimate the systematic risk of the project and use the CAPM to determine the appropriate required rate of return. For example, in Fig. 7.5, the

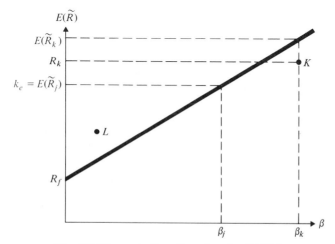

Fig. 7.5 The cost of equity using the CAPM

expected rate of return on project k is higher than the cost of equity for the firm. But the project also is riskier than the firm because it has greater systematic risk. If the managers of the firm were to demand that it earn the same rate as the firm (k_e), the project would be accepted since its anticipated rate of return, R_k, is greater than the firm's cost of equity. However, this would be incorrect. The market requires a rate of return, $E(R_k)$, for a project with systematic risk of β_k, but the project will earn less. Therefore, since $R_k < E(R_k)$, the project is clearly unacceptable. (Is project L acceptable? Why?)

Because the CAPM allows decision makers to estimate the required rate of return for projects of different risk, it is an extremely useful concept. Although we have assumed no debt or taxes in the above simple introduction, Chapter 11 shows how the model can be extended to properly conceptualize more realistic capital budgeting and cost of capital decisions.

G. EXTENSIONS OF THE CAPM

Virtually every one of the assumptions under which the CAPM is derived is violated in the real world. If so, then how good is the model? There are two parts to this question: (1) Is it possible to extend the model to relax the unrealistic assumptions without drastically changing it? (2) How well does the model stand up to empirical testing? The first part is the subject of this section of the chapter. Surprisingly, the model is fairly robust to various extensions of it.

1. No Riskless Asset
First, how will the model change if investors cannot borrow and lend at the risk-free rate? In other words, how is the CAPM affected if there is no risk-free asset which has constant returns in every state of nature? This problem was solved by Black [1972]. His argument is illustrated in Fig. 7.6. Portfolio M is identified by all in-

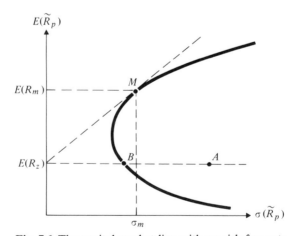

Fig. 7.6 The capital market line with no risk-free rate

vestors as the market portfolio which lies on the efficient set. Now, suppose that we can identify all portfolios which are uncorrelated with the true market portfolio.[5] This means that their returns have zero covariance with the market portfolio, and that they have the same systematic risk (i.e., they have zero beta). Therefore, because they have the same risk they must have the same return. Portfolios A and B in Fig. 7.6 are both uncorrelated with the market portfolio M and have the same expected return, $E(R_z)$. However, only one of them, portfolio B, lies on the opportunity set. It is the minimum-variance zero-beta portfolio and it is unique. Portfolio A also has zero beta, but it has a higher variance and therefore does not lie on the minimum variance opportunity set.

We can derive the slope of the line $E(R_z)M$ by forming a portfolio with $a\%$ in the market portfolio and $(1 - a)\%$ in the zero-beta portfolio. The mean and standard deviation of such a portfolio can be written as follows:

$$E(R_p) = aE(R_m) + (1 - a)E(R_z),$$
$$\sigma(R_p) = [a^2\sigma_m^2 + (1 - a)^2\sigma_z^2 + 2a(1 - a)r_{zm}\sigma_z\sigma_m]^{1/2}.$$

But since the zero-beta portfolio is uncorrelated with the market portfolio, r_{zm}, the correlation between the zero-beta portfolio and the market portfolio, is zero, and the last term drops out. The slope of a line tangent to the portfolio at point m, where 100% of the investor's wealth is invested in the market portfolio, can be found by taking the partial derivatives of the above equations and evaluating them where $a = 1$. The partial derivative of the mean portfolio return is

$$\frac{\delta E(R_p)}{\delta a} = E(R_m) - E(R_z),$$

---

[5] As an example of how to calculate the vector of weights in a world with only two assets, see Problem 7.14. For portfolios with many assets, we are interested in identifying the portfolio which (a) has zero covariance with the market portfolio and (b) has the minimum variance. The solution will be the vector of weights which satisfies the following quadratic programming problem.

$$\text{Min } \sigma_p^2 = W_1' \sum W_1$$
$$\text{Subject to} \quad W_1' \sum W_m = \sigma_{1m} = 0,$$
$$W_1'\mathbf{e} = 1,$$

where

σ_p^2 = the variance of the zero beta portfolio.
W_1' = the row vector of weights in the minimum-variance zero-beta portfolio (W_1 is a column vector with the same weights).
$\sum$ = the variance/covariance matrix for all N assets in the market.
W_m = the vector of weights in the market portfolio.
σ_{1m} = the covariance between the zero-beta portfolio and the market. It must equal zero.
$\mathbf{e}$ = a column vector of ones.

and the partial derivative of the standard deviation is

$$\frac{\delta\sigma(R_p)}{\delta a} = \tfrac{1}{2}[a^2\sigma_m^2 + (1-a)^2\sigma_z^2]^{-1/2}[2a\sigma_m^2 - 2\sigma_z^2 + 2a\sigma_z^2].$$

Taking the ratio of these partials and evaluating where $a = 1$, we obtain the slope of the line $E(R_z)M$ in Fig. 7.6:

$$\left.\frac{\delta E(R_p)/\delta a}{\delta\sigma(R_p)/\delta a}\right|_{a=1} = \frac{E(R_m) - E(R_z)}{\sigma_m}. \tag{7.22}$$

Furthermore, since the line must pass through the point $[E(R_m), \sigma(R_m)]$, the intercept of the tangent line must be $E(R_z)$. Consequently, the equation of the line must be

$$E(R_p) = E(R_z) + \frac{E(R_m) - E(R_z)}{\sigma_m}\,\sigma_p. \tag{7.23}$$

This is exactly the same as the capital market line (Eq. (6.27)), except that the expected rate of return on the zero-beta portfolio, $E(R_z)$, has replaced the risk-free rate.

Given the above result, it is not hard to prove that the expected rate of return on *any* risky asset, whether or not it lies on the efficient set, must be a linear combination of the rate of return on the zero-beta portfolio and the market portfolio. To show this, recall that in equilibrium the slope of a line tangent to a portfolio composed of the market portfolio and any other asset at the point represented by the market portfolio must be equal to Eq. (7.8):

$$\left.\frac{\delta E(R_p)/\delta a}{\delta\sigma(R_p)/\delta a}\right|_{a=0} = \frac{E(R_i) - E(R_m)}{(\sigma_{im} - \sigma_m^2)/\sigma_m}. \tag{7.8}$$

If we equate the two definitions of the slope of a line tangent to point M [that is, if we equate (7.8) and (7.22)], we have

$$\frac{E(R_m) - E(R_z)}{\sigma_m} = \frac{[E(R_i) - E(R_m)]\sigma_m}{\sigma_{im} - \sigma_m^2}.$$

Solving for the required rate of return on asset i, we have

$$E(R_i) = (1 - \beta_i)E(R_z) + \beta_i E(R_m), \tag{7.24}$$

where

$$\beta = \sigma_{im}/\sigma_m^2 = \text{COV}(R_i, R_m)/\sigma_m^2.$$

Equation (7.24) shows that the expected rate of return on any asset can be written as a linear combination of the expected rate of return of two assets—the market portfolio, and the unique minimum-variance, zero-beta portfolio (which is chosen to be uncorrelated with the market portfolio). Interestingly, the weight to be invested in the market portfolio is the beta of the ith asset. If we rearrange (7.24), we see that it is exactly equal to the CAPM (Eqs. (7.9) and (7.21)) except that the expected rate of return on the zero-beta portfolio has replaced the rate of return on the risk-free asset:

$$E(R_i) = E(R_z) + [E(R_m) - E(R_z)]\beta_i. \tag{7.25}$$

The upshot of this proof is that the major results of the CAPM do not require the existence of a pure riskless asset. Beta is still the appropriate measure of systematic risk for an asset and the linearity of the model still obtains. The version of the model given by Eq. (7.25) is usually called the two-factor model.

2. Returns not Jointly Normal

Obviously, returns on assets cannot be normally distributed because the largest negative return possible, given limited liability of the investor, is minus 100%. But the assumption of normally distributed returns implies that there is a finite possibility that returns will be less than 100% and that asset prices will be negative. However, as a practical matter, the probability of observing returns as low as minus 100% may be so small that it has no impact on the empirical validity of the CAPM.

Another implication of the normality assumption is that only two parameters are needed to completely describe the distribution: its mean and its variance. Fama [1965a] has investigated the empirical distribution of daily returns on New York Stock Exchange securities and discovered that they are distributed symmetrically but that the empirical distribution has "fat tails" and no finite variance.[6] In Fig. 7.7 the dashed line represents the empirical distribution of stock prices. The important question which arises is how can investors make choices based on mean and variance if the actual distribution of security prices is such that a variance does not exist? Fama [1965b] has shown that as long as the distribution is symmetric (and stable), investors can use measures of dispersion other than the variance and the theory of portfolio choice is still valid.

If security returns are measured over longer periods of time, their distribution is better approximated by a lognormal distribution which has positive skewness.

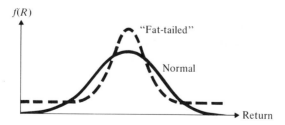

$f(R)$

"Fat-tailed"

Normal

Return

Fig. 7.7 The empirical distribution of daily stock returns

---

[6] There are various theories which explain the empirical distribution of daily returns. The interested reader is referred to Fama [1965a] for the stable Paretian hypothesis, and to Clark [1972] for the subordinated stochastic process hypothesis.

Figure 7.8 compares a normal with a lognormal distribution. There is no limit to the positive returns which may be realized on a successful investment but the maximum negative return is minus 100%. This explains why the distribution of annual returns, for example, tends to be lognormal. The CAPM makes no provision for investor preference for skewness; it is therefore an empirical question whether or not the model fits reality well enough to permit us to ignore the fact that the empirical distribution of returns is not normal. The empirical evidence is reviewed in the next section of this chapter.

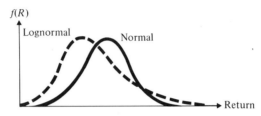

Fig. 7.8 Over long intervals of time, security returns are lognormal

3.   The Existence of Nonmarketable Assets

Suppose the cost of transactions on an asset is infinite or that by law or regulation the asset is not marketable. Perhaps the most important example of such an asset is human capital. You can rent your skills in return for wages, but you cannot sell yourself or buy anyone else. Slavery is forbidden. This has the effect of introducing a nondiversifiable asset into your portfolio—your human capital. Because you cannot divide up your skills and sell them to different investors, you are forced into making portfolio decisions where you are constrained to hold a large risky component of your wealth in the form of your own human capital. What impact does this have on portfolio decisions and the CAPM?

We saw earlier that if there are no transaction costs and if all assets are perfectly divisible, two-fund separation obtains (see Chapter 6). Every investor, regardless of the shape of his indifference curve, will hold one of two assets: the risk-free asset or the market portfolio. This implies that everyone holds exactly the same portfolio of risky assets: the market portfolio. Of course, casual empiricism tells us that this is not what actually happens. People do hold different portfolios of risky assets. There are many reasons why this may be true and the existence of nonmarketable assets is a good possibility.

Mayers [1972] shows that when investors are constrained to hold nonmarketable assets which have risky rates of return, $\tilde{R}_H$, the CAPM takes the following form:

$$E(\tilde{R}_j) = R_f + \lambda \, \text{COV}(\tilde{R}_j, \tilde{R}_m + \tilde{R}_H), \qquad (7.26)$$

where

$$\lambda = \frac{E(\tilde{R}_m) - R_f}{\text{COV}(\tilde{R}_m, \tilde{R}_m + \tilde{R}_H)}$$

$$= \frac{E(\tilde{R}_m) - R_f}{V_m \sigma_m^2 + \text{COV}(\tilde{R}_m, \tilde{R}_H)},$$

V_m = the current market value of all marketable assets,

$\tilde{R}_H$ = the total dollar return on all nonmarketable assets.

In this version of the model, λ may be interpreted as the market price per unit risk where risk contains not only the market variance, σ_m^2, but also the covariance of return between marketable and nonmarketable assets. This result is obtained by first deriving an individual's demand curves for holding marketable assets, then aggregating them to obtain Eq. (7.26), which is the return on a marketable asset required by the market equilibrium. There are three important implications: First, individuals will hold different portfolios of risky assets. Second, the market equilibrium price of a risky asset may still be determined independently of the shape of the individual's indifference curves, which implies that the separation principle still holds. Third, the appropriate measure of risk is still the covariance, but we must now consider the covariance between the jth risky asset and a portfolio of both marketable and nonmarketable assets.[7]

4. The Model in Continuous Time

Merton [1973] has derived a version of the CAPM which assumes (among other things) that trading takes place continuously over time, and that asset returns are distributed lognormally. If the risk-free rate of interest is nonstochastic over time, then (regardless of individual preferences, the distribution of individuals' wealth, or their time horizon), the equilibrium returns must satisfy

$$E(R_i) = r_f + [E(R_m) - r_f]\beta_i. \tag{7.27}$$

Equation (7.27) is the continuous-time analogy to the CAPM. In fact, it is exactly the same as the CAPM except that instantaneous rates of return have replaced rates of return over discrete intervals of time, and the distribution of returns is lognormal instead of normal.

If the risk-free rate is not constant over time, investors are exposed to another kind of risk, namely the risk of unfavorable shifts in the investment opportunity set. Merton shows that investors will hold portfolios chosen from three funds: the riskless asset, the market portfolio, and a portfolio chosen so that its returns are perfectly negatively correlated with the riskless asset. This model exhibits three-fund

---

[7] See Fama and Schwert [1977] for an empirical test of the model set forth by Mayers.

separation. The third fund is necessary to hedge against unforeseen changes in the future risk-free rate. The required rate of return on the jth asset is

$$E(R_j) = r_f + \gamma_1[E(R_m) - r_f] + \gamma_2[E(R_N) - r_f], \qquad (7.28)$$

where

R_N = the instantaneous rate of return on a portfolio which has perfect negative correlation with the riskless asset.

$$\gamma_1 = \frac{\beta_{jm} - \beta_{jN}\beta_{Nm}}{1 - \rho_{Nm}^2}, \qquad \gamma_2 = \frac{\beta_{jN} - \beta_{jm}\beta_{Nm}}{1 - \rho_{Nm}^2}.$$

ρ_{Nm} = the correlation between portfolio N and the market portfolio, M.

$$\beta_{ik} = \frac{\text{COV}(R_i, R_k)}{\sigma_k^2}.$$

Merton argues that the sign of γ_2 will be negative for high beta assets and positive for low beta assets. As we shall see, in the next section, which discusses the empirical tests of the CAPM, Merton's argument is consistent with the empirical evidence.

5.   The Existence of Heterogeneous Expectations and Taxes

If investors do not all have the same information about the distribution of future returns, they will perceive different opportunity sets and will obviously choose different portfolios. Lintner [1969] has shown that the existence of heterogeneous expectations does not critically alter the CAPM except that expected returns and covariances are expressed as complex weighted averages of investor expectations. However, if investors have heterogeneous expectations, then the market portfolio is not necessarily efficient. This makes the CAPM nontestable. In fact, as we shall see when we discuss Roll's critique later in this chapter, the only legitimate test of the CAPM is a joint test to determine whether or not the market portfolio is efficient.

No one has investigated the equilibrium model in a world with personal as well as corporate taxes. However, Brennan [1970] has investigated the effect of differential tax rates on capital gains and dividends. Although he concludes that beta is the appropriate measure of risk, his model includes an extra term which causes the expected return on an asset to depend on dividend yield as well as systematic risk:

$$E(R_j) = \gamma_1 R_f + \gamma_2 \beta_j + \gamma_3 D_j, \qquad (7.29)$$

where

D_j = the dividend yield on asset j.

We shall leave a complete discussion of the Brennan model to Chapters 13 and 14, which cover the theory and empirical evidence related to the corporate dividend policy decision.

H. EMPIRICAL TESTS OF THE CAPM

The CAPM is a simple linear model which is expressed in terms of expected returns and expected risk. In its *ex ante* form, we have

$$E(R_j) = R_f + [E(R_m) - R_f]\beta_j. \tag{7.30}$$

Although many of the aforementioned extensions of the model support this simple linear form, others suggest that it may not be linear, that factors other than beta are needed to explain $E(R_j)$, or that R_f is not the appropriate riskless rate. Therefore, with so many alternative possibilities, a great deal of energy has been devoted to the empirical question: How well does the model fit the data?

There have been numerous empirical tests of the CAPM, so many in fact that it would be fruitless to mention all of them. Also, the literature is interwoven with many serious and difficult econometric problems which must be confronted in order to provide the best empirical tests of the model.[8] Most of the econometric subtleties are beyond the scope of this text and are therefore ignored. However, in the opinion of the authors, the tests of the CAPM which are summarized below represent the best of the work which has been done to date.

The first step necessary to empirically test the theoretical CAPM is to transform it from expectations or *ex ante* form (expectations cannot be measured) into a form which uses observed data. This can be done by assuming that the rate of return on any asset is a fair game.[9] In other words, on average, the expected rate of return on an asset is equal to the realized rate of return. We can write the fair game as follows:

$$R_{jt} = E(R_{jt}) + \beta_j \delta_{mt} + \epsilon_{jt}, \tag{7.31}$$

where

$$\delta_{mt} = R_{mt} - E(R_{mt}),$$
$$E(\delta_{mt}) = 0,$$
$$\epsilon_{jt} = \text{a random-error term},$$
$$E(\epsilon_{jt}) = 0,$$
$$\text{COV}(\epsilon_{jt}, \delta_{mt}) = 0,$$
$$\text{COV}(\epsilon_{jt}, \epsilon_{j,t-1}) = 0,$$
$$\beta_{jt} = \text{COV}(R_{jt}, R_{mt})/\text{VAR}(R_{mt}).$$

---

[8] For an excellent discussion of the econometric problems involved in testing the CAPM, the reader is referred to Miller and Scholes [1972].
[9] Chapter 8 explains the theory of efficient capital markets which describes a fair game at length.

Equation (7.31) is seen to be a fair game because if we take the expectation of both sides, the average realized return is equal to the expected return. In other words, on average, you get the return which you expected:

$$E(R_{jt}) = E(R_{jt}).$$

If we use the CAPM assumption that asset returns are jointly normal, then β_j in the fair-game model is defined in exactly the same way as β_j in the CAPM. By substituting $E(R_j)$ from the CAPM into Eq. (7.31), we obtain

$$R_{jt} = R_{ft} + [E(R_{mt}) - R_{ft}]\beta_j + \beta_j[R_{mt} - E(R_{mt})] + \epsilon_{jt}$$
$$= R_{ft} + (R_{mt} - R_{ft})\beta_j + \epsilon_{jt}.$$

Finally, by subtracting R_{ft} from both sides, we have

$$R_{jt} - R_{ft} = (R_{mt} - R_{ft})\beta_j + \epsilon_{jt}, \tag{7.32}$$

which is the *ex post* form of the CAPM. We derived it by simply assuming that returns are normally distributed and that capital markets are efficient in a fair-game sense. Now we have an empirical version of the CAPM which is expressed in terms of *ex post* observations of return data instead of *ex ante* expectations.

One important difference between the *ex post* empirical model and the *ex ante* theoretical model is that the former can have a negative slope while the latter cannot. After the fact we may have experienced a state of nature where the market rate of return was negative. When this happens the empirical security market line will slope downward as in Fig. 7.9(a). On the other hand, the theoretical CAPM always requires the expected return on the market to be higher than the risk-free rate of return, as shown in Fig. 7.9(b). This is because prices must be established in such a way that riskier assets have higher expected rates of return. Of course, it may turn out that after the fact their return was low or negative, but that is what is meant by risk. If a risky asset has a beta of 2.0, it will lose 20% when the market goes down by 10%.

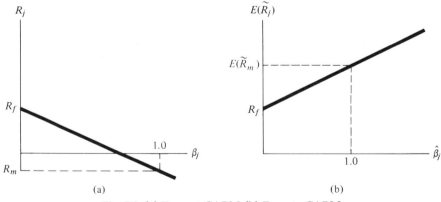

Fig. 7.9 (a) Ex post CAPM (b) Ex ante CAPM

When the CAPM is empirically tested, it is usually written in the following form:

$$R'_{pt} = \gamma_0 + \gamma_1 \beta_p + \epsilon_{pt}, \tag{7.33}$$

where

$\gamma_1 = R_{mt} - R_{ft}$,
$R'_{pt} =$ the excess return on portfolio p, $R_{pt} - R_{ft}$.

This is the same as Eq. (7.32) except that a constant term, γ_0, has been added. Exactly what predictions made by the CAPM are tested in Eq. (7.33)? The predictions should meet the following criteria:

a. The intercept term, γ_0, should not be significantly different from zero. If it is different from zero, then there may be something "left out" of the CAPM which is captured in the empirically estimated intercept term.

b. Beta should be the only factor which explains the rate of return on a risky asset. If other terms such as residual variance or beta squared are included in an attempt to explain return, they should have no explanatory power.

c. The relationship should be linear in beta.

d. The coefficient of beta, γ_1, should be equal to $R_{mt} - R_{ft}$.

e. When the equation is estimated over very long periods of time, the rate of return on the market portfolio should be greater than the risk-free rate. Because the market portfolio is riskier, on average it should have a higher rate of return.

The major empirical tests of the CAPM were published by Blume and Friend [1970, 1973]; Black, Jensen, and Scholes [1972]; Miller and Scholes [1972]; and Fama and Macbeth [1973]. Most of the studies use monthly total returns (dividends are reinvested) on listed common stocks as their data base. The usual technique is to estimate the betas of every security during a five-year holding period, by computing the covariance between return on the security and a market index which is usually an equally weighted index of all listed common stocks. The securities are then ranked by beta and placed into N portfolios (where N is usually 10, 12, or 20). By grouping the individual securities into large portfolios chosen to provide the maximum dispersion in systematic risk, it is possible to avoid a good part of the measurement error in estimating betas of individual stocks. Next, the portfolio betas and returns are calculated over a second five-year period and a regression similar to Eq. (7.33) is run.

With few exceptions, the empirical studies agree on the following conclusions:

a. The intercept term, γ_0, *is* significantly different from zero, and the slope, γ_1, is less than the difference between the return on the market portfolio minus the risk-free rate.[10] The implication is that low beta securities earn more than the CAPM would predict and high beta securities earn less.

---

[10] Empirical studies have used a 90-day Treasury bill rate as a proxy for the risk-free rate and they have also laboriously calculated the return on the zero-beta portfolio. Either approach results in an intercept term significantly different from zero.

b. Beta is the only measure of risk which adequately explains risk. Versions of the model which include a squared term or unsystematic risk find that at best these explanatory factors are useful only in a small number of the time-periods sampled.

c. The simple linear empirical model (Eq. (7.33)) fits the data best. It is linear in beta. Also, over long periods of time, the rate of return on the market portfolio is greater than the risk-free rate (that is, $\gamma_1 > 0$).

Figure 7.10 shows the average monthly returns on 10 portfolios vs. their systematic risk for the 35-year period 1931–1965 (taken from the Black-Jensen-Scholes study [1972]). The results shown here are typical. The empirical market line is linear with a positive trade-off between return and risk, but the intercept term is significantly different from zero. In fact, it is 9.79 standard deviations away. This forces us to reject the CAPM, given the empirical techniques of the previously mentioned studies.

The empirical evidence has led scholars to conclude that the pure theoretical form of the CAPM does not agree well with reality. However, the empirical form of the model, which has come to be known as the *empirical market line*,

$$R_{it} = \hat{\gamma}_{0t} + \hat{\gamma}_{1t}\beta_{it} + \epsilon_{it}, \tag{7.34}$$

does provide the best model of security returns. The practitioner who wishes to have unbiased estimates of the empirical market-line parameters, $\hat{\gamma}_{0t}$ and $\hat{\gamma}_{1t}$, estimated

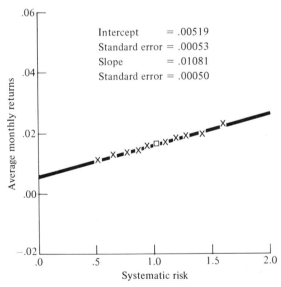

Fig. 7.10 Average monthly returns versus systematic risk for ten portfolios 1931–1965 (From *Studies in the Theory of Capital Markets*, edited by Michael C. Jensen. Copyright © 1972 by Praeger Publishers, Inc. Reprinted by permission of Holt, Rinehart and Winston.)

each month from January 1935 through June 1968, is referred to Fama [1976]. Obviously, if one can estimate a security's beta for a given time period, then by knowing the empirical market-line parameters he can estimate the security's required rate of return from Eq. (7.34).

I. THE PROBLEM OF MEASURING PERFORMANCE: ROLL'S CRITIQUE

One of the potentially most useful applications of the securities market line in its *ex post* form (Eq. (7.32)) or the empirical market line (Eq. (7.34)) is that they might be used as benchmarks for security performance. The residual term ϵ_{jt} has been interpreted as abnormal performance because, as shown in Fig. 7.11, it represents return in excess of what is predicted by the securities market line.

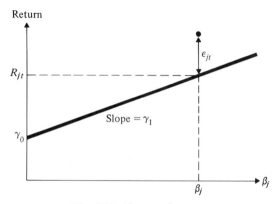

Fig. 7.11 Abnormal return

Roll [1977] takes exception to this interpretation of cross-section abnormal performance measures and to empirical tests of the CAPM in general. In brief, his major conclusions are:

1. The only legitimate test of the CAPM is whether or not the market portfolio (which includes *all* assets) is mean-variance efficient.

2. If performance is measured relative to an index which is *ex post* efficient, then from the mathematics of the efficient set, no security will have abnormal performance when measured as a departure from the security market line.[11]

3. If performance is measured relative to an *ex post* inefficient index, then any ranking of portfolio performance is possible depending on which inefficient index has been chosen.

---

[11] It is important to note that he does not take exception to time series measures of abnormal performance such as those described by the market model in Chapter 9.

This is a startling statement. It implies that even if markets are efficient and the CAPM is valid, then the cross-section securities market line cannot be used as a means of measuring the *ex post* performance of portfolio selection techniques. Furthermore, the efficiency of the market portfolio and the validity of the CAPM are joint hypotheses which are almost impossible to test because of the difficulty of measuring the true market portfolio.

To understand Roll's critique, we must go back to the derivation of the zero-beta portfolio. Recall that if there is no risk-free asset, it is still possible to write the securities market line as a combination of the market portfolio and a zero-beta portfolio which is uncorrelated with the market index. Therefore, the expected return on any asset could be written as

$$E(R_i) = E(R_z) + [E(R_m) - E(R_z)]\beta_i. \tag{7.35}$$

Roll points out that there is nothing unique about the market portfolio. The zero-beta relationship applies to *any* efficient portfolio. It is always possible to choose an efficient portfolio as an index, then find the minimum variance portfolio which is uncorrelated with the selected efficient index. This is shown in Fig. 7.12. Once this has been done, then Eq. (7.35) can be derived and written as

$$E(R_i) = E(R_{z,I}) + [E(R_I) - E(R_{z,I})]\beta_{i,I}. \tag{7.36}$$

Note that the market portfolio, R_m, has been replaced by any efficient index, R_I, and that beta is measured relative to the selected efficient index, $\beta_{i,I}$. Also, the zero-beta portfolio is measured relative to the index, $R_{z,I}$. Because the expected return on any asset can be written as a linear function of its beta measured relative to any efficient index, then it is not necessary to know the market index. One only need know the

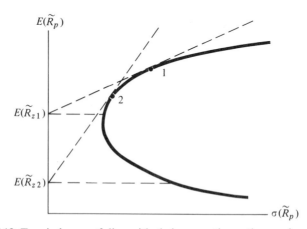

Fig. 7.12 Two index portfolios with their respective orthogonal portfolios

composition of any efficient index in order to write Eq. (7.36). Furthermore, if the index turns out to be *ex post* efficient, then every asset will fall exactly on the securities market line. There will be no abnormal returns. If there are systematic abnormal returns, it simply means that the index which has been chosen is not *ex post* efficient.

The Roll critique does not imply that the CAPM is an invalid theory. However, it does mean that tests of the CAPM must be interpreted with great caution. The fact that portfolio residuals exhibited no significant departures from linearity merely implies that the market index which was selected (usually an equally weighted index of all listed shares of common stock) was *ex post* efficient. In fact, the only way to test the CAPM directly is to see whether or not the true market portfolio is *ex post* efficient. Unfortunately, because the market portfolio contains all assets (marketable or nonmarketable, e.g., human capital, coins, houses, bonds, stocks, options, land, etc.) it is impossible to observe.

Mayers and Rice [1978] show, by using a choice and information theoretic framework, that residual analysis and portfolio performance tests *can* yield meaningful results for a wide class of information structures. Their argument refutes Roll's contention that the CAPM cannot be meaningfully used to measure abnormal performance (as in Fig. 7.11, for example). Mayers and Rice define one individual as superior with respect to the information he holds. The better informed individual is able to buy more future consumption than does the uninformed in states of nature that are more likely to occur. Consequently, the informed individual earns a higher average return than the uninformed expects him or her to. Since the uninformed individual expects the informed individual to plot directly on the security market line, using the uninformed estimate of beta, the informed individual will beat the (uninformed's) security market line. Thus, if the uninformed is analogous to the market, then it is reasonable to expect residual analysis techniques which employ the security market line to detect positive abnormal performance.

Although Mayers and Rice show that the CAPM can be used to detect abnormal risk-adjusted performance, we are still left with the fundamental conclusion of Roll's critique, namely that the validity of the CAPM and of market efficiency are joint hypotheses. This implies, for example, that if we find abnormal performance as measured by the CAPM we cannot necessarily conclude that capital markets are inefficient. Some other (as yet unknown) equilibrium model may come along which can explain the (CAPM-measured) abnormal performance in a way which is consistent with market efficiency.

J. SUMMARY

This chapter has derived a model which enables us to price risky assets in equilibrium and to establish that the appropriate measure of risk is the covariance of returns between the risky asset in question and the market portfolio of all assets.

The CAPM was shown to provide a useful conceptual framework for capital budgeting and the cost of capital. It is also reasonably untouched by the relaxation of many of the unrealistic assumptions which made its derivation simpler. Finally, although the model is not perfectly validated by empirical tests, its main implications are upheld, namely that systematic risk (beta) is the only valid measure of risk, that the model is linear, and that the trade-off between return and risk is positive.

Appendix to Chapter 7

An Alternative Derivation of the CAPM

The Sharpe [1964] derivation of the CAPM is appealing because it does not rely on constrained optimization techniques of differential calculus. However, it has the disadvantage of omitting explicit consideration of the individual's portfolio problem. The advanced student will want to be familiar with alternative derivations of the CAPM. The one given below assumes that all investors are risk-averse single-period maximizers of expected utility whose consumption decisions are made independently of their portfolio composition decisions.[1]

We assume that portfolio cash flows for the ith individual are generated at the end of the period and that they are normally distributed with mean, e_i, and variance, σ_i^2. The ith individual's utility is a function of the mean and variance of his end-of-period cash flows. His utility function is written

$$U_i(e_i, \sigma_i^2). \tag{A.1}$$

We further assume that the marginal utility of expected cash flows is positive, and the marginal utility of the variance of cash flows is negative.

$$\delta U_i/\delta e_i > 0, \qquad \delta U_i/\delta \sigma_i^2 < 0. \tag{A.2}$$

Finally, all assets are marketable and infinitely divisible, transactions costs and taxes are zero, and there are no constraints on short sales. The expected end-of-period cash flows to an individual are the payments from risky assets less any interest on debt:

$$e_i = \sum_j X_{ij} E(\tilde{D}_j) - r d_i, \tag{A.3}$$

---

[1] See Jensen [1972].

where

X_{ij} = the fraction of the jth firm held by the ith individual.
 $r = (1 + R_f)$, where R_f is the one-period risk-free borrowing/lending rate.
 d_i = the net personal debt issued by the ith individual.
 $\tilde{D}_j$ = the end-of-period cash flow paid by the jth firm.

The variance of end-of-period cash flows for the ith individual is

$$\sigma_i^2 = \sum_j \sum_k X_{ij} X_{ik} \sigma_{jk}, \tag{A.4}$$

where

σ_{jk} = the covariance of cash payments by the jth and kth firms.

The individual investor's problem is to find the set of weights, X_{ij}, and borrowing, d_i, which maximize his expected end-of-period utility subject to his budget constraint.

$$\text{MAX } EU_i(e_i, \sigma_i^2) \tag{A.5a}$$
$$\underset{X_{ij}, d_i}{}$$

$$\text{subject to } \sum_j X_{ij} V_j - d_i = W_i, \tag{A.5b}$$

where

V_j = the total market value of the jth firm at the beginning of the period.
W_i = the total wealth of the individual at the beginning of the period.

Assuming that all investors see the same opportunity set (i.e., have homogeneous expectations regarding e_i and σ_i^2), we can solve the individual's constrained optimization by forming the Lagrangian, ψ:

$$\psi = EU_i(e_i, \sigma_i^2) + \lambda_i \left[W_i - \sum_j X_{ij} V_j + d_i \right]. \tag{A.6}$$

Taking the partials with respect to X_{ij}, d_i, and λ_i, and equating them to zero, we have

$$\frac{\delta \psi}{\delta X_{ij}} = \frac{\delta EU_i}{\delta e_i} \frac{\delta e_i}{\delta X_{ij}} + \frac{\delta EU_i}{\delta \sigma_i^2} \frac{\delta \sigma_i^2}{\delta X_{ij}} - \lambda_i V_j = 0$$

$$= \frac{\delta EU_i}{\delta e_i} [E(\tilde{D}_j)] + \frac{\delta EU_i}{\delta \sigma_i^2} \left(2 \sum_k X_{ik} \sigma_{jk} \right) - \lambda_i V_j = 0 \tag{A.6a}$$

$$\frac{\delta \psi}{\delta d_i} = \frac{\delta EU_i}{\delta e_i} \frac{\delta e_i}{\delta d_i} + \frac{\delta EU_i}{\delta \sigma_i^2} \frac{\delta \sigma_i^2}{\delta d_i} + \lambda_i = 0.$$

$$= \frac{\delta EU_i}{\delta e_i} (-r) + \lambda_i = 0 \tag{A.6b}$$

$$\frac{\delta \psi}{\delta \lambda_i} = W_i - \sum_j X_{ij} V_j + d_i = 0.$$

From (A.6b) we note that

$$\lambda_i = r \frac{\delta EU_i}{\delta e_i}.$$

Substituting this into (A.6a) we have

$$\frac{\delta EU_i}{\delta e_i} E(\tilde{D}_j) + \frac{\delta EU_i}{\delta \sigma_i^2} \left(2 \sum_k X_{ik} \sigma_{jk} \right) - r \frac{\delta EU_i}{\delta e_i} V_j = 0,$$

$$\frac{\delta EU_i}{\delta e_i} [E(\tilde{D}_j) - rV_j] + \frac{\delta EU_i}{\delta \sigma_i^2} \left(2 \sum_k X_{jk} \sigma_{jk} \right) = 0. \qquad (A.7)$$

Equation (A.7) is an equilibrium relationship which must hold for all individuals, i, and all firms, j. Suppose that we take the ratios of a pair of equations (Eqs. (A.7)) for two assets, j and t, for individual i. Then we have

$$\frac{(\delta EU_i/\delta e_i)[E(\tilde{D}_j) - rV_j]}{(\delta EU_i/\delta e_i)[E(\tilde{D}_t) - rV_t]} = \frac{-(\delta EU_i/\delta \sigma_i^2)(2 \sum_k X_{ik} \sigma_{jk})}{-(\delta EU_i/\delta \sigma_i^2)(2 \sum_k X_{ik} \sigma_{tk})},$$

which reduces to

$$\frac{E(\tilde{D}_j) - rV_j}{E(\tilde{D}_t) - rV_t} = \frac{\sum_k X_{ik} \sigma_{jk}}{\sum_k X_{ik} \sigma_{tk}} \quad \text{for all } i. \qquad (A.8)$$

We know that in market equilibrium, all assets must be held by investors; therefore the sum of weights held by all individuals for a given firm, j, must add to one. This condition is written below.

$$\sum_i X_{ij} = 1 \quad \text{for all } j. \qquad (A.9)$$

Summing (A.8) across all i, applying (A.9), and rearranging terms we have, for all assets,

$$\frac{E(\tilde{D}_j) - rV_j}{\sum_k \sigma_{jk}} = \frac{E(\tilde{D}_t) - rV_t}{\sum_k \sigma_{tk}} = \theta, \qquad (A.10)$$

where

θ = a common ratio for all assets.

Summing (A.10) over all assets, t, we have

$$\frac{\sum_t [E(\tilde{D}_t) - rV_t]}{\sum_t \sum_k \sigma_{tk}} = \frac{E(\tilde{D}_m) - rV_m}{\sigma_m^2} = \theta, \qquad (A.11)$$

where

$\tilde{D}_m$ = the cash payouts by all firms in the market.
V_m = the value of the market portfolio at the beginning of the period.
σ_m^2 = the variance of the total cash paid by all firms.

Substituting the right-hand side of (A.11) into (A.10) and solving for V_j, we have

$$\frac{E(\tilde{D}_j) - rV_j}{\sum_k \sigma_{jk}} = \frac{E(\tilde{D}_m) - rV_m}{\sigma_m^2},$$

$$V_j = \left[E(\tilde{D}_j) - \frac{E(\tilde{D}_m) - rV_m}{\sigma_m^2} \sum_k \sigma_{jk} \right] \frac{1}{r}$$

$$V_j = \frac{1}{r} [E(\tilde{D}_j) - \theta \, \text{COV}(\tilde{D}_j, \tilde{D}_m)], \qquad (A.12)$$

where

$$\theta = [E(\tilde{D}_m) - rV_m]/\sigma_m^2, \qquad \text{COV}(\tilde{D}_j, \tilde{D}_m) = \sum_k \sigma_{jk}.$$

Equation (A.12) is a certainty-equivalent formula for the market value of all assets, evaluated at the beginning of the period. The certainty equivalent is the expected end-of-period cash flow minus the "price of risk" multiplied by the risk factor which is the covariance between the cash flows on the jth asset and the market portfolio. The discount rate is $r = 1 + R_f$.

Equation (A.12) can be converted into rates of return if we define the rate of return on the jth asset as

$$\tilde{R}_j = (\tilde{D}_j - V_j)/V_j. \qquad (A.13)$$

Using (A.13) in (A.12), we obtain

$$E(\tilde{R}_j) = R_f + \lambda \, \text{COV}(\tilde{R}_j, \tilde{R}_m), \qquad (A.14)$$

where

$$\lambda = [E(\tilde{R}_m) - R_f]/\sigma_m^2, \qquad E(\tilde{R}_m) = \sum_j Z_j E(\tilde{R}_j), \qquad Z_j = V_j/V_m.$$

Equation (A.14) is the familiar CAPM.

PROBLEM SET

7.1 Let us assume a normal distribution of returns and risk-averse utility functions. Under what conditions will all investors demand the same portfolio of risky assets?

7.2 The following data have been developed for the Donovan Company, the manufacturer of an advanced line of adhesives:

State	Probability	Market return, R_m	Return for the firm, R_j
1	.1	−.15	−.30
2	.3	.05	.00
3	.4	.15	.20
4	.2	.20	.50

The risk-free rate is 6%. Calculate the following:

a) The expected market return.
b) The variance of the market return.
c) The expected return for the Donovan Company.
d) The covariance of the return for the Donovan Company with the market return.
e) Write the equation of the security market line.
f) What is the required return for the Donovan Company? How does this compare with its expected return?

7.3 The following data have been developed for the Milliken Company:

Year	Market return	Company returns
1978	.27	.25
1977	.12	.05
1976	−.03	−.05
1975	.12	.15
1974	−.03	−.10
1973	.27	.30

The yield to maturity on Treasury bills is .066 and is expected to remain at this point for the foreseeable future. Calculate the following:

a) The expected market return.
b) The variance of the market return.
c) The expected return for the Milliken Company.
d) The covariance of the return for the Milliken Company with the return on the market.
e) Write the equation of the security market line.
f) What is the required return for the Milliken Company?

7.4 For the data in Table Q7.1, perform the indicated calculations.

7.5 For the data in Table Q7.2, calculate the items indicated.

7.6 What are the assumptions sufficient to guarantee that the market portfolio is an efficient portfolio?

7.7 Prove that $\text{COV}(\tilde{R}_j, \tilde{R}_k) = \beta_j \beta_k \sigma_m^2$.

7.8 In the CAPM, is there any way to identify the investors who are more risk averse? Explain. How would your answer change if there were not a riskless asset?

7.9 Given risk-free borrowing and lending, efficient portfolios have no unsystematic risk. True or false? Explain.

7.10 What is the beta of an efficient portfolio with $E(R_j) = 20\%$ if $R_f = 5\%$, $E(R_m) = 15\%$, and $\sigma_m = 20\%$? What is its σ_j? What is its correlation with the market?

7.11 Given the facts of Problem 7.10 and that the common stock of the Rapid Rolling Corporation has $E(R_k) = 25\%$ and $\sigma_k^2 = 52\%$, what is the systematic risk of the common stock? What is its unsystematic risk?

7.12

a) If the expected rate of return on the market portfolio is 14% and the risk-free rate is 6%, find the beta for a portfolio which has an expected rate of return of 10%. What assump-

Table Q7.1 Estimates of market parameters

Year	S&P 500 price index	Percent change in price	Dividend yield	Percent return	Return deviation	Market variance	
	P_t	$\dfrac{P_t}{P_{t-1}} - 1$	$\dfrac{D_t}{P_t}$	R_{mt} $(3+4)$	$(R_{mt} - \bar{R}_m)$ $(5 - \bar{R}_m)$	$(R_{mt} - \bar{R}_m)^2$ (6^2)	R_f
(1)	(2)	(3)	(4)	(5)	(6)	(7)	(8)
1960	55.85						
1961	66.27		.0298				.03
1962	62.38		.0337				.03
1963	69.87		.0317				.03
1964	81.37		.0301				.04
1965	88.17		.0300				.04
1966	85.26		.0340				.04
1967	91.93		.0320				.05
1968	98.70		.0307				.05
1969	97.84		.0324				.07
1970	83.22		.0383				.06

a) $\bar{R}_m = ?$ b) $VAR(R_m) = ?$ c) $\sigma(R_m) = ?$

Table Q7.2 Calculation of beta for General Motors

Year	GM price	Percent change in price	Dividend yield	Percent return	Deviation of returns	Variance of returns	Covariance with market
	P_t	$\dfrac{P_t}{P_t-1} - 1$	$\dfrac{D_t}{P_t}$	R_{jt} $(3+4)$	$(R_{jt} - \bar{R}_j)$ $(5 - \bar{R}_j)$	$(R_{jt} - \bar{R}_j)^2$ (6^2)	$(R_{jt} - \bar{R}_j)(R_{mt} - \bar{R}_m)$ (Col. 6 × Q7.1 Col. 6)
(1)	(2)	(3)	(4)	(5)	(6)	(7)	(8)
1960	48						
1961	49		.05				
1962	52		.06				
1963	74		.05				
1964	90		.05				
1965	102		.05				
1966	87		.05				
1967	78		.05				
1968	81		.05				
1969	74		.06				
1970	70		.05				

a) $\bar{R}_j = ?$ b) $VAR(R_j) = ?$ c) $COV(R_j, R_m) = ?$ d) $\beta_j = ?$

tions concerning this portfolio and/or market conditions do you need to make to calculate the portfolio's beta?

b) What percentage of this portfolio must an individual put into the market portfolio in order to achieve an expected return of 10%?

7.13 You believe that the Beta Alpha Watch Company will be worth $100 per share one year from now. How much are you willing to pay for one share today if the risk-free rate is 8%, the expected rate of return on the market is 18%, and the company's beta is 2.0?

7.14 Given the following variance-covariance matrix and expected returns vector (for assets X and Y respectively) for a two-asset world:

$$\Sigma = \begin{bmatrix} .01 & 0 \\ 0 & .0064 \end{bmatrix}, \qquad \bar{R}_I' = [.2 \quad .1]$$

a) What is the expected return of a zero-beta portfolio given that 50% of the index portfolio is invested in asset X and 50% in asset Y?

b) What is the vector of weights in the global minimum-variance portfolio?

c) What is the covariance between the global minimum-variance portfolio and the zero-beta portfolio?

d) What is the equation of the market line?

7.15 Given the following variance-covariance matrix, calculate the covariance between portfolio A which has 10% in asset 1 and 90% in asset 2, and portfolio B which has 60% in asset 1 and 40% in asset 2:

$$\Sigma = \begin{bmatrix} .01 & -.02 \\ -.02 & .04 \end{bmatrix}.$$

7.16 Suppose that securities are priced as if they are traded in a two-parameter economy. You have forecast the correlation coefficient between the rate of return on Knowlode Mutual Fund and the market portfolio at .8. Your forecast of the standard deviations of the rates of return are .25 for Knowlode, and .20 for the market portfolio. How would you combine the Knowlode Fund and a riskless security to obtain a portfolio with a volatility (beta) of 1.6?

7.17 You currently have 50% of your wealth in a risk-free asset, and 50% in the four assets below:

Asset	Expected return on asset i	β_i	Percent invested in asset i
$i = 1$	7.6%	.2	10%
$i = 2$	12.4%	.8	10%
$i = 3$	15.6%	1.2	10%
$i = 4$	18.8%	1.6	20%

If you want an expected rate of return of 12%, you can obtain it by selling some of your holdings of the risk-free asset and using the proceeds to buy the market portfolio. If this is the way you decide to revise your portfolio, what will the set of weights in your revised portfolio be? If you hold only the risk-free asset and the market portfolio, what set of weights would give you an expected 12% return?

7.18 The market price of a security is \$40, the security's expected rate of return is 13%, the riskless rate of interest is 7%, and the market risk premium is 8%. What will be the security's price if the covariance of its rate of return with the market portfolio doubles?

7.19 Suppose you are the manager of an investment fund in a two-parameter economy. Given the following forecast:

$$E(R_m) = .16, \qquad \sigma(R_m) = .20, \qquad R_f = .08.$$

a) Would you recommend investment in a security with $E(R_j) = .12$ and $\mathrm{COV}(R_j, R_m) = .01$? What percentage change in the security's price would be required to reverse your investment decision? [*Note:* Assume that this price change has no significant effect on the position of the security market line.]

b) Suppose that in the next period, security R_j has earned only 5% over the preceding period. How would you explain this *ex post* return?

7.20 Why is the separation principle still valid in a world with
a) nonmarketable assets?
b) a nonstochastic risk-free rate?

REFERENCES

BLACK, F., "Capital Market Equilibrium with Restricted Borrowing," *Journal of Business*, July 1972, 444–455.

———, M. C. JENSEN, and M. SCHOLES, "The Capital Asset Pricing Model: Some Empirical Tests," reprinted in M. C. Jensen, Ed., *Studies in the Theory of Capital Markets*. Praeger, New York, 1972, 79–124.

BLUME, M., "Portfolio Theory: A Step Toward Its Practical Application," *Journal of Business*, April 1970, 152–173.

———, "On the Assessment of Risk," *Journal of Finance*, March 1971, 1–10.

———, and I. FRIEND, "A New Look at the Capital Asset Pricing Model," *Journal of Finance*, March 1973, 19–34.

BRENNAN, M. J., "Taxes, Market Valuation and Corporation Financial Policy," *National Tax Journal*, December 1970, 417–427.

CLARK, P. K., "A Subordinated Stochastic Process Model with Finite Variance for Speculative Prices," *Econometrica*, January 1973, 135–155.

FAMA, E. F., "The Behavior of Stock Market Prices," *Journal of Business*, January 1965a, 34–105.

———, "Portfolio Analysis in a Stable Paretian Market," *Management Science*, January 1965b, 404–419.

———, "Risk, Return and Equilibrium: Some Clarifying Comments," *The Journal of Finance*, March 1968, 29–40.

———, "Risk, Return and Equilibrium," *Journal of Political Economy*, January/February 1971, 30–55.

———, *Foundations of Finance*. Basic Books, New York, 1976.

———, and J. MACBETH, "Risk, Return and Equilibrium: Empirical Test," *Journal of Political Economy*, May/June 1973, 607–636.

———, and G. W. SCHWERT, "Human Capital and Capital Market Equilibrium," *The Journal of Financial Economics*, January 1977, 95–125.

FRIEND, I., and M. BLUME, "Measurement of Portfolio Performance under Uncertainty," *American Economic Review*, September 1970, 561–575.

HAMADA, R. S., "The Effect of the Firm's Capital Structure on the Systematic Risk of Common Stocks," *The Journal of Finance*, May 1972, 435–452.

JENSEN, M. C., "Capital Markets: Theory and Evidence," *The Bell Journal of Economics and Management Science*, Autumn 1972, 357–398.

LINTNER, J., "The Valuation of Risk Assets and the Selection of Risky Investments in Stock Portfolios and Capital Budgets," *The Review of Economics and Statistics*, February 1965, 13–37.

———, "Security Prices and Maximal Gains from Diversification," *Journal of Finance*, December 1965, 587–616.

———, "The Aggregation of Investor's Diverse Judgments and Preferences in Purely Competitive Security Markets," *Journal of Financial and Quantitative Analysis*, December 1969, 347–400.

MAYERS, D., "Non-Marketable Assets and the Capital Market Equilibrium under Uncertainty," reprinted in M. C. Jensen, Ed., *Studies in the Theory of Capital Markets*. Praeger, New York, 1972, 223–248.

MAYERS, D., and E. RICE, "Measuring Portfolio Performance and the Empirical Content of Asset Pricing Models," *The Journal of Financial Economics*, Vol. 7, no. 1.

MERTON, R., "An Intertemporal Capital Asset Pricing Model," *Econometrica*, September 1973, 867–888.

MILLER, M., and M. SCHOLES, "Rates of Return in Relation to Risk: A Re-examination of Some Recent Findings," in M. C. Jensen, Ed., *Studies in the Theory of Capital Markets*. Praeger, New York, 1972, 47–78.

MODIGLIANI, F., and G. POGUE, "An Introduction to Risk and Return," *Financial Analysts Journal*, March/April 1974 and May/June 1974, 68–80 and 69–85.

MOSSIN, J., "Equilibrium in a Capital Asset Market," *Econometrica*, October 1966, 768–783.

ROLL, R., "A Critique of the Asset Pricing Theory's Tests," *Journal of Financial Economics*, March 1977, 129–176.

RUBINSTEIN, M. E., "A Mean-Variance Synthesis of Corporate Financial Theory," *Journal of Finance*, March 1973, 167–182.

SHARPE, W. F., "A Simplified Model for Portfolio Analysis," *Management Science*, January 1963, 277–293.

———, "Capital Asset Prices: A Theory of Market Equilibrium Under Conditions of Risk," *Journal of Finance*, September 1964, 425–442.

TREYNOR, J., "Toward a Theory of the Market Value of Risky Assets." Unpublished manuscript, 1961.

VASICEK, O. A., "Capital Market Equilibrium with No Riskless Borrowing," March 1971, mimeograph available from the Wells Fargo Bank.

Chapter 8

Efficient Capital Markets: Theory

In a world of uncertainty, information becomes a useful commodity—acquisition of information to eliminate uncertainty should then be considered as an alternative to productive investment subject to uncertainty.

J. Hirshleifer, *Investment, Interest and Capital*,
Prentice Hall, Englewood Cliffs, N.J., 1970, p. 311

A. DEFINING CAPITAL MARKET EFFICIENCY

The purpose of capital markets is to efficiently transfer funds between lenders (savers) and borrowers (producers). Individuals or firms may have an excess of productive investment opportunities with anticipated rates of return which exceed the market-determined borrowing rate but not enough funds to take advantage of all these opportunities. However, if capital markets exist, they can borrow the needed funds. Lenders, who have excess funds after exhausting all their productive opportunities with expected returns greater than the borrowing rate, will be willing to lend their excess funds because the borrowing/lending rate is higher than what they might otherwise earn. Therefore both borrowers and lenders are better off if efficient capital markets are used to facilitate fund transfers. The borrowing/lending rate is used as an important piece of information by each producer. He will accept projects until the rate of return on the least profitable project just equals the opportunity cost of external funds (the borrowing/lending rate): Thus a market is said to be *allocationally efficient* when prices are determined in a way which equates the *marginal* rates of return (adjusted for risk) for all producers and savers. In an allocationally efficient market, scarce savings are optimally allocated to productive investments in a way which benefits everyone.

In order to describe *efficient capital markets* it is useful, first of all, to contrast them with *perfect capital markets*. The following conditions are necessary for perfect capital markets:

- Markets are frictionless, i.e., there are no transaction costs or taxes, all assets are perfectly divisible and marketable, and there are no constraining regulations.
- There is perfect competition in product and securities markets. In product markets, this means that all producers supply goods and services at minimum average cost, and in securities markets, it means that all participants are price takers.
- Markets are informationally efficient, i.e., information is costless, and it is received simultaneously by all individuals.
- All individuals are rational expected utility maximizers.

Given these conditions both product and securities markets will be both allocationally and operationally efficient. Allocational efficiency has already been defined, but what about operational efficiency? *Operational efficiency* deals with the cost of transferring funds. In the idealized world of perfect capital markets, transactions costs are assumed to be zero; therefore we have perfect operational efficiency.[1] However, we shall see later, when we focus on empirical studies of real-world phenomena, that operational efficiency is, indeed, an important consideration.

Capital market efficiency is much less restrictive than the notion of perfect capital markets outlined above. In an efficient capital market, prices fully and instantaneously reflect all available relevant information. This means that when assets are traded, prices are accurate signals for capital allocation.

To show the difference between perfect markets and efficient capital markets we can relax some of the perfect market assumptions. For example, we can still have efficient capital markets if markets are not frictionless. Prices will still fully reflect all available information if, for example, securities traders have to pay brokerage fees, or if an individual's human capital (which after all is an asset) cannot be divided into a thousand parts and auctioned off. More important, there can be imperfect competition in product markets and we still have efficient capital markets. Hence, if a firm can reap monopoly profits in the product market, the efficient capital market will determine a security price which fully reflects the present value of the anticipated stream of monopoly profits. Hence we can have allocative inefficiencies in product markets but still have efficient capital markets. Finally, it is not necessary to have costless information in efficient capital markets.

Still, in a somewhat limited sense, efficient capital markets imply operational efficiency as well as asset prices which are allocationally efficient. Asset prices are correct signals in the sense that they fully and instantaneously reflect all available relevant information and are useful for directing the flow of funds from savers to investment projects which yield the highest return (even though the return may reflect monopolistic practices in product markets). Capital markets are operationally

---

[1] Note that even in perfect markets the minimum cost of transferring funds may not be zero if the transfer of funds also involves risk bearing.

efficient if intermediaries, who provide the service of channeling funds from savers to investors, do so at the minimum cost which provides them a fair return for their services.

Fama [1970, 1976] has done a great deal to operationalize the notion of capital market efficiency. He defines three types of efficiency each of which is based on a different notion of exactly what type of information is understood to be relevant in the phrase "all prices fully reflect all *relevant* information."

1. *Weak-form efficiency.* No investor can earn excess returns if he develops trading rules based on historical price or return information. In other words, the information in past prices or returns is not useful or relevant in achieving excess returns.

2. *Semistrong-form efficiency.* No investor can earn excess returns from trading rules based on any publicly available information. Examples of publicly available information are: annual reports of companies, investment advisory data such as "Heard on the Street" in *The Wall Street Journal,* or ticker tape information.

3. *Strong-form efficiency.* No investor can earn excess returns using any information, whether publicly available or not.

Obviously, the last type of market efficiency is very strong indeed. If markets were efficient in their strong form, prices would fully reflect all information even though it might be held exclusively by a corporate insider. Suppose, for example, he knows that his company has just discovered how to control nuclear fusion. Even before he has a chance to trade based on the news, the strong form of market efficiency predicts that prices will have adjusted so that he cannot profit.

B. A FORMAL DEFINITION OF THE VALUE OF INFORMATION

The notion of efficient capital markets depends on the precise definition of information and the value of information. An information structure may be defined as a message about various events which may happen. For example, the message "there are no clouds in the sky" provides a probability distribution for the likelihood of rain within the next 24 hours. This message may have various values to different people depending on (1) whether or not they can take any actions based on the message and (2) what net benefits (gain in utility) will result from their actions. For example, a message which is related to rainfall can be of value to a farmer because he can take actions which increase his wealth. If there is to be no rain, he might decide that it is a good time to harvest his hay. On the other hand, a deep-pit coal miner probably will not alter his actions at all. Hence messages about rainfall have no value to him.

A formal expression of the above concept defines the value of an information structure, $V(\eta)$, as

$$V(\eta) \equiv \sum_m q(m) \; \text{MAX}_a \sum_e p(e \mid m)U(a, e), \tag{8.1}$$

where

$q(m)$ = the marginal probability of receiving a message m.
$p(e|m)$ = the conditional probability of an event e given a message m.
$U(a, e)$ = the utility resulting from an action a if an event e occurs. We shall call this a *benefit function*.

According to Eq. (8.1) a decision maker will evaluate an information structure (which, for the sake of generality, is defined as a set of messages) by choosing an action which will maximize his expected utility given the arrival of a message. For example, if he receives a message (one of many that he could have received) that there is a 20% chance of rain, he may carry an umbrella because of the high "disutility" of getting drenched and the low cost of carrying it. For each possible message he can determine his optimal action. Mathematically, this is the solution to the problem

$$\text{MAX} \sum_a \sum_e p(e|m)U(a, e).$$

Finally, by weighting the expected utility of each optimal action (in response to all possible messages) by the probability, q_m, of receiving the message which gives rise to the action, the decision maker knows the expected utility of the entire set of messages, which we call the *expected utility* (or *value*) of an information set, $V(\eta)$.

The following example applies the value-of-information concept to the theory of portfolio choice. The investor will choose his optimal portfolio as a combination of two funds: either the risk-free asset which yields 6%, or the market portfolio which may yield 16%, or 10%, or -5%.[2] We assume that the standard deviation of the market portfolio, σ_m, is known with certainty. Figure 8.1 shows the linear efficient set (the capital market line) for each of the three possible states of the world. A risk-averse investor will maximize his expected utility by choosing the portfolio where his indifference curve is tangent to the efficient set.

In order to calculate the value of an information set we need to know the payoff function $U(a, e)$, which tells us the utility of having taken a course of action, a, when an event or state of the world, e, occurs. For the sake of convenience, we will label the three states of the world by their market returns: $e_3 = 16\%$, $e_2 = 10\%$, and $e_1 = -5\%$.

If the market return were 16%, the investor would choose portfolio 3 in Fig. 8.1 which is where indifference curve U_7 is tangent to the capital market line e_3. On the other hand, he would put all of his portfolio in the risk-free asset (portfolio 1) if the market return were known to be -5%. This occurs where indifference curve U_4 passes through R_f. If he chooses portfolio 3, and if the market rate of return really is 16%, then his payoff is $U_7 = 40$. But if he makes a mistake and chooses portfolio 3 when the market rate of return turns out to be -5%, his portfolio is suboptimal.

---

[2] A more general, but also more complicated, example would assign a continuous probability distribution to the possible returns offered by the market portfolio.

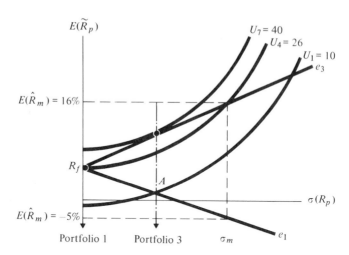

Fig. 8.1 Optimal choices for two states of the world

After the fact, he would have been much better off with portfolio 1, the risk-free asset. His utility for holding portfolio 3 when state 1 obtains (point A in Fig. 8.1) is $U_1 = 10$ less his regret, which is the difference between where he actually is and where he would have liked to be.[3] In this case his regret is the difference between U_4 and U_1. Therefore, his net utility is $U_1 - (U_4 - U_1) = 2U_1 - U_4 = -6$. When the investor receives a message which provides estimates of the likelihood of future states of the world, he will choose an action (in our example this amounts to choosing a portfolio) which will maximize his expected utility given that message. The utility provided by each portfolio choice (i.e., each action) in each state of the world can be taken from Fig. 8.2, which is similar to Fig. 8.1 except that it gives all possible portfolios and states of the world. The corresponding benefit function, $U(a, e)$, is given in Table 8.1.

Table 8.1 Benefit function $U(a, e)$

Action	$e_1(R_M = -5\%)$	$e_2(R_M = 10\%)$	$e_3(R_M = 16\%)$
Portfolio 1 (action a_1)	$U_4 = 26$	$2U_4 - U_5 = 22$	$2U_4 - U_7 = 12$
Portfolio 2 (action a_2)	$2U_2 - U_4 = 14$	$U_5 = 30$	$2U_6 - U_7 = 24$
Portfolio 3 (action a_3)	$2U_1 - U_4 = -6$	$2U_3 - U_5 = 20$	$U_7 = 40$

In addition to a benefit matrix it is also necessary to have an information structure (a Markov matrix) which gives the probability that an event will actually occur

---

[3] Needless to say, the computation of "regret" as suggested here is not necessarily accurate and is only for purposes of illustration. However, it is consistent with the fact that utilities are stage contingent. (See Chapter 5, state-preference theory.)

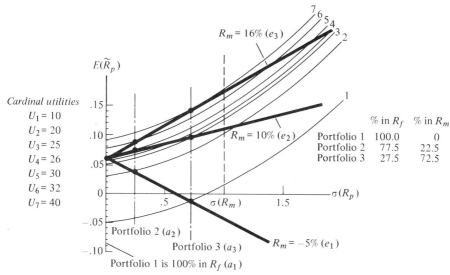

Fig. 8.2 Optimal actions given various states of the world

given that a particular message has been received. The two obvious polar cases are perfect information and no information. Their matrices are given in Table 8.2. If the information structure is perfect, receipt of a message implies that a given state of the world will occur with certainty. This makes it easy to select a course of action which results in the highest utility. If you receive m_1, then the state of world e_1 will obtain with certainty; therefore the best action is a_1 with expected utility $U_4 = 26$. Thus, for each message, it is possible to find the optimal action. Implicitly this procedure amounts to solving Eq. (8.1), which tells us the utility value of information. Given perfect information, the optimal action (and its utility) for each message is seen to be:

Message	Optimal action	Utility
m_1	a_1 (invest in portfolio 1)	26
m_2	a_2 (invest in portfolio 2)	30
m_3	a_3 (invest in portfolio 3)	40

Table 8.2 Information structures

	η_2 = perfect information			η_0 = no information			η_1 = noisy information		
	m_1	m_2	m_3	m_1	m_2	m_3	m_1	m_2	m_3
e_1	1.0	0	0	$\frac{1}{3}$	$\frac{1}{3}$	$\frac{1}{3}$	.6	.3	.1
e_2	0	1.0	0	$\frac{1}{3}$	$\frac{1}{3}$	$\frac{1}{3}$	.2	.5	.3
e_3	0	0	1.0	$\frac{1}{3}$	$\frac{1}{3}$	$\frac{1}{3}$	.2	.2	.6

These actions represent the solution to the first part of the value of information, Eq. (8.1)

$$\text{MAX}_a \sum_e p(e\,|\,m)U(a, e).$$

Finally, the utility of each action which results from a message is weighted by the probability of the message. In our example, each of the three messages is assumed to be equally likely; therefore, using the notation of Eq. (8.1), we have $q(m_1) = \frac{1}{3}$, $q(m_2) = \frac{1}{3}$, and $q(m_3) = \frac{1}{3}$. The utility value of perfect information is

$$V(\eta_2) = \tfrac{1}{3}(26) + \tfrac{1}{3}(30) + \tfrac{1}{3}(40) = 32.$$

Next, consider the value of no information. In Table 8.2 we see that no information means that all messages are identical. Each says the same thing: "All events are equally likely." For example, suppose you asked a friend whether or not a movie was worth seeing. If he always replies "yes," whether or not the movie is good, then the message contains no information. If he always says "no," the result is the same—no information. In the example at hand, when asked about the probability of a state of the world, he always answers "one-third." In order to compute the value of no information, we begin just as before, by selecting the optimal action for each message. For example, let us assume that we receive message 1:

If we take action	the expected utility is
a_1 (invest in portfolio 1)	$\tfrac{1}{3}(26) + \tfrac{1}{3}(22) + \tfrac{1}{3}(12) = 20$
a_2 (invest in portfolio 2)	$\tfrac{1}{3}(14) + \tfrac{1}{3}(30) + \tfrac{1}{3}(24) = 22.67$
a_3 (invest in portfolio 3)	$\tfrac{1}{3}(-6) + \tfrac{1}{3}(20) + \tfrac{1}{3}(40) = 18$

Suppose we receive message 2:

If we take action	the expected utility is
a_1 (invest in portfolio 1)	$\tfrac{1}{3}(26) + \tfrac{1}{3}(22) + \tfrac{1}{3}(12) = 20$
a_2 (invest in portfolio 2)	$\tfrac{1}{3}(14) + \tfrac{1}{3}(30) + \tfrac{1}{3}(24) = 22.67$
a_3 (invest in portfolio 3)	$\tfrac{1}{3}(-6) + \tfrac{1}{3}(20) + \tfrac{1}{3}(40) = 18$

And if we receive message 3, the expected utilities of our actions are the same (obviously, since the three messages are the same). Regardless of the message our optimal action is always the same—invest in portfolio 2; and our expected utility is 22.67. As with perfect information the selection of optimal actions, given various messages, is the first part of the problem. The second part is to weight the expected utility of an action, given a message, by the probability of the message. The result is the utility value of information. The value of no information is

$$V(\eta_0) = \tfrac{1}{3}(22.67) + \tfrac{1}{3}(22.67) + \tfrac{1}{3}(22.67) = 22.67.$$

The difference between perfect information and no information is the maximum gain from information

$$V(\eta_2) - V(\eta_0) = 9.33.$$

Finally, consider the third information structure in Table 8.2. In this case the messages received are noisy. The first message says that there is a .6 probability that the first state of the world might obtain, but .4 of the time the message will err, with a .2 probability that e_2 will actually occur and a .2 probability that e_3 will obtain. In order to value the noisy information, we proceed as before. We choose the optimal action given a message. For example, let us assume that m_1 is received:

If we take action	the expected utility is
a_1 (invest in portfolio 1)	$.6(26) + .2(22) + .2(12) = 22.4$
a_2 (invest in portfolio 2)	$.6(14) + .2(30) + .2(24) = 19.2$
a_3 (invest in portfolio 3)	$.6(-6) + .2(20) + .2(40) = 8.4$

Therefore the optimal action is to invest in portfolio 1 if message 1 is received. Similarly,

If we receive	the optimal action is	with expected utility
m_2	a_2	24
m_3	a_3	29.4

Finally, if we weight the utility of the optimal actions, given the three messages, by the probability of the messages, we have the utility value of the noisy information structure:

$$V(\eta_1) = \tfrac{1}{3}(22.4) + \tfrac{1}{3}(24) + \tfrac{1}{3}(29.4) = 25.27.$$

C. THE RELATIONSHIP BETWEEN THE VALUE OF INFORMATION AND EFFICIENT CAPITAL MARKETS

Equation (8.1) can be used to evaluate any information structure. It also points out some ideas which are only implicit in the definition of efficient markets. Fama [1976] defines efficient capital markets as those where the joint distribution of security prices, $f_m(P_{1t}, P_{2t}, \ldots, P_{nt} | \eta_{t-1}^m)$, given the set of information that the *market uses* to determine security prices at $t - 1$, is identical to the joint distribution of prices which would exist if *all relevant information* available at $t - 1$ were used, $f(P_{1t}, P_{2t}, \ldots, P_{nt} | \eta_{t-1})$. Mathematically, this is

$$f(P_{1t}, \ldots, P_{nt} | \eta_{t-1}^m) = f(P_{1t}, \ldots, P_{nt} | \eta_{t-1}). \tag{8.2}$$

If an information structure is to have value, it must accurately tell you something you do not already know. If the distribution of prices in time period t (which was predicted in the previous time period $t - 1$ and based on the information structure which the market uses) is not different from the prices predicted by using all relevant information from the previous time period, then there must be no difference between the information which the market uses and the set of all relevant information. This is the essence of an efficient capital market—it instantaneously and fully reflects all relevant information. Using information theory, this also means that, *net of costs*, the value of the gain from information must be zero.

$$V(\eta_i) - V(\eta_0) \equiv 0. \tag{8.3}$$

For example, consider capital markets which are efficient in their weak form. The relevant information structure, η_i, is defined to be the set of historical prices on all assets. If capital markets are efficient, then Eq. (8.2) says that the distribution of security prices today has already incorporated past price histories. In other words, it is not possible to develop trading rules (courses of action) based on past prices which will allow anyone to beat the market. Equation (8.3) says that no one would pay anything for the information set of historical prices. The value of the information is zero.

It is important to emphasize that the value of information is determined net of costs. These include the cost of undertaking courses of action and the costs of transmitting and evaluating messages. Some of these costs in securities markets are transactions costs: for example, brokerage fees, bid-ask spreads, costs involved in searching for the best price (if more than one price is quoted), and taxes, as well as data costs and analysts' fees.

It is necessary to evaluate the efficiency of capital markets and information markets simultaneously. The capital market is efficient relative to a given information set only after consideration of the costs of acquiring messages and taking actions pursuant to a particular information structure. This distinction is especially important for strong-form efficiency which hypothesizes that no investor can earn excess returns regardless of the information structure he uses. Jaffe [1974] has tested the performance of insider trading and found that even after reasonable transactions costs, insiders can earn abnormal profits because they possess information which the market does not have. However, this does not necessarily imply that capital markets are inefficient. Instead it may mean that insiders have monopolistic access to information about their firms and are able to profit by their special position. This may represent an inefficiency in the information market—not in capital markets.

D. STATISTICAL TESTS UNADJUSTED FOR RISK

Historically it was possible to test certain predictions of the efficient markets hypothesis even before a theory of risk-bearing allowed comparison of risk-adjusted returns. For example, if the riskiness of an asset does not change over time or if its risk changes randomly over time, then there should be no pattern in the time series of security returns. If there were a recurring pattern of any type, investors who recognize it can use it to predict future returns and make excess profits. However, in their very efforts to use the patterns, they eliminate them.

Three theories of the time series behavior of prices can be found in the literature: (1) the fair-game model, (2) the martingale or submartingale, and (3) the random walk. The fair-game model is based on the behavior of average returns (not on the entire probability distribution). Its mathematical expression is

$$\epsilon_{j,t+1} = \frac{P_{j,t+1} - P_{jt}}{P_{jt}} - \frac{E(P_{j,t+1}|\eta_t) - P_{jt}}{P_{jt}} \tag{8.4}$$

$$= \frac{P_{j,t+1} - E(P_{j,t+1}|\eta_t)}{P_{jt}},$$

where:

$P_{j,t+1}$ = the actual price of security j next period.
$E(P_{j,t+1}|\eta_t)$ = the predicted end-of-period price of security j given the current information structure, η_t.
$\epsilon_{j,t+1}$ = the difference between actual and predicted returns.

Note that (8.4) is really written in returns form. If we let the one-period return be defined as

$$r_{j,t+1} = \frac{P_{j,t+1} - P_{jt}}{P_{jt}},$$

then (8.4) may be rewritten as

$$\epsilon_{j,t+1} = r_{j,t+1} - E(r_{j,t+1}|\eta_t)$$

and

$$E(\epsilon_{j,t+1}) = E(r_{j,t+1} - E(r_{j,t+1}|\eta_t)) = 0. \tag{8.5}$$

A fair game means that, on average, across a large number of samples, the expected return on an asset equals its actual return. An example of a fair game would be games of chance in Las Vegas. Because of the house percentage you should expect to lose, let's say 10%, and, sure enough, on the average that's what people actually lose. A fair game does not imply that you will earn a positive return, only that expectations are not biased.

Given the definition of a fair game as in Eq. (8.4), a *submartingale* is a fair game where tomorrow's price is expected to be greater than today's price. Mathematically, a submartingale is

$$E(P_{j,t+1}|\eta_t) > P_{jt}.$$

In returns form this implies that expected returns are positive. This may be written as follows:

$$\frac{E(P_{j,t+1}|\eta_t) - P_{jt}}{P_{jt}} = E(r_{j,t+1}|\eta_t) > 0. \tag{8.6a}$$

A *martingale* is also a fair game, however, with a martingale tomorrow's price is expected to be the same as today's price. Mathematically, this is

$$E(P_{j,t+1}|\eta_t) = P_{jt},$$

or in returns form, it is written as

$$\frac{E(P_{j,t+1}|\eta_t) - P_{jt}}{P_{jt}} = E(r_{j,t+1}|\eta_t) = 0. \tag{8.6b}$$

A submartingale has the following empirical implication: Because prices are expected to increase over time, any test of the abnormal return from an experimental portfolio must compare its return with that from a buy-and-hold strategy for a control portfolio of the same composition. If the market is an efficient submartingale, both portfolios will have a positive return, and the difference between their returns will be zero. In other words, we will observe a fair game with positive returns: a submartingale.

Finally, a random walk says that there is no difference between the distribution of returns conditional on a given information structure and the unconditional distribution of returns. Equation (8.2) is a random walk in prices. Equation (8.7) is a random walk in returns:

$$f(r_{1,t+1}, \ldots, r_{n,t+1}) = f(r_{1,t+1}, \ldots, r_{n,t+1}|\eta_t). \tag{8.7}$$

Random walks are much stronger conditions than fair games or martingales because they require all the parameters of a distribution (for example, mean, variance, skewness, and kurtosis) to be the same with or without an information structure. Furthermore, successive drawings over time must (1) be independent and (2) be taken from the same distribution. If returns follow a random walk, then the mean of the underlying distribution does not change over time, and a fair game will result.

Most empirical evidence indicates that security returns do not follow a process that has all the properties of a random walk. This makes sense because the condition that the entire underlying probability distribution of returns remain stationary through time is simply too strong. It is reasonable to believe that because of changes in the risk of a firm, the variance of stock returns will change over time. This, in fact, appears to be the case. The fair-game model makes no statement about the variance of the distribution of security returns and consequently the nonstationarity of return variances is irrelevant to its validity.[4]

A statistical difference between fair games and random walks is that the latter hypothesis requires that all drawings be independently taken from the same distribution while the former does not. This means that the random walk requires that serial covariances between returns for any lag must be zero. However, positive serial covariances of one-period returns are not inconsistent with a fair game. To see this, suppose that the relevant information structure consists of past returns. In other words, assume weak-form market efficiency. When Eq. (8.4) is written in returns

---

[4] For example, consider a situation where random drawings are taken randomly from two normal distributions both having a mean return of zero but different return variances. The expected value of a large sample of alternative drawings would be zero, therefore we have a fair game. However, the experiment violates the random walk requirement that all drawings be taken from the same distribution.

form, we have

$$\epsilon_{jt+1} = r_{jt+1} - E(r_{jt+1} | r_{jt}, r_{jt-1}, \ldots, r_{jt-n}).$$

Note that the fair-game model does not require individual observations of ϵ_{jt} to be zero, but it does require the average of the ϵ_{jt} to be zero. Next note that the serial covariance for one-period returns is[5]

$$E[(r_{jt+1} - E(r_{jt+1}))(r_{jt} - E(r_{jt}))] = COV(r_{jt+1}, r_{jt})$$

$$= \int_{r_{jt}} [r_{jt} - E(r_{jt})][r_{jt+1} - E(r_{jt+1})] f(r_{jt}) \, dr_{jt}. \quad (8.8)$$

But from (8.4) in its returns form we know that

$$r_{jt+1} = \epsilon_{jt+1} + E(r_{jt+1} | r_{jt}),$$

$$r_{jt} = \epsilon_{jt} + E(r_{jt} | r_{jt-1}).$$

Therefore (8.8) can be written as

$$COV(r_{jt+1}, r_{jt}) = \int_{r_{jt}} \epsilon_{jt} \epsilon_{jt+1} f(r_{jt}) \, dr_{jt} \neq 0. \quad (8.9)$$

Therefore, serial covariance of one-period returns are not inconsistent with a fair-game model, but they are inconsistent with a random walk because the latter requires that successive drawings be independent (a serial covariance of zero).[6]

Fama [1965] has presented evidence to show that the serial correlations of one-day changes in the natural logarithm of price are significantly different from zero for 11 out of 30 of the Dow Jones Industrials.[7] Furthermore, 22 of the 30 estimated

---

[5] The reader who is unfamiliar with covariances is referred to Chapter 6. In general, the covariance between two random variables, x and y, is

$$COV(x, y) = E[(x - E(x))(y - E(y))].$$

[6] The relationship between a fair game and one-period serial correlation is subtle. If we have a fair game, then we *must* have zero serial covariance. However, non-zero serial covariance does not imply that we do not have a fair game. More formally we can say that a fair game is a sufficient but not necessary condition for zero serial covariance. Diagramatically, this is

Fair game $\rightleftarrows$ zero serial covariance

As an example of a random process which has serial correlation and is also a fair game, suppose we alternately choose returns from one of two normal distributions with different means and variances. There would be serial covariance in returns, but the fair game condition of Eq. (8.4) would not be violated.

[7] To show that the logarithm of successive price changes is a good approximation of returns, assume one-period continuous compounding:

$$P_{t+1} = P_t e^{rt}, \quad \text{where } t = 1,$$

$$\ln P_{t+1} - \ln P_t = \frac{P_{t+1} - P_t}{P_t}, \quad \text{where } r = \frac{P_{t+1} - P_t}{P_t}.$$

serial correlations are positive. This, as well as evidence collected by other authors, shows that security returns are not, strictly speaking, random walks. However, the evidence is not inconsistent with fair-games models or, in particular, the submartingale.

Direct tests of the fair-game model were provided by Alexander [1961] and Fama and Blume [1970]. They used a technical trading filter rule which states: Using price history buy a stock if the price rises $x\%$, hold it until the security falls $x\%$, then sell and go short. Maintain the short position until the price rises $x\%$, then cover the short position, and establish a long position. This process is repeated for a fixed time interval, and the performance according to the filter rule is then compared with a buy-and-hold strategy in the same security. Because each security is compared with itself, there is no need to adjust for risk.

Filter rules are designed to make the investor a profit if there are any systematic patterns in the movement of prices over time. It is only a matter of trying enough different filters so that one of them picks up any serial dependencies in prices and makes a profit which exceeds the simple buy-and-hold strategy.

The filter rule tests have three important results. First they show that even before subtracting transactions costs, filters greater than 1.5% cannot beat a simple buy-and-hold strategy. Second, filters below 1.5%, on the average, make very small profits which, because of frequent trading, can beat the market. This is evidence of a very short-term serial dependence in price changes. However, it is not necessarily evidence of capital market inefficiency. First one must subtract from gross profits the cost of taking action based on the filter rule. Fama and Blume [1970] show that even a floor trader (the owner of a seat on the NYSE) must pay at least $.1\%$ per transaction. Once these costs are deducted from the profits of filters that are less than 1.5%, the profits vanish. Therefore, the capital market is allocationally efficient down to the level of transactions costs. The smaller the transactions costs are, the more operationally efficient the market is, and smaller price dependencies are eliminated by arbitrage trading. Capital markets are efficient in their weak form because the return on a portfolio managed with price-history information is the same as a buy-and-hold strategy which uses no information. Therefore, the value of messages provided by filter rules is zero. Technical trading doesn't work.

The third inference which can be drawn from filter tests is that the market appears to follow a submartingale. All the securities tested had average positive returns. This makes sense because risky assets are expected to yield positive returns to compensate investors for the risk they undertake.

E. THE JOINT HYPOTHESIS OF MARKET EFFICIENCY AND THE CAPM

Statistical tests and filter rules are interesting and present evidence of weak-form efficiency but are limited by the fact that they cannot compare assets of different risk. The CAPM provides a theory which allows the expected return of a fair-game model to be conditional on a relevant costless measure of risk. If the CAPM is written as a fair game, we have

$$\epsilon_{jt} = R_{jt} - E(R_{jt}|\hat{\beta}_{jt}),$$

$$E(R_{jt}|\hat{\beta}_{jt}) = R_{ft} + [E(R_{mt}|\hat{\beta}_{mt}) - R_{ft}]\hat{\beta}_{jt}, \tag{8.10}$$

$$E(\epsilon_{jt}) = 0, \tag{8.11}$$

where

$E(R_{jt}|\hat{\beta}_{jt})$ = the expected rate of return on the jth asset during this time period, given a prediction of its systematic risk, $\hat{\beta}_{jt}$.

R_{ft} = the risk-free rate of return during this time period.

$E(R_{mt}|\hat{\beta}_{mt})$ = the expected market rate of return, given a prediction of its systematic risk, $\hat{\beta}_{mt}$.

$\hat{\beta}_{jt}$ = the estimated systematic risk of the jth security based on last time period's information structure η_{t-1}.

The CAPM is graphed in Fig. 8.3. According to the theory, the only relevant parameter necessary to evaluate the expected return for every security is its systematic risk.[8] Therefore, if the CAPM is true *and* if markets are efficient, the expected return of every asset should fall exactly on the security market line. Any deviation from the expected return is interpreted as an abnormal return, ϵ_{jt}, and can be taken as evidence of market inefficiency *if* the CAPM is correct.

The CAPM is derived from a set of assumptions which are very similar to those of market efficiency. For example, the Sharpe-Lintner-Mossin derivation of the CAPM assumes:

- All investors are single-period expected-utility-of-wealth maximizers whose utility functions are based on the mean and variance of return.

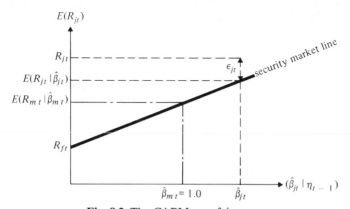

Fig. 8.3 The CAPM as a fair game

---

[8] For a detailed explanation of the CAPM and empirical tests of it, see Chapter 7.

- All investors can borrow or lend an indefinite amount at the risk-free rate, and there are no restrictions on short sales.
- All investors have homogeneous expectations of the end-of-period joint distributions of returns.
- Securities markets are frictionless and perfectly competitive.

In Chapter 9, we shall report the results of several empirical studies which use the CAPM as a tool for analyzing capital market efficiency. However, one should always keep in mind the fact that the CAPM and capital market efficiency are joint and inseparable hypotheses. If capital markets are inefficient, then the assumptions of the CAPM are invalid and a different model is required. And if the CAPM is inappropriate, even though capital markets are efficient, then the CAPM is the wrong tool to use in order to test for efficiency.

Various sophisticated empirical tests of the CAPM by Black, Jensen, and Scholes [1972], Black and Scholes [1974], and Fama and MacBeth [1973] show that the CAPM fits reality surprisingly well. However, because the theoretical CAPM assumes market efficiency, any empirical results which show that on the average there are no significant deviations from the model are merely consistent with market efficiency. They do not necessarily prove market efficiency because the model might be wrong. Therefore, any test of market efficiency which uses the CAPM to adjust for risk is, as mentioned before, a joint test of the CAPM which assumes market efficiency for its derivation and of market efficiency itself.

One may also ask the question: "If I can accurately predict systematic risk, $\hat{\beta}_{jt}$, I can also predict the expected rate of return on an asset; doesn't this mean that I can beat the market?" The answer, of course, is: "Probably not." If the information necessary to estimate $\hat{\beta}_{jt}$ is publicly available and if markets are efficient in their semistrong form, then prices will instantaneously and fully reflect all the information relevant for estimating $\hat{\beta}_{jt}$, the expected return of the security will fall exactly on the security line, and no abnormal returns will be observed.

Perhaps the most interesting use of the CAPM is to examine historical situations to see whether or not the market was efficient for a particular set of information. If the CAPM is valid (we shall assume it is, but keep in mind that it is a joint hypothesis with market efficiency), then any evidence of persistent deviations from the security market line can be interpreted as evidence of capital market inefficiency with regard to a particular information set. Chapter 9 is devoted to tests of market efficiency with regard to various information sets.

F. SUMMARY

The hypothesis of capital market efficiency has attracted a great deal of interest and critical comment during the late 1960s and early 1970s. This is somewhat surprising because capital market efficiency is a fairly limited concept. It says that the prices of securities instantaneously and fully reflect all available relevant information. It does not imply that product markets are perfectly competitive or that markets for information are perfect.

Capital market efficiency relies on the ability of arbitrageurs to recognize that prices are out of line and to make a profit by driving them back to an equilibrium value which is consistent with available information. Given this type of behavioral paradigm, one often hears the following questions: "If capital market efficiency implies that no one can beat the market (i.e., make an abnormal profit), then how can arbitrageurs be expected to exist since they too cannot beat the market?" "If capital markets are efficient, how can we explain the existence of a multibillion dollar security analysis industry?" The answer, of course, is that neither of these questions is inconsistent with efficient capital markets. First, arbitrageurs can and do make profits. However, they compete with each other to do so. If the profit to arbitrageurs becomes abnormally large, then new individuals will enter the arbitrage business until, on average, the return from arbitrage equals the cost (which, by the way, includes a fair return to the resources which are employed). The same thing is true of the security analysis industry. However, the product of the security analysis industry is information. Not only do security analysts provide information about expected future returns, but they also provide a great deal of expertise about tax laws and portfolio diversification techniques. For these, and other reasons, one can easily argue that there is nothing inconsistent with the notion of capital market efficiency and the existence of arbitrageurs and security analysis.

As we shall see in the next chapter, the concept of capital market efficiency is important in a wide range of applied topics, for example accounting information, new issues of securities, and mergers and acquisitions. By and large, the evidence seems to indicate that capital markets are efficient in their weak and semistrong forms.

PROBLEM SET

8.1 Suppose you know with certainty that the Clark Capital Corporation will pay a dividend of $10 per share on every January 1 forever. The continuously compounded risk-free rate is 5% (also forever).

a) Graph the price path of the Clark Capital common stock over time.

b) Is this (highly artificial) example a random walk? A martingale? A submartingale? (Why?)

8.2 Given the following situations, determine in each case whether or not the hypothesis of an efficient capital market (semistrong form) is contradicted.

a) Through the introduction of a complex computer program into the analysis of past stock price changes, a brokerage firm is able to predict price movements well enough to earn a consistent 3% profit, adjusted for risk, above normal market returns.

b) On the average, investors in the stock market this year are expected to earn a positive return (profit) on their investment. Some investors will earn considerably more than others.

c) You have discovered that the square root of any given stock price multiplied by the day of the month provides an indication of the direction in price movement of that particular stock with a probability of .7.

d) An SEC suit was filed against Texas Gulf Sulfur Company in 1965 because its corporate employees had made unusually high profits on company stock which they had purchased after exploratory drilling had started in Ontario (in 1959), and before stock prices rose dramatically (in 1964) with the announcement of the discovery of large mineral deposits in Ontario.

8.3 The First National Bank has been losing money on automobile consumer loans, and is considering the implementation of a new loan procedure which requires a credit check on loan applicants. Experience indicates that 82% of the loans were paid off while the remainder defaulted. However, if the credit check is run, the probabilities can be revised as follows:

	Favorable credit check	Unfavorable credit check
Loan is paid	.9	.5
Loan is defaulted	.1	.5

An estimated 80% of the loan applicants receive a favorable credit check. Assume that the bank earns 18% on successful loans, loses 100% on defaulted loans, suffers an opportunity cost of 18% when the loan is not granted but would have been successful, and an opportunity cost of 0% when the loan is not granted and would have defaulted. If the cost of a credit check is 5% of the value of the loan, should the bank go ahead with the new policy?

8.4 The efficient-market hypothesis implies that abnormal returns are expected to be zero. Yet in order for markets to be efficient, arbitrageurs must be able to force prices back into equilibrium. If they earn profits in doing so, is this fact inconsistent with market efficiency?

8.5

a) In a poker game with six players, you can expect to lose 83% of the time. How can this still be a martingale?

b) In the options market, call options[9] expire unexercised over 80% of the time. Thus, the option holders frequently lose all their investment. Does this imply that the options market is not a fair game? not a martingale? not a submartingale?

8.6 If securities markets are efficient, what is the NPV of any security, regardless of its risk?

8.7 From time to time the federal government considers passing into law an excess profits tax on U.S. corporations. Given what you know about efficient markets and the CAPM, how would you define excess profits? What would be the effect of an excess profits tax on the investor?

8.8 State the assumptions inherent in this statement: A condition for market efficiency is that there be no second-order stochastic dominance.

---

[9] See Chapter 15 for a description of call options.

REFERENCES

ALEXANDER, S. S., "Price Movements in Speculative Markets: Trends or Random Walks," *Industrial Management Review*, May 1961.

BLACK, F., M. JENSEN, and M. SCHOLES, "The Capital Asset Pricing Model: Some Empirical Tests," in M. Jensen, Ed., *Studies in the Theory of Capital Markets.* Praeger, New York, 1972, 79–124.

BLACK, F., and M. SCHOLES, "The Effects of Dividend Yield and Dividend Policy on Common Stock Prices and Returns," *Journal of Financial Economics*, May 1974, 1–22.

FAMA, E. F., "Efficient Capital Markets: A Review of Theory and Empirical Work," *The Journal of Finance*, May 1970, 383–417.

——, *Foundations of Finance.* Basic Books, New York, 1976.

——, and M. BLUME, "Filter Rules and Stock Market Trading Profits," *The Journal of Finance*, May 1970, 383–417.

——, and J. MACBETH, "Risk, Return, and Equilibrium: Empirical Tests," *Journal of Political Economy*, May/June 1973, 607–636.

JAFFE, J., "The Effect of Regulation Changes on Insider Trading," *The Bell Journal of Economics and Management Science*, Spring 1974, 93–121.

MARSCHAK, J., *Economic Information, Decision, and Prediction, Selected Essays*, vol. II. Reidel, Boston, 1974.

Part II

Corporate Policy: Theory, Evidence, and Applications

The first half of this text has laid the foundations for the microeconomics of decision-making under uncertainty. For the most part, we relied on the assumption of joint normal distributions of returns in order to reduce investor objects of choice to mean and variance. However, this oversimplification is not necessary. The same results may also be obtained in a state-preference framework.

We began Part I with a discussion of the consumption-investment decision in a one-period world with certainty. The major result was that once capital markets are introduced, Fisher separation obtains. In other words, there is a separation between shareholders' subjective rates of time preference and the optimal amount of investment which will maximize shareholders' wealth. Shareholders will unanimously agree that the optimal investment decision rule is to undertake new investment up to the point where the marginal rate of return equals the objective, market-determined rate of interest. Chapters 2 and 3 showed that in a world with no uncertainty the NPV criterion is equivalent to shareholder wealth maximization, and therefore is consistent with the Fisher separation principle even in a multiperiod context. Chapter 10 will show the set of conditions necessary to extend the multiperiod investment decision into a world with uncertainty.

Chapter 4 introduced decision-making under uncertainty by discussing a theory of investor choice. Given a set of axioms to define rational behavior, we saw that investors will seek to maximize their expected utility of wealth when faced with uncertain outcomes. This finding in turn gave rise to the definition of a risk premium and to measures of risk aversion. First- and second-order stochastic dominance were seen to be consistent with expected utility maximization regardless of the underlying probability distribution of returns. Then we assumed that returns were normally distributed in order to develop mean-variance indifference curves which express the subjective marginal rates of substitution between return and risk for an individual investor.

215

Chapter 5 introduced the fundamental objects of choice for investors, namely different patterns of payoff across different states of nature. An asset with the same payoff in every state of nature is risk free. Other assets with different payoffs in different states of nature are partially diversified and will be priced according to payoffs weighted by the prices of the underlying pure securities that they represent. Thus the prices of pure securities allow a decomposition of the utility maximization problem so that a general equilibrium solution can be expressed in means and variances, as discussed in Chapter 6.

Chapter 6 restated the objects of choice that exist in a world with a joint normal distribution of returns. All combinations of risky assets could be identified by portfolio mean and variance of return. Although less general than the state-preference approach, the mean-variance approach has the advantage of lending itself more readily to empirical tests. Once the mean-variance opportunity set was established we saw that all risk-averse investors chose expected utility maximizing portfolios along the efficient set, which is the upper half of the opportunity set. Next, we introduced capital markets by stipulating the opportunity to borrow or lend at the risk-free rate. This resulted in two-fund separation. Thus the Fisher separation principle was extended into a world with uncertainty. Investors will unanimously support an investment rule which equates the marginal rate of substitution between return and risk along the opportunity set with the objective market-determined price of risk.

Chapter 7 discussed the implications of market equilibrium in a mean-variance world. The appropriate measure of risk for an individual asset is seen to be covariance risk—its contribution to the variance of a portfolio. In equilibrium, given that the market portfolio is efficient, the rate of return on all assets is the risk-free rate plus a risk premium. And the risk premium is the market price per unit risk (the marginal rate of substitution between return and risk) multiplied by the covariance risk of the asset. The simple linearity of the capital asset pricing model is unchanged when we assume there is no risk-free asset. However, other extensions of the model introduce factors other than covariance in order to explain the rate of return on risky assets. Most of the empirical tests of the CAPM agree that although the evidence does not validate the theory, it does confirm many of the important predictions. Namely, that covariance risk appears to be the only significant factor in explaining the required rate of return and that the best empirical model is linear in beta. Finally, Roll's critique shows that the CAPM cannot be empirically validated without measuring the market portfolio and proving that it is efficient.

The concept of market efficiency, which is inextricably related to market equilibrium, was discussed in Chapter 8. We saw that there is a difference between perfect markets and efficient markets. Capital market efficiency is related to the value of information and to efficiency in markets for information. Efficient markets must be fair games but not necessarily random walks. Also, if the CAPM is valid as a fair game, then it may be used to test for abnormal returns on a risk-adjusted basis.

The first part of the text covers most of what has come to be recognized as a unified theory of decision-making under uncertainty as applied to the field of finance. However, our presentation is far from complete. The treatment of state-preference theory is at an introductory level. Furthermore, option pricing theory is not mentioned at all. The reader who wishes to study option pricing theory will probably want to turn to Chapter 15 before starting into the second part of the text which focuses on applications of finance theory to corporate finance.

*   *   *

The theory of finance, as presented in the first half of the text, is applicable to a wide range of finance topics. The theoretical foundations are prerequisite to almost any of the traditional subject areas in finance curricula, for example, portfolio management, corporation finance, commercial banking, money and capital markets, financial institutions, security analysis, international finance, investment banking, speculative markets, insurance, and case studies in finance. Since all these topics require a thorough understanding of decision-making under uncertainty, all use the theory of finance.

The second half of this text focuses, for the most part, on applications of the theory of finance to a corporate setting. The fundamental issue is: Does financing matter? Does the type of financing (debt or equity) have any real effect on the value of the firm? Does the form of financial payment (dividends or capital gains) have any effect on the value of claims held by various classes of security holders?

Because these issues are usually discussed in the context of corporate finance they may seem to be narrow. This is not the case. First of all, the definition of a corporation is very broad. The class of corporations includes not only manufacturing firms, but also commercial banks, savings and loan associations, many brokerage houses, some investment banks, and even the major security exchanges. Second, the debt equity decision applies to all individuals as well as all corporations. Therefore, although the language is narrow, the issues are very broad indeed. They affect almost every economic entity in the private sector of the economy.

As we shall see, the theoretical answer to the question "Does financing matter?" is often a loud and resounding "Maybe." Often, the answer depends on the assumptions of the model which is employed to study the problem. Under different sets of assumptions, different and even opposite answers are possible. This is extremely disquieting to the student of finance. Therefore, we have presented empirical evidence related to each of the theoretical hypotheses. Frequently, but not always, the preponderance of evidence supports a single conclusion.

It is important to keep in mind that hypotheses cannot be tested by the realism of the assumptions used to derive them. What counts for a positive science is the development of theories which yield valid and meaningful predictions about observed phenomena. On the first pass, what counts is whether or not the hypothesis is consistent with the evidence at hand. Further testing involves deducing new facts capable of being observed but not previously known, then checking those deduced facts against additional empirical evidence. As students of finance, which seeks to be a positive science, we must not only understand the theory, but also study the empirical evidence in order to determine which hypothesis is validated.

Chapter 9 is devoted to various empirical studies related to the efficient market hypothesis. Most of the evidence is consistent with the weak and semistrong forms of market efficiency, but inconsistent with the strong form. In certain situations, individuals with inside information appear to be able to earn abnormal returns. In particular, corporate insiders can beat the market when trading in the securities of their firm. Also, block traders can earn abnormal returns when they trade at the block price, as can purchasers of new equity issues. The last two situations will surely lead to further research because current theory cannot explain why, in the absence of barriers to entry, there appear to be inexplicable abnormal rates of return.

Chapter 10 returns to the theoretical problem of how to evaluate multiperiod investments in a world with uncertainty. It shows the set of assumptions necessary in order to extend the simple one-period CAPM rules into a multiperiod world. It also discusses two interesting applied issues: the abandonment problem, and the technique for discounting uncertain costs.

Chapter 11 explores the theory of capital structure and the cost of capital. This is the first of the corporate policy questions which relate to whether or not the value of the firm is affected by the type of financing it chooses. Also, we define a cost of capital which is consistent with the objective of maximizing the wealth of the current shareholders of the firm. This helps to complete, in a consistent fashion, the theory of project selection. Capital-budgeting decisions which are consistent with shareholder wealth maximization require use of the correct technique (the NPV criterion), the correct definition of cash flows (operating cash flows after taxes) and the correct cost of capital definition.

Chapter 12 discusses empirical evidence on whether or not the debt-to-equity ratio (i.e., the type of financing) affects the value of the firm. This is one of the most difficult empirical issues in finance. Although not conclusive, the evidence is consistent with increases in the value of the firm resulting from increasing debt (up to some range) in the capital structure. However, much work remains to be done in this area. Chapter 12 also provides a short example of how to actually compute the cost of capital using real data for an actual corporation.

Chapter 13 looks at the relationship between dividend policy and the value of the firm. There are several competing theories. However, the dominant argument seems to be that the value of an all-equity firm depends on the expected returns from current and future investment and not on the form in which the returns are paid out. If investment is held constant, it makes no difference whether the firm pays out high or low dividends. On the other hand, a firm's announcement of an increase in dividend payout may be interpreted as a signal by shareholders that the firm anticipates permanently higher levels of return from investment, and, of course, higher returns on investment will result in higher share prices.

Chapter 14 presents empirical evidence on the relationship between dividend policy and the value of the firm which, for the most part, seems to be consistent with the theory—namely, that dividend policy does not affect shareholders' wealth. The chapter also applies the valuation models (presented in Chapter 13) to a real world example.

Chapters 15 and 16 introduce the reader to the theory of option pricing and to the recent empirical evidence on options. This topic has been the most rapidly advancing area in the field of finance, and it provides new insights into the nature of common stock and bonds. For example, common stock can be thought of as a call option written on the underlying value of the firm.

Chapters 17 and 18 consider the widespread phenomenon of mergers. They begin with the proposition that without synergy, value additivity holds in mergers as it does in other types of capital budgeting analysis. Mergers do not affect value unless the underlying determinants of value—the patterns of future cash flows or the applicable capitalization factors—are changed by combining firms. Empirical tests of mergers indicate that the shareholders of acquired firms benefit, on the average, but the shareholders of acquiring firms experience neither significant benefit nor harm.

Chapters 19 and 20 conclude the book by placing finance in its increasingly important international setting. A framework for analyzing the international financial decisions of business firms is developed by summarizing the applicable fundamental propositions. The Fisher effect which states that nominal interest rates reflect anticipated rates of inflation is carried over to its international implications. This leads to the Interest Rate Parity Theorem which states that the current forward exchange rate for a country's currency in relation to the currency of another country will reflect the present interest rate differentials between the two countries. The Purchasing Power Parity Theory states that the difference between the current spot exchange rate and the future spot exchange rate of a country's currency in relation to the currency of another country will reflect the ratio of the rates of price changes of their internationally traded goods. These fundamental theorems provide the principles to guide firms in adjusting their policies to the fluctuations in the exchange rate values of the currencies in which their business is conducted.

Chapter 9

Efficient Capital Markets: Evidence

The only valid statement is that the current price embodies all knowledge, all expectations and all discounts that infringe upon the market.

C. W. J. Granger and O. Morgenstern,
Predictability of Stock Market Prices,
Heath Lexington Books, Lexington, Mass., 1970, p. 20

Empirical evidence for or against the hypothesis that capital markets are efficient takes many forms. This chapter is arranged by topic rather than chronological order, degree of sophistication, or type of market efficiency. Not all the articles mentioned completely support the efficient-market hypothesis. However, most agree that capital markets are efficient in the weak and semistrong forms, but not in the strong form. The majority of the studies are very recent, dating from the late 1960s and continuing up to the most recently published papers. Usually capital market efficiency has been tested in the large and sophisticated capital markets of developed countries. Therefore, one must be careful to limit any conclusions to the appropriate arena from which they are drawn. Research into the efficiency of capital markets is an ongoing process, and the work is being extended to include assets other than common stock as well as to smaller and less sophisticated marketplaces.

A. EMPIRICAL MODELS USED FOR RESIDUAL ANALYSIS

Before discussing the empirical tests of market efficiency it is useful to review the three basic types of empirical models which are frequently employed. The differences between them are important. The simplest model, called the market model, simply argues that returns on security j are linearly related to returns on a "market" portfolio. Mathematically, the *market model* is described by

$$R_{jt} = a_j + b_j R_{mt} + \epsilon_{jt}.$$

The market model is not supported by any theory. It assumes that the slope and intercept terms are constant over the time period during which the model is fit to the available data. This is a strong assumption, particularly if the time series is long.

The second model uses the capital asset pricing theory. It requires the intercept term to be equal to the risk free rate, or the rate of return on the minimum variance zero-beta portfolio, both of which change over time. The model, the $CAPM$, is written

$$R_{jt} = R_{ft} + [R_{mt} - R_{ft}]\beta_j + \epsilon_{jt}.$$

Note, however, that systematic risk is assumed to remain constant over the interval of estimation. The use of the CAPM for residual analysis was explained at the end of Chapter 8.

Finally, we sometimes see the *empirical market line*, which was explained in Chapter 7 and is written as

$$R_{jt} = \hat{\gamma}_{0t} + \hat{\gamma}_{1t}\beta_{jt} + \epsilon_{jt}.$$

Although related to the CAPM, it does not require the intercept term to equal the risk-free rate. Instead, both the intercept, $\hat{\gamma}_{0t}$, and the slope, $\hat{\gamma}_{1t}$, are the best linear estimates taken from cross-section data each time period (typically each month). Furthermore, it has the advantage that no parameters are assumed to be constant over time.

All three models use the residual term, ϵ_{jt}, as a measure of risk-adjusted abnormal performance. However, only one of the models, the second, relies exactly on the theoretical specification of the Sharpe-Lintner capital asset pricing model.

In each of the empirical studies which are discussed, we shall mention the empirical technique by name.

B. ACCOUNTING INFORMATION

Market efficiency requires that security prices instantaneously and fully reflect all available relevant information. But what information is *relevant*? And how *fast* do security prices really react to new information? The answers to these questions are of particular interest to corporate officers who report the performance of their firm to the public, to the accounting profession which audits these reports, and to the Securities and Exchange Commission which regulates securities information.

The market value of assets is the present value of their cash flows discounted at the appropriate risk-adjusted rate. Investors should care only about the cash-flow implications of various corporate decisions. However, corporations report accounting definitions of earnings, not cash flow, and frequently the two are not related. Does an efficient market look at the effect of managerial decisions on earnings per share (eps) or cash flow? This is not an unimportant question, because frequently managers are observed to maximize eps rather than cash flow because they believe that the market value of the company depends on reported eps, when in fact (as we shall see), it does not.

Inventory accounting provides a good example of a situation where managerial decisions have opposite effects on eps and cash flow. During an inflationary economy the cost of producing the most recent inventory continues to rise. On the books, inventory is recorded at cost so that in the example in Table 9.1 the fourth item added to the inventory costs more to produce than the first. If management elects to use first-in-first-out (FIFO) accounting, it will record a cost of goods sold of $25 against a revenue of $100 when an item is sold from inventory. This results in eps of $.45. On the other hand, if LIFO (last-in-first-out) is used, eps is $.06. The impact of the two accounting treatments on cash flow is in exactly the opposite direction. Because the goods were manufactured in past time periods, the actual costs of production are sunk costs and irrelevant to current decision-making. Therefore, current cash flows are revenues less taxes. Cost-of-goods sold is a noncash charge. Therefore, with FIFO, cash flow per share is $.70 while with LIFO it is $.96. LIFO provides more cash flow because taxes are lower.

Table 9.1 FIFO versus LIFO

	LIFO	FIFO	Inventory at cost	
Revenue	100	100		
Cost of goods sold	90	25	Fourth item	90 → LIFO
Operating income	10	75	Third item	60
Taxes at 40%	4	30	Second item	40
Net income	6	45	First item	25 → FIFO
eps (100 shares)	.06	.45		
Cash flow per share	.96	.70		

If investors really value cash flow and not eps, we should expect to see stock prices rise when firms announce a switch from FIFO to LIFO accounting during inflationary periods. Sunder [1973, 1975] collected a sample of 110 firms which switched from FIFO to LIFO between 1946 and 1966 and 22 firms which switched from LIFO to FIFO. His procedure was to look at the pattern of cumulative average residuals from the market model. A residual return is the difference between the actual return and the return estimated by the model:

$$\epsilon_{jt} = R_{jt} - E(R_{jt} \mid \hat{\beta}_{jt}).$$

The usual technique is to estimate ϵ_{jt} over an interval surrounding the economic event of interest. Taking monthly data, Sunder used all observations of returns except for those occurring plus or minus 12 months around the announcement of the inventory-accounting change. He then used the estimated $\hat{\beta}_{jt}$, the actual risk-free rate, and the actual market return during the 24-month period around the split date to predict the expected return.[1] Differences between estimated and actual returns

---

[1] Sunder used a moving-average beta technique in his second study [1975]. However, it did not substantially change his results.

were then averaged across all companies for each month. The average abnormal return in a given month is

$$AR_t = \frac{1}{N} \sum_{j=1}^{N} \epsilon_{jt}, \qquad \text{where} \quad N = \text{the number of companies.}$$

The cumulative average return is the sum of average returns over all months from the start of the data up to and including the current month, T.

$$\text{CAR} = \sum_{t=1}^{T} AR_t$$

where

T = the number of months being summed $(T = 1, 2, \ldots, M)$
M = the total number of months in the sample

If there were no abnormal change in the value of the firm associated with the switch from FIFO to LIFO, we should observe no pattern in the residuals. They would fluctuate around zero and on the average would equal zero. In other words, we would have a fair game. Figure 9.1 shows Sunder's results. Assuming that risk does not change during the 24-month period, the cumulative average residuals for the firms switching to LIFO rise by 5.3% during the 12 months prior to the announcement of the accounting change. This is consistent with the fact that shareholders actually value cash flow, not eps. However, it does not necessarily mean that a switch

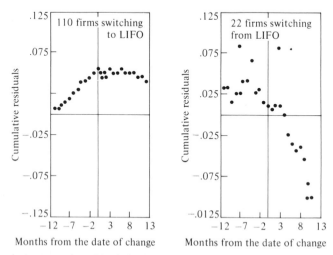

Fig. 9.1 Cumulative average residuals for 24 months around the accounting change (Sunder, S., "Relationship Between Accounting Changes and Stock Prices: Problems of Measurement and Some Empirical Evidence," reprinted from *Empirical Research in Accounting: Selected Studies*, 1973, 18.)

to LIFO causes higher value. Almost all studies of this type, which focus on a particular phenomenon, suffer from what has come to be known as post-selection bias. In this case, firms may decide to switch to LIFO because they are already doing well and their value may have risen for that reason, not because of the switch in accounting method. Either way, Sunder's results are inconsistent with the fact that shareholders look only at changes in eps in order to value common stock. There is no evidence that the switch to LIFO lowered value even though it did lower eps.

Kaplan and Roll [1972] investigated two types of accounting changes which have the effect of increasing reported eps but have no effect on cash flows. In 1964 companies were allowed to report to shareholders the entire amount of the investment tax credit for an investment in the year it was made, instead of taking the tax saving into income spread over the life of the asset as they were still required to do for tax purposes. Three hundred and thirty-two companies elected this approach. It increased their eps but had no effect on their tax books or cash flows. Figure 9.2 shows the pattern of cumulative average residuals using weekly data. It's hard to tell whether or not there are any statistically significant departures from a fair game. Changes of $\pm 2\%$ are not large and are within the range of deviations which may be wiped out by transactions costs. But even if one considers the positive residuals following the reported accounting change of higher eps to be significant, it appears that people were only temporarily fooled because cumulative residuals return to zero approximately 25 weeks after the announcement.

Fig. 9.2 Cumulative average residuals for 60 weeks around a change to the flow-through method of reporting investment tax credits (Kaplan, R. S., and R. Roll, "Investor Evaluation of Accounting Information: Some Empirical Evidence," reprinted from *The Journal of Business*, April 1972, 237.)

The second type of accounting change was a switchback from reporting accelerated to straight-line depreciation which was permitted on the annual report but not on the tax books. Again, the effect is to increase reported eps while there is no change in cash flow. The pattern of cumulative average residuals for a sample of 71 firms is shown in Fig. 9.3. The residuals are negative because firms using the depreciation change were, in general, doing worse than the market. Furthermore, there is no evidence that the accounting change which increased reported eps had any positive effect on the value of the firm. Again, the evidence is consistent with the

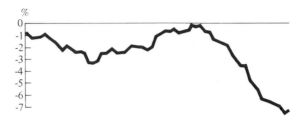

Fig. 9.3 Cumulative average residuals for 60 weeks around a switch-back to reporting straight-line depreciation (Kaplan, R. S., and R. Roll, "Investor Evaluation of Accounting Information: Some Empirical Evidence," *reprinted from The Journal of Business*, April 1972, 239.)

fact that investors actually discount cash flows and disregard changes in eps which do not reflect real economic events.

The above two studies indicate that investors in efficient markets attempt to evaluate news about the effect of managerial decisions on cash flows—not on eps. This fact has direct implications for the accounting treatment of mergers and acquisitions. Two types of accounting treatment are possible: pooling or purchase. In a pooling arrangement the income statements and balance sheets of the merging firms are simply added together. On the other hand, when one company purchases another, the assets of the acquired company are added to the acquiring company's balance sheet along with an item called goodwill. Goodwill is the difference between the purchase price and the book value of the acquired company's assets. Regulations require that goodwill be written off as a charge against earnings *after taxes* in a period not to exceed 40 years. Because the writeoff is after taxes, there is no effect on cash flows but reported eps decline. The fact that there is no difference in cash flows between pooling and purchase and the fact that cash flows, not eps, are the relevant information used by investors to value the firm should convey to management the message that the accounting treatment of mergers and acquisitions is a matter of indifference.[2] Yet many managements prefer pooling, presumably because they don't like to see eps decline due to the writeoff of goodwill. No economically rational basis for this type of behavior can be cited.

In a recent empirical study Hong, Kaplan, and Mandelker [1978] tested the effect of pooling and purchase techniques on stock prices of acquiring firms. Using monthly data between 1954 and 1964, they compared a sample of 122 firms which used pooling and 37 which used purchase. The acquired firm had to be at least 3% of the net asset value of the acquiring firm. Mergers were excluded from the sample if

---

[2] The IRS allows the book value of the assets of the acquired firm to be written up before purchase. This reduces the amount of goodwill created, but even more important, it creates a depreciation tax shield which would not exist in a pooling arrangement. Therefore, in many cases cash flows for purchase will be higher than pooling. In these cases purchase is actually preferable to pooling.

another merger took place within 18 months, if the acquiring firm was not NYSE listed, or if the merger terms were not based on an exchange of shares. (This last criterion rules out taxable mergers.)

Using the simple time-series market model given below, they calculated cumulative abnormal residuals:

$$\ln R_{jt} = \alpha_j + \beta_j \ln R_{mt} + u_{jt},$$

where

R_{jt} = return on the jth security in time period t,
α_j = an intercept term assumed to be constant over the entire time period,
β_j = systematic risk assumed to be constant over the entire time period,
R_{mt} = market return in time period t,
u_{jt} = abnormal return for the jth security in time period.

When the cumulative average residuals were centered around the month of the actual merger, the patterns revealed no evidence of abnormal performance for the sample of 122 poolings. This is shown in Fig. 9.4. Therefore there is no evidence that "dirty pooling" raises the stock prices of acquiring firms. Investors are not fooled by the accounting convention.

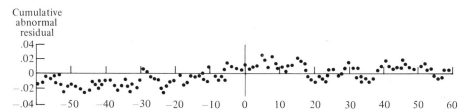

Fig. 9.4 Cumulative abnormal residuals for 122 poolings with market value greater than book value in the month relative to merger (Hong, H., R. S. Kaplan, and G. Mandelker, "Pooling vs. Purchase: the Effects of Accounting for Mergers on Stock Prices," reprinted with permission of *The Accounting Review*, January 1978, 42.)

These results are just as important for acquiring firms which had to write off goodwill against their after-tax earnings because they used the purchase technique. As shown in Fig. 9.5, there is no evidence of negative abnormal returns, which is what we would expect if investors looked at eps. Instead, there is weak evidence that shareholders of acquiring firms experienced positive abnormal returns when the purchase technique was used. This is consistent with the hypothesis that investors value cash flows and that they disregard reported eps.

The empirical studies of Sunder [1973, 1975], Kaplan and Roll [1972], and Hong, Kaplan, and Mandelker [1978] provide evidence on what is meant by relevant accounting information. By relevant we mean any information about the *expected*

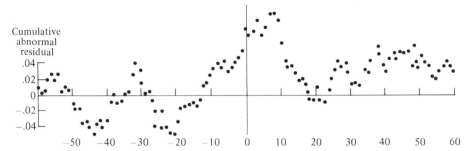

Fig. 9.5 Thirty-seven purchases with market value greater than book value in the month relative to merger (Hong, H., R. S. Kaplan, and G. Mandelker, "Pooling vs. Purchase: the Effects of Accounting for Mergers on Stock Prices," reprinted with permission of *The Accounting Review*, January 1978, 42.)

distribution of future cash flows. Next a study by Ball and Brown [1968] provides some evidence about the speed of adjustment of efficient markets to new information.

Earnings data and cash flows are usually highly correlated. The examples discussed above merely serve to point out some situations where they are not related and therefore allow empiricists to distinguish between the two. Ball and Brown [1968] use monthly data for a sample of 261 firms between 1946 and 1965 to evaluate the usefulness of accounting income numbers (eps). First, they separated the sample into companies which had earnings that were either higher or lower than those predicted by a naive time-series model. The model for change in earnings was

$$\Delta I_{jt} = \hat{a} + \hat{b}_j \Delta m_t + \epsilon_{jt}, \tag{9.1}$$

where

ΔI_{jt} = the change in earnings per share for the jth firm,
Δm_t = the change in the average eps for all firms (other than firm j) in the market.

Next, this regression was used to predict next year's change in earnings, $\widehat{\Delta I}_{j,t+1}$:

$$\widehat{\Delta I}_{jt+1} = \hat{a} + \hat{b}_j \Delta m_{t+1}, \tag{9.2}$$

where

$\hat{a}, \hat{b}$ = coefficients estimated from time-series fits of Eq. (9.1) to the data,
Δm_{t+1} = the actual change in market average eps during the $(t + 1)$th time period.

Finally, estimated earnings changes were compared with actual earnings changes. If the actual change was greater than the estimated one, the company was put into a portfolio where returns were expected to be positive, and vice versa.

Figure 9.6 plots an abnormal performance index (API) which represents the value of one dollar invested in a portfolio 12 months before an annual report and

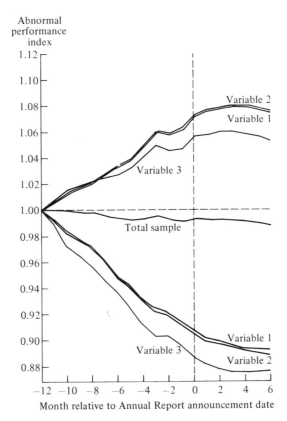

Fig. 9.6 Abnormal performance index of portfolios chosen on the basis of differences between actual and predicted accounting income (Ball, R., and P. Brown, "An Empirical Evaluation of Accounting Income Numbers," reprinted with permission of *The Journal of Accounting Research*, Autumn 1968, 169.)

held for T months (where $T = 1, 2, \ldots, 12$). It is computed as follows:

$$\text{API} = \frac{1}{N} \sum_{j=1}^{N} \prod_{t=1}^{T} (1 + \epsilon_{jt}),$$

where

$N = $ the number of companies in a portfolio,

$T = 1, 2, \ldots, 12,$

$\epsilon_{jt} = $ abnormal performance measured by deviations from the market model.

A quick look at Fig. 9.6 shows that when earnings are higher than predicted, returns are abnormally high. Furthermore, returns appear to adjust gradually until, by the time of the annual report, almost all the adjustment has occurred. Most of the information contained in the annual report is anticipated by the market *before* the annual report is released. In fact, anticipation is so accurate that the actual income number does not appear to cause any unusual jumps in the API in the announcement month. Most of the content of the annual report (about 85% to 90%) is captured by more timely sources of information. Apparently market prices adjust continuously to new information as it becomes publicly available throughout the year. The annual report has little new information to add.

These results suggest that prices in the marketplace continuously adjust in an unbiased manner to new information. Two implications for the corporate treasurers are: (1) significant new information, which will affect the future cash flows of the firm, should be announced as soon as it becomes available so that shareholders can use it without the (presumably greater) expense of discovering it from alternative sources, and (2) it probably doesn't make any difference whether cash flow effects are reported in the balance sheet, the income statement, or footnotes—the market can evaluate the news as long as it is publicly available, whatever form it may take.

C. BLOCK TRADES

During a typical day for an actively traded security on a major stock exchange thousands of shares will be traded, usually in round lots ranging between one hundred and several hundred shares. However, occasionally a large block, say 10,000 shares or more, is brought to the floor for trading. The behavior of the marketplace during the time interval around the trading of a large block provides a "laboratory" where the following questions can be investigated: (1) Does the block trade disrupt the market? (2) If the stock price falls when the block is sold, is the fall a liquidity effect, an information effect, or both? (3) Can anyone earn abnormal returns from the fall in price? (4) How fast does the market adjust to the effects of a block trade?

In perfect (rather than efficient) capital markets all securities are perfect substitutes for each other. Because all individuals are assumed to possess the same information and because markets are assumed to be frictionless, the number of shares traded in a given security should have no effect on its price. If markets are less than perfect, the sale of a large block may have two effects (see Fig. 9.7). First, if it is believed to carry with it some new information about the security, the price will change (permanently) to reflect the new information. As illustrated in parts (c) and (d) of Fig. 9.7, the closing price is lower than the opening price. Second, if buyers must incur extra costs when they accept the block, there may be a (temporary) decline in price to reflect what has been in various articles described as a price pressure, or distribution, or liquidity premium, as shown in parts (a) and (c). Figure 9.7 depicts how hypothesized information or price pressure effects can be expected to show up in continuous transactions data. For example, if the sale of a large block has both effects (Fig. 9.7(c)) we may expect the price to fall from the price before the trade $(-T)$ to the block price (BP), then recover quickly from any price pressure effect

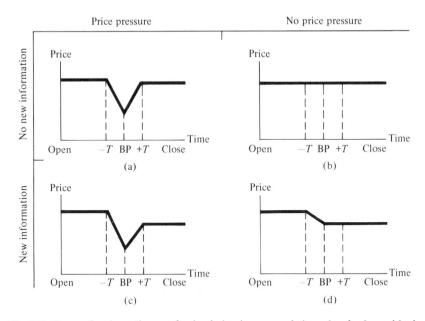

Fig. 9.7 Competing hypotheses of price behavior around the sale of a large block

by the time of the next trade $(+T)$ but to remain at a permanently lower level which reflects the impact of new information on the value of the security.

Scholes [1972] and Kraus and Stoll [1972] provided the first empirical evidence about the price effects of block trading. Scholes used daily returns data to analyze 345 secondary distributions between July 1961 and December 1965. Secondary distributions, unlike primary distributions, are not initiated by the company but by shareholders who will receive the proceeds of the sale. The distributions are usually underwritten by an investment banking group which buys the entire block from the seller. The shares are then sold on a subscription basis *after* normal trading hours. The subscriber pays only the subscription price and not stock exchange or brokerage commissions. Figure 9.8 shows an abnormal performance index based on the market model and calculated for 40 trading days around the date of a secondary distribution. The abnormal performance index falls from an initial level of 1.0 to a final value of .977 14 days after the sale, a decline of 2.2%. On the day of the secondary distribution, the average abnormal performance was $-.5\%$. Because this study uses only close to close daily returns data, it focuses only on permanent price changes. We have characterized these as information effects (Fig. 9.7(c) and (d)). Further evidence that the permanent decline in price is an information effect is revealed when the API is partitioned by vendor classification. These results appear in Table 9.2.

On the day of the offering the vendor is not usually known but we may presume that the news becomes available soon thereafter. One may expect that an estate

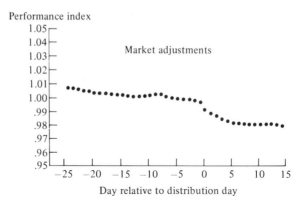

Fig. 9.8 Abnormal performance index on days around a secondary distribution (Scholes, M., "The Market for Securities: Substitution vs. Price Pressure and the Effects of Information on Share Prices," reprinted with permission of *The Journal of Business*, April 1972, 193.)

Table 9.2 Abnormal performance index for secondary distributions partitioned by vendor category

No. of observations in sample	Category	API	
		− 10 to + 10 days	0 to + 10 days
192	Investment companies and mutual funds	−2.5%	−1.4%
31	Banks and insurance companies	− .3	−0.0
36	Individuals	− 1.1	− .7
23	Corporations and officers	− 2.9	− 2.1
50	Estates and trusts	− .7	− .5

Scholes, M., "The Market for Securities: Substitution vs. Price Pressure and the Effects of Information on Share Prices," reprinted with permission of *The Journal of Business*, April 1972, 202.

liquidation or a portfolio rebalancing by a bank or insurance company would not be motivated by information about the performance of the firm. On the other hand, corporate insiders as well as investment companies and mutual funds (with large research staffs) may be selling on the basis of adverse information. The data seem to support these suppositions. Greater price changes after the distribution are observed when the seller is presumed to have a knowledgeable reason for trading.[3]

---

[3] A second test performed by Scholes showed that there was no relationship between the size of the distribution (as a percentage of the firm) and changes in the API on the distribution date. This would lead us to reject the hypothesis that investment companies and mutual funds may have had an impact because they sold larger blocks.

The data available to Kraus and Stoll [1972] were a little more complete. They examined price effects for all block trades of 10,000 shares or more carried out on the NYSE between July 1, 1968 and September 30, 1969. They had prices for the close the day before the block trade, the price immediately prior to the transaction, the block price, and the closing price the day of the block trade. Abnormal performance indices based on daily data were consistent with Scholes' results. More interesting were intraday price effects which are shown in Fig. 9.9. There is clear evidence of a price-pressure or distribution effect. The stock price recovers substantially from the block price by the end of the trading day. The recovery averages .713%. For example, a stock which sold for $50.00 before the block transaction would have a block price of $49.43, but by the end of the day the price would have recovered to $49.79.

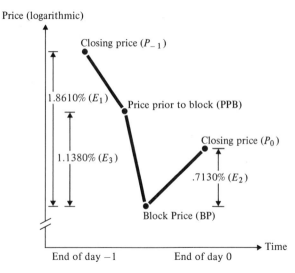

Fig. 9.9 Intra-day price impacts of block trading (Kraus, A., and H. R. Stoll, "Price Impacts of Block Trading on the New York Stock Exchange," reprinted with permission of *The Journal of Finance*, June 1972, 575.)

The Scholes and Kraus-Stoll studies find evidence of a permanent price decline which is measured by price drops from the closing price the day before the block trade to the closing price the day of the block transaction. These negative returns seem to persist for at least a month after the block trade. In addition, Kraus and Stoll found evidence of temporary intraday price pressure effects. The implications of these findings are discussed by Dann, Mayers, and Raab [1977], who collected continuous transactions data during the day of a block trade for a sample of 298 blocks between July 1968 and December 1969. The open-to-block price decline was at least 4.56% for each block in the sample. The reason for restricting the sample to blocks with large price declines was to provide the strongest test of market efficiency. If an individual or a group of investors can establish a trading rule which allows them to buy a block whose open-to-block price change is at least 4.56%, then sell at the end of the day, they may be able to earn abnormal profits. This would be evidence of capital market inefficiency.

Testing a trading rule of this type takes great care. Normally, a block trade is not made publicly available until the trade has already been consummated and the transaction is recorded on the ticker. The semistrong form of market efficiency is based on the set of publicly available information. Therefore, a critical issue is: Exactly how fast must an individual react after he observes that his -4.56% trading rule has been activated by the first publicly available announcement which occurs on the ticker tape? Figure 9.10 shows annualized rates of return using the -4.56% rule with the purchase made x minutes after the block and the stock then sold at the close.

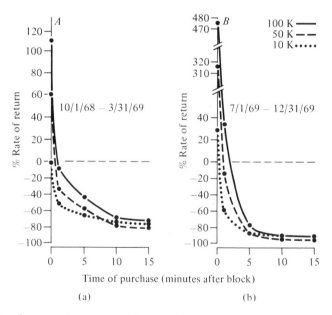

Annualized[a] rates of return on initial wealth, -4.56 percent rule; purchase at first price at least x minutes after block, sell at close[b] (using only first block per day). Gross returns less actual commissions and NY State transfer taxes (curves represent levels of initial wealth).

[a] Annualized rates of return are calculated by squaring the quantity one plus the respective six-month return.

[b] Blocks occurring within x minutes of the close were assumed not to have been acted upon.

Fig. 9.10 Annualized rates of return on the -4.56 percent rule (Dann, L., D. Mayers, and R. Raab, "Trading Rules, Large Blocks, and the Speed of Adjustment," reprinted from *The Journal of Financial Economics*, January 1977, 18.)

Returns are net of actual commissions and New York State transfer taxes. For both time periods which are reported, an individual would have to react in less than five minutes in order to earn a positive return. Such a rapid reaction is, for all practical purposes, impossible. It seems that no abnormal returns are available to individuals who trade on publicly available information about block trades because prices react so quickly. Fifteen minutes after the block trade, transaction prices have completely adjusted to unbiased estimates of closing prices. This gives some idea of how fast the market adjusts to new, unexpected information like a block trade.

What about people who can transact at the block price? Who are they and don't they earn an abnormal return? Usually, the specialist, the floor trader (a member of the NYSE), brokerage houses, and favored customers of the brokerage houses can participate at the block price. Dann, Mayers, and Raab show that with a -4.56% trading rule, an individual participating in every block with purchases of $100,000 or more could have earned a net annualized rate of return of 203% for the 173 blocks which activated the filter rule. Of course, this represents the maximum realizable rate of return. Nevertheless, it is clear that even after adjusting for risk, transaction costs, and taxes, it is possible to earn rates of return in excess of what any existing theory would call "normal." This can be interpreted as evidence that capital markets are inefficient in their strong form. Individuals who are notified of the pending block trade and who can participate at the block price before the information becomes publicly available do, in fact, appear to earn excess profits.

However, Dann, Mayers, and Raab caution us that we may not properly understand all the costs which a buyer faces in a block trade. One possibility is that the specialist (or anyone else) normally holds an optimal utility-maximizing portfolio. In order to accept part of a block trade, which forces him away from that portfolio, he will charge a premium rate of return. In this way, what appear to be abnormal returns, may actually be fair, competitively determined fees for a service rendered— the service of providing liquidity to a seller.

To date, the empirical research into the phenomenon of price changes around a block trade shows that block trades do not disrupt markets, that markets are efficient in the sense that they very quickly (less than 15 minutes) fully reflect all publicly available information. There is evidence of both a permanent information effect and a (very) temporary liquidity or price pressure effect as illustrated in Fig. 9.7(c). The market is efficient in its semistrong form, but the fact that abnormal returns are earned by individuals who participate at the block price may indicate strong form inefficiency.

D. INSIDER TRADING

A direct test of strong-form efficiency is whether or not insiders with access to information which is not publicly available can outperform the market. Jaffe [1974] collected data on insider trading from the *Official Summary of Security Transactions and Holdings* published by the Securities and Exchange Commission. He then defined an intensive trading month as one during which there were at least three more sellers than buyers or vice versa. If a stock was intensively traded during a given month, it was included in an intensive-trading portfolio. Using the empirical market line, Jaffe then calculated cumulative average residuals. If the stock had intensive selling, its residual (which would presumably be negative) was multiplied by −1 and added to the portfolio returns, and conversely for intensive buying. For 861 observations during the 1960s, the residuals rose approximately 5% in eight months following the intensive trading event with 3% of the rise occurring in the last six months. These returns are statistically significant and are greater than transaction costs. A sample of insider trading during the 1950s produces similar results. These findings suggest that insiders do earn abnormal returns and that the strong-form hypothesis of market efficiency does not hold.

Jaffe also investigated the effect of regulation changes on insider trading. Two of the most significant changes in security regulation resulted from (1) the Cady-Roberts decision in November 1961, when the SEC first exercised its power to punish insider trading and thus established the precedent that corporate officials trading on inside information were liable for civil prosecution, and (2) the Texas Gulf Sulphur case in August 1966, when the courts upheld the earlier (April 1965) SEC indictment of company officials who had suppressed and traded on news about a vast mineral strike. After examining abnormal returns from intensive insider-trading samples around the dates of these historic decisions, Jaffe was forced to the following conclusion: the data could not reject the null hypothesis that the enforcement of SEC regulations in these two cases had no effect on insider trading in general. At best the regulations prohibit only the most flagrant examples of speculation based on inside information.

A study by Finnerty [1976] corroborates Jaffe's conclusions. The major difference is that the Finnerty data sample was not restricted to an intensive trading group. By testing the entire population of insiders, the empirical findings allow an evaluation of the "average" insider returns. The data include over 30,000 individual insider transactions between January 1969 and December 1972. Abnormal returns computed from the market model indicate that insiders are able to "beat the market" on a risk-adjusted basis, both when selling and when buying.

E. NEW ISSUES

There has been a long history of articles which have studied the pricing of the common stock of companies which is issued to the public for the first time. To mention a few, the list includes papers by the Securities and Exchange Commission [1963], Reilly and Hatfield [1969], Stickney [1970], McDonald and Fisher [1972], Logue [1973], Stigler [1964], and Shaw [1971]. They all faced a seemingly insoluble problem: How could returns on unseasoned issues be adjusted for risk if time-series data on pre-issue prices were nonexistent? Any estimate of systematic risk, for example, requires the computation of the covariance between time-series returns for a given security and returns on a market portfolio. But new issues are not priced until they become public. An ingenious way around this problem was employed by Ibbotson [1975]. Portfolios of new issues with identical seasoning (defined as the number of months since issue) were formed. The monthly return on the *XYZ* Company, say two months after its issue, in March of 1964 was matched with the market return that month, resulting in one pair of returns for a portfolio of two months seasoning. By collecting a large number of return pairs for new issues which went public in different calendar months but which all had two months seasoning, it was possible to form a vector of returns of issues of two months seasoning for which Ibbotson could compute a covariance with the market. In this manner, he estimated the systematic risk of issues with various seasoning. Using the empirical market line, he was able to estimate abnormal performance indices in the month of initial issue (initial performance from the offering date price to the end of the first month), and in the aftermarket (months following the initial issue). From 2650 new issues between 1960 and 1969 Ibbotson randomly selected one new issue for each of the 120 calendar months.

The estimated systematic risk (beta) in the month of issue was 2.26 and the abnormal return was estimated to be 11.4%. Even after transaction costs, this represents a statistically significant positive abnormal return. Therefore, either the offering price is set too low or investors systematically overvalue new issues at the end of the first month of seasoning. Later evidence shows that the aftermarket is efficient; therefore Ibbotson focused his attention on the possibility that offering prices determined by the investment banking firm are systematically set below the fair market value of the security. Regulations of the SEC require a maximum offering price for a new issue which is usually filed two weeks in advance of the actual offering, although it can be adjusted in some cases.[4] The actual offering price is set immediately before the offering. The existence of a regulation which requires the actual offering price to be fixed creates the possibility of a "heads I lose, tails you win" situation for the underwriter. Table 9.3 shows the four possibilities which can occur in a firm commitment offering (the underwriting syndicate buys the issue from the firm for the offering price less an underwriting spread, then sells the issue to the public at the fixed

Table 9.3 Gain and loss situations for a new issue

	Situation	Investors	Investment banker
I	Maximum offering price ≥ Market price ≥ Offering price	Gain	Parity
II	Maximum offering price ≥ Offering price ≥ Market price	Parity	Loss
III	Maximum offering price = Offering price ≥ Market price	Parity	Loss
IV	Market price ≥ Maximum offering price = Offering price	Gain	Parity

---

[4] In most cases, the maximum offering price is set high enough to cause little concern that it may actually constrain the actual offering price.

offering price). The best the underwriter can do is achieve a parity situation with no gain or loss. This happens whenever the market price turns out to be above the offering price (situations I and IV). Obviously, the investment banker does not want the market price to equal or exceed the *maximum* offering price (situations III and IV). This would infuriate the issuing firm and lead to a loss of future underwriting business. Therefore, we usually observe situations I and II. But if the investment banker receives adequate compensation from his underwriting spread for the risk he undertakes and if he cannot gain by setting the offer price lower than the market price, then why don't we observe offer prices (which, after all, are established only moments before the issues are sold to the public) set equal to the market value? Why can investors systematically earn an abnormal return of 11.4% during the first month of issue? This conundrum, like the difference between the block price and the closing price on the day of the block, cannot easily be explained by existing finance theory.

What about new issue performance in the aftermarket, that is for prices from the first market price onward? Figure 9.11 shows abnormal returns (based on the empirical market line) in the aftermarket for six-month holding periods and the significance tests (*t*-tests). The nine periods other than the initial offering period include only two periods with results which are statistically different from zero (and returns in these two periods are negative). Ibbotson concludes that the evidence cannot allow us to reject the null hypothesis that aftermarkets are efficient, although it is interesting to note that returns in seven out of nine periods show negative returns.

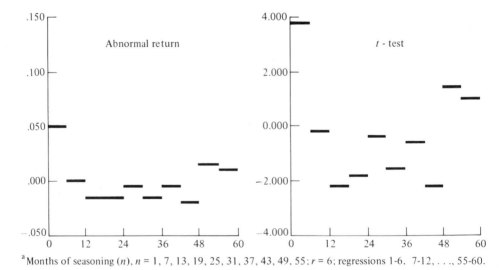

^aMonths of seasoning (n), $n = 1, 7, 13, 19, 25, 31, 37, 43, 49, 55$; $r = 6$; regressions 1-6, 7-12, . . ., 55-60.

Fig. 9.11 Abnormal returns for issues of different seasoning (Ibbotson, R., "Price Performance of Common Stock New Issues," reprinted from *The Journal of Financial Economics,* September 1975, 254.)

Figure 9.12 shows plots of changes in systematic risk in the aftermarket. Note the downward decline. The results show that the systematic risk of new issues is greater than the systematic risk of the market (which always has a beta equal to one) and that their systematic risk is not stable in that it drops as the new issues become seasoned.

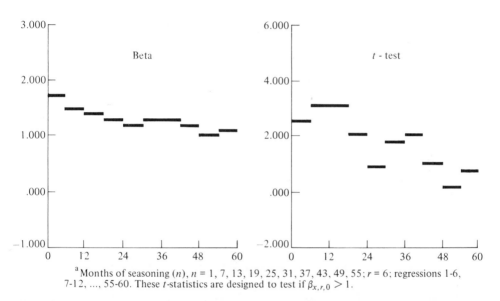

[a] Months of seasoning (n), $n = 1, 7, 13, 19, 25, 31, 37, 43, 49, 55$; $r = 6$; regressions 1-6, 7-12, ..., 55-60. These t-statistics are designed to test if $\beta_{x,r,0} > 1$.

Fig. 9.12 Systematic risk of issues with different seasoning (Ibbotson, R., "Price Performance of Common Stock New Issues," reprinted from *The Journal of Financial Economics*, September 1975, 260.)

F. STOCK SPLITS

Why do stocks split and what effect, if any, do splits have on shareholder wealth? The best known study of stock splits was conducted by Fama, Fisher, Jensen, and Roll [1969]. Cumulative average residuals were calculated from the simple market model using monthly data for an interval of 60 months around the split date for 940 splits between January 1927 and December 1959. Figure 9.13 shows the results. Positive abnormal returns are observed before the split but not afterward. This would seem to indicate that splits are the cause of the abnormal returns. But such a conclusion has no economic logic to it. When the stock splits, there is no change whatsoever in the distribution of expected future cash flows which can be attributed to the split *per se*. Stock splits and stock dividends are merely paper transactions with no real economic meaning.

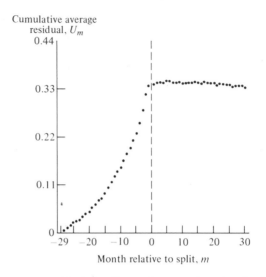

Fig. 9.13 Cumulative average residuals for 60 months around stock splits (Fama, E., L. Fisher, M. Jensen, and R. Roll, "The Adjustment of Stock Prices to New Information," reprinted with permission of *The International Economic Review*, February 1969, 13. © *The International Economic Review*.)

Fama *et al.* [1969] speculated that stock splits might be interpreted by investors as a message about future changes in the firm's expected cash flows. They hypothesized that stock splits might be interpreted as a message about dividend increases, which in turn imply that the managers of the firm feel confident that it can maintain a permanently higher level of cash flows. In order to test this hypothesis, the sample was divided into those firms which increased their dividends beyond the average for the market in the interval following the split and those which paid out lower dividends. The results, shown in Fig. 9.14, reveal that stocks in the dividend "increased" class have slightly positive returns following the split. This is consistent with the hypothesis that splits are interpreted as messages about dividend increases.[5] Of course, a dividend increase does not always follow a split. Hence the slightly positive abnormal return for the dividend-increase group reflects small price adjustments which occur when the market is absolutely sure of the increase. On the other hand, split-up stocks with poor dividend performance experience declines in cumulative average residuals until about a year after the split by which time it must be very clear that the anticipated dividend increase is not forthcoming. Taken together, these

---

[5] This does not imply that higher dividend payout *per se* causes an increase in the value of the firm. In Chapter 13 (Dividend Policy) we shall see that higher dividends are interpreted as signals that the future cash flows from the firm will increase.

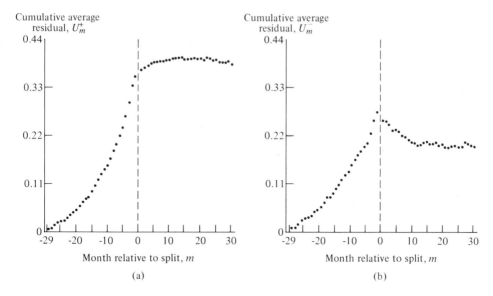

Fig. 9.14 Cumulative average residuals for splits with dividend increases (a) and decreases (b) (Fama, E., L. Fisher, M. Jensen, and R. Roll, "The Adjustment of Stock Prices to New Information," reprinted with permission of *The International Economic Review*, February 1969, 15. © *The International Economic Review*.)

results are consistent with the hypothesis that on the average the market makes unbiased dividend forecasts for split-up securities and these forecasts are fully reflected in the price of the security by the end of the split month.

The results of Fama, Fisher, Jensen, and Roll [1969] are consistent with the semistrong form of market efficiency. Prices appear to fully reflect information about expected cash flows. The split *per se* has no effect on shareholder wealth. Rather it merely serves as a message about dividend changes. There seems to be no way to use a split to increase one's expected returns, unless, of course, inside information concerning the split or subsequent dividend behavior is available.

One often hears that stocks split because there is an "optimal" price range for common stocks. Moving the security price into this range makes the market for trading in the security "wider" or "deeper," hence there is more trading liquidity. Copeland [1978] reports that contrary to the above argument, market liquidity is actually lower following a stock split. Trading volume is proportionately lower than its presplit level, brokerage revenues (a major portion of transaction costs) are proportionately higher, and bid-ask spreads are higher as a percentage of the bid price. Taken together, these empirical results point to lower post-split liquidity. Hence, we can say that the market for split-up securities has lower operational efficiency relative to its presplit level.

G. MUTUAL FUND PERFORMANCE

Mutual funds allege that they can provide two types of service to their clients. First, they may minimize the amount of unsystematic risk an investor must face. This is done through efficient diversification in the face of transactions costs. Second, they may be able to use their professional expertise to earn abnormal returns through successful prediction of future security prices. This second claim is contradictory to the semistrong form of capital market efficiency unless, for some reason, mutual fund managers can consistently obtain information which is not publicly available.

A number of studies have focused their attention on the performance of mutual funds. A partial list includes Friend and Vickers [1965], Sharpe [1966], Treynor [1965], Farrar [1962], Friend, Blume, and Crockett [1970], Jensen [1968], and Mains [1977]. Various performance measures are used. Among them are:

$$\text{Reward to variability ratio} = \frac{R_{jt} - R_{ft}}{\sigma_j}, \tag{9.3}$$

$$\text{Treynor index} = \frac{R_{jt} - R_{ft}}{\hat{\beta}_j}, \tag{9.4}$$

$$\text{Abnormal performance} = \alpha_{jt} = (R_{jt} - R_{ft}) - [\hat{\beta}_j(R_{mt} - R_{ft})], \tag{9.5}$$

where

R_j = the return on the jth mutual fund,
R_f = the return on a risk-free asset (usually Treasury bills),
σ_j = the standard deviation of return on the jth mutual fund,
$\hat{\beta}_j$ = the estimated systematic risk of the jth mutual fund.

Of these, the abnormal performance measure (9.5) makes the best use of the CAPM. It was developed by Jensen [1968], who used it to test the abnormal performance of 115 mutual funds using annual data between 1955 and 1964. If the performance index, α, is positive, it means that after adjusting for risk and for movements in the market index, the abnormal performance of a portfolio is also positive. The average α for returns measured "net of costs" such as research costs, management fees, and brokerage commissions was -1.1% per year over the 10-year period. This suggests that, on the average, the funds were not able to forecast future security prices well enough to cover their expenses. When returns were measured "gross of expenses" (excepting brokerage commissions), the average α was $-.4\%$ per year. Apparently, the gross returns were not sufficient to recoup even brokerage commissions.

In sum, Jensen's study of mutual funds provides evidence that the 115 mutual funds, on the average, were not able to predict security prices well enough to outperform a buy-and-hold strategy. In addition, there was very little evidence that any individual fund was able to do better than what might be expected from mere random chance. These conclusions held even when fund returns were measured gross of management expenses and brokerage costs. Results obtained are consistent with the hypothesis of capital market efficiency in its semistrong form, because we may assume that, at the very least, mutual fund managers have access to publicly available information. However, they do not necessarily imply that mutual funds will not be held by rational investors. On the average, the funds do an excellent job of diversification. This may, by itself, be a socially desirable service to investors.

More recently, Mains [1977] has reexamined the issue of mutual fund performance. He criticizes Jensen's work on two accounts: (1) the rates of return were underestimated, (a) because dividends were assumed to be reinvested at year end rather than during the quarter they were received and (b) because when expenses were added back to obtain gross returns, they were added back at year end instead of continuously throughout the year. By using monthly data instead of annual data, Mains is able to better estimate both net and gross returns. (2) Jensen assumed that mutual fund betas were stationary over long periods of time (note that $\hat{\beta}_j$ has no time subscript in Eq. 9.5). Using monthly data, Mains obtains lower estimates of $\hat{\beta}_j$ and argues that Jensen's estimates of risk were too high.

The abnormal performance results calculated for a sample of 70 mutual funds indicate that as a group, the mutual funds had neutral risk-adjusted performance on a net return basis. On a gross-return basis (i.e., before operating expenses and transactions costs), 80% of the funds sampled performed positively. This suggests that mutual funds are able to outperform the market well enough to earn back their operating expenses.

H. SUMMARY

All the evidence suggests that capital markets are efficient in their weak and semistrong forms, that security prices conform to a fair-game model but not precisely to a random walk because of small first-order dependencies in prices and nonstationarities in the underlying price distribution over time, and that the strong-form hypothesis does not hold. However, any conclusions about the strong form of market efficiency need be qualified by the fact that capital-market efficiency must be considered jointly with competition and efficiency in markets for information. If insiders have monopolistic access to information, this fact may be considered an inefficiency in the market for information rather than in capital markets. Filter rules (described in Chapter 8) have shown that security prices exhibit no dependencies over time, at least down to the level of transaction costs. Thus capital markets are allocationally efficient up to the point of operational efficiency. If transactions costs amounted to a greater percentage of value traded, price dependencies for filter rules greater than 1.5% might have been found.

At least in two instances, special types of "abnormal" returns could not be explained. Block traders who can buy at the block price and sell at the market close could earn annual abnormal returns of over 200% per year even after transaction costs. Individuals who could buy new issues at the subscription price and sell at the end of the month could earn an abnormal return of 11.4% per month (this is over 350% per year). Although both of these results may be interpreted as strong-form inefficiencies, the authors were quick to point out that they may simply represent fair returns for services provided by the block positioner or the investment banker. It is best to say at this point that we do not know.

All the studies reviewed in this chapter have used data from the stock market. However, there is evidence that other markets are also efficient. Roll [1970] showed that prices in the Treasury bill market obey a fair-game model. Schwert [1977] concludes that the prices of New York Stock Exchange seats follow a multiplicative random walk. Stein [1977] examines the auction market for art and finds it efficient. Larson [1960] looks at corn futures, and Mandelbrot [1964] investigates spot prices in cotton. In addition to these studies, we should mention in passing that there are many other topics related to the question of market efficiency which have not been discussed here.

PROBLEM SET

9.1 Roll's critique of tests of the CAPM shows that if the index portfolio is *ex post* efficient, it is mathematically impossible for abnormal returns, as measured by the empirical market line, to be statistically different from zero. Yet, the Ibbotson study on new issues uses the cross-section empirical market line and finds significant abnormal returns in the month of issue and none in the following months. Given Roll's critique, this should have been impossible. How can the empirical results be reconciled with the theory?

9.2 In a recent study on corporate disclosure by a special committee of the Securities and Exchange Commission, we find the following statement (1977, p. D6):

The "efficient market hypothesis"—which asserts that the current price of a security reflects all publicly available information—even if valid, does not negate the necessity of a mandatory disclosure system. This theory is concerned with how the market reacts to disclosed information and is silent as to the optimum amount of information required or whether that optimum should be achieved on a mandatory or voluntary basis; market forces alone are insufficient to cause all material information to be disclosed, ...

Two questions that arise are:
a) What is the difference between efficient markets for securities and efficient markets for information?
b) What criteria define "material information"?

9.3 In your own words, what does the empirical evidence on block trading tell us about market efficiency?

9.4 Which of the following types of information provides a likely opportunity to earn abnormal returns on the market:
a) The latest copy of a company's annual report.
b) News coming across the NYSE ticker tape that 100,000 shares of Lukens Steel Company were just traded in a single block.
c) Advance notice that the *XYZ* Company is going to split its common stock three for one, but not increase dividend payout.
d) Advance notice that a large new issue of common stock in the *ABC* Company will be offered soon.

9.5 Mr. *A* has received, over the last three months, a solicitation to purchase a service which claims to be able to forecast movements in the Dow Jones Industrial Index. Normally, he doesn't believe in such things, but the service provides evidence of amazing accuracy. In each of the last three months, it was always right in predicting whether or not the index would move up more than 10 points, stay within a 10-point range, or go down by more than 10 points. Would you advise him to purchase the service? Why or why not?

9.6 The Ponzi Mutual Fund (which is not registered with the SEC) guarantees a 2% per month (24% per year) return on your money. You have looked into the matter and found that they have indeed been able to pay their shareholders the promised return for each of the 18 months they have been in operation. What implication does this have for capital markets? Should you invest?

9.7 Empirical evidence indicates that mutual funds which have abnormal returns in a given year are successful in attracting abnormally large numbers of new investors the following year. Is this inconsistent with capital market efficiency?

9.8 The Value Line Investment Survey publishes weekly stock performance forecasts. Stocks are grouped into five portfolios according to expected price performance, with Group 1 comprising the most highly recommended stocks. The chart of each portfolio's actual performance over a 10-year period (Fig. Q8.1) assumes that each of the five portfolios was adjusted on a weekly basis in accordance with Value Line's stock ratings. The chart shows that the portfolios' actual performances are consistent with Value Line's forecasts. Is this evidence against an efficient securities market?

9.9 In each of the following situations, explain the extent to which the empirical results offer reliable evidence for (or against) market efficiency.

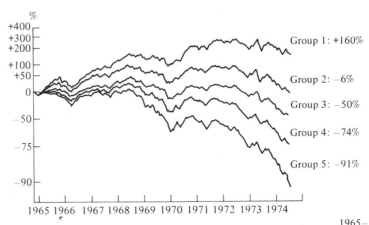

	1965*	1966	1967	1968	1969	1970	1971	1972	1973	1974	1965–1974
Group 1	+28.8%	− 5.5%	+53.4%	+37.1%	−10.4%	+ 7.3%	+30.6%	+12.6%	−19.1%	−11.1%	+160%
Group 2	+18.5	− 6.2	+36.1	+26.9	−17.5	− 3.2	+13.7	+ 7.4	−28.9	−29.5	− 6
Group 3	+ 6.7	−13.9	+27.1	+24.0	−23.8	− 8.0	+ 9.3	+ 3.5	−33.6	−34.1	− 50
Group 4	− .4	−15.7	+23.8	+20.9	−33.3	−16.3	+ 8.4	− 7.1	−37.9	−40.6	− 74
Group 5	− 3.2	−18.2	+21.5	+11.8	−44.9	−23.3	− 5.5	−13.4	−43.8	−55.7	− 91

*April through December − all other years cover a 12-month period.

Q8.1 Ten-year record of actual forecast assumes all rank changes had been followed (Bernhard, A., "The Value Line Investment Survey," *Investing in Common Stock*, Arnold Bernhard and Company, Inc., 1975. Reprinted with permission of the author.)

a) A research study using data for firms continuously listed on the Compustat computer tapes from 1953–1973 finds no evidence of impending bankruptcy costs reflected in stock prices as a firm's debt/equity ratio increases.
b) One thousand stock brokers are surveyed via questionnaire, and their stated investment preferences are classified according to industry groupings. The results can be used to explain rate of return differences across industries.
c) A study of the relationships between size of type in the *New York Times* headline and size of price change (in either direction) in the subsequent day's stock index reveals a significant positive correlation. Further, when independent subjects are asked to qualify the headline news as good, neutral, or bad, the direction of the following day's price change (up or down) is discovered to vary with the quality of news (good or bad).
d) Using 25 years of data in exhaustive regression analysis, a *Barron's* writer develops a statistical model that explains the 25-year period of stock returns (using 31 variables) with minuscule error.

REFERENCES

ALEXANDER, S. S., "Price Movements in Speculative Markets: Trends or Random Walks," *Industrial Management Review*, May 1961, 7–26.

BALL, R., and P. BROWN, "An Empirical Evaluation of Accounting Income Numbers," *Journal of Accounting Research*, Autumn 1968, 159–178.

BERNHARD, A., *Investing in Common Stocks*. Arnold Bernhard & Co., Inc., New York, 1975.

BLACK, F., M. JENSEN, and M. SCHOLES, "The Capital Asset Pricing Model: Some Empirical Tests," in M. Jensen, Ed., *Studies in the Theory of Capital Markets*. Praeger, New York, 1972, 79–121.

———, and M. SCHOLES, "The Effects of Dividend Yield and Dividend Policy on Common Stock Prices and Returns," *Journal of Financial Economics*, May 1974, 1–22.

COPELAND, T. E., "Liquidity Changes Following Stock Splits," *The Journal of Finance*, March 1979.

DANN, L., D. MAYERS, and R. RAAB, "Trading Rules, Large Blocks and the Speed of Adjustment," *The Journal of Financial Economics*, January 1977, 3–22.

FAMA, E. F., "The Behavior of Stock Market Prices," *The Journal of Business*, January 1965, 34–105.

———, "Efficient Capital Markets: A Review of Theory and Empirical Work," *The Journal of Finance*, May 1970, 383–417.

———, *Foundations of Finance*. Basic Books, New York, 1976.

———, L. FISHER, M. JENSEN, and R. ROLL, "The Adjustment of Stock Prices to New Information," *International Economic Review*, February 1969, 1–21.

———, and M. BLUME, "Filter Rules and Stock Market Trading Profits," *The Journal of Finance*, May 1970, 226–241.

———, and J. MACBETH, "Risk, Return, and Equilibrium: Empirical Test," *Journal of Political Economy*, May/June 1973, 607–635.

FARRAR, D. E., *The Investment Decision Under Uncertainty*. Prentice-Hall, Englewood Cliffs, N.J., 1962.

FINNERTY, J. E., "Insiders and Market Efficiency," *Journal of Finance*, September 1976, 1141–1148.

FRIEND, I., M. BLUME, and J. CROCKETT, *Mutual Funds and Other Institutional Investors*. McGraw Hill, New York, 1970.

——, F. E. BROWN, E. S. HERMAN, and D. VICKERS, *A Study of Mutual Funds*. U.S. Govt. Printing Office, Washington, D.C., 1962.

——, and D. VICKERS, "Portfolio Selection and Investment Performance," *Journal of Finance*, September 1965, 391–415.

HONG, H., R. S. KAPLAN, and G. MANDELKER, "Pooling vs. Purchase: The Effects of Accounting for Mergers on Stock Prices," *The Accounting Review*, January 1978, 31–47.

IBBOTSON, R., "Price Performance of Common Stock New Issues," *Journal of Financial Economics*, September 1975, 235–272.

JAFFE, J., "The Effect of Regulation Changes on Insider Trading," *The Bell Journal of Economics and Management Science*, Spring 1974, 93–121.

JENSEN, M., "The Performance of Mutual Funds in the Period 1945-64," *The Journal of Finance*, May 1968, 389–416.

——, "Risk, the Pricing of Capital Assets, and the Evaluation of Investment Portfolios," *The Journal of Business*, April 1969, 167–247.

——, "Capital Markets: Theory and Evidence," *The Bell Journal of Economics and Management Science*, Autumn 1972, 357–398.

KAPLAN, R. S., and R. ROLL, "Investor Evaluation of Accounting Information: Some Empirical Evidence," *Journal of Business*, April 1972, 225–257.

KRAUS, A., and H. R. STOLL, "Price Impacts of Block Trading on the New York Stock Exchange," *The Journal of Finance*, June 1972, 569–588.

LARSON, A. B., "Measurement of a Random Process in Futures Prices," reprinted in Cootner, Ed., *The Random Character of Stock Market Prices*, MIT Press, Cambridge, Mass., 1964, 219–230.

LINTNER, J., "The Valuation of Risk Assets and the Selection of Risky Investments in Stock Portfolios and Capital Budgets," *Review of Economics and Statistics*, February 1965, 13–37.

LOGUE, D. E., "On the Pricing of Unseasoned Equity Offerings: 1965–1969," *Journal of Financial and Quantitative Analysis*, January 1973, 91–104.

MAINS, N. E., "Risk, the Pricing of Capital Assets, and the Evaluation of Investment Portfolios: Comment," *Journal of Business*, July 1977, 371–384.

MANDELBROT, B., "The Variation of Certain Speculative Prices," reprinted in Cootner, Ed., *The Random Character of Stock Market Prices*, MIT Press, Cambridge, Mass., 1964, 307–332.

MCDONALD, J. G., and A. K. FISHER, "New Issue Stock Price Behavior," *The Journal of Finance*, March 1972, 97–102.

MOSSIN, J., "Security Pricing and Investment Criteria in Competitive Markets," *American Economic Review*, December 1969, 749–756.

REILLY, F. K., and K. HATFIELD, "Investor Experience with New Stock Issues," *Financial Analysts Journal*, September/October 1969, 73–80.

Report of the Advisory Committee on Corporate Disclosure to the Securities and Exchange Commission, U.S. Government Printing Office, Washington, D.C., November 1977.

ROLL, R., *The Behavior of Interest Rates*. Basic Books, New York, 1970.

SCHOLES, M., "The Market for Securities: Substitution versus Price Pressure and the Effects of Information on Share Prices," *Journal of Business*, April 1972, 179–211.

SCHWERT, W., "Stock Exchange Seats as Capital Assets," *Journal of Financial Economics*, January 1977, 51–78.

Securities and Exchange Commission, *Report of the Special Study on Securities Markets*. U.S. Government Printing Office, Washington, D.C., 1963.

SHARPE, W. F., "Mutual Fund Performance," *Journal of Business*, January 1966, 119–138.

SHAW, D., "The Performance of Primary Stock Offerings: A Canadian Comparison," *The Journal of Finance*, December 1971, 1103–1113.

STEIN, J. P., "The Monetary Appreciation of Paintings," *Journal of Political Economy*, October 1977, 1021–1036.

STICKNEY, C. P., Jr., *A Study of the Relationships of Accounting Principles and Common Stock Prices of Firms Going Public*. Ph.D. Thesis, Florida State University, Tallahassee.

STIGLER, G., "Public Regulation of Security Markets," *Journal of Business*, April 1964, 117–142.

SUNDER, S., "Relationship between Accounting Changes and Stock Prices: Problems of Measurement and some Empirical Evidence," *Empirical Research in Accounting: Selected Studies*, 1973, 1–45.

SUNDER, S., "Stock Price and Risk Related to Accounting Changes in Inventory Valuation," *Accounting Review*, April 1975, 305–315.

TREYNOR, J. L., "How to Rate Mutual Fund Performance," *Harvard Business Review*, January/February 1965, 63–75.

Chapter 10

Capital Budgeting Under Uncertainty: The Multiperiod Case

Former Student: Professor, this is the same examination that you gave to my class when I was a student twenty years ago. Don't you ever change the questions?
Professor: The questions don't change, just the answers.

A. INTRODUCTION

Chapters 2 and 3 discussed capital budgeting given the assumption that all future cash flows were known with certainty. The appropriate discount rate was assumed to be the risk-free rate, and the chapters focused on selection of discounting techniques consistent with the goal of maximizing the net present value of shareholders' wealth. Subsequent chapters introduced uncertainty in the context of a one-period equilibrium pricing model, the capital asset pricing model.

In this chapter we introduce some of the difficulties implicit in the use of the CAPM to determine the appropriate multiperiod risk-adjusted discount rate for capital budgeting purposes. Given multiperiod uncertainty, under what conditions can one use the following formula to determine the NPV of risky projects?

$$\text{NPV}_j = \sum_{t=0}^{N} \frac{\text{NCF}_{jt}}{[1 + E(R_j)]^t}, \qquad (10.1)$$

where

$\text{NPV}_j = $ the net present value of project j
$\text{NCF}_{jt} = $ the net cash flow of project j in time t,
$E(R_j) = $ the risk-adjusted required rate of return for project j.

In particular, we are interested in the conditions under which the required rate of return on the project, frequently called the *weighted average cost of capital*, can be determined by the CAPM as written below:

$$E(R_j) = R_f + [E(R_m) - R_f]\beta_j. \tag{10.2}$$

Presumably, one would use *current* estimates of the risk-free rate, R_f, the expected rate of return on the market, $E(R_m)$, and the systematic risk of the project, β_j, in order to determine the multiperiod discount rate, $E(R_j)$.

In the first half of this chapter, which deals mainly with theoretical issues, we review the results of two articles. First, Bogue and Roll [1974] show that the problem may not be as simple as suggested in Eq. (10.1). They show that a much more complex procedure becomes necessary if we consider a world where the risk-free rate in future time periods is not known with certainty. Later Fama [1977] shows that given the type of uncertainty admissible in the capital asset pricing world, it *is* reasonable to use the risk-adjusted discounting procedure of Eq. (10.1).

The second half of the chapter deals with two applied issues. Both assume that the risk-adjusted discount rate may be used for multiperiod capital budgeting under uncertainty. The simpler of the two problems shows how to adjust the risk-adjusted discount rate when comparing cost (rather than total income) data for mutually exclusive projects. We demonstrate that the correct technique is to use a lower discount rate for riskier cost cash flows. The second issue has come to be known as the *abandonment problem*. How should one evaluate the residual value of investment assets?

B. MULTIPERIOD CAPITAL BUDGETING WITH "IMPERFECT" MARKETS FOR PHYSICAL CAPITAL

Bogue and Roll [1974] analyze capital budgeting of risky projects in a multiperiod framework and conclude that it may be incorrect to discount cash flows by using the single-period risk-adjusted discount rate. However, under specified conditions, the investment decision for a multiperiod project can be made with a one-period forecast. If appropriate secondary markets exist for the project, only a one-period analysis is required for a decision. The firm makes a comparison between the current investment outlay and the value of the forecast of cash flows during the first period plus the forecasted end-of-period secondary market price.

In addition, even with imperfect secondary markets for physical capital, some investment decisions can still be made with one-period forecasts. If the machine is acceptable on the basis of its one-period cash flow plus its net salvage value after the first period, the possibility of values in subsequent periods will only add to the acceptability of the project. Because the single-period analysis is important in its own right and also because it will be used in a dynamic programming framework to solve the multiperiod problem, Bogue and Roll start the analysis with a single-period valuation model. They begin with the CAPM in value form. We derive their basic valuation expression by starting with the CAPM in return form as shown in Eq. (10.3).

$$E(\tilde{R}_1) = r_{f0} + [E(\tilde{R}_{m1}) - r_{f0}] \frac{\mathrm{COV}(\tilde{R}_1, \tilde{R}_{m1})}{\sigma^2(\tilde{R}_{m1})}. \tag{10.3}$$

By definition,

$$\tilde{R}_{m1} = \frac{\tilde{V}_{m1} - V_{m0}}{V_{m0}} = \frac{\tilde{V}_{m1}}{V_{m0}} - 1, \qquad \tilde{R}_1 = \frac{\tilde{V}_1 - V_0}{V_0} = \frac{\tilde{V}_1}{V_0} - 1,$$

$$\sigma^2(\tilde{R}_{m1}) = \sigma^2\left(\frac{\tilde{V}_{m1}}{V_{m0}} - 1\right) = \sigma^2\left(\frac{\tilde{V}_{m1}}{V_{m0}}\right) = \frac{1}{(V_{m0})^2}\, \sigma^2(\tilde{V}_{m1}),$$

$$\text{COV}(\tilde{R}_1, \tilde{R}_{m1}) = \text{COV}\left(\frac{\tilde{V}_1}{V_0} - 1, \frac{\tilde{V}_{m1}}{V_{m0}} - 1\right) = \frac{1}{V_0 V_{m0}}\, \text{COV}(\tilde{V}_1, \tilde{V}_{m1}),$$

where

$V_0 =$ the certain current value of the firm,
$\tilde{V}_1 =$ the uncertain end-of-period value of the firm (including any dividends paid over the period),
$\tilde{V}_{m1} =$ the uncertain end-of-period value of the market portfolio,
$r_{f0} =$ the risk-free rate of interest over the period.

Then the security market line (SML) is

$$\frac{E(\tilde{V}_1)}{V_0} - 1 = r_{f0} + \left[\frac{E(\tilde{V}_{m1})}{V_{m0}} - 1 - r_{f0}\right]\left(\frac{V_{m0}}{V_0}\right)\frac{\text{COV}(\tilde{V}_1, \tilde{V}_{m1})}{\sigma^2(\tilde{V}_{m1})}. \qquad (10.4)$$

Substituting and rearranging, we can obtain a certainty-equivalent value for the firm. First, we multiply both sides by V_0:

$$E(\tilde{V}_1) - V_0 = V_0 r_{f0} + [E(\tilde{V}_{m1}) - (1 + r_{f0})V_{m0}][\text{COV}(\tilde{V}_1, \tilde{V}_{m1})/\sigma^2(\tilde{V}_{m1})].$$

Next, we subtract $V_0 r_{f0}$ and $E(\tilde{V}_1)$ from both sides and change signs:

$$(1 + r_{f0})V_0 = E(\tilde{V}_1) - [E(\tilde{V}_{m1}) - (1 + r_{f0})V_{m0}][\text{COV}(\tilde{V}_1, \tilde{V}_{m1})/\sigma^2(\tilde{V}_{m1})].$$

Solving for V_0, we have

$$V_0 = \frac{E(\tilde{V}_1) - [E(\tilde{V}_{m1}) - (1 + r_{f0})V_{m0}][\text{COV}(\tilde{V}_1, \tilde{V}_{m1})/\sigma^2(\tilde{V}_{m1})]}{1 + r_{f0}}.$$

Using λ_0, the market price per unit risk, to simplify, we obtain the certainty-equivalent value of the firm:

$$V_0 = \frac{E(\tilde{V}_1) - \lambda_0\, \text{COV}(\tilde{V}_1, \tilde{V}_{m1})}{1 + r_{f0}}, \qquad (10.5)$$

where

$$\lambda_0 \equiv \frac{E(\tilde{V}_{m1}) - (1 + r_{f0})V_{m0}}{\sigma^2(\tilde{V}_{m1})} = \text{the market price per unit of risk.}$$

Now let $\tilde{X}_1$ be an incremental end-of-period net cash inflow from a project requiring current cash outlay of X_0. With the addition of the project, the end-of-period value of the firm will be $\tilde{V}_1 + \tilde{X}_1$. The new value of the firm is expressed by

$$V_0 + \Delta V_0 = \frac{E(\tilde{V}_1 + \tilde{X}_1) - \lambda_0 \, \text{COV}(\tilde{V}_1 + \tilde{X}_1, \tilde{V}_{m1})}{1 + r_{f0}}. \tag{10.6}$$

When V_0 is subtracted from both sides of Eq. (10.6), we obtain

$$\Delta V_0 = \frac{E(\tilde{X}_1) - \lambda_0 \, \text{COV}(\tilde{X}_1, \tilde{V}_{m1})}{1 + r_{f0}}, \tag{10.7}$$

which is the certainty-equivalent value of a project. If the left-hand side of Eq. (10.7) exceeds the right-hand side, the project is acceptable and should be undertaken. The methodology is to begin with an uncertain cash flow from which a certainty-equivalent value is constructed. The end-of-period certainty-equivalent value should be discounted at the risk-free rate to obtain its current value. This one-period result is used as the basis of generalization to the multiperiod case which is considered next.

The firm is considering a project lasting over n periods. The net uncertain cash flows from the project are $\tilde{X}_t$, leading to increments to the value of the firm for each time period t of $\Delta \tilde{V}_t$. To solve the problem we start at the end where for the last period of the project we have[1]

$$\Delta \tilde{V}_n = \tilde{X}_n.$$

The next-to-last period represents a one-period valuation problem. Assuming that the capital market for equities is in equilibrium, the one-period valuation model can be used to find the value of the final cash flow at the end of the next-to-last period. This will enable us to obtain the discounted certainty equivalent of $\tilde{X}_n$ for period $n - 1$ as expressed by

$$\frac{E(\tilde{X}_n | \tilde{e}_{n-1}) - \tilde{\lambda}_{n-1} \, \widehat{\text{COV}}(\tilde{X}_n, \tilde{V}_{mn} | \tilde{e}_n)}{1 + \tilde{r}_{f(n-1)}}, \tag{10.8}$$

where

$$\tilde{e}_{n-1} = \text{state of the world at time } n - 1,$$
$$\tilde{\lambda}_{n-1} = \text{market price of risk at } n - 1,$$
$$\tilde{r}_{f(n-1)} = \text{risk-free rate at } n - 1 \text{ (assumed to be stochastic)},$$
$$\tilde{E}(\tilde{X}_n | \tilde{e}_{n-1}) = \text{conditional expectation at } n - 1 \text{ of cash flows at } n.$$

This enables us to obtain the incremental value at $n - 1$:

$$\Delta V_{n-1} = X_{n-1} + \frac{\tilde{E}(\tilde{X}_n | \tilde{e}_{n-1}) - \tilde{\lambda}_{n-1} \, \widehat{\text{COV}}(\tilde{X}_n, \tilde{V}_{mn} | \tilde{e}_n)}{1 + \tilde{r}_{f(n-1)}}. \tag{10.9}$$

The result in Eq. (10.9) can be generalized to the recursive relationship for the incremental value at any time k:

$$\Delta \tilde{V}_k = \tilde{X}_k + \frac{\tilde{E}(\Delta \tilde{V}_{k+1} | \tilde{e}_k) - \tilde{\lambda}_k \, \widehat{\text{COV}}[\Delta \tilde{V}_{k+1}, \tilde{V}_{m(k+1)} | \tilde{e}_k]}{1 + \tilde{r}_{fk}}. \tag{10.10}$$

---

[1] Note that there is the implicit assumption that the project returns cash only in the nth time period.

From Eq. (10.10) we see that for an n-period project, an n-period infinite-state dynamic programming problem must be solved. Each step involves an application of the one-period valuation model with the parameters depending on the state of the world at the beginning of that particular period. Next, the nature of this solution is illustrated for the special case of a project with a single cash inflow two periods in the future. Using Eq. (10.10) with the risk-free interest-rate expression placed on the left-hand side, we can obtain the incremental value for period 1 and for period 0 as shown below:

$$\Delta \tilde{V}_1 (1 + \tilde{r}_{f1}) = \tilde{E}(\tilde{X}_2 | \tilde{\epsilon}_1) - \tilde{\lambda}_1 \ \widetilde{\mathrm{COV}}(\tilde{X}_2, \ \tilde{V}_{m2} | \tilde{\epsilon}_1), \tag{10.11}$$

$$\Delta V_0 (1 + r_{f0}) = E(\Delta \tilde{V}_1) - \lambda_0 \ \mathrm{COV}(\Delta \tilde{V}_1, \ \tilde{V}_{m1}). \tag{10.12}$$

Note that the second-period risk-free rate, $\tilde{r}_{f1}$, is currently uncertain and will not be revealed until the end of the first period. Next we take expectations of Eq. (10.11) and making use of the covariance identity,

$$\mathrm{COV}(\tilde{X}, \ \tilde{Y}) = E(\tilde{X}, \ \tilde{Y}) - E(\tilde{X})E(\tilde{Y}),$$

we have[2]

$$E(\Delta \tilde{V}_1)E(1 + \tilde{r}_{f1}) + \mathrm{COV}(\Delta \tilde{V}_1, \tilde{r}_{f1}) = E(\tilde{X}_2) - E[\tilde{\lambda}_1 \ \widetilde{\mathrm{COV}}(\tilde{X}_2, \ \tilde{V}_{m2} | \tilde{\epsilon}_1)].$$

We then solve Eq. (10.12) for $E(\Delta \tilde{V}_1)$ and substitute in the preceding expression and arrange terms. The result is

$$V_0(1 + r_{f0})E(1 + \tilde{r}_{f1}) = E(\tilde{X}_2) - E[\tilde{\lambda}_1 \ \widetilde{\mathrm{COV}}(\tilde{X}_2, \ \tilde{V}_{m2} | \tilde{\epsilon}_1)]$$
$$- \lambda_0 \ \mathrm{COV}(\Delta \tilde{V}_1, \ \tilde{V}_{m1})E(1 + \tilde{r}_{f1}) - \mathrm{COV}(\Delta \tilde{V}_1, \tilde{r}_{f1}) \tag{10.13}$$

Equation (10.13) can also be written in the following form: ΔV_0, the present value of the single uncertain cash flow two periods in the future is equal to

$$\Delta V_0 = \frac{E(\tilde{X}_2)}{(1 + r_{f0})E(1 + \tilde{r}_{f1})} - \frac{E[\tilde{\lambda}_1 \ \widetilde{\mathrm{COV}}(\tilde{X}_2, \ \tilde{V}_{m2} | \tilde{\epsilon}_1)]}{(1 + r_{f0})E(1 + \tilde{r}_{f1})} - \frac{\lambda_0 \ \mathrm{COV}(\Delta \tilde{V}_1, \ \tilde{V}_{m1})}{(1 + r_{f0})}$$
$$- \frac{\mathrm{COV}(\Delta \tilde{V}_1, \tilde{r}_{f1})}{(1 + r_{f0})E(1 + \tilde{r}_{f1})}. \tag{10.14}$$

---

[2] The covariance identity follows directly from the definition of covariance:

$$\mathrm{COV}(X, Y) = E[(X - E(X))(Y - E(Y))]$$
$$= E[XY - E(X)Y - E(Y)X + E(X)E(Y)]$$
$$= E(XY) - E(X)E(Y) - E(Y)E(X) + E(X)E(Y)$$
$$= E(XY) - E(X)E(Y).$$

This result is applied to the left-hand side of Eq. (10.11) because it is the expectation of the product of two random variables.

The first of the four terms on the right-hand side of (10.14) is the two-period discounted current expectation of the uncertain cash flow two periods in the future. Subtracted from it are three risk premiums: (1) covariation risk within the second period—i.e., beta risk, (2) covariation risk of the intermediate value of the project which may be thought of as a reinvestment opportunity cost related to the sale of rights to the cash flow after one period has elapsed, and (3) the risk premium for interest rate fluctuations over the two time periods which could cause changes in the project's value at intermediate periods.

In its rearranged form, Eq. (10.13) is in the same form and spirit as the single-period pricing model (Eq. 10.7). However, it contains two additional risk premia that have to be deducted from the two-period discounted current expectation of the single uncertain cash flow two periods in the future. The first is the covariation risk of the intermediate value of the project. And the second is the risk premium charged for the risk of interest fluctuations over the two time periods.

Bogue and Roll conclude by observing that if the errors in probability assessments of the cash flows over the multiple time periods are not systematically biased, stockholders can diversify away most of the error as the number of projects becomes large. Thus, unbiased misassessments can be diversified away in the personal portfolios of stockholders, whereas the use of a wrong capital-budgeting criterion will result in aggregate errors that stockholders will not be able to reduce by diversification. In concept, the multiperiod capital budgeting problem must utilize a valuation expression which includes two additional risk measures over and above the discounted current expectation of cash flows and the usual covariation of those flows with total market values.

C. AN EXAMINATION OF ADMISSIBLE UNCERTAINTY IN A MULTIPERIOD CAPITAL ASSET PRICING WORLD

In the previous section we presented Bogue and Roll's suggestion that in a two-period context, the present value of the firm (Eq. (10.14)) cannot be calculated by simply discounting the certainty-equivalent cash flows at the end of the second time period back to the present. In addition, it is necessary to subtract two additional risk premia: (1) a term for the covariation risk of the intermediate value of the project and (2) a term for the risk of fluctuations in the risk-free rate over the two time periods.

Fama [1977] reexamines the multiperiod capital-budgeting problem under uncertainty and clarifies the Bogue and Roll analysis by showing that within a CAPM world, certain types of uncertainty which are allowed by Bogue and Roll are inadmissible. He then shows that given the CAPM assumptions, the last two terms of Eq. (10.14) vanish, and it is possible to use the discounted rate of return approach to capital budgeting as suggested in Eq. (10.1).

If we assume that the firm has net cash earnings, $\tilde{X}_t$, at time t and no cash flows at any other time, the recursive relationship for the value of the firm at $t - 1$ can be written in a form similar to Eq. (10.5):

$$V_{t-1} = \frac{E(\tilde{X}_t) - \phi_t \, \mathrm{COV}(\tilde{X}_t, \tilde{R}_{mt})}{1 + R_{ft}},$$
(10.15)

where $\phi_t = [E(\tilde{R}_{mt}) - R_{ft}]/\sigma^2(\tilde{R}_{mt})$. This is a certainty-equivalent expression for the value of the firm at $t - 1$. The firm's value at $t - 1$ can also be expressed using the risk-adjusted discount rate to compute the present value of the expected end-of-period cash flows:

$$V_{t-1} = \frac{E(\tilde{X}_t)}{1 + E(\tilde{R}_t)},$$
(10.16)

where $E(\tilde{R}_t) = R_{ft} + [E(\tilde{R}_{mt}) - R_{ft}]\beta_t$.

So far all we have is a one-period expression for the value of cash flows at t, evaluated at $t - 1$. The way we write the value of the firm in a two-period context, at $t - 2$, depends on where we admit uncertainty into expression (10.16). Bogue and Roll allow uncertainty in the parameters of the market opportunity set, namely (1) a stochastic risk-free rate, $\tilde{R}_{ft}$, and (2) uncertainty in the intermediate value of the firm, $\mathrm{COV}(\Delta\tilde{V}^{(1)}, \tilde{V}_m^{(1)})$. However, Fama points out that in a world where securities are priced according to the CAPM, relationships between uncertainty in the returns realized at $t - 1$ and the characteristics of the portfolio opportunity set are ruled out. Were such relationships to exist, they would provide initiative for investors to use their portfolio opportunities at $t - 2$ to hedge against uncertainty in portfolio opportunities at $t - 1$. The result is a pricing process different from the CAPM. The alternative pricing model which results has been discussed by Merton [1973] and Long [1974].[3] Therefore, if we assume that the CAPM is the appropriate model, then any variation through time in the market parameters R_{ft} and ϕ_t is nonstochastic.

Having ruled out uncertainty about R_{ft} and ϕ_t, we can see from (10.15) that any uncertainty about V_{t-1} must arise from uncertainty about the values of $E(\tilde{X}_t)$ and $\mathrm{COV}(\tilde{X}_t, \tilde{R}_{mt})$ assessed as of $t - 1$. The strongest assumption is that there is no intermediate uncertainty about $E(\tilde{X}_t)$ and $\mathrm{COV}(\tilde{X}_t, \tilde{R}_{mt})$. If so, then the value in period $t - 2$ becomes

$$V_{t-2} = \frac{V_{t-1}}{1 + R_{f,t-1}},$$

and at $t = 0$ it is

$$V_0 = \prod_{k=1}^{t-1} \left(\frac{1}{1 + R_{fk}}\right) V_{t-1}.$$

Finally, using (10.16), we obtain

$$V_0 = \prod_{k=1}^{t-1} \left(\frac{1}{1 + R_{fk}}\right)\left(\frac{E(\tilde{X}_t)}{1 + E(R_t)}\right).$$
(10.17)

---

[3] The Merton [1973] study is discussed briefly in Chapter 7.

In this case, the appropriate discount rates prior to period t are the risk-free rates because there is no uncertainty until period t. For period t, the risk-adjusted rate is given by the CAPM relationships.

Of course, the previous assumption is unreasonably strong. However, if V_{t-1} is to be uncertain prior to $t-1$, the uncertainty must be introduced in a fashion consistent with the CAPM. Suppose that the cash flow in period t is estimated in an unbiased fashion in period $t-1$ conditional on all information available at that time. This process can be expressed as

$$\tilde{X}_t = E_{t-1}(\tilde{X}_t)(1 + \tilde{\epsilon}_t) = E_{t-1}(\tilde{X}_t) + E_{t-1}(\tilde{X}_t)\tilde{\epsilon}_t, \qquad (10.18)$$

where $E_{t-1}(\tilde{X}_t)$ is the expected value of $\tilde{X}_t$ and $\tilde{\epsilon}_t$ is a random variable with expected value equal to zero. Prior to $t-1$ the expected value itself is a random variable. This process evolves in the following fashion:

$$\tilde{E}_\tau(\tilde{X}_t) = E_{\tau-1}(\tilde{X}_t)(1 + \tilde{\epsilon}_\tau) = E_{\tau-1}(\tilde{X}_t) + E_{\tau-1}(\tilde{X}_t)\tilde{\epsilon}_\tau. \qquad (10.19)$$

Again, the expected value of $\tilde{\epsilon}_\tau$, conditional on the availability of information at $\tau - 1$, is equal to zero. Therefore, given rational expectations, the value of cash flow at time t, $\tilde{X}_t$, evolves as a martingale.[4] Note that $\tilde{\epsilon}_\tau$ is the change in the expected value of $\tilde{X}_t$ per unit of $E_{t-1}(\tilde{X}_t)$.

$$\tilde{\epsilon}_\tau = \frac{\tilde{E}_\tau(\tilde{X}_t) - E_{\tau-1}(\tilde{X}_t)}{E_{\tau-1}(\tilde{X}_t)} = \frac{\tilde{E}_\tau(\tilde{X}_t)}{E_{\tau-1}(\tilde{X}_t)} - 1. \qquad (10.20)$$

Substituting (10.18) into (10.15), we have the value of the firm as of $t-1$:

$$V_{t-1} = E_{t-1}(\tilde{X}_t)\left[\frac{1 - \phi_t\, \mathrm{COV}(\tilde{\epsilon}_t, \tilde{R}_{mt})}{1 + R_{ft}}\right] = E_{t-1}(\tilde{X}_t)\left[\frac{1}{1 + E(\tilde{R}_t)}\right]. \qquad (10.21)$$

Note that because $\tilde{V}_t = \tilde{X}_t$, we have the following:

$$\frac{\mathrm{COV}(\tilde{V}_t, \tilde{R}_{mt})}{E_{t-1}(\tilde{V}_t)} = \frac{\mathrm{COV}(\tilde{X}_t, \tilde{R}_{mt})}{E_{t-1}(\tilde{X}_t)} = \mathrm{COV}(\tilde{\epsilon}_t, \tilde{R}_{mt}). \qquad (10.22)$$

In (10.21) the return expected from the firm, $E(\tilde{R}_t)$, is part of the portfolio opportunity set perceived by investors at $t-1$. Any stochastic change in this expected return between $t-2$ and $t-1$ is likely to affect the value of the firm at $t-1$. If such a stochastic relationship were to exist, the return realized at $t-1$, $\tilde{R}_{t-1}$, would not be independent of the expected return, $E(\tilde{R}_t)$, from $t-1$ to t, a result which would be inconsistent with the CAPM. Therefore uncertainty at $t-2$ about the risk-adjusted discount rate, $E(\tilde{R}_t)$, in Eq. (10.21) is inadmissible in the multiperiod version of the CAPM. Since uncertainty about ϕ_t and R_{ft} have already been ruled out, the implication is that uncertainty about $\mathrm{COV}(\tilde{\epsilon}_t, \tilde{R}_{mt})$ in Eq. (10.21) is also inadmissible. Consequently, the expected earnings, $E_{t-1}(\tilde{X}_t)$, are the only parameter whose value can be uncertain at $t-2$. This fact will allow us to simplify things considerably.

---

[4] See Chapter 8 for a discussion of martingales.

If $E(\tilde{R}_t)$ is certain, then by substituting (10.19) into (10.21) we have

$$\tilde{V}_{t-1} = [E_{t-2}(\tilde{X}_t) + E_{t-2}(\tilde{X}_t)\tilde{\epsilon}_{t-1}] \left[\frac{1}{1 + E(\tilde{R}_t)} \right]. \tag{10.23}$$

The implication of (10.23) is that the value of the firm at $t - 1$ is perfectly correlated with $E_{t-1}(\tilde{X}_t)$, which is the assessment of the expected value of earnings turning up at $t - 1$.

Taking the expectation of (10.23), we see that the expected value of $\tilde{V}_{t-1}$ as of $t - 2$ is

$$E_{t-2}(\tilde{V}_{t-1}) = E_{t-2}(\tilde{X}_t) \left[\frac{1}{1 + E(\tilde{R}_t)} \right], \tag{10.24}$$

and using (10.22), we see that

$$\text{COV}(\tilde{V}_{t-1}, \tilde{R}_{mt-1}) = E_{t-2}(\tilde{X}_t) \left[\frac{1}{1 + E(\tilde{R}_t)} \right] \text{COV}(\tilde{\epsilon}_{t-1}, \tilde{R}_{mt-1}). \tag{10.25}$$

Finally, taking the ratio of (10.24) and (10.25), we have

$$\frac{\text{COV}(\tilde{V}_{t-1}, \tilde{R}_{mt-1})}{E_{t-2}(\tilde{V}_{t-1})} = \text{COV}(\tilde{\epsilon}_{t-1}, \tilde{R}_{mt-1}) \tag{10.26}$$

and from (10.20),

$$\frac{\text{COV}[\tilde{E}_{t-1}(\tilde{X}_t), \tilde{R}_{mt-1}]}{E_{t-2}(\tilde{X}_t)} = \text{COV}(\tilde{\epsilon}_{t-1}, \tilde{R}_{mt-1}). \tag{10.27}$$

Therefore the covariance between the value of the firm at $t - 1$ and the market portfolio per unit of $E_{t-2}(\tilde{V}_{t-1})$ is identical to the covariance between the expected value of earnings and the market portfolio per unit of $E_{t-2}(\tilde{X}_t)$.

Now the value of the firm as of $t - 2$ may be written as

$$V_{t-2} = \frac{E_{t-2}(\tilde{V}_{t-1}) - \phi_{t-1} \text{COV}(\tilde{V}_{t-1}, \tilde{R}_{mt-1})}{1 + R_{ft-1}}$$

$$= E_{t-2}(\tilde{V}_{t-1}) \left[\frac{1 - \phi_{t-1} \text{COV}(\tilde{V}_{t-1}, \tilde{R}_{mt-1})/E_{t-2}(\tilde{V}_{t-1})}{1 + R_{ft-1}} \right],$$

and using (10.26), we have

$$V_{t-2} = E_{t-2}(\tilde{V}_{t-1}) \left[\frac{1 - \phi_{t-1} \text{COV}(\tilde{\epsilon}_{t-1}, \tilde{R}_{mt-1})}{1 + R_{ft-1}} \right]$$

$$= E_{t-2}(\tilde{V}_{t-1}) \left[\frac{1}{1 + E(\tilde{R}_{t-1})} \right]. \tag{10.28}$$

We can rewrite $E_{t-2}(\tilde{V}_{t-1})$ by using (10.24) to obtain

$$V_{t-2} = E_{t-2}(\tilde{X}_t) \left[\frac{1}{1 + E(\tilde{R}_t)} \right] \left[\frac{1}{1 + E(\tilde{R}_{t-1})} \right],$$

and in general, we obtain the recursive relationship

$$V_\tau = E_\tau(\tilde{X}_t) \left[\frac{1}{1 + E(\tilde{R}_{\tau+1})} \right] \cdots \left[\frac{1}{1 + E(\tilde{R}_t)} \right]. \tag{10.29}$$

The market value of the firm at τ is the expected value at τ of the earnings to be realized at time t, discounted at the risk-adjusted discount rates for each of the periods between τ and t.

Fama points out that if the CAPM is assumed to hold, only uncertainty about $\tilde{E}_\tau(\tilde{X}_t)$ is admissible. Uncertainty about the risk-adjusted discount rates, $E(\tilde{R}_{\tau+1})$, ..., $E(\tilde{R}_t)$, is not admissible. The risk adjustments in the discount rates arise because of the uncertain evolution through time of the expected value of cash flow.

If we are to obtain the usual solution to the multiperiod capital-budgeting problem, we must also assume that the risk-free rate, R_{ft}, the covariance, $\text{COV}(\tilde{\varepsilon}_t, \tilde{R}_{mt})$, and the risk-adjusted rate, $E(\tilde{R}_t)$, are constant through time. If so, we obtain

$$V_0 = \frac{E_0(\tilde{X}_t)}{[1 + E(\tilde{R})]^t},$$

which, of course, is equal to Eq. (10.1) for an example with cash flow only in the last time period.

Bogue and Roll [1974] show that if the expected risk-free rate and therefore the expected portfolio opportunity set are stochastic, then the multiperiod capital-budgeting problem is not easily solved. Not only must the investor consider systematic risk in the usual CAPM sense, but he must also take into account two additional factors: (1) the risk of fluctuations in the risk-free rate and (2) the covariation risk of the intermediate value of the project. These results are consistent with various multiperiod versions of the CAPM (e.g., Merton [1973] and Long [1974]) which assume a stochastic risk-free rate.

Fama [1977] carefully examines the types of variability admissible under a stationary CAPM which assumes that the portfolio opportunity set is nonstochastic. In general, the only admissible form of uncertainty is in the expected cash earnings in time t, assessed as of time $\tau < t$. The risk-adjusted discount rates in each future time period are known with certainty at time τ. Given the somewhat unpalatable assumptions of the stationary multiperiod CAPM, we have the result that the usual textbook treatment of multiperiod capital budgeting under uncertainty is reasonable.

Although the issues discussed in this chapter may seem exceedingly academic to the reader, they are no less important than the issue of whether to use the NPV or the IRR criterion as discussed in Chapter 2. Proper use of capital-budgeting techniques is not a trivial issue. Until the question was posed by Bogue and Roll, little formal consideration had been given to the problems involved in the complex issue of multiperiod capital budgeting under uncertainty. Although the Fama article does much to clarify matters, we see that the standard solution to the problem requires a set of fairly restrictive assumptions.

D. COMPARING RISKY COST STRUCTURES

Applied capital budgeting problems are almost always multiperiod and frequently it is reasonable to assume that the revenues from two mutually exclusive projects will be identical. For example, this is the usual assumption in machine replacement problems. The revenues of the firm will be invariant to the choice of equipment. Therefore the usual capital-budgeting process simply discounts the various in-cremental costs associated with the mutually exclusive alternatives and chooses the project with the lowest discounted cost.

Assuming that the multiperiod risk-adjusted rate of return is the appropriate technique for capital budgeting, how should it be used to compare cash outflows on a risk-adjusted basis? As we shall see, the correct approach discounts the expected costs at a lower rate when the project has greater risk. In order to develop this result let's look at a simple one-period case. At the end of the period, the after-tax cash flows from operations may be written as follows:

$$\widetilde{CF} = (\tilde{R} - \widetilde{VC})(1 - \tau_c) + \tau_c \, dep,$$

where

CF = after-tax cash flows for capital-budgeting purposes,
$\ R$ = end-of-period revenues,
VC = end-of-period variable cash costs,
$\ \tau_c$ = the corporate tax rate,
dep = depreciation.

The rate of return, $\tilde{r}_j$, on the project is the return on investment (where investment is I_0):

$$\tilde{r}_j = \frac{(\tilde{R} - \widetilde{VC})(1 - \tau_c) - \tau_c \, dep - I_0}{I_0}.$$

If we assume that the project is fully depreciated during the period, then $I_0 = dep$, and we have

$$\tilde{r}_j = \frac{(\tilde{R} - \widetilde{VC})(1 - \tau_c) - I_0(1 - \tau_c)}{I_0}$$

$$= \frac{(1 - \tau_c)}{I_0} \tilde{R} - \frac{(1 - \tau_c)}{I_0} \widetilde{VC} - (1 - \tau_c).$$

Using the properties of random variables derived in Chapter 5, we can write the covariance between the return on the project and the return on the market portfolio as

$$\text{COV}(\tilde{r}_j, \tilde{r}_m) = \frac{(1 - \tau_c)}{I_0} \text{COV}(\tilde{R}, \tilde{r}_m) - \frac{(1 - \tau_c)}{I_0} \text{COV}(\widetilde{VC}, \tilde{r}_m). \quad (10.30)$$

Equation (10.30) shows that the covariance risk of a project can be partitioned into two parts: the covariance risk of its revenue stream, and the covariance risk of its cost stream. Note that if the costs have positive covariance with the market in the sense that they are high when the market return is high and vice versa, then the covariance risk will be large and negative. This implies that the cost streams of riskier projects should be discounted at lower (and even negative) discount rates in order to properly adjust for risk. Note also that Eq. (10.30) can be rewritten in terms of systematic risk by dividing both sides by the variance of market return. This yields

$$\beta_j = \left(\frac{1 - \tau_c}{I_0}\right)\beta_{jR} - \left(\frac{1 - \tau_c}{I_0}\right)\beta_{jVC}, \quad (10.31)$$

where

β_j = the systematic risk of the project where $j = 1, 2,$
β_{jR} = the systematic risk of the revenue stream,
β_{jVC} = the systematic risk of the variable cost stream.

As an illustration, consider the following example. The two mutually exclusive projects given in Table 10.1 have identical revenue streams but different costs. In addition to the project cash flows, the table also provides the rate of return on the market portfolio, $\tilde{r}_m$, and the risk-free rate, r_f, in each of the three equally likely states of the world. The cost of the project, I_0, is $100 and the corporate tax rate is 50%. The rate of return, r_j, on each project (columns 7 and 11) is calculated as follows:

$$\tilde{r}_j = \frac{\widetilde{CF}_j - I_0}{I_0}.$$

By inspecting the cash flows in Table 10.1 we see that the revenue streams are positively correlated with the market return, and so are the variable cost streams of

Table 10.1 Projects with different risky costs

				Project 1				Project 2			
	Proba-bility	$\tilde{r}_m$	r_f	$\tilde{R}_1$	$\widetilde{VC}_1$	$\widetilde{CF}_1$	$\tilde{r}_1$	$\tilde{R}_2$	$\widetilde{VC}_2$	$\widetilde{CF}_2$	$\tilde{r}_2$
State 1	.33	.26	.04	610	500	105	.05	610	495	107.5	.075
State 2	.33	.14	.04	600	470	115	.15	600	500	100.0	0
State 3	.33	.20	.04	610	520	95	−.05	610	505	102.5	.025

the projects. However, the correlation between the variable cost stream of project 1 and the market return is so strong that it causes the project's net cash flow, CF_1, to be negatively correlated with the market. The higher risk of the first project requires that its cash costs be discounted at a lower rate.

Table 10.2 shows the results of computations of various statistics necessary for the calculation of the risk-adjusted rate of return. By using the CAPM and the statistics in Table 10.2, we can calculate the appropriate discount rates for the projects' net cash flow streams, or their cost streams. Using project 1 as an example, we employ the CAPM

$$E(r_j) = r_f + [E(r_m) - r_f]\beta_j,$$

and use Eq. (10.31) to compute the correct, *adjusted betas*:

$$\beta_j = \left(\frac{1 - \tau_c}{I_0}\right)\beta_{jR} - \left(\frac{1 - \tau_c}{I_0}\right)\beta_{jVC}.$$

Substituting data from Table 10.2, we see that the systematic risk for the project is a weighted average of the adjusted betas for the revenue and cost streams.

$$-.833 = \left(\frac{1 - .5}{100}\right)(83.33) - \left(\frac{1 - .5}{100}\right)(250)$$

$$= .4167 - 1.25.$$

Now we have $\beta_1 = -.833$, $\beta_{1,R} = .4167$, and $\beta_{1,VC} = -1.25$.

Table 10.2 A list of relevant statistics

	Mean			Covariance with r_m			β		
	r	R	VC	r	R	VC	r	R	VC
Project 1	.050	603.33	496.67	−.0020	.20	.60	−.833	83.33	250.00
Project 2	.033	603.33	500.00	.0015	.20	−.10	.625	83.33	−41.67
Market return	.200	—	—	.0024	—	—	1.000	—	—

Figure 10.1 graphs the security market line given by the CAPM and shows the betas and required rates of return for the project's cash flows, its revenue stream, and its cost stream.[5] Note that the cost stream should be discounted at -16%. Similar calculations show that for project 2 the cost stream should be discounted at 7.33%.

---

[5] It may seem unusual to discount cash flows at negative rates of return. Normally, this would not be the case because real-world projects are almost always positively correlated with the market. However, in the artificially constructed example above, it is perfectly consistent with the CAPM to require negative rates on projects with negative betas.

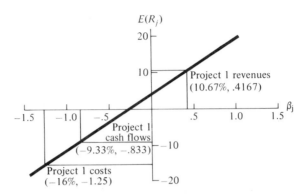

Fig. 10.1 Systematic risk and required rate of return for Project 1

Thus we have demonstrated the result that the riskier cash stream should be discounted at the lower rate. The results for both projects are summarized in Table 10.3.

A word of caution to the practitioner is appropriate at this point. It is never advisable to totally ignore revenues or the riskiness of the revenue stream (even though this is frequent practice). In the above example, the market required rate of return on project 2 is 14%, and the expected rate of return (the mean return in Table 10.2) is only 3.3%. Therefore, project 2 is unacceptable under any circumstances. This may have been true for both projects. The practitioner who ignores revenues and chooses the project with the lower discounted cost may easily accept a project with negative NPV. Costs tell only half the story. Decision-making on the basis of cost comparisons alone is inappropriate unless the decision maker is absolutely sure that the mutually exclusive projects all have positive net present value.

Table 10.3 Discount rates and adjusted betas

	Discount rates			Adjusted β		
	CF	R	VC	CF	R	VC
Project 1	−9.33%	10.67%	−16.00%	−.833	.4167	−1.2500
Project 2	14.00%	10.67%	7.33%	.625	.4167	.2083

Given the results of Fama [1977], which were discussed in the previous section, it is possible to extend the one-period cost comparison procedure into a multiperiod framework. So long as the market parameters are assumed *ex ante* to be stationary over time, we still have the result that riskier cost streams should be discounted at lower rates.

E. ABANDONMENT VALUE

A critical aspect of the capital-budgeting decision is the consideration of the residual value of the investment assets. The residual values will be known only at some future date so they are necessarily uncertain at the time investments are being made. However, for investments such as land and buildings, values may actually increase with inflation in future years. For machinery and equipment, subject to a high rate of obsolescence, the residual value may drop to virtually nothing even before the end of the expected life of the machine used in the initial capital-budgeting analysis.

Clearly, the residual value of an investment asset may be substantial. Hence to make a capital-budgeting decision without taking residual value into account may lead to serious errors. In addition, for a number of reasons, the sales value or *abandonment value* of an asset may be greater than the present value of the continued use of the asset by the firm which owns the asset.

Thus there are two aspects of the abandonment decision. One aspect is to take the resale value or abandonment value of the asset into account in the capital-budget analysis. The second is the requirement that the analysis consider the optimal period at which abandonment of the asset or its sale at its current market value should take place.

The first article emphasizing the importance of taking abandonment value into account was published by Robichek and Van Horne [1967], who proposed that the project be abandoned in the first year that its abandonment value exceeds the present value of the remaining expected cash flows associated with the continued operation of the investment. They pointed out that considering abandonment before the end of the life of a project could increase the project's NPV so that an otherwise unacceptable project would become desirable.

In a comment on the Robichek-Van Horne analysis, Dyl and Long [1969] point out that there may be an even greater advantage to abandonment in a period subsequent to the first instance when abandonment value exceeds the present value of continued operations. They argue that it is necessary to consider future abandonment possibilities in addition to the year in which abandonment value may exceed the present value of continued operations. Consideration of future abandonment values will provide a measure of maximum present value resulting from the selection of the optimum abandonment timing.

Robichek-Van Horne acknowledge that deferred abandonment may be preferred to present abandonment. However, they observe that future operating cash flows and abandonment values are not known with certainty. They suggest that a practical operational procedure does not require a forecast over the full estimated economic life of the investment, and go on to offer a revised formulation which requires only one period for which the present value of continued operation exceeds abandonment value. If such an instance exists, the project is held another year and then reevaluated. The reevaluation would be based on the new formulation of expectations made at that time. Thus it is not required that the decision maker provide a complete enumeration of all possible present values of continued operations and of abandonment values in future years. The benefits of a sequential decision process can be obtained.

Joy [1976] has formulated a clear statement of the revised Robichek-Van Horne abandonment value algorithm. Let

C_t = expected operating cash flow in year t,

k_0 = cost of capital,

n = maximum expected feasible life of project,

AV_a = expected abandonment value in period a.

Step 1. Set $a = 1$.

Step 2. Compute NPV_a, where

$$NPV_a = \sum_{t=0}^{a} \frac{C_t}{(1 + k_0)^t} + \frac{AV_a}{(1 + k_0)^a} - I_0$$

= NPV of project, given abandonment in

period a.

Step 3. If $NPV_a > 0$, accept. If $NPV_a < 0$, go to step 4.

Step 4. Repeat steps 2 and 3 for $a = 2, 3, \ldots, n$ until

either $NPV_a > 0$ for some a: accept,

or $NPV_a < 0$ for all a: reject.

Joy points out that the basic decision is whether to relinquish the asset now or to hold it for one more period. A decision to keep the asset requires only one instance where the present value of continuing to hold the asset exceeds the abandonment value. The same analysis applies to currently owned assets. The decision to abandon leads to immediate abandonment. Otherwise the asset will be held for one additional year and a keep-vs.-abandon decision will then again be made. At that time revisions in estimates of expected future operating cash flows and abandonment values may be made.

Joy then points out that the foregoing analysis is applicable to accept-reject decisions for independent investments. However, if mutually exclusive projects are being compared, it is necessary to make the analysis over the full planning horizon for each to determine which of the projects dominates. Hence an exhaustive search for abandonment possibilities over a full planning horizon will be required utilizing the Dyl-Long approach. Joy formulates this abandonment algorithm as follows:

Step 1. Compute NPV_a for $a = 1, 2, \ldots, n$ for each project.

Step 2. Select the maximum value of NPV_a for each project, and select that project with the largest positive maximum value of NPV_a.

A comparison of the accept-reject decision approach with the mutually exclusive choice decision approach is illustrated utilizing the data presented in Table 10.4. The investment costs of the project are assumed to be $10,000. Present value estimates are made for two series of flows. Line 1 is the estimated present value of the project in period a if operated for its remaining years of life and then abandoned. Line 2 is the estimated present value of the project if abandoned in period a. A plausible real-world counterpart to such a pattern of flows could be an investment in a fruit or citrus orchard. With such an investment there is always the alternative of selling the annual product from the orchard or to sell the orchard at various time periods. The values from selling the product of the orchard may fluctuate with estimates of demand and supply conditions in those markets in particular years. In addition, there may be a demand for the trees for decorative or other purposes which will be sensitive to fluctuations in demand conditions in individual years, and over longer periods of time supply conditions may change as well. Thus a wide variety of patterns in gains from selling the product of the orchard, selling the orchard for future product yields, or selling the orchard for immediate decorative-tree purposes could create a wide variety of year-by-year present value estimates.

Let us first illustrate the accept-reject decision. The first column of figures in Table 10.4 provides a basis for undertaking the investment and deferring the abandonment decision for at least one year. The estimated present value of the project at the beginning of period 1 if operated for five additional periods and then abandoned is $11,000. Hence the net value of the project is positive. In addition, the NPV of the project with deferred abandonment is greater than the estimated present value of abandonment of the project in period 1. At the beginning of period 2, another assessment of future prospects could be made. If the estimates are as indicated in column 2, the decision would be to continue to operate the project another year.

At the beginning of the third year another analysis is made with the estimates as indicated in the column for period 3. Now the estimated present value of the project given abandonment in period 3 is $12,000. The estimated present value of the project in period 3 if operated for the remaining years of its life and then abandoned is seen to be only $11,000. According to the Robichek-Van Horne formulation as revised by Joy, the project would then be abandoned in the third year. However, in our judgment the Dyl-Long criticism is still valid. Before such a determination could be

Table 10.4

	Period				
Series of flows	1	2	3	4	5
1. Estimated present values of project in period a if operated for remaining years of life and then abandoned	11,000	11,000	11,000	10,000	9,000
2. Estimated present value of abandonment in period a	4,000	6,000	12,000	10,000	8,000

made, a complete enumeration would be required over the remaining years of the investment planning horizon. For example, if in the fourth year the estimated present value of abandonment in period 4 were $13,000, then it would have been even more favorable to defer the abandonment until the fourth year rather than to abandon the project in the third year. Thus the Dyl-Long comment remains valid even when the accept-reject decision is involved. Complete enumeration can be avoided for any individual year until the year in which a tentative decision to abandon the project is made. Then it is still necessary to make an analysis for the remaining years of the planning horizon to determine the year in which abandonment will yield the highest present value.

Thus far in the analysis the discussion has been in terms of best estimates of the cash flows over the time pattern of years. The analysis could be extended by an additional step which would consider estimates of probabilities of various levels of cash flow in each year and then show the calculations of expected values and their standard deviations. However, in terms of the central issues of the role of abandonment value and the optimal timing of abandonment covered in the literature, the discussion to this point covers both issues.

With the rise in replacement or market values of investments that has developed as a result of the high rate of inflation in the United States which began in 1966, the issue of abandonment value takes on increasingly greater significance for the planning and control of existing operations. Management is under increased pressure to improve revenue levels and more effectively control cost increases in order to justify not only new investments but also the continued operation of present investments instead of selling them in the open market where a greater NPV could be realized. Thus the issue is whether to continue operations or to abandon by selling at higher current present values. This issue is developed in the following illustrative example.

The Cincinnati Company operates a cement factory. The historical depreciated cost of the factory and equipment is $10,000,000. It has an expected life of another 10 years. The effective corporate tax rate is 40%, and the applicable cost of capital is 12%. The current replacement cost of the plant is $20,000,000.

Over a 10-year planning horizon, it is estimated that revenues will be $10,000,000 per year and total costs (excluding depreciation) will be $6,600,000 per year. The Cincinnati Company will use the double-declining balance method of depreciation.

On the basis of the present estimates of revenues and costs, what is the NPV of the cement factory? The solution is given below,[6]

$$\text{NPV} = [3,400,000(1 - \tau_c) + \tau_c \text{ dep}] \text{ PVIF}_a$$

$$= 2,040,000(5.650) + .4(10,000,000)(.643)$$

$$= 11,526,000 + 2,572,000$$

$$= 14,098,000,$$

---

[6] *Note:* PVIF$_a$ is the present-value factor for an annuity with payments at the end of each year for a years.

that is, Cincinnati Company can sell the plant for $20,000,000, which exceeds the present value of future net flows by $5,902,000.

Thus we see that the present value of the new cement factory is positive. However, in relation to the plant's current replacement cost of $20 million, the investment in continued operation is simply not justifiable. In other words, the present value derived from continuing to operate the cement factory is $14.1 million. However, the plant could be sold in the open market at something like $20 million. Thus there is a larger addition to present value to be achieved by "abandoning" the plant rather than to continue its operation.

This illustrates a general problem facing many business firms today. Inflation has pushed up the replacement costs of plant and equipment. Also, materials and wage costs continue to rise. As a consequence, there is a squeeze on profits even in nominal terms and profits have to rise in nominal terms for profit ratios to be maintained. Market values of shares have not kept up with inflation.

On the average the market values of nonfinancial corporations are 70% to 80% of the current replacement values of their assets. Often firms can buy other companies below replacement values while new investments in their own line of business do not offer prospects of NPV's that would be positive. This is one of the reasons why new investments in the economy as a whole have lagged. Profit margins capitalized at applicable discount factors result in present values that are below current replacement values of the investment projects.

SUMMARY

By considering the relations between periods recursively, Bogue and Roll [1974] develop an equation for multiperiod capital budgeting. In addition to the usual beta risk, the resulting equation contains two additional risk premia: the covariation risk of the intermediate values of the project and the risk premium related to the risk of interest fluctuations. Fama [1977] points out that in a world in which securities are priced according to the CAPM, the only admissible form of uncertainty is the expected cash earnings in time t assessed one period earlier. The risk-free rate, the covariance, and the risk-adjusted rate are then constant through time and the traditional capital budgeting model can be employed.

In most equipment replacement problems, it is plausible that revenues from two mutually exclusive types of equipment will be identical. However, the riskiness of the cost streams may be different. We are accustomed to increasing the amount of risk-adjustment in the capitalization factor applied to riskier net cash flow streams. This has the effect of penalizing riskier investments. When the streams under comparison are costs alone, we need to have higher present values for riskier cost streams. This is accomplished by lowering the discount rate, rather than increasing it.

Another important aspect of the assessment of risky investments is to estimate residual values. In addition, the sales or abandonment value of an asset may be greater than the present value of the continued use of the asset. The initial criterion proposed abandonment in the first year that abandonment value exceeded the present value of continued use of the asset. Later studies pointed out the necessity of consideration of abandonment possibilities in future years to obtain the maximum present value from the selection of the optimal time for abandonment.

PROBLEM SET

10.1 Which of the following types of uncertainty are inadmissible in a multiperiod model if we are using the CAPM? Why?

a) $COV(\tilde{\varepsilon}_t, \tilde{R}_{m,t})$

b) $\tilde{R}_{ft}$

c) $E_{t-1}(\tilde{X}_t)$

d) $COV(\tilde{V}_{t-1}, \tilde{R}_{m,t-1})$

e) $(E(\tilde{R}_{m,t}) - R_{ft})/\sigma^2(\tilde{R}_{m,t})$

10.2 The Ramsden Company is installing 10 new forklift trucks. Electric trucks cost $8000 each, while gas-powered trucks cost $5000 each. The operating costs for the electric trucks would be $5200 per truck per year compared with $6000 per gas truck for the 8-year expected life of each vehicle. Expected salvage value is zero and straight-line depreciation is to be used. Ramsden will apply a 10% discount factor for analysis of the electric trucks and a 2% differential to the gas trucks due to their higher operating risks. The applicable tax rate is 40%. Should electric or gas forklift trucks be purchased by Ramsden?

10.3 Your firm is trying to choose between two mutually exclusive projects. Both cost $10,000, have a five-year life and no salvage value. The company uses straight-line depreciation and the corporate tax rate is 40%. Over the life of the project the annual expected rate of return on the market portfolio is 15% and the risk-free rate is 5%. The first project has expected revenues of $5000 per year with an adjusted β_R of 1.5 and expected variable costs of $2333 per year with an adjusted β_{VC} of -1.4 (i.e., both the revenues and variable costs are positively correlated with the market). The second project has expected revenues of $6067 per year with an adjusted β_R of 1.3 and expected variable costs of $2400 with an adjusted β_{VC} of .3 (i.e., revenues are positively correlated with the market, and variable costs are negatively correlated with the market). Which project should the firm accept? [*Note:* Adjusted β's are discussed in Section D of Chapter 10.]

10.4 The following investment decision is being considered by Citrus Farms. For $7000 the company can acquire ownership of 10 acres of 15-year-old orange trees and a 15-year lease on the land. The productive life of an orange tree is divided into stages as follows:

State	Age of trees, years	Expected annual profit from 10 acres, $
Peak	16–20	1000
Adult	21–25	900
Mature	26–30	800

There is a market for decorative orange trees. Suppliers will buy trees and remove them according to a schedule based on the age of the tree. Expected prices that can be obtained for the 10-acre harvest are: $9000 at end of age 20, $12,000 at age 25, and $8000 at age 30. Citrus Farms has a 10% cost of capital.

a) What is the present value of each alternative? Since the land and anything on it will belong to the leasor in 15 years, assume that once the trees are harvested the land will not be replanted by Citrus.

b) As an alternative to this investment, Citrus can use the $7000 to buy a new orange-sorting machine. The machine would reduce sorting expenses by $1300 a year for 15 years. Which investment would you make? Why? Assume that all other investment opportunities for the next 15 years will earn the cost of capital.

c) In the 10th year Citrus discovers that everyone else with 25-year-old trees has sold them. As a consequence, the price the firm can get for the trees is only $8000. Since so many trees have been sold for decoration, small orange crops are expected for the next five years. As a result, the price of oranges will be higher. Your acreage will yield $1200 a year. The selling price of your trees in another five years is expected to be still depressed to $6000. What should you do?

d) Given the situation in (c), what was the NPV of your actual investment over the 15-year period?

e) What would the NPV be if the trees had been sold in year 10 for $8000?

10.5 *Southern Electric Power Company*[7]

The State Public Service Commission (PSC) is charged with the responsibility of regulating the two large public utility companies in the state. The PSC is comprised of seven persons; four elected, one gubernatorial appointee and one representative each from the two public utilities.

The PSC is currently considering a capacity expansion program submitted by Southern Electric Power (SE). SE operates three power plants as shown in Table 10.5. The population in the area served by SE has been growing 2% per year. This trend is expected to continue for at least the next 10 years. Industrial growth is even more rapid, about 4% per year. As a result, demand for electricity is growing at approximately 3% per year. Peakload demand is very near SE's capacity, so it is necessary to begin some expansion within the year.

Table 10.5

Type of plant	Date constructed	Percent of current power needs supplied	Remaining life in years
Coal	1946	25	30
Hydroelectric	1958	10	35
Natural gas generating	1963	65	45

Another problem the company is confronted with is the growing shortage of natural gas. Last year SE was unable to buy enough natural gas to meet the full electric power needs of the area. The company was able to buy electricity generated by a company in an adjoining state which was coal, but there is no assurance that this source of power can be relied on in the future.

Given the uncertainty of future natural gas supplies, and the fact that hydroelectric power is already being fully utilized, SE feels the only sensible course is to expand its own coal generating capacity. This would be especially desirable since it would use the large soft coal deposits in the northern part of the state.

---

[7] This is really a short case, rather than a problem in the usual sense of the word. It does not necessarily have a simple, cut and dried solution.

There are two alternatives for increasing the capacity for coal generation. For $40,000,000 it would be possible to double the generating capacity of the existing plant. This would fully satisfy the growing demand for electricity for the next six to eight years, after which time additional capacity would be needed. The expansion would have a useful life of 30 years.

The existing plant is located 20 miles from the center of the largest city in the state. In 1946, when the plant was originally built, the location was selected specifically to be at a considerable distance from any populated area so that the smoke produced by burning coal would not be an environmental nuisance.

In 30 years the city has grown considerably. Heavily populated suburbs are now located within four miles of the plant, and pollution created by SE is a growing political issue. The company believes it probable that within the next five years political pressure will require that smoke scrubbers be installed at the existing plant (Table 10.6). Scrubbers can be installed any time at the existing plant for $4,000,000. If plant capacity is doubled and scrubbers are installed at that time, the total cost would be $5,500,000. (This would be in addition to the base cost of the new plant discussed below.) If the installation of scrubbers is postponed, and carried out as a separate capital investment, the total cost is estimated to be $8,000,000 subject to the same probability that installation might never occur (see Table 10.6).

Table 10.6 Probability that scrubbers will be required

Time frame	Probability
within 2 years	0%
within 3 years	10%
within 4 years	50%
within 5 years	40%

The alternative to expanding the capacity of the old plant is to build an entirely new plant. Such a plant would cost $110,000,000 and would have a maximum capacity of three times the existing coal plant. With the new capacity in addition to the existing plant, energy needs could be met for the next 18 to 20 years. The useful life of the plant would be 40 years. If desired, the capacity of the new plant could be increased to the point that the old plant could be abandoned and capacity would still be adequate for the same period. The additional cost of the extra capacity would be $22,082,000, which would be depreciated over the full life of the plan. If the old plant is abandoned, equipment worth $7,000,000 could be used in the new plant, and sale of the land would provide additional capital of $3,000,000.

Annual operating costs of the old plant are $2,000,000. If its capacity is doubled, operating costs will rise by $1,500,000. Cost of operating the new plant will be $4,000,000 per year. If the old plant is abandoned, operating costs of the new plant will increase by $450,000 per year for the remaining life of the old plant.

SE uses straight-line depreciation to zero salvage value on all capital investments discussed here. The cost of scrubbers is amortized over the remaining life of the plant in which they are installed. Book value of the existing coal plant is $10,000,000.

SE has an effective tax rate of 40%. SE's weighted average cost of capital is 10%. Revenues and other costs will be the same under either alternative. Excess capacity can be sold outside the state at the same rate as within the state.

1. As a representative of the utility company, you are concerned with maximizing the present value of the project. Analyze the alternatives and indicate your recommendation.

2. Keeping in mind that you are working only with costs, how would you adjust the discount rate to account for: (a) the extra uncertainty for any alternative which includes delayed installation of smoke scrubbers; (b) the pollution that would result from operating the old plant without smoke scrubbers?

3. How would these factors affect your recommendation? As an elected member of the PSC, what factors would you include in your analysis of the project? How would each of these factors bear on your decision?

REFERENCES

BOGUE, M. C., and R. R. ROLL, "Capital Budgeting of Risky Projects with 'Imperfect' Markets for Physical Capital," *The Journal of Finance*, May 1974, 601–613.

BRENNAN, M., "An Approach to the Valuation of Uncertain Income Streams," *The Journal of Finance*, June 1973, 661–674.

DYL, E. A., and H. W. LONG, "Abandonment Value and Capital Budgeting: Comment," *Journal of Finance*, March 1969, 88–95.

FAMA, E. F., "Multiperiod Consumption-Investment Decisions," *American Economic Review*, March 1970, 163–174.

———, "Risk-Adjusted Discount Rates and Capital Budgeting Under Uncertainty," *The Journal of Financial Economics*, August 1977, 3–24.

———, and J. D. MACBETH, "Tests of the Multiperiod Two-Parameter Model," *The Journal of Financial Economics*, May 1974, 43–66.

JOY, O. M., "Abandonment Values and Abandonment Decisions: A Clarification," *Journal of Finance*, September 1976, 1225–1228.

LONG, J. B., Jr., "Stock Prices, Inflation and the Term Structure of Interest Rates," *The Journal of Financial Economics*, July 1974, 131–170.

MERTON, R. C., "An Intertemporal Capital Asset Pricing Model," *Econometrica*, September 1973, 867–887.

MYERS, S. C., "Procedures for Capital Budgeting Under Uncertainty," *Industrial Management Review*, Spring 1968, 1–20.

———, and S. M. TURNBULL, "Capital Budgeting and the Capital Asset Pricing Model: Good News and Bad News," *Journal of Finance*, May 1977, 321–332.

ROBICHEK, A. A., and J. C. VAN HORNE, "Abandonment Value and Capital Budgeting," *Journal of Finance*, December 1967, 577–590.

Chapter 11

Capital Structure and the Cost of Capital: Theory

The average cost of capital to any firm is completely independent of its capital structure and is equal to the capitalization rate of a pure equity stream of its class.

F. Modigliani and M. Miller, "The Cost of Capital, Corporation Finance, and the Theory of Investment," *The American Economic Review*, June 1958, p. 268

Funds for investment are provided to the firm by investors who hold various types of claims on the cash flows returned by investments. Debt holders hold contracts (bonds) which promise to pay them fixed schedules of interest in the future in exchange for their cash now. Equity holders provide retained earnings (internal equity provided by *existing* shareholders) or purchase new shares (external equity provided by *new* shareholders). They do so in return for claims on the residual earnings of the firm in the future. Also, shareholders retain control of the investment decision while bondholders have no direct control except for various types of indenture provisions in the bond which may constrain the decision-making of shareholders. In addition to these two basic categories of claimants, there are others such as holders of convertible debentures, leases, preferred stock, nonvoting stock, and warrants.

Each investor category is confronted with a different type of risk and therefore each requires a different expected rate of return in order to provide funds to the firm. The required rate of return is the opportunity cost to the investor of investing his scarce resources elsewhere in projects of equivalent risk. As we shall see, the fact that shareholders are the ones who decide whether to accept or reject new projects is critical to understanding the cost of capital. They will accept only those projects which increase their expected utility of wealth. Each project must earn, on a risk-adjusted basis, enough net cash flow to pay investors (bondholders and shareholders) their expected rates of return, to repay the principal amount which they originally provided, and to have something left over which will increase the wealth of existing shareholders. The cost of capital is the minimum risk-adjusted rate of return which a project must earn in order to be acceptable to shareholders.

The investment decision cannot be made without knowledge of the cost of capital. Consequently many textbooks introduce the concept of the cost of capital before they discuss investment decisions. It probably does not matter which topic comes first. Both topics are important and they are interrelated. Figure 11.1 shows the investment decision as the intersection of the demand and supply of investment capital. All projects are assumed to have equivalent risk. Also, fund sources have equal risk (in other words, in the figure, we make no distinction between equity and debt). Chapters 2, 3, and 10 discussed the ranking of projects assuming that the appropriate cost of capital was known. The schedule of projects with their rates of return is sometimes called the marginal efficiency of investment schedule and is shown as the demand curve in Fig. 11.1. The supply of capital, represented as the marginal cost of capital curve, is assumed to be infinitely elastic. Implicitly, the projects are assumed to have equal risk. Therefore, the firm faces an infinite supply of capital at the rate $E(R_j)$ because it is assumed that the projects it offers are only a small portion of all investment in the economy. They affect neither the total risk of the economy nor the total supply of capital. The optimal amount of investment for the firm is I_j^*, and the marginally acceptable project must earn at least $E(R_j)$. All other projects, of course, earn more than the marginal cost of capital.

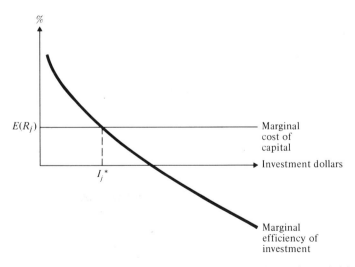

Fig. 11.1 Demand and supply of investment for projects of equal risk

Figure 11.1 is an oversimplified explanation of the relationship between the cost of capital and the amount of investment. However, it demonstrates the inter-relatedness of the two concepts. For a given schedule of investments, a rise in the cost of capital will result in less investment. This chapter shows how the firm's mix of debt and equity financing affects the cost of capital, it explains how the cost of capital is related to shareholders' wealth, and it shows how to extend the cost of capital concept to the situation where projects do not all have the same risk. Chapter 12 discusses the empirical evidence regarding capital structure and the cost of capital and provides a realistic application.

A. THE COST OF CAPITAL WITH PROJECTS OF EQUAL RISK

1. The Value of the Levered Firm

Modigliani and Miller [1958, 1963] wrote the seminal paper on cost of capital, corporate valuation, and capital structure. They assumed that:

- Capital markets are frictionless.
- Individuals can borrow and lend at the risk-free rate.
- There are no costs to bankruptcy.
- Firms issue only two types of claims: risk-free debt and (risky) equity.
- Corporate taxes are the only form of government levy (i.e., there are no wealth taxes on corporations and no personal taxes).
- All cash flow streams are perpetuities (i.e., no growth).

It goes without saying that many of these assumptions are unrealistic, but later we can show that relaxing them does not really change the major conclusions of the model of firm behavior which Modigliani and Miller provide.

One of the assumptions requires greater clarification. What is meant when we say that all firms have the same risk class? The implication is that the expected risky future net operating cash flows vary by, at most, a scale factor. Mathematically this is

$$\widetilde{NOI}_i = \lambda \widetilde{NOI}_j$$

where

$\widetilde{NOI}$ = the risky net cash flow from operations (cash flow before interest and taxes),
λ = a constant scale factor.

This implies that the expected future cash flows from the two firms (or projects) are perfectly correlated. Recalling the definition of correlation from Chapter 6,

$$r_{xy} \equiv \frac{\text{COV}(X, Y)}{\sigma_x \sigma_y},$$

and recalling from the properties of random variables (property 4, Chapter 6) that

$$\sigma(\widetilde{NOI}_i) = \sigma(\lambda \widetilde{NOI}_j) = \lambda\sigma(\widetilde{NOI}_j)$$

$$\sigma(\lambda \widetilde{NOI}_j) = \lambda\sigma(\widetilde{NOI}_j),$$

$$COV(\widetilde{NOI}_i, \lambda \widetilde{NOI}_j) = COV(\lambda \widetilde{NOI}_j, \lambda \widetilde{NOI}_j) = \lambda^2\, VAR(\widetilde{NOI}_j),$$

where

$\sigma(\cdot) = $ standard deviation,
$VAR(\cdot) = [\sigma(\cdot)]^2 = $ variance,
$r_{xy} = $ correlation coefficient between $\tilde{X}$ and $\tilde{Y}$,

we can see that the correlation coefficient between two random variables which differ by, at most a scale factor, is equal to 1. They are perfectly correlated:

$$r_{ij} = \frac{COV(\widetilde{NOI}_i, \widetilde{NOI}_j)}{\sigma(\widetilde{NOI}_i)\sigma(\widetilde{NOI}_j)}$$

$$= \frac{COV(\lambda \widetilde{NOI}_j, \widetilde{NOI}_j)}{\lambda\sigma(\widetilde{NOI}_j)\sigma(\widetilde{NOI}_j)} = 1.$$

If, instead of focusing on the level of NOI, we focus on the returns, the perfect correlation becomes obvious because the returns are identical, as shown below:

$$\tilde{R}_{i,t} = \frac{\widetilde{NOI}_{i,t} - NOI_{i,t-1}}{NOI_{i,t-1}},$$

and because $\widetilde{NOI}_{i,t} = \lambda\widetilde{NOI}_{j,t}$, we have

$$\tilde{R}_{i,t} = \frac{\lambda\widetilde{NOI}_{j,t} - \lambda NOI_{j,t-1}}{\lambda NOI_{j,t-1}} = \tilde{R}_{j,t}.$$

Therefore, if two streams of cash flow differ by, at most, a scale factor, they will have the same distributions of returns, the same risk, and will require the same expected return.

Suppose the assets of a firm return the same distribution of net operating cash flows each time period for an infinite number of time periods. This is a no-growth situation because the average cash flow does not change over time. We can value this after-tax stream of cash flows by discounting its expected value at the appropriate risk-adjusted rate. The value of an unlevered firm will be

$$V^U = \frac{E(\widetilde{NOI})(1 - \tau_c)}{\rho} \tag{11.1}$$

where

V^U = the present value of an unlevered firm (i.e., all equity),
$E(\widehat{NOI})$ = the average cash flow before interest and taxes,
τ_c = the corporate income tax rate,
ρ = the discount rate for an all equity firm.

This is the value of an unlevered firm because it represents the discounted value of a perpetual, non-growing stream of net operating cash flows after taxes which would accrue to shareholders if the firm had no debt. To clarify this point, let us look at the following *pro forma* cash flow statement:

R	Revenues
$-VC$	Variable costs of operations
$-F$	Fixed costs (i.e., administrative costs and depreciation)
NOI	Net operating income
$-rD$	Interest on debt (interest rate, r, times principal, D)
EBT	Earnings before taxes
$-T$	Taxes $= \tau_c(EBT)$, where τ_c is the corporate tax rate
NI	Net income

It is extremely important to distinguish between cash flows and the accounting definition of profit. After-tax cash flows from operations may be calculated as follows. Net operating income less taxes is

$$NOI - \tau_c(NOI).$$

Rewriting this using the fact that $NOI = R - VC - F$, we have

$$(R - VC - F)(1 - \tau_c).$$

This is operating income after taxes, but it is not yet a cash flow definition because a portion of fixed costs are noncash expenses such as depreciation and deferred taxes. Let us suppose that fixed costs can be partitioned in two parts: let F^* be the cash-fixed costs and "dep" be the noncash-fixed costs, therefore $F = F^* + \text{dep}$.

In order to convert after-tax operating income into cash flows, we must add back depreciation and other noncash expenses. Doing this, we have

$$(R - VC - F^* - \text{dep})(1 - \tau_c) + \text{dep},$$

which can be simplified to

$$(R - VC - F^*)(1 - \tau_c) + \tau_c \text{ dep}.$$

This is what is meant by *net operating cash flows after taxes*. (The same definition can be found in Chapter 2, p. 37.)

The derivations which follow are considerably simpler if we ignore the tax shield (τ_c dep) provided by depreciation and other noncash expenses. However, the reader should always keep in mind that hereafter when we write NOI, we always mean that it is defined in terms of the appropriate cash flows. It is *not*, strictly speaking, the same as accounting profit.

If there is no debt outstanding, interest costs are zero and shareholders receive $NOI - \tau_c(NOI) = NI$, which is the cash flow discounted in Eq. (11.1).

Next let us assume that the firm issues debt. The after-tax cash flows must be split up between debt holders and shareholders. Shareholders receive NI, net cash flows after interest and taxes, and bondholders receive interest on debt, rD. Mathematically, this is equivalent to

$$\widetilde{NI} + rD = (\widetilde{NOI} - rD)(1 - \tau_c) + rD$$
$$= \widetilde{NOI}(1 - \tau_c) + rD\tau_c. \tag{11.2}$$

The first part of this stream, $\widetilde{NOI}(1 - \tau_c)$, is exactly the same as the numerator of (11.1), with exactly the same risk. Therefore, recalling that it is a perpetual stream, we can discount it at the rate appropriate for an unlevered firm, ρ. The second part of the stream, $rD\tau_c$, is assumed to be risk free. Therefore, we shall discount it at the cost of risk-free debt, k_d. Consequently, the value of the levered firm is the sum of the discounted value of the two types of cash flow which it provides:

$$V^L = \frac{E(\widetilde{NOI})(1 - \tau_c)}{\rho} + \frac{rD\tau_c}{k_d}. \tag{11.3}$$

Note that rD is the perpetual stream of risk-free payments to bondholders and that k_d is the current market-required rate of return for the risk-free stream. Therefore, since the stream is perpetual, the market value of the bonds, B, is

$$B = rD/k_d. \tag{11.4}$$

Now we can rewrite Eq. (11.3) as

$$V^L = V^U + \tau_c B. \tag{11.5}$$

The value of the levered firm, V^L, is equal to the value of an unlevered firm, V^U, plus the tax shield provided by debt, $\tau_c B$. This is perhaps the single most important result in the theory of corporation finance obtained in the last 25 years. It says that in the absence of any market imperfections including corporate taxes (i.e., if $\tau_c = 0$), the value of the firm is completely independent of the type of financing used for its projects. Without taxes, we have

$$V^L = V^U, \quad \text{if } \tau_c = 0. \tag{11.5'}$$

However, when the government subsidizes interest payments to providers of debt capital by allowing the corporation to deduct interest payments on debt as an expense, the market value of the corporation can increase as it takes on more and more (risk-free) debt. Ideally (given the assumptions of the model) the firm should take on 100% debt.[1]

2. The Weighted Average Cost of Capital

Next, we can determine the cost of capital by using the fact that shareholders will require the rate of return on new projects to be greater than the opportunity cost of the funds supplied by them and bondholders. This condition is equivalent to requiring that original shareholders' wealth increase. From Eq. (11.3) we see that the change in the value of the levered firm, ΔV^L, with respect to a new investment, ΔI, is[2]

$$\frac{\Delta V^L}{\Delta I} = \frac{(1 - \tau_c)}{\rho} \frac{\Delta E(\widehat{NOI})}{\Delta I} + \tau_c \frac{\Delta B}{\Delta I}. \tag{11.6}$$

If we take the new project, the change in the value of the firm, ΔV^L, will also be equal to the change in the value of original shareholder's wealth, ΔS^o, plus the new equity required for the project, ΔS^n, plus the change in the value of bonds outstanding, ΔB^o, plus new bonds issued, ΔB^n:

$$\Delta V^L = \Delta S^o + \Delta S^n + \Delta B^o + \Delta B^n. \tag{11.7a}$$

Alternatively, the changes with respect to the new investment are

$$\frac{\Delta V^L}{\Delta I} = \frac{\Delta S^o}{\Delta I} + \frac{\Delta S^n}{\Delta I} + \frac{\Delta B^o}{\Delta I} + \frac{\Delta B^n}{\Delta I}. \tag{11.7b}$$

Because the old bondholders hold a contract which promises fixed payments of interest and principal, because the new project is assumed to be no riskier than those already outstanding, and especially because both old and new debt are assumed to be risk free, the change in the value of outstanding debt is zero ($\Delta B^o = 0$). Furthermore, the new project must be financed with either new debt, new equity, or both. This implies that[3]

$$\Delta I = \Delta S^n + \Delta B^n. \tag{11.8}$$

Using this fact (11.7b) can be rewritten as

$$\frac{\Delta V^L}{\Delta I} = \frac{\Delta S^o}{\Delta I} + \frac{\Delta S^n + \Delta B^n}{\Delta I} = \frac{\Delta S^o}{\Delta I} + 1. \tag{11.9}$$

---

[1] We shall see later in this chapter that this result is modified when we consider a world with both corporate and personal taxes, or one where bankruptcy costs are non-trivial.

[2] Note that τ_c and ρ do not change with ΔI. The cost of equity for an all-equity firm doesn't change because new projects are assumed to have the same risk as old ones do.

[3] Note that (11.8) does not require new issues of debt or equity to be positive. It is conceivable, for example, that the firm might issue $4000 in stock for a $1000 project and repurchase $3000 in debt.

In order for a project to be acceptable to original shareholders, it must increase their wealth. Therefore, they will require that

$$\frac{\Delta S^o}{\Delta I} = \frac{\Delta V^L}{\Delta I} - 1 > 0, \qquad (11.10)$$

which is equivalent to the requirement that $\Delta V^L/\Delta I > 1.$

When this condition is imposed on Eq. (11.6) we are able to determine the cost of capital[4]

$$\frac{\Delta V^L}{\Delta I} = \frac{(1 - \tau_c)}{\rho} \cdot \frac{\Delta E(\widetilde{NOI})}{\Delta I} + \tau_c \frac{\Delta B}{\Delta I} > 1,$$

or, by rearranging terms, we have

$$\frac{(1 - \tau_c) \, \Delta E(\widetilde{NOI})}{\Delta I} > \rho \left(1 - \tau_c \frac{\Delta B}{\Delta I}\right). \qquad (11.11)$$

The left-hand side of (11.11) is the after-tax change in net operating cash flows brought about by the new investment, in other words, the after-tax return on the project.[5] The right-hand side is the opportunity cost of capital applicable to the project. As long as the anticipated rate of return on investment is greater than the cost of capital, current shareholders' wealth will increase.

Note that if the corporate tax rate is zero the cost of capital is independent of capital structure (the ratio of debt to total assets). This result is consistent with Eq. (11.5'), which says that the value of the firm is independent of capital structure. On the other hand, if corporate taxes are paid, the cost of capital declines steadily as the proportion of new investment financed with debt increases. The value of the levered firm reaches a maximum when there is 100% debt financing (so long as all of the debt is risk free).

3. Two Definitions of Market Value Weights

Equation (11.11) defines what has often been called the weighted average cost of capital, WACC$^\tau$, for the firm:

$$\text{WACC}^\tau = \rho \left(1 - \tau_c \frac{\Delta B}{\Delta I}\right). \qquad (11.12)$$

An often debated question is the correct interpretation of $\Delta B/\Delta I$. Modigliani and Miller [1963, p. 441] interpret it by saying that

If B^*/V^* denotes the firm's long run "target" debt ratio ... then the firm can assume, to a first approximation at least, that for any particular investment $dB/dI = B^*/V^*$.

---

[4] Note that $\Delta B = \Delta B^n$ because ΔB^o is assumed to be zero.
[5] Chapter 2, the investment decision, stressed the point that the correct cash flows for capital budgeting purposes were always defined as net cash flows from operations after taxes. Equation (11.11) reiterates this point and shows that it is the *only* definition of cash flows which is consistent with the opportunity cost of capital for the firm.

Two questions arise in the interpretation of the leverage ratio, $\Delta B/\Delta I$. First, is the leverage ratio marginal or average? Modigliani and Miller, in the above quote, set the marginal ratio equal to the average by assuming the firm sets a long-run target ratio, which is constant. Even if this is the case, we still must consider a second issue, namely: Is the ratio to be measured as *book value leverage, replacement value leverage*, or *reproduction value leverage*? The last two definitions, as we shall see, are both market values. At least one of these three measures, book value leverage, can be ruled out immediately as being meaningless. In particular, there is no relationship whatsoever between book value concepts, such as retained earnings, and the economic value of equity.

The remaining two interpretations, replacement and reproduction value, make sense because they are both market value definitions. (First, what are they?) By replacement value, we mean the economic cost of putting a project in place. For capital projects, a large part of this cost is usually the cost of purchasing plant and equipment. In the Modigliani-Miller formulation, replacement cost is the market value of the investment in the project under consideration, ΔI. It is the denominator on both sides of the cost-of-capital inequality (11.11). On the other hand, reproduction value, ΔV, is the total present value of the stream of goods and services expected from the project. The two concepts can be compared by noting that the difference between them is the NPV of the project, that is,

$$\text{NPV} = \Delta V - \Delta I.$$

For a marginal project, where NPV = 0, replacement cost and reproduction value are equal.

Haley and Schall [1973, pp. 306–311] introduce an alternative cost of capital definition where the "target" leverage is the ratio of debt to reproduction value, as shown below:

$$\text{WACC}^\tau = \rho\left(1 - \tau_c\,\frac{\Delta B}{\Delta V}\right). \tag{11.13}$$

If the firm uses a reproduction value concept for its "target" leverage, it will seek to maintain a constant ratio of the market value of debt to the market value of the firm.

With the foregoing as background, we can now reconcile the apparent conflict in the measurement of leverage applicable to the determination of the relevant cost of capital for a new investment project. Modigliani and Miller define the target L^* as the average, in the long run, of the debt-to-value ratio or B^*/V^*. Then regardless of how a particular investment is financed, the relevant leverage ratio is dB/dI. For example, a particular investment may be financed entirely by debt. But the cost of that particular increment of debt is not the relevant cost of capital for that investment. The debt would require an equity base. How much equity? This is answered by the long run target B^*/V^*. So procedurally, we start with the actual amount of investment increment for the particular investment, dI. The L^* ratio then defines the amount of dB

assigned to the investment. If the NPV from the investment is positive, then dV will be greater than dI. Hence, the debt capacity of the firm will have been increased by more than dB. However, the relevant leverage for estimating the WACC will still be dB/dI, which will be equal to B^*/V^*. We emphasize that the latter is a policy target decision by the firm, based on relevant financial economic considerations. The dI is an amount assigned to the analysis to be consistent with L^*.

Haley and Schall are correct that the relevant leverage *ratio* is $\Delta B/\Delta V$ equal to B^*/V^*. However, the incremental investment made is valued at replacement cost, not at reproduction cost. Hence for calculating the NPV from the investment, ΔI is the correct denominator.[6] Otherwise, we would have NPV $= \Delta V - \Delta V$. The correct formulation, of course, is NPV $= \Delta V - \Delta I$.

Haley and Schall give a misleading impression in stating that we do not know how much debt can be used to finance the new investment project until we know ΔV. Procedurally, at the time of the *ex ante* investment decision, we do not know ΔV. As a practical matter, a particular investment might be financed with an increment of debt or of equity, or some combination of the two. But the relevant ratio to be used for determining dB/dI is B^*/V^*. And also, *ex post*, if ΔV is greater than ΔI, the debt capacity of the firm has been increased. The full ΔB that can be created *ex post*, will define a $\Delta B/\Delta V$ ratio also equal to B^*/V^*. The reconciliation of the alternative concepts can be illustrated by a numerical example.

Postulate that the firm's B^*/V^* has been set at 50%. The firm now makes an investment of $100,000. The dB that would be assigned to define the debt capacity associated with the new investment, *ex ante*, is $50,000. Hence dB/dI is 50%. *Ex post* the value of the investment is determined to be $130,000 so that the NPV is $30,000. The debt capacity associated with the net investment is now determined to be $65,000 so that ΔB is $65,000 and an additional $15,000 has been added to the debt capacity of the firm.

In summary, it is dB/dI $(= B^*/V^*)$ that is relevant for the analytical derivation of the relevant weighted cost of capital for investment decisions. Other measures of the relationship of new debt capacity to investment which measure the new investment differently can be reconciled with the (dB/dI)-measure but are technically inferior to it.

4. The Cost of Equity

If Eqs. (11.12) and (11.13) are the weighted average cost of capital, how do we determine the cost of the two components, debt and equity? The cost of debt is the risk-free rate, at least given the assumptions of this model. (We shall discuss risky debt later on.) The cost of equity capital is the change in the return to equity holders with respect to the change in their investment, $\Delta S^n + \Delta S^o$. The return to equity holders is the net cash flow after interest and taxes, NI. Therefore, their rate of return

---

[6] For a more complete discussion of this issue, see Beranek [1977].

is $\Delta NI/(\Delta S^n + \Delta S^o)$. In order to solve for this, we begin with identity (11.2),

$$NI + rD = NOI(1 - \tau_c) + rD\tau_c.$$

Next we divide by ΔI, the new investment, and obtain

$$\frac{\Delta NI}{\Delta I} + \frac{\Delta(rD)}{\Delta I} - \frac{\tau_c \Delta(rD)}{\Delta I} = (1 - \tau_c)\frac{\Delta NOI}{\Delta I}. \tag{11.14}$$

Substituting the left-hand side of (11.14) into (11.6), we get

$$\frac{\Delta V^L}{\Delta I} = \frac{\Delta NI/\Delta I + (1 - \tau_c)\,\Delta(rD)/\Delta I}{\rho} + \tau_c\,\frac{\Delta B}{\Delta I}. \tag{11.15}$$

From (11.7), we know that

$$\frac{\Delta V^L}{\Delta I} = \frac{\Delta S^o + \Delta S^n}{\Delta I} + \frac{\Delta B^n}{\Delta I}, \qquad \text{since} \quad \Delta B^o \equiv 0. \tag{11.16}$$

Consequently, by equating (11.15) and (11.16) we get

$$\frac{\Delta V^L}{\Delta I} = \frac{\Delta S^o + \Delta S^n}{\Delta I} + \frac{\Delta B}{\Delta I} = \frac{\Delta NI/\Delta I + (1 - \tau_c)\,\Delta(rD)/\Delta I}{\rho} + \tau_c\,\frac{\Delta B}{\Delta I}.$$

Then, multiplying both sides by ΔI, we have

$$\Delta S^o + \Delta S^n + \Delta B = \frac{\Delta NI + (1 - \tau_c)\,\Delta(rD) + \rho\tau_c\,\Delta B}{\rho}.$$

Subtracting ΔB from both sides gives

$$\Delta S^o + \Delta S^n = \frac{\Delta NI + (1 - \tau_c)\,\Delta(rD) + \rho\tau_c\,\Delta B - \rho\,\Delta B}{\rho}$$

$$\rho(\Delta S^o + \Delta S^n) = \Delta NI - (1 - \tau_c)(\rho - k_d)\,\Delta B, \qquad \text{since} \quad \Delta(rD) = k_d\,\Delta B.$$

And finally,

$$\frac{\Delta NI}{\Delta S^o + \Delta S^n} = \rho + (1 - \tau_c)(\rho - k_d)\frac{\Delta B}{\Delta S^o + \Delta S^n}. \tag{11.17}$$

The change in new equity plus old equity equals the change in the total equity of the firm $(\Delta S = \Delta S^o + \Delta S^n)$. Therefore, the cost of equity, $k_e = \Delta NI/\Delta S$, is written

$$k_e = \rho + (1 - \tau_c)(\rho - k_d)\frac{\Delta B}{\Delta S}. \tag{11.18}$$

The implication of Eq. (11.18) is that the opportunity cost of capital to shareholders increases linearly with changes in the market value ratio of debt to equity. If the firm has no debt in its capital structure, the cost of equity capital, k_e, is equal to the cost of equity for an all equity firm, ρ.

5.   A Graphical Presentation for the Cost of Capital

Figure 11.2 graphs the cost of capital and its components as a function of the ratio of debt to equity. The weighted average cost of capital is invariant to changes in capital structure in a world without corporate taxes; however, with taxes it declines as more and more debt is used in the firm's capital structure. In both cases, the cost of equity capital increases with higher proportions of debt. This makes sense because increasing financial leverage implies a riskier position for shareholders as their residual claim on the firm becomes more variable. They require a higher rate of return to compensate them for the extra risk they take.

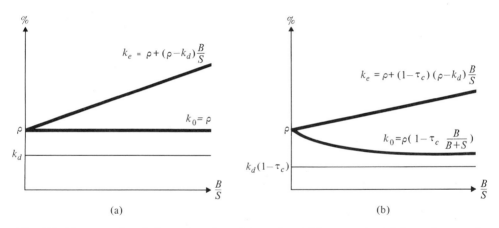

Fig. 11.2 The cost of capital as a function of the ratio of debt to equity (a) Assuming $\tau_c = 0$
(b) Assuming $\tau_c > 0$

The careful reader will have noticed that in Fig. 11.2 B/S is on the horizontal axis while Eqs. (11.13) and (11.18) are written in terms of $\Delta B/\Delta S$ or $\Delta B/\Delta V$, which are changes in debt with respect to changes in equity or value of the firm. The two are equal only when the firm's average debt-to-equity ratio is the same as its marginal debt-to-equity ratio. This will be true as long as the firm establishes a "target" debt-to-value ratio equal to B/S and then finances all projects with the identical proportion of debt and equity so that $B/S = \Delta B/\Delta S$.

The usual definition of the weighted average cost of capital is to weight the after-tax cost of debt by the percentage of debt in the firm's capital structure and add the result to the cost of equity multiplied by the percentage of equity. The equation is

$$\text{WACC}^\tau = (1 - \tau_c)k_d \frac{B}{B+S} + k_e \frac{S}{B+S}. \tag{11.19}$$

We can see that this is the same as (11.13) by substituting (11.18) into (11.19) and assuming that $B/S = \Delta B/\Delta S$. This is done below:

$$\text{WACC}^\tau = (1 - \tau_c)k_d \ \frac{B}{B+S} + \left[\rho + (1 - \tau_c)(\rho - k_d)\frac{B}{S}\right]\frac{S}{B+S}$$

$$= (1 - \tau_c)k_d \ \frac{B}{B+S} + \rho\frac{S}{B+S} + (1 - \tau_c)\rho\frac{B}{S}\frac{S}{B+S} - (1 - \tau_c)k_d \ \frac{B}{S}\frac{S}{B+S}$$

$$= k_d(1 - \tau_c) \ \frac{B}{B+S} + \rho\left(\frac{S}{B+S} + \frac{B}{B+S}\right) - \rho\tau\frac{B}{B+S} - (1 - \tau_c)k_d \ \frac{B}{B+S}$$

$$= \rho\left(1 - \tau_c \ \frac{B}{B+S}\right) \quad \text{QED.}$$

There is no inconsistency between the two definitions of the cost of capital (Eqs. (11.13) and (11.19)). They are identical.

B. THE VALUE OF THE FIRM IN A WORLD WITH PERSONAL AND CORPORATE TAXES

In the original model, the gain from leverage, G, is the difference between the value of the levered and unlevered firms, which is the product of the corporate tax rate and the market value of debt:

$$G = V^L - V^U = \tau_c B. \tag{11.20}$$

Miller [1977] modifies this result by introducing personal as well as corporate taxes into the model. In addition to making the model more realistic, the revised approach adds considerable insight into the effect of leverage on value in the real world. We do not, after all, observe firms with 100% debt in their capital structure as the original Modigliani-Miller model suggests.

Assume for the moment that there are only two types of personal tax rates: the rate on income received from holding shares of stock, τ_{ps}, and the rate on income from bonds, τ_{pB}. The expected after-tax stream of cash flows to shareholders of an all-equity firm would be $(\text{NOI})(1 - \tau_c)(1 - \tau_{ps})$. By discounting this perpetual stream at the cost of equity for an all-equity firm we have the value of the unlevered firm:

$$V^U = \frac{E(\text{NOI})(1 - \tau_c)(1 - \tau_{ps})}{\rho}. \tag{11.21}$$

Alternatively, if the firm has both bonds and shares outstanding, the earnings stream is partitioned into two parts. Cash flows to shareholders after corporate and personal taxes are:

$$\text{payments to shareholders} = (\text{NOI} - rD)(1 - \tau_c)(1 - \tau_{ps}),$$

and payments to bondholders, after personal taxes, are

$$\text{payments to bondholders} = rD(1 - \tau_{pB}).$$

Adding these together and rearranging terms, we have:

total cash payments
to suppliers of capital $= \text{NOI}(1 - \tau_c)(1 - \tau_{ps}) - rD(1 - \tau_c)(1 - \tau_{ps})$
$$+ rD(1 - \tau_{pB}). \quad (11.22)$$

The first term on the right-hand side of (11.22) is the same as the stream of cash flows to owners of the unlevered firm and its expected value can be discounted at the cost of equity for an all-equity firm. The second and third terms are risk free and can be discounted at the risk-free rate, k_d. The sum of the discounted streams of cash flow is the value of the levered firm:

$$V^L = \frac{E(\text{NOI})(1 - \tau_c)(1 - \tau_{ps})}{\rho} + \frac{rD[(1 - \tau_{pB}) - (1 - \tau_c)(1 - \tau_{ps})]}{k_d}$$

$$= V^U + \left[1 - \frac{(1 - \tau_c)(1 - \tau_{ps})}{(1 - \tau_{pB})}\right] B, \quad (11.23)$$

where $B = rD(1 - \tau_{pB})/k_d$, the market value of debt. Consequently, with the introduction of personal taxes, the gain from leverage is the second term in (11.23):

$$G = \left[1 - \frac{(1 - \tau_c)(1 - \tau_{ps})}{(1 - \tau_{pB})}\right] B. \quad (11.24)$$

Note that when personal tax rates are set equal to zero, the gain from leverage in (11.24) equals the gain from leverage in (11.20), the earlier results. This finding also obtains when the personal tax rate on share income equals the rate on bond income. In the United States, it is reasonable to assume that the effective tax rate on common stock is lower than that on bonds.[7] The implication is that the gain from leverage when personal taxes are considered (Eq. (11.24)) is lower than $\tau_c B$ (Eq. (11.20)).

If the personal income tax on stocks is less than the tax on income from bonds, then the before-tax return on bonds has to be high enough, other things being equal, to offset this disadvantage. Otherwise no investor would want to hold bonds. While it is true that owners of a levered corporation are subsidized by the interest deductibility of debt, this advantage is counterbalanced by the fact that the required interest payments have already been "grossed up" by any differential bondholders must pay on their interest income. In this way, the advantage of debt financing may be lost. In fact, whenever the following condition is met in Eq. (11.24),

$$(1 - \tau_{pB}) = (1 - \tau_c)(1 - \tau_{ps}), \quad (11.25)$$

the advantage of debt vanishes completely.

Suppose that the personal tax rate on income from common stock is zero. We may justify this by arguing that (1) no one has to realize a capital gain until after death, (2) gains and losses in well-diversified portfolios can offset each other, thereby

---

[7] The tax rate on stock is thought of as being lower than that on bonds because of the $100 dividend exclusion, and because of a relatively higher capital gains component of return.

eliminating the payment of capital gains taxes, (3) the first several hundred dollars of dividend income received by individuals is not taxed, (4) 85% of dividends received by taxable corporations can be excluded from taxable income, or (5) many types of investment funds pay no taxes at all (nonprofit organizations, pension funds, trust funds, etc.).[8] Figure 11.3 portrays the supply and demand for corporate bonds. The rate paid on the debt of tax-free institutions (municipal bonds, for example) is r_0. If all bonds paid only r_0, no one would hold them with the exception of tax-free institutions which are not affected by the tax disadvantage of holding debt when $\tau_{pB} > \tau_{ps}$. An individual with a marginal tax rate on income from bonds equal to τ_{pB}^i will not hold corporate bonds until they pay $r_0/(1 - \tau_{pB}^i)$, that is, until their return is "grossed up." Since the personal income tax is progressive, the interest rate which is demanded has to keep rising to attract investors in higher and higher tax brackets.[9] The supply of corporate bonds is perfectly elastic, and bonds must pay a rate of $r_0/(1 - \tau_c)$ in equilibrium. To see that this is true, let us recall that the personal tax rate on stock is assumed to be zero ($\tau_{ps} = 0$) and rewrite the gain from leverage:

$$G = \left(1 - \frac{(1 - \tau_c)}{(1 - \tau_{pB})}\right) B. \tag{11.26}$$

If the rate of return on bonds supplied by corporations is $r_s = r_0/(1 - \tau_c)$, then the gain from leverage, in Eq. (11.26), will be zero. The supply rate of return equals the demand rate of return in equilibrium:

$$r_s = \frac{r_0}{1 - \tau_c} = r_D = \frac{r_0}{1 - \tau_{pB}}.$$

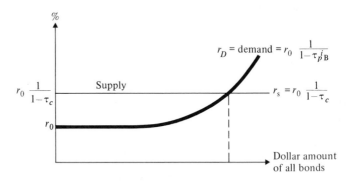

Fig. 11.3 Aggregate supply and demand for corporate bonds (before tax rates)

---

[8] Also, as will be shown in Chapter 14, it is possible to completely shield dividend income from taxes.
[9] Keep in mind the fact that the tax rate on income from stock is assumed to be zero. Therefore, the higher an individual's tax bracket becomes, the higher the before tax rate on bonds must be in order for the after tax rate on bonds to equal the after tax rate on stock (after adjusting for risk).

Consequently,

$$(1 - \tau_c) = (1 - \tau_{pB}),$$

and the gain from leverage in (11.26) will equal zero. If the supply rate of return is less than $r_0/(1 - \tau_c)$, then the gain from leverage will be positive, and all corporations will try to have a capital structure containing 100% debt. On the other hand, if the supply rate of return is greater than $r_0/(1 - \tau_c)$, the gain from leverage will be negative and no debt will be issued. Thus we see that in equilibrium, taxable debt must be supplied to the point where the before-tax cost of corporate debt must equal the rate which would be paid by tax-free institutions "grossed up" by the corporate tax rate.

The implications of Miller's argument are that: (1) in equilibrium, under a set of fairly realistic assumptions, there is no optimal leverage from the point of view of the firm, and (2) there may be an equilibrium amount of aggregate debt outstanding in the economy which is determined by relative corporate and personal tax rates.

In Chapter 12, we shall discuss several empirical studies which provide some evidence about the gain from leverage.

C. THE COST OF CAPITAL WHEN PROJECTS HAVE DIFFERENT RISKS

The CAPM discussed in Chapter 7 provides a natural theory for the pricing of risk. When combined with the cost of capital definitions derived by Modigliani and Miller [1958, 1963], it provides a unified approach to the cost of capital. The work which we shall describe was first published by Hamada [1969] and synthesized by Rubinstein [1973].

The CAPM may be written as

$$E(R_j) = R_f + [E(R_m) - R_f]\beta_j, \tag{11.27}$$

where

$E(R_j)$ = the expected rate of return on asset j,
  R_f = the (constant) risk-free rate,
$E(R_m)$ = the expected rate of return on the market portfolio,
  $\beta_j = COV(R_j, R_m)/VAR(R_m)$.

Figure 11.4 illustrates the difference between the Modigliani-Miller cost of capital and the CAPM. Modigliani and Miller assumed that all projects within the firm had the same business or operating risk (mathematically, they assumed that $NOI_i = \lambda NOI_j$). This was expedient because in 1958, when the paper was written, there was no accepted theory which allowed adjustments for differences of this type. Consequently, the Modigliani-Miller theory is represented by the horizontal line in Fig. 11.4. The WACC for the firm (implicitly) does not change as a function of systematic risk, β. The systematic risk of a firm is a weighted average of the systematic risk of its

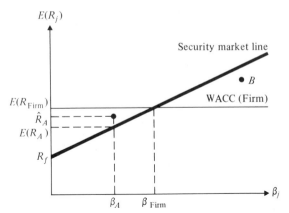

Fig. 11.4 CAPM, the cost of capital, and capital budgeting

projects.[10] As long as a new project has exactly the same systematic risk as the entire firm, the appropriate required rate of return is the WACC for the firm as a whole. However, only rarely will new projects have exactly the same risk as the firm. Consider project A in Fig. 11.4. Its estimated rate of return, $\hat{R}_A$, is less than the firm's weighted average cost of capital $[\text{WACC(firm)} = E(R_{\text{firm}})]$. Does this mean that the project should be rejected? The answer is no. The project may earn a rate of return which is less than for investment in the firm as a whole, but it is also less risky than the firm. It has lower systematic risk (that is, $\beta_A < \beta_{\text{firm}}$). Therefore, it is inappropriate to use the weighted average cost of capital for the firm when we evaluate a project whose risk differs from that of the firm as a whole. Instead, we should use the CAPM. It provides an estimate of the required rate of return for any project. In the case of project A the required rate of return, $E(R_A)$, given the estimated systematic risk of the project, β_A, is less than the anticipated rate of return, $\hat{R}_A$. If the anticipated rate is higher than the rate required by investors in the securities market, the project should be accepted. (Should project B be accepted or rejected?) Thus, we see that it is important to combine the CAPM with the Modigliani-Miller concept of the cost of capital in order to correctly evaluate new projects.

By using the fact that the correlation between two random variables is the covariance between them divided by the product of their standard deviations (see Chapter 6), we have:

$$r_{jm} = \frac{\text{COV}(R_j, R_m)}{\sigma(R_j)\sigma(R_m)}, \tag{11.28}$$

where

$r_{jm} =$ the correlation between asset j and the market portfolio,
$\text{COV}(R_j, R_m) =$ the covariance between asset j and the market portfolio,
$\sigma(\cdot) =$ the standard deviation.

---

[10] For proof, see Chapter 7.

Therefore, the CAPM may be rewritten as

$$E(R_j) = R_f + [E(R_m) - R_f] \frac{r_{jm}\sigma(R_j)\sigma(R_m)}{\sigma^2(R_m)}$$

$$= R_f + \lambda^* r_{jm}\sigma(R_j) \tag{11.29}$$

where $\lambda^* \equiv [E(R_m) - R_f]/\sigma(R_m)$.

Figure 11.5 shows both definitions of the security market line. Recall that if capital markets are efficient and if the CAPM is valid, then in equilibrium every risky asset must be priced so that it falls exactly on the securities market line. Consequently, if we know an asset's risk, we also know exactly what its required rate of return must be. This notion can be used directly to estimate the cost of capital for a firm with a given business risk and financial leverage.

The systematic risk of equity for a levered firm is the beta coefficient, β_e^L, which is estimated from the covariance between returns on the firm's common stock and the market index divided by the variance of the market. Therefore, the cost of equity capital for a levered firm is

$$k_e = R_f + [E(R_m) - R_f]\beta_e^L, \tag{11.30}$$

where β_e^L = the systematic risk of the equity of a levered firm.

If we still maintain the assumption that the corporation issues risk-free debt (that is, $k_d = R_f$), the after-tax weighted average cost of capital is[11]

$$\text{WACC}^\tau = (1 - \tau_c)k_d \frac{B}{B+S} + k_e \frac{S}{B+S}. \tag{11.31}$$

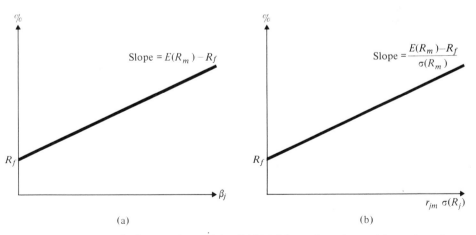

Fig. 11.5 Two equivalent versions of the CAPM (a) Eq. (11.27) and (b) Eq. (11.29)

---

[11] We also return to the assumption that there are corporate taxes but no personal taxes.

This result is useful in estimating the cost of capital for a firm as it actually is, but it doesn't shed any light on the relationship between the CAPM and the Modigliani-Miller cost of capital definitions. Nor is it useful as a means of telling us how to evaluate the cost of capital if the firm decides to change its capital structure. Answers to these questions require a more detailed look at the cost of capital.

1.   The Value of the Levered Firm

In order to see that the value of the levered firm is greater than the value of the unlevered firm (Eq. (11.5)) when the CAPM is combined with the Modigliani-Miller valuation model, we note that the value of the shares of an unlevered firm (which is also the value of the firm) is

$$V^U = \frac{E(\widehat{NOI})(1 - \tau_c)}{\rho}, \tag{11.32}$$

and the value of the shares of a levered firm, S^L, is their expected stream of after-tax cash flows discounted at the cost of equity, k_e:

$$S^L = \frac{(E(\widehat{NOI}) - rD)(1 - \tau_c)}{k_e}$$

$$= \frac{(E(\widehat{NOI}) - R_f B)(1 - \tau_c)}{k_e}, \qquad \text{because} \quad rD = R_f B \tag{11.33}$$

where

k_e = the cost of equity capital for a levered firm,
ρ = the cost of equity capital for an unlevered firm,
D = book value of debt,
B = market value of debt.

From the CAPM we know that all assets are priced so that they lie on the security market line. Therefore they all have the same slope, λ^*, in common. From (11.29) we can solve for λ^*:

$$\lambda^* = \frac{E(R_j) - R_f}{r_{jm}\sigma(R_j)}. \tag{11.34}$$

The levered and unlevered firms must both have the same λ^*; therefore

$$\frac{k_e - R_f}{r_{L,M}\sigma_L} = \frac{\rho - R_f}{r_{U,M}\sigma_U} = \lambda^*, \tag{11.35}$$

where

$r_{L,M}$ = correlation between the levered firm and the market,
$r_{U,M}$ = correlation between the unlevered firm and the market,
σ_L = standard deviation of the return on equity of the levered firm,

σ_U = standard deviation of the return on equity of the unlevered firm,

k_e = the expected rate of return on the equity of the levered firm, its cost of equity capital,

ρ = the expected rate of return on the unlevered firm (which is the cost of equity for an all-equity firm).

From the properties of random variables (see Chapter 6) we can solve for the standard deviation of k_e and ρ. However, first we note that

$$\rho = \frac{(E(\widetilde{NOI})(1 - \tau_c)}{V^U} \qquad \text{(from Eq. (11.32)),} \qquad (11.36)$$

and that,

$$E(\widetilde{NOI}) = \frac{V^U \rho}{1 - \tau_c}.$$

The standard deviation of the 100% equity rate of return, ρ, is denoted as σ_U; therefore

$$\sigma(\widetilde{NOI}) = \frac{V^U}{1 - \tau_c} \sigma_U \qquad \text{(from property 4, Chapter 6).} \qquad (11.36a)$$

Also, from Eq. (11.33) we have the return on levered equity

$$k_e = \frac{(E(\widetilde{NOI}) - rD)(1 - \tau_c)}{S^L}. \qquad (11.37)$$

The standard deviation of the return on levered equity is designated as σ_L:

$$\sigma_L = \frac{1 - \tau_c}{S^L} \sigma(\widetilde{NOI}) \qquad \text{(from property 4, Chapter 6)} \qquad (11.37a)$$

$$= \frac{1 - \tau_c}{S^L} \frac{V^U}{1 - \tau_c} \sigma_U \qquad \text{(from Eq. (11.36a))} \qquad (11.38)$$

$$\sigma_L = \frac{V^U}{V^L - B} \sigma_U \qquad \text{because} \quad V^L = S^L + B. \qquad (11.39)$$

Substituting (11.36), (11.37), and (11.38) into Eq. (11.35), we have

$$\frac{[(E(\widetilde{NOI}) - rD)(1 - \tau_c)/S^L] - R_f}{r_{L,M}(V^U/S^L)\sigma_U} = \frac{[E(\widetilde{NOI})(1 - \tau_c)/V^U] - R_f}{r_{U,M}\sigma_U}.$$

Noting that $S^L = V^L - B$, that $rD = R_f B$, and that $r_{L,M} = r_{U,M}$,[12] we obtain

$$\frac{(E(\widetilde{NOI}) - R_f B)(1 - \tau_c) - R_f(V^L - B)}{V^U} = \frac{E(\widetilde{NOI})(1 - \tau_c) - R_f V^U}{V^U},$$

$$E(\widetilde{NOI})(1 - \tau_c) - R_f B + R_f B\tau_c - R_f V^L + R_f B = E(\widetilde{NOI})(1 - \tau_c) - R_f V^U,$$

$$V^L = V^U + \tau_c B. \tag{11.40}$$

This result is exactly the same as Eq. (11.5). The value of the levered firm is equal to the value of the unlevered firm plus the gain from leverage. Therefore, we see that the Modigliani-Miller results hold equally well in a world where assets are allowed to have different risk classes. If the marginal tax rate, τ_c, is zero, the value of the levered firm equals the value of the unlevered firm.

2. The Cost of Equity

Next, we derive an expression for the cost of equity capital. Substituting (11.40) into (11.39), we have

$$\sigma_L = \frac{V^L - \tau_c B}{V^L - B}\sigma_U$$

$$= \frac{S^L + B - \tau_c B}{S^L}\sigma_U$$

$$= \left[1 + \frac{B}{S^L}(1 - \tau_c)\right]\sigma_U. \tag{11.41}$$

---

[12] Proof that $r_{LM} = r_{UM}$ follows from the definition of correlation and the definitions of k_e and ρ:

$$r_{L,M} = \frac{COV(k_e, R_M)}{\sigma_L \sigma_M} = r_{U,M} = \frac{COV(\rho, R_M)}{\sigma_U \sigma_M}, \tag{a}$$

$$COV(k_e, R_M) = E\left\{\left[\frac{(\widetilde{NOI} - R_f B)(1 - \tau_c)}{S^L} - E\left[\frac{(\widetilde{NOI} - R_f B)(1 - \tau_c)}{S^L}\right]\right][\tilde{R}_M - E(\tilde{R}_M)]\right\}$$

$$= \frac{(1 - \tau_c)}{S^L}COV(\widetilde{NOI}, \tilde{R}_M),$$

$$COV(\rho, R_M) = E\left\{\left[\frac{\widetilde{NOI}(1 - \tau_c)}{V^U} - E\left[\frac{\widetilde{NOI}(1 - \tau_c)}{V^U}\right]\right][\tilde{R}_M - E(\tilde{R}_M)]\right\}$$

$$= \frac{(1 - \tau_c)}{V^U}COV(\widetilde{NOI}, \tilde{R}_M).$$

Therefore, substituting back into (a), and using Eqs. (11.36a) and (11.37a), we get

$$\frac{[(1 - \tau_c)/S^L]COV(\widetilde{NOI}, \tilde{R}_M)}{[(1 - \tau_c)/S^L]\sigma(\widetilde{NOI})\sigma_M} = \frac{[(1 - \tau_c)/V^U]COV(\widetilde{NOI}, \tilde{R}_M)}{[(1 - \tau_c)/V^U]\sigma(\widetilde{NOI})\sigma_M}, \qquad \text{QED.}$$

Substituting (11.41) into the market line equation (Eq. (11.29)), we get

$$E(R_j) = R_f + \frac{E(R_M) - R_f}{\sigma_M} r_{L,M} \left[1 + \frac{B}{S^L}(1 - \tau_c)\right] \sigma_U$$

$$k_e = E(R_j) = R_f + \frac{E(R_M) - R_f}{\sigma_M} r_{L,M}\sigma_U + \frac{E(R_M) - R_f}{\sigma_M} r_{L,M}\sigma_U(1 - \tau_c)\frac{B}{S^L}.$$

$$(11.42)$$

This is exactly the same as the Modigliani-Miller cost of equity capital, Eq. (11.18). To see the relationship, we observe that the required rate of return on an unlevered firm is given by the security market line as

$$\rho = E(R_j) = R_f + \frac{E(R_M) - R_f}{\sigma_M} r_{U,M}\sigma_U. \qquad (11.43)$$

But we already know that $r_{L,M} = r_{U,M}$; therefore the first two terms in (11.42) are the cost of equity capital for an unlevered firm. Consequently (11.42) can be rewritten as

$$k_e = \rho + (\rho - k_d)(1 - \tau_c)(B/S),$$

which is exactly the same as Eq. (11.17). Therefore, what we have done in Eq. (11.42) amounts to adding an adjustment for business risk to the original Modigliani-Miller cost of equity capital which assumed that all projects had equal business risk. Furthermore, the adjustment for risk follows naturally from the CAPM.

3.   The Weighted Average Cost of Capital

Finally, in order to complete the picture, we can derive an expression for the weighted average cost of capital. To do so, we begin with the traditional definition, Eq. (11.19):

$$\text{WACC}^\tau = (1 - \tau_c)R_f \frac{B}{B + S} + k_e \frac{S}{B + S}.$$

We then substitute in the definition of k_e in Eq. (11.42):

$$\text{WACC}^\tau = R_f \frac{B}{B + S} - R_f \tau_c \frac{B}{B + S}$$

$$+ \left[R_f + \frac{E(R_M) - R_f}{\sigma_M} r_{U,M}\sigma_U + \frac{E(R_M) - R_f}{\sigma_M} r_{U,M}\sigma_U(1 - \tau_c)\frac{B}{S}\right]\frac{S}{B + S},$$

and obtain

$$\text{WACC}^\tau = R_f + \frac{E(R_M) - R_f}{\sigma_M} r_{U,M}\sigma_U - \tau_c\left[R_f + \frac{E(R_M) - R_f}{\sigma_M} r_{U,M}\sigma_U\right]\frac{B}{B + S}.$$

$$(11.44)$$

Once again, if we observe that the cost of equity capital for an all-equity firm is given by Eq. (11.43), then

$$\text{WACC}^\tau = \rho - \rho\tau_c \frac{B}{B+S} = \rho\left(1 - \tau_c \frac{B}{B+S}\right).$$

Not surprisingly, this is exactly the same as the Modigliani-Miller definition of the weighted average cost of capital. Once again, we have demonstrated the consistency between the Modigliani-Miller results and the CAPM.

Before turning to a sample problem which will help to pull together the theory, it will be useful to compare the systematic risk of a levered firm with an unlevered firm. Equation (11.42) gives the cost of equity capital for a levered firm:

$$k_e = R_f + \frac{E(R_M) - R_f}{\sigma_M} r_{U,M}\sigma_U + \frac{E(R_M) - R_f}{\sigma_M} r_{U,M}\sigma_U(1 - \tau_c) \frac{B}{S}.$$

The definition of systematic risk for an unlevered firm is

$$\beta_U = \frac{\text{COV}(\rho, R_M)}{\sigma_M^2}.$$

If we recall that $r_{U,M} = \text{COV}(\rho, M)/\sigma_U \sigma_M$, then we can rewrite (11.42) as

$$k_e = R_f + [E(R_M) - R_f]\beta_U + [E(R_M) - R_f]\beta_U(1 - \tau_c) \frac{B}{S}$$

$$= R_f + [E(R_M) - R_f]\beta_U[1 + (1 - \tau_c)] \frac{B}{S}.$$

But we know from the CAPM that the cost of equity capital for a levered firm can be observed directly if we can estimate β_L, the systematic risk of the levered firm. This was defined as β_e^L in Eq. (11.30):

$$k_e = R_f + [E(R_M) - R_f]\beta_L.$$

Comparing the above two equations makes it clear that the relationship between the betas of the levered and unlevered firms is

$$\beta_L = \beta_U \left[1 + (1 - \tau_c) \frac{B}{S}\right]. \tag{11.45}$$

D. A SIMPLE EXAMPLE

The usefulness of the theoretical results can be demonstrated by considering the following problem. The United Southern Construction Company currently has a market value capital structure of 20% debt to total assets. The company's treasurer believes that more debt can be taken on, up to a limit of 35% debt, without losing the firm's ability to borrow at 7%, the prime rate (also assumed to be the risk-free rate).

The firm has a marginal tax rate of 50%. The expected return on the market next year is estimated to be 17% and the systematic risk of the company's equity, β_L, is estimated to be .5.

- What is the company's current weighted average cost of capital, and its current cost of equity?
- What will the new weighted average cost of capital be if the "target" capital structure is changed to 35% debt?
- Should a project with a 9.25% expected rate of return be accepted if its systematic risk is the same as that of the firm?

In order to calculate the company's current cost of equity capital we can use the CAPM:

$$k_e = R_f + [E(R_M) - R_f]\beta_L$$
$$= .07 + [.17 - .07].5 = .12.$$

Therefore, the weighted average cost of capital is

$$\text{WACC}^\tau = (1 - \tau_c)R_f \frac{B}{B+S} + k_e \frac{S}{B+S}$$
$$= (1 - .5).07(.2) + .12(.8) = 10.3\%.$$

The weighted average cost of capital with the new capital structure is shown in Fig. 11.6.[13] Note that the cost of equity increases with increasing leverage. This simply reflects the fact that shareholders face more risk with higher financial leverage and that they require a higher return to compensate them for it. Therefore, in order to calculate the new weighted average cost of capital we have to use the Modigliani-Miller definition to estimate the cost of equity for an all equity firm:

$$\text{WACC}^\tau = \rho\left(1 - \tau_c \frac{B}{B+S}\right),$$

$$\rho = \frac{\text{WACC}^\tau}{1 - \tau_c[B/(B+S)]} = \frac{.103}{1 - .5(.2)} = 11.44\%.$$

As long as the firm does not change its business risk, its unlevered cost of equity capital, ρ, will not change. Therefore, we can use ρ to estimate the weighted average cost of capital with the new capital structure:

$$\text{WACC}^\tau = .1144(1 - .5(.35)) = 9.438\%.$$

Therefore, the new project with its 9.25% rate of return will not be acceptable even if the firm increases its ratio of debt to total assets from 20% to 35%.

---

[13] Note that if debt to total assets is 20%, then debt to equity is 25%. Also, 35% converts to 53.85% in Fig. 11.6.

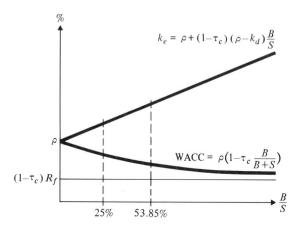

Fig. 11.6 Changes in the cost of capital as leverage increases

A common error made in this type of problem is to forget that the cost of equity capital will increase with higher leverage. Had we estimated the weighted average cost of capital, using 12% for the old cost of equity and 35% debt as the target capital structure, we would have obtained 9.03% as the estimated weighted average cost of capital and we would have accepted the project.

A more difficult problem is to decide what to do if the project's risk is different from that of the firm. Suppose the new project would increase the replacement market value of the assets of the firm by 50% and that the systematic risk of the operating cash flows it provides is estimated to be 1.2. What rate of return must it earn in order to be profitable if the firm has (a) 20% or (b) 35% debt in its capital structure?

Figure 11.7 shows that the CAPM may be used to find the required rate of return given the beta of the project without leverage, $\beta_{U,p}$, which has been estimated to be

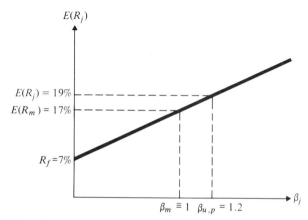

Fig. 11.7 Using the CAPM to estimate the required rate of return on a project

1.2. This is the beta for the *unlevered* project, because the beta is defined as the systematic risk of the operating cash flows. By definition this is the covariance between the cash flows *before* leverage and taxes and the market index, $COV(\widetilde{NOI}, \tilde{R}_M)$. The required rate of return on the project, if it is an all-equity project, will be

$$E(R_j) = R_f + [E(R_M) - R_f]\beta_{U,p}$$
$$= .07 + [.17 - .07]1.2 = 19\%.$$

Next we must "add in" the effect of the firm's leverage. If we recognize that 19% is the required rate if the project were all equity, we can find the required rate with 20% leverage by using the Modigliani-Miller weighted average cost of capital, Eq. (11.12):

$$WACC^\tau = \rho\left(1 - \tau_c \frac{B}{B + S}\right)$$
$$= .19(1 - .5(.2)) = 17.1\%.$$

And if the leverage is increased to 35%, the required return falls to 15.675%:

$$WACC^\tau = .19(1 - .5(.35)) = 15.675\%.$$

The above examples serve to illustrate the usefulness of the risk-adjusted cost of capital for capital-budgeting purposes. Each project must be evaluated at a cost of capital which reflects the systematic risk of its operating cash flows as well as the financial leverage of the firm as a whole. Estimates of the correct opportunity cost of capital are derived from a thorough understanding of the Modigliani-Miller cost of capital and the CAPM.

E.   THE SEPARABILITY OF INVESTMENT AND FINANCING DECISIONS

The preceding example shows that the required rate of return on a new project is dependent on the firm's weighted average cost of capital, which in turn may or may not be a function of the capital structure of the firm. What implications does this have for the relationship between investment and financing decisions; that is, how independent is one of the other? The simplest possibility is that, after adjusting for project specific risk, we can use the same capital structure—the capital structure of the entire firm—to estimate the cost of capital for all projects. However, this may not be the case. In order to clarify the issue we shall investigate two different suppositions.

1.   If the weighted average cost of capital is invariant to changes in the firm's capital structure (i.e., if $WACC^\tau = \rho$ in Eq. (11.12) because $\tau_c = 0$), then the investment and financing decisions are completely separable. This might actually be the case if Miller's [1977] paper is empirically valid. The implication is that we can use Eq. (11.44) and set $\tau_c = 0$ when estimating the appropriate cutoff rate for capital-budgeting decisions. In other words, it is unnecessary to consider the financial leverage of the firm. Under the above assumptions, it is irrelevant.

2.   If there really is gain from leverage, as would be suggested by the Modigliani-Miller theory if $\tau_c > 0$, then the value of a project is not independent of the capital structure assumed for it. In the preceding simple example we saw that the required rate of return on the project was 19% if the firm had no debt, 17.1% if it had 20% debt, and 15.675% if it had 35% debt in its capital structure. Therefore, the project has greater value as the financial leverage of the firm increases. As a practical matter, this problem is usually "handled" by assuming that the firm has decided on an "optimal" capital structure and that all projects are financed, at the margin, with the optimal ratio of debt to equity. The relevant factors which may be used to determine the optimal capital structure are discussed in the following chapter. However, assuming that an optimum does exist, and assuming that all projects are financed at that optimum, we may treat the investment decision *as if* it were separable from the financing decision. First the firm decides what optimal capital structure to use, then it applies the same capital structure to all projects. Under this set of assumptions the decision to accept or reject a particular project does not change the "optimal" capital structure. We could use Eq. (11.44) with $B/(B + S)$ set equal to the optimal capital structure in order to determine the appropriate cost of capital for a project. This is precisely what we did in the example.

But suppose projects carry with them the ability to change the optimal capital structure of the firm as a whole. Suppose that some projects have more debt capacity than others. Then the investment and financing decisions cannot even be "handled as if" they were independent. There is very little in the accepted theory of finance which admits of this possibility, but it cannot be disregarded. One reason that projects may have separate debt capacities is the simple fact that they have different collateral values in bankruptcy. However, since the theory in this chapter has proceeded on the assumption that bankruptcy costs are zero, we shall refrain from further discussion of this point until the next chapter.

F. SUMMARY

The cost of capital is seen to be a rate of return whose definition requires a project to improve the wealth position of the *current* shareholders of the firm. The original Modigliani-Miller work has been extended by using the CAPM so that a risk-adjusted cost of capital may be obtained for each project. When the expected cash flows of the project are discounted at the correct risk-adjusted rate, the result is the NPV of the project.

In a world without taxes, the value of the firm is independent of its capital structure. However, there are several important extensions of the basic model. With the introduction of corporate taxes, the optimal capital structure becomes 100% debt. Finally, when personal taxes are also introduced, the value of the firm is unaffected by the choice of financial leverage. Financing is irrelevant! The next chapter takes a more careful look at the question of optimal capital structure and summarizes some of the empirical work which has been done.

PROBLEM SET

11.1 The Modigliani-Miller theorem assumes that the firm has only two classes of securities, perpetual debt and equity. Suppose that the firm has issued a third class of securities—preferred stock—and that $X\%$ of preferred dividends may be written off as an expense $(0 \le X \le 1)$.

a) What is the appropriate expression for the value of the levered firm?
b) What is the appropriate expression for the weighted average cost of capital?

11.2 The Acrosstown Company has an equity beta, β_L, of .5 and 50% debt in its capital structure. The company has risk-free debt which costs 6% before taxes, and the expected rate of return on the market is 18%. Acrosstown is considering the acquisition of a new project in the peanut-raising agribusiness which is expected to yield 25% on after-tax operating cash flows. The Carternut Company, which is in the same product line (and risk class) as the project being considered, has an equity beta, β_L, of 2.0 and has 10% debt in its capital structure. If Acrosstown finances the new project with 50% debt, should it be accepted or rejected? Assume that the marginal tax rate, τ_c, for both companies is 50%.

11.3 The XYZ Company has a current market value of $1,000,000, half of which is debt. Its current weighted average cost of capital is 9%, and the corporate tax rate is 40%. The treasurer proposes to undertake a new project, which costs $500,000, and which can be financed completely with debt. The project is expected to have the same operating risk as the company and to earn $8\frac{1}{2}\%$. The treasurer argues that the project is desirable because it earns more than 5%, which is the before-tax marginal cost of the debt used to finance it. What do you think?

11.4 Given a world with corporate taxes, τ_c, a personal tax rate paid on bonds, τ_{pB}, and a personal tax rate on income from equity, τ_{pS}, what would be the effect of a decrease in the corporate tax rate on

a) the aggregate amount of debt in the economy, and
b) the optimal capital structure of firms?

11.5 Congress has proposed to eliminate "double taxation" on dividends by reducing the personal tax on dividend income. At the same time, a compensating increase in taxes on capital gains (traditionally taxed at a much lower percentage than dividend income) has been proposed.

a) What effect would this joint proposal have on the optimal capital structure of a firm, according to the Miller model?
b) What effect would it have on the aggregate amount of corporate debt outstanding?

11.6 Consider firm B as an unlevered firm, and firm C as a levered firm with target debt-to-equity ratio $(B/S)^* = 1$. Both firms have exactly the same perpetual net operating income, $NOI_1 = 180$, before taxes. The before-tax cost of debt, k_d, is the same as the risk-free rate. The corporate tax rate = .5. Given the following market parameters,

$$E(R_m) = .12, \qquad \sigma_m^2 = .0144, \qquad R_F = .06, \qquad \beta_B = 1, \qquad \beta_C = 1.5.$$

a) Find the cost of capital and value for each firm. (Ignore any effect from personal income taxes.)
b) Evaluate the following four projects to determine their acceptance (or rejection) by firms B and C. What do the results of this evaluation tell you about leverage in a world with corporate, but no personal, taxes? (Note: for firm B, r_{jm} is the correlation between the

unlevered equity return and the market. For firm C, it is the correlation between the levered equity return and the market.)

Project$_j$	Cost$_j$	$E(\widetilde{NOI}_j)$ (after tax)	σ_j	r_{jm} correlation of j with the market
1	100	9	.10	.6
2	120	11	.11	.7
3	80	9	.12	.8
4	150	18	.20	.9

11.7 A firm with $1,000,000 in assets and 50% debt in its capital structure is considering a $250,000 project. The firm's after-tax weighted average cost of capital is 10.4%, the marginal cost of debt is 8% (before taxes), and the marginal tax rate is 40%. If the project does not change the firm's operating risk and is financed exclusively with new equity, what is the rate of return it must earn to be acceptable?

11.8 The firm's cost of equity capital is 18%, the market value of the firm's equity is $8 million, the firm's cost of debt capital is 9%, and the market value of debt is $4 million. The firm is considering a new investment with an expected rate of return of 17%. This project is 30% riskier than the firm's average operations. The riskless rate of return is 5%; the variance of the market return is .08. Is the project profitable? [Assume a world without taxes.]

11.9 Susan Varhard, Treasurer of the Gammamax Company, has proposed that the company should sell equity and buy back debt in order to maximize its value. As evidence, she presents the financial statements given in Table 11.1. The company currently has a price-earnings ratio of 50. Before the change in capital structure it has 10 shares outstanding; therefore its earnings per share are $1.00, and the price per share is $50. If 10 new shares are issued at $50 each, $500 is collected and used to retire $500 of debt (which pays a coupon rate

Table 11.1

Income statement	Before	After
Net operating income	100	100
Interest expense	80	40
Earnings before taxes	20	60
Taxes at 50%	10	30
Net income	10	30

Balance Sheet

Before		After	
Assets	Liabilities	Assets	Liabilities
	Debt 1000		Debt 500
	Equity 500		Equity 1000
Total = 1500	Total = 1500	Total = 1500	Total = 1500

of 8%). After the capital-structure change, earnings per share have increased to $1.50 (since there are now 20 shares outstanding); and with a price-earnings ratio of 50, presumably the price per share will increase from $50 before the capital-structure change to $75 afterward. Given your understanding of modern finance theory, discuss the above proposal.

11.10 Community Bank is faced with the decision of whether or not to open a new branch. The current market value of the bank is $2,500,000. According to company policy (and industry practice), the bank's capital structure is highly leveraged. The present (and optimal) ratio of debt to total assets is .9. Community Bank's debt is almost exclusively in the form of demand, savings, and time deposits. The average return on these deposits to the bank's clients has been 5% over the past five years. However, recently interest rates have climbed sharply, and as a result Community Bank presently pays an average annual rate of $6\frac{1}{4}\%$ on its accounts in order to remain competitive. In addition, the bank incurs a service cost of $2\frac{3}{4}\%$ per account. Because federal "Regulation Q" puts a ceiling on the amount of interest paid by banks on their accounts, the banking industry at large has been experiencing disintermediation—a loss of clients to the open money market (Treasury bills, etc.), where interest rates are higher. Largely because of the interest-rate situation (which shows no sign of improving), Community Bank's president has stipulated that for the branch project to be acceptable, its entire cost of $500,000 will have to be raised by an issue of new equity. The bank's cost of equity capital, k_e, is 11%. Community Bank's marginal tax rate is .48. Market analysis indicates that the new branch may be expected to return net cash flows according to the following schedule:

Year	0	1	2	3	4	5
$	−500,000	25,000	35,000	45,000	45,000	50,000

Should Community Bank open the new branch?

11.11 A not-for-profit organization, such as a ballet company or a museum, usually carries no debt. Also, since there are no shareholders, there is no equity outstanding. How would you go about determining the appropriate weighted average cost of capital for not-for-profit organizations given that they have no debt or equity?

REFERENCES

BAXTER, N. D., "Leverage, Risk of Ruin and the Cost of Capital," *Journal of Finance*, September 1967, 395–403.

BERANEK, W., "The WACC Criterion and Shareholder Wealth Maximization," *The Journal of Financial and Quantitative Analysis*, March 1977, 17–32.

FAMA, E. F., and M. H. MILLER, *The Theory of Finance*. Holt, Rinehart and Winston, New York, 1972.

FARRAR, D. E., and L. SELWYN, "Taxes, Corporate Financial Policies and Returns to Investors," *National Tax Journal*, December 1967, 444–454.

HALEY, C. W., and L. D. SCHALL, *The Theory of Financial Decisions*. McGraw Hill, New York, 1973.

HAMADA, R. S., "The Effect of the Firm's Capital Structure on the Systematic Risk of Common Stocks," *Journal of Finance*, May 1972, 435–452.

MILLER, M. H., "Debt and Taxes," *The Journal of Finance*, May 1977, 261–275.

MODIGLIANI, F., and M. H. MILLER, "The Cost of Capital, Corporation Finance, and the Theory of Investment," *American Economic Review*, June 1958, 261–297.

———, "Corporate Income Taxes and the Cost of Capital," *American Economic Review*, June 1963, 433–443.

———, "Some Estimates of the Cost of Capital to the Electric Utility Industry 1954–57," *American Economic Review*, June 1966, 333–348.

RUBINSTEIN, M. E., "A Mean-Variance Synthesis of Corporate Financial Theory," *Journal of Finance*, March 1973, 167–181.

STIGLITZ, J. E., "On the Irrelevance of Corporate Financial Policy," *American Economic Review*, December 1974, 851–866.

———, "A Re-Examination of the Modigliani-Miller Theorem," *American Economic Review*, December 1969, 784–793.

Chapter 12

Capital Structure: Empirical Evidence and Applications

One kind of evidence in favor of the traditional position is that companies in various industry groups appear to use leverage as if there is some optimal range appropriate to each group. While significant intercompany differences in debt ratios exist within each industry, the average use of leverage by broad industrial groups tends to follow a consistent pattern over time.

E. Solomon, *The Theory of Financial Management*,
Columbia University Press, New York, 1963, p. 98

A. INTRODUCTION

The theories presented in the previous chapter provide some fairly unsettling conclusions about capital structure. On one hand, it is argued that capital structure has no effect on the value of the firm (Modigliani and Miller [1958] or Miller [1977]), and on the other hand, it is suggested that the firm carry 100% debt (Modigliani and Miller [1963]). Neither result is consistent with what seem to be cross-section regularities in the observed capital structures of U.S. firms. For example, the electric utility and steel industries have high financial leverage while service industries like accounting firms or brokerage houses have almost no long-term debt.

The first part of this chapter looks at some possible explanations for why there might be such a thing as an "optimal" capital structure which contains both debt and equity. First, we shall examine the argument that risky debt is the cause of an optimal capital structure and conclude that it does not change any of the previous results. Second, we look at bankruptcy costs. It turns out that if they are nontrivial, then it is possible that an optimal capital structure can be obtained as the tax advantages of debt are traded off against the likelihood of incurring bankruptcy costs. Third, we discuss two theories of optimal capital structure which are novel because they require neither taxes nor bankruptcy costs.

Next, the discussion turns to the empirical evidence. The central issue is whether or not the value of the firm is affected by changes in its debt-equity ratio. Important related questions are: (1) Does the cost of equity increase as financial leverage does? (2) Are bankruptcy costs really nontrivial?

Finally, in an attempt to give a realistic example of how to calculate the cost of capital, we use a case study based on Bethlehem Steel.

B. POSSIBLE REASONS FOR AN "OPTIMAL" MIX OF DEBT AND EQUITY

1. The Effect of Risky Debt

The fundamental theorem set forth by Modigliani and Miller is that given complete and perfect capital markets it doesn't make any difference how one splits up the stream of operating cash flows. The percentage of debt or equity doesn't change the total value of the cash stream provided by the productive investments of the firm. Therefore, so long as there are no costs of bankruptcy (paid to third parties like trustees and law firms), it shouldn't make any difference whether or not debt is risk free or risky. The value of the firm should be equal to the value of the discounted cash flows from investment. A partition which divides these cash flows into risky debt and risky equity has no impact on value. Stiglitz [1969] first proved this result, using a state-preference framework, and Rubinstein [1973] provided a proof, using a mean-variance approach.

Risky debt, just like any other security, must be priced in equilibrium so that it falls on the security market line. Therefore, if we designate the return on risky debt as $\tilde{R}_{dj}$, its expected return is

$$E(\tilde{R}_{dj}) = R_f + [E(\tilde{R}_M) - R_f]\beta_{dj} \qquad (12.1)$$

where $\beta_{dj} = \text{COV}(\tilde{R}_{dj}, \tilde{R}_M)/\sigma_M^2$. The return on the equity of a levered firm, k_e, is similar to Eq. (11.33) except that risky debt replaces risk-free debt:

$$k_e = \frac{(\text{NOI} - \tilde{R}_{dj}B)(1 - \tau_c)}{S^L}. \qquad (12.2)$$

Using the CAPM, we find that the expected return on equity will be[1]

$$E(k_e) = R_f + \lambda^* \text{COV}(k_e, R_M). \qquad (12.3)$$

---

[1] Recall that $\lambda^* \equiv (E(R_M) - R_f)/\sigma_M^2$.

The covariance between the expected rate of return on equity and the market index is

$$\text{COV}(k_e, R_M) = E\left\{\left[\frac{(\text{NOI} - R_{dj}B)(1 - \tau_c)}{S^L} - E\left[\frac{(\text{NOI} - R_{dj}B)(1 - \tau_c)}{S^L}\right]\right]\right.$$

$$\left. \times [R_M - E(R_M)]\right\}$$

$$= \frac{1 - \tau_c}{S^L} \text{COV}(\text{NOI}, R_M) - \frac{(1 - \tau_c)B}{S^L} \text{COV}(R_{dj}, R_M). \qquad (12.4)$$

Substituting this result into (12.3) and the combined result into (12.2), we have the following relationship for a levered firm:

$$R_f S^L + \lambda^*(1 - \tau_c) \text{COV}(\text{NOI}, R_M) - \lambda^*(1 - \tau_c)B \text{COV}(R_{dj}, R_M)$$

$$= E(\text{NOI})(1 - \tau_c) - E(R_{dj})B(1 - \tau_c). \qquad (12.5)$$

By following a similar line of logic for the unlevered firm (where $B = 0$, and $S^L = V^U$) we have

$$R_f V^U + \lambda^*(1 - \tau_c) \text{COV}(\text{NOI}, R_M) = E(\text{NOI})(1 - \tau_c). \qquad (12.6)$$

Substituting (12.6) for $E(\text{NOI})(1 - \tau_c)$ in the right-hand side of (12.5) and using the fact that $V^L = S^L + B$, we have

$$R_f S^L + \lambda^*(1 - \tau_c) \text{COV}(\text{NOI}, R_M) - \lambda^*(1 - \tau_c)B \text{COV}(R_{dj}, R_M)$$

$$= R_f V^U + \lambda^*(1 - \tau_c) \text{COV}(\text{NOI}, R_M) - E(R_{dj})B(1 - \tau_c),$$

$$R_f(V^L - B) - \lambda^*(1 - \tau_c)B \text{COV}(R_{dj}, R_M)$$

$$= R_f V^U - [R_f + \lambda^* \text{COV}(R_{dj}, R_M)]B(1 - \tau_c),$$

$$V^L = V^U + \tau_c B.$$

This is exactly the same Modigliani-Miller result that we obtained when the firm was assumed to issue only risk-free debt. Therefore, the introduction of risky debt cannot, by itself, be used to explain the existence of an optimal capital structure.

2.   The Effect of Bankruptcy Costs
When we consider bankruptcy costs, the value of the firm in bankruptcy is reduced by the fact that payments must be made to third parties other than bond- or share-holders. Trustee fees, legal fees, and other costs of reorganization or bankruptcy are deducted from the net asset value of the bankrupt firm and from the proceeds which should go to bondholders. Consequently, the "dead-weight" losses associated with bankruptcy may cause the value of the firm in bankruptcy to be less than the discounted value of the expected cash flows from operations. This fact can be used to explain the existence of an optimal capital structure. Baxter [1967] was one of the

first to suggest this possibility. Since then more sophisticated treatments have been offered by Stiglitz [1972], Kraus and Litzenberger [1973], and Kim [1978]. The interested reader is referred to these papers for explicit mathematical treatment of optimal capital structure. Figure 12.1 summarizes the results: Figure 12.1(a) shows the effects on various costs of capital. The dashed lines are the, by now familiar, Modigliani-Miller results where the weighted average cost of capital (in a world with only corporate taxes) declines with leverage. The solid lines show what might happen if nontrivial bankruptcy costs are introduced. As the proportion of debt in the firm's capital structure is increased, the probability of bankruptcy also increases. Consequently, the rate of return required by bondholders (the solid line, R_{dj}, in Fig. 12.1(a)) increases with leverage. This, in turn, results in a "U-shaped" weighted average cost of capital (solid line $\text{WACC}^{\tau'}$) and an optimal capital structure. The optimal ratio of debt to equity is determined by taking on increasing amounts of debt until the marginal gain from leverage is equal to the marginal expected loss from bankruptcy costs.

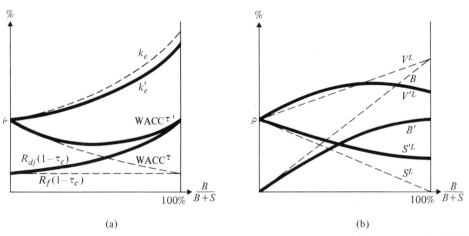

Fig. 12.1 Optimal capital structure in the presence of bankruptcy costs: (a) The cost of capital (b) The value of claims

Figure 12.1(b) shows the same results in terms of the market values of the firm, its equity, and its debt. The dashed lines indicate that in a world with corporate taxes and no bankruptcy costs the value of the levered firm is maximized by 100% debt financing. The solid lines show that with nontrivial bankruptcy costs there is an interior optimal capital structure.

An important question for the existence of optimal capital structure brought about by the dead-weight losses of bankruptcy is: Exactly how large are bankruptcy costs? If they are trivial, some other explanation for optimal capital structure is needed. Warner [1977a] collects data for 11 railroad bankruptcies which occurred between 1933 and 1955. He measures only direct costs such as lawyers' and accountants' fees, other professional fees, and the value of managerial time spent in administering the bankruptcy. He does not estimate indirect costs to creditors such as the opportunity cost of funds tied up during bankruptcy proceedings and losses in asset value due to forced capital structure changes, or indirect costs to shareholders such as lost profits created by decreased sales in anticipation of bankruptcy or from disruptions in production during reorganization. The evidence indicates that direct costs are trivial, averaging about 1% of the market value of the firm prior to bankruptcy. Furthermore, direct costs as a percent of value seem to decrease as a function of the size of the bankrupt firm. This would suggest that bankruptcy costs are less important for the capital-structure decisions of large firms than of small firms. Although Warner's evidence is inconclusive because indirect costs are not measured, it does suggest that bankruptcy costs may not be sufficiently large to cause optimal leverage.

In a second paper, Warner [1977b] examines the effect of bankruptcy on the market returns of 73 defaulted bonds of 20 separate railroads, each of which was in bankruptcy at some time during the period from 1930 through 1955. None of the railroads was actually liquidated, although there were mergers, spinoffs, and abandonments of operations. The following effects were observed:

- The systematic risk of bonds increased prior to filing for bankruptcy. A reasonable explanation is that as the market value of equity, relative to bonds, falls prior to bankruptcy, the bondholders' claim becomes more like that of the shareholders of an all-equity firm, and hence their risk rises.
- After adjusting for risk, the performance of the bonds in the month of the bankruptcy petition was significantly negative.
- Investors who purchased a portfolio of bonds on the date of the bankruptcy petition appeared to earn significant risk-adjusted abnormal returns in the post-bankruptcy period. One possible explanation is that the courts approved capital structure simplifications which had been unanticipated and which benefited bondholders.

It is hard to argue that conclusions based on a study of the railroad industry can be generalized because federal regulations encourage the continued operation of railroad service even though the firm is in bankruptcy. Nevertheless, if one views the bondholders' position as being the residual claim at the time of bankruptcy, the significant negative return to bondholders on the date of the bankruptcy petition is evidence of nontrivial bankruptcy costs. Because the empirical evidence is mixed and somewhat limited, more research is necessary before the real importance of bankruptcy costs is fully understood.

3. Other Possible Causes of Optimal Capital Structure

We have just seen that if there is a gain from leverage because of the tax deductibility of interest expenses, and if bankruptcy costs are nontrivial, then it is possible to construct a theory of optimal capital structure. One troublesome aspect of this approach is that even before income taxes existed in the United States, firms used debt in their capital structure. Furthermore, the same cross-sectional regularities in financial leverage which exist today can also be observed in data prior to the introduction of corporate taxes. This suggests that optimal leverage (if it exists) may be explained by causes other than debt tax shields and bankruptcy costs. Two possibilities are discussed below.

Jensen and Meckling [1976] use the notion of agency costs to argue that the probability distribution of cash flows provided by the firm is not independent of its ownership structure and that this fact may be used to explain optimal leverage. First, there is an incentive problem associated with the issuance of new debt. Consider an example where unbeknownst to lenders, the firm has two different investment projects (see Table 12.1), both having the same systematic risk but difference variances. The first has a 50/50 chance of yielding an end-of-period cash flow of $9,000 or $11,000. The second has a 50/50 chance of yielding $2,000 or $18,000. Both cost $8,000 and both have the same expected return. Suppose the firm shows only project 1 to lenders and asks to borrow $7,000. From the lenders' point of view this request seems reasonable because project 1 will always earn enough to pay off the loan. Of course, if creditors lend $7,000 and if the owners of the firm have the ability to switch to project 2, they will do so. (Why?) The result is the transfer of wealth from bondholders to shareholders.

Table 12.1 Two investment projects

Probability	Project 1	Project 2
.5	$9,000	$2,000
.5	11,000	18,000

To prevent such machinations, bondholders may insist on various types of protective covenants and monitoring devices in order to protect their wealth from raids made on it by shareholders. However, the costs of writing and enforcing such covenants may well be nontrivial. Furthermore, these costs may increase with the percent of financing supplied by bondholders.

On the other hand, there are agency costs associated with external equity. Suppose we begin with a firm owned exclusively by a single individual, the owner-manager. He will obviously take every action possible to increase his own wealth. However, if he sells a portion of the ownership rights by selling external equity to new shareholders, there will arise conflicts in interest. Now he is co-owner with the new shareholders. If at their expense he can maximize his wealth by purchasing an executive jet and taking long vacations he will do so. Co-ownership of equity implies agency problems. The new shareholders will have to incur monitoring costs of one form or another in order to ensure that the original owner-manager acts in their interest.

Jensen and Meckling suggest that given increasing agency costs with higher proportions of equity on the one hand and higher proportions of debt on the other, there is an optimum combination of outside debt and equity which will be chosen because it minimizes total agency costs. In this way it is possible to argue for the existence of an optimum capital structure even in a world without taxes or bankruptcy costs.

Scott [1976] shows that optimal leverage may be related to the collateral value of the tangible assets held by the firm. If a firm goes bankrupt, the losses of bondholders are limited by the salvage value of the property held in the firm. If the corporate tax rate is zero, the optimal amount of debt in the capital structure is the discounted value of the liquidation price of the firm's assets in bankruptcy. This approach fits in with that of Jensen and Meckling if the bondholders simply require that the loan be tied to the salvage value of specific assets. Such a scheme considerably reduces monitoring costs.

C. EMPIRICAL EVIDENCE ON OPTIMAL CAPITAL STRUCTURE

For the most part, the empirical literature on capital structure and the cost of capital has focused on the theory provided by Modigliani and Miller [1958, 1963]. The issue is whether or not the value of the firm can be changed by changing its capital structure. This may seem to be a relatively straightforward question, but the empirical testing is difficult and complex. For example, the Modigliani-Miller model assumes perpetual expected streams of cash flow which are not growing. How shall growth be included in the analysis? Even worse, the correct variable is anticipated *future* growth which is impossible to measure. A second difficulty is that flotation costs for external debt and equity are higher for smaller firms. Therefore, size may be related to economies of scale in the cost of capital. This possibility must be considered. Third, the theory assumes that all companies have the same business risk. But even for an industry as homogeneous as electric utilities, this may not be true (see Boness and Frankfurter [1977]). Also, firms do not choose a capital structure in isolation. Usually new financing simultaneously implies new investment with changes in the asset structure of the firm and (possibly) risk. Finally, much of the empirical work has used cross-section regressions which are likely to have highly correlated residuals across firms. This tends to exaggerate the significance of the regression coefficients, thereby weakening any conclusions which might be drawn. All of these problems make empirical tests troublesome to conduct and difficult to interpret.

There have been many empirical studies of the cost of capital. We shall report on only a few in order to keep to a concise summary. The empirical questions are whether the weighted average cost of capital (1) does not change with changes in financial leverage, as would be predicted by the earliest Modigliani-Miller theory (Eq. 11.12 with zero corporate tax rate) or by the most recent Miller paper (Eq. 11.24 with condition 11.25) in a world with both corporate and personal taxes; (2) declines with increasing leverage, as would be predicted by the Modigliani-Miller theory where corporate taxes provide a gain to leverage (Eq. 11.12 with $\tau_c > 0$); or (3) is a "U-shaped" function of leverage which would indicate an optimal capital structure.

Modigliani and Miller [1958] use cross-section regression equations on data taken from 43 electric utility companies during 1947–48 and 42 oil companies during 1953. They estimate the weighted average cost of capital as net operating cash flows after taxes divided by the market value of the firm.[2] When regressed against financial leverage (measured as the ratio of the market value of debt to the market value of the firm) the results were[3]

$$\text{Electric utilities:} \quad \text{WACC} = 5.3 + .006d, \quad r = .12,$$
$$(\pm.008)$$

$$\text{Oil companies:} \quad \text{WACC} = 8.5 + .006d, \quad r = .04,$$
$$(\pm.024)$$

where

$$\text{WACC} = \frac{\text{NOI}(1 - \tau_c)}{V^L} = \frac{\text{NI} + k_d D}{V^L} = \text{weighted average cost of capital,}$$

$$r = \text{the correlation coefficient,}$$

$$d = \frac{B}{B + S} = \text{financial leverage.}$$

These results suggest that the cost of capital is not affected by capital structure because the t-statistics (the ratio of the slope coefficients to the standard errors, given in parentheses) cannot allow rejection of the null hypothesis that the weighted average cost of capital is unrelated to capital structure.

Weston [1963] criticizes the Modigliani-Miller results on two counts. First, the oil industry is not even approximately homogeneous in business risk, and second the valuation model from which the cost of capital is derived assumes that cash flows are perpetuities which do not grow. Mathematically,

$$V_L = \frac{E(\text{NOI})(1 - \tau_c)}{\text{WACC}}. \tag{12.7}$$

However, the stream of cash flows usually is expected to grow over time. Proper estimates of the cost of capital must attempt to measure anticipated future earnings, not earnings today. When growth is added to the cross-section regression the results are[4]

---

[2] Net operating cash flows after taxes were actually estimated as net income after taxes plus interest payments on debt. This assumes that there is no growth in earnings and that replacement investment equals depreciation expense.

[3] Standard errors are given in parentheses.

[4] Weston's sample was the same sample of 43 electric utilities that Modigliani and Miller used but the cross-section was estimated in 1959 instead of 1947–48. Standard errors are in parentheses.

Electric utilities:

$$\text{WACC} = 5.91 - .0265d + \underset{(\pm.0079)}{.00A} - \underset{(\pm.0001)}{.0822E}, \quad r = .5268,$$
$$\phantom{\text{WACC} = 5.91 - .0265d}(\pm.0079) \quad (\pm.0001) \quad (\pm.0024)$$

where

A = total book value of assets (a proxy for firm size),
E = compound growth in earnings per share 1949–1959.

Weston's results are consistent with the Modigliani-Miller view of the cost of capital in a world where the tax shield provided by the deductibility of interest expenses causes the weighted average cost of capital to decline with leverage.

Modigliani and Miller [1966] also found results which appear to be consistent with a gain from leverage. The valuation model which they use (which is discussed in Chapter 13) assumes, among other things, that the firm grows more rapidly than the economy for a finite period of time, T, and that there are corporate taxes but no personal taxes. The valuation model is given below:

$$V^L = \frac{[E(\widetilde{NOI}_1)](1 - \tau_c)}{\rho} + \tau_c B + K[E(\widetilde{NOI})](1 - \tau_c)\left[\frac{r - \text{WACC}}{\text{WACC}(1 - \text{WACC})}\right]T,$$

(12.8)

where

K = the percent of earnings invested in new assets, $K \geq 1$,
r = the tax-adjusted rate of return on new assets, $r > \text{WACC}$,
T = the number of years where $r > \text{WACC}$.

The first term in (12.8) can be thought of as the capitalized value of the anticipated *level* of cash flows from operations. The second term is the gain from leverage. If it is greater than zero, the weighted average cost of capital falls with increasing leverage. The third term is a growth term. It is far from simple, and is represented by the product of three elements: the profitability of future growth opportunities (measured by the difference between r and WACC), the size of these opportunities $(K[E(NOI)(1 - \tau_c)])$, and the length of duration of these opportunities, T.

Cross-section multiple regressions based on the above model were run on a sample of 63 electric utility firms in 1954, 1956, and 1957. Table 12.2 summarizes the contribution of the three above-mentioned variables as well as firm size to the value of the firm. For our purposes, the important result is that the empirical evidence indicates that the tax subsidy from debt does contribute a significant amount to the value of the firm. This is consistent with the notion that the WACC falls as leverage increases.

As was mentioned earlier, all the aforementioned empirical tests suffer from the impossibility of measuring future earnings and the fact that changes in the ratio of debt to assets usually is accompanied by changes in the asset structure of the firm, which in turn may imply changes in risk. None of the above papers attempts to

Table 12.2 Sources contributing to the value of the firm

	Absolute contribution			Percentage contribution		
	1957	1956	1954	1957	1956	1954
1. Capitalized earnings on assets currently held	.758	.808	.914	68.1	72.0	75.9
2. Tax subsidy on debt	.262	.254	.258	23.5	22.6	23.7
3. Growth potential	.112	.072	.028	10.0	6.4	2.3
4. Size of firm	− .019	− .008	− .021	− 1.7	− .7	− 1.7
$\dfrac{\text{Average market value}}{\text{book value}}$	1.113	1.123	1.204	100.0	100.0	100.0

Miller, M., and F. Modigliani, "Some Estimates of the Cost of Capital to the Electric Utility Industry, 1954–57," *The American Economic Revue*, June 1966, 373. Reprinted by permission of the authors.

adjust for risk directly. Instead, they rely on assumptions about the homogeneity of business risk across different firms within the electric utility industry. In a study which avoids most of these difficulties, Masulis [1977] uses a phenomenon known as corporate exchange offers to study the effects of capital-structure changes on security prices. This is a situation where one class of securities is exchanged in return for another. The most important feature is that with exchange offers, there is no simultaneous change in the asset structure of the firm. Therefore, they represent a relatively pure type of financial event which allows the researcher to isolate the effects of changes in capital structure on value.

If protective covenants written into bond indenture provisions are incomplete because the cost of monitoring and enforcing them exceeds their likely benefit, then it may be possible for management to occasionally alter the firm's capital structure in such a way that a redistribution of wealth among the various classes of security holders may result. If, for example, debt is issued to retire equity, existing bond-holders may suffer a wealth loss if the claim of the new debt on the assets of the firm is not subordinated. The effect is to make existing debt riskier without any compensation. Consequently, the market value of the debt claim will fall. Simultaneously, shareholders may benefit in two ways: (1) directly from the redistribution effect, and (2) from any tax shield provided by the new debt.

For a sample containing 163 exchanges between equity and debt during the period of 1962 through 1976, after removing general market movements and adjusting for risk, Masulis found abnormal two-day rates of return of 6.9% on common stock for the day of the announcement of an exchange offering and the following day. This was over 15 standard deviations from the mean and therefore statistically significant. For a subsample, where debt had incomplete protective covenants (27 events), the two-day abnormal loss to existing bondholders was .77%, which was over three standard deviations from the mean (again significant). These results are consistent with a tax benefit from leverage. To separate the tax shield effects from possible redistribution effects on share price changes, a cross-section regression was run. Results showed that the tax effect in recapitalizations was statistically significant and that it amounted to between 14% and 20% of the change in share prices which occurred in the two-day announcement period.

An important part of the Modigliani-Miller theory is that the cost of equity capital increases with higher leverage. Hamada [1972] tests this proposition empirically by combining the Modigliani-Miller theory and the CAPM. He reconstructs the return on common stock for a firm as if it had been unlevered and measures the unlevered return, R_t^U, as follows:

$$R_t^U = \frac{D_t + \Delta S_t + k_p P_t + k_d D_t (1 - \tau_c)}{(V^L - \tau_c B)_{t-1}}, \tag{12.9}$$

where

D_t = dividends;
ΔS_t = capital gains;
$k_p P_t$ = yield on preferred, k_p, times the amount of preferred outstanding, i.e., preferred dividends;
$k_d D_t$ = interest on debt, k_d, times the face value of debt outstanding, i.e., interest on debt;
τ_c = the corporate tax rate;
V^L = the value of a levered firm;
B = the market value of debt outstanding.

Note that the denominator of (12.9) is the value of an unlevered firm if the Modigliani-Miller theory (Eq. 11.5) is correct and if the tax effect of leverage is nonzero. The observed rate of return on common stock of the levered firm is

$$R_t^L = \frac{D_t + \Delta S_t}{S_{t-1}}. \tag{12.10}$$

By using the market model, that is, by regressing the common stock returns on the market portfolio, it is possible to obtain an estimate of the systematic risk for the unlevered and levered equity (β_{jt}^U and β_{jt}^L, respectively):

$$R_{jt}^U = \alpha_j + \beta_j^U R_{mt} + \epsilon_{jt}, \tag{12.11}$$

$$R_{jt}^L = \alpha_j' + \beta_j^L R_{mt} + \epsilon_{jt}, \tag{12.12}$$

where

ϵ_{jt} = a random error term,
α_j = a fixed intercept term.

Hamada finds that on the average the systematic risk of the levered firm is greater than that for the unlevered firm:

$$\hat{\beta}^L = .91, \qquad \hat{\beta}^U = .70.$$

This, of course, is consistent with the increased risk associated with higher leverage. But recall that in order to construct the return on equity for an unlevered firm the Modigliani-Miller theory was assumed to be correct. Suppose that it is not correct. Namely, what would happen if the return on equity, i.e., the cost of equity capital, did not increase with increasing leverage? We would expect that for a sample of firms with the same operating risk, there would be no increase in systematic risk with higher financial leverage. Because it is almost impossible to find firms with identical operating risk, Hamada suggests that within an industry, if the β^U-values of individual firms are closer or less scattered than their β^L-values, then the Modigliani-Miller theory would be supported. Greater variability in the β^L-values implies that the cost of equity changes with financial leverage. In nine industries examined, β^L was greater than β^U in all cases, and the standard deviation of the β^L-values was greater than eight out of nine of the β^U-values. This may be taken as indirect evidence that the Modigliani-Miller proposition is valid.

D. REVIEW OF EMPIRICAL EVIDENCE ON CAPITAL STRUCTURE

Optimal capital structure, if it exists, cannot be explained by the presence of risky debt alone. However, if there are significant costs involved in bankruptcy, then there may be a tradeoff between possible tax advantages of using debt capital and the probability of incurring bankruptcy costs. The optimal capital structure will attain the minimum cost of capital. Furthermore, if an optimal capital structure exists, then investment will not be independent of financing.

The empirical evidence on capital structure and the cost of capital is inconclusive. Warner [1977] argues that direct costs of bankruptcy are insignificant. However, his study is limited to the railroad industry. Other studies will surely expand in scope to examine other industries as well as indirect costs. Modigliani and Miller [1958, 1966], Weston [1963], and Masulis [1977] all have looked at the relationships among the cost of capital, capital-structure changes, and the value of the firm's securities. Although the evidence partially supports the existence of a tax benefit from leverage, more work needs to be done. Hamada [1972] shows that the cost of equity increases with leverage which is consistent with the Modigliani-Miller cost-of-capital propositions.

There are many other studies which are not reported here. Some of them find no leverage effect or even opposite effects. It is fair to say that the academic community is divided on the issue. A great deal of work needs to be done before a consensus about the effect of capital structure on the cost of capital will be reached.

E. COST OF CAPITAL: APPLICATIONS

Even when one is very familiar with the theoretical concept of the cost of capital it is not a straightforward or easy task to apply the theory to practice. Too often one is confronted with questions not made explicit because theoretical expositions are deliberately oversimplified. For example, how do unusual liabilities such as accruals, preferred debt, convertibles, or accounts payable affect the cost of capital? How should the market value weights of various sources of capital be estimated? How can one tell whether or not the firm is at its long-run target capital structure?

This section further develops some of the cost-of-capital example calculations given in Chapter 11. However, first a simple example shows how firms with high price-earnings ratios may choose to carry no debt—for the wrong reason. Second, a detailed cost of capital calculation is given for Bethlehem Steel. And finally, capital structure is discussed.

1. The Wrong Reason for Carrying No Debt. An Example

Companies with high price-earnings ratios can increase their earnings per share by issuing new equity and using the funds to buy back debt. Carried to the extreme, this process results in an optimal capital structure which contains zero debt. Much of the theory in Chapter 11 and the empirical evidence earlier in this chapter suggest that this idea is wrong. In fact, just the opposite is true. If there is a tax advantage to carrying debt, then shareholders' wealth will be increased if there is at least some debt. Nothing in the theory suggests that zero debt is optimal. Yet consider the following example, and see whether you can identify the error in its logic.

Betamax currently has a price-earnings ratio of 50. Before the change in capital structure it has 10 shares outstanding; therefore its earnings per share is $1.00, and the price per share is $50. If 10 new shares are issued at $50 each, $500 is collected and used to retire $500 of debt (which pays a coupon rate of 8%). After the capital-

Table 12.3 Higher Earnings per Share with Lower Leverage

Income statement	Before	After
Net operating income	100	100
Interest expense	− 80	− 40
Earnings before taxes	20	60
Taxes at 50%	− 10	− 30
Net income	10	30
Earnings per share	$1.00	$1.50

Balance Sheet

Before				After			
Assets		Liabilities		Assets		Liabilities	
Current	200	Debt	1,000	Current	200	Debt	500
Long-term	1,300	Equity	500	Long-term	1,300	Equity	1,000
	1,500		1,500		1,500		1,500

structure change, earnings per share have increased to $1.50 per share (since there are now 20 shares outstanding), and with a price-earnings ratio of 50, presumably the price per share will increase from $50 before the capital-structure change to $75 afterward.

The above example shows that if a firm with a high price-earnings ratio seeks to maximize earnings per share, it will carry little or no debt. The problem, of course, is that shareholders care about net cash flows (and the gain from leverage), not earnings per share. In the above example, the change in operating cash flows is zero. Before debt is retired, cash flow (neglecting depreciation, which is not given anyway) is equal to net income, $10, plus interest on debt after taxes $(1 - \tau_c)\Delta(rD)$, $40, or a total of $50.[5] After the swap of stock for bonds the cash flow is still $50. If there were no gain from leverage, the value of the firm would be unchanged. However, because there is a leverage effect in a world with corporate taxes, the value of the firm will actually fall, because leverage declines.

Using the Modigliani-Miller valuation model, Eq. (11.3), we can calculate the decrease in the value of the firm. The value of the firm before the change is

$$V^L = \frac{E(\text{NOI})(1 - \tau_c)}{\rho} + \left(\frac{rD}{k_d}\right)\tau_c, \tag{11.3}$$

where

V^L = the market value of debt, B, plus the market value of equity, S,
$E(\text{NOI})$ = the expected operating income,
τ_c = the marginal corporate tax rate,
ρ = the cost of equity for an all-equity firm,
r = the coupon rate on bonds,
k_d = the market rate on new debt,
D = the book value of debt.

Using the numbers in the Betamax example, we have

$$500 + 1000 = \frac{100(1 - .5)}{\rho} + \left(\frac{.08(1000)}{.08}\right).5.$$

Solving for ρ, the cost of equity for the unlevered firm, we have

$$\rho = 5\%.$$

We can use the fact that ρ does not change when capital structure changes to determine the value of the firm after the repurchase of debt. Substituting the new, lower amount of debt into Eq. (11.3), we have

$$V^L = \frac{100(1 - .5)}{.05} + \left(\frac{.08(500)}{.08}\right).5 = \$1250.$$

---

[5] This method for computing cash flows is covered in Chapter 2, footnote 11.

Therefore, the value of the firm has fallen from \$1500 to \$1250. Since $V^L = B + S$, the new value of equity is \$1250 − 500 = \$750, and with 20 shares outstanding, the price per share is \$37.50, while the new price-earnings ratio is 25.

This example serves to enforce a point which has been made several times earlier in the text, namely that management should not set financial policy in terms of earnings per share or the growth of earnings per share. Discounted cash flow to shareholders (and the gain from leverage) is all that matters. The Modigliani-Miller definition of the cost of capital is based on precisely this concept. Therefore it is hardly surprising that a proposal which decreases the tax shield from debt will also lower the value of the firm and raise the cost of capital. The price per share will fall from \$50 to \$37.50, and the price earnings ratio declines from 50 to 25.

2. The Cost of Capital: An Example Calculation (Bethlehem Steel)

From Chapter 11 we have two seemingly different, yet equivalent, definitions of the weighted average cost of capital. Equation (11.12), given below, is the Modigliani-Miller requirement that projects earn enough cash flow to increase the wealth of the original shareholders.

$$\text{WACC} = \rho\left(1 - \tau_c \frac{\Delta B}{\Delta I}\right),\tag{11.12}$$

where

ρ = the cost of equity for an all-equity firm,
τ_c = the marginal corporate tax rate,
ΔB = the market value of new debt,
ΔI = the replacement cost of new investment.

Given that the firm is at its long-run "optimal capital structure," we can say that an equivalent definition of the weighted average cost of capital is the weighted average of the marginal costs of various sources of capital, Eq. (11.19):

$$\text{WACC} = (1 - \tau_c)k_d \frac{B}{B + S} + k_e \frac{S}{B + S}.\tag{11.19}$$

In order to compute the weighted average cost of capital by means of Eq. (11.19), we must know (1) the marginal cost of debt and equity, k_d and k_e, and (2) the market-value capital structure used by the firm.

Although we use the term weighted average cost of capital to mean the cost of a mixture of sources of funds, it is important to emphasize that the costs of these funds must be measured as *marginal* costs. Hence the weighted average cost of capital is a weighted average of the marginal costs of the firm's various sources of capital. In this context, the word "marginal" has two meanings. Foremost is that marginal cost means the cost of *new* financing at current market equilibrium rates of return—not historical cost. Second, and implied in the rate of return required by the market, is the impact of new financing on the perceived capital structure of the firm. For example, if the percentage of debt is perceived to be rising, the marginal cost of debt must include its impact on the weighted average cost of capital. We shall ignore this second possibility by adopting the convention that the firm establishes a target capital structure and sticks with it. Given this assumption, Eqs. (11.12) and (11.19) are identical. Consequently, there are no changes in leverage to complicate matters.

Some of the complexities which arise while we estimate the cost of capital are illustrated by the following example, the cost of capital for Bethlehem Steel Corporation during December of 1976. Because market-equilibrium conditions change from day to day, so does the cost of capital. Therefore, the estimate which is given below is only an historical number, valid at the end of 1976.

Bethlehem Steel is the second-largest producer of steel in the United States. It manufactures steel products for markets in construction, transportation, service centers, and machinery. It also produces minerals and plastic products for industrial use. Table 12.4 provides a simplified *pro forma* balance sheet.[6] In order to estimate a weighted average cost of capital we need the marginal cost of each capital source and the appropriate weighting scheme.

a.   The Cost of Long-Term Debt

The first problem is estimating the current market rate of return which would be required if the firm issued new long-term debt. Almost all of Bethlehem Steel's long-term debt has had a maturity of 25 to 30 years when first issued. Therefore, we will assume that any new long-term debt will also be issued with a 30-year maturity and an Aa bond rating. What rate of return would the market require for a new issue with this risk? The "yield" provided by *The Wall Street Journal* is not useful because it assumes an infinite maturity for the debt. For

Table 12.4 *Pro forma* balance sheet, Bethlehem Steel, December 1976 (in thousands of dollars)

Assets		Liabilities	
Cash	45,600	Accounts payable	274,800
Marketable securities	355,600	Notes payable	—
Receivables	421,500	Accruals	948,600
Inventories	834,100	Long-term debt*	1,023,100
Long-term assets (net)	3,007,600	Common stock at par**	576,000
Total assets	4,939,100	less Treasury stock	69,300
		Retained earnings	2,185,900
		Total liabilities	4,939,100

* Long-term debt is detailed in Table 12.5.
** 43,665,578 shares outstanding with a market price of $40⅝ per share on December 31, 1976.

[6] Data taken from *Moody's Industrial Manual*.

Table 12.5 Composition of long-term debt (in thousands of dollars) in Table 12.4

Issue	Rating	Amount	Call price	Recent price	Yield	Year of issue
Consol. Mtge. S.F. 3s, K, 1979	Aa	21,800	$100\frac{1}{8}$	NA	NA	1949
Debenture $3\frac{1}{4}$s, 1980	Aa	3,100	100	$89\frac{1}{2}$	3.6	1955
Debenture 5.40s, 1992	Aa	109,200	$102\frac{1}{2}$	$84\frac{3}{8}$	6.4	1967
Debenture $6\frac{7}{8}$s, 1999	Aa	85,800	$104\frac{1}{4}$	$94\frac{1}{4}$	6.6	1969
Debenture 9s, 2000	Aa	144,000	$105\frac{1}{4}$	$106\frac{1}{2}$	8.5	1970
Debenture 8.45s, 2005	Aa	250,000	107.45	$103\frac{1}{2}$	8.2	1975
Debenture $8\frac{3}{8}$s, 2001	Aa	200,000	106.63	$105\frac{1}{2}$	7.9	1976
Subord. Deb. $4\frac{1}{2}$s, 1990	A	94,500	102.40	$76\frac{1}{4}$	5.9	1965
Notes payable	—	30,000	—	NA	NA	NA
Subsidiary debt	—	3,200	—	NA	NA	NA
Revenue bonds $5\frac{1}{4}$s–6s, 2002	—	100,000	—	NA	NA	NA

example, take the $3\frac{1}{4}\%$ debentures which are due in 1980. The "yield" is the coupon divided by the market price:

$$\text{Yield} = \frac{32.50}{895.00} = 3.6\%.$$

This number is completely unrealistic. The required market rate of return is the rate which equates the discounted value of the expected future cash flows with the current market price of the security. We can find this rate by solving Eq. (12.13) for the before-tax cost of debt, k_{dj}:

$$B_j = \sum_{t=1}^{T} \frac{E(\text{coupon})_t}{(1 + k_{dj})^t} + \frac{E(\text{face value})}{(1 + k_{dj})^T}, \qquad (12.13)$$

where

$E(\text{coupon})_t$ = the expected coupon payment in year t (assumed to be $32.50),
$E(\text{face value})$ = the expected face value (assumed to be $1000),
  T = number of years to maturity,
  B_j = market value of the jth debt issue.

Note that we have assumed that the bond rated Aa will actually pay its full face value of $1000 when it matures. This may not always be a valid assumption. If the bond is very risky, the expected payout may be less than $1000. (Or if the bond is callable, the expected payout may be more than $1000 and the time to maturity may be less than T if the bond is called early.) Given the above assumptions about the expected payout of the $3\frac{1}{4}\%$ debentures, the current required rate of return from them is approximately 8%. At the end of 1976, this was the appropriate interest rate for an

Aa-rated debenture due to mature in around four years.[7] Bonds with the same rating but longer maturities are slightly riskier and therefore yield higher rates. For example, the 8.45s maturing in the year 2005 yield approximately 8.3%. In our judgment, if Bethlehem Steel had decided to issue new long-term debt in December of 1976 with an Aa bond rating and a maturity of between 25 and 30 years, the company would have had to pay approximately 8.3%. We shall use this as the before-tax cost, k_d, of long-term debt, because it is the best estimate of the marginal cost of *new* debt. Next, we need an estimate of the percent of long-term debt, $B/(B + S)$, used by Bethlehem in its target capital structure. Table 12.6 shows the market value weights of various capital sources.

Table 12.6 Market value weights of capital sources

	Market value (in thousands of dollars)	Percent	Cost
Short-term liabilities	1,223,400	32.1	4.9%
Long-term debt	815,945	21.4	8.3%
Equity	1,773,914	46.5	13.5%
		100.0	

b. Market Value Weights   The market value weights of long-term debt and equity are obvious. For long-term debt, we use the market values from Table 12.6 and when they are unavailable, we use book value. The market value of equity is simply the number of shares outstanding multiplied by the price per share. Short-term liabilities are calculated at book value. This is not an unreasonable assumption because, under normal circumstances, the market value of short-term debt rarely deviates much from its book value. We assume that the current market value weights are a reasonable estimate of the firm's long-run "optimal" target capital structure. A quick, but somewhat unreliable, way of checking this assumption is to observe that the book value of long-term debt to that of total long-term debt plus equity is currently 27.5%. Its high between 1970 and 1976 was 27.5%, the average was 23.4%, and the low was 20.67%. Therefore the current capital structure is not too far from the normal pattern obtaining in recent years.

---

[7] Coupon payments of $16.25 per $1000 are made every May first and November first. The issue matures on May 1, 1980. Therefore, the actual computation is more complicated than Eq. (12.13). Students familiar with the actuarial complexities of discounting formulas will find the exact calculation to be

$$\frac{895.00}{(1 + k_{dj})^{1/6}} = \frac{32.50}{2} \left[\frac{1 - (1 + k_{dj}/2)^{-6}}{k_{dj}/2} \right] + \frac{1016.25}{(1 + k_{dj}/2)^7},$$

where $k_{dj}/2$ is a semiannual nominal rate. The solution to this problem provides an annual effective rate of approximately 8%.

c.   The Cost of Short-Term Liabilities   The cost of short-term liabilities is an often debated topic. One technique is to ignore it completely by arguing that payables and accruals may be thought of as "free" capital because in the capital-budgeting process, such spontaneously generated funds may be netted out against the required investment outlay. The alternative, which we prefer, is to include short-term liabilities in the cost of capital and also to include working capital requirements as part of the investment outlay in the capital-budgeting decision. This approach forces us to face pragmatic questions such as What is the real cost of accounts payable or accrued taxes? Both are short-term obligations, usually with a maturity of less than 90 days. Although neither has interest payments, both have opportunity costs to the "lender." With accounts payable, the lender is another firm. The opportunity cost of credit is implicit in the net price of the goods or services purchased. The opportunity cost of accruals is more difficult to justify, but the lender, whether it be the government or an unpaid worker, almost surely has an opportunity cost which is accounted for in tax or wage rates. For the sake of convenience, we shall assume that the opportunity cost of lenders of short-term liabilities is the same as the interest rate on other short-term obligations of equal risk. A good approximation is the commercial paper rate, which in December of 1976 was 4.91%.

d.   The Cost of Equity   The cost of equity capital, unfortunately, is still more an art than a science. We can use the CAPM to estimate the cost of equity, but two of the important parameters are judgmental. Equation (12.14) gives the CAPM equation for the cost of equity

$$k_e = R_f + [E(R_M) - R_f]\beta_e^L. \tag{12.14}$$

The expected future rate of return on the market cannot be measured. However, a good way of guessing what it might be is to add three components: (1) the real rate of growth of the economy, 3–4%, (2) an adjustment for inflation next year (in December of 1976 a good guess might have been 6%–7%), and (3) a risk premium for the riskiness of the market portfolio (say 4%–5%). Using the mean of each of these components, we estimate the expected rate of return as 14.5%. The risk-free rate may be approximated by the 90-day rate on U.S. Government Treasury bills, which in December of 1976 was 4.67%. Finally, we need an estimate of the systematic risk of the common stock of the company, which was .9.[8] This is really an estimate of the future systematic risk of Bethlehem Steel, and it is as much a guess as is the future rate of return on the market index. Substituting these parameter estimates into Eq. (12.14), we estimate the cost of equity capital to be 13.52%.

e.   The Weighted Average Cost of Capital   Finally, by using the market-value weights and capital costs in Table 12.6 we can estimate the weighted average cost of capital for Bethlehem Steel as of December 1976 by using Eq. (11.19) and a marginal

---

[8] There are several companies which publish estimates of the systematic risk of individual firms. We used an estimate provided by Wilshire Associates, Santa Monica, California.

corporate tax rate assumed to be 48%. The weighted average cost of capital is 8.02%. The calculation is given below:

$$\text{WACC} = (1 - \tau_c) \sum k_{dj} \left[\frac{B_j}{\sum B_j + S} \right] + k_e \frac{S}{\sum B_j + S},$$

where

k_{dj} = the before-tax cost of the jth nonequity liability (for example, k_{d1} is short-term liabilities and k_{d2} is long-term debt),
B_j = the market value of the jth nonequity liability,
k_e = the cost of equity,
S = the market value of equity.

Thus

$$\text{WACC} = (1 - .48)(.321)(.049) + (1 - .48)(.214)(.083) + .135(.465) = 8.02\%.$$

F. SUMMARY

The cost of capital, the capital structure of the firm, and the capital-budgeting decision are all inextricably linked. The theory of finance provides equations which may be applied to the solution of the weighted average cost of capital under a variety of assumptions. Although no completely satisfactory theory has yet been found to explain the existence of optimal capital structure, casual empiricism suggests that firms behave as though it does exist. Therefore, for the time being, suggested techniques for estimating the weighted average cost of capital usually assume that each firm has a target capital structure. This target is then applied to the cost of capital formulas.

A major empirical issue is the impact of capital structure on the value of the firm and on the weighted average cost of capital. Although the evidence is mixed, the articles which were summarized seem to indicate that there is, in fact, a gain from leverage which seems to be around 20%. Of course, this is less than the marginal corporate tax rate (48%) and we could have used a tax rate of 20% in estimating the cost of capital for Bethlehem Steel. If so, the weighted average cost of capital would have been 8.96%.

No mention has been made of the problem involved in estimating the cost of preferred stock, convertible debt, leases, or warrants. Nor has there been any mention of the cost of retained earnings versus the cost of new equity capital—a popular topic in most textbooks. The topic usually arises when the author brings attention to the fact that firms must incur flotation costs when issuing new equity but not while using retained earnings. The easiest way to solve the problem is to include any flotation costs as cash outflows in the capital-budgeting decision instead of trying to adjust the cost of capital.

PROBLEM SET

12.1 The puzzle of optimal capital structure is that there appear to be cross-sectional regularities in the observed ratios of debt to equity of U.S. firms. For example, the steel industry appears to carry a higher percentage of debt than the public accounting industry does. These same regularities appeared even before the existence of corporate income taxes. How can optimal leverage be explained without relying on the tax shield of debt?

12.2 What are the empirical problems involved in testing for the effect of capital structure on the value of the firm?

12.3 Assume a world without taxes. How would the weighted average cost of capital vary with the ratio of debt to total assets, $B/(B + S)$, if the cost of equity remained constant, that is, $k_e = \rho > k_d$?

12.4 During recent years your company has made considerable use of debt financing, to the extent that it is generally agreed that the percent of debt in the firm's capital structure (either in book or market-value terms) is too high. Further use of debt will likely lead to a drop in the firm's bond rating. You would like to recommend that the next major capital investment be financed with a new equity issue. Unfortunately, the firm hasn't been doing very well recently (nor has the market). In fact, the rate of return on investment has been just equal to the cost of capital. As shown in the financial statement in Table 12.7, the market value of the firm's equity is less than its book value. This means that even a profitable project will decrease earnings per share if it is financed with new equity. For example, the firm is considering a project which costs $400 but has a value of $500 (i.e., an NPV of $100), and which will increase total earnings by $60 per year. If it is financed with equity, the $400 will require approximately 200 shares, thus bringing the total shares outstanding to 1200. The new earnings will be $660, and earnings per share will fall to $.55. The president of the firm argues that the project should be delayed for three reasons.

a) It is too expensive for the firm to issue new debt.
b) Financing the project with new equity will reduce earnings per share because the market value of equity is less than book value.
c) Equity markets are currently depressed. If the firm waits until the market index improves, the market value of equity will exceed the book value and equity financing will no longer reduce earnings per share.

Critique the president's logic.

Table 12.7 Balance sheet as of December 31, 19xx

Assets		Liabilities	
Short-term assets	2,000	Debt	6,000
Plant and equipment	8,000	Equity	4,000
	10,000	Total	10,000

Total market value of equity = $2,000.00
Number of shares outstanding = 1,000.00
Price per share = 2.00
Total earnings for the year 19xx = 600.00
Earnings per share = .60

12.5 *Southwestern Electric Company.*[9] John Hatteras, the financial analyst for Southwestern Electric Company, is responsible for preliminary analysis of the company's investment projects. He is currently trying to evaluate two large projects which management has decided to consider as a single joint project, because it is felt that the geographical diversification the joint project provides would be advantageous.

Southwestern Electric was founded in the early 1930s and has operated profitably ever since. Growing at about the same rate as the population in its service area, the company has usually been able to forecast its revenues with a great deal of accuracy. The stable pattern in revenues and a favorable regulatory environment have caused most investors to view Southwestern as an investment of very low risk.

Hatteras is concerned because one of the two projects uses a new technology which will be very profitable, assuming that demand is high in a booming economy, but will do poorly in a recessionary economy. However, the expected cash flows of the two projects, supplied by the engineering department, are identical. The expected after-tax cash flows on operating income for the joint project is given in Table 12.8. Both projects are exactly the same size so that the cash flows for one is simply half the joint cash flow.

Table 12.8

Year	Outflows	Inflows	Interest
1	250	10	7.5
2	250	20	15.0
3	250	25	22.5
4	250	60	30.0
5–30	0	110	30.0
31–40	0	80	30.0
41	0	40	0

In order to better evaluate the projects, Hatteras applies his knowledge of modern finance theory. He estimates that the beta of the riskier project is .75 while the beta for the less risky project is .4375. These betas, however, are based on the covariance between the return on after-tax operating income and the market. Hatteras vaguely recalls that any discount rate he decides to apply to the projects should consider financial risk as well as operating (or business) risk. The beta for the equity of Southwestern is .5. The company has a ratio of debt to total assets of 50% and a marginal tax rate of 40%. Because the bonds of Southwestern are rated Aaa, Hatteras decides to assume that they are risk free. Finally, after consulting his investment banker, Hatteras believes that 18% is a reasonable estimate of the expected return on the market.

The joint project, if undertaken, will represent 10% of the corporation's assets. Southwestern intends to finance the joint project with 50% debt and 50% equity.

---

[9] This problem is really a short case. It has a definite answer but requires knowledge of cash flows, discounting, the CAPM, and risky cost of capital.

Hatteras wants to submit a report which answers the following questions:

a) What is the appropriate required rate of return for the new project?
b) What are the cost of equity capital and the weighted average cost of capital for South-western Electric before it takes the project?
c) Should the joint project be accepted?
d) What would the outcome be if the projects are considered separately?
e) If the joint project is accepted, what will the firm's new risk level be?

REFERENCES

BARGES, A., *The Effect of Capital Structure on the Cost of Capital.* Prentice-Hall, Englewood Cliffs, N.J., 1963.

BAXTER, N., "Leverage, Risk of Ruin and the Cost of Capital," *The Journal of Finance,* September 1967, 395–403.

BERANEK, W., *The Effect of Leverage on the Market Value of Common Stock.* Bureau of Business Research and Service, Madison, Wisconsin, 1964.

BONESS, A. J., and G. M. FRANKFURTER, "Evidence of Non-Homogeneity of Capital Costs Within 'Risk-Classes'," *The Journal of Finance,* June 1977, 775–787.

HALEY, C., and L. SCHALL, *The Theory of Financial Decisions.* McGraw-Hill, New York, 1973.

HAMADA, R. S., "The Effect of the Firm's Capital Structure on the Systematic Risk of Common Stocks," *The Journal of Finance,* May 1972, 435–452.

JENSEN, M., and W. MECKLING, "Theory of the Firm: Managerial Behavior, Agency Costs, and Ownership Structure," *Journal of Financial Economics,* October 1976, 305–360.

KIM, E. H., "A Mean Variance Theory of Optimal Capital Structure and Corporate Debt Capacity," *Journal of Finance,* March 1978, 45–64.

KRAUS, A., and R. LITZENBERGER, "A State-Preference Model of Optimal Financial Leverage," *The Journal of Finance,* September 1973, 911–922.

MASULIS, R., "Effects of Capital Structure Change on Security Prices" (PhD thesis), The University of Chicago, 1977.

MILLER, M., "Debt and Taxes," *The Journal of Finance,* May 1977, 261–275.

————, and F. MODIGLIANI, "Some Estimates of the Cost of Capital to the Electric Utility Industry, 1954–57," *The American Economic Review,* June 1966, 333–348.

————, "Some Estimates of the Cost of Capital to the Electric Utility Industry, 1954–57: Reply," *American Economic Review,* December 1967, 1288–1300.

MODIGLIANI, F., and M. MILLER, "The Cost of Capital, Corporation Finance and The Theory of Investment," *American Economic Review,* June 1958, 261–297.

————, "Taxes and the Cost of Capital: A Correction," *The American Economic Review,* June 1963, 433–443.

MYERS, S. C., "Determinants of Corporate Borrowing," *Journal of Financial Economics,* November 1977, 147–176.

ROBICHEK, A., J. MCDONALD, and R. HIGGINS, "Some Estimates of the Cost of Capital to the

Electric Utility Industry, 1954–57: Comment," *American Economic Review*, December 1967, 1278–1288.

RUBINSTEIN, M., "A Mean-Variance Synthesis of Corporate Financial Theory," *The Journal of Finance*, March 1973, 167–181.

SCOTT, J. H. JR., "A Theory of Optimal Capital Structure," *The Bell Journal of Economics*, Spring 1976, 33–54.

STIGLITZ, J., "A Re-Examination of the Modigliani-Miller Theorem," *American Economic Review*, December 1969, 784–793.

———, "On the Irrelevance of Corporate Financial Policy," *American Economic Review*, December 1974, 851–866.

———, "Some Aspects of the Pure Theory of Corporate Finance: Bankruptcies and Take-Overs," *Bell Journal of Economics and Management Science*, Autumn 1972, 458–482.

WARNER, J., "Bankruptcy Costs: Some Evidence," *The Journal of Finance*, May 1977a, 337–347.

———, "Bankruptcy, Absolute Priority, and the Pricing of Risky Debt Claims," *Journal of Financial Economics*, May 1977b, 239–276.

WESTON, J. F., "A Test of Capital Propositions," *Southern Economic Journal*, October 1963, 105–112.

Chapter 13

Dividend Policy: Theory

The one thing that shareholders cannot do through their purchase and sale transactions is negate the consequences of investment decisions by management.

J. E. Walter, "Dividend Policy: Its Influence on the Value of the Enterprise," *The Journal of Finance*, May 1963, p. 284

Is the value of shareholders' wealth affected by the dividend policy of the firm? This is another variation on the basic question, Can any financing decision affect the value of the firm? The previous chapters looked at the relationship between capital structure and the value of the firm, using a fairly simple valuation model which assumed a nongrowing stream of cash flows from investment. Capital-structure theory shows that in a world without taxes, repackaging the firm's net operating cash flows into fixed cash flows for debt and residual cash flows for shareholders has no effect on the value of the firm. This chapter develops valuation models which include growth opportunities, thereby adding a greater element of realism. Even so, we shall show that, in a world without taxes, it makes no difference whether or not shareholders receive their cash flows as dividends or capital gains. Thus in the absence of taxes, dividend policy is irrelevant. It does not affect shareholders' wealth. The argument is then extended to a valuation model which includes growth and corporate taxes, but the result does not change. Dividend payout does not affect the value of the firm. Only when personal as well as corporate taxes are included does the possibility arise that dividends may affect value.

Empirical tests of dividend policy and applications of corporate valuation are discussed in Chapter 14.

A. THE IRRELEVANCE OF DIVIDEND POLICY IN A WORLD WITHOUT TAXES

Miller and Modigliani [1961] present a cogent argument for the fact that the value of the firm is unaffected by dividend policy in a world without taxes or transactions costs. They begin by assuming that two firms are identical in every respect except for their dividend payout in the current time period. Their streams of future cash flows from operations are identical, their planned investment outlays are identical, and all future dividend payments from the second time period on are also identical. We can represent this mathematically as follows:

$$\widetilde{NOI}_1(t) = \widetilde{NOI}_2(t), \qquad t = 0, 1, \ldots, \infty,$$

$$\tilde{I}_1(t) = \tilde{I}_2(t), \qquad t = 0, 1, \ldots, \infty,$$

$$\tilde{D}_1(t) = \tilde{D}_2(t), \qquad t = 1, \ldots, \infty,$$

$$D_1(0) \neq D_2(0)$$

where

$\widetilde{NOI}_i(t) =$ the random future cash flows from operations for the ith firm in time period t,

$\tilde{I}_i(t) =$ the variable investment outlay for the ith firm in time period t,

$\tilde{D}_i(t) =$ the random dividend payout for firms in period t,

$D_i(0) =$ the dividend payout for the ith firm during the current time period.

1. A Recursive Valuation Formula

The important question is whether or not the two firms will have different value if their current dividend payouts are different. In order to supply an answer we first need a simple valuation model. Let us begin by assuming that the market-required rates of return for firms in the same risk class are identical.[1] The two firms above obviously have the same risk because their streams of operating cash flows are identical. The rate of return is defined as dividends plus capital gains,

$$\rho(t + 1) = \frac{d_i(t + 1) + P_i(t + 1) - P_i(t)}{P_i(t)} \tag{13.1}$$

where

$\rho(t + 1) =$ the market-required rate of return during time period t,

$d_i(t + 1) =$ dividends per share paid at the end of time period t,

$P_i(t + 1) =$ price per share at the end of time period t,

$P_i(t) =$ price per share at the beginning of time period t.

---

[1] For the sake of simplicity, we assume that both firms are 100% equity. This avoids the problem of confusing capital-structure effects with possible dividend-policy effects.

If the numerator and denominator of (13.1) are multiplied by the current number of shares outstanding, $n(t)$, then by rearranging terms, we have

$$V_i(t) = \frac{D_i(t+1) + n(t)P(t+1)}{1 + \rho(t+1)},$$ (13.2)

where

$D_i(t+1) =$ total dollar dividend payment $= n(t)d_i(t+1)$,
$\quad V_i(t) =$ the market value of the firm $= n(t)P_i(t)$.

Hence the value of the firm is seen to be equal to the discounted sum of two cash flows: any dividends paid out, $D_i(t+1)$, and the end-of-period value of the firm. In order to show that the value of the firm is independent of dividend payout, we shall examine the sources and uses of funds for the two firms in order to rewrite (13.2) in a way that is independent of dividends.

2. Sources and Uses of Funds

There are two major sources of funds for an all-equity firm. First, it receives cash from operations, $\widetilde{NOI}_i(t+1)$, and second, it may issue new shares, $m_i(t+1)\tilde{P}_i(t+1)$, where $m_i(t+1)$ is the number of new shares. There are also two major uses of funds: dividends paid out, $\tilde{D}_i(t+1)$, and planned cash outlays for investment, $\tilde{I}_i(t+1)$.[2] By definition, sources and uses must be equal. Therefore, we have the following identity:

$$\widetilde{NOI}_i(t+1) + m_i(t+1)\tilde{P}_i(t+1) \equiv \tilde{I}_i(t+1) + \tilde{D}_i(t+1).$$ (13.3)

We can use this fact to rewrite the numerator of the valuation equation (13.2). Calling the numerator of (13.2) the dollar return to shareholders, $\tilde{R}_i(t+1)$, we have

$$\tilde{R}_i(t+1) = \tilde{D}_i(t+1) + n_i(t)\tilde{P}_i(t+1).$$ (13.4)

We know that if new shares are issued, the total number of shares outstanding at the end of the period, $n(t+1)$, will be the sum of current shares, $n(t)$, and new shares $m(t+1)$:

$$n_i(t+1) = n_i(t) + m_i(t+1).$$ (13.5)

Using (13.5), we can rewrite (13.4) as

$$\tilde{R}_i(t+1) = \tilde{D}_i(t+1) + n_i(t+1)\tilde{P}_i(t+1) - m_i(t+1)\tilde{P}_i(t+1).$$ (13.6)

Finally, taking Eq. (13.3), which establishes the identity of the sources and uses of funds, to substitute for $m_i(t)\tilde{P}_i(t+1)$ in the above equation, we obtain

$$\tilde{R}_i(t+1) = \tilde{D}_i(t+1) + \tilde{V}_i(t+1) - \tilde{I}_i(t+1) + \widetilde{NOI}_i(t+1) - \tilde{D}_i(t+1)$$
$$= \widetilde{NOI}_i(t+1) - \tilde{I}_i(t+1) + \tilde{V}_i(t+1),$$ (13.7)

---

[2] This argument assumes, for the sake of convenience, that sources and uses of funds from balance sheet items (e.g., changes in inventories or accounts receivable) are negligible.

where $\tilde{V}_i(t + 1) = n_i(t + 1)\tilde{P}_i(t + 1)$. Therefore, the valuation equation (13.2) may be rewritten

$$\tilde{V}_i(t) = \frac{\widehat{NOI}_i(t + 1) - \tilde{I}_i(t + 1) + \tilde{V}_i(t + 1)}{1 + \rho(t + 1)}. \tag{13.8}$$

3.   Valuation and the Irrelevancy of Dividend Payout

It is no accident that dividends do not appear in the valuation equation (13.8). The firm can choose any dividend policy whatsoever without affecting the stream of cash flows received by shareholders. It could, for example, elect to pay dividends in excess of cash flows from operations and still be able to undertake any planned investment. The extra funds needed are supplied by issuing new equity. On the other hand, it could decide to pay dividends less than the amount of cash left over from operations after making investments. The excess cash would be used to repurchase shares. It is the availability of external financing in a world without transactions costs which makes the value of the firm independent of dividend policy.

We can use Eq. (13.8) to prove that two firms which are identical in every respect except for their current dividend payout must have the same value. The equation has four terms. First, the market required rate of return, ρ, must be the same because both firms have identical risk, $\widehat{NOI}_1(t) = \widehat{NOI}_2(t)$, for all t. Second, current cash flows from operations and current investment outlays for the two firms have been assumed to be identical:

$$\widehat{NOI}_1(1) = \widehat{NOI}_2(1), \qquad \tilde{I}_1(1) = \tilde{I}_2(1).$$

Finally, the end-of-period values of the two firms depend only on *future* investments, dividends, and cash flows from operations, which also have been assumed to be identical. Therefore, the end-of-period values of the two firms must be the same:

$$\tilde{V}_1(1) = \tilde{V}_2(1).$$

Consequently, the present values of the two firms must be identical regardless of their current dividend payout. Dividend policy is irrelevant because it has no effect on shareholders' wealth in a world without taxes or transactions costs.

Note that the proof of the irrelevancy of dividend policy was made using a multiperiod model whose returns were uncertain. Therefore, it is an extremely general argument. In addition to providing insight into what does not affect the value of the firm, it provides considerable insight into what *does* affect value. The value of the firm depends only on the distribution of future cash flows provided by investment decisions. The key to the Miller-Modigliani argument is that investment decisions are completely independent of dividend policy. The firm can pay any level of dividends it wishes without affecting investment decisions. If dividends plus desired investment outlays use more cash flow than is provided from operations, the firm should issue new equity. The desire to maintain a level of dividends should never affect the investment decision.

B. VALUATION, GROWTH, AND DIVIDEND POLICY

The Miller-Modigliani argument that the value of the firm is independent of dividend policy also extends into a world with corporate taxes but without personal taxes. In this section, the valuation model (Eq. (13.8)) is extended to include corporate taxes and a growing stream of cash flows. The result is a valuation model which has realistic features and hence may be usefully applied to real-world valuation problems. Chapter 14 will expand on the usefulness of the valuation model by means of an example.

1. The Valuation of an All-Equity Firm with Growth

Figure 13.1 uses a time line as a graphic representation of the pattern of cash flows earned by a growing firm. Note that there is a current level of cash flow, NOI_1, which is assumed to be received at the end of each year forever. If the firm made no new investments and only maintained its current level of capital stock, it would receive cash flows each year equal to NOI_1, but it would not be growing. Growth comes from new investment, not replacement investment. The value of new investment depends on the amount of investment, I_t, and its rate of return, r_t.

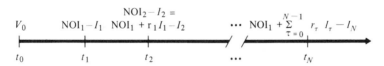

Fig. 13.1 Time pattern of cash flows for a growing firm

We can extend the valuation equation (13.8) by assuming that the discount rate, ρ, does not change from time period to time period. This is reasonable if all new projects have the same risk as those which the firm currently holds. Equation (13.8) is[3]

$$V_0 = \frac{NOI_1 - I_1}{1 + \rho} + \frac{V_1}{1 + \rho}. \tag{13.8}$$

Given a constant discount rate, ρ, it can be extended to an N-period model as follows:

$$V_0 = \frac{NOI_1 - I_1}{1 + \rho} + \frac{NOI_2 - I_2}{(1 + \rho)^2} + \cdots + \frac{NOI_N - I_N}{(1 + \rho)^N} + \frac{V_N}{(1 + \rho)^N}. \tag{13.9}$$

---

[3] The tildes ($\tilde{\ }$) are dropped for notational convenience. Also note that:

$$NOI_2 = NOI_1 + r_1 I_1.$$

A reasonable assumption is that in any time period the value of the firm, V_t, is finite.[4] Therefore, given a model with an infinite horizon, we have

$$\lim_{N \to \infty} V_0 = \sum_{t=1}^{N} \frac{\text{NOI}_t - I_t}{(1+\rho)^t}. \tag{13.10}$$

Equation (13.10) is the same formula used in Chapter 2 on capital budgeting. The present value of the firm is the sum of the discounted cash flows from operations less the new investment outlays necessary to undertake them.

Referring to Fig. 13.1, we can see that the average return on investment, r_t, is assumed to continue forever at a constant rate. This is a perfectly reasonable assumption because if the capital budgeting decision is made correctly, each project will return enough cash to cover payments to suppliers of capital and to recover the initial investment. Thus the cash flows are sufficient to provide any needed replacement investment to sustain the project at a constant level forever. The stream of cash flows for the growing firm in Fig. 13.1 are given in Table 13.1 (also Eq. (13.11)).

Table 13.1

Time period	Cash inflow	Cash outflow
1	NOI_1	$-I_1$
2	$\text{NOI}_2 = \text{NOI}_1 + r_1 I_1$	$-I_2$
3	$\text{NOI}_3 = \text{NOI}_1 + r_1 I_1 + r_2 I_2$	$-I_3$
⋮	⋮	⋮
N	$\text{NOI}_N = \text{NOI}_1 + \sum_{\tau=1}^{N} r_\tau I_\tau$	$-I_N$

$$\tag{13.11}$$

Substituting (13.11) into (13.10), we can express the present value of the growing firm as

$$V_0 = \frac{\text{NOI}_1 - I_1}{1+\rho} + \frac{\text{NOI}_1 + r_1 I_1 - I_2}{(1+\rho)^2} + \frac{\text{NOI}_1 + r_1 I_1 + r_2 I_2 - I_3}{(1+\rho)^3}$$

$$+ \cdots + \frac{\text{NOI}_1 + \sum_{\tau=1}^{N-1} r_\tau I_\tau - I_N}{(1+\rho)^N}. \tag{13.12}$$

---

[4] After all, no one has observed a firm with infinite value as yet.

This extended equation can be simplified greatly. First, rewrite it by rearranging terms as follows.

$$V_0 = \frac{NOI_1}{1 + \rho} + \frac{NOI_1}{(1 + \rho)^2} + \cdots + \frac{NOI_1}{(1 + \rho)^N}$$

$$+ I_1 \left[\frac{r_1}{(1 + \rho)^2} + \frac{r_1}{(1 + \rho)^3} + \cdots + \frac{r_1}{(1 + \rho)^N} - \frac{1}{1 + \rho} \right]$$

$$+ I_2 \left[\frac{r_2}{(1 + \rho)^3} + \frac{r_2}{(1 + \rho)^4} + \cdots + \frac{r_2}{(1 + \rho)^N} - \frac{1}{(1 + \rho)^2} \right] + \cdots.$$

This result can be generalized as

$$V_0 = \sum_{t=1}^{N} \frac{NOI_1}{(1 + \rho)^t} + \sum_{t=1}^{N} I_t \left[\left(\sum_{\tau=t+1}^{N} \frac{r_t}{(1 + \rho)^\tau} \right) - \frac{1}{(1 + \rho)^t} \right]. \tag{13.13}$$

We can simplify Eq. (13.13) by recognizing that the first term is an infinite annuity with constant payments of NOI_1 per period. Therefore

$$\lim_{N \to \infty} \sum_{t=1}^{N} \frac{NOI_1}{(1 + \rho)^t} = \frac{NOI_1}{\rho}. \tag{13.14}$$

Next, the second term in (13.13) can be simplified as follows:

$$\sum_{\tau=t+1}^{N} \frac{r_t}{(1 + \rho)^\tau} = \frac{1}{(1 + \rho)^t} \sum_{\tau=1}^{N} \frac{r_t}{(1 + \rho)^\tau},$$

$$\frac{1}{(1 + \rho)^t} \lim_{N \to \infty} \sum_{\tau=1}^{N} \frac{r_t}{(1 + \rho)^\tau} = \frac{1}{(1 + \rho)^t} \frac{r_t}{\rho}. \tag{13.15}$$

Substituting (13.14) and (13.15) back into (13.13), we obtain a simplified expression for the present value of the firm:

$$V_0 = \frac{NOI_1}{\rho} + \sum_{t=1}^{\infty} I_t \left[\left(\frac{r_t}{\rho(1 + \rho)^t} \right) - \frac{1}{(1 + \rho)^t} \right]$$

$$= \frac{NOI_1}{\rho} + \sum_{t=1}^{\infty} \frac{I_t(r_t - \rho)}{\rho(1 + \rho)^t}. \tag{13.16}$$

2. Why Growth Maximization is an Inappropriate Goal

This form of valuation equation provides important insights into the much abused term "growth stock." The first term in Eq. (13.16) is the present value of a firm which makes no new investments. It is the present value of an infinite stream of constant cash flows. In other words, it is the value of a firm which is not growing. But what about the firm which makes new investments? The present value of new investment is shown in the second term of Eq. (13.16). The *value* of new investment depends on two things: (1) the amount of investment made and (2) the difference between the average rate of return on the investment, r_t, and the market-required rate of return, ρ. The assets of a firm may grow, but they don't add anything to value unless they earn a rate of return greater than what the market requires for assets of equivalent risk. For example, supposing that the market requires a 10% rate of return, that is, $\rho = 10\%$, consider the three situations given in Table 13.2. Firm 3 has the greatest "growth" in cash flows (ΔNOI = 5000). But which firm has the greatest increase in value? Obviously, firm 1 does. The reason is that it is the only firm which has new investments which earn more than the required-market rate of return of 10%. Therefore, the objective of a firm should *never* be to simply maximize growth in earnings or cash flows. The objective should be to maximize the market value of the firm which is equivalent to maximizing shareholders' wealth.

Table 13.2

	ΔI, \$	r, %	ΔNOI, \$	ΔV_0, \$
Firm 1	10,000	20	2,000	9,090
Firm 2	30,000	10	3,000	0
Firm 3	100,000	5	5,000	− 45,454

Another feature of Eq. (13.16) is that it is derived directly from Eq. (13.8), and in both we have the result that dividend policy is irrelevant in a world without taxes or transactions costs.

3. The Value of an All-Equity Firm Which Grows at a Constant Rate Forever

Equation (13.16) is elegant, but somewhat cumbersome to use. It has two useful variations. The first, which is developed below, assumes that the firm experiences a constant rate of growth forever. We shall call it the infinite constant-growth model. The second, developed later on, assumes that the firm can maintain a supernormal rate of growth for a finite period of time, T, and realizes a normal rate of growth thereafter. It is called the finite supernormal growth model.

The constant-growth model can be derived from Eq. (13.16) if we assume that a constant fraction, K, of earnings is retained for investment and the average rate of return, r_t, on all projects is the same. The fraction of earnings to be retained for investment is usually called the retention ratio; however, there is no reason to restrict it to be less than 100% of cash flows from operations. Rather than calling K the retention rate, we shall call it the *investment rate*. As was mentioned in the first section of this chapter, the firm can invest more than cash flow from operations if it provides for the funds by issuing new equity. If investment is a constant proportion of cash flows, we have

$$I_t = K(\text{NOI}_t). \tag{13.17}$$

And if the rate of return on investment, r_t, is the same for every project, then

$$\text{NOI}_t = \text{NOI}_{t-1} + r I_{t-1},$$
$$= \text{NOI}_{t-1} + rK\ \text{NOI}_{t-1},$$
$$= \text{NOI}_{t-1}(1 + rK).$$

By successive substitution, we have

$$\text{NOI}_t = \text{NOI}_1(1 + rK)^{t-1}. \tag{13.18}$$

Note that rK is the same as the rate of growth, g, for cash flows. In other words, NOI in the tth time period is the future value of NOI in the first time period assuming that cash flows grow at a constant rate, g:

$$\text{NOI}_t = \text{NOI}_1(1 + g)^{t-1}.$$

By substituting (13.17) into (13.16) and maintaining the assumption that $r_t = r$, we have

$$V_0 = \frac{\text{NOI}_1}{\rho} + \sum_{t=1}^{\infty} \frac{K\ \text{NOI}_t(r - \rho)}{\rho(1 + \rho)^t}. \tag{13.19}$$

Then by using (13.18) in (13.19) we obtain

$$V_0 = \frac{\text{NOI}_1}{\rho} + K\ \text{NOI}_1 \left(\frac{r - \rho}{\rho} \right) \sum_{t=1}^{\infty} \frac{(1 + rK)^{t-1}}{(1 + \rho)^t}$$
$$= \frac{\text{NOI}_1}{\rho} \left[1 + \frac{K(r - \rho)}{1 + rK} \sum_{t=1}^{\infty} \left(\frac{1 + rK}{1 + \rho} \right)^t \right]. \tag{13.20}$$

If $rK < \rho$, then the last term in (13.20) will have a finite limit[5]

$$\lim_{N \to \infty} \sum_{t=1}^{N} \left(\frac{1 + rK}{1 + \rho} \right) = \frac{1 + rK}{\rho - rK} \qquad \text{iff} \qquad \rho > rK. \tag{13.20a}$$

---

[5] For proof let $(1 + rK)/(1 + \rho) = U$. This can be written as

$$S = U + U^2 + \cdots + U^N.$$

Multiplying this by U and subtracting the result from the above, we have

$$S = U/(1 - U) - U^{N+1}/(1 - U).$$

The second term approaches zero in the limit as N approaches infinity. By substituting back the definition of U, we get (13.20a).

Substituting (13.20a) into (13.20) and simplifying, we have an equation for the value of the firm, assuming infinite growth at a rate less than the market rate of return, ρ.

$$V_0 = \frac{\text{NOI}_1}{\rho}\left[1 + \frac{K(r - \rho)}{1 + Kr}\frac{1 + Kr}{\rho - rK}\right]$$

$$= \frac{\text{NOI}_1(1 - K)}{\rho - Kr}. \tag{13.21}$$

Equation (13.21), rewritten in a somewhat different form, is frequently referred to as the *Gordon growth model*. Note that since K is the investment rate (although K need not be less than one), the numerator of (13.21) is the same as dividends paid at the end of the first time period:

$$\text{NOI}_1(1 - K) = D_1.$$

Also, as was shown earlier, the product of the investment rate and the average rate of return on investment is the same as the growth rate, g, in cash flows; therefore

$$Kr = g.$$

Given these facts and the necessary condition that $g < \rho$, the infinite growth model, Eq. (13.21), can be rewritten as

$$V_0 = \frac{D_1}{\rho - g}, \tag{13.21a}$$

which is the *Gordon growth model*.

4. Independence between Investment Plans and Dividend Payout

This form of the valuation model can be used to illustrate the relationship between the result that the value of the firm is independent of dividend policy and the assumption that investment decisions should never be affected by dividend payout. A commonly made error is to implicitly assume that there is some relationship between the amount of cash flow retained and the amount of investment which the firm undertakes. Suppose we take the partial derivative of Eq. (13.21) with respect to changes in the investment rate, K:

$$\frac{\delta V_0}{\delta K} = \frac{\text{NOI}_1(r - \rho)}{(\rho - rK)^2} > 0.$$

This suggests that if the rate of return on investments, r, is greater than the market-required rate of return, ρ, the value of the firm will increase as more cash flow is retained, and presumably the increased amount of retained cash flow implies lower dividend payout. This line of reasoning is incorrect for two reasons. First, the amount of cash flow retained has nothing to do with dividend payout. As was shown in the sources and uses of funds, identity (13.3), the firm can arbitrarily set dividend payout at any level whatsoever, and if the sum of funds used for dividends and investment is greater than cash flows from operations, the firm will issue new equity. Second, the investment decision which maximizes shareholder wealth depends only on the market-required rate of return. The amount of cash flow retained could exceed the amount of investment, which would imply that shares would be repurchased. Therefore there is no relationship between the value of the firm and either dividend payout or cash flow retention.

5. The Bird-in-Hand Fallacy

A more sophisticated argument for a relationship between the value of the firm and dividend payout is that although the dividend decision cannot change the present value of cash payments to shareholders, it can affect the temporal pattern of payouts. Suppose that investors view distant dividend payments as riskier than current payments, might they not prefer a bird in the hand to two in the bush? We can represent this argument mathematically by assuming that higher investment rates mean lower current dividend payout, more risk, and therefore an increase in the market rate of return, ρ, as a function of the investment rate, K. A simple example would be to specify the relationship as

$$\rho = \alpha + \beta K^2.$$

Then we would have

$$\frac{\delta V_0}{\delta K} = \frac{\text{NOI}_1(\beta K^2 - 2\beta K + r - \alpha)}{(\alpha + \beta K^2 - rK)^2}.$$

This function will have a maximum where

$$\text{NOI}_1(\beta K^2 - 2\beta K + r - \alpha) = 0.$$

In order to see the error in this line of reasoning, we need only to return to our understanding of valuation under uncertainty. The risk of the firm is determined by the riskiness of the cash flows from its projects. An increase in dividend payout today will result in an equivalent drop in the ex-dividend price of the stock. It will not increase the value of the firm by reducing the riskiness of future cash flows.

6. Finite Supernormal Growth Model for an All-Equity Firm

Perhaps the most useful variation of the valuation equation is one which assumes that the rate of return on investment is greater than the market-required rate of return for a finite number of years, T, and from then on is equal to the market-required rate of return. In other words, the firm experiences supernormal growth for a short period of time, then settles down, and grows at a rate which is equal to the rate of growth in the economy. Obviously a firm cannot grow faster than the economy forever or it would soon be larger than the economy.

In order to derive the finite growth model we start with Eq. (13.20). Note that the summation is no longer infinite:

$$V_0 = \frac{\text{NOI}_1}{\rho}\left[1 + \frac{K(r - \rho)}{1 + rK} \sum_{t=1}^{T}\left(\frac{1 + rK}{1 + \rho}\right)^t\right]. \tag{13.20}$$

Instead, growth lasts for only T years. After year T, we assume that $r = \rho$, which means that the second term adds nothing to the present value of the firm. The summation term in Eq. (13.20) can be evaluated as follows. Let

$$U = [(1 + rK)/(1 + \rho)].$$

We can then expand the sum:

$$S = U + U^2 + \cdots + U^T.$$

By multiplying S by U and subtracting the result, we have

$$S - US = U - U^{T+1}.$$

Solving for S and substituting back for U, we obtain

$$S = \frac{U - U^{T+1}}{1 - U} = \frac{[(1 + Kr)/(1 + \rho)] - [(1 + Kr)/(1 + \rho)]^{T+1}}{1 - [(1 + Kr)/(1 + \rho)]}$$

$$= \frac{(1 + Kr)[1 - [(1 + Kr)/(1 + \rho)]^T]}{\rho - Kr}. \tag{13.21b}$$

Substituting (13.21b) into (13.20) yields

$$V_0 = \frac{\text{NOI}_1}{\rho} \left[1 + \frac{Kr - \rho K}{\rho - Kr} \left[1 - \left(\frac{1 + Kr}{1 + \rho} \right)^T \right] \right]. \tag{13.22}$$

As long as Kr is approximately equal to ρ, and T is small, we can approximate the last term as[6]

$$\left(\frac{1 + Kr}{1 + \rho} \right)^T \approx 1 - T \left(\frac{\rho - Kr}{1 + \rho} \right). \tag{13.23}$$

---

[6] The binomial expansion can be used to derive the approximation in the following way. Let $(1 + Kr)/(1 + \rho) = 1 + \Delta$. Then, recalling that $Kr = g$, we have:

$$\left(\frac{1 + g}{1 + \rho} \right)^T = (1 + \Delta)^T = \sum_{K=0}^{T} \binom{T}{K} (1)^{T-K} \Delta^K$$

$$= 1 + T\Delta + \sum_{K=2}^{T} \binom{T}{K} \Delta^K \approx 1 + T\Delta.$$

Solving for Δ, we have

$$\Delta = \frac{1 + Kr}{1 + \rho} - 1 = \frac{Kr - \rho}{1 + \rho}.$$

Therefore the correct approximation is

$$1 + T\Delta = 1 - T \left(\frac{\rho - Kr}{1 + \rho} \right).$$

By substituting the approximation (13.23) into the valuation equation (13.22), we have an approximate valuation formula for finite supernormal growth:[7]

$$V_0 = \frac{\text{NOI}_1}{\rho} + \frac{K(r-\rho)}{\rho - Kr} T\left(\frac{\rho - Kr}{1+\rho}\right)\frac{\text{NOI}_1}{\rho}$$

$$= \frac{\text{NOI}_1}{\rho} + K(\text{NOI}_1)T\left[\frac{r-\rho}{\rho(1+\rho)}\right]. \tag{13.24}$$

7. Finite Growth Model for a Firm with Debt and Taxes

Up to this point, we have maintained the assumption that we are dealing with an all-equity firm in a world without taxes. In order to extend the above valuation equation into a world where firms have debt as well as equity and where there are corporate taxes, we can rely on the results obtained in Chapter 11. The value of a levered firm with finite supernormal growth can be written as follows:

$$V_0 = \frac{\text{NOI}_1(1-\tau_c)}{\rho} + \tau_c B + K(\text{NOI}_1(1-\tau_c))T\left[\frac{r-k_0}{k_0(1+k_0)}\right], \tag{13.25}$$

where

NOI_1 = end-of-year net operating profits,
k_0 = weighted average cost of capital = $\rho(1 - \tau_c B/(B+S))$,
B = market value of debt,
K = investment rate,
T = the number of years that $r > k_0$,
r = the average rate of return on investment,
ρ = the cost of equity capital for an all-equity firm.

The first two terms in (13.25) are the value of a levered firm with no growth. They are the same as Eq. (11.3), the Modigliani-Miller result which assumes that firms pay

---

[7] To simulate the validity of the approximation assume that the retention rate, K, is 50%, the rate of return on investment, r, is 20%, and the market-required rate of return is 5%. Figure 13.A is a plot of $[(1 + Kr)/(1 + \rho)]^T$. We can see visually that the linear approximation is reasonable.

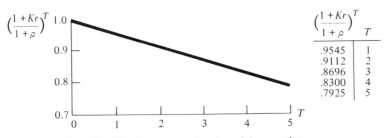

Fig. 13.A The linear approximation of the growth term

corporate taxes, but are not growing. The third term in Eq. (13.25) is the effect of growth on the value of a levered firm. It depends on the amount of investment, $I_t = K(\text{NOI}_t)$, the difference between the expected average rate of return on investment and the weighted average cost of capital, $r - k_0$, and the length of time, T, that the new investment is expected to earn more than the weighted average cost of capital.

Equation (13.25) is used in Chapter 14 as the basis for the valuation of Bethlehem Steel. Note, however, that even in this model (which is the most realistic of those developed so far in this chapter), dividend payout is not relevant to determining the value of the firm.

C. DIVIDEND POLICY IN A WORLD WITH PERSONAL AND CORPORATE TAXES

Up to this point the models of firms which have been introduced assume a world with only corporate taxes. What happens when personal taxes are considered? In particular, how is dividend policy affected by the important fact that in the United States, the capital gains tax is less than the personal income tax? An answer to this question is provided by Farrar and Selwyn [1967] and extended into a market equilibrium framework by Brennan [1970].[8]

Farrar and Selwyn [1967] use partial equilibrium analysis and assume that individuals attempt to maximize their after-tax income. Shareholders have two choices. They can own shares in an all-equity firm and borrow in order to provide personal leverage, or they can buy shares in a levered firm. Therefore the first choice is the amount of personal versus corporate leverage which is desired. The second choice is the form of payment to be made by the firm. It can pay out earnings as dividends or it can retain earnings and allow shareholders to take their income in the form of capital gains. Shareholders must choose whether they want dividends or capital gains.

If the firm pays out all of its cash flows as dividends, the ith shareholder will receive the following after-tax income, $\tilde{Y}_i^d$.

$$\tilde{Y}_i^d = [(\widetilde{\text{NOI}} - rD_c)(1 - \tau_c) - rD_{pi}](1 - \tau_{pi}), \qquad (13.26)$$

where

$\tilde{Y}_i^d =$ the uncertain income to the ith individual if corporate income is received as dividends,
$\widetilde{\text{NOI}} =$ the uncertain cash flows from operations provided by the firm,
$r =$ the borrowing rate which is assumed to be equal for individuals and firms,
$D_c =$ corporate debt,
$D_{pi} =$ personal debt held by the ith individual,
$\tau_c =$ the corporate tax rate,
$\tau_{pi} =$ the personal income tax rate of the ith individual.

---

[8] More recently Miller and Scholes [1977] have also considered a world with dividends and taxes. The implications of this paper are discussed in the next chapter.

The first term within the brackets is the after-tax cash flow of the firm, $(\widetilde{NOI} - rD)$ $(1 - \tau_c)$, all of which is assumed to be paid out as dividends. The before-tax income to the shareholder is the dividends received minus the interest on debt used to buy shares. After subtracting income taxes on this income we are left with Eq. (13.26).

Alternatively, the firm can decide to pay no dividends, in which case we assume that all gains are realized *immediately* by investors and taxed at the capital gains rate.[9] In this event, the after-tax income of a shareholder is

$$\tilde{Y}_i^q = (\widetilde{NOI} - rD_c)(1 - \tau_c)(1 - \tau_{gi}) - rD_{pi}(1 - \tau_{pi}), \tag{13.27}$$

where

$\tilde{Y}_i^q =$ the uncertain income to the ith individual if corporate income is received as capital gains,

$\tau_{gi} =$ the capital gains rate for the ith individual.

Now the individual pays a capital gains tax rate on the income from the firm and deducts after-tax interest expenses on personal debt. The corporation can implement the policy of translating cash flows into capital gains by simply repurchasing its shares in the open market.

We can rewrite Eq. (13.27) as follows:

$$\tilde{Y}_i^q = [(\widetilde{NOI} - rD_c)(1 - \tau_c) - rD_{pi}](1 - \tau_{gi}) + rD_{pi}(\tau_{pi} - \tau_{gi}). \tag{13.28}$$

From Eqs. (13.26) and (13.28) the advantage to investors of receiving returns in the form of capital gains rather than dividends should be obvious. So long as the tax rate on capital gains is less than the personal tax rate $(\tau_{gi} < \tau_{pi})$, individuals will prefer capital gains to dividends for any positive operating cash flows, rate of interest, and level of debt (personal or corporate). The ratio of the two income streams,

$$\frac{\tilde{Y}_i^q}{\tilde{Y}_i^d} = \frac{[(\widetilde{NOI} - rD_c)(1 - \tau_c) - rD_{pi}](1 - \tau_{gi}) + rD_{pi}(\tau_{pi} - \tau_{gi})}{[(\widetilde{NOI} - rD_c)(1 - \tau_c) - rD_{pi}](1 - \tau_{pi})} > 1, \tag{13.29}$$

is greater than one if $\tau_{gi} < \tau_{pi}$. In general, the best form of payment is the one which is subject to least taxation. The implication, of course, is that corporations should never pay dividends. If payments are to be made to shareholders, they should always be made via share repurchase. This allows shareholders to avoid paying income tax rates on dividends. Instead, they receive their payments in the form of capital gains which are taxed at a lower rate.

What about debt policy? Again the same principle holds. The debt should be held by the party which can obtain the greatest tax shield from the deductible interest payments. This is the party with the greatest marginal tax rate. If the firm pays out all its cash flow in the form of dividends, the favorable tax treatment of capital gains is irrelevant. In this case, we have the familiar Modigliani-Miller [1963] result that the

---

[9] Obviously there is the third possibility that earnings are translated into capital gains and the capital gains taxes are deferred to a later date. This possibility is considered in Farrar and Selwyn [1967]; it does not change their conclusions.

value of the firm is maximized by taking on the maximum amount of debt (see Chapter 11). Proof is obtained by taking the partial derivative of Eq. (13.26) with respect to personal and corporate debt and comparing the results.

Debt policy becomes more complex when the corporation repurchases shares instead of paying dividends. Taking the partial derivatives of the capital gains income equation, (13.27), we obtain

$$\text{Corporate debt:} \quad \frac{\delta \tilde{Y}_i^q}{\delta D_c} = -r(1 - \tau_c)(1 - \tau_{gi}) \tag{13.30}$$

$$\text{Personal debt:} \quad \frac{\delta \tilde{Y}_i^q}{\delta D_{pi}} = -r(1 - \tau_{pi}) \tag{13.31}$$

If the effective tax rate on capital gains is zero (as Miller [1977] suggests), then personal debt will be preferred to corporate debt by those individuals who are in marginal tax brackets higher than the marginal tax bracket of the firm. This result allows the possibility of clientele effects where low-income investors prefer corporate debt and high-income investors prefer personal debt. Miller [1977] takes this argument even further. He shows that if the borrowing rate on debt is "grossed up" so that the after-tax rate on debt equals the after-tax rate on other sources of capital, the marginal investor will be indifferent between personal and corporate debt.[10]

Brennan [1970] extends the work of Farrar and Selwyn into a general equilibrium framework where investors are assumed to maximize their expected utility of wealth. Although this framework is more robust, Brennan's conclusions are not much different from those of Farrar and Selwyn. With regard to dividend payout he concludes that "for a given level of risk, investors require a higher total return on a security the higher its prospective dividend yield is, because of the higher rate of tax levied on dividends than on capital gains." As we shall see in the next chapter, this statement has empirical implications for the CAPM. It suggests that dividend payout should be included as a second factor to explain the equilibrium rate of return on securities. If true, the empirical CAPM would become

$$R_{jt} = \delta_0 + [R_{mt} - r_f]\beta_j + \delta_1 D_{jt} + \epsilon_{jt},$$

where

δ_0 = a constant,
δ_1 = influence of dividend payout on R_{jt},
R_{mt} = the rate of return on the market portfolio,
β_j = the systematic risk of the jth security,
D_{jt} = the dividend payout of the jth security,
ϵ_{jt} = a random error term,
r_f = the risk-free rate.

If the dividend payout factor turns out to be statistically significant, then we might conclude that dividend policy is not irrelevant.

---

[10] The reader is referred to Chapter 11 for a complete discussion of this point.

D. OTHER DIVIDEND POLICY ISSUES

1. Dividends and Share Repurchase from a Bondholder's Point of View

Debt contracts, particularly when long-term debt is involved, frequently restrict a firm's ability to pay cash dividends. Such restrictions usually state (1) that future dividends can be paid only out of earnings generated after the signing of the loan agreement (that is, future dividends cannot be paid out of past retained earnings), and (2) that dividends cannot be paid when net working capital (current assets minus current liabilities) is below a prespecified amount.

Bondholders want to restrict the firm's ability to pay dividends or to repurchase shares because the value of their debt depends on the market value of the firm's assets. In an extreme case, it would be theoretically possible for the shareholders to pay themselves a liquidating dividend or to repurchase all outstanding shares. Without any restrictions on share repurchase or dividends, such a move would leave the bondholders holding a bankrupt firm with no assets. Therefore bond indenture provisions routinely contain restrictions on dividends and repurchases.

It is an interesting (and as yet unanswered) empirical question whether or not any dividend payment, no matter how large it is, will affect the market value of bonds. One would expect that the market price of bonds would reflect the risk that future dividend payments would lower the asset base which secures debt.[11] However, as changes in the dividend payments are actually realized, there may be changes in the expectations of the bondholders which in turn would be reflected in the market price of bonds. All other things being equal, we may expect that higher dividend payments or share repurchases will be associated with a decline in the market value of debt. However, rarely do we have a situation where all other things are equal. For example, if announcements about dividend changes are interpreted as information about future cash flows, then a dividend increase means that current debt will be more secure because of the anticipated higher cash flows, and we would observe dividend increases to be positively correlated with increases in the market value of debt.

2. Dividends and the Incentive-Signaling Process

Ross [1977] suggests that implicit in the Miller-Modigliani dividend irrelevancy proposition is the assumption that the market *knows* the (random) return stream of the firm and values this stream to set the value of the firm. What is valued in the marketplace, however, is the *perceived* stream of returns for the firm. Putting the issue this way raises the possibility that changes in the capital structure (or dividend payout) may alter the market's perception. In the old terminology of Modigliani and

---

[11] Dividend payments do not necessarily change the assets side of the balance sheet. When cash balances are reduced in order to pay dividends, there is an asset effect. However, it is not necessary. Dividends can also be paid by issuing new debt or equity. In this case, assets remain unaffected, and the dividend decision is purely financial in nature.

Miller, by changing its financial structure (or dividend payout) the firm alters its perceived risk class, even though the actual risk class remains unchanged.

Managers, as insiders who have monopolistic access to information about the firm's expected cash flows, will choose to establish unambiguous signals about the firm's future if they have the proper incentive to do so. In order to show how this incentive-signaling process works, let us assume that managers are prohibited (perhaps by SEC regulations) from trading in the securities of their own firm. This keeps them from profiting by issuing false signals, such as announcing bad news and selling short even though they know the firm will do well.

In a simple one-period model the manager's compensation, M, paid at the end of the period, may be

$$M = (1 + r)\gamma_0 V_0 + \gamma_1 \begin{cases} V_1 & \text{if} \quad V_1 \geq D, \\ V_1 - L & \text{if} \quad V_1 < D, \end{cases} \tag{13.32}$$

where

$\gamma_0, \gamma_1 =$ positive weights,
   $r =$ the one-period interest rate,
$V_0, V_1 =$ the current and future value of the firm,
   $D =$ the face value of debt,
   $L =$ a penalty paid if bankruptcy occurs, i.e., if $V_1 < D$.

This result can be used to establish a signaling equilibrium if we further assume that investors use D, the face value of debt, to tell them whether a firm is successful (type A) or unsuccessful (type B). If $D > D^*$, the market perceives the firm to be successful, and vice versa. Assume that D^* is the maximum amount of debt that an unsuccessful firm can carry without going bankrupt. For the signaling equilibrium to be established, (1) the signals must be unambiguous (that is, when investors observe $D > D^*$, the firm is always type A), and (2) managers must have incentive to always give the appropriate signal.

If the end-of-period value of a successful type-A firm is V_{1a} and is always greater than the value of an unsuccessful type-B firm, V_{1b}, then the compensation of the management of a type-A firm is

$$M_a = \begin{cases} \gamma_0(1 + r) \dfrac{V_{1a}}{1 + r} + \gamma_1 V_{1a} & \text{if} \quad D^* < D \leq V_{1a} \quad \text{(tell the truth)}, \\[2ex] \gamma_0(1 + r) \dfrac{V_{1b}}{1 + r} + \gamma_1 V_{1a} & \text{if} \quad D < D^* \quad \text{(lie)}. \end{cases} \tag{13.33}$$

Clearly management of a type-A firm has incentive to establish a level of debt greater than D^* in order to earn maximum compensation. Therefore it will give the correct signal. But what about the management of a type-B firm? Doesn't it have incentive to lie by falsely signaling that its firm is type A? The answer is found by looking at the management-incentive scheme.

$$
M_b = \begin{cases} \gamma_0(1 + r)\dfrac{V_{1a}}{1 + r} + \gamma_1(V_{1b} - L) & \text{if } D^* < D < V_{1a} \quad \text{(lie)} \\[2ex] \gamma_0(1 + r)\dfrac{V_{1b}}{1 + r} + \gamma_1 V_{1b} & \text{if } D < D^* \quad \text{(tell the truth).} \end{cases} \tag{13.34}
$$

In order for management of a type-B firm to have incentive to signal that the firm will be unsuccessful, the payoff from telling the truth must be greater than that produced by telling lies. Mathematically,

$$
\gamma_0 V_{1a} + \gamma_1(V_{1b} - L) < \gamma_0 V_{1b} + \gamma_1 V_{1b},
$$

which can be rewritten as

$$
\gamma_0(V_{1a} - V_{1b}) < \gamma_1 L. \tag{13.35}
$$

This condition says that management will give the correct signal if the marginal gain from a false signal, $V_{1a} - V_{1b}$, weighted by management's share, γ_0, is less than the bankruptcy costs incurred by management, L, weighted by its share, γ_1.

The incentive-signaling approach suggests that management might choose real financial variables such as financial leverage or dividend policy as a means of sending unambiguous signals to the public about the future performance of the firm. These signals cannot be mimicked by unsuccessful firms because they do not have sufficient cash flow to back them up and because managers have incentives to tell the truth.

The concept is easily applied to dividend policy as well as to financial structure. A firm which increases dividend payout is signaling that it has expected future cash flows which are sufficiently large to meet debt payments and dividend payments without increasing the probability of bankruptcy. Therefore we may expect to find empirical evidence which shows that the value of the firm increases because dividends are taken as signals that the firm is expected to have permanently higher future cash flows. Chapter 14 reviews the empirical evidence.

3.   Stock Dividends and Share Repurchase

Stock dividends are often mentioned as part of the dividend policy of the firm. However, a stock dividend is nothing more than a small stock split. It simply increases the number of shares outstanding without changing any of the underlying risk or return characteristics of the firm. Therefore it has no effect on shareholders' wealth except for the losses associated with the clerical and transactions costs which accompany the stock dividend. The reader who is interested in empirical studies of stock splits is referred to Chapter 9.

Another question which often arises is whether share repurchase is preferable to dividend payments as a means of distributing cash to shareholders. Share repurchase allows shareholders to receive the cash payment as a capital gain rather than as dividend income. Any shareholder who pays a higher tax rate on income than on capital gains would prefer share repurchase to dividend payment. But not all classes of shareholders have this preference. Some, like tax-free university endowment funds, are indifferent to income versus capital gains, while others, such as corporations with their dividend exclusions, would actually prefer dividends.

To see that share repurchase and dividends can result in the same benefit per share, consider the following example. The United Canadian Brewery earns $4.4 million in 1978 and decides to pay out 50%, or $2.2 million, either as dividends or repurchase. The company has 1,100,000 shares outstanding with a market value of $20 per share. It can pay dividends of $2 per share or repurchase shares at $22 each. We know that the market price for repurchase is $22 rather than $20 because this will be the price per share after repurchase. To demonstrate this statement we know that the current earnings per share are $4, and the price earnings ratio is 5. At $22 per share the firm can repurchase 100,000 shares. This leaves 1,000,000 shares outstanding with earnings of $4.4 million, or $4.40 per share after the repurchase. If the same price-earnings ratio applies, the new price per share, after repurchase, will be $22. Therefore, the shareholders can receive a dividend of $2 per share or a capital gain of $2 per share. The form of preferred payment will depend on their tax rates.

E. SUMMARY

Several valuation models with or without growth, and with or without corporate taxes have been developed. Dividend policy is irrelevant in all instances. It has no effect on shareholders' wealth. Only when personal taxes are introduced do we have a result where dividends matter. For shareholders who pay higher taxes on dividends than on capital gains, the preferred dividend payout is zero; they would rather have the company distribute cash payments via the share repurchase mechanism. Yet corporations do pay dividends. The next chapter presents empirical evidence which examines the relationship between the level of dividend payout, the value of the shares, and the amount of investment undertaken by the firm. Also changes in dividend payout are studied in relation to their effect on share value. These studies provide greater insight into the empirical validity of the theory discussed here.

PROBLEM SET

13.1 The chairman of the board of Alphanull Corporation has announced that the corporation will change its dividend policy from paying a fixed dollar dividend per share. Instead dividends will be paid out as a residual. That is, any cash flows left over after the firm has undertaken all profitable investments will be paid out to shareholders. This new policy will obviously increase the variability of dividends paid. How do you think it will affect the value of the firm?

13.2 The *XYZ* Company (an all-equity firm) currently has after-tax operating cash flows of $3.00 per share and pays out 50% of its earnings in dividends. If it expects to keep the same payout ratio, and to earn 20% on future investments forever, what will its current price per share be? Assume the cost of capital is 15%.

13.3 The Highrise Investment Co. (an all-equity firm) currently pays a dividend of $2.00 per share, which is 75% of its after-tax cash flows from operations. It is currently selling for $16 a share and earns 40% on invested capital. Its equity β is 2.0, the expected market rate of return is 12.5%, and the risk-free rate is 5%. How long will its supernormal rate of growth last before it levels off to equal the normal rate for a company with its risk?

13.4 The balance sheet of the Universal Sour Candy Company is given in Table 13.3. Assume that all balance sheet items are expressed in terms of market values. The company has decided to pay a $2000 dividend to shareholders. There are four ways to do it:

1) Pay a cash dividend.
2) Issue new debt and equity in equal proportions ($1000 each) and use the proceeds to pay the dividend.
3) Issue $2000 of new equity and use the proceeds to pay the dividend.
4) Use the $2000 of cash to repurchase equity.

What impact will each of the four policies above have on the following:

a) the systematic risk of the portfolio of assets held by the firm,
b) the market-value of original bondholders' wealth,
c) the market-value ratio of debt to equity,
d) the market value of the firm in a world without taxes.

Table 13.3 Balance sheet as of December 31, 19xx

Assets		Liabilities	
Cash	$ 2,000	Debt	$ 5,000
Inventory	2,000	Equity	5,000
Property, plant, and equipment	6,000		
Total assets	$10,000	Total liabilities	$10,000

13.5 According to the valuation model (Eq. (13.25)) with finite supernormal growth and corporate taxes, there are six variables which affect the value of the firm.

a) What are they?
b) Why can't the president of a firm cause the firm's market value to increase simply by reporting anticipated favorable changes in the six variables, for example, an increase in expected return on investment?

13.6 Prove the following for a firm with no supernormal growth (in a world with only corporate taxes)

$$V^L = \frac{E(\text{NOI}_1)(1 - \tau_c)}{k_0} = V^U + \tau_c B.$$

13.7 Calculate the value of a company that earned $50,000 this year, has a 40 % investment rate, K, and a tax rate of 40 %; has $200,000 in debt outstanding, and a weighted average cost of capital of 12 %; and is expected to earn 40 % on invested capital for the next five years, then 25 % for the following five years, before the rate of return declines to a normal rate of growth.

13.8 How does an increase in the investment (retention) rate affect the anticipated stream of investments that a company will undertake?

REFERENCES

BAR-YOSEF, S., and R. KOLODNY, "Dividend Policy and Market Theory," *The Review of Economics and Statistics*, May 1976, 181–190.

BLACK, F., and M. SCHOLES, "The Effects of Dividend Yield and Dividend Policy on Common Stock Prices and Returns," *Journal of Financial Economics*, May 1974, 1–22.

————, M. JENSEN, and M. SCHOLES, "The Capital Asset Pricing Model: Some Empirical Tests," in M. Jensen, Ed., *Studies in the Theory of Capital Markets*, Praeger, New York, 1972, 79–124.

BRENNAN, M., "Taxes, Market Valuation and Corporate Financial Policy," *National Tax Journal*, December 1970, 417–427.

BRITTAIN, J. A., *Corporate Dividend Policy*. Brookings Institute, Washington, D.C., 1966.

DARLING, P., "The Influence of Expectations and Liquidity on Dividend Policy," *Journal of Political Economy*, June 1957, 209–224.

DOBROVOLSKY, S., *The Economics of Corporation Finance*. McGraw-Hill, New York, 1971.

FAMA, E., "The Empirical Relationships Between the Dividend of Investment Decisions of Firms," *The American Economic Review*, June 1974, 304–318.

————, and H. BABIAK, "Dividend Policy: An Empirical Analysis," *Journal of the American Statistical Association*, December 1968, 1132–1161.

————, and M. H. MILLER, *The Theory of Finance*. McGraw-Hill, New York, 1971.

FARRAR, D., and L. SELWYN, "Taxes, Corporate Financial Policy and Return to Investors," *National Tax Journal*, December 1967, 444–454.

FRIEND, I., and M. PUCKETT, "Dividends and Stock Prices," *The American Economic Review*, September 1964, 656–682.

GORDON, M., "Dividends, Earnings, and Stock Prices," *Review of Economics and Statistics*, May 1959, 99–105.

————, "The Savings, Investment and Valuation of a Corporation," *Review of Economics and Statistics*, February 1962, 37–51.

KHOURY, N., and K. SMITH, "Dividend Policy and the Capital Gains Tax in Canada," *Journal of Business Administration*, Spring 1977.

LINTNER, J., "Distribution of Incomes of Corporations among Dividends, Retained Earnings and Taxes," *The American Economic Review*, May 1956, 97–113.

————, "Optimal Dividends and Corporate Growth Under Uncertainty," *The Quarterly Journal of Economics*, February 1964, pp. 49–95.

————, "The Valuation of Risk Assets and the Selection of Risky Investments in Stock Portfolios and Capital Budgets," *Review of Economics and Statistics*, February 1965, 13–37.

MILLER, M., and F. MODIGLIANI, "Dividend Policy, Growth, and the Valuation of Shares," *The Journal of Business*, October 1961, 411–433.

————, and M. SCHOLES, "Dividends and Taxes," working paper, University of Chicago, Chicago, IL, 1977.

PETTIT, R. R., "Dividend Announcements, Security Performance, and Capital Market Efficiency," *The Journal of Finance*, December 1972, 993–1007.

ROSS, S. A., "The Determination of Financial Structure: The Incentive-Signalling Approach," *The Bell Journal of Economics*, Spring 1977, 23–40.

————, "Some Notes on Financial Incentive—Signalling Models, Activity Choice and Risk Preferences," *The Journal of Finance*, June 1978, 777–792.

WALTER, J. E., *Dividend Policy and Enterprise Valuation*, Wadsworth, Belmont, Calif., 1967.

WATTS, R., "The Information Content of Dividends," *The Journal of Business*, April 1973, 191–211.

Chapter 14

Dividend Policy: Empirical Evidence and Applications

... in the real world a change in the dividend rate is often followed by a change in the market price (sometimes spectacularly so). Such a phenomenon would not be incompatible with irrelevance to the extent that it was merely a reflection of what might be called the "informational content" of dividends ...

M. Miller and F. Modigliani,
"Dividend Policy, Growth, and the Valuation of Shares,"
The Journal of Business, October 1961, p. 431

Our discussion first deals with models which simply explain the behavior of corporate dividend policy over time. Evidence indicates that U.S. corporations behave as if they had some target dividend payout in mind and that they move toward it with a lag. They also show reluctance to lower dividends.

Second, we look at the possibility of clientele effects. Do people in high tax brackets avoid investing in high-dividend companies in order to escape higher income taxes on dividend income? On this question, the empirical evidence is mixed, although it does lean toward the existence of a clientele effect.

Third, we focus on the relationship between dividend payout and the market value of equity. The best empirical evidence indicates that dividend payout is not related to the value of the firm. Several explanations are given for why this result is plausible, even with our current tax system.

Fourth, the information content of dividend increases is tested. Although not conclusive, the evidence leans toward validation of the signaling hypothesis.

Finally, we apply the Miller-Modigliani valuation model to the case of Bethlehem Steel in order to demonstrate the relevance of the different factors which determine the value of a firm.

A. BEHAVIORAL MODELS OF DIVIDEND POLICY

Lintner [1956] conducted interviews with 28 carefully selected companies to investigate their thinking on the determination of dividend policy. His field work suggested that (1) managers focused on the change in the existing rate of dividend payout, not on the amount of the newly established payout as such; (2) most managements sought to avoid making changes in their dividend rates that might have to be reversed within a year or so; (3) major changes in earnings "out of line" with existing dividend rates were the most important determinants of the company's dividend decisions; and (4) investment requirements generally had little effect on modifying the pattern of dividend behavior. Taken together, these observations suggest that most companies had somewhat flexible but nevertheless reasonably well-defined standards regarding the speed with which they would try to move toward a full adjustment of dividend payout to earnings. Lintner suggests that corporate dividend behavior can be described on the basis of the following equation:

$$\Delta D_{it} = a_i + c_i(D_{it}^* - D_{i,t-1}) + U_{it}, \tag{14.1}$$

where

ΔD_{it} = the change in dividends per share,
    c_i = the speed of adjustment to the difference between a target dividend payout and last year's payout,
    D_{it}^* = the target dividend payout,
$D_{i,t-1}$ = last period's dividend payout per share,
a_i, U_{it} = a constant and a normally distributed random error term.

The target dividend payout, D_{it}^*, is a fraction, r_i, of this period's earnings, E_{it}. Upon fitting the equations to annual data from 1918 through 1941, Lintner found that the model explained 85% of the changes in dividends for his sample of companies. The average speed of adjustment was approximately 30% per year, and the target payout was 50% of earnings.

Fama and Babiak [1968] investigated many different models for explaining dividend behavior. They used a sample of 201 firms with 19 years of data (1947–1964), then tested each explanatory model by using it to (1) explain dividend policy for a holdout sample of 191 firms and (2) predict dividend payments one year hence. Of the many models which they tried, the two best are Lintner's model (Eq. (14.1)) and a similar model which suppresses the constant term and adds a term for the lagged level of earnings. The second model did slightly better than Lintner's.

One can conclude that U.S. corporations seem to increase dividends only after they are reasonably sure that they will be able to maintain them permanently at the new level. However, this does not help to answer the question of why corporations pay dividends in the first place.

B. CLIENTELE EFFECTS

The clientele effect was originally suggested by Miller and Modigliani [1961]:

> *If for example the frequency distribution of corporate payout ratios happened to correspond exactly with the distribution of investor preferences for payout ratios, then the existence of these preferences would clearly lead ultimately to a situation whose implications were different, in no fundamental respect, from the perfect market case. Each corporation would tend to attract to itself a "clientele" consisting of those preferring its particular payout ratio, but one clientele would be as good as another in terms of the valuation it would imply for firms.*

The clientele effect is a possible explanation for management reluctance to alter established payout ratios because such changes might cause current shareholders to incur unwanted transactions costs.

Elton and Gruber [1970] attempt to measure clientele effects by observing the average price decline when a stock goes ex-dividend. If a current shareholder were to sell his stock the instant before it goes ex-dividend, he would receive its price, P_B, and pay the capital gains rate, t_g, on the difference between the selling price and the price at which it was purchased, P_c. Alternatively, he could sell the stock after it goes ex-dividend. In this case, he would receive the dividend, D, and pay the ordinary tax rate, t_0, on it. In addition, he would pay a capital gains tax on the difference between its ex-dividend price, P_A, and the original purchase price P_c. To prevent arbitrage profits, his gain from either course of action must be the same, namely

$$P_B - t_g(P_B - P_c) = P_A - t_g(P_A - P_c) + D(1 - t_0). \qquad (14.2)$$

Rearranging (14.2), we get

$$\frac{P_B - P_A}{D} = \frac{1 - t_0}{1 - t_g}. \qquad (14.3)$$

Therefore the ratio of the decline in stock price to the dividend paid becomes a means of estimating the marginal tax rate of the average investor, if we assume that the capital gains rate is half the ordinary income rate.

Using 4148 observations between April 1, 1966 and March 31, 1967, Elton and Gruber discovered that the average price decline as a percent of dividend paid was 77.7%. This implied that the marginal tax bracket of the average investor was 36.4%. They continued by arguing that

> *...the lower a firm's dividend yield the smaller the percentage of his total return that a stockholder expects to receive in the form of dividends and the larger the percentage he expects to receive in the form of capital gains. Therefore, investors who held stocks which have high dividend yields should be in low tax brackets relative to stockholders who hold stocks with low dividend yield.*

Table 14.1 shows that dividend payout ranked from the lowest to highest deciles along with (1) the average drop in price as a percent of dividends and (2) the implied

Table 14.1 Dividend yield statistics ranked by decile

		$\dfrac{P_B - P_A}{D}$ *				
Decile	D/P mean	Mean	Standard deviation	Z value	Probability true mean is one or more	Implied tax bracket
1	.0124	.6690	.8054	.411	.341	.4974
2	.0216	.4873	.2080	2.465	.007	.6145
3	.0276	.5447	.1550	2.937	.002	.5915
4	.0328	.6246	.1216	3.087	.001	.5315
5	.0376	.7953	.1064	1.924	.027	.3398
6	.0416	.8679	.0712	1.855	.031	.2334
7	.0452	.9209	.0761	1.210	.113	.1465
8	.0496	.9054	.0691	1.369	.085	.1747
9	.0552	1.0123	.0538	.229	.591	†
10	.0708	1.1755	.0555	3.162	.999	†

* Spearman's rank correlation coefficient between D/P and $(P_B - P_A)/D$ is .9152 which is significant at the 1% level.
† Indeterminate.

Source: Elton, E. J., and M. J. Gruber, "Marginal Stockholders' Tax Rates and the Clientele Effect," reprinted from *The Review of Economics and Statistics*, February 1970, 72.

tax bracket. Note that the implied tax bracket decreases when dividend payout increases. Elton and Gruber conclude that the evidence suggests that Miller and Modigliani were right in hypothesizing a clientele effect.

A possible counterargument to this interpretation is that arbitrage may also be carried out by traders who do not own the stock initially. They would not receive favored capital gains treatment but would have to pay ordinary income taxes on short-term gains. Their arbitrage profit, π, may be stated mathematically as

$$\pi = -P_B + D - t_0 D + P_A + t_0(P_B - P_A). \tag{14.4}$$

They spend P_B to acquire the stock before it goes ex-dividend, then receive the dividend and pay ordinary income taxes on it, and finally sell the stock after it goes ex-dividend (receiving P_A dollars) and receive a tax shield from their short-term loss. Rearranging (14.4), we see that their profit is

$$\pi = (1 - t_0)[P_A - P_B + D]. \tag{14.5}$$

In order to prevent arbitrage profits, the price decline must equal the amount of dividend payout, that is, $P_B - P_A = D$.

The above condition is completely different from Eq. (14.3) proposed by Elton and Gruber. Of course neither model has taken transactions costs into account. Nor have we considered other classes of investors, such as tax-free investors. Therefore no strong conclusion can be made regarding the existence of a clientele effect.

More recently, Pettit [1977] has tested for clientele effects by examining the portfolio positions of approximately 914 individual accounts handled by a large retail brokerage house between 1964 and 1970. He argues that stocks with low dividend yields will be preferred by investors with high income, by younger investors, by investors whose ordinary and capital gains tax rates differ substantially, and by investors whose portfolios have high systematic risk. His empirical results are presented below:[1]

$$DY_i = a_1 + a_2\beta_i + a_3 \, AGE_i + a_4 \, INC_i + a_5 \, DTR_i + \epsilon_i, \tag{14.6}$$

where

DY_i = dividend yield for the ith individual's portfolio in 1970,
β_i = the systematic risk of the ith individual's portfolio,
AGE_i = the age of the individual,
INC_i = the gross family income averaged over the last three years,
DTR_i = the difference between the income and capital gains tax rates for the ith individual,
ϵ_i = a normally distributed random error term.

He finds that

$$DY_i = .042 - .021\beta_i + .031 \, AGE_i - .037 \, INC_i + .006 \, DTR_i.$$
$$(11.01) \quad (-16.03) \quad (6.15) \quad (-2.25) \quad (1.57)$$

This evidence suggests that there is a clientele effect because a significant portion of the observed cross-sectional variation in individual portfolio dividend yields can be explained. However, the study in no way suggests that the market price of a security is determined by the dividend policy followed by the firm.

C. THE RELATIONSHIP BETWEEN DIVIDENDS AND VALUE

In Chapter 13 we saw that in a world with only corporate taxes, the Miller-Modigliani proposition suggests that dividend policy is irrelevant to value. However, when personal taxes are introduced with a capital gains rate which is less than the rate on ordinary income, the picture changes. Under this set of assumptions, the firm should not pay any dividends. One way to test these theories is to look directly at the relationship between dividend payout and the price per share of equity.

Friend and Puckett [1964] use cross-section data to test the effect of dividend payout on share value. Prior to their work, most studies had related stock prices to current dividends and retained earnings, and reported that higher dividend payout was associated with higher price-earnings ratios. The "dividend multiplier" was found to be several times the "retained earnings multiplier." The usual cross-section equation was

$$P_{it} = a + bD_{it} + cR_{it} + \epsilon_{it}, \tag{14.7}$$

---

[1] t-statistics are given in parentheses. The r^2 was .3 for 914 observations.

where

P_{it} = the price per share,
D_{it} = aggregate dividends paid out,
R_{it} = retained earnings,
ϵ_{it} = the error term.

Friend and Puckett criticize the above approach on three major points. First, the equation is misspecified because it assumes that the riskiness of the firm is uncorrelated with dividend payout and price-earnings ratios. However, a look at the data suggests that riskier firms have both lower dividend payout and lower price-earnings ratios. Consequently, the omission of a risk variable may cause an upward bias in the dividend coefficient in Eq. (14.7). Second, there is almost no measurement error in dividends but there is considerable measurement error in retained earnings. It is well known that accounting measures of income often imprecisely reflect the real economic earnings of the firm. The measurement error in retained earnings will cause its coefficient to be biased downward. Third, Friend and Puckett argue that even if dividends and retained earnings *do* have different impacts on share prices, we should expect their coefficients in (14.7) to be equal. In equilibrium, firms would change their dividend payout until the marginal effect of dividends is equal to the marginal effect of retained earnings. This will provide the optimum effect on their price per share.

No theory had been developed to allow the pricing of risk when they wrote their paper, but Friend and Puckett were able to eliminate the measurement error on retained earnings by calculating a normalized earnings variable based on a time series fit of the following equation:

$$\frac{(E/P)_{it}}{(E/P)_{kt}} = a_i + b_i t + e_{it}, \tag{14.8}$$

where

$(E/P)_{it}$ = the earnings-price ratio for the firm,
$(E/P)_{kt}$ = the average earnings price ratio for the industry,
t = a time index,
e_{it} = the error term.

When normalized retained earnings were calculated by subtracting dividends from normalized earnings and then used in Eq. (14.7), the difference between the dividend and retained earnings coefficients was reduced. Unfortunately, no test was performed to see whether the differences between the impact of retained earnings and dividends were significantly different after Friend and Puckett had normalized earnings and controlled for firm effects.

A much more recent study by Black and Scholes [1974] uses capital-asset pricing theory to control for risk.[2] Their conclusion is quite strong. "It is not possible to demonstrate, using the best empirical methods, that the expected returns on high

---

[2] See Chapter 7 for a complete development of the capital asset pricing model.

yield common stocks differ from the expected returns on low yield common stocks either before or after taxes." They begin by pointing out that the assumption that capital gains tax rates are lower than income tax rates does not apply to all classes of investors. Some classes of investors might logically prefer high dividend yields. They include (a) corporations, because they usually pay higher taxes on realized capital gains than on dividend income (because of the 85% exclusion of dividends), (b) certain trust funds in which one beneficiary receives the dividend income and the other receives capital gains, (c) endowment funds from which only the dividend income may be spent, and (d) investors who are spending from wealth and may find it cheaper and easier to receive dividends than to sell or borrow against their shares. Alternatively, investors who prefer low dividend yield will be those who pay higher taxes on dividend income than on capital gains. Finally, there is a large group of tax-exempt investors (for example, university endowments) who will be indifferent between dividends and capital gains. With all of these diverse investors, it is possible that there are clientele effects which imply that if a firm changes its dividend payout, it may lose some shareholders but they will be replaced by others who prefer the new policy. Thus, dividend payout will have no effect on the value of an individual firm.[3]

An even more recent argument by Miller and Scholes [1977] is that even with existing tax laws (where the tax on ordinary personal income is greater than the capital gains tax), there is no need for individuals ever to pay more than the capital gains rate on dividends. The implication is that individuals will be indifferent between payments in the form of dividends or capital gains (if the firm decides to repurchase shares). Thus the firm's value will be unrelated to its dividend policy.

To clarify their argument, Miller and Scholes provide the following simple example. Let us suppose we have an initial net worth of $25,000 which is represented wholly by an investment of 2500 shares worth $10 each in a company which earns $1.00 per share. At the end of the year the company pays $.40 per share in dividends and retains $.60. Consequently its end-of-year price per share is $10.60. In order to neutralize our dividend income for tax purposes, we borrow $16,667 at 6% and invest the proceeds in a risk-free project (such as life insurance or a Keough account) which pays 6% of tax-deferred interest. Our opening and closing balance sheets and our income statement are given in Table 14.2. Note that by investing in risk-free assets we have not increased the risk of our wealth position. The riskless cash inflows from insurance exactly match the required payments on debt. Our true economic income could be $1500 in *unrealized* capital gains plus the $1000 of tax-deferred interest from life insurance or our Keough account.

Of course, federal tax laws are complex and these transactions cannot be carried out without some transactions costs. Nevertheless, the above argument is a clever way to demonstrate the fact that ordinary income taxes on dividends can be avoided.

---

[3] This does not rule out the possibility that in aggregate there is a desired equilibrium amount of dividend payout. For example, in the United States, there are obviously a far greater number of companies with generous dividend payout than without.

Table 14.2

Opening balance sheet				Closing balance sheet			
Assets		Liabilities		Assets		Liabilities	
2,500 shares				2,500 shares			
at $10 = 25,000	Loan		16,667	at $10.60 = 26,500	Loan		16,667
Insurance	16,667	Net worth	25,000	Accrued		Accrued	
	41,667		41,667	dividends	1,000	interest	1,000
				Insurance	16,667	Net worth	26,500
					44,167		44,167

Ordinary income		Capital gains	
Dividends received	$1,000	Sale of 2,500 shares at $10.60 = $26,500	
Less interest expense	1,000	Less original basis	25,000
	0		1,500
Nontaxable income	1,000		
	1,000		

The Black and Scholes [1974] study presents strong empirical evidence that the before-tax returns on common stock are unrelated to corporate dividend payout policy. They adjust for risk by using the CAPM.

The CAPM predicts that the expected return on any asset is a linear function of its systematic risk:

$$E(\tilde{R}_j) = R_f + [E(\tilde{R}_m) - R_f]\beta_j. \tag{14.9}$$

However, it is derived by assuming, among other things, that there are no differential tax effects which would affect investors' demands for different securities. Brennan [1970] has shown that if effective capital gains tax rates are lower than effective rates on dividend income, investors will demand a higher return on securities with higher dividend payout. Black and Scholes test this hypothesis by adding a dividend payout term to an empirical version of the CAPM:

$$\tilde{R}_j = \gamma_0 + [\tilde{R}_m - \gamma_0]\beta_j + \gamma_1(\delta_j - \delta_m)/\delta_m + \epsilon_j, \tag{14.10}$$

where

$\tilde{R}_j$ = the rate of return on the jth portfolio,
γ_0 = an intercept term which should be equal to the risk-free rate, R_f, according to the CAPM,
$\tilde{R}_m$ = the rate of return on the market portfolio,
β_j = the systematic risk of the jth portfolio,
γ_1 = the dividend impact coefficient,

δ_j = the dividend yield on the jth portfolio,
δ_m = the dividend yield on the market portfolio,
 ϵ_j = the error term.

If the coefficient, γ_1, of the dividend yield term is significantly different from zero, we would reject the null hypothesis that dividend payout has no impact on the required rate of return for securities. The results of Black and Scholes are summarized in Table 14.3. Note that the dividend yield coefficient, $\hat{\gamma}_1$, is not significantly different from zero (since the t-test is less than the level required to make it significant at the 95% confidence level) across the entire time period, 1936 through 1966, or in any subperiod. This means that the expected returns on high-yield securities are not significantly different from the expected returns on low-yield securities, other things being equal. For the investor, this implies that he cannot tell whether high-yield stocks have higher or lower expected returns than low-yield stocks with the same risk. Therefore, it may make sense for him to simply ignore dividend yield in making his investment decisions.[4]

Table 14.3 Results of the Black-Scholes test for dividend effects

The portfolio estimators for γ_1 (part A) and γ_0 (part B)

Part A

Period	$\alpha_1 = \hat{\gamma}_1$	t_α	$\hat{\beta}_1$	δ_1	δ_m
1936–66	0.0009	0.94	−0.01	0.044	0.048
1947–66	0.0009	0.90	0.08	0.047	0.049
1936–46	0.0011	0.54	−0.01	0.036	0.046
1947–56	0.0002	0.19	0.11	0.054	0.060
1957–66	0.0016	0.99	−0.14	0.040	0.038
1940–45	0.0018	0.34	0.15	0.051	0.052

Part B

Period	$\alpha_0 = \hat{\gamma}_0$	t_α	$\hat{\beta}_0$	δ_0	δ_m
1936–66	0.0060	3.02	0.02	0.048	0.048
1947–66	0.0073	3.93	0.03	0.049	0.049
1936–46	0.0033	0.72	−0.01	0.046	0.046
1947–56	0.0067	2.55	0.12	0.060	0.060
1957–66	0.0065	2.37	0.10	0.038	0.038

Source: Black, F., and M. Scholes, "The Effects of Dividend Yield and Dividend Policy on Common Stock Prices and Returns," reprinted from *The Journal of Financial Economics*, May 1974, 14.

---

[4] The lower half of Table 15.2 shows that γ_0 *is* significantly different from the risk-free rate. This is not important for the conclusions about dividend policy but is consistent with other empirical work (e.g., Black, Jensen, and Scholes [1972]) which shows that the intercept term in the CAPM is different from what theory would predict.

Both the Friend and Puckett, and Black and Scholes studies tend to support the conclusion that the value of the firm is independent of dividend yield. However, according to the Miller-Modigliani irrelevancy proposition, it is also important to know whether or not dividend policy can affect the investment decisions made by managers of the firm. This is a particularly difficult empirical question because the Miller-Modigliani theorem requires only that *dividend payout not affect investment decisions*. However, the opposite causality is not ruled out by Miller and Modigliani That is, investment decisions can affect dividends. For example, the firm may simply choose to treat dividends as a residual payout after all profitable investment projects have been undertaken. This would not be inconsistent with the Miller-Modigliani proposition that the value of the firm is unaffected by dividend policy.

Fama [1974] uses a sophisticated two-stage least-squares econometric technique in order to determine the direction of causality, if any, between dividend and investment decisions. Because a description of two-stage least-squares is beyond the scope of this book, we refer the interested reader to Fama's article for a detailed exposition. His conclusion, however, is consistent with the Miller-Modigliani assumption that the period-by-period investment decisions of the firm are separable from its dividend decisions. There appears to be no causality in either direction. The data could not reject the hypothesis that investment and dividend decisions are completely independent from each other.

Although the foregoing studies appear to support the Miller-Modigliani irrelevancy proposition from the point of view of an individual firm, they do not necessarily rule out the possibility that there may exist an aggregate equilibrium supply of dividends which will increase if the difference between the ordinary income rate and the capital gains rate declines. This type of situation is implicit in Miller's [1977] paper "Debt and Taxes," which was discussed at length in Chapter 11.

Some empirical evidence which is consistent with the thesis that the aggregate supply of dividends is sensitive to the differential between the ordinary income and capital gains rates is contained in a study by Khoury and Smith [1977]. They observed that Canadian corporations significantly increased their dividend payout after a capital gains tax was introduced for the first time in 1972.

D. DIVIDEND ANNOUNCEMENT EFFECTS ON THE VALUE OF THE FIRM: THE SIGNALING HYPOTHESIS

Although Fama discovered no contemporaneous relationship between investment and dividend decisions, the evidence does not rule out a relationship between current dividends and future investment opportunities. Most firms which pay dividends exhibit behavior which results in constant dividend payouts which are increased only when management is relatively certain that the higher dividend payout can be maintained indefinitely. Given this type of management behavior, it is likely that investors will interpret an increase in current dividend payout as a message that management anticipates permanently higher levels of cash flows from investment. We may, therefore, expect to observe an increase in share prices associated with public announcement of a dividend increase. The dividend *per se* does not affect the value of the firm. Instead it serves as a message from management that the firm is anticipated to do better.

If dividend changes are to have an impact on share values, it is necessary that they convey information about future cash flows, but it is not sufficient. The same information may be provided to investors via other sources.[5] Therefore, it becomes an empirical question whether or not announcements of dividend changes actually affect share value. Pettit [1972] and Watts [1973] have studied this issue. Their conclusions are somewhat mixed. Watts finds a positive dividend announcement effect, but concludes that the information content is of no economic significance because it would not enable a trader with monopolistic access to the information to earn abnormal returns after transactions costs. On the other hand, Pettit finds clear support for the proposition that the market uses dividend announcements as information for assessing security values. Their methodologies are also different. Watts proceeds in two stages. First, he develops a model to predict dividend changes. It is the same model which Fama and Babiak [1968] found to provide the best prediction of next period's dividends. It may be written as follows:

$$\Delta D_t = \beta_1 D_{t-1} + \beta_2 E_t + \beta_3 E_{t-1} + Z_t, \tag{14.11}$$

where

ΔD_t = the change in dividends in period t,
D_{t-1} = the previous period's dividends,
E_t = this period's earnings,
E_{t-1} = last period's earnings,
Z_t = unanticipated dividend changes (the error term).

Using this equation, we are able to estimate unanticipated dividend changes, Z_t. Next, an abnormal performance index which measures departures from the risk-adjusted rate of return can be constructed from the market model,

$$R_{jt} = \alpha + \beta_j R_{mt} + \epsilon_{jt}, \tag{14.12}$$

where

R_{jt} = the total return (dividends and capital gains) on the common stock of the jth firm,
α = a constant term,
β_j = systematic risk,
R_{mt} = the rate of return on a market index,
ϵ_{jt} = the abnormal performance of the jth security.

---

[5] Ross [1977] argues that an increase in dividend payout is an unambiguous message because (1) it cannot be mimicked by firms which do not anticipate higher earnings and (2) because management has an incentive to "tell the truth."

The abnormal performance index for a security is computed as the product of its one-month abnormal returns.

$$\text{API} = \prod_{t=1}^{T} (1 + \epsilon_{jt}), \qquad T = 1, \ldots, N.$$

Watts looked at the abnormal performance index averaged across 310 firms. The abnormal performance index for 24 months around the dividend announcement for the subsamples of firms which had unanticipated dividend increases or decreases is given in Table 14.4. The performance of firms with dividend increases is better than that of firms with dividend decreases, but the greatest difference between the two

Table 14.4 Abnormal performance indices for subsamples of firms with unanticipated dividend changes

Month relative to last month of fiscal year	API $\hat{z}_{i,t} > 0$	API $\hat{z}_{i,t} < 0$	χ^2 statistic for sign of stock return residual for month and dividend residual for year	Total API
−11	0.996	0.995	0.2	0.995
−10	0.998	0.997	0.3	0.998
− 9	1.003	1.002	1.9	1.002
− 8	1.002	1.002	4.0	1.002
− 7	1.004	1.001	2.5	1.002
− 6	1.004	0.999	2.6	1.001
− 5	1.003	1.000	0.6	1.002
− 4	1.001	0.999	0.3	1.000
− 3	1.000	0.997	0.0	0.998
− 2	1.003	1.001	2.6	1.002
− 1	1.006	1.001	4.0	1.004
0	1.009	1.002	0.1	1.006
1	1.003	0.996	0.0	1.000
2	1.005	0.999	0.6	1.002
3	1.010	1.005	0.0	1.008
4	1.011	1.004	1.4	1.007
5	1.011	1.004	0.0	1.008
6	1.012	1.003	3.3	1.008
7	1.011	1.003	0.2	1.007
8	1.010	1.001	0.2	1.006
9	1.007	1.000	0.4	1.004
10	1.011	1.002	1.5	1.007
11	1.012	1.006	3.4	1.009
12	1.014	1.006	1.2	1.010

Note: Probability $(\chi^2 > 3.84 \,|\, x^2 = 0) = .05$ for 1 df; probability $(\chi^2 > 6.64 \,|\, x^2 = 0) = .01$ for 1 df.

Source: Watts, R., "The Information Content of Dividends," reprinted from *The Journal of Business*, April 1973, 206.

samples in the six months around the dividend change is only .7% in the month of the dividend. This is a trivial difference.

Pettit used both monthly and daily data to investigate the abnormal performance index of firms which had dividend changes of -1% to -99%, 1% to 10%, 10% to 25%, and over 25%. Figure 14.1 shows the cumulative abnormal performance index using daily data for 135 firms. Most of the price adjustment takes place very quickly either on the dividend announcement date or the following day. Furthermore, the price changes appear to be significant. This leads Pettit to conclude that substantial information is conveyed by the announcement of dividend changes.

Although the empirical evidence seems to indicate that dividend changes do convey some unanticipated information to the market, it is inconclusive. We do not know with certainty whether or not a trader who has monopolistic access to information about dividend announcements could make an abnormal gain after transactions costs. The Watts monthly data would seem to suggest that abnormal gains are not available, while the Pettit results based on daily data seem to have sufficiently large abnormal returns to cover transactions costs. Unfortunately no trading rules were tested.

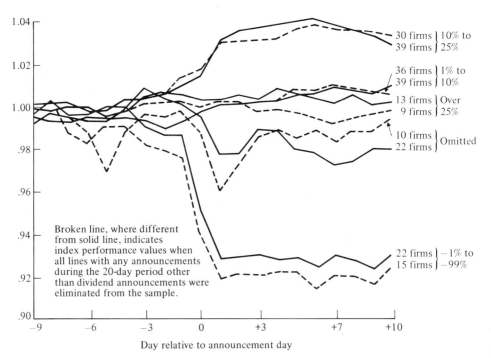

Fig. 14.1 Abnormal performance index for dividend accouncement effects (using daily data) (Pettit, R., "Dividend Announcements, Security Performance and Capital Market Efficiency," reprinted with permission of *The Journal of Finance*, December 1972, 1004.)

E. OVERVIEW OF EMPIRICAL EVIDENCE

The theory of finance clearly demonstrates that in the absence of taxes dividend policy has no effect on the value of the corporation. However, if taxes are introduced, then the firm can maximize the value of shareholders' wealth by paying no dividends so long as the personal tax rate on dividend income is higher than that on capital gains. However, this is not true for all types of shareholders; hence there exists the possibility of clientele effects with shareholders choosing the firm with the payout they prefer. The empirical evidence seems to indicate that dividend payout has no marked effect on the value of individual firms, but that changes in dividend payout can be interpreted as new information about the future cash flows of the firm.

F. VALUATION AND CORPORATE POLICY

The valuation models developed in Chapter 13 have many useful applications. For example, fundamental analysis techniques use them as a tool for estimating the impact of various types of new information on the value of the firm. Although the valuation models cannot aid in attempts to "beat" the market, they do provide a useful framework for concentrating on relevant information. When a corporate president asks "How much should we pay to acquire Company X?" the valuation model is a useful tool. When a company is going public for the first time or when it becomes necessary to value a privately held company, again the valuation model provides a relevant framework for analysis.

In the next section we continue the Bethlehem Steel example which was started in Chapter 12. The object is to see how to apply the Miller-Modigliani finite-growth model. In so doing, it becomes possible to analyze six factors which affect corporate value.

1. Review of the Finite-Growth Valuation Formula
The most complicated, and the most realistic, valuation model discussed in Chapter 13 assumed that the firm grows at a rate, g, for a finite number of years, T, and at the same rate as the economy thereafter.

The model is written below:[6]

$$V^L = \frac{E(NOI_1)(1 - \tau_c)}{\rho} + \tau_c B + K[E(NOI_1)(1 - \tau_c)]T \left[\frac{r - k_0}{k_0(1 + k_0)} \right], \quad (14.13)$$

where

V^L = the market value of the levered firm, i.e., the market value of equity, S, plus the market value of debt, B,

$E(NOI_1)$ = the expected net cash flows from operations during the current year, net of capitalized maintenance,

---

[6] Remember that we derive this version of the model by assuming, among other things, that corporate taxes are the only form of government levy. Personal taxes do not exist.

$\rho =$ the cost of equity for the firm if it had no debt, i.e., the cost of equity for an all-equity firm,

$\tau_c =$ the marginal corporate tax rate,

$B =$ the market value of debt,

$r =$ the expected rate of return on new projects,

$K =$ the firm's investment rate,

$k_0 =$ the firm's weighted average cost of capital

$T =$ the number of years that r, the rate of return, is expected to be different from k_0, the market-determined weighted average cost of capital.

The first term in (14.13) is the capitalized value of the expected level of after-tax cash flows from investment which is currently in place. The second term is the value added by tax deductible financial leverage. And the third term is the present value of the growth in cash flows from new investment.

It is also useful to recall a few of the relationships between the parameters of Eq. (14.13). For example, the rate of growth in the firm's cash flows is Kr, the product of the investment rate, K, and the rate of return on new projects, r. Also, the anticipated amount of new investment, I, is equal to the investment rate times the firm's expected after-tax cash flow, $E(NOI_1)$. In other words, $I_1 = K[E(NOI_1)]$.

Equation (14.13) is a useful construct which uses modern finance theory for valuation. However, realistically it is at best only a crude tool. No one should be advised that it is the only approach to valuation or that it provides perfect answers. Yet it does point out precisely which pieces of information are relevant. Interestingly, none of them is provided in the annual report of the corporation. The only relevant parameters are forward-looking. Although some can be estimated from historic accounting data, the most important information is hardly ever reported by corporate management to shareholders.

2. A Valuation Example: Bethlehem Steel
What are the six relevant valuation parameters? And how can they be estimated?

a. *Expected After-tax Cash Flows from Current Operations*   Perhaps the most important factor is the level of cash flows earned on the projects which the firm has already undertaken. It is assumed that this level of cash flows will be maintained into perpetuity. Furthermore, it is assumed that depreciation allowances are sufficient to allow the current level of equipment to be maintained indefinitely.

Table 14.5 is a *pro forma* income statement for Bethlehem Steel for the years 1973–1976. We are attempting to estimate the value of the company as of December 31, 1976. (That is the date of our estimate of the cost of capital in Chapter 12.) The expected after-tax cash flows from operations during 1977, $E(NOI_1)(1 - \tau_c)$, can be estimated by computing 1976 cash flows and assuming that they will grow during 1977.

Table 14.5 *Pro forma* income statements, Bethlehem Steel (in thousands of dollars)

	1976	1975	1974	1973
Net billings and other income	5,304,700	5,028,300	5,448,709	4,174,833
Cost of billings	4,082,100	3,854,300	4,052,478	3,138,048
Provisions for:				
depreciation	275,600	234,200	210,912	196,086
pensions	261,200	198,400	153,842	115,533
misc. taxes	179,400	175,000	169,616	150,982
Selling and administrative expenses	234,700	220,000	210,842	178,641
Earnings before interest and taxes	271,700	346,400	660,019	395,543
Interest expense	77,700	63,400	43,985	38,934
Income taxes*	26,000	41,000	274,000	150,000
Net income	168,000	242,000	342,034	206,609
Dividends paid to common	87,400	120,000	100,172	72,431

* During 1976 this includes current taxes (federal, foreign, and state) of −$9,000,000; and deferred taxes (federal and state) of $35,000,000. Note that deferred taxes are a noncash charge.

Cash flows for 1976 from operations, NOI_0, can be calculated from the income statement in one of two equivalent ways. For example, consider the *pro forma* income statement in Table 14.6. The equation for net income can be rearranged as follows:

$$(R - VC - F - rD)(1 - \tau_c) = NI,$$

$$(R - VC - F)(1 - \tau_c) = NI + rD(1 - \tau_c). \qquad (14.14)$$

By adding back noncash charges, such as depreciation expenses (and deferred income taxes), we have two definitions of cash flow from operations:[7]

$$(R - VC)(1 - \tau_c) + \tau_c(\text{dep}) = NI + rD(1 - \tau_c) + \text{dep}. \qquad (14.15)$$

Table 14.6

$100	R		Revenues
− 60	−VC	−	Cash costs of operations
− 20	−F	−	Noncash costs (depreciation)
20	EBIT		Earnings before interest and taxes
− 10	−rD	−	Interest expense
10	EBT		Earnings before taxes
− 5	−T	−	Taxes at 50%
5	NI		Net income

[7] Recall that we have assumed $F = \text{dep}$.

The left-hand side starts at the top of the income statement in Table 14.6 and works down while the right-hand side starts at the bottom and works up. In order to obtain the correct definition of cash flows, one further adjustment must be made. Recall that the model assumes that depreciation is adequate to replace worn-out equipment. In other words, cash outflows used to replace equipment each year are exactly equivalent to depreciation. The two cancel each other. Therefore, because depreciation is used for replacement investment, it is not part of the *free cash flow* available to investors. Consequently, it is necessary to subtract depreciation from both sides of (14.15). The result is the correct definition of after-tax free cash flows from operations which can be maintained into perpetuity, $NOI_0(1 - \tau_c)$.

$$NOI_0(1 - \tau_c) = (R - VC)(1 - \tau_c) - dep(1 - \tau_c) = NI + rD(1 - \tau_c). \quad (14.16)$$

For the simple example above (if $\tau_c = .5$),

$$NOI_0(1 - \tau_c) = (100 - 60)(1 - .5) - 20(1 - .5) = 5 + 10(1 - .5) = 10.$$

For Bethlehem Steel the estimates are given in Table 14.7. Note that for 1976 estimates, we also have to add deferred taxes of $35 million, a noncash charge (discovered in the footnotes to the income statement). This makes our estimate of $NOI_0(1 - \tau_c)$ add up to be $243,404.

Table 14.7 Various valuation statistics for Bethlehem Steel ($ given in thousands)

	1976	1975	1974	1973
Net income	$168,000	$242,000	$342,034	$206,609
$+ rD(1 - \tau_c)$	40,404	32,968	22,872	20,246
$NOI_0(1 - \tau_c)$	$208,404	$274,968	$364,906	$226,855
Dividends	$87,400	$120,100	$100,172	$72,431
Dividends/$NOI_0(1 - \tau_c)$	.419	.437	.275	.319
(Investment rate) $= K$	58.1%	56.3%	72.5%	68.1%
Book value of assets	4,939,100	4,591,500	4,512,617	3,919,264
$(NOI_0(1 - \tau_c)/BV) = r$	4.22%	5.99%	8.09%	5.79%
Growth $= Kr$	2.75%	3.63%	6.10%	4.16%

b. The investment rate   The reason for estimating the investment rate, K, is that it is useful in estimating two more fundamental parameters: (1) the expected dollar amount of new investment $I_1 = K(NOI_1)(1 - \tau_c)$, and (2) the expected rate of growth in the firm, $g = Kr$. There is no reason that the investment rate must be less than 100% of cash flows. A higher investment rate simply means that the firm will be issuing new equity in order to undertake new investment in excess of current cash flows. This is certainly feasible for any firm with $r > k_0$.

From Table 14.6 we can estimate the investment rate by subtracting the dividend payout (dividends $\div NOI_0(1 - \tau_c)$) from 100%. Bethlehem did not issue new equity during the period 1973–1976. The average investment rate is 63.8%.

c.   The Rate of Return on New Investment   It is very difficult to come up with a reasonable projection of the rate of return on new investment. In Table 14.7 it has been estimated as the ratio of after-tax cash flows to the book value of assets. But the book value of assets is a number with little meaning, particularly during an inflationary economy. Also, what is really needed is not an historic estimate of return on capital in place, but rather an estimate of future return on investment. This information simply cannot be found in the accounting statements of the firm. The community of financial analysts make their living, at least in part, by trying to estimate the impact of future investment possibilities on the market value of the firm.

For lack of anything better to use, we have assumed that future growth is likely to be the same as that during the past four years. Estimated in Table 14.7, the average rate of return, r, on book value is 6.02%.

Once given the investment rate, $K = .638$, and the rate of return, $r = .0602$, we can estimate the rate of growth:

$$g = Kr = .0384.$$

d.   The Target Capital Structure   The target capital structure is useful for two purposes. First, as we saw in Chapter 12, it is needed in order to estimate the weighted average cost of capital. And second, when used in combination with the investment rate, it determines the extent to which the company will issue new equity.

In Chapter 12 we saw that Bethlehem Steel has had a fairly stable ratio of debt to total assets of around 53.5%. Also, the market value of debt, B, was estimated to be $2,039,345.

e.   The Weighted Average Cost of Capital   Assuming that new projects undertaken by the firm will have the same risk as current projects, then the current estimate of the weighted average cost of capital represents the required rate of return on new investment. If the expected rate of return, r, is greater than the required rate, k_0, a quick glance at the third term in Eq. (14.13) reveals that new investment will add to the market value of the firm. If new investment does not meet this criterion, it cannot possibly increase value (although, as was shown in Chapter 13, it might cause growth in earnings per share).

We assume that Bethlehem Steel will take on new investments with approximately the same risk as its existing projects. Therefore, we can use the weighted average cost of capital, estimated in Chapter 12. It was $k_0 = 8.02\%$. In addition, we need to know the cost of equity capital if Bethlehem Steel were an all-equity firm. This can be computed by using the Modigliani-Miller definition of cost of capital, Eq. (11.12):

$$k_0 = \text{WACC} = \rho \left(1 - \tau_c \frac{B}{B + S}\right),$$

$$\rho = \frac{\text{WACC}}{\left(1 - \tau_c \dfrac{B}{B + S}\right)}, \tag{11.12}$$

where

ρ = the cost of equity for the all-equity firm,
τ_c = the corporate tax rate = .48,
$B/(B + S)$ = the percent of debt in the capital structure of the firm = 53.5% (using market value weights),
WACC = the weighted average cost of capital = 8.02% = k_0.

Solving for ρ, we have

$$\rho = \frac{.0802}{1 - .48(.535)} = 10.76\%.$$

f.   The Duration of Abnormal Growth   The final important question is how long the firm will be able to undertake new investment projects which earn abnormally high rates of return, that is, projects which earn more than the rate required for investments of equal risk. How long will r be greater than k_0?

In the case of Bethlehem Steel the estimated future rate return, 6.02%, is less than the rate which the market requires, 8.02%. This means that we need to estimate the length of time it will take them to get out of trouble. This is a matter of judgment, and we have assumed that the current "growth" pattern shall persist for three years ($T = 3$).

g.   The Value of Bethlehem Steel   All that remains is to use the estimates of the six valuation parameters in the valuation equation. For convenience it is rewritten below

$$V^L = \frac{E(NOI_1)(1 - \tau_c)}{\rho} + \tau_c B + K[E(NOI_1)(1 - \tau_c)]T \left[\frac{r - k_0}{k_0(1 + k_0)}\right]. \quad (14.13)$$

Note that the expected 1977 after-tax cash flows from operations, $E(NOI_1)(1 - \tau_c)$, is equal to the estimated 1976 figure multiplied by the estimated growth rate ($g = Kr$):

$$E(NOI_1)(1 - \tau_c) = NOI_0(1 - \tau_c)(1 + Kr)$$

$$= 243,404(1 + .638(.0602))$$

$$= 243,404(1.0384076) = \$252,753.$$

Substituting the values of the remaining parameters into (14.13), we have

$$V^L = \frac{252,753}{.1079} + .48(2,039,345) + .638(252,753)3 \left[\frac{.0602 - .0802}{.0802(1.0802)}\right]$$

$$= 2,342,475 + 978,886 - 111,684$$

$$= \$3,299,677 \quad \text{(thousands of dollars).}$$

The actual market value of Bethlehem Steel at the end of December 1976 was $3.812 billion. Therefore, the estimate provided by the valuation model is around $.512 billion too low, an error of around 13.4%. The discrepancy may be due to any number of reasons. Most likely, our estimates of the anticipated operating cash flows and the rate of return on future investment (which were based on historical accounting data) were too low.

The valuation model does serve to point out the contribution of the three major components. Most of the market value of Bethlehem Steel comes from the stream of cash flows provided by investments which are already in place. Some extra value is provided by the tax shield from debt. And almost no value, or more accurately, negative value, results from the profitability of anticipated growth opportunities.

3. Implications for Accounting Information

The valuation example given above is useful for two reasons. First, it shows an investor how to evaluate the effect of new information on the market value of the firm. Second, it provides a shopping list of relevant information.

Investors gain little benefit from historic accounting data because they contain no new information. Therefore, although the annual report may serve as a useful device for monitoring the performance of management, it has little value to the investment community. Relevant data are forward-looking. Investors seek out information about the six parameters mentioned in Section 2.

An interesting related issue is the behavior of the Securities and Exchange Commission. By charter, its chief function is to monitor the disclosure of information. Yet many of its rules are concerned with the quality of historic accounting data. For example, it supports the publication of segment-based revenue data. Companies are asked to break down their total sales by line of business. The justification is presumably that the line-of-business reporting improves the shareholder stewardship function and allows investors to better estimate future returns. As we have already argued, historic accounting data, whatever their form, are of little benefit to investors. Consequently, it is hard to understand why the SEC should ask companies to bear the added cost of meeting its requirement of reporting segmented sales revenue.

What investors would like to know is what the management estimates future performance to be. This kind of information can be supplied in the company president's letter in the annual report without legal liability in the event that things don't turn out as well as anticipated. In particular, investors would benefit from unbiased estimates of the rate of return on future investment, the dollar amount of new investment, the length of time supernormal growth is expected to persist, and the percent of new capital which will be provided from equity sources.

Once again, it is important to keep in mind that the valuation model used in the above example is only as good as the assumptions used in its derivation. Also it is limited by the inevitable inaccuracies in estimating future cash flows. At best, it is only a framework for analysis which is useful for structuring the way we conceptualize corporate valuation.

Not only is it useful to understand which parameters determine value, but it is also important to understand those which do not. For example, accounting conventions which do not affect cash flows are irrelevant.

PROBLEM SET

14.1 Under what conditions might dividend policy affect the value of the firm?

14.2 According to federal tax law, corporations need not pay taxes on 85% of dividends received from shares held in other corporations. In other words, only 15% of the dividends received by a corporate holder are taxable. Given this fact, how much must the price of a stock fall on the ex-dividend date in order to prevent a corporate holder from making arbitrage profits? Assume that the capital gains rate equals the corporate tax rate, $\tau_c = .5$.

14.3 Empirical evidence supports the existence of a clientele effect. This implies that every time a company revises its dividend policy to pay out a greater (or smaller) percentage of earnings, the characteristics of its shareholders also change. For example, a firm with a higher payout ratio may expect to have more shareholders in lower tax brackets. Suppose that lower-income people are also more risk averse. Would this have an effect on the value of the firm?

14.4 Miller and Scholes [1977] suggest that it is possible to shelter income from taxes in such a way that capital gains rates are paid on dividend income. Furthermore, since capital gains need never be realized, the effective tax rate will become zero. Why wouldn't this scheme be used to shelter all income, instead of just dividend income? The implication would be that no one has to pay taxes—ever!

14.5 The Pettit study suggests an increase in the price per share of common stock commensurate with an increase in dividends. Can this be taken as evidence that the value of the firm is, in fact, affected by dividend policy?

REFERENCES

BAR-YOSEF, S., and R. KOLODNY, "Dividend Policy and Market Theory," *The Review of Economics and Statistics*, May 1976, 181–190.

BLACK, F., and M. SCHOLES, "The Effects of Dividend Yield and Dividend Policy on Common Stock Prices and Returns," *Journal of Financial Economics*, May 1974, 1–22.

———, M. JENSEN, and M. SCHOLES, "The Capital Asset Pricing Model: Some Empirical Tests" in M. Jensen, Ed. *Studies in the Theory of Capital Markets*. Praeger, New York, 1972, pp. 79–124.

BRENNAN, M., "Taxes, Market Valuation and Corporate Financial Policy," *National Tax Journal*, December 1970, 417–427.

BRITTAIN, J. A., *Corporate Dividend Policy*. Brookings Institute, Washington, D.C., 1966.

DARLING, P., "The Influence of Expectations and Liquidity on Dividend Policy," *Journal of Political Economy*, June 1957, 209–224.

ELTON, E. J., and M. J. GRUBER, "Marginal Stockholders' Tax Rates and the Clientele Effect," *Review of Economics and Statistics*, February 1970, 68–74.

FAMA, E., "The Empirical Relationships Between the Dividend and Investment Decisions of Firms," *The American Economic Review*, June 1974, 304–318.

———, and H. BABIAK, "Dividend Policy: An Empirical Analysis," *Journal of the American Statistical Association*, December 1968, 1132–1161.

FARRAR, D. and L. SELWYN, "Taxes, Corporate Financial Policy and Return to Investors," *National Tax Journal*, December 1967, 444–454.

FRIEND, I., and M. PUCKETT, "Dividends and Stock Prices," *The American Economic Review*, 1964, 656–682.

GORDON, M., "Dividends, Earnings, and Stock Prices," *Review of Economics and Statistics*, May 1959, 99–105.

———, "The Savings, Investment and Valuation of a Corporation," *Review of Economics and Statistics*, February 1962, 37–51.

KALAY, A., "Essays in Dividend Policy," Ph.D. thesis, University of Rochester, 1977.

KHOURY, N., and K. SMITH, "Dividend Policy and the Capital Gains Tax in Canada," *Journal of Business Administration*, Spring 1977.

LAUB, P. M., "On the Informational Content of Dividends," *The Journal of Business*, January 1976, 73–80.

LINTNER, J., "Distribution of Incomes of Corporations Among Dividends, Retained Earnings and Taxes," *The American Economic Review*, May 1956, 97–113.

———, "Optimal Dividends and Corporate Growth Under Uncertainty," *The Quarterly Journal of Economics*, February 1964, 49–95.

———, "The Valuation of Risk Assets and the Selection of Risky Investments in Stock Portfolios and Capital Budgets," *Review of Economics and Statistics*, February 1965, 13–37.

MILLER, M., and F. MODIGLIANI, "Dividend Policy, Growth, and the Valuation of Shares," *The Journal of Business*, October 1961, 411–433.

———, and M. SCHOLES, "Dividends and Taxes," working paper, University of Chicago, 1977.

PETTIT, R. R., "Dividend Announcements, Security Performance, and Capital Market Efficiency," *The Journal of Finance*, December 1972, 993–1007.

———, "The Impact of Dividend and Earnings Announcement: A Reconciliation," *The Journal of Business*, January 1976, 86–96.

———, "Taxes, Transactions Costs and Clientele Effect of Dividends," *The Journal of Financial Economics*, December 1977, 419–436.

ROSS, S. A., "The Determination of Financial Structure: The Incentive-Signalling Approach," *The Bell Journal of Economics*, Spring 1977, 23–40.

VAN HORNE, J., and J. G. McDONALD, "Dividend Policy and New Equity Financing," *Journal of Finance*, May 1971, 507–520.

WALTER, J. E., *Dividend Policy and Enterprise Valuation.* Wadsworth, Belmont, Calif., 1967.

WATTS, R., "The Information Content of Dividends," *The Journal of Business*, April 1973, 191–211.

———, "Comments on the Informational Content of Dividends," *The Journal of Business*, January 1976, 81–85.

———, "Comments on 'The Impact of Dividend and Earnings Announcements: a Reconciliation,'" *The Journal of Business*, January 1976, 97–106.

Chapter 15

Pricing Contingent Claims: Option Pricing Theory

The Black and Scholes option pricing model results in some ways can be viewed as an intertemporal analogue of the Modigliani-Miller theory.

J. C. Cox and S. A. Ross, "The Valuation of Options for Alternative Stochastic Processes," *Journal of Financial Economics,* January/March 1976, p. 145

A. INTRODUCTION

The theory of option pricing has undergone rapid advances in recent years. Simultaneously, organized option markets have developed in the United States. On April 26, 1973, the Chicago Board of Options Exchange (CBOE) became the first organized exchange for trading standardized options contracts. By the end of 1974, in terms of share equivalents, volume on the CBOE was larger than that on the American Stock Exchange. By the end of 1976 there were 1,337 registered CBOE exchange members and the bid-ask price for a seat was $55,000 to $62,000.[1] This phenomenal growth in option trading has been catalyzed, at least in part, by the standardization of contracts which has had the effect of lowering the transaction costs of option trading.

There are many types of options, and at first, the terminology is confusing with calls, puts, straps, strips, straddles, spreads, in-the-money options, out-of-the-money options, and so forth. This nomenclature can be greatly simplified if we recognize that all contracts are made up of four basic securities: puts, calls, stocks (the underlying asset), and default-free bonds. A *call option* is a contract which is contingent on

---

[1] By comparison, during December 1976, nine seats on the New York Stock Exchange exchanged hands at prices ranging from $58,000 to $80,000.

the value of an underlying asset. For example, a call option on the CBOE allows its holder to purchase a share of stock in the underlying company at a fixed price, usually called the *exercise price* or the *striking price*, for a fixed length of time. Table 15.1 is a clipping from *The Wall Street Journal* of October 4, 1977. We see, for example, that three Bethlehem Steel call options are being traded based on the value of its common stock, which closed that day at $19\frac{7}{8}$ per share. The first option has an exercise price of $20 and three maturity dates, the third Friday in October 1977, January 1978, and April 1978.

Should the price of the common stock climb above $20 per share, a trader who holds the call option with an exercise price of $20 could exercise his option and keep the difference between the exercise price and the stock price. A *put* is exactly the opposite of a call option. The holder of a put has the right to sell the stock at the exercise price any time up to and including the maturity date of the put. For example, the holder of a January put option on Avon with the exercise price of $45 can make a profit if the stock, which is now selling for $47 per share, falls below $45 before the third Friday in January.

B. A DESCRIPTION OF THE FACTORS WHICH AFFECT PRICES OF EUROPEAN OPTIONS

In order to keep the theory simple for the time being, we assume that all options can be exercised only on their maturity date and that there are no cash payments (such as dividends) made by the underlying asset. Options of this type are called *European* options. They are considerably easier to price than their *American* option counterparts which can be exercised at any date up to maturity.

A quick look at the option prices in Table 15.1 shows that at least three factors are important for the market value of an option. Since most of the options on the CBOE are call options, we shall, for the moment, confine our discussion to the determination of their value. Obviously, the higher the value of the underlying asset, S, the greater the value of an option written on it, *ceteris paribus*. Alcoa, American Express, Burlington Northern, Digital Equipment, and Walt Disney all have call options with an exercise price of $40 and a maturity date on the third Friday in January. Figure 15.1 clearly shows that the value of the call increases as a function of the value of the stock for a given exercise price and maturity date. Note also that the option still has a positive value even though the stock price is less than the exercise price. As long as investors believe that there is a chance that the stock price will exceed the exercise price before the option matures, the option will be valuable. Three of these companies, American Express, Digital Equipment, and Disney, have a second option with a lower exercise price of $35. Note that the relationship between the call price and the stock price has shifted upward. The lower the exercise price, the greater the value of a call option. The third obvious factor which affects call prices is the length of time to maturity. A quick look at any option in Table 15.1 shows that the longer the time to maturity, the higher the value of the option. The reason is that

Table 15.1 CBOE option price listing

Chicago Board

Option &	price	— Oct — Vol. Last	— Jan — Vol. Last	— Apr — Vol. Last	N.Y. Close

Listed Options Quotations

Tuesday, October 4, 1977

Closing prices of all options. Sales unit usually is 100 shares. Security description includes exercise price. Stock close is New York Stock Exchange final price. p-Put option. o-Old shares.

Option &	price	— Oct — Vol. Last	— Jan — Vol. Last	— Apr — Vol. Last	N.Y. Close

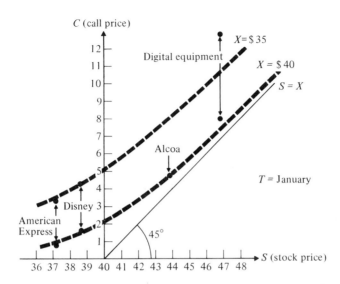

Fig. 15.1 The relationship between the call price and the stock price

with more time to maturity, there is a greater chance that the stock price will climb higher above the exercise price. Hence options with longer maturity have higher prices. In fact, a call option which has an infinite maturity date will have the same value as the stock, regardless of its exercise price. This is because the option will never be exercised. (Why not?)

In addition to the stock price, the exercise price, and the time to maturity, there are two other important, but less obvious, factors which affect the option's value: the instantaneous variance rate on the price of the underlying asset (the common stock), and the risk-free rate of return. The holder of a call option will prefer more variance in the price of the stock to less. The greater the variance, the greater the probability that the stock price will exceed the exercise price, and this is of value to the call holder. A call option is a type of contingent claim. In other words, the option holder gains only under the condition that the stock price exceeds the exercise price at the maturity date. Suppose an option holder is faced with the two hypothetical stock price distributions shown in Fig. 15.2. Both distributions have identical means but one has a larger variance. Which would the option holder prefer if both have an identical exercise price, X? When we recall that option holders gain only when the stock price is greater than the exercise price, it becomes clear that they will prefer the option on the security which has the higher variance because the cumulative probability of receiving a gain is greater for a security of this sort.[2] This points out an important difference between the value of options and the value of the underlying

---

[2] This example is given merely as an illustration, and the result holds only if $X > E(S)$. The example which follows is more accurate and more general.

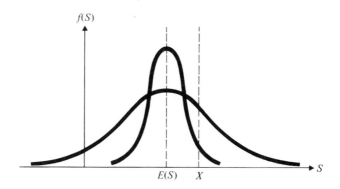

Fig. 15.2 Hypothetical distributions of stock prices

asset. If we hold the asset, we receive payoffs offered by the entire probability distribution of outcomes. If we are risk averse, we will dislike higher variance which means
that we must accept low returns along with high returns. On the other hand, if we
hold an option, we receive payoffs only from one tail of the distribution. The contingent claim feature of options makes higher variance desirable.

The value of higher variance is also illustrated in the following example. Suppose
that a company has borrowed long-term debt with fixed interest payments of $8000
per year and that it finds itself with one of the two investment projects below:

Project 1		Project 2	
Probability	Cash flow	Probability	Cash flow
.2	4,000	.4	0
.6	5,000	.2	5,000
.2	6,000	.4	10,000

Both projects have identical expected cash flows of $5000. However, if the sharehold-
ers accept project 1, the firm will surely go bankrupt because all possible cash flows
are less than the debt commitment of $8000. On the other hand, if they accept project
2, which has higher variance, there is a 40% chance that they will be able to pay off
their debt obligation and have $2000 left over. Obviously they will choose the riskier
project because it offers them a 40% chance of a positive value. This example further
illustrates the fact that holders of contingent claims, that is holders of options, will
prefer more variance to less. It also introduces the notion that the shareholders of a
firm are really holders of call options on the market value of the firm. If the value of
the firm is less than the required debt payoff (the exercise price on the option),
shareholders will allow their option to expire unexercised and turn over the assets of
the firm to bondholders. If the value of the firm exceeds the debt payoff, they will
exercise their option by paying off the debt holders and keeping any excess for

themselves. In Chapter 16 we shall explore in greater detail the implications of option pricing theory for corporate financial policy.

The final factor in determining the value of an option is the risk-free rate of interest. Of all the factors it is the least intuitive. Black and Scholes [1973] have shown that it is possible to create a risk-free hedged position consisting of a long position in the stock and a short position (where the investor writes a call) in the option. This insight allows them to argue that the rate of return on the equity in the hedged position is nonstochastic. Therefore the appropriate rate is the risk-free rate, and as it increases so does the rate of return on the hedged position. This implies that the value of the call option will increase as a function of the risk-free rate of return. The mechanics of forming the risk-free hedge, as well as a more precise exposition of the logic, will be given later in the chapter.

The preceding intuitive description shows that five factors are important in determining the value of a European option: the price of the underlying asset, S; the exercise price of the option, X; the instantaneous variance of the price of the underlying asset, σ^2; the time to maturity of the option, T; and the risk-free rate, r_f. This may be written in functional form as

$$c = f(S, X, \sigma^2, T, r_f),\tag{15.1}$$

and the partial derivatives of the call price, c, with respect to its various arguments are:

$$\frac{\delta c}{\delta S} > 0, \quad \frac{\delta c}{\delta X} < 0, \quad \frac{\delta c}{\delta \sigma^2} > 0, \quad \frac{\delta c}{\delta T} > 0, \quad \frac{\delta c}{\delta r_f} > 0.\tag{15.2}$$

C. COMBINING OPTIONS, A GRAPHIC PRESENTATION

One of the most fascinating features of options is that they can be combined in many different ways to provide almost any desired pattern of payoffs. For the sake of simplicity, assume that European put and call options have the same maturity date, the same underlying asset, and that the exercise price is set equal to the asset price.[3] A graphic representation of the value of buying or selling a call option as a function of changes in the stock price is given in Fig. 15.3. When selling a call, we receive the call price now. If the stock price stays the same or falls, the option will mature unexpired and we keep the sale price, $+C$. This is the horizontal portion of the dashed line in Fig. 15.3(a) with an intercept at $+C$. If the stock price rises, we lose one dollar for each dollar that it rises. This is the portion of the dashed line with an intercept at $+C$ and a slope of -1. Buying a call is the opposite of selling a call. If we sell a put, we receive $+P$ dollars now and lose a dollar for every dollar that the stock price falls below the exercise price. This is represented by the dashed line in Fig. 15.3(b). The solid line, which represents buying a put, is just the opposite.

---

[3] We also assume that capital markets are frictionless and there are no taxes. This implies, among other things, that the risk-free borrowing rate equals the risk-free lending rate.

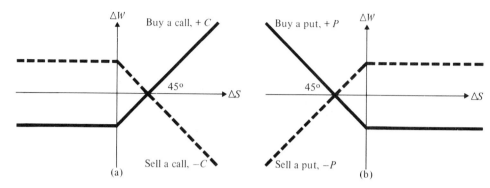

Fig. 15.3 Payoffs from put and call options where $S = X$

The payoffs for long and short positions for stocks and bonds are shown in Fig. 15.4. If we hold a long position in a stock we gain or lose one dollar for every dollar that the stock price changes. If we hold a bond, we receive the same payoff regardless of changes in the stock price because a risk-free bond is presumed to have identical payoffs irrespective of which state of the world obtains.

These elemental securities may be combined in various ways according to the following relationship:

$$S + P = B + C. \qquad (15.3)$$

Buying a share of stock and buying a put written on that share yield the same payoff as holding a bond and buying a call. Alternatively, holding a portfolio made up of long positions in the stock and the put and a short position in the call is equivalent to the perfectly risk-free payoff offered by holding the bond. This can be seen by simply rearranging Eq. (15.3) as follows:

$$S + P - C = B. \qquad (15.4)$$

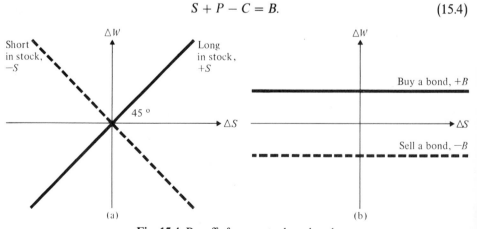

Fig. 15.4 Payoffs from a stock or bond

Figure 15.5 shows how the payoffs can be combined graphically by adding the payoffs. The dashed line is the payoff from holding a put and a share of stock. On the graph it is the vertical sum of the payoffs of the two securities. Note that there is no risk if the stock price falls, because the put gains a dollar in value for every dollar that the stock loses. In the terminology of Wall Street we say that the put insures against downside losses. If we also sell a call, any upside variability is eliminated too, and the result is a perfectly risk-free payoff. Thus a portfolio composed of a long position in a stock, a put on the stock, and a short position in a call on the stock is completely risk free.

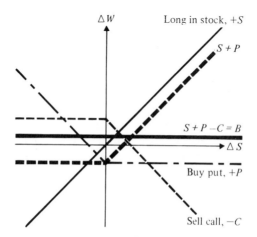

Fig. 15.5 Graphical representation of $S + P - C = B$

The reader may use the above graphic analysis to investigate the payoff patterns of many different securities. One often hears of straddles, spreads, straps and strips. They are defined as follows:

- *Spread.* A combination of put and call options in a single contract, with the exercise price of the put usually less than the exercise price of the call. Because of the put-call parity relationship (discussed in the next section) the value of a spread is less than for a straddle.

- *Straddle.* A combination of put and call options in the same contract where the exercise price and maturity date are identical for both options. A straddle is graphed in Fig. 15.6.

- *Straps and strips.* Combinations of two calls and one put, and two puts and one call, respectively.

A straddle loses money for small changes in the stock price and gains money for large changes. This may seem to be "a good deal," but let us keep in mind that the

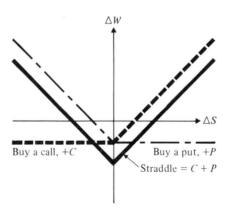

Fig. 15.6 Payoff on a straddle

market values of the put and call options are determined in a way which already incorporates the market's best estimate of the instantaneous variance in the price of the underlying security. The greater the variance, the more we have to pay for the put and call options. Therefore greater price fluctuations will be needed to make a profit. In the final analysis, given efficient capital markets, the securities will always be priced to yield a fair return for their riskiness.

D. COMBINING OPTIONS, AN ALGEBRAIC REPRESENTATION

The same analysis of payoffs from combinations of options can be represented by piecewise linear functions, in other words, an algebra of option payoffs. This form of analysis is particularly useful because it can be easily extended to include transactions costs and taxes.[4] We continue to assume that all options have the same maturity date, the same exercise price, and are written on the same underlying security. Furthermore, they are European options, and there are no cash disbursements from the underlying security during the life of the option. In the preceding graphic analysis we have seen that the end-of-period payoffs of the securities can be expressed as piecewise linear functions of the end-of-period price of the underlying security. It is possible to express all possible piecewise linear functions as linear combinations of two functions: a step or Heaviside function, and a slope or ramp function. Let us define S as the end-of-period price of the underlying security and $\{b_1, b_2, \ldots, b_n\}$ as the set of breakpoints where a profitability function (defined on S) either is discontinuous or has a discontinuous first derivative (changes slope). Furthermore, we adopt the convention that breakpoints are ordered as follows:

$$0 = b_1 < b_2 < \cdots < b_n.$$

---

[4] The interested reader is referred to Garman [1976] for an excellent presentation of the algebra of hedge portfolios.

Figure 15.7 shows a Heaviside function, $h(b, S)$ and a ramp function $m(b, S)$. The mathematical definitions of the Heaviside and ramp functions are:

$$h(b, S) \equiv \begin{cases} 0 & \text{if} \quad S < b \\ 1 & \text{if} \quad S \geq b \end{cases}$$

$$m(b, S) \equiv \begin{cases} 0 & \text{if} \quad S < b \\ S - b & \text{if} \quad S \geq b \end{cases}$$

The end-of-period payoff of every hedge portfolio may be derived by postmultiplying an option vector by a basis function vector. The easiest way to explain this is by example. Let us consider writing a call option:

Option profitability function = Option vector × Basis function vector.   (15.5)

The writer receives C_0 dollars now which will be worth $C_0(1 + r)$ dollars at the expiration date of the option. At expiration there are two possibilities: (1) If the price of the underlying security, S, is less than or equal to the exercise price, X, the call expires worthless. (2) If the security price exceeds the exercise price the option is exercised against the call writer, and he loses one dollar for every dollar that S exceeds X. There are two breakpoints in this example. The first breakpoint is always zero because the value of the underlying asset, S, cannot become negative. The second breakpoint is the exercise price, X. The option vector is derived from the Heaviside and ramp components of the end-of-period payoff. We will see that it turns out to be equal to

$$(1 + r)C_0 h(b_1, S) - m(b_2, S), \quad \text{where} \quad b_1 = 0, \quad b_2 = X.$$

In this example, note that at the first breakpoint there is no ramp component. At $b_1 = 0$ the only thing which happens is that the value of the option at maturity jumps from a value of zero to a value of $(1 + r)C_0$ (see Fig. 15.8). At the second breakpoint there is no Heaviside (step) component. However, the slope of the function changes from 0 to -1. Therefore, at b_2 the ramp function is -1. Using the

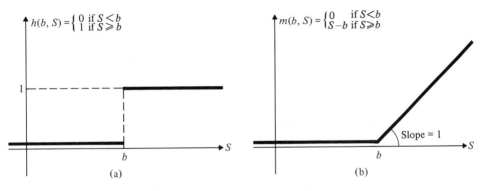

Fig. 15.7 Heaviside (a) and ramp (b) functions

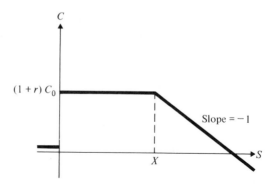

Fig. 15.8 Piecewise linear function for writing a call

definitions of the Heaviside and ramp functions, we obtain

$$(1 + r)C_0(0) - (S - X)(0) = 0 \qquad\qquad \text{if} \quad S < b_1 = 0;$$
$$(1 + r)C_0(1) - (S - X)(0) = (1 + r)C_0 \qquad \text{if} \quad b_1 \leq S \leq b_2 = X;$$
$$(1 + r)C_0(1) - (S - X) = (1 + r)C_0 - (S - X) \quad \text{if} \quad b_2 \leq S.$$

Therefore the option vector which fully describes the call sale is

$$[(1 + r)C_0, 0, 0, -1].$$

In other words, at the first breakpoint $(b_1 = 0)$ the Heaviside component is $(1 + r)C_0$, while at the second breakpoint $(b_2 = X)$ it is 0. These are the first two elements in the row vector. The second two elements are the values taken by the ramp function at the two breakpoints. At the first breakpoint it is 0, while at the second the ramp component (the change in slope) is -1. The basis vector, given the two breakpoints, $b_1 = 0$ and $b_2 = X$, is

$$[h(b_1, S), h(b_2, S), m(b_1, S), m(b_2, S)]'.$$

The prime denotes the vector transpose.

Postmultiplying the option vector by the basis function vector, we obtain the piecewise linear function for writing a call,

$$[(1 + r)C_0, 0, 0, -1] \begin{bmatrix} h(0, S) \\ h(X, S) \\ m(0, S) \\ m(X, S) \end{bmatrix} = [(1 + r)C_0]h(0, S) - m(X, S),$$

which is graphed in Fig. 15.8. This analysis improves on the previous graphic approach because it recognizes the time value of money $(1 + r)$, it allows the use of any exercise price, X, and it can easily be extended to include transaction costs and taxes.

The piecewise linear function for a call option, as described above, can be used to calculate the end-of-period profit from a particular call position. For example, suppose that the call price is $5, the exercise price is $50, and the time value of money, $(1 + r)$, is 1.05. What will be the end-of-period portfolio position if the final stock price is $60? The option profitability function for writing a call is

$$[(1 + r)C_0]h(0, S) - m(X, S).$$

If the stock price is greater than the exercise price, the Heaviside function takes the value $+1$, and the ramp function takes the value $S - X$. Therefore

$$\text{the end-of-period position} = [(1 + r)C_0][1] - [S - X]$$
$$= (1.05)(5) - (60 - 50) = -4.75.$$

In this example, the call writer loses $4.75 because the call is exercised against him.

We can use the algebra of hedge portfolios to quickly analyze almost any combination of assets. Table 15.2 summarizes the various option functions.

Table 15.2 Summary of option functions*

Description	b_1	b_2	h_1	h_2	m_1	m_2
				Option function		
Buy stock	0	None	$-S_0 d$	0	$+1$	0
Short stock	0	None	$S_0 d$	0	-1	0
Buy call	0	X	$-C_0 d$	0	0	$+1$
Sell call	0	X	$C_0 d$	0	0	-1
Buy put	0	X	$-P_0 d$	0	-1	$+1$
Sell put	0	X	$P_0 d$	0	$+1$	-1
Buy bond	0	None	$-B_0 d$	0	0	0
Sell bond	0	None	$B_0 d$	0	0	0

* Note: The symbols appearing in the table have the following meaning: $d = 1 + r$, where r is the borrowing and lending rates, $P_0 =$ current price of a put option, $C_0 =$ current price of a call option, $S_0 =$ current price of stock, $B_0 =$ current price of bond, $B =$ end-of-period bond price = $B_0(1 + r) = B_0 d$, and $X =$ the exercise price of the option.

In order to show how they are applied, let us consider a straddle position, i.e., we buy a call and a put with the same exercise price and time to maturity. The payoff function for a straddle will be the sum of the call and put payoff functions. Mathematically, this is written as

$$[-C_0 d, 0, 0, +1] \begin{bmatrix} h(0, S) \\ h(X, S) \\ m(0, S) \\ m(X, S) \end{bmatrix} + [-P_0 d, 0, -1, +1] \begin{bmatrix} h(0, S) \\ h(X, S) \\ m(0, S) \\ m(X, S) \end{bmatrix},$$

which equals

$$[-(C_0 + P_0)d, 0, -1, +2] \begin{bmatrix} h(0, S) \\ h(X, S) \\ m(0, S) \\ m(X, S) \end{bmatrix},$$

and multiplying the two vectors yields the payoff function

$$[-(C_0 + P_0)dh(0, S) - m(0, S) + 2m(X, S)].$$

This says that the payoffs are equal to

$$-(C_0 + P_0)d - (S - X) \qquad \text{if} \qquad 0 < S \le X,$$
$$-(C_0 + P_0)d - (S - X) + 2(S - X) \qquad \text{if} \qquad S > X.$$

This result is shown in Fig. 15.6.

E. PUT-CALL PARITY

Table 15.1 shows some securities with both put and call options written against them. For example, Avon has puts and calls with exercise prices of $45 and $50. We show below that, for European options, there is a fixed relationship between the price of put and call options with the same maturity date which are written on a single underlying security. This relationship, derived by Stoll [1969], is called *put-call parity*. It is particularly useful, because if we know how to compute the value of a European call, we automatically know the price of the corresponding put.

Suppose we have a portfolio where we purchase one share of stock, one put option, and sell (write) one call option. Both options are written on the share of stock. Also, they have the same maturity date, T, and the same exercise price, X. At maturity all states of the world can be divided into those where the stock price is less than the exercise price, $S < X$, and those where it is greater than or equal to the exercise price, $S \ge X$. The payoffs from the portfolio in either state are listed below.

If $S < X$:

a) you hold the stock S
b) the call option is worthless 0
c) the put option is worth $X - S$
d) therefore, your net position is X

If $S \ge X$

a) you hold the stock S
b) the call option is worth $-(S - X)$
c) and the put option is worthless 0
d) therefore, your net position is X

No matter what state of the world obtains at maturity, the portfolio will be worth X. Consequently, the payoff from the portfolio is completely risk-free, and we can discount its value at the risk-free rate, r_f. Using discrete discounting, this is

$$S_0 + P_0 - C_0 = \frac{X}{1 + r_f}$$

This can be rearranged to give the put-call parity formula

$$(C_0 - P_0) = \frac{(1 + r_f)S_0 - X}{1 + r_f}. \tag{15.6}$$

Note that the interest rate, r, is a one-period rate but that the time period need not equal a calendar year. For example, if the option expires in six months and r is an annual rate, then we can replace $(1 + r)$ in Eq. (15.7) with $(1 + r)^{1/2}$. Equation (15.6) is referred to as the *put-call parity* relationship for European options. A special case occurs when the exercise price, X, is set equal to the current stock price, S_0. When $S_0 = X$, we have

$$C_0 - P_0 = \frac{r_f S_0}{1 + r_f} > 0. \tag{15.7}$$

This shows that when all the valuation parameters are identical (the same stock price, instantaneous variance, exercise price, time to expiration, and risk free rate) and the exercise price equals the stock price, the call option will have greater present value than the put option.

An equivalent continuous compounding formula for put-call parity is

$$C_0 - P_0 = S_0 - Xe^{-r_f T} \tag{15.8}$$

where r_f is the annual risk-free rate and T is the time to maturity of the put and call options. The put-call parity relationship is extremely useful for the valuation of European options because if we know the value of a call, the put-call parity relationship also gives the value of a corresponding put.

F. SOME DOMINANCE THEOREMS WHICH BOUND THE VALUE OF A CALL OPTION

The value of a call option has been described as a function of five parameters: the price of the underlying asset, S; the instantaneous price variance of the asset, σ^2; the exercise price, X; the time to expiration, T; and the risk-free rate, r_f:

$$c = f(S, \sigma^2, X, T, r_f). \tag{15.1}$$

Perhaps even more interesting are some factors which do not affect the value of an option. For example, the option price does not depend on investor attitudes toward risk nor does it depend on the expected rate of return of the underlying security. This section of the chapter provides a logical, rather than descriptive or intuitive, framework for understanding why the above five parameters affect option value and why investor attitudes toward risk and the rate of return on the underlying security do not.

All the following theorems are based on the notion of stochastic dominance, which was introduced in Chapter 4. We shall use first-order stochastic dominance which says that one asset will be preferred by all investors (be they risk averse, risk neutral, or risk loving) if the return which it offers is superior in every state of nature to the return offered by a second asset. If this is true, we say that the first asset is stochastically dominant over the second. Clearly, if all the following theorems are based on this simple notion, the value of a call option will not depend on individual risk preferences.

Before developing the theorems it is useful to spell out in detail the assumptions which have been used in developing valuation models for options:

- Frictionless capital markets with no transactions costs or taxes and with information simultaneously and costlessly available to all individuals.
- No restrictions on short sales.
- Asset trading is continuous, with all asset prices[5] following continuous and stationary stochastic processes.
- The risk-free rate is nonstochastic (constant over time).[6]
- No dividends.[7]

Most of these assumptions are self-explanatory and are consistent with efficient capital markets. By continuous stochastic processes we mean that the price of the underlying asset can vary over time but does not have any discontinuities or jumps. In other words, we could graph the price movement over time without lifting our pen from the paper. A stationary stochastic process is one which is determined in the same way for all time periods of equal length. In particular, the instantaneous price variance does not change over time. If the underlying asset is a common stock, we assume no dividend payments so that there are no jumps in the stock price. It is well known that the stock price falls by approximately the amount of the dividend on the ex-dividend date.

Theorem 15.1 Call prices are nonnegative.

This is obvious for a European call because the option can be exercised only on its expiration date. Its value at that time is either zero if $S < X$, or $S - X$ if $S > X$. The value at expiration may be written as

$$\text{MAX}[0, S - X] \geq 0. \tag{15.9}$$

---

[5] Cox and Ross [1975] have relaxed this assumption.
[6] Merton [1973] has relaxed this assumption.
[7] Geske [1977] has relaxed this assumption.

This is always equal to or greater than zero, and therefore the current call price is nonnegative. The same argument holds for an American call for any time, t, before the expiration date, T.

Theorem 15.2   An American option must sell for at least the difference between the stock price and the exercise price at any date before expiration. If we adopt the convention that American calls are written with a capital C and European calls with a small c, Theorem 15.2 is

$$C(S, T - t, X) \geq \text{MAX}[0, S - X] \geq 0. \tag{15.10}$$

Proof of the theorem is based on the fact that if the option price ever falls below $S - X$, it can be exercised. Since the call price would be less than $S - X$, an immediate arbitrage profit could be made by investors who bought the call and exercised it immediately.

Theorem 15.3   If two American calls differ only with regard to their maturity date, the one with more time to expiration will be more valuable:

$$C(S, T - t_1, X) \geq C(S, T - t_2, X) \qquad \text{iff} \qquad t_1 < t_2. \tag{15.11}$$

From (15.9) we know that the value of the shorter-lived option must be at least zero or $S - X$. By (15.10), this then is the minimum price of the longer-term option. Therefore, in order to prevent dominance, (15.11) must hold.

Theorem 15.4   An American call must be priced no lower than an identical European call:

$$C(S, T - t, X) \geq c(S, T, X). \tag{15.12}$$

This is obvious because an American call is identical to a European call except that it offers the additional advantage of premature exercise. Therefore to avoid dominance, (15.12) must hold.

Theorem 15.5   If two options are identical except that one has a higher exercise price, then in order to avoid dominance, it must have a lower value than a similar option with a lower exercise price.

Let the exercise prices of the two options be X_1 and X_2, respectively, where $X_1 > X_2$. Table 15.3 illustrates the payoffs from the two options for each possible

Table 15.3 Comparison of options with different exercise prices $(X_1 > X_2)$

Portfolio	Current value	Portfolio value, given stock price at T		
		$S \leq X_2$	$X_2 < S < X_1$	$X_1 < S$
A	$C(S, T - t, X_2)$	0	$S - X_2$	$S - X_2$
B	$C(S, T - t, X_1)$	0	0	$S - X_1$
Relationship between terminal values of A and B		$V_a = V_b$	$V_a > V_b$	$V_a > V_b$

stock price at the maturity date, T. Because, at expiration, the value of A is greater than or equal to the value of B in every state of nature, it is necessary for the current value of A to be greater than B in order to prevent dominance. If the opposite were true, then A would cost less and also provide a higher terminal value. It would then clearly dominate B. However, we assume that in efficient capital markets, in equilibrium there can be no dominance because any dominance profits will be immediately arbitraged away.

Therefore, in order to prevent dominance, we know that Theorem 15.5 must obtain:

$$C(S, T - t, X_1) \le C(S, T - t, X_2), \qquad X_1 > X_2,$$
$$c(S, T, X_1) \le c(S, T, X_2), \qquad X_1 > X_2. \tag{15.13}$$

Theorem 15.6   The underlying asset has value greater than or equal to a perpetual call with a zero exercise price:

$$S \ge C(S, \infty, 0) \ge C(S, T - t, X). \tag{15.14}$$

From Theorem 15.3, the option with a longer time to expiration will be more valuable, and from Theorem 15.5, the option with a lower exercise price must be more valuable. The reason that common stock (if it is the underlying asset) may be more valuable than a perpetual option with zero exercise price is that the holder of common stock has voting rights in the firm. Theorem 15.6 also says that if the underlying asset is worthless (that is, $S = 0$), then the option will also be worthless.

The preceding theorems have the effect of bounding possible values which option prices may take relative to the stock price. Theorem 15.1 shows that call prices will be nonnegative. Theorem 15.2 requires the call price to be greater than the stock price minus the exercise price. This fact is represented by the 45° line labeled $C \ge S - X$ in Fig. 15.9. It also shows that the call price is a negative function of the exercise price and a positive function of the stock price. If the exercise price is zero but the option has a finite life T, Theorem 15.6 requires the call price to be less than the stock price.

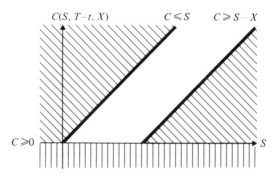

Fig. 15.9 Boundaries for the value of a call option

Therefore, the call price must lie to the right of the line labeled $C \le S$ in the figure. As more theorems are developed, the feasible values for the call price will be limited even further.

Theorem 15.7 An American call on a nondividend paying stock will not be exercised before the expiration date.

In order to prove this, we first assume that $B(\tau)$ is the current price of a risk-free pure discount bond. A pure discount bond pays no coupons. Given positive interest rates and assuming that the bond pays one dollar upon maturity, we have[8]

$$B(\tau) = (\$1)e^{-r_f\tau}, \tag{15.15}$$

where r_f is the one-year risk-free rate and τ is the number of years (or fraction of a year) to maturity. We shall adopt the convention that $\tau_1 > \tau_2 > \cdots > \tau_n$; therefore

$$0 = B(\infty) < B(\tau_1) < B(\tau_2) < \cdots < B(0) = \$1. \tag{15.16}$$

Now let us consider two portfolios. Portfolio A represents the purchase of one European call for $c(S, T, X)$ dollars and X bonds for $XB(\tau)$ dollars. Portfolio B is the purchase of one share of stock for S dollars. Table 15.4 demonstrates the relationship between the terminal values for the two portfolios. If the stock price is less than the exercise price at the expiration date, the option will expire unexercised, with no value, and portfolio A will be worth X dollars. But since $X > S$, portfolio A will be worth more than portfolio B, which is one share of stock. On the other hand, when the stock price is greater than the exercise price, portfolios A and B have the same payoff. In any state of nature portfolio A pays an amount greater than or equal to portfolio B. Therefore, in order to prevent dominance, portfolio A must have a higher price than portfolio B:

$$c(S, T, X) + XB(T) \ge S.$$

Table 15.4 Relationship between the value of a share of stock and a portfolio made up of a European call and X risk-free bonds

Portfolio	Current value	Portfolio value, given stock price at T	
		$S < X$	$S \ge X$
A	$c(S, T, X) + XB(T)$	$0 + X$	$S - X + X$
B	S_0	S	S
Relationship between terminal values of A and B		$V_a > V_b$	$V_a = V_b$

[8] This is the continuous discounting version of the more familiar discrete discounting formula

$$B(\tau) = \frac{\$1}{(1 + r_f)^\tau} = (\$1)(1 + r_f)^{-\tau}.$$

This restriction may be rearranged to obtain

$$c(S; T, X) \geq \text{MAX}[0, S - XB(T)].$$

Finally from (15.15), we have

$$c(S, T, X) \geq \text{MAX}[0, S - e^{-r_f T}X]. \tag{15.17}$$

Equation (15.17) applies to a European call, but it has already been demonstrated, in Theorem 15.4, that an American call is always at least as valuable as an equivalent European call; therefore

$$C(S, T - t, X) \geq c(S, T, X) \geq \text{MAX}[0, S - e^{-r_f T}X]. \tag{15.18}$$

Furthermore, if exercised, the value of an American call is $\text{MAX}[0, S - X]$, which is less than $\text{MAX}[0, S - XB(T)]$, since $B(T) = e^{-r_f T}$, which is less than one, for positive r_f. Consequently, the holder of an American option can always do better by selling it in the marketplace rather than exercising it prior to expiration. This is an important result because European options are much simpler than American options.

Theorem 15.7 further limits the set of feasible prices for call options because the requirement that

$$c(S, T, X) \geq \text{MAX}[0, S - XB(T)]$$

is more restrictive than

$$c(S, T, X) \geq \text{MAX}[0, S - X].$$

This is shown in Fig. 15.10. Also, it is now possible to demonstrate, in a plausible fashion, that the call price will increase when the risk-free rate increases. Suppose the stock price is $50, the exercise price is $30, and the option expires in one year. If the risk-free rate is 5%, the lower bound on the option price will be $21.46. If the risk-free rate changes to 10%, the lower bound increases to $22.85. Intuitively, the call option is worth more because an investor has to pay less today to acquire the risk-free

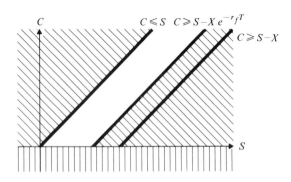

Fig. 15.10 Further limitation of the feasible set of call prices

discount bond which guarantees one dollar at the end of the year. This makes portfolio A in Table 15.4 more valuable relative to portfolio B.

Theorem 15.8   A perpetual option on a nondividend paying stock must sell for the same price as the stock.[9]

This result follows directly from Eq. (15.18):

$$C(S, \infty, X) \geq MAX[0, S - Xe^{-r_f T}].$$

As T approaches infinity, $e^{-r_f T}$ approaches zero; therefore

$$C(S, \infty, X) \geq MAX[0, S],$$

and from Theorem 15.6, the call price is not greater than the stock price. Therefore, we have the following equality:

$$C(S, \infty, X) = S. \tag{15.19}$$

Theorem 15.8 merely serves to more firmly establish $C = S$ as the upper bound for call prices in Fig. 15.10.

Theorem 15.9   Premature exercise of an American call may occur if the underlying security (common stock) pays dividends (and if the option is inadequately protected against the dividend payment).

In December of 1976, General Motors stock was selling at around $75 per share. Call options were outstanding with an exercise price of $60. On the next day the company was scheduled to go ex-dividend with a dividend of $3 per share. This implied that the stock price would fall to approximately $72 per share. CBOE call options provide no protection against dividend payments, and hence option holders found themselves with the following dilemma. Before the ex-dividend date the option price could not fall below $S - X$, or $15. (Why?) On the following day everyone knew the stock price would fall to around $72 per share, and that the option price would also fall (it fell to around $12\frac{5}{8}$). On one day their option was worth $15 and on the next they knew it would have a lower price. Obviously, the rational thing to do was to exercise the option just before the stock went ex-dividend.

The rationality of the above example can be demonstrated by assuming that a security makes a certain dividend payment, D, on the expiration date of an option. Consider two portfolios. Portfolio A is one European call and $X + D$ bonds. Portfolio B is one share of stock. Table 15.5 shows the terminal values of the two portfolios. The value of A is greater than that of B when the stock price is less than the exercise price and equal to it otherwise. Therefore

$$C(S, T - t, X) + (X + D)B(T) \geq S.$$

---

[9] A nondividend paying stock can have positive value if the cash payments to shareholders take the form of repurchase rather than dividends. See Chapter 13.

Table 15.5 Options on dividend-paying stocks may be exercised prematurely

Portfolio	Current value	Portfolio value given on stock price at T	
		$S < X$	$S \geq X$
A	$C(S, T - t, X) + (X + D)B(T)$	$0 + X + D$	$S - X + X + D$
B	S	$S + D$	$S + D$
Relationship between terminal values of A and B		$V_a > V_b$	$V_a = V_b$

By rearranging this and using Eq. (15.15), we obtain

$$C(S, T - t, X) \geq \text{MAX}[0, S - (X + D)e^{-r_f T}]. \tag{15.20}$$

Depending on the size of the dividend payment and the risk-free rate, it is possible to have the following situation,

$$(X + D)e^{-r_f T} > S,$$

in which case the value of the call in (15.20) is zero, at best. Therefore, in some cases it may be advantageous to exercise an American option prematurely.[10]

The theorems presented above serve to bound the possible values of call prices as shown in Fig. 15.10. They do so without any mention whatsoever of the risk preferences of different individuals. The dominance arguments used to prove the theorems are very robust. They require only that arbitrage opportunities in efficient capital markets do not result in dominated securities. Further, the theorems provide considerable insight into the relationship between option prices, the price of the underlying asset, S; the exercise price, X; the time to maturity, T; and the risk-free rate, r_f. In the next section, we demonstrate the call valuation formula which can be used to determine the price of a European call, given that we know the above four parameters and the instantaneous variance of the price of the underlying asset.

G. THE EUROPEAN CALL VALUATION FORMULA

Black and Scholes [1973] were the first to provide a closed-form solution for the valuation of European calls. They recognized that given the assumption of frictionless markets and continuous trading opportunities, it is possible to form a risk-free hedge portfolio consisting of a long position in the stock and a short position in the European call written on that stock. If the stock price changes over time, the risk-free hedge can be maintained by continuously readjusting the proportions of

---

[10] The reader who is interested in the valuation of call options written on dividend-paying stocks is referred to Roll [1977].

stock and calls. The value of the hedge portfolio, V_H, can be expressed as the number of shares of stock, Q_s, times the price per share, S, plus the quantity of calls, Q_c, times their price:

$$V_H = SQ_s + cQ_c. \tag{15.21}$$

The change in the value of the hedge portfolio is the total derivative of (15.21).

$$dV_H = Q_s \, dS + Q_c \, dc. \tag{15.22}$$

Of course, the stock price moves randomly over time. We assume that it follows a geometric Brownian motion process. Its rate of return can be described as

$$\frac{dS}{S} = \mu \, dt + \sigma \, dz, \tag{15.23}$$

where

$\mu =$ the instantaneous expected rate of return (it measures the drift in the random walk through time, dt),
$\sigma =$ the instantaneous standard deviation of the rate of return,
$dt =$ a small increment of time,
$dz =$ a Wiener process.

Since the option's price is a function of the stock's price, its movement over time must be related to the stock's movement over time. Black and Scholes [1973] show that if the stock price follows a geometric Brownian motion process such as (15.23), then using stochastic calculus (which is far beyond the mathematical capabilities assumed for this text) and employing a technique known as Ito's lemma, one can express the change in the option price by the following stochastic differential equation:

$$dc = \frac{\delta c}{\delta S} \, dS + \frac{\delta c}{\delta t} \, dt + \frac{1}{2} \frac{\delta^2 c}{\delta S^2} \sigma^2 S^2 \, dt. \tag{15.24}$$

Note that the only stochastic term in the expression for dc is dS. The others are deterministic.

Substituting (15.24) into (15.22), we obtain

$$dV_H = Q_s \, dS + Q_c \left[\frac{\delta c}{\delta S} \, dS + \frac{\delta c}{\delta t} \, dt + \frac{1}{2} \frac{\delta^2 c}{\delta S^2} \sigma^2 S^2 \, dt \right]. \tag{15.25}$$

As mentioned earlier, the insight which Black and Scholes provided was to notice that it is possible to continuously adjust the hedge portfolio, V_H, so that it becomes risk free. How this may be done is illustrated in Fig. 15.11. The curved line, labeled $c(S, T, X)$, represents the theoretical relationship between the call price and the stock price. If we buy one share of stock and sell a number of call options equal to the inverse of the slope of a line tangent to the curve $c(S, T, X)$, we can create a riskless hedge. For example, let us suppose that the current stock price is $15, and the option

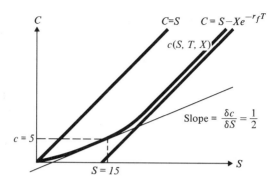

Fig. 15.11 Forming a continually adjusted riskless hedge portfolio

price is $5. We form a hedge portfolio by selling two calls (for which we receive $10) and by buying one share of stock for $15. Our net equity position would be $5. This is illustrated in Table 15.6. Next, for the sake of argument, let us assume that the stock price rises to $20 and the option price to $7⅞. We gain $5 from the stock and lose $5¾ on the two call options. Our net equity has decreased by $.75. A similar small loss may be expected if the stock price falls by $5. Of course, for smaller changes in the stock price, our equity loss is even smaller. And if we continuously adjust our hedge portfolio to maintain a ratio of stock to call options of $1/(\delta c/\delta S)$, the hedge will be perfectly risk free. Therefore, the risk-free hedge portfolio will earn the risk-free rate in equilibrium if capital markets are efficient. This is really the main insight. It is possible, given continuous trading, to form risk-free hedges with only two securities, the underlying asset and a call option. This equilibrium relationship is expressed as

$$\frac{dV_H}{V_H} = r_f \, dt. \tag{15.26}$$

This fact and the fact that the riskless hedge is maintained by purchasing one share of stock and selling $1/(\delta c/\delta S)$ calls,

$$Q_s = 1, \qquad Q_c = -\frac{1}{(\delta c/\delta S)}, \tag{15.27}$$

allows us to substitute (15.26) and (15.27) into (15.25) in order to simplify it. This is done below:

$$dV_H = r_f \, dt V_H = (1) \, dS - \frac{\delta S}{\delta c} \left[\frac{\delta c}{\delta S} \, dS + \frac{\delta c}{\delta t} \, dt + \frac{1}{2} \frac{\delta^2 c}{\delta S^2} \, \sigma^2 S^2 \, dt \right],$$

$$\frac{\delta c}{\delta t} = r_f V_H \left(-\frac{\delta c}{\delta S} \right) - \frac{1}{2} \frac{\delta^2 c}{\delta S^2} \, \sigma^2 S^2.$$

Table 15.6 An example of a riskless hedge

	$\Delta S = -5$	Initial	$\Delta S = +5$
Stock price S	$10	$15	$20
Call price c	$ 2\frac{7}{8}$	$ 5	$ 7\frac{7}{8}$
Short two calls	$ 5\frac{3}{4}$	$10	$15\frac{3}{4}$
Equity position	$ 4\frac{1}{4}$	$ 5	$ 4\frac{1}{4}$

Substituting (15.21) for V_H and using (15.27) again, we have

$$\frac{\delta c}{\delta t} = r_f(SQ_s + cQ_c)\left(-\frac{\delta c}{\delta S}\right) - \frac{1}{2}\frac{\delta^2 c}{\delta S^2}\sigma^2 S^2$$

$$= r_f c - r_f S\frac{\delta c}{\delta S} - \frac{1}{2}\frac{\delta^2 c}{\delta S^2}\sigma^2 S^2. \tag{15.28}$$

Equation (15.28) is a nonstochastic differential equation for the value of the option. By using the notion of a riskless hedge, Black and Scholes eliminate the only stochastic term, dS. Now the nonstochastic differential equation may be solved subject to the boundary conditions that at the terminal date the option price must be

$$c = \text{MAX}[0, S - X]$$

and that, for any date,

$$c(S = 0, T, X) = 0.$$

Black and Scholes [1973] transform the equation into the heat exchange equation from physics to find the following solution:[11]

$$c = S \cdot N\left|\frac{\ln(S/X) + [r_f + (\sigma^2/2)T]}{\sigma\sqrt{T}}\right| - e^{-r_f T}X \cdot N\left|\frac{\ln(S/X) + [r_f - (\sigma^2/2)T]}{\sigma\sqrt{T}}\right|,$$
$$\tag{15.29}$$

where all variables are as defined previously except that

$N(\cdot)$ = the cumulative normal probability of a unit normal variable; where, for example, $N(-\infty) = 0$, $N(0) = .5$, and $N(\infty) = 1.0$;

$N(\cdot) = \int_{-\infty}^{z} f(z)\,dz$, where $f(z)$ is distributed normally with mean zero and standard deviation one.

---

[11] Note that once we are given the call pricing solution (Eq. (15.29)), we see that the hedge ratio in terms of the number of calls per share is

$$Q_c = -1/(\delta c/\delta S) = -1/N(d_1),$$

where $N(d_1)$ is the first term in braces in Eq. (16.29). This fact is needed in order to continuously construct risk-free hedges (see the problem set at the end of this chapter).

A more intuitive solution to the problem was suggested by Cox and Ross [1975]. Because the price of the option is determined by riskless arbitrage in perfect capital markets, the risk preferences of investors are irrelevant. Therefore, it is easiest to assume that investors are neutral to risk. The present value of a call option is simply the discounted expected terminal price, c^*:

$$c = e^{-r_f T} E(c^*)$$

$$= e^{-r_f T} \int_X^\infty (S - X) L(S) \, dS. \tag{15.30}$$

If $L(S)$ is a lognormal density function, then the solution to (15.30) is the Black-Scholes option pricing model, Eq. (15.29).

The option pricing model (OPM) is a closed-form solution to the pricing of contingent claim assets. If one takes the partial derivatives of the call price, it is an increasing function of the stock price, the time to maturity, the instantaneous variance of the stock price, and the risk-free rate, and it is a decreasing function of the exercise price. Of these five parameters only the instantaneous variance is difficult to estimate, as we shall see in the next section. In Chapter 16, we shall see that the option-pricing framework has numerous applications for the theory of the firm. It has already been suggested that the equity of the firm may be thought of as a call option on the value of the firm's assets.

H. VALUATION OF AN AMERICAN CALL WITH NO DIVIDEND PAYMENTS

At first, we can use a simple example, where all of the parameters are given in order to understand the mechanics of using the OPM. Then we can proceed to a problem which uses real-world data.

Suppose that the current stock price is $50, that the exercise price of an American call written on the stock is $45, that the annual risk-free rate is 6%, that the option matures in three months, and that the instantaneous variance of the stock price is estimated to be 20%. Given these facts and the assumption that the stock will pay no dividends or undertake any other capital distributions, we can use the OPM, Eq. (15.29), to value the call:

$$c = S \cdot N \left| \frac{\ln(S/X) + (r_f + \sigma^2/2)T}{\sigma\sqrt{T}} \right| - e^{-r_f T} X \cdot N \left| \frac{\ln(S/X) + (r_f - \sigma^2/2)T}{\sigma\sqrt{T}} \right|.$$

$$\tag{15.29}$$

We can simplify the notation in (15.29) if we let

$$d_1 = \frac{\ln(S/X) + r_f T}{\sigma\sqrt{T}} + \tfrac{1}{2}\sigma\sqrt{T}, \qquad d_2 = d_1 - \sigma\sqrt{T}. \tag{15.31}$$

Substituting (15.31) into (15.29), we have

$$c = SN(d_1) - e^{-r_f T} X N(d_2). \tag{15.32}$$

To evaluate (15.32), we first calculate the value of d_1. The time to maturity, three months, must be expressed as a fraction of a year, that is one-fourth of a year. Setting $T = .25$, and substituting in the values of the other parameters, we get

$$d_1 = \frac{\ln(50/45) + .06(.25)}{\sqrt{.2}\sqrt{.25}} + \tfrac{1}{2}(\sqrt{.2})\sqrt{.25}$$

$$= \frac{.12036}{.2236} + .1118 = .65.$$

Using (15.31), we can solve for d_2:

$$d_2 = d_1 - \sigma\sqrt{T} = .65 - \sqrt{.2}\sqrt{.25} = .4264.$$

Substituting these values back into (15.32), we have

$$c = SN(.65) - e^{-r_f T} X N(.4264).$$

Recall that $N(\cdot)$ are cumulative probabilities for a unit normal variable. Therefore $N(d_1)$ is the cumulative probability from minus infinity to $+.65$ standard deviations above the mean (which is defined to be zero for a unit normal distribution). The probability contained in the shaded area of Fig. 15.12 will give us the value of $N(d_1)$. Table 15.9, Areas under the normal curve (on page 401), shows that if $d_1 = .65$, the cumulative probability from the mean ($\mu = 0$) to .65 is approximately .242. If we add this to the cumulative probability from minus infinity to zero (which equals .5), we get

$$N(d_1) = \int_{-\infty}^{0} f(z)\, dz + \int_{0}^{d_1} f(z)\, dz$$

$$= .5 + .242 = .742.$$

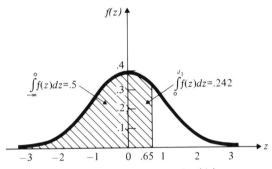

Fig. 15.12 Illustration of $N(d_1)$

Repeating this procedure for $N(d_2)$, we get $N(d_2) = .6651$. Substituting these probabilities into the call valuation formula, we have

$$c = 50(.742) - e^{-.06(.25)}(45)(.6651)$$

$$= 37.10 - .9851(45)(.6651)$$

$$= 37.10 - 29.48 = \$7.62.$$

Table 15.7 gives the value of the call option for various stock prices and Fig. 15.13 plots the call price as a function of the stock price.

Table 15.7 $c(S, T, \sigma^2, X, r_f)$ for different stock prices

Stock price	d_1	$N(d_1)$	d_2	$N(d_2)$	Call price	Given
$30	− 1.63	.052	− 1.85	.032	$ .14	
40	− .35	.363	− .57	.284	$ 1.93	$T = 3$ months
50	.65	.742	.43	.665	$ 7.62	$r_f = .06$
60	1.47	.929	1.24	.893	$16.15	$\sigma^2 = 20\%$
70	2.15	.984	1.93	.973	$25.75	$X = \$45$

Note that the call has little value until the stock price rises to the point where it is near the exercise price $(X = \$45)$. When the stock price is well below the exercise price, the option is said to be "out-of-the-money" and the call will not be worth much. On the other hand, when the stock price is above the exercise price, the option is "in-the-money" and its value increases until in the limit it reaches $S - Xe^{-r_f T}$ for very high stock prices.

When pricing a real-world call it is important to keep in mind that (1) the Black-Scholes formula cannot be used if the common stock is expected to pay a dividend during the life of the option, (2) a CBOE call option is not really a simple

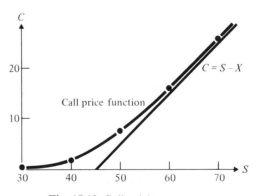

Fig. 15.13 Call pricing example

option, but rather an option on an option, and (3) the instantaneous variance is not stationary over time. If the common stock of a firm is really an option on the assets of the firm, then a call option written against the common stock is really an option on an option. The Black-Scholes formula tends to underprice deep out-of-the-money options and overprice deep in-the-money options. One possible reason is that the simple OPM does not accurately price compound options, and that the bias increases as the stock price moves away from the exercise price.

Of the options listed in Table 15.1 only one, Digital Equipment, pays no dividend. For close-to-the-money calls on Digital Equipment, the assumptions of the Black-Scholes model are closely approximated. Therefore, we should be able to use it to give reasonable estimates of the price of the calls. Table 15.8 provides most of the information needed to value the call. The stock price, the exercise price, and the number of days to maturity are given for each option. The risk-free rate is estimated by using the average of the bid and ask quotes on U.S. Treasury bills of approximately the same maturity as the option. The only missing piece of information is the instantaneous variance of the stock price. There are several different techniques which have been suggested for estimating it (for example, see Latane and Rendleman [1976] or Parkinson [1977]). We shall use the implicit variance estimated from one call price in valuing the others. The implicit variance is calculated by simply using the actual call price and the four known exogenous parameters in the Black-Scholes formula, Eq. (15.29), to solve for an estimate of the instantaneous variance. We did

Table 15.8 Data needed to price Digital Equipment calls

Exercise price	Call price, 4 Oct.			Closing stock price
	Oct.	Jan.	Apr.	
35	$11\frac{7}{8}$	$12\frac{7}{8}$	NA	$46\frac{3}{4}$
40	$6\frac{7}{8}$	8	NA	$46\frac{3}{4}$
45	$2\frac{5}{16}$	$4\frac{1}{4}$	6	$46\frac{3}{4}$
50	$\frac{1}{4}$	$1\frac{3}{4}$	3	$46\frac{3}{4}$
Maturity date	21 Oct.	20 Jan.	21 April	
Days to maturity	17	108	199	

Treasury bill rates on 4 Oct.

Maturity date	Bid	Ask	Average	r_f
20 Oct., 1977	6.04	5.70	5.87	5.9
19 Jan., 1978	6.15	6.07	6.11	6.1
4 Apr., 1978	6.29	6.21	6.25	6.2
2 May, 1978	6.20	6.12	6.16	

this, using the January 45s on Digital Equipment, which were priced at $4\frac{1}{4}$ on October 4th. The estimate of instantaneous variance was approximately 7.84% (this is a standard deviation of 28%).

Substituting our estimates of the five parameters into the Black-Scholes valuation equation, we can estimate the price of the April 45s as follows:

$$c = SN(d_1) - e^{-r_f T} XN(d_2),$$

where

$$r_f = .062, \qquad T = \tfrac{199}{365}, \qquad S = \$46.75, \qquad X = \$45, \qquad \sigma = .28,$$

$$d_1 = \frac{\ln(S/X) + r_f T}{\sigma \sqrt{T}} + \tfrac{1}{2}\sigma\sqrt{T}, \qquad d_2 = d_1 - \sigma\sqrt{T}.$$

The estimated call price turns out to be $5.58 while the actual call price is $6.00. If we repeat the procedure for the October 45s (now $r_f = .059$ and $T = \tfrac{17}{365}$), the estimated call price is $2.28 while the actual price is $2.94. Since both of the estimated prices are lower than the actual prices, our estimate of the instantaneous variance is probably too low.

The above examples show how the Black-Scholes valuation model may be used to price call options on nondividend paying stocks. Recent work by Roll [1977] has solved the problem of valuing American calls when the common stock is assumed to make known dividend payments before the option matures. However, the mathematics involved in the solution is beyond the level of this text.

I.   SUMMARY

The closed form solution for pricing options has only recently been developed. Yet its potential for application to problems in finance is tremendous. Almost all financial assets are really contingent claims. The next chapter will explore the implications of this concept. For example, common stock is really a call option on the underlying assets of a firm. Similarly, risky debt, insurance, warrants, and convertible debt may all be thought of as options. Also, option pricing theory has implications for the capital structure of the firm, for mergers and acquisitions, and for dividend policy.

We have established that option prices are functions of five parameters: the price of the underlying security, its instantaneous variance, the exercise price on the option, the time to maturity, and the risk-free rate. Only one of these variables, the instantaneous variance, is not directly observable. Even more interesting is the fact that the option price does not depend on (1) individual risk preferences or (2) the expected rate of return on the underlying asset. Both results follow from the fact that option prices are determined from pure arbitrage conditions available to the investor who establishes perfectly hedged portfolios.

Table 15.9 Areas under the normal curve

Areas under the standard normal distribution function $\int_0^z f(z)\, dz$.

z	.00	.01	.02	.03	.04	.05	.06	.07	.08	.09
0.0	.0000	.0040	.0080	.0120	.0160	.0199	.0239	.0279	.0319	.0359
0.1	.0398	.0438	.0478	.0517	.0557	.0596	.0636	.0675	.0714	.0753
0.2	.0793	.0832	.0871	.0910	.0948	.0987	.1026	.1064	.1103	.1141
0.3	.1179	.1217	.1255	.1293	.1331	.1368	.1406	.1443	.1480	.1517
0.4	.1554	.1591	.1628	.1664	.1700	.1736	.1772	.1808	.1844	.1879
0.5	.1915	.1950	.1985	.2019	.2054	.2088	.2123	.2157	.2190	.2224
0.6	.2257	.2291	.2324	.2357	.2389	.2422	.2454	.2486	.2517	.2549
0.7	.2580	.2611	.2642	.2673	.2704	.2734	.2764	.2794	.2823	.2852
0.8	.2881	.2910	.2939	.2967	.2995	.3023	.3051	.3078	.3106	.3133
0.9	.3159	.3186	.3212	.3238	.3264	.3289	.3315	.3340	.3365	.3389
1.0	.3413	.3438	.3461	.3485	.3508	.3531	.3554	.3577	.3599	.3621
1.1	.3643	.3665	.3686	.3708	.3729	.3749	.3770	.3790	.3810	.3830
1.2	.3849	.3869	.3888	.3907	.3925	.3944	.3962	.3980	.3997	.4015
1.3	.4032	.4049	.4066	.4082	.4099	.4115	.4131	.4147	.4162	.4177
1.4	.4192	.4207	.4222	.4236	.4251	.4265	.4279	.4292	.4306	.4319
1.5	.4332	.4345	.4357	.4370	.4382	.4394	.4406	.4418	.4429	.4441
1.6	.4452	.4463	.4474	.4484	.4495	.4505	.4515	.4525	.4535	.4545
1.7	.4554	.4564	.4573	.4582	.4591	.4599	.4608	.4616	.4625	.4633
1.8	.4641	.4649	.4656	.4664	.4671	.4678	.4686	.4693	.4699	.4706
1.9	.4713	.4719	.4726	.4732	.4738	.4744	.4750	.4756	.4761	.4767
2.0	.4772	.4778	.4783	.4788	.4793	.4798	.4803	.4808	.4812	.4817
2.1	.4821	.4826	.4830	.4834	.4838	.4842	.4846	.4850	.4854	.4857
2.2	.4861	.4864	.4868	.4871	.4875	.4878	.4881	.4884	.4887	.4890
2.3	.4893	.4896	.4898	.4901	.4904	.4906	.4909	.4911	.4913	.4916
2.4	.4918	.4920	.4922	.4925	.4927	.4929	.4931	.4932	.4934	.4936
2.5	.4938	.4940	.4941	.4943	.4945	.4946	.4948	.4949	.4951	.4952
2.6	.4953	.4955	.4956	.4957	.4959	.4960	.4961	.4962	.4963	.4964
2.7	.4965	.4966	.4967	.4968	.4969	.4970	.4971	.4972	.4973	.4974
2.8	.4974	.4975	.4976	.4977	.4977	.4978	.4979	.4979	.4980	.4981
2.9	.4981	.4982	.4982	.4982	.4984	.4984	.4985	.4985	.4986	.4986
3.0	.4987	.4987	.4987	.4988	.4988	.4989	.4989	.4989	.4990	.4990

PROBLEM SET

15.1 What is the value of a European call option with an exercise price of $40 and a maturity date six months from now if the stock price is $28, the instantaneous variance of the stock price is .5, and the risk-free rate is 6%?

15.2 What is the price of a European put if the price of the underlying common stock is $20, the exercise price is $20, the risk-free rate is 8%, the variance of the price of the underlying stock is .36 (that is, $\sigma = .6$), and the option expires six months from now?

15.3

a) Graph changes in wealth, ΔW, against changes in the price of the underlying security, ΔS, for a portfolio where you sell one call option and sell one put option (both with the same X, T, σ, and r_f). Would this be a good strategy if you have inside information which leads you to expect the instantaneous variance of the underlying security will increase?

b) Graph ΔW against ΔS for a portfolio where you buy a call and sell a put. Would this be a good strategy if you expect an increase in the instantaneous variance?

15.4 Assume you are a senior financial analyst at Morgan Stanley. You are asked by a client to determine the maximum price he should be willing to pay to purchase Honeywell call options having an exercise price of $45 and expiring in 156 days. The current price of Honeywell stock is $44\frac{3}{8}$, the riskless interest rate is 7%, and the estimated rate of return variance of the stock is $\sigma^2 = .0961$. No dividends are expected to be declared over the next six months.

15.5 Given two identical European put options except that the exercise price of the first put, X_1, is greater than the exercise price of the second put, X_2, use first-order stochastic dominance and equilibrium in a perfect capital market to prove that one of the puts must have a higher price than the other. Which put option has the higher price? [*Hint:* Determine the relevant states of the world.]

15.6 Consider a firm with current value of $5,000,000 and outstanding debt of $4,000,000 which matures in 10 years. The firm's asset rate-of-return variance is .5. The interest on the debt is paid at maturity, and the firm has a policy of not paying cash dividends. Use the OPM to determine the change in the prices of the firm's debt and equity if there is an unanticipated rise in the rate of inflation of 5% which raises the riskless nominal interest rate from 5% to 10%. Which class of security holders benefits from the rise in R_F?

15.7 Figure 15.4 graphs the value of a call option as a function of the value of the underlying stock. Graph the value of a call option (vertical axis) against

a) σ, the instantaneous standard deviation of the returns on the underlying asset;

b) R_f, the risk-free rate;

c) T, the time to maturity.

15.8 What are the conditions under which an American put would be exercised early on a stock that pays no dividends?

15.9 Consider the case of a firm with secured debt, subordinated debentures, and common stock, where the secured debt and subordinated debentures mature at the same time. Find the equations for the values of the three classes of securities using the OPM framework. Assume no dividends or interest payments prior to the debt's maturity and a lognormal distribution of the future value of the firm's assets, $\tilde{V}_t$, as shown in Fig. Q15.1, where V = market value of the firm, S = market value of the stock, B_s = market value of the senior debt, B_j = market value of the junior debt, D_s = face value of the senior debt, D_j = face value of the junior debt.

15.10 Why will the value of an American put always be greater than or equal to the value of a corresponding European put?

15.11 Use the algebra of hedge portfolios to prove that $S_0 + P_0 - C_0 = B_0$.

15.12 Using the algebra of hedge portfolios, compute the end-of-period payoff for a portfolio of two puts and one call written on a stock with an exercise price of $55, given $R_f = .06$ for the six month options and that the final stock price is $50.

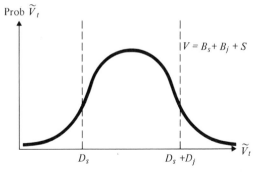

Prob $\tilde{V}_t$

$|V = B_s + B_j + S$

D_s $D_s + D_j$ $\tilde{V}_t$

V = market value of the firm
S = market value of the stock
B_s = market value of the senior debt
B_j = market value of the junior debt
D_s = face value of the senior debt
D_j = face value of the junior debt

Figure Q15.1

15.13 Options listed for Digital Equipment were used in the text as an example of option price estimation using implicit variance. The implicit variance from the January 45 option resulted in estimated call prices lower than actual call prices for the April 45 and October 45 options. Assuming the Black-Scholes OPM is correct, and that all assumptions of the model are met in the marketplace: What hedge (i.e., riskless) portfolio can be formed to make arbitrage profits with Digital Equipment April 45 options?

15.14 The share price of Honeybear Inc. is $44.75. Call options written on Honeybear have an exercise price of $40 and mature in 71 days. The risk-free rate is $6\frac{1}{2}\%$, and the instantaneous price variance of Honeybear is 9.61% (that is, $\sigma = .31$). What actions must you take in order to create a perfect hedge in the following situations:

a) If you own 100 shares of Honeybear stock, how many call options must you buy (sell)?
b) If you own five put option contracts, how many shares of stock do you need?
c) If you own one call contract, how many put contracts do you need?

REFERENCES

BLACK, F., and M. SCHOLES, "The Pricing of Options and Corporate Liabilities," *Journal of Political Economy*, May/June 1973, 637–659.

———, "The Valuation of Option Contracts and a Test of Market Efficiency," *The Journal of Finance*, May 1972, 399–418.

COX, J., and S. ROSS, "The Valuation of Options for Alternative Stochastic Processes," *Journal of Financial Economics*, January/March 1976, 637–659.

GALAI, D., and R. MASULIS, "The Option Pricing Model and the Risk Factor of Stock," *Journal of Financial Economics*, January/March 1977, 53–82.

GARMAN, M., "An Algebra for Evaluating Hedge Portfolios," *Journal of Financial Economics*, October 1976, 403–428.

GESKE, R., "The Valuation of Compound Options," Ph.D. thesis, The University of California, Berkeley, 1977.

KRUIZENGA, R. J., "Introduction to the Option Contract," reprinted in P. Cootner, Ed., *The Random Character of Stock Market Prices*. MIT Press, Cambridge, Mass., 1964, 377–391.

LATANE, H., and R. J. RENDLEMAN, Jr., "Standard Deviations of Stock Price Ratios Implied in Option Prices," *The Journal of Finance*, May 1976, 369–382.

MERTON, R., "The Theory of Rational Option Pricing," *The Bell Journal of Economics and Management Science*, Spring 1973, 141–183.

———, "On the Pricing of Corporate Debt: The Risk Structure of Interest Rates," *Journal of Finance*, May 1974, 449–470.

PARKINSON, M., "Option Pricing: The American Put," *The Journal of Business*, January 1977, 21–36.

ROLL, R., "An Analytic Valuation Formula for Unprotected American Call Options on Stocks with Known Dividends," *Journal of Financial Economics*, November 1977, 251–258.

ROSS, S., "Options and Efficiency," *Quarterly Journal of Economics*, February 1976, 75–89.

SMITH, C., "Option Pricing Review," *Journal of Financial Economics*, January/March 1976, 1–51.

STOLL, H. R., "The Relationship Between Put and Call Option Prices," *The Journal of Finance*, December 1969, 802–824.

Chapter 16

Option Pricing: Empirical Evidence and Implications for Corporate Financial Policy

It is not generally realized that corporate liabilities other than warrants may be viewed as options. Under [certain] conditions, it is clear that the stockholders have the equivalent of an option on their company's assets.

F. Black and M. Scholes, "The Pricing of Options and Corporate Liabilities," *Journal of Political Economy*, May/June 1973, p. 649

A. INTRODUCTION

The previous chapter introduced the Black-Scholes option pricing formula under a fairly restrictive set of assumptions. The empirical evidence, presented below, indicates that the model seems to fit reality fairly well, although as yet no attempts have been made to see whether or not other models do even better.

Following a discussion of the empirical evidence, Section C shows that the equity in a firm may be viewed as a call option on the value of the firm. This point of view provides a number of useful insights into the role of debt and equity in the capital structure of the firm. For example, we shall see that if bondholders do not have perfect foresight and if they cannot write perfect protective covenants, it is possible for shareholders to benefit from increased leverage, even in a world without taxes.

B. EMPIRICAL EVIDENCE

Tests of the option pricing model (OPM), like those of the capital asset pricing model (CAPM), are faced with the problem that two hypotheses are being tested simultaneously: first that the model is valid, and second, that the market is efficient. The usual procedure is to employ the pricing model to identify over- or underpriced securities, then to form trading rules which will earn abnormally high risk-adjusted returns. If no profitable trading rule exists, the market is said to be efficient. If profitable trading rules are discovered, the market is presumed to be inefficient.

1.   The Black-Scholes Study

To date there have been two major studies of market efficiency and the OPM. The first, by Black and Scholes [1972], uses price data from the over-the-counter option market (OTCOM) for contracts written on 545 securities between 1966 and 1969. Options traded on the OTCOM did not have standardized exercise prices or maturity dates; however, they were "dividend protected."[1] Whenever the common stock went ex-dividend, the exercise price on outstanding options was lowered by the amount of the dividend.

The secondary market in nonstandardized OTCOM options was virtually non-existent. Therefore, Black and Scholes adopted a test procedure which uses the OPM to generate the expected prices of each option on each trading day. By comparing the model prices with actual prices at the issuing date they divide options into those "overvalued" and those "undervalued" by the market. For each option bought (if undervalued) or sold (if overvalued), a perfectly risk-free hedged portfolio is formed by selling or buying shares in the underlying stock. The excess dollar return on the hedged portfolio is defined as

$$\left(\Delta C - \frac{\delta C}{\delta S} \, \Delta S \right) - \left(C - \frac{\delta C}{\delta S} \, S \right) r_f \, \Delta t.$$

The first expression is the dollar return on the hedged portfolio (see Chapter 15, pp. 393–395, for a discussion), where ΔC is the change in the value of a call option and where $\delta C / \delta S = N(d_1)$ is the number of shares which is multiplied by ΔS, the change in the price per share. The second expression, which is subtracted from the first in order to obtain *excess* returns, is the dollar return on a risk-free position. Theoretically, the difference between the two terms should be equal to zero because the portfolio is chosen to be hedged. Therefore it should have zero beta and earn the risk-free rate.

The option position is maintained throughout the life of the option. The risk-free hedge is adjusted daily by buying or selling shares of stock in order to maintain the proportion $\delta C / \delta S = N(d_1)$. At the end of each day, the hedged position is assumed to be liquidated so that the daily dollar return can be calculated. The option position is then immediately reestablished and a new hedge position constructed.

---

[1] Of course, there is no such thing as perfect dividend protection. For example, if shareholders were to issue a liquidating dividend equal to the value of the firm's assets, the value of common stock would fall to zero, and no amount of dividend protection could keep the value of a call option from falling to zero.

Black and Scholes compute the systematic risk of the hedged portfolio by regressing its excess returns against a market index. The results verify that it has a beta which is not significantly different from zero (even though the hedge was not adjusted continuously).

Their results show that in the absence of transaction costs, buying "undervalued" contracts and selling "overvalued" contracts at model prices, given *ex post* estimates of actual variances of the returns on the underlying stock over the holding period, produces insignificant average profits. However, when *ex ante* variances are estimated from past stock price histories, buying "undervalued" contracts and selling "overvalued" contracts at model prices results in significant negative excess portfolio returns. The same procedure, when repeated using market prices, yields substantial positive excess returns. These results indicate that the market uses more than past price histories to estimate the *ex ante* instantaneous variance of stock returns. But when actual variances are used in the model, it matches actual option prices quite accurately.

When the transaction costs of trading in options were included, the implied profits vanished. Therefore, even though the option market does not appear to be efficient before transaction costs are taken into account, there is no opportunity for traders to take advantage of this inefficiency.

2. The Galai Study

Galai [1977] uses data from the Chicago Board Options Exchange (CBOE) for each option traded between April 26, 1973 and November 30, 1973. Option contracts on the CBOE have standardized striking prices and expiration dates. Although the options are not "dividend protected," the standardization of contracts has resulted in a substantial volume of trading and lower transaction costs.

The fact that option prices are listed every day allows Galai to extend the Black-Scholes procedure. Black and Scholes established an initial option position and then maintained a hedge position by buying or selling shares of stock. They could not adjust the option position because they did not have market prices for the options. They were unable to exploit all the information available in the daily deviation of the option's actual prices from the model prices.

Galai duplicates the Black-Scholes tests and extends them by adusting the option position each day. Undervalued options are bought and overvalued options are sold at the end of each day, and, in addition, the hedged position is maintained by buying or selling the appropriate number of shares of common stock. Galai uses two tests: (1) an *ex post* test which assumes that traders can use the closing price on day t to determine whether the option is over- or undervalued and that they can transact at the closing prices on day t, and (2) a more realistic *ex ante* test which assumes that the trading rule is determined from closing prices on day t but the transaction is not executed until the closing price at day $t + 1$. Both tests use various estimates of the variance of common stock rates of return which are based on data gathered *before* the trading rule is executed.

The main results of the test are:

1. Using *ex post* hedge returns, trading strategies (in the absence of transaction costs) which are based on the Black-Scholes model earn significant excess returns.
2. Given 1% transaction costs, the excess returns vanished.
3. The results are robust to changes in various parameters such as the risk-free rate or instantaneous variance.
4. The results are sensitive to dividend adjustment. Trading in options written on common stocks paying high dividends yielded lower profits than trading in options written on low-dividend stocks. This result, however, simply reflects the fact that the Black-Scholes formula assumes no dividend payments.
5. Deviations from the model's specifications led to worse performance.
6. Tests of spreading strategies yield results similar to those produced by the hedging strategies described above.

Taken together, the two studies mentioned above seem to indicate that the Black-Scholes OPM predicts option prices very well indeed. So well in fact, that excess returns can be earned in the absence of transaction costs. However, once transaction costs are introduced into the trading strategies, excess profits vanish. This confirms the usual result that nonmember traders cannot beat the market. Prices are efficiently determined down to the level of transaction costs.

C. IMPLICATIONS OF OPTION PRICING FOR THE THEORY OF CORPORATE FINANCE

Black and Scholes [1973] suggest that the equity in a levered firm can be thought of as a call option. When shareholders issue bonds, it is equivalent to selling the assets of the firm (but not control over those assets) to the bondholders in return for cash (the proceeds of the bond issues) and a call option.

In order to reduce the analogy to its simplest form, assume that (1) the firm issues pure discount bonds[2] which prohibit any capital disbursements (such as dividend payments) until after the bonds mature T time periods hence, (2) there are no transaction costs or taxes so that the value of the firm is unaffected by its capital structure (in other words, Modigliani-Miller Proposition I is assumed to be valid), (3) there is a known nonstochastic risk-free rate of interest, and (4) there are homogeneous expectations about the stochastic process which describes the value of the firm's assets. Given these assumptions we can imagine a simple firm which issues

---

[2] All accumulated interest on pure discount bonds is paid at maturity, hence $B(T)$, the current market value of debt with maturity T, must be less than its face value, D, assuming a positive risk-free rate of discount.

only one class of bonds secured by the assets of the firm. From the shareholders' point of view, cash is received from the sale of the bonds. The value of the shareholders' position is equal to the discounted value of the bonds and a call option. If, on the maturity date, the value of the firm, V, exceeds the face value of the bonds, D, the shareholders will exercise their call option by paying off the bonds and keeping the excess. On the other hand, if the value of the firm is less than the face value of the bonds, the shareholders will default on the debt by failing to exercise their option. Therefore, at maturity, the shareholders' wealth, S, is

$$S = \text{MAX}[0, V - D]. \tag{16.1}$$

This is, of course, a European call option, and we can use the Black-Scholes formula to value it. Bondholder's wealth is $B = \text{MIN}[V, D]$.

Galai and Masulis [1976] take the insight provided by Black and Scholes and show how it may be applied to many of the traditional issues in corporate finance such as dividend policy, acquisitions and divestitures, conglomerate mergers, and investment decisions. First, however, it is useful to show how the CAPM and the OPM are related. Merton [1973] has derived a continuous time version of the CAPM which is given below:

$$E(R_i) = R_f + [E(R_m) - R_f]\beta_i, \tag{16.2}$$

where

$E(R_i) =$ the instantaneous expected rate of return on asset i,
$\beta_i =$ the instantaneous systematic risk of the ith asset, $\beta_i = \text{COV}(R_i, R_m)/\text{VAR}(R_m)$,
$E(R_m) =$ the expected instantaneous rate of return on the market portfolio,
$R_f =$ the nonstochastic instantaneous rate of return on the risk-free asset.

Although the continuous-time version of the CAPM appears to be no different than the traditional one-period model derived in Chapter 7, it is important to prove that the CAPM also exists in continuous time because the Black-Scholes OPM requires continuous trading, and the assumptions underlying the two models must be consistent.

In order to relate the OPM to the CAPM, we begin with the differential equation (15.24), but recognize that the call option is now the value of the common stock in the firm, S, which is written on the value of the firm, V. Therefore (15.24) may be rewritten as

$$dS = \frac{\delta S}{\delta V} dV + \frac{\delta S}{\delta t} dt + \frac{1}{2} \frac{\delta^2 S}{\delta V^2} \sigma^2 V^2 \, dt. \tag{16.3}$$

Dividing by S, we have, in the limit as dt approaches zero,

$$\lim_{dt \to 0} \frac{dS}{S} = \frac{\delta S}{\delta V} \frac{dV}{S} = \frac{\delta S}{\delta V} \frac{dV}{V} \frac{V}{S}. \tag{16.4}$$

We recognize dS/S as the rate of return on the common stock, r_s, and dV/V as the rate of return on the firm's assets, r_V, therefore

$$r_S = \left(\frac{\delta S}{\delta V}\right)\frac{V}{S}\, r_V. \tag{16.5}$$

If the instantaneous systematic risk of common stock, β_S, and that of the firm, β_V, are defined as

$$\beta_S \equiv \frac{\text{COV}(r_S, r_m)}{\text{VAR}(r_m)}, \qquad \beta_V \equiv \frac{\text{COV}(r_V, r_m)}{\text{VAR}(r_m)}, \tag{16.6}$$

then we can use (16.5) and (16.6) to rewrite the instantaneous covariance as

$$\beta_S = \frac{\delta S}{\delta V}\frac{V}{S}\frac{\text{COV}(r_V, r_m)}{\text{VAR}(r_m)} = \frac{\delta S}{\delta V}\frac{V}{S}\,\beta_V. \tag{16.7}$$

Now write the Black-Scholes OPM where the call option is the equity of the firm:

$$S = VN(d_1) - e^{-r_f T}DN(d_2), \tag{16.8}$$

where

S = the market value of equity,
V = the market value of the firm's assets,
r_f = the risk-free rate,
T = the time to maturity,
D = the face value of debt (book value),
$N(\cdot)$ = the cumulative normal probability of the unit normal variate, d_1,
$$d_1 = \frac{\ln(V/D) + r_f T}{\sigma\sqrt{T}} + \tfrac{1}{2}\sigma\sqrt{T}, \qquad d_2 = d_1 - \sigma\sqrt{T}.$$

Finally, the partial derivative of the equity value, S, with respect to the value of the underlying asset is

$$\frac{\delta S}{\delta V} = N(d_1), \qquad \text{where} \qquad 0 \le N(d_1) \le 1. \tag{16.9}$$

Substituting this into (16.7) we obtain

$$\beta_S = N(d_1)\frac{V}{S}\,\beta_V. \tag{16.10}$$

This tells us the relationship between the systematic risk of the equity, β_S, and the systematic risk of the firm's assets, β_V. The value of S is given by the OPM, Eq. (16.8); therefore we have

$$\beta_S = \frac{VN(d_1)}{VN(d_1) - De^{-r_f T}N(d_2)}\,\beta_V$$

$$= \frac{1}{1 - (D/V)e^{-r_f T}[N(d_2)/N(d_1)]}\,\beta_V. \tag{16.11}$$

We know that $D/V \le 1$, that $e^{-r_f T} < 1$, that $N(d_2) \le N(d_1)$, and hence that $\beta_S \ge \beta_V > 0$. This shows that the systematic risk of the equity of a levered firm is greater than the systematic risk of an unlevered firm, a result which is consistent with the results found elsewhere in the theory of finance. Note also that the beta of the levered firm increases monotonically with leverage.

The OPM provides insight into the effect of its parameters on the systematic risk of equity. We may assume that the risk characteristics of the firm's assets, β_V, are constant over time. Therefore, it can be shown that the partial derivatives of (16.11) have the following signs:

$$\frac{\delta\beta_S}{\delta V} < 0, \qquad \frac{\delta\beta_S}{\delta D} > 0, \qquad \frac{\delta\beta_S}{\delta r_f} < 0, \qquad \frac{\delta\beta_S}{\delta\sigma^2} < 0, \qquad \frac{\delta\beta_S}{\delta T} < 0. \quad (16.12)$$

Most of these have readily intuitive explanations. The systematic risk of equity falls as the market value of the firm increases, and it rises as the amount of debt issued increases. When the risk-free rate of return increases, the value of the equity option increases and its systematic risk decreases. The fourth partial derivative says that as the variance of the value of the firm's assets increases, the systematic risk of equity decreases. This result follows from the contingent claim nature of equity. The equity holders will prefer more variance to less because they profit from the probability that the value of the firm will exceed the face value of the debt. Therefore their risk actually decreases as the variance of the value of the firm's assets increases.[3] Finally, the fifth partial says that the systematic risk of equity declines as the maturity date of the debt becomes longer and longer. From the shareholders' point of view the best situation would be to never have to repay the face value of the debt.

It is also possible to use Eq. (16.10) to view the cost of equity capital in an OPM framework and to compare it with the Modigliani-Miller results of Chapter 11. Substituting β_S from (16.10) into the CAPM, we obtain from Eq. (16.2) an expression for k_e, the cost of equity capital:

$$k_e = R_f + (R_m - R_f)N(d_1)\frac{V}{S}\beta_V. \quad (16.13)$$

Note that from Eq. (16.10), $\beta_S = N(d_1)(V/S)\beta_V$. Substituting this into (16.13) yields the familiar CAPM relationship $k_e = R_f + (R_m - R_f)\beta_S$. Furthermore, the CAPM can be rearranged to show that

$$\beta_V = \frac{R_V - R_f}{R_m - R_f},$$

which we substitute into (16.13) to obtain

$$k_e = R_f + N(d_1)(R_V - R_f)\frac{V}{S}. \quad (16.14)$$

---

[3] Note that since the value of the firm, V, and the debt equity ratio D/V are held constant, any change in total variance, σ^2, must be nonsystematic risk.

Equation (16.14) shows that the cost of equity capital is an increasing function of financial leverage.

In order to compare the option pricing definition of the cost of equity with the Modigliani-Miller definition, it is necessary that $N(d_1) = 1$ in Eq. (16.14). If so, then Eq. (16.14) reduces to equal

$$k_e = R_f + (R_V - R_f)\frac{V}{S}$$

$$= R_f + (R_V - R_f)\frac{B}{S} + (R_V - R_f)\frac{S}{S}$$

$$= R_V + (R_V - R_f)\frac{B}{S}. \tag{16.15}$$

Equation (16.15) is exactly the same as Eq. (11.18), the Modigliani-Miller definition of the cost of equity capital in a world without taxes.

Similarly, when the firm has no debt, then in Eq. (16.14), $V = S$ and $N(d_1) = 1$. Therefore, the cost of equity for an all equity firm is equal to R_V. In Chapter 11, in discussing the cost of capital, we used the symbol ρ instead of R_V. Both symbols have the same meaning and therefore $\rho = R_V$.

It has been argued above that the OPM definition of the cost of equity is mathematically identical to the Modigliani-Miller definition only if $N(d_1) = 1$. If we rewrite d_1 below and note that if d_1 is infinite, then $N(d_1) = 1$, we see that there are only two ways that the necessary condition can be achieved:

$$d_1 = \frac{\ln(V/D) + (r_f - \sigma^2/2)T}{\sigma\sqrt{T}}.$$

First, if the instantaneous variance, σ^2, of the value of the firm's assets is zero, then $N(d_1) = 1$. But this implies that the market value of the firm is nonstochastic. Hence both debt and equity claims would be risk free. Therefore, the first condition is unreasonable. The second possibility is that debt is completely risk free and that it is perpetual, i.e., it never matures. Given these assumptions, $N(d_1) = 1$ because T, the time to maturity, is infinite. However, also note that the present value, $B(T)$, of a discount bond which pays no coupons and never matures is equal to zero.[4] If the market value of debt is zero, then the firm has no financial leverage. Consequently, the second condition is also unreasonable.

Fortunately, if we allow debt to be risky instead of risk free and assume that bankruptcy costs (i.e., losses to third parties other than creditors or shareholders) are zero, then the OPM, the CAPM, and the Modigliani-Miller propositions can be shown to be consistent. The simple algebraic approach given below was proved by Hsia [1978].

---

[4] Modigliani and Miller allow debt to pay annual coupons, however, the Black-Scholes option pricing model assumes no intermediate cash flows on European options.

First, note that the systematic risk, β_B, of risky debt capital in a world without taxes can be written as[5]

$$\beta_B = \beta_V \frac{\delta B}{\delta V} \frac{V}{B}.$$ (16.16)

We know that in a world without taxes, the value of the firm is invariant to changes in its capital structure. Also, from Eq. (16.9), we know that if the common stock of a firm is thought of as a call option on the value of the firm, then

$$\frac{\delta S}{\delta V} = N(d_1).$$

These two facts imply that

$$\frac{\delta B}{\delta V} = N(-d_1) = 1 - N(d_1).$$ (16.17)

In other words, any change in the value of equity is offset by an equal and opposite change in the value of risky debt.

Next, the required rate of return on risky debt, k_d, can be expressed by using the CAPM, Eq. (16.2):

$$k_d = R_f + (R_m - R_f)\beta_B.$$ (16.18)

Substituting Eqs. (16.16) and (16.17) into (16.18), we have

$$k_d = R_f + (R_m - R_f)\beta_V N(-d_1) \frac{V}{B}.$$

From the CAPM, we know that

$$R_V - R_f = (R_m - R_f)\beta_V.$$

Therefore

$$k_d = R_f + (R_V - R_f)N(-d_1) \frac{V}{B}.$$

And since $R_V \equiv \rho$,

$$k_d = R_f + (\rho - R_f)N(-d_1) \frac{V}{B}.$$ (16.19)

Note that Eq. (16.19) expresses the cost of risky debt in terms of the OPM. The required rate of return on risky debt is equal to the risk-free rate, R_f, plus a risk premium, θ, where

$$\theta = (\rho - R_f)N(-d_1) \frac{V}{B}.$$

---

[5] See Galai and Masulis [1976, footnote 15].

In order to arrive at a weighted average cost of capital, we multiply Eq. (16.19), the cost of debt, by the percent of debt in the capital structure, B/V, then add this result to the cost of equity, Eq. (16.14) multiplied by B/S, the percent of equity in the capital structure. The result is

$$k_d \frac{B}{V} + k_e \frac{S}{V} = \left[R_f + (\rho - R_f)N(-d_1) \frac{V}{B} \right] \frac{B}{V} + \left[R_f + N(d_1)(\rho - R_f) \frac{V}{S} \right] \frac{S}{V}$$

$$= R_f \left(\frac{B+S}{V} \right) + (\rho - R_f)[N(-d_1) + N(d_1)]$$

$$= R_f + (\rho - R_f)(1 - N(d_1) + N(d_1))$$

$$= \rho. \tag{16.20}$$

Equation (16.20) is exactly the same as the Modigliani-Miller proposition that in a world without taxes, the weighted average cost of capital is invariant to changes in the capital structure of the firm. Also, simply by rearranging terms, we have

$$k_e = \rho + (\rho - k_d) \frac{B}{S}. \tag{16.21}$$

This is exactly the same as Eq. (11.18), the Modigliani-Miller definition of the cost of equity capital in a world without taxes. Therefore, if we assume that debt is risky, the OPM, the CAPM, and the Modigliani-Miller definition are all consistent with one another.

Next we turn our attention to the insight offered by the OPM for various corporate decisions under a slightly different set of assumptions. More often than not, the following arguments are made intuitively rather than mathematically. The reader who is interested in the additional insight provided by a mathematical presentation is referred to Galai and Masulis [1976]. In each of the following cases we rely on the Modigliani-Miller result that in the absence of transaction costs or taxes, the value of the firm remains constant regardless of the financial decisions made by management. Furthermore, we assume that any changes which affect the systematic risk of various securities, or their expected rate of return, are *unanticipated* changes. To the extent that changes in the value of securities is unanticipated, it is possible that there may be a redistribution of wealth from one class of security holders to another.

We also assume that two-fund separation does not apply. Two-fund separation implies, among other things, that all individuals hold the same portfolio of risky assets, namely, the market portfolio. If an individual holds both the equity and risky debt of a firm, then any offsetting change in the market value of the debt and equity claims against the firm will not change his wealth position. Therefore, he would be indifferent to the redistribution effects which we are about to discuss. It is necessary, then, to rule out two-fund separation and discuss the wealth of shareholders and bondholders as if they were separate and distinct.

1.   Investment Decisions Which Do Not Change the Size of the Firm

Assume that two firms have the same face value of debt, $D_A = D_B$, the same market value, $V_A = V_B$, and the same systematic risk

$$\text{COV}(V_A, V_m) = \text{COV}(V_B, V_m),$$

but that firm A has greater total variance than firm B $(\sigma_A^2 > \sigma_B^2)$. We know, from the CAPM that this is possible because the marketplace takes only systematic risk into account when valuing assets. Firm A can have the same systematic risk as firm B but higher total variance if it has greater unsystematic risk uncorrelated with the market portfolio.

   In the context of a single firm, this situation may arise if management purchases a risky asset with cash. The total assets of the firm remain constant, and it is possible that the risky asset can increase the firm's variance without changing its covariance with the market portfolio. If so, the market value of equity will increase and the market value of debt will decrease. The market value of the debt-equity ratio for firm A will be less than that for firm B:

$$B_A/S_A < B_B/S_B,$$

where

B_A, B_B = the market value of debt for firms A and B respectively,
S_A, S_B = the market value of equity for firms A and B respectively.

   This result follows from the fact that in (16.12), $\delta\beta_S/\delta\sigma^2 < 0$. The systematic risk of the equity holders declines with an increase in the variance of return on the firm's assets, and consequently the market value of their wealth increases. But since the market value of the firm is constant, the debt holders will experience a decline in wealth—they must bear the cost of the greater total variance of the firm. The risk of bankruptcy has increased. Shareholders can actually benefit from the greater risk of bankruptcy because they hold a contingent claim, a call option. Their chances of having greater gains have increased while their losses are still bounded by the fact that they cannot be less than zero.

   This example highlights the importance of indenture restrictions in bond contracts. Obviously, the bondholders want to protect themselves against possible shareholder attempts to expropriate, without compensation, portions of bond value. In a world without any monitoring costs, it would be possible to construct contracts with perfect "me first" rules. Then bondholders, or their agents, could costlessly monitor the actions of shareholders. However, it is not possible to foresee every possible contingency so that it can be written into a contract, nor are monitoring costs nontrivial. Consequently, bondholders cannot protect themselves perfectly. Still, if they have perfect foresight, they can correctly price the bonds to account for the risk of shareholder decisions. This is certainly a possibility. However, as we began the analysis, we assumed that any changes which affect the systematic risk of securities are *unanticipated* changes. Therefore, we have ruled out even the possibility of perfect foresight.[6]

The inability to write perfect, costlessly monitored bond indentures and the lack of perfect foresight are the important differences between the implication of the Modigliani-Miller theory of the firm and those of option pricing. Modigliani and Miller assume that bondholders cannot be "fooled," so that debt is always correctly priced, *ex ante*. The OPM explores some of the implications which follow from relaxing this assumption. For example, in Section 4 below, we shall see that without perfect "me first" rules, shareholders' wealth is increased by an increase in financial leverage, even in a world without taxes. First, however, we discuss conglomerate mergers and dividend policy.

2. Conglomerate Mergers

A pure conglomerate merger is presumed to have no real economic benefits such as economies of scale or synergy. Therefore, we examine the purely financial effects of conglomerate merger. If the cash flows of the two merging firms are less than perfectly correlated, then the total variance of the resulting firm will be less than the sum of the two separate variances. Do shareholders benefit or lose?

If the total variance decreases, everything else being held constant, shareholders' systematic risk increases and bondholders' risk decreases. The probability of default will decline, and bondholders are better off. The sum of the market values of debt in the merged firm will be greater than that of the two separate firms. Shareholders lose.

Why then do we observe so many conglomerate mergers if shareholders do not benefit? One answer, of course, is that in the real world not everything else is held constant. Conglomerate mergers are often accompanied by increases in the ratio of the face value of debt to the value of the firm. In other words, shareholders use the increased debt capacity to take on more debt.

3. Capital Distributions (Dividend Policy)

When the assets of a corporation are paid out to shareholders in any type of capital distribution the effect is to "steal away" a portion of the bondholders' collateral. In effect, some of the assets which bondholders could claim, in the event that shareholders decide to default, are paid out to shareholders. This diminishes the value of debt and increases the wealth of shareholders.

---

[6] Perfect foresight does not imply that investors are clairvoyant. It simply means that they cannot be "fooled." This requires that all economic agents (individuals, managers, and firms) have the same information which allows them to properly assess the probabilities of expropriation in different states of the world.

The most common type of capital distribution is a dividend payment. A portion of the firm's assets is paid out in the form of cash dividends to shareholders.[7] The most extreme example of defrauding bondholders would be to simply liquidate the assets of the firm and pay out a single, final dividend to shareholders, thereby leaving bondholders with a claim to nothing. For this very reason, most bond indentures explicitly restrict the dividend policy of shareholders. Usually dividends cannot exceed the current earnings of the firm, and they cannot be paid out of retained earnings.

Other types of capital distributions are share repurchase and spinoffs. Share repurchase has exactly the same effect as dividend payment except that the form of payment is capital gains instead of dividend income (see Chapter 13, "Dividend Policy: Theory"). The conventional procedure for a spinoff is to take a portion of a firm's assets, often a division relatively unrelated to the rest of the firm, and create an independent firm with these assets. The important fact is that the shares of the new entity are distributed solely to the *shareholders* of the parent corporation. Therefore, like dividend payment or share repurchase, this is a technique for taking collateral from bondholders.

4. Capital Structure

If shareholders are not constrained by the indenture provisions of debt from issuing new debt with an equal claim on the assets of the firm, then current bondholders will experience a loss of wealth when new debt is issued. It is possible to increase the book value debt-to-equity ratio by issuing new debt and using the proceeds to repurchase equity. In this way the assets of the firm remain unchanged. If the new debt has equal claim on those assets, then the current bondholders end up with only a partial claim to the assets of the firm, whereas before the new debt was issued, they had complete claim on the assets. Clearly, this approach puts current bondholders in a riskier position, and they are unable to charge more for the extra risk because the discounted value of their bonds has already been paid (in other words, they cannot raise their coupon payments once the bonds have been issued). Consequently, the market value of their bonds will fall. At the same time, the value of the firm remains unchanged, and new bondholders pay a fair market price for their position. Therefore the value which is expropriated from current bondholders must accrue to shareholders, who are the residual claimants of the firm. Their wealth increases.

The theory of option pricing argues that in a world with no transaction costs or taxes the wealth of shareholders is increased by greater financial leverage. In Chapter

---

[7] When dividends are paid in cash, the effect is to change the assets side of the balance sheet. This is seen to really be an investment decision, and as such, it will change the value of debt and equity claims. The dividend decision can also be strictly financial (as assumed by Modigliani and Miller) if the dividends are paid from new debt or equity. In this way the assets side of the balance sheet (and investment) remains unchanged and so too will the value of the firm (assuming no expropriation).

11, the Modigliani-Miller propositions argue that under the same set of assumptions the value of shareholders' wealth is unaffected by changes in capital structure. How can the seemingly contradictory conclusions of the two theories be explained? The crucial difference is that option pricing assumes that *unanticipated* redistributions of wealth are possible. To the extent that bondholders can appropriately assess the probability of shareholders' ability to expropriate their wealth, they can charge a rate of return which adequately compensates them for their risk or they can carefully write bond indenture provisions which restrict the actions of shareholders. Either way they can protect themselves against anticipated redistribution effects. Whether or not such protection is actually possible is an empirical question. Some of the empirical evidence was discussed in Chapter 12.

D. SUMMARY

The OPM provides a closed-form solution for pricing contingent claim assets. This is an extremely useful result because it allows us to price European puts and calls. We have just seen that the equity of a firm may be viewed as a call option, and that this point of view provides considerable insight into the theory of the firm. There are many other useful applications of option-pricing theory which we haven't had the time or space to mention. For example, insurance can be viewed as a put option. You pay a fee now for the right to claim the face value of the insurance policy if the value of the asset falls below its insured value. A personal loan, for example the mortgage on a house, may be thought of as giving ownership of an asset (i.e., the collateral) to the bank in return for cash and a call option. If the market value of the house falls below the value of the loan, a rational borrower will default on the loan. Corporations often issue warrants which give their holder the right to purchase shares of stock at a predetermined price as long as the warrant remains outstanding. Thus, the warrant is similar to a call option, but is somewhat more difficult to price because when the warrant is exercised, the firm receives cash, which changes its asset structure, and new equity is created which also changes its capital structure. Convertible bonds may also be thought of as options. The holder has the right to keep the value of the bond or to convert it into equity at a fixed price per share.

The theory and application of option pricing are relatively new and are changing rapidly as scholars apply the ideas to more and more concepts. This section has presented only a brief overview of this versatile new tool in corporate financial policy.

PROBLEM SET

16.1 Firms A and B are each considering an unanticipated new investment opportunity which will marginally increase the value of the firm and will also increase the firm's level of diversification. Firm A is unlevered, and firm B has a capital structure of 50% debt. Assuming that the shareholders control the firm, will either firm make the investment?

16.2 Consider a levered firm with $10 million face value of debt outstanding, maturing in one year. The riskless rate is 6% and the expected rate of return on the market is 12%. The systematic risk of the firm's assets is $\beta_V = 1.5$, the total risk of these assets is $\sigma_V = 1.3$, and their market value is $25 million.

a) Determine the market value of the firm's debt and equity.

b) Determine the cost of debt and equity capital (assuming a world without taxes).

16.3

a) True or false: The Modigliani-Miller model of cost of equity is equivalent to the OPM definition of cost of equity for an all-equity firm. Explain.

b) If we assume that $N(d_1) = 1$ in the OPM, what does this imply about $\delta S/\delta V$? about the firm's capital structure?

16.4 After a call contract is created, the outcome must be a zero-sum game; that is, the call writer may win or lose N, but the call buyer will experience an opposite return of exactly N and consequently their aggregate payoff is zero. Given this fact, can you explain how they could both enter into the contract anticipating a positive return?

16.5 In a world without taxes or transaction costs, the Modigliani-Miller model predicts shareholders' wealth invariant to changes in capital structure, while the OPM predicts increased shareholder wealth with increased leverage. Given what you know about option pricing, is a 20% increase in the variance of return on the firm's assets more likely to benefit shareholders in a low-leverage or in a high-leverage firm?

16.6 In Chapter 14 it was suggested that if the firm announces its intention to increase its dividends (paid from cash), the price of common stock increases, presumably because the higher dividend payout represents an unambiguous signal to shareholders that anticipated cash flows from investment are permanently higher. A higher level of cash flows is also beneficial to bondholders because it diminishes the probability of default.

If dividends are paid from cash, what does the OPM suggest will happen to the market value of debt? How does this contrast with the prediction in the above paragraph?

16.7 The Sharpe version of the CAPM results in the principle of two-fund separation. Every individual holds the same portfolio of risky assets, namely, the market portfolio. Therefore, individuals will be indifferent to redistribution effects caused by imperfect "me-first" rules. True or false? Why?

For Problems 16.8 through 16.12 assume the following:

i) We are dealing with a world where there are no taxes.

ii) The changes in the parameters affecting value are unanticipated; therefore redistribution effects are possible.

iii) Firms A and B initially have the following parameters:

$\sigma_A = \sigma_B = .2$	Instantaneous standard deviation
$T_A = T_B = 4$ years	Maturity of debt
$V_A = V_B = \$2,000$	Value of the firm, $V = B + S$
$R_f = .06$	Risk-free rate
$D_A = D_B = \$1,000$	Face value of debt

16.8 What is the initial market value of debt and equity for firms A and B?

16.9 Firm A decides to use some of its cash in order to purchase marketable securities. This has the effect of leaving its value, V_A, unchanged but increasing its instantaneous standard deviation from .2 to .3. What are the new values of debt and equity?

16.10 The correlation between the cash flows of firms A and B is .6. If they merge, the resultant firm will be worth $\$4,000 = V_A + V_B$, but its new instantaneous variance will be

$$\sigma_{AB}^2 = (\tfrac{1}{2})^2\sigma_A^2 + 2(\tfrac{1}{2})(\tfrac{1}{2})r_{AB}\sigma_A\sigma_B + (\tfrac{1}{2})^2\sigma_B^2$$
$$= (.25)(.2)^2 + 2(.5)(.5)(.6)(.2)(.2) + (.25)(.2)^2$$
$$= .01 + .012 + .01 = .032$$
$$\sigma_{AB} = .179.$$

What will the market value of debt and equity in the merged firm be? If there were no other merger effects, would shareholders agree to the merger?

16.11 Given the results of Problem 16.10, suppose that the merged firm has 1,000 shares outstanding. Furthermore, suppose that the shareholders decide to issue $1,000 of new debt (which is not subordinate to outstanding debt), maturing in four years, and invest the proceeds in marketable securities, so that the new value of the merged firm is $5,000. What will be the new price per share? Assume the merged firm's instantaneous variance is unchanged by this investment.

16.12 Using the original pre-merger parameters for firm A, what will be the change in the market value of debt if the shareholders of firm A decide to pay themselves a $500 dividend out of cash. [*Note:* The dividend payment will have two effects. First, it will decrease the market value of the firm to $1,500. Second, since cash has little or no risk, the instantaneous standard deviation of the firm's assets will increase to .25.]

REFERENCES

BLACK, F., and M. SCHOLES, "The Pricing of Options and Corporate Liabilities," *Journal of Political Economy*, May/June 1973, 637–659.

FAMA, E. F., "The Effects of a Firm's Investment and Financing Decisions on the Welfare of its Security Holders," *American Economic Review*, June 1978, 272–284.

FINNERTY, J., "The Chicago Board Options Exchange and Market Efficiency," *Journal of Financial and Quantitative Analysis*, March 1978, 29–38.

GALAI, D., "Tests of Market Efficiency of the Chicago Board Options Exchange," *Journal of Business*, April 1977, 167–197.

———, "On the Boness and Black-Scholes Models for the Valuation of Call Options," *Journal of Financial and Quantitative Analysis*, March 1978, 15–27.

———, and R. MASULIS, "The Option Pricing Model and the Risk Factor of Stock," *The Journal of Financial Economics*, January/March 1976, 53–82.

HSIA, C., "Relationships Among the Theories of MM, CAPM, and OPM," Mimeograph, UCLA, 1978.

MERTON, R., "An Intertemporal Capital Asset Pricing Model," *Econometrica*, September 1973, 867–887.

Chapter 17

Mergers and Acquisitions: Theory

Let me not to the marriage of true minds
Admit impediments ...

Shakespeare, Sonnet 116

The issues and literature on mergers are so voluminous that a framework must be formulated to provide an organizational structure for the subject. We have organized our analysis of the merger literature within the basic plan of this book so that each topic is discussed in terms of theory, tests, and managerial applications. To provide an overview, we list the individual topics we plan to present in this and the following chapter:

A. Merger Theories
   1. Synergy or no synergy
   2. Operating effects
   3. Market share and market power
   4. Financial effects of mergers

B. Theories of Conglomerate Mergers and Managerialism

C. Tests of Merger Theories
   1. Tests of terms of mergers
   2. Tests of merger profitability
   3. Tests of market power issues

D. Managerial Policies in a Valuation Framework

Merger theories and theories of conglomerate mergers are covered in the present chapter. In Chapter 18, we present tests of merger theories and develop the implications for managerial policies.

A. MERGER THEORIES

The business literature discusses various types of possible gains or economies from mergers. The theoretical literature of finance focuses on the issue of whether or not synergy is achieved by mergers. If synergy occurs, the value of the combined firm, V_{AB}, exceeds the value of the individual firms brought together by the mergers. With synergy,

$$V_{AB} > V_A + V_B.$$

Because much of the theoretical literature was stimulated in response to the dramatic conglomerate merger movement of the 1960s and because true social gains from conglomerate mergers were not readily perceived, much of the formal analysis in the scholarly literature assumed no synergy:

$$V_{AB} = V_A + V_B.$$

Myers [1968], Schall [1972], and Mossin [1973] have all argued that value is conserved (value additivity obtains) under addition of income streams (mergers). Nielsen [1974], however, pointed out that Myers paralleled the earlier Modigliani-Miller [1958] formulation by using a partial equilibrium approach in which prices and other parameters are assumed to be constant. Nielsen also called attention to the Schall assumption that the capital markets are complete and perfect, and to the Mossin assumption that the equilibrium allocation of income (hence also the marginal utilities of all investors) is invariant with respect to a change in the number of trading instruments due to merger. Thus, at the theoretical level, the conditions under which value is conserved (even assuming the absence of synergy) are more restrictive than generally acknowledged.

Thus the dominant theme in the theoretical literature is that the value additivity principle holds in still another setting, the area of combining business entities through mergers or acquisitions. Much of the journal literature has sought to determine whether, in the absence of synergy, any theoretical justification for a merger could be found. However, the justification for mergers given by the executives engaging in mergers and some of the general literature as well argued that there were at least potential real gains from combining business firms. Some arguments for mergers will be considered next.

1. Potential Operating Gains from Mergers

The most general theory of mergers that can be formulated involves differential efficiency. In theory, if the management of firm A is more efficient than the management of firm B and if after firm A acquires firm B, the efficiency of firm B is brought up to the level of efficiency of firm A, efficiency is increased by merger. Note that this would be a social gain as well as a private gain. The level of efficiency in the economy would be raised by such mergers.

One difficulty in the differential efficiency theory is that if carried to its ultimate extreme, it would result in only one firm in the economy, indeed in the world—the firm with the greatest managerial efficiency. Clearly, problems of coordination would arise before that extreme result was reached. Hence another formulation of the differential efficiency theory of mergers is that there are always many firms with below-average efficiency or not operating up to their potentials, however defined. It is further suggested that firms operating in similar kinds of business activity would be most likely to be the potential acquirers. They would have the background for detecting below-average or less-than-full-potential performance and have the managerial knowhow for improving the performance of the acquired firm. The latter scenario is plausible, but in practice, acquiring firms may be overoptimistic in their judgments of their impact on the performance of the acquired firms. As a consequence, they may either pay too much for the acquired firm or fail to improve the performance of the acquired firm to the degree reflected in the acquisition value placed upon the acquired firm.

Manne [1965] extended the differential efficiency argument into a more general theory of the role of mergers in keeping the market for capital assets competitive. He saw mergers as a threat of takeover by more efficient managements if a firm's management lagged in performance. Another aspect of the role of mergers in the market for capital assets is that they provide an incentive for entrepreneurs to form firms, develop them until their potential is attractive, and sell out for the capital gains returns.

Thus tax considerations are also involved in mergers. One such tax consideration is to substitute capital gains taxes for ordinary income taxes by acquiring a growth firm with a small or no dividend payout and then selling it to realize capital gains. Also, when the growth of a firm has slowed so that earnings retention cannot be justified to the Internal Revenue Service, an incentive for sale to another firm is created. Rather than pay out future earnings as dividends subject to the ordinary personal income tax, future earnings can be capitalized in a sale to another firm. Most substantial mergers are tax-free exchanges. Not only is a lower capital gains tax applicable, but it is also postponed until the securities received in the tax-free exchange are liquidated for cash.

Another tax factor is the sale of firms with accumulated tax losses. Although a business purpose must also be demonstrated, a firm with tax losses can shelter the positive earnings of a firm with which it is joined. Still other tax effects are associated with inheritance taxes. A closely held firm may be sold as the owners become older because of the uncertainty of the value placed on the firm in connection with estate taxes. Or a sale may be made to provide greater liquidity for the payment of estate taxes.

Even if the differential efficiency theory is plausible, it implies some degree of excess executive capacity on the management team of the acquiring firm. It suggests that the managers of the relatively more efficient firms have time left over to give attention to the acquired firms, as though they had been underutilized prior to the mergers. This hypothesis leads to a third theory of mergers—that operating economies of scale may be achieved. This theory is based on a number of major assumptions. It assumes that economies of scale do exist in the industry and that prior to the merger, the firms are operating at levels of activity that fall short of achieving the potentials for economies of scale.

Basically, economies of scale involve "indivisibilities," such as people, equipment, and overhead, which provide increasing returns if spread over a larger number of units of output. Thus, in manufacturing operations, heavy investments in plant and equipment typically produce such economies; for example, costly machinery such as the large presses used to produce automobile bodies requires optimal utilization. Similarly, in the area of financing, data on flotation costs indicate that the cost of floating a larger issue amounts to a smaller percentage of the issue floated because the fixed costs of investigation and compliance with SEC regulations are spread over a larger dollar amount. And the same principle applies to the research and development departments of chemical and pharmaceutical companies which often have to have a large staff of highly competent scientists who, if given the opportunity, could develop and oversee a larger number of product areas. Finally, in marketing, having one organization cover the entire United States may yield economies of scale because of the increase in the ratio of calling-on-customer time to traveling time, which in turn is due to the higher density of customers who can be called on by the same number of salesmen.

One potential problem in merging firms with existing organizations is the question of how to combine and coordinate the good parts of the organizations and eliminate what is not required. Often the merger announcement will say that firm A is strong in research and development but weak in marketing, while firm B is strong in marketing but weak in R&D, and the two firms combined will complement each other. Analytically, this implies underutilization of some existing factors and inadequate investment in other factors of production. (Since the economies are jointly achieved, the assignment of the contributions of each firm to the merger is difficult both in theory and in practice.)

Economies in production, research, marketing, or finance are sometimes referred to as economies in the specific management functions. It has also been suggested that economies may be achieved in the generic management activity such as the planning and control functions of the firm. It is argued that firms of even moderate size need at least a minimum number of corporate officers. The corporate staff with capabilities for planning and control is therefore assumed to be underutilized to some degree. Acquisitions of firms just approaching the size where they need to add corporate staff would provide for fuller utilization of the corporate staff of the acquiring firm and avoid the necessity of adding such staff for the other firm.

A third area in which operating economies may be achieved is in vertical integration. Combining firms at different stages of an industry may achieve more efficient coordination of the different levels. The argument here is that costs of communication and various forms of bargaining can be avoided by vertical integration [Williamson, 1971; Arrow, 1975].

Thus differential efficiency, economies of scale, and vertical integration are all potential sources of gains or economies from mergers and acquisitions. If these potentials do exist, they do not tell us how the gains, if any, will be shared among the participants in mergers. Further financial analysis is required and ultimately is settled only by the empirical materials treated below.

2. Market Share and Market Power

A reason often given for mergers is that it will increase a firm's market share, but it is not clear how increasing the market share will achieve economies or synergies. If increasing the firm's market share simply means that the firm will be larger, then we are essentially talking about economies of scale, which we have already discussed. Increasing market share really means increasing the size of the firm *relative* to other firms in an industry. But it is not made clear why increasing the firm's relative size will provide economies or other social gains.

Indeed, this poses a challenge to the arguments for merger emphasizing economies of scale and vertical integration. These could also be achieved by the internal expansion of the firm. Why is the external acquisition of another firm necessary to achieve these economies if indeed they do exist? A number of possible explanations may be offered such as acquiring a larger volume of operations sooner. But it is not clear whether the price required by the selling firm (the firm to be acquired) will really make the acquisition route the more economical method of expanding a firm's capacity either horizontally or vertically.

An objection that is often raised against permitting a firm to increase its market share by merger is that the result will be "undue concentration" in the industry. Indeed, public policy in the United States holds that when four or fewer firms account for 40% or more of the sales in a given market or line of business, an undesirable market structure or "undue concentration" exists. The argument in brief is that if four or fewer firms account for a substantial percentage of an industry's sales, these firms will recognize the impact of their actions and policies upon one another. This recognized interdependence will lead to a consideration of actions and reactions to changes in policy that will tend toward "tacit collusion." As a result, the prices and profits of the firms will contain monopoly elements. Thus, if economies from mergers cannot be established, it is assumed that the resulting increases in concentration may lead to monopoly returns. If economies of scale can be demonstrated, then a comparison of efficiencies versus the effects of increased concentration must be made.

While some economists hold that high concentration causes some degree of monopoly, other economists hold that increased concentration is generally the *result* of active and intense competition. They argue further that the intense competition continues among large firms in concentrated industries because the dimensions of decision-making over prices, outputs, types of product, quality of product, service, etc., are so numerous and of so many gradations that collusion simply is not feasible. This is an area where the issues continue to be unresolved.

3. Financial Effects of Mergers

Several financial gains from mergers have been proposed. Arguments claiming financial economies from mergers other than the possible advantage of economies of scale in financing are of dubious validity. As presented in most basic finance texts, it can readily be demonstrated that a differentially higher price-earnings ratio can achieve gains in earnings per share for acquiring firms. If merger terms represent a differentially higher price-earnings ratio for the acquiring firm, its earnings per share after the acquisition will be higher and the earnings per share of the acquired firm will be lower. The acquiring firm achieves earnings accretion while the acquired firm suffers earnings dilution.

But it can be readily demonstrated that the higher price-earnings ratio must reflect differentially more favorable earnings growth prospects. The effect of acquiring firms with low price-earnings ratios and lower earnings growth prospects will be to depress the average rate of future growth in earnings of the combined firm. The new price-earnings ratio should reflect this change in the outlook for the growth in earnings of the merged firm so that there should be no gain in the value of the combined firm over the values of the two separate firms. Hence the differential price-earnings ratio theory and its immediate effects on earnings per share have no validity as a theory for measuring the potential gains of a merger, since it is valuation, not earnings per share, that is the relevant test.

The second financial advantage of mergers that has been cited is that the merged firm may more fully utilize the unused debt capacity of one of the firms. This assumes that debt capacity can be identified within some measurable range. If this is the case, then it can be determined that one of the firms involved in the merger was operating substantially below its debt capacity, and hence was not fully utilizing the tax shelter benefits of debt. If, after the merger, the amount of its debt is increased up to its debt capacity, we know from our previous discussion on financial structure that the increase in debt could result in an increased value of the firm.

While reducing unused debt capacity will increase the value of a firm, it has not been established that a merger is the necessary and only method capable of bringing about this result. The firm with unused debt capacity is perfectly able to increase the amount of its borrowing without the merger. Merger activity is certainly not a necessary ingredient for reducing the unused debt capacity which a firm may have.

A similar argument made by others applies to firms which have an excess amount of funds invested in marketable securities such as Treasury bills. The excess investment in marketable securities may be regarded as negative debt so that the firm may be said to have an excessive amount of negative debt (i.e., loans). By eliminating excessive negative debt, the firm will eliminate this negative tax shield, and the value of the firm will increase. Again, if the argument is valid that excess marketable securities can be identified and that they represent excess negative tax shields, a merger which liquidates the excess marketable securities will result in increased value. But, even if valid (and we doubt it), the financial management of the firm can achieve this result without any merger. There is nothing in the merger that is essential to improving financial management by eliminating or reducing an error in financial policy.

We are unaware of any arguments establishing that economies can be achieved through purely financial effects of the type we have been describing. Since conglomerate mergers appeared to place a heavy emphasis on financial stratagems for achieving higher market prices, they were especially criticized as devoid of financial or economic justification. Hence our next section will deal with conglomerate mergers.

B. CONGLOMERATE MERGERS AND MANAGERIALISM

One concern about conglomerate mergers was that they represented efforts to achieve market power. This concern resulted in a number of studies of the conglomerate merger movement by the United States Federal Trade Commission. Its *Staff Report* of November 1972 presented over 50 tables of data to test a number of hypotheses about the effects of conglomerate merger activity during the 10-year period from 1960–1969. The FTC Report found that 82% of the acquisitions by the conglomerates, from 1963 to 1969, represented a "toe-hold" acquisition defined by a market share of less than 5%. Indeed 54% of the acquisitions represented product classes in which the market share in the year prior to acquisition was less than 1%. The postacquisition changes in market positions acquired by conglomerates were predominantly decreases. Hence, after the massive merger activity of the 1960s, the market share of the conglomerate firms in 1969 was less than 5% in more than 80% of the product classes in which they operated. The FTC Report concluded, "Finally, they do not appear to have become significant market forces in large sectors of our economy. They are located in a number of industries in which their individual market shares are relatively small and have shown no particular tendency to increase." Nor were other apprehensions such as reciprocity, deep-pocket power, and forbearance supported by the evidence.

But while the concern about the potential anticompetitive consequences of conglomerate mergers subsided, there was a widespread judgment that conglomerate mergers were exercises in financial self-levitation. As indicated above, financial stratagems alone are not likely to produce any real gains for the conglomerate firms. Later we will consider other reasons for conglomerate mergers. But if they are the results of predominantly financial motivations of the type described above, it should have been readily predictable that conglomerate firms would achieve no real financial gains.

If conglomerates did not benefit their owners, whom did they benefit? One explanation is that conglomerate mergers were carried out by and for the managers of the firms. The "managerialism" explanation for conglomerate mergers was set forth most fully by Mueller [1969]. The central core of Mueller's theory is illustrated in Fig. 17.1. The motivations of a smaller growth firm and a larger, more mature firm are contrasted in the two parts of the figure. In part (a), the schedule of marginal rates of return on investments for the growing firm is shown to be somewhat higher and somewhat flatter (more elastic) than for the relatively more mature firm. The marginal cost of capital for the smaller growth firm is shown to be somewhat higher than for the larger, more mature firm. Also, we can see that the greater growth requirement for the smaller growth firm has the result that the marginal rate-of-return function and the marginal cost-of-capital function intersect at a point on the upward-sloping section of the marginal cost-of-capital function.

This is contrasted with the situation of the larger, more mature firm depicted in Fig. 17.1(b). Because of the large internal cash flows of this type of firm, its marginal cost-of-capital function is parallel to the horizontal axis over a substantial amount of investment. But relative to the size of its internal cash flows, the investment opportunities within the traditional business activities of the firm are more restricted. As a consequence, the schedule of marginal rates of return on investments for the mature firm is likely to intersect well within the horizontal segment of its marginal cost-of-capital function (as defined by the criterion of stockholder opportunity).

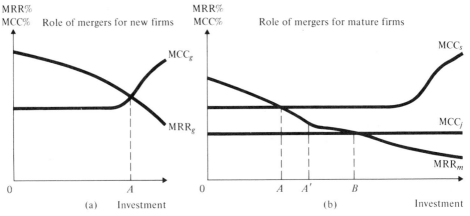

MRR_g = schedule of marginal rates of return on investments for growing firm.
MRR_m = schedule of marginal rates of return on investments for mature firm.
MCC_g = marginal cost of capital for growing firm.
MCC_s = marginal cost of capital for mature firm by stockholder opportunity cost criterion to maximize stockholder welfare.
MCC_j = marginal cost of capital as viewed by management seeking to maximize growth; operates as a constraint, but is below opportunity cost level for stockholders.

Fig. 17.1 (a) Role of mergers for new firms (b) Role of mergers for mature firms (Based on Dennis C. Mueller, "A Theory of Conglomerate Mergers," *Quarterly Journal of Economics*, November 1969, 643–659.)

Mueller hypothesizes that managers are motivated to increase the size of their firms further. He assumes that the compensation to managers is a function of the size of the firm and he argues, therefore, that managers adopt a lower investment hurdle rate as illustrated in Fig. 17.1(b). But in a study critical of earlier evidence, Lewellen and Huntsman [1970] present findings that managers' compensation is significantly correlated with the firm's profit rate, not its level of sales. Thus the basic premise of the Mueller theory is doubtful.

In Mueller's theory, the lower investment hurdle rate prompts the managers of older, larger, more mature firms to invest more heavily than they would if they were confronted with a higher hurdle and represents a basic motivation for the conglomerate merger movement. The schedule for the marginal rate of return on investments for the mature firm begins to flatten out at the point indicated by A' in Fig. 17.1(b) because managers then begin to invest by making acquisitions outside the mature firm.

Thus, instead of following the economic principle of equating the relevant marginal curves to determine the rate of investment, the managers in the more mature firm invest the larger amount OB. Of this amount, OA represents investments internal to the firm, and the segment $A'B$ represents amounts of investment external to the firm gained through acquisitions. This latter segment, it is argued, represents inefficient investment. In addition, the segment AA' of internal investment is also inefficient since the marginal rate of return on investment is below the relevant marginal cost of capital for stockholders.

In addition to doubt cast on the basic premise of the Mueller theory by the evidence presented by Lewellen and Huntsman, his theory is contradicted by the basic facts of merger activity. Of the 200 largest industrial corporations in 1968, 141 were among the 200 largest in 1954 as well. [Bock, 1970, pp. 10–11.] In 1954, the average size of these 200 firms, as measured by total assets, was $600 million. In the period 1954–1968, large acquisitions amounted to 9% of their change in assets. Of the 59 newcomers to the top 200 in 1968, asset data were available for 43 in 1954. The average size of total assets of these 43 firms, in 1954, was approximately $60 million, and during the 1954–1968 period, large acquisitions amounted to 34% of their change in assets. Thus the large acquirers during the 1954–1968 period were about one-tenth the average size of the larger, more mature nonacquirers. The initial size of the active conglomerate acquirers was small, rather than large. The large, mature firms did little acquiring.

Not only do the basic facts contradict Mueller's theory of conglomerate mergers, but his theory contradicts itself. If the managers in firms were making investment decisions using an investment hurdle rate below a market equilibrium rate and therefore below the alternative returns available to stockholders, stockholders would shift their investment to firms offering higher rates of return. Basic capital market forces would not permit different firms to follow a "two-tier" investment hurdle rate policy. Furthermore, managers would seek merger opportunities whose prospective rates of return would be higher than the rates of return from internal investments.

The returns from external investments would be represented by a curve above and to the right of the MRR_m curve in Fig. 17.1(b).

1. Pure Financial Theories of Conglomerate Firms

The popular justification of conglomerate mergers was synergy—the $2 + 2 = 5$ effect. But other theories of conglomerate firms were set forth which did not require the assumption of synergy. Lewellen [1971], for example, offered a purely financial rationale for conglomerate mergers. His theory may be summarized initially in terms of the numerical examples he provides, concluding with his general statement of conditions.

Let us consider two firms, A and B, whose annual cash flows are independent (correlation coefficient is zero) and each distributed as shown in columns (1) through (3) of Table 17.1.

Table 17.1*

(1) State (s_1)	(2) $P(s_1)$	(3) Y_1
1	.1	100
2	.2	250
3	.7	500

* Note: s_1 = alternative future state of the world, $P(s_1)$ = probability of alternative states, Y_1 = annual cash flow outcomes under alternative states.

It is assumed that each firm has incurred borrowings to the point that its annual cash contractual obligation amounts to $240. The probability, $P(D)$, that one or both firms will be unable to meet their debt service obligations of $240 each is shown below:

$$P(D) = P(Y_A < 240) + P(Y_B < 240) - P(Y_A < 240, \ Y_B < 240)$$
$$= .1 + .1 - (.1)(.1) = .19.$$

If the two firms merge, the distribution of their joint returns can be calculated as shown in the matrix in Table 17.2. The distribution of their joint returns would therefore become

Y_m	200	350	500	600	750	1,000
$P(Y_m)$	.01	.04	.04	.14	.28	.49

Since their aggregate debt burden would become $480 per annum, the probability of default now drops to .05 as compared with .19 before the merger.

The foregoing was based on the assumption of zero correlation between the two returns. If the correlation were -1, the gains from merger would be even greater. If the correlation were $+1$, reducing the probability of default would require other

Table 17.2

		.1	.2	.7
.1	Joint probability	.01	.02	.07
	Amount	200	350	600
.2	Joint probability	.02	.04	.14
	Amount	350	500	750
.7	Joint probability	.07	.14	.49
	Amount	600	750	1,000

differences such as differences in the size of debt obligations. Thus if we assume the same distribution of returns for the two firms as before, but assume a correlation of $+1$ between the two and the debt obligations of A and B to be \$255 and \$240, respectively, the before-merger probability of default would be

$$P(D) = .3 + .1 - .1 = .3.$$

After merger, the total debt obligations would be \$495, and it would be related to the following combined cash flow pattern:

Y_m	200	500	1,000
$P(Y_m)$	.1	.2	.7

The probability of default would therefore fall to only 0.1.

Levy and Sarnat [1970] set forth a similar argument. They state, "A somewhat stronger case can be made for conglomerate mergers when economies in capital costs are considered ... large firms have better access to the capital markets and also enjoy significant cost savings when securing their financing needs ... These cost savings presumably reflect, at least in part, the reduction in lenders' risk achieved through diversification." (p. 801)

Galai and Masulis [1976] point out the confusion involved between the value of the merged firm and the positions of the debt and equity holders. They argue that the value of the merged firm is the simple sum of the constituent firms. "This can be seen once one recognizes that investors in the marketplace could have created an identical financial position by purchasing equal proportions of the debt and equity of the two firms." (p. 68). The OPM establishes that the relative position of the creditors and the equity holders of the firms will be changed. If the correlation between the returns of the merging firms is less than 1, the variance in the rate of return of the merged firm will be lower than the variance of the rates of return of the merging firms (assumed to be equal).

It follows from the OPM that the value of the equity of the merged firm will be less than the sum of the constituent equity values and the value of the debt will be higher. According to the OPM, increased variability increases the value of the option and conversely. Since the equity is an option on the face value of the debt outstanding, its value will fall with a decrease in volatility. "What is taking place, as Rubinstein points out, is that the bondholders receive more protection since the stockholders of each firm have to back the claims of the bondholders of both companies. The stockholders are hurt since their limited liability is weakened." [Galai and Masulis, 1976, p. 68]

A number of alternatives could be used to return the wealth of different classes of security holders to the original position they held prior to the merger. One solution would be to increase the amount of the face value of debt and use the proceeds to retire equity. This process is continued until the original bondholders' holdings have a market value equal to their constituent sum prior to the merger. The debt-to-equity ratio of the merged firm can be increased to offset the decrease in the volatility of the merged firm's rate of return. The tax shelter effect of increasing the face value of the merged firm's debt will increase the *after-tax* value of the firm.

Thus a pure diversification rationale for conglomerate mergers is not valid. Reducing the risk to bondholders represents a redistribution of value from shareholders, leaving the total value of the firm unchanged.

2. Potential Sources of Synergy in Conglomerate Mergers

From the mid-1950s through 1968, economists and managers offered a number of reasons other than the ones discussed above to explain how economies might be achieved in conglomerate mergers. During this period, formal long-range enterprise planning developed, and computer technology began to be adapted to the management of the firm. Financial planning and control systems were extended with further improvements in the use of balanced, centralized-decentralized management-control systems. Further, World War II and the Korean conflict had stimulated new technologies resulting in an uneven diffusion of and wide variations in advanced technological capabilities among firms.

The major conceptual point here is that the role of the general management functions (planning, control, organizing, information systems) and functions centralized at top management levels (research, finance, legal) increased in importance in the management of enterprises. As a consequence, the costs of managing large, diversified firms were substantially reduced relative to potential operating economies. This is the broader theoretical basis explaining the formation of conglomerates.

3. Tests of the Performance of Conglomerate Firms

Empirical studies of conglomerate performance have been of two kinds. The first was a concern with their operating characteristics. In a study whose data ended in the early 1960s, Reid [1968] concluded that conglomerate mergers satisfied the desires of managers for larger firms, but did not increase earnings or market prices. For a later period, 1958–1968, Weston and Mansinghka [1971] found that conglomerates as a group raised the depressed premerger rates of return on total assets up to the average for all firms. In the Melicher and Rush study [1974] for 1960–1969, conglomerates acquired more profitable firms than nonconglomerate acquirers did, a fact which casts doubt on synergy, and increased the utilization of latent debt capacity, a fact which is consistent with the Galai and Masulis theory using the OPM.

A second type of empirical study focused on conglomerate performance within the context of the CAPM. Weston et al. [1972] compared conglomerates with mutual funds (using annual data for 1960–1969), finding that conglomerates provided higher ratios of return to systematic risk. Melicher and Rush [1973] analyzed conglomerates against a matched sample of nonconglomerates. Operating comparisons were based on annual data, while market comparisons utilized monthly data over the period 1965–1971. Conglomerates exhibited higher levels of systematic risk, but did not achieve significantly different rates of return or other performance measures. Joenk and Nielsen [1974] compared levels of systematic risks and coefficients of determination for 21 conglomerates and 23 nonconglomerates (1962–1969). The market response for three years before and three years after each merger was not significantly different. Mason and Goudzwaard [1976] compared 22 conglomerates against randomly selected portfolios having similar asset structures for the years 1962–1967. They concluded that conglomerates performed statistically worse, on the basis of both return on assets and return on equity, compared to an unmanaged portfolio of similar industry investments.

In a later study, Smith and Weston [1977] retested their 1972 results, using monthly data and extending the coverage through 1973. Their research broadened the comparisons of Melicher and Rush [1973] by including mutual funds and closed-end investment companies as well as nonconglomerate firms. They studied a sample of 38 conglomerate firms. Conglomerates from their 1972 study were included for which complete data of monthly prices and dividends were available for the 10 years from 1964 through 1973 (38). Similar data were available for 35 nonconglomerate firms that were part of a larger sample (matched by major industry) as developed by Melicher and Rush [1973]. Standard and Poor's Composite Stock Price Index was used as a surrogate for the overall stock market. For comparisons of managed portfolios, they compiled data for 104 mutual funds and also for 17 closed-end investment companies.

The risk-adjusted performance of conglomerates was found to be significantly better than that of the mutual funds. The higher-beta conglomerates performed better during the rising market, but less well during the flat market. However, on theoretical grounds, the risk-adjusted performance measure should not show better performance for higher-risk securities during an up-market or worse performance during a down-market situation. As discussed by Friend and Blume [1970] and Black et al. [1972], a possible reason for the early differentially better performance of conglomerates is that the CAPM from which the risk-adjusted performance measures are derived is misspecified. An alternative explanation is expectation errors coupled with institutional changes. The attitudes toward conglomerates changed considerably over time, exhibiting overoptimism about their potential during 1964–1968. During the second period, 1969–1973, some unfavorable institutional changes took place. Accounting rules were changed, adverse tax treatment was legislated, and antitrust suits were filed by the Department of Justice. Also the aerospace industry, which spawned many of the conglomerates as a form of defensive diversification, suffered from excess capacity and sharp product shifts with the escalation of the Vietnam war. Tests of operating effectiveness suggest an initial overoptimism about the potentials for management performance of conglomerates. Following 1969, conglomerates began to be viewed with considerable pessimism. These expectation changes are consistent with the risk-adjusted performance exhibited by the conglomerates.

As experience with conglomerates grew, investors were able to develop a more dependable basis for forming expectations with respect to their performance. We would expect conglomerates to continue to exhibit high betas because of the characteristics of the product-markets of conglomerate firms. Risk-adjusted measures of conglomerate performance are not likely to be significantly different from those of other firms and portfolios. These results are consistent with the premise of no continuing gains from synergy in conglomerate mergers.

4. The Merger Binge of 1976–77

While the frenzied merger movement of the 1960s peaked in the last two years of that decade, mergers of major magnitude have continued to take place in the 1970s. It was reported that merger activity in 1976 was up 30% over the previous year [*Business Week*, July 19, 1976]. In addition, between 1971 and 1975 approximately 40 companies with assets exceeding $100 million were merged into acquiring companies. The years 1976 and 1977 have been characterized as a "merger binge" of companies of substantial size. Twelve major mergers took place during 1976 and 1977, and the total value of the transactions amounted to $6.3 billion. While the explanations of the 1976–78 takeover activity have not been documented in any rigorous way, the financial press has presented the following rationale.

The major reason given for the increase in takeovers in 1976–77 is that the replacement values of corporate assets have been rising with inflation while inflation has depressed real earnings, resulting in lower stock prices. It has been estimated that by the end of 1977, the replacement costs of corporate net assets (for nonfarm, nonfinancial corporations) were about 25% higher than the market values of the corporate securities representing ownership of the corporate assets [*Business Week*, November 14, 1977, p. 179]. Because selling prices of products have been based on the historical costs of assets, the prospective returns on new investments at current, higher replacement costs have been unattractively low. With the market values of other companies substantially below their replacement costs, acquisitions provide the opportunity of higher returns than would be earned by investments in physical assets either in the firm's own line of business or in new areas.

But this implies that the prices of products have risen less than the increase in the prices of capital goods. It also implies that similar assets are selling at different prices. Also, why should a firm valued by the market at less than the replacement value of its assets be worth more than its market price to the acquiring firms? No answer can be given that flows from a rigorous theoretical model. Only a number of conjectures can be offered: The acquiring firm may be making assumptions about more favorable developments such as product price increases that lead to higher present value estimates by acquiring firms; or the acquiring firm may need to add production capacity to keep a balance with its general management organization, the capacity of its marketing and distribution organization, etc. If the market value of additional capacity represented by another firm is below the cost of installing new capacity, it is rational to take the lower cost alternative. Another possibility is that when a firm in a different line of business makes the acquisition, it is overpessimistic about prospects in its own markets, but is overoptimistic about the prospects for the different industries about which it has less complete information. Still another explanation is that the market is unduly pessimistic about the prospects for some firms, and the acquirers are simply making what they consider to be sound long-run investments. We are uncomfortable about all these rationalizations and raise the question whether future empirical studies will find the merger binge of 1976–77 to have been soundly conceived.

C. SUMMARY

A number of theories of mergers have been offered. The synergy theory of mergers holds that the combined value of the merged firms is increased by the merger. Most studies of mergers have assumed that there is no synergy and have been concerned with identifying theoretical justifications for merger without synergy.

Mergers may occur to replace inefficient management. This type of merger is most likely to be between firms of similar kinds since similarity makes inefficiency easier to detect and remedy. The threat of takeover is one of the pressures for efficiency in firms. Merger may also be undertaken for tax reasons such as to substitute capital gains for ordinary income. Merger may produce (1) operating scale economies if some departments in the firms are underutilized prior to merger due to indivisibilities, (2) economies in generic management functions, or (3) information efficiencies from vertical integration.

The market power theory of mergers holds that mergers lead to concentration which enables firms to behave monopolistically. The concern that this is the motivation behind many mergers leads policy makers to discourage merger activity when efficiency gains are difficult to establish. Whether concentration reduces competition is an issue which remains unresolved.

A number of financial gains have been attributed to merger, including a theory that price-earnings ratio differentials can be used to increase earnings. Arguments have also been made that mergers can increase efficient use of debt capacity or of surplus investable funds. But except for the possibility that merger lowers the flotation cost of new capital, the pure financial arguments for merger generally do not hold up under analysis.

Starting in the early sixties there has been a marked increase in conglomerate merger activity. This is difficult to comprehend since efficiency gains from such mergers are not obvious. Studies have shown that such mergers were not anti-competitive since typically they involved a small fraction of the market of any given industry. Also, acquiring firms did not appear to have gained from these mergers. Continued efforts to find a reason for the merger activity have led to a theory of managerialism, which holds that the managers believe their rewards to depend on firm size and hence endeavor to maximize size to the detriment of the shareholders. There is, however, both empirical evidence and strong theoretical reasoning that the managerial theory of mergers is not valid.

One justification of conglomerate merger is that mergers of firms with less than perfectly correlated earnings could lower risk. The counterargument to this is that there is no reason for firms to do what the investor can do at lower cost in the financial markets. The one qualification to this argument is that managers may have superior knowledge of the combined risk or that substantial bankruptcy costs could be avoided by merger.

In fact it may be that conglomerate mergers are a natural outgrowth of the computer age. Improved information systems have expanded the generic managerial capabilities of many firms, and this has led them to view conglomerate merger as a natural extension of their existing activities. Studies of market relationships have found that the performance of conglomerates is not significantly different from the performance of other firms, a result consistent with market efficiency.

PROBLEM SET

17.1 Discuss the assumptions and implications of the proposition that value is conserved (value additivity obtains) under the addition of income streams (mergers).

17.2 Summarize the sources of synergy or operating gains from mergers that have been presented in the literature. Evaluate the validity of the arguments for synergy.

17.3 Explain and illustrate how differential price-earnings ratios reflected in the terms of mergers result in increases or decreases in earnings per share of the merging firms. Do such effects on price-earnings ratios also have effects on the valuation of the firms resulting from mergers?

17.4 Explain and evaluate the managerialism theory of conglomerate mergers set forth by Mueller.

17.5 Explain the pure financial theories of conglomerate firms and evaluate their validity.

17.6 You are given the following information:

	Firm *A*	Firm *B*
Value prior to merger	$1,000	$1,000
Face value of debt	$ 500	$ 500

In addition, the value of equity for firm *A* equals the value of equity for firm *B*, and the variance of returns for firm *A* and firm *B* are also equal. Using a risk-free rate of 8%, an appropriate time horizon of 5 years, and a variance for each firm of 10%, apply the OPM to calculate the value of equity of the two firms before the merger. Under the further assumption that the correlation between the percentage returns on firms A and B is zero, calculate the value of equity and the value of debt of the merged firm, using the OPM. How does the new market value of equity and of debt of the merged firm compare with the sum of the values of equity and debt of the constituent firms which combined in the merger?

17.7 Empirical studies have established that the betas of conglomerate firms have been significantly above 1. What does this imply about diversification as a strong motive for conglomerate mergers?

17.8 Over a long period of time would you expect the risk-adjusted performance of conglomerate firms to be significantly different from the risk-adjusted performance of a broad market index? Why?

17.9 Galai and Masulis argue that if two firms merge and thus decrease the probability of default on their debt along the lines of Lewellen's scenario, then the stockholders are actually hurt, since they have assumed some of the risk previously borne by the bondholders. Why might nonowner managers of a firm be motivated to transfer risk from bondholders to stockholders in this manner?

REFERENCES*

ALCHIAN, A., and H. DEMSETZ, "Production, Information Costs, and Economic Organizations," *The American Economic Review*, December 1972, 777–795.

ARROW, K. J., "Vertical Integration and Communication," *Bell Journal of Economics*, Spring 1975, 173–183.

BEMAN, L., "What We Learned from the Great Merger Frenzy," *Fortune*, April 1973, 70ff.

BLACK, F., M. JENSEN, and M. SCHOLES, "The Capital Asset Pricing Model: Some Empirical Tests," in M. Jensen (Ed.), *Studies in the Theory of Capital Markets*. Praeger, New York, 1972.

BLUME, M., "Portfolio Theory: A Step Toward Its Practical Application," *Journal of Business*, April 1970.

BOCK, B., *Statistical Games and the "200 Largest" Industrials: 1954 and 1968*. The Conference Board, Inc., New York, 1970.

CELLER, E., *Investigation of Conglomerate Corporations Hearings* before the Antitrust Subcommittee of the Committee on the Judiciary, House of Representatives, 1969–1970, Parts 1–7. U.S. Government Printing Office, Washington, D.C., 1971.

CELLER COMMITTEE STAFF REPORT, *Investigation of Conglomerate Corporations*. U.S. Government Printing Office, Washington, D.C., June 1, 1971.

COASE, R. H., "The Nature of the Firm," *Economica*, November 1937, 386–405.

DEWING, A. S., "A Statistical Test of the Success of Consolidations," *Quarterly Journal of Economics*, November 1921, 84–101.

---

* Since Chapters 17 and 18 are closely related in subject matter, the reader is urged to consult the reference sections for both chapters.

FAMA, E., "Efficient Capital Markets: A Review of Theory and Empirical Work," *Journal of Finance*, May 1970, 383–417.

———, "Perfect Competition and Optimal Production Decisions Under Uncertainty," *Bell Journal of Economics*, Autumn 1972, 509–530.

FRIEND, I., and M. BLUME, "Measurement of Portfolio Performance under Uncertainty," *American Economic Review*, September 1970, 561–575.

GALAI, D., and R. W. MASULIS, "The Option Pricing Model and the Risk Factor of Stock," *Journal of Financial Economics*, January/March 1976, 53–82.

GORT, MICHAEL, "An Economic Disturbance Theory of Mergers," *Quarterly Journal of Economics*, November 1969, 624–642.

HAUGEN, R. A., and J. G. UDELL, "Rates of Return to Stockholders of Acquired Companies," *Journal of Financial and Quantitative Analysis*, January 1972, 1387–1398.

HIGGINS, R. C., "Discussion," *Journal of Finance*, May 1971, 543–545.

JENSEN, M., and J. LONG, "Corporate Investment Under Uncertainty and Pareto Optimality in the Capital Markets," *Bell Journal of Economics*, Spring 1972, 151–174.

JOEHNK, M. D., and J. F. NIELSEN, "The Effects of Conglomerate Merger Activity on Systematic Risk," *Journal of Financial and Quantitative Analysis*, March 1974, 215–225.

LEVY, H., and M. SARNAT, "Diversification, Portfolio Analysis and the Uneasy Case for Conglomerate Mergers," *Journal of Finance*, September 1970, 795–802.

LEWELLEN, W. G., "A Pure Financial Rationale for the Conglomerate Merger," *Journal of Finance*, May 1971, 521–545.

———, and B. HUNTSMAN, "Managerial Pay and Corporate Performance," *American Economic Review*, September 1970, 710–720.

LINTNER, J., "Conglomerate and Vertical Responses to Market Imperfection: Expectations, Mergers and Equilibrium in Purely Competitive Markets," *American Economic Review*, May 1971, 101–111.

LIVERMORE, S., "The Success of Industrial Mergers," *Quarterly Journal of Economics*, November 1935, 63–96.

MANNE, H. G., "Mergers and the Market for Corporate Control," *Journal of Political Economy*, April 1965, 110–120.

MARKHAM, J. W., "Market Structure and Decision-Making in the Large Diversified Firm," in J. F. Weston and S. I. Ornstein, Eds., *The Impact of Large Firms on the U.S. Economy*, Chapter 14. D. C. Heath, Lexington, Mass., 1973.

MASON, R. H., and M. B. GOUDZWAARD, "Performance of Conglomerate Firms: A Portfolio Approach," *Journal of Finance*, March 1976, 39–48.

MELICHER, R. W., and D. F. RUSH, "The Performance of Conglomerate Firms: Recent Risk and Return Experience," *Journal of Finance*, May 1973, 381–388.

———, "Evidence on the Acquisition-Related Performance of Conglomerate Firms," *Journal of Finance*, March 1974, 141–149.

———, and T. H. HARTER, "Stock Price Movements of Firms Engaged in Large Acquisition," *Journal of Financial and Quantitative Analysis*, March 1972, 1469–1475.

MERTON, R., and M. SUBRAHMANYAN, "The Optimality of a Competitive Stock Market," *Bell Journal of Economics*, Spring 1974, 145–170.

MODIGLIANI, F., and M. H. MILLER, "The Cost of Capital, Corporation Finance, and the Theory of Investment," *American Economic Review*, June 1958, 261–297.

MOSSIN, J., *Theory of Financial Markets*. Prentice-Hall, Englewood Cliffs, N.J., 1973.

MUELLER, D. C., "A Theory of Conglomerate Mergers," *Quarterly Journal of Economics*, November 1969, 643–659. (See also comment by Dennis E. Logue and Philippe A. Naert, November 1970, 663–667; comment by David R. Kanerschen, 668–673, and reply by Dennis C. Mueller, 674–679.)

MYERS, S. C., "Procedures for Capital Budgeting under Uncertainty," *Industrial Management Review*, Spring 1968, 1–19.

NIELSEN, N. C., *The Firm as an Intermediary between Consumers and Production Functions under Uncertainty*. Doctoral dissertation, Graduate School of Business, Stanford University, Palo Alto, Calif., 1974.

REID, S. R., *Mergers, Managers and the Economy*. McGraw-Hill, New York, 1968.

REINHARDT, U. E., *Mergers and Consolidations: A Corporate Financial Approach*. General Learning Press, Morristown, New Jersey, 1972.

SCHALL, L. D., "Asset Valuation, Firm Investment, and Firm Diversification," *Journal of Business*, January 1972, 11–28.

SHICK, R. A., "The Analysis of Mergers and Acquisitions," *The Journal of Finance*, May 1972, 495–502.

SMITH, K. V., and J. F. WESTON, "Further Evaluation of Conglomerate Performance," *Journal of Business Research*, March 1977, 5–14.

U.S. FEDERAL TRADE COMMISSION, Staff Report: *Economic Report on Conglomerate Merger Performance*. U.S. Government Printing Office, Washington, D.C., November 1972.

———, Staff Report: *Economic Report on Corporate Mergers*. U.S. Government Printing Office, Washington, D.C., August 28, 1969.

———, *Statistical Report on Mergers and Acquisitions*. Bureau of Economics, November 1977.

WESTERFIELD, R., "A Note on the Measurement of Conglomerate Diversification," *Journal of Finance*, September 1970, 909–914.

WESTON, J. F., "The Determination of Share Exchange Ratios," in W. W. Alberts and J. E. Segal, Eds., *The Corporate Merger*, pp. 117–138. University of Chicago Press, 1966.

WESTON, J. F., and S. K. MANSINGHKA, "Tests of the Efficiency Performance of Conglomerate Firms," *Journal of Finance*, September 1971, 919–936.

———, "Discussion," *The American Economic Review*, May 1971, 125–127.

———, "ROI Planning and Control," *Business Horizons*, August 1972, 35–42.

———, and EDWARD M. RICE, "Discussion," *Journal of Finance*, May 1976, 743–747.

———, K. V. SMITH, and R. E. SCHRIEVES, "Conglomerate Performance Using the Capital Asset Pricing Model," *The Review of Economics and Statistics*, November 1972, pp. 357–363.

WILLIAMSON, O. E., *Corporate Control and Business Behavior*. Prentice-Hall, Englewood Cliffs, N.J., 1970.

———, "The Vertical Integration of Production: Market Failure Considerations," *The American Economic Review*, May 1971, 112–123.

Chapter 18

Mergers:
Tests and Applications

A. TESTS OF MERGER THEORIES

The preceding chapter dealt with theories of mergers and considered some empirical tests of conglomerate merger theories. We now consider three additional tests of other merger theories: (1) tests of terms of mergers, (2) tests of merger returns, and (3) tests of market power issues.

1. Tests of Terms of Mergers

Larson and Gonedes [1969] set forth a model of exchange-ratio determination. They reject the effect of mergers on earnings per share as a test and argue that the effects of mergers on market value would be an appropriate test. The market values of common stocks are used to determine the precombination wealth positions of the parties involved in a merger, and the result is compared with the postmerger wealth positions of the parties. Since the Larson-Gonedes decision horizon is the immediate postmerger market values, the postmerger price-earnings ratio of the merged firm receives their greatest emphasis. They observe that the earnings multiple of a combined firm will be a weighted average of the earnings multiple of the constituent firms if (1) the growth rate of the combined entity is a weighted average of its constituents' growth rates, and (2) the riskiness of earnings stream of the combined entities is a weighted average of the earnings streams (p. 722). The earnings multiple of a merged firm will exceed the average of its constituents' earnings multiples if the new growth rate exceeds the average of the constituents' growth rates. The earnings multiple of a combined entity will also be affected by its risk. The risk of the combined firm will be decreased, increased, or remain the same depending upon whether the covariance of the earnings stream with the market is increased, decreased or remains the same.

The Larson-Gonedes model holds that the exchange ratio will be determined by each firm's assessment of the postmerger price-earnings multiple and postulates that each firm requires that its equivalent price per share be at least maintained as a result of the merger. Their model is summarized algebraically and graphically by Conn and Nielsen [1977], using the following symbols:

ER = exchange ratio (i.e., the number of the acquiring firm's shares exchanged for each share of the acquired firm's equity),
P = price per share,
EPS = earnings per share,
PE = price-earnings multiple,
E = earnings,
S = number of common shares outstanding,
AER = actual exchange ratio.

In the formulations which follow, subscripts 1, 2, and 12 are used to refer to the acquiring, acquired, and combined firms, respectively.

An exchange ratio is determined depending upon postmerger advantages expected from the combined firm subject to the stockholder wealth constraint. This is expressed as follows:

$$P_{12} \geq P_1, \tag{18.1}$$

We use the equality relationship. The market price per share for the combined firm is defined in terms of earnings and the price-earnings ratio as

$$P_{12} \equiv (\mathrm{PE}_{12})(\mathrm{EPS}_{12}) \equiv P_1. \tag{18.2}$$

The expression for the earnings per share of the combined firm is then detailed as follows:

$$\mathrm{EPS}_{12} = \frac{E_1 + E_2}{S_1 + S_2(\mathrm{ER}_1)}. \tag{18.3}$$

In this equation, ER_1 represents the exchange ratio of shares of firm 2 for shares of firm 1 from the perspective of firm 1. In Eq. (18.4), Eq. (18.3) is used to restate Eq. (18.2):

$$P_1 = \frac{(\mathrm{PE}_{12})(E_1 + E_2)}{S_1 + S_2(\mathrm{ER}_1)}. \tag{18.4}$$

Equation (18.4) is then solved for ER_1 to yield Eq. (18.5a):

$$\mathrm{ER}_1 = -\frac{S_1}{S_2} + \frac{(E_1 + E_2)}{P_1 S_2} \mathrm{PE}_{12}. \tag{18.5a}$$

Table 18.1

	Total earnings, E	Number of shares of common stock, S	Earnings per share, EPS	Price-earnings ratio, PE	Market price per common share, P
Firm 1	$200	100	$2.00	10	$20
Firm 2	$200	100	$2.00	20	$40

An example will illustrate the nature of Eq. (18.5a) and some subsequent relationships. Let us assume that firm 1 and firm 2 are contemplating a merger in which firm 1 will acquire firm 2. Table 18.1 contains the information gathered about the two firms.

In the following discussion related to this example, let subscripts 1 and 2 refer to the individual firms. Let ER_1 stand for the exchange ratio from the standpoint of firm 2; AER is the actual exchange ratio; PE_{12} will be the price-earnings ratio for the merged firm, after the merger.

Using the above data in Eq. (18.5a), we obtain

$$ER_1 = -\tfrac{100}{100} + \tfrac{400}{2000}PE_{12}, \tag{18.5b}$$

which is expressed in simplified form as

$$ER_1 = -1 + \tfrac{1}{5}PE_{12}. \tag{18.5c}$$

We then use some illustrative values of PE_{12} to indicate the required maximum exchange ratio that firm 1 may offer the shareholders of firm 2 if the wealth constraint for the shareholders of firm 1 is to be satisfied:

PE_{12}	0	7	11	12	15	20	30
Max. ER_1	-1	0.4	1.2	1.4	2.0	3.0	5.0

These data, of course, plot on a straight line as illustrated in Fig. 18.1. We have discussed the maximum ER_1. Let us now consider the minimum ER_2 that may be accepted by the shareholders of firm 2 if their wealth constraint is to be satisfied. Their basic requirement is

$$P_{12} \geq P_2/ER_2 \tag{18.6}$$

Using the equality form of Eq. (18.6), we rewrite it utilizing the accounting determination of P_1. This is simply the price-earnings ratio times the earnings per share for the combined firm,

$$P_{12} = (PE_{12})(EPS_{12}) = \frac{P_2}{ER_2}, \tag{18.7a}$$

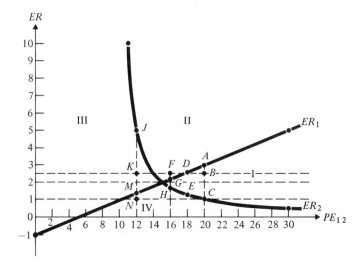

Fig. 18.1 Influence of AER and PE_{12} on merger gains and losses

and substituting for the earnings per share from Eq. (18.3),

$$P_{12} = \frac{P_2}{ER_2} = \frac{(PE_{12})(E_1 + E_2)}{S_1 + S_2(ER_2)} \tag{18.7b}$$

We then solve for ER_2:

$$\frac{P_2 S_1 + P_2 S_2(ER_2)}{ER_2} = (PE_{12})(E_1 + E_2),$$

$$ER_2 = \frac{P_2 S_1}{(PE_{12})(E_1 + E_2) - P_2 S_2}. \tag{18.8a}$$

Substituting the numerical values of our example, we obtain

$$ER_2 = \frac{4000}{400PE_{12} - 4000} = \frac{10}{PE_{12} - 10}. \tag{18.8b}$$

Again, we show the nature of the relationship conveyed by Eq. (18.8a) by calculating values of ER_2 for a range of values of PE_{12}.

PE_{12}	11	12	15	20	30
Min. ER_2	10	5	2	1	0.5

The above data are plotted in Fig. 18.1; as indicated, ER_2 is in the form of a hyperbola. Two relationships of significance are portrayed in the figure. One is the intersection of the two ER-lines. The other is the four quadrants formed by the two lines. The two ER-lines intersect at a PE_{12} of 15, and $ER_1 = ER_2 = 2$. Thus, at an exchange ratio of 2 and a PE_{12} of 15, neither firm will have immediate gains or losses from the merger. The PE_{12} that brings about this result represents a weighted average of the two PE-ratios. The weighted average can be expressed in two forms as shown below:

$$PE_{12}^* = \frac{P_1 S_1 + P_2 S}{E_1 + E_2} = \frac{2000 + 4000}{400} = 15 \tag{18.9a}$$

$$= \frac{(P_1/E_1)S_1 + (P_2/E_2)S_2}{S_1 + S_2} = \frac{1000 + 2000}{200} = 15. \tag{18.9b}$$

By the shareholder wealth constraint formulated by Larson-Gonedes, the actual exchange ratio (AER) should be bounded by quadrant I, in which the shareholders of both firms gain from the merger. In the other three quadrants, the shareholders of one or both firms will suffer a wealth loss. The calculation of merger premiums and discounts can be illustrated using the data of our example both numerically as shown in Table 18.2 and graphically as in Fig. 18.1. Four cases are presented in the table illustrating results for each of the four quadrants. For various combinations of the actual exchange ratio and illustrative values of PE_{12}, the resulting equivalent prices for the shareholders of firm 1 and firm 2 are shown in the columns headed by P_{12} and P_2^*, respectively. In the following two columns, the premium or discount for the shareholder of each firm is calculated. The corresponding merger premium in graphic terms as measured in Fig. 18.1 is then shown in the final two columns of Table 18.2.

Table 18.2 Calculation of merger premiums or discounts

Case	AER	PE_{12}	P_{12}	P_2^*	Premium or (discount)		Merger premium to	
					$(P_{12} - P_1)/P_1$	$(P_2^* - P_2)/P_2$	1	2
1	2.5	20	22.86	57.15	$+14.3\%$	$+42.9\%$	AB	BC
2	2.5	16	18.29	45.72	-8.6%	$+14.3\%$	$-FG$	FH
3	2.5	12	13.71	34.28	-31.4%	-14.3%	$-KM$	$-JK$
4	1.0	12	24.00	24.00	$+20.0\%$	-40.0%	MN	$-JN$

$$P_2^* = \text{value of } P_2 \text{ on the basis of the AER} = P_{12}\text{AER}$$

$$P_{12} = (PE_{12})(EPS_{12}) = \frac{(PE_{12})(E_1 + E_2)}{S_1 + S_2(ER)}$$

$$\text{Case 1: } P_{12} = \frac{20(400)}{100 + 100(2.5)} = \frac{8000}{350} = \$22.86.$$

$$\text{Case 2: } P_{12} = \frac{16(400)}{350} = \frac{6400}{350} = \$18.29.$$

$$Case\ 3:\ P_{12} = \frac{12(400)}{350} = \frac{4800}{350} = \$13.71.$$

$$Case\ 4:\ P_{12} = \frac{12(400)}{100 + 100(1.0)} = \frac{4800}{200} = \$24.00.$$

Conn and Nielsen calculated the premium or discount combinations for major mergers defined as involving an acquired firm with assets of at least $10 million prior to the merger. The period covered was 1960 through 1969 for a sample of 131 mergers. To avoid premerger announcement effects, the variables P_1 and P_2 were calculated using an average of monthly high and low share prices during the period three to five months prior to the month of merger announcement. The postmerger results were calculated for the month following the consummation of the merger.

Conn and Nielsen make the calculations with reference to announcement date, merger consummation date, and for the month following the consummation of the merger. The results are summarized in Table 18.3.

Table 18.3 Number of mergers by ex post quadrant and changes in quadrant status from month of announcement to month following merger consummation

From period of	Announcement				Consummation				Month following consummation			
	I	II	III	IV*	I	II	III	IV	I	II	III	IV
Announcement												
I	78				66	8	3	1	60	14	3	1
II		36			4	25	7	0	5	23	8	0
III			12		0	3	8	1	1	3	5	3
IV				5	2	0	1	2	1	0	2	2
Consummation												
I					72				64	7	0	1
II						36			2	32	2	0
III							19		1	1	15	2
IV								4	0	0	1	3
Month following consummation												
I									67			
II										40		
III											18	
IV												6

* The roman numerals I, II, III, IV refer to the quadrants in which the *ex post* price-earnings ratios fall based on the prior decision rules.
Source: R. L. Conn and J. F. Nielsen, "An Empirical Test of the Larson-Gonedes Exchange Ratio Determination Model," *Journal of Finance*, June 1977, 754.

Two statistical tests were developed by Conn and Nielsen. A nonparametric chi-square test of the hypothesis of equal likelihood that a merger will fall in any one of the four quadrants is rejected at the 1% level. A first-difference test of the Larson-Gonedes model was also statistically significant. Conn and Nielsen observed that the statistical tests supported the Larson-Gonedes model, but they also noted and were concerned about the relatively large 40% of the mergers which did not fall into quadrant I. But rarely did the stockholders of the acquiring firm gain while the acquired stockholders lost. This result is similar to those obtained by Halpern and Mandelker which we'll discuss later. In any event, the pattern suggests a competitive market among acquiring firms in merger activity.

Conn and Nielsen noted that a large number of mergers fell into quadrant III; in these mergers, the postmerger market valuation of the combined entity was less than the sum of the valuations of the acquiring and acquired firms prior to the merger announcement. However, Conn and Nielsen acknowledged that leakages of merger information might occur even earlier than the three to five months lead time they used in their study. They also recognized that analyzing the effects of the merger only one month after the consummation date might be too restrictive. It would be of interest to analyze the results over longer periods of time subsequent to the merger. Finally Conn and Nielsen did not provide any numerical measures of possible changes in risk resulting from the merger.

B. TESTS OF MERGER RETURNS[1]

In a somewhat different spirit, another series of empirical studies of mergers have used comparative studies of merger performances to test for synergy from mergers. Progressive improvements in methodology were developed leading to the use of asset pricing models and explicit recognition of the role of possible changes in risks resulting from the mergers.

Kelly [1967] was the first to study merger profitability by means of security market measures. Using a sample of 21 firms for which acquisitions yielded at least a 20% increase in sales, Kelly also compiled a second sample of 21 "nonmerging" firms (having no more than a 5% increase in sales due to merger) which, in all other respects, matched the original 21 one for one. The period covered was from 1946 to 1960. Five measures of profitability (percentage change in price of common stock, in price-earnings ratio, in earnings per share, in net sales per common share, and in profit margin) were developed. The percentage change was computed from the average values of the respective parameters during the premerger period to the average of the postmerger period. (The premerger period was defined as the five years preceding the merger, the postmerger period as the five years following the merger.)

Nonmerging companies yielded insignificantly higher profit margin increases

---

[1] This section draws heavily on Krouse [1975].

and gains in earnings per share; merging companies were somewhat better in comparisons based on price-earnings ratios and sales per share. In terms of capital gains (changes in stock prices), neither merging nor nonmerging companies were superior. In net, Kelly's conclusion was that mergers had little impact on the profitability (to shareholders) of acquiring companies and hence yielded little or no synergy.

While better than earlier studies, Kelly's work has shortcomings: in particular, his small sample and "matching technique" raise questions about the scope of his analysis and the adequacy of his comparison standard. Nonetheless, Kelly's work is important in that he measured changes in capital market values, and a standard of comparison, or control for other factors, is part of the test of merger gains.

Hogarty [1970] comes much closer in developing evidence on investment returns to test for merger synergy. For 43 firms, he develops an investment performance index based on changes in stock market values (adjusted for dividends). He then compares these indexes for acquiring firms with similarly constructed indexes for their respective industries. On an annual basis, the mean difference between the "investment performance" of acquiring firms in mergers and their industry average was a negative 5%—the "gain" of merging was 5% per year less (and significant at a 10% level). This result implies negative synergy. While Hogarty attempts to control for other factors affecting market-value changes by comparing each merging firm with the average performance of its industry, this method is open to a variety of obvious criticisms.

Lev and Mandelker [1972] employ an explicit paired-comparison experimental design which potentially could alleviate some of the objections one may make regarding the appropriateness of comparing the market-value performance of selected firms with their industry averages as a test of merger synergy. Measuring profitability by the annual rate of return of the market (with dividends reinvested and adjusting for stock splits), they calculated the difference between the postmerger five-year average and premerger five-year average for 69 firms. Subtracting the respective pre- and postmerger average of a matching firm from that of an acquiring firm, they tested difference in the mean residuals. (Measuring differences before and after the merger in this fashion corrects, or controls, for other factors which are presumed to identically affect the market value of the matching firm.) The market valuation of the acquiring firm increased an average of 5.6% more than that of the matching control firms, and this difference was significant at a 10% level. The practical problem of selecting a match to a merging firm which is adequately comparable both before and after the merger severely attenuates the results obtained by Lev and Mandelker.

In summary to this point, the evidence on capital market gains made by acquiring firms in mergers is conflicting, and is confounded by legitimate criticisms of the samples, methodologies, and control devices used to account for excluded variables. It is in this setting that the studies of Halpern [1973] and Mandelker [1974] appear. These two analyses have a somewhat common and particular experimental design which, while introducing other subtle problems, attempts to meet systematically the principal criticisms of earlier studies.

1. Halpern

Halpern attempts to directly measure buyer and seller premiums in mergers in a sample of approximately 75 acquisitions. Basically his method is to adjust the observed market prices of acquiring and acquired firms for general market variations during the period when merger information affects their share prices: the price change which remains unexplained by market variations is that attributable to the merger.

Two estimates are required to make the proposed share-price adjustments and measurements. First, Halpern needs a base period, the interval before the announcement date during which merger information is reflected in the stock prices. To determine this, he employs the "residual technique" developed by Fama, Fisher, Jensen, and Roll, and runs the following time-series regression:

$$_jR_{i,t} = \alpha_i + \beta_{1j}R_{m,t*} + \beta_{2j}R_{I,t*} + \epsilon_{i,t}, \tag{18.10}$$

where $_jR_{i,t}$ is the *price relative* for company i in industry j during the month t, $_jR_{I,t*}$ is the industry price relative, and $_jR_{m,t*}$, the market price relative. The regression yields estimates of $\hat{\alpha}_i$, $\hat{\beta}_i$, and $\hat{\beta}_2$. Substituting these, he rewrites the regression equation in the form:

$$\epsilon_{i,t} = {_jR_{i,t}} - \hat{\beta}_{1j}R_{I,t*} - \hat{\beta}_{2j}R_{m,t*} - \alpha_i. \tag{18.11}$$

Halpern then notes that if all of company i's price relative in month t could be explained by industry or market price relatives, the value of the merger, as measured by $\epsilon_{i,t}$, would be zero. Thus, a nonzero $\epsilon_{i,t}$ indicates that firm i's share price is not entirely accounted for by "normal" factors. Since mergers are unusual events, we would expect the estimated residuals to display unusual behavior during the merger adjustment period. A base date can then be chosen as that date before which "abnormal" residuals were observed. Because of extraneous influences, cross-sectional residuals (over merging firms) were calculated over time relative to the announcement date.

Halpern's analysis indicates that on the average, merger information is available for seven months before the *announcement* date. From the twenty-third until the eighth month prior to announcements, the cumulative average of Halpern's residuals are randomly increasing and decreasing. From the seventh month onward, they increase steadily. Average residual values are small and vary in size until the large positive value is encountered in the seventh month. Also, a large proportion of positive residuals in the seventh month seems to strengthen this result.

The second element of Halpern's analysis is calculating adjusted security prices. Excluding data from the 12 months prior to the merger, Halpern runs the following equation for each firm using five years of monthly observations:

$$R^b_{k,t} = \alpha^b_k + B_1 R^b_{m,t} + B^b_2 R^b_{I,t} + \epsilon. \tag{18.12}$$

From the estimates $\hat{\alpha}^b_k$, $\hat{\beta}^b_1$, and $\hat{\beta}^b_2$ and the actual price relative in the market and industry for the adjustment interval, Halpern calculates the unbiased estimates of the expected price relative for each firm. Multiplying this relative by the base period price and adjusting for dividends paid during the adjustment period, he then obtains an unbiased estimate of the adjusted price. After calculating the gains to "buyers" and "sellers," the firms were classified as "larger" or "smaller" on the basis of their equity value at the base date. Halpern finds that the mean gain prior to dividend adjustment of larger firms exceeded those of smaller firms by a factor of 4. After the dividend adjustment, the gains were smaller for both firm types and approximately equal in absolute amount. Adjustments also had a tendency to make negative gains less negative and at times turned negative "gains" into positive ones.

Subsequently Halpern calculates price premiums, the gain relative to a base price, for both acquiring and acquired firms. While the premium accruing to smaller firms was significantly greater than zero (at 5%), the premium accruing to larger firms was not. His results suggest synergy or improvement in the performance of the smaller firms which is reflected in prices paid by acquirers.

2. Mandelker

Mandelker [1974] used the Fama and MacBeth [1973] methodology to examine the testable implications of what we have termed the "empirical market line,"

$$R_{it} = \hat{\gamma}_{0t} + \hat{\gamma}_{it} \beta_{it} + \epsilon_{it}, \tag{7.34}$$

presented in Chapter 7.

First, Fama and MacBeth estimate betas with seven years of monthly data for individual securities using the regression analog of our Eq. (7.32):

$$R_{jt} - R_{ft} = (R_{mt} - R_{ft})\beta_j + \epsilon_{jt}, \tag{7.32}$$

which is the *ex post* form of the CAPM equation. The individual betas are ranked and placed in 20 portfolios with maximum dispersion of systematic risk in the attempt to minimize the measurement error in the beta estimates.

Second, they use the next five years to recalculate the betas and average them to obtain the portfolio betas. The betas for individual securities are updated every 10 months on the basis of the return data for the preceding five years.

Third, using monthly data for the next four years, they run cross-sectional regressions for each month across the 20 portfolios utilizing Eq. (7.34), the empirical market line. These provide estimates of γ_0 and γ_1, which have been used as measures of the empirical market line parameters in a number of other studies.

Mandelker used the Fama and MacBeth procedures, adding two additional steps for his study of mergers.

Fourth, he estimated the betas for individual firms involved in mergers, using the *ex post* form of the asset pricing relation, Eq. (7.32). The time period measured covered months prior to the merger as well as months following it.

Fifth, he calculated residuals for each month, using the gamma values from Eq. (7.34) and utilizing the values of returns and betas calculated in the fourth step.

Mandelker tested two hypotheses. One was that acquisitions took place in a market under conditions of perfect competition. The other was the hypothesis of efficient capital markets with respect to information on acquisitions. The stockholders of the acquired firms received cumulative average residuals that were positive, indicating that they earned abnormal gains from the mergers. This suggests that the acquired firms may have had unique resources whose values are realized to a greater degree by mergers. Alternatively, the acquired firms may have been operating at below their optimal levels of efficiency, and the mergers were seen as increasing the effectiveness of their operations. The possible benefits to be derived from the acquired firms are apparently perceived by a number of potential acquirers. The competition in the market for acquisitions results in competitive prices for the acquired firms. The acquiring firms appear to operate in a competitive market so that the prices they pay for the acquired firm's stock result in normal returns on the acquisitions. The acquiring firms earn a rate of return equal to other investment or production activities of similar risks. The average residuals for the acquiring firms are generally positive, but not statistically significant. This finding controverts the argument that acquiring firms overpay and lose from mergers.

With respect to the hypothesis of efficient capital markets, Mandelker's findings are consistent with the view that the stock market operates efficiently with respect to information on mergers. The price movements which take place at the time of the merger announcement and even before reflect all valuable information about the merger preceding the effective date of the transaction. The stock prices of the constituent firms at the date when the merger is consummated reflect the economic gains expected. The stock prices of the merged firms do not undergo postmerger adjustments. While significant changes in betas were observed, the rates of return adjusted efficiently to the changes in risk. Stockholders were not misled by accounting manipulations in mergers or by the artificial increase in earnings per share resulting from the differential price-earnings ratio game played by acquiring firms. The view that mergers reflect the desires of managers to control larger firms and their emphasis on growth maximization imply losses to the acquiring stockholders. But the finding of positive average residuals for the acquiring firms is inconsistent with the managerialism hypothesis. There are also public policy implications of the findings of the Mandelker study which were developed more fully by Ellert, whose results are covered in the following section.

3.   Tests of Market Power Issues

One view of mergers is that by gaining monopoly power from acquisitions acquiring firms are then able to achieve higher returns. Ellert's studies [1975, 1976] provide data on this issue by measuring the impact of regulatory activities of government agencies. His findings are combined with the earlier studies to provide an empirical basis for testing the monopolization theory of mergers. Ellert's data, like the earlier findings of Halpern [1973] and Mandelker [1974], indicate that the impact on the market prices of merging firms takes place 7 to 12 months prior to the actual merger.

For acquiring firms, the evidence indicates that while the cumulative average residual (CAR) is generally positive during this period it is either not significant or the magnitude of the change in CAR during this period is small. This evidence is inconsistent with the managerial theory and its related growth maximization prediction. It is also inconsistent with the monopolistic exploitation theory, at least in providing monopoly gains to acquiring firms.

Both Mandelker and Ellert find that very substantial increases in the CAR of acquiring firms take place during the period from 4 to 8 years prior to the merger activity. This is consistent with the hypothesis set forth by both Mandelker and Ellert that the differentially higher efficiency of acquiring firms prior to mergers leads to their subsequent expansion both externally and internally. With respect to acquired firms, both Mandelker and Ellert find that their CARs are significantly negative in the years and months running up to the period when information about their upcoming acquisition by others becomes available. In the subsequent 7 to 12 months through the actual merger date, the CARs turn strongly positive and are highly significant by statistical tests.

The finding of positive residuals for the acquired firms in the 7 to 12 months preceding the merger is consistent with the theory of monopoly control with all the gains going to the acquired firms. However, the evidence of negative CARs in the period running up to the time information on the mergers becomes available is consistent with an alternative explanation. The inefficient utilization of economic resources by the management of the firms prior to the merger leads to their acquisition by firms with a record of above-average performance. Hence the evidence leans in the direction of efficiency and/or synergy as the explanation rather than the managerial or monopoly theories.

If differential efficiency between acquired and acquiring firms were the explanation for mergers, it is likely that there would be a number of acquiring firms bidding for an individual acquired firm. Competition among acquiring firms would, on the average, eliminate gains to the acquiring firm from the merger activity. This is consistent with the general findings of Mandelker and Ellert. If the acquiring firms had a unique synergistic relationship with an individual acquired firm, the gains from the merger would be attributable to both and could not be allocated individually. This is consistent with Halpern's finding that the absolute dollar amount of the gains is equally divided between acquiring and acquired firms. However, Halpern, Mandelker and Ellert find that while the absolute gains of acquired firms were statistically significant, neither the percentage premium returns nor CARs for the acquiring firms were statistically significant.

These results are also consistent with synergy that is not dependent on a one-to-one relationship with a specific firm. If a number of acquiring firms regard themselves as having a synergistic relation with the firm not using its resources efficiently, then competition among the acquiring firms would wipe out the synergy gains for the acquiring firms. Hence the finding of no significant gains for acquiring firms is consistent with differential efficiency as well as nonfirm specific synergy. But no direct tests of the alternative explanations were performed. However, the evidence is unambiguously consistent with the hypothesis of a perfectly competitive acquisitions market. Thus the empirical findings of Ellert add to a growing body of evidence that helps to distinguish between alternative hypotheses of mergers as well as provide tests of stock market efficiency and the competitiveness of the market for corporate acquisitions.

C. MANAGERIAL POLICIES IN A VALUATION FRAMEWORK

In the perspective of alternative merger theories and empirical tests, the foundation has been provided for guides to managerial policies toward merger and acquisition decisions. From an operational standpoint, mergers and acquisitions should be related to a firm's general planning framework. These requirements have been set forth in detail in other studies [Weston, 1970]. Here we focus on merger policies in a valuation framework. We make the concepts explicit by using an illustrative case example to convey the ideas.

The Allison Corporation is a manufacturer of materials handling equipment with heavy emphasis on forklift trucks. Because of a low internal profitability rate and lack of favorable investment opportunities in its existing line of business, Allison is considering merger to achieve more favorable growth and profitability opportunities. It has made an extensive search of a large number of corporations and has narrowed the candidates to two firms, for a number of considerations. The Connors Corporation is a manufacturer of agricultural equipment and is strong in research and marketing. It has had high internal profitability and substantial investment opportunities. The Dorden Company is a manufacturer of plastic toys. It has a better profitability record than Connors.

Some relevant data on the three firms are summarized in Table 18.4.

Additional information on market parameters includes a risk-free rate, R_f, of 6% and an expected return on the market, $E(R_m)$, of 11%. Each firm pays a 10% interest rate on its debt. The tax rate, τ_c, of each is 50%. A period of 10 years is estimated for the duration of supernormal growth, T.

From the information provided we can first formulate the accounting balance sheets for the three firms (Table 18.5).

Table 18.4 Comparative statistics for the year ended 1978

	Book value per share	Price/ earnings ratio (P/E)	Number of shares (millions)	Debt ratio, % (B/S_A)	Beta for existing leverage	Internal profit- ability rate (r)	Invest- ment rate (K)	Growth rate (g)
Allison	$10.00	5.40	5	30	1.2	.04	0.1	.004
Connors	40.00	11.70	1	30	1.4	.12	1.5	.18
Dorden	40.00	9.88	1	30	1.6	.14	1.0	.14

Table 18.5 Accounting balance sheets (millions)

	Allison	Connors	Dorden
Debt	$15	$12	$12
Equity	50	40	40
Total assets	$65	$52	$52

Dividing the internal profitability rate r by $(1 - \tau_c)$ and multiplying by total assets, we get the net operating income. From the net operating income we can obtain the market price per share and the total market value that would have to be paid for each of the three companies (Table 18.6).

Table 18.6 Market price per share

		Allison	Connors	Dorden
1)	Total assets (millions)	$65	$52	$52
2)	Earning rate, $r \div (1 - \tau_c)$	.08	.24	.28
3)	Net operating income (1) × (2) (millions)	$5.2	$12.48	$14.56
4)	Interest on debt (millions)	1.5	1.20	1.20
5)	Profit before tax (millions)	3.7	11.28	13.36
6)	Taxes at 50% (millions)	1.85	5.64	6.68
7)	Net income (millions)	1.85	5.64	6.68
8)	Number of shares of common stock (millions)	5	1	1
9)	Earnings per share of common stock, (7) ÷ (8)	$ .37	$ 5.64	$ 6.68
10)	Price-earnings ratio (information provided)	5.4 ×	11.7 ×	9.88 ×
11)	Market price per share, (9) × (10)	$ 2.00	$66.00	$66.00
12)	Total market value of equity, (11) × (8) (millions)	$10	$66	$66

We now have earnings per share, market values per share, and total market values of equity for use in the subsequent analysis.

One popular criterion for evaluating desirability of making acquisitions from the standpoint of the acquiring company is to determine the effect on its earnings per share. Table 18.7 illustrates these effects based on the data in the present example.

It can be seen that the merger effects on Allison's earnings per share is a substantial decline. The percentage dilution in Allison's earnings per share would be 47% if Connors were acquired and 39% if Dorden were acquired. We believe that this

Table 18.7

| | Effects on Allison's Earnings per Share if it Merges: | |
	With Connors	With Dorden
1) Number of new shares* (millions)	33	33
2) Existing shares (millions)	5	5
3) Total new shares (millions)	38	38
4) Earnings after taxes (millions of dollars)	5.64	6.68
5) *Add* Allison's after-tax earnings (millions of dollars)	1.85	1.85
6) Total new earnings (millions of dollars)	7.490	8.530
7) New earnings per share, (6) ÷ (3), $	.197	.225
8) *Less* Allison's old earnings per share, $	.370	.370
9) Net effect	(.173)	(.145)
10) Percent dilution [(9 ÷ 8)100]	47%	39%

* Each share of Connors and Dorden has a market value 33 times that of Allison. Hence 33 shares times the 1 million existing shares of Connors and Dorden is the total number of new Allison shares required.

widely used criterion is in error. It is the effect on market value that is relevant, not the effect on earnings per share.

In a valuation framework it is necessary to make a forecast of the key variables affecting value after the merger has taken place. This requires an in-depth business analysis of each proposed merger in terms of its impact on the key valuation factors. From the background provided, we observe that Allison is a manufacturer of materials-handling equipment. Connors is a manufacturer of agricultural equipment with strength in research and marketing. Dorden is a manufacturer of plastic toys. While Dorden has a better profitability record than Connors, the toy industry is under the pressure of continuously creating new ideas and concepts if growth and profitability of a toy manufacturing firm are to continue. In addition, there seems to be less potential for favorable interaction of management capabilities in a merger between Allison and Dorden than there would be in a merger between Allison and Connors. Connors is known to have a strong research organization which may be able to develop new products in Allison's area of materials-handling equipment. This merely sketches the kind of favorable carry-over of capabilities that may be achieved in a merger between Allison and Connors. Reflecting these qualitative considerations, the following estimates are made of the new financial parameters of the combined firms.

	NOI	r	K	g
Allison/Connors (AC)	18	.14	1.0	.14
Allison/Dorden (AD)	16	.13	1.0	.13

We can now proceed to evaluate the two alternative acquisition prospects, using a valuation analysis. First, we calculate the new beta for the merged company under the two alternatives. The beta for the combined companies is a market-value weighted average of the betas of the constituent companies. We use the new betas in the security market line equation to obtain the cost of equity capital for each of the two combined firms:

$$\beta_{AC} = 1.2\left(\frac{10}{10 + 66}\right) + 1.4\left(\frac{66}{10 + 66}\right)$$

$$= .1579 + 1.2158 = 1.374 = 1.37$$

$$k_e(AC) = R_f + [E(R_m) - R_f]\beta_{AC}$$

$$= .06 + [.05]1.37 = .1285 = 12.85\%$$

$$\beta_{AD} = 1.2\left(\frac{10}{10 + 66}\right) + 1.6\left(\frac{66}{10 + 66}\right)$$

$$= .1579 + 1.3895 = 1.547 = 1.55$$

$$k_e(AD) = .06 + .05(1.55),$$

$$= .1375 = 13.75\%$$

Given the debt cost of 10% and the cost of equity capital as calculated, we can then proceed to determine the weighted average cost of capital for the two combined firms.

	AC	AD
Debt, B	27	27
Equity, S	76	76
Value, V^L	103	103

We now continue our calculations:

$$\text{WACC} = k_0 = k_e(S/V) + k_d(1 - \tau_c)(B/V)$$

$$k_0(AC) = .1285\left(\tfrac{76}{103}\right) + .05\left(\tfrac{27}{103}\right)$$

$$= .0948 + .0131 = .1079 = 10.8\%;$$

$$k_0(AD) = .1375\left(\tfrac{76}{103}\right) + .05\left(\tfrac{27}{103}\right)$$

$$= .1016 + .0131 = .1147 = 11.5\%.$$

We now have all the information required to calculate the valuation of the two alternative combinations. We will use the Modigliani-Miller valuation model, Eq.

(12.7) in the expressions below:

$$V^L = \frac{[E(\widetilde{NOI})](1 - \tau_c)}{\rho} + \tau_c B + K[E(\widetilde{NOI})](1 - \tau_c)\left[\frac{r - WACC}{WACC(1 - WACC)}\right]T,$$

(12.7)

where

K = the percent of earnings invested in new assets, $K \gtrless 1$,

r = the tax-adjusted rate of return on new assets, $i > WACC$,

T = the number of years during which $r > WACC$ (i.e., the number of years during which the firm experiences a rate of growth greater than the economy).

For ease of computation, we shall combine the first two terms in the equation. Equation (11.5) defined V^L as

$$V^L = \frac{E(\widetilde{NOI})(1 - \tau_c)}{\rho} + \tau_c B.$$

(11.5)

In addition, Eq. (12.6a) defined V^L as

$$V^L = \frac{E(\widetilde{NOI})(1 - \tau_c)}{WACC} = \frac{E(\widetilde{NOI})(1 - \tau_c)}{k_0}.$$

(12.6a)

The two are equivalent formulations of V^L, so we can use the simpler, (12.6a). We can now insert the numerical values to determine the value of the combined firm if Allison merges with Connors (AC) or alternatively with Dorden (AD). The results are shown below:

Merger AC:

$$V^L = \frac{18(.5)}{.108} + 1[18(.5)]\left[\frac{.14 - .108}{.108(1 - .108)}\right]10$$

$$= 83.33 + 9\left(\frac{.032}{.096336}\right)10$$

$$= 83.33 + 90(.3322)$$

$$= 83.33 + 30.00$$

$$= 113.33 \approx 113.$$

Merger AD:

$$V^L = \frac{16(.5)}{.115} + 1[16(.5)]\left[\frac{.13 - .115}{.115(1 - .115)}\right]10$$

$$= 69.57 + 8\left(\frac{.015}{.101775}\right)10$$

$$= 69.57 + 80(.1474)$$

$$= 69.57 + 11.79$$

$$= 81.36 \approx 81.$$

Table 18.8 Comparison of two mergers

	Allison/Connors (millions)	Allison/Dorden (millions)
Postmerger value, V	$113	$81
Less amount of debt, B	− 27	27
Value of equity, S	86	54
Less Allison's premerger market value	10	10
Gain in equity value	76	44
Cost if acquired at market price	66	66
Gain in value (loss)	10	(22)

Using the results obtained, we make a summary comparison of the gains or losses from the two alternative mergers. The data are summarized in Table 18.8.

The data show that, based on estimates of the key parameters, a gain in value of $10 million would result from a merger between Allison and Connors. However, the merger between Allison and Dorden would result in a loss in valuation amounting to $22 million. We believe that comparing the effects on value represents the conceptually correct way of approaching merger analysis from a managerial standpoint. The results of this comparison permit some margin of error, yet clearly indicate that a merger between Allison and Connors is preferable to a merger between Allison and Dorden. Indeed, the gain in value of $10 million could be divided between the shareholders of Allison and those of Connors. Allison could pay a premium over the current market price of Connors and still achieve a gain in net value that would go to its shareholders.

The foregoing illustrative case example provides a general methodology for the management analysis of merger activity, which utilizes a number of principles: The acquiring firm is considering other firms as alternative merger candidates. To come up with a rational basis for analysis, prospective returns and risk from alternative merger combinations must be estimated. While historical data may be used as inputs, a forecast or estimate must be made of the returns and risk that may arise after alternative merger combinations have taken place.

Thus the forecast of the variables that measure prospective returns and risk for alternative postmerger combinations is critical to a sound evaluation of merger alternatives. The estimates of net operating earnings and of their potential growth may or may not reflect synergy between the combining firms depending on the nature and potential of the combined operations. Analysis in depth of the relevant product markets and the results of combining the organizations of the two firms is required. The resulting forecasts are subject to prediction errors which are sometimes of substantial magnitude.

We may obtain the measures of risk by market-value weighted averages of the betas (the systematic risk) of the combining firms. With the estimates of the new betas, along with a selection of market parameters, we can calculate the new relevant cost of capital for the merged firm, utilizing the security market line relationship. We must also estimate the effect of alternative merger combinations on the cost of debt. With estimates of the cost of equity capital and the cost of debt, we must formulate appropriate capital structure targets for the combined firm and use these to estimate a cost of capital.

Having obtained an estimate of the applicable cost of capital and the estimates of returns discussed earlier, we can apply valuation principles to formulate estimates of the value of alternative merger combinations. From these, we deduct the value of the acquiring firm in the absence of the merger to determine the total value remaining, which we next compare with the cost of acquiring the firm or firms with which a merger is being considered. If the value contributed by the merger exceeds the cost of the acquisition, the acquiring firm has a basis for making an offer that includes a premium to the shareholders of the acquired firm, yet still provides an increase in value for the shareholders of the acquiring firm.

Merger analysis thus involves the application of the same basic principles of cost of capital and valuation discussed in earlier chapters. However, the problems of application are more difficult. While merger analysis is fundamentally a form of capital budgeting analysis, the magnitudes of the alternative projects are usually quite large. Unlike standard capital budgeting projects in fields related to the firm's past experience, some mergers involve the analysis of industrial activities quite different from the firm's own experience. Prediction errors can therefore be substantial. Our emphasis has been to avoid compounding large potential errors of forecasting with unsound valuation procedures. What we have done in the foregoing illustration has been to utilize the predictions of the relevant return and risk data and apply sound valuation procedures to the process of determining whether the costs of a prospective acquisition result in commensurate increases in prospective values.

D. SUMMARY

A number of economists have performed various empirical tests of alternative merger theories. Larson and Gonedes constructed a model specifying a region of mutually beneficial mergers. Conn and Nielsen used this model to measure market value changes in order to test the hypothesis that mergers were undertaken to increase values. They found some support for the hypothesis. They also observed that information about the intended merger appeared to be capitalized in the market well in advance of the actual merger announcement.

Studies of merger profitability have yielded inconsistent results, probably due to econometric problems of selecting a basis for comparison. Kelly found that profit margins of merged firms were not significantly different from other firms and concluded that mergers had little impact on profitability. Another study by Hogarty indicated that there was negative synergy in most mergers. Lev and Mandelker found the opposite result—that, on the average, the values of merging firms increased more than those of other firms.

Halpern used a linear regression model to identify the approximate instant when the news of the merger reached the market, and found it to be as much as seven months prior to the formal announcement. Using this result, he found that there were significant positive gains to mergers, particularly for smaller (acquired) firms.

Mandelker found that the stockholders of acquired firms experienced positive cumulative average residuals, indicating that they gained from mergers. The acquiring firms also experienced positive residuals, but these were not statistically significant. Mandelker's results support the hypothesis of market efficiency in that price movements reflect information "leaks" about mergers which occur in advance of the formal announcements. Rates of return also adjust efficiently to changes in risk that result from mergers. The competitive acquisitions market hypothesis was also supported since the prices paid by acquiring companies result in normal returns on the acquisitions. Ellert's findings are similar, supporting efficiency or synergy as results of mergers rather than the managerial and monopoly theories.

In the perspective of alternative merger theories and tests, we developed a framework for managerial analysis of prospective mergers. Basically, good forecasts of postmerger returns and risks are required as a starting point. Standard capital budgeting procedures, cost of capital analysis and valuation principles presented in the preceding chapters are then applied. The aim is to determine whether the value of the merged firm exceeds the value of the constituent firms. If it does, the merger has a valid social and private justification.

PROBLEM SET

18.1 Firm 1 and firm 2 are contemplating a merger in which firm 1 will acquire firm 2. The information in Table 18.9 has been developed on the two firms. In the questions and answers related to this case, let subscripts 1 and 2 refer to the individual firms. Let ER_1 stand for the exchange ratio from the standpoint of firm 1 and ER_2 stand for the exchange ratio from the standpoint of firm 2. AER is the actual exchange ratio. PE_{12} will be the price-earnings ratio for the merged firm, after the merger.

a) The managements of the two firms are negotiating the terms of the merger, specifically the number of shares of firm 1 that will be exchanged for one share of common stock of firm 2. Three alternative criteria are under consideration:

i) The effect on each firm's earnings per share after the merger.
ii) The expected market value of the merged firm's common stock per one original share immediately after the merger.

Table 18.9

	Total earnings, E	Number of shares of common stock, S	Earnings per share, EPS	Price-earnings ratio, PE	Market price per common share, P
Firm 1	$400	100	$4.00	15	$60
Firm 2	$200	400	$0.50	30	$15

iii) The expected market value of the holdings per one original share after synergistic effects have been developed, for example, three years after the merger.

Of the three criteria, which would it be most rational for the management and shareholders of the firms to emphasize?

b) Using the estimates of the following range of post-merger PE_{12} values, determine which of ER_1 will equate P_1 to $P_{12}\%$.

Range of possible PE_{12} values: 12, 15, 20, 25, 30.

Make a graph on which ER_1 is plotted against PE_{12} and label the curve ER_1.

c) Calculate the ER_2 that will equate P_2 to P_{12} for the PE_{12} estimates given in part (b). Plot the curve ER_2 on the graph begun in part (b).

d) At what PE_{12} do the two curves intersect? What is the significance of this point of intersection?

e) For the following combinations, calculate and graph the premium or loss to each firm.

Actual exchange ratio (AER)	0.4	0.4	0.4	0.4	0.2	0.1
Post-merger price-earnings ratio (PE_{12})	30	26	22	18	16	18

18.2 The Jordan Corporation is a manufacturer of heavy-duty trucks. Because of a low internal profitability rate and lack of favorable investment opportunities in the existing line of business, Jordan is considering merger to achieve more favorable growth and profitability opportunities. It has made an extensive search of a large number of corporations and has narrowed the candidates to two firms. The Konrad Corporation is a manufacturer of materials handling equipment and is strong in research and marketing. It has had higher internal profitability than the other firm being considered, and has substantial investment opportunities.

The Loomis Company is a manufacturer of food and candies. It has a better profitability record than Konrad. Data on all three firms are given in Table 18.10.

Table 18.10

	Book value per share $	Price-earnings ratio, PE	Shares (millions of dollars)	Debt ratio, B/S	β for existing leverage	Internal profit-ability rate, r	Invest-ment rate, K	Growth rate, g
Jordan	20.00	6	4	1	1.4	.06	0.5	.03
Konrad	20.00	15	2	1	1.2	.12	1.5	.18
Loomis	20.00	12	2	1	1.5	.15	1.0	.15

Additional information on market parameters includes a risk-free rate of 6% and an expected return on the market, $E(R_m)$, of 11%. Each firm pays a 10% interest rate on its debt. The tax rate, τ_c, of each is 40%. Ten years is estimated for the duration of supernormal growth.

a) Prepare the accounting balance sheets for the three firms.

b) If each company earns the before-tax r on total assets in the current year, what is the net operating income for each company?

c) Given the indicated price-earnings ratios, what is the market price of the common stock for each company?
d) What will be the immediate effects on the earnings per share of Jordan if it acquired Konrad or Loomis at their current market prices by the exchange of stock based on the current market prices of each of the companies?
e) Compare Jordan's new beta and required return on equity if it merges with Konrad with the same parameters that would result from its merger with Loomis.
f) Calculate the new required cost of capital for a Jordan-Konrad combination and for a Jordan-Loomis combination, respectively.
g) Compare the increase in value of Jordan as a result of a merger at market values with the cost of acquiring either Konrad or Loomis if the combined firms have the following financial parameters:

	NOI	r	WACC	K	g
Jordan/Konrad	32	.16	9.3%	1.0	.16
Jordan/Loomis	36	.13	10%	1.0	.13

18.3 Tables 18.11 through 18.13 provide financial information on three well-known conglomerate firms for which data adjusted for stock splits, etc., were readily available for 1962–77. Data for the Dow-Jones Industrial Average are also presented for the same time period in Table 18.14.

Table 18.11 International Telephone & Telegraph Corporation

Year	Earnings per share $	Dividends per share $	Dividend payout, %	Price range	PE ratio	Average yield %
1962	1.21	0.50	41	29– 16	19.0	2.2
1963	1.35	0.50	37	27– 20	18.0	2.1
1964	1.58	0.53	33	30– 26	18.0	1.8
1965	1.79	0.60	34	35– 24	16.6	2.0
1966	2.04	0.68	33	39– 29	16.9	2.0
1967	2.27	0.75	33	62– 36	21.6	1.5
1968	2.58	0.85	33	62– 44	20.8	1.6
1969	2.90	0.95	33	60– 45	18.4	1.8
1970	3.17	1.05	33	60– 30	14.3	2.3
1971	3.45	1.15	33	67– 45	16.4	2.0
1972	3.80	1.19	31	64– 48	14.8	2.1
1973	4.17	1.28	31	60– 25	10.2	3.0
1974	3.63	1.43	39	29–124	5.7	6.9
1975	3.20	1.52	47	25– 14	6.2	7.7
1976	4.00	1.60	40	34– 22	7.0	5.7
1977	4.14	1.76	43	36– 28	7.9	5.4

Table 18.12 Textron, Inc.

Year	Earnings per share, $	Dividend per share, $	Dividend payout %	Price range	PE ratio	Average yield %
1961	0.52	0.31	51	7– 5	12.4	4.9
1962	0.74	0.31	43	7– 5	9.1	4.6
1963	0.86	0.34	40	10– 7	10.3	3.9
1964	1.02	0.39	38	13– 9	11.4	3.3
1965	1.31	0.44	34	23–13	14.0	2.4
1966	1.77	0.53	30	26–19	13.1	2.3
1967	2.06	0.63	31	55–25	19.5	1.6
1968	2.26	0.73	32	57–40	21.7	1.5
1969	2.31	0.83	36	45–23	14.8	2.4
1970	1.99	0.90	45	26–15	10.5	4.3
1971	2.06	0.90	44	32–23	13.7	3.2
1972	2.32	0.92	40	36–30	14.4	2.7
1973	2.65	0.97	37	34–16	9.6	3.8
1974	2.83	1.08	38	22–11	6.1	6.3
1975	2.58	1.10	43	26–12	7.5	5.7
1976	3.23	1.15	36	31–20	8.0	4.4
1977	3.65	1.35	37	29–24	7.4	5.0

Table 18.13 City Investing Company

Year	Earnings per share, $	Dividend per share, $	Dividend payout, %	Price range	PE ratio	Average yield, %
1961	0.20	0.10	50	8– 3	30.9	1.6
1962	0.21	0.10	48	7– 3	25.9	1.8
1963	0.17	0.10	59	5– 4	29.0	2.0
1964	0.17	0.11	65	5– 4	27.9	2.3
1965	0.19	0.11	58	7– 4	32.9	1.8
1966	0.59	0.12	20	12– 6	15.5	1.2
1967	1.07	0.12	11	28– 9	17.7	0.6
1968	1.97	0.14	7	39–18	14.6	0.5
1969	2.35	0.26	11	35–21	12.1	0.9
1970	1.44	0.45	31	27–10	13.3	2.4
1971	1.98	0.50	25	25–14	10.1	2.5
1972	1.98	0.52	26	22–13	9.1	2.9
1973	2.28	0.57	25	16– 8	5.3	4.7
1974	1.24	0.65	52	14– 4	7.4	7.1
1975	0.97	0.66	63	9– 4	6.2	9.4
1976	2.04	0.66	32	14– 7	5.2	6.2
1977	3.01	0.77	26	16–11	4.7	5.5

Table 18.14 Dow-Jones Industrial Average (DJIA)

End of calendar year, Dec. 31	Price (end of year)	Earnings (for preceding 12 months)	PE
1962	652	36.43	17.9
1963	763	41.21	18.5
1964	874	46.43	18.8
1965	969	53.67	18.1
1966	786	57.66	13.6
1967	905	53.87	16.8
1968	944	57.89	16.3
1969	800	57.02	14.0
1970	839	51.02	16.4
1971	890	55.09	16.2
1972	1020	67.11	15.3
1973	851	86.17	9.9
1974	616	99.04	6.2
1975	852	75.66	11.3
1976	1005	96.72	10.4
1977	831	89.10	9.3

The year 1968 is generally regarded as the peak of the conglomerate merger movement. Subsequently changes in the tax laws treating mergers, in accounting rules, and in the antitrust climate took place.

a) Compare the growth rates in earnings for the three conglomerates and for the DJIA for the two time periods 1962–68 vs. 1969–77.
b) Compare the price-earnings ratios of the DJIA with price-earnings ratios of the three conglomerates for the years 1962, 1968, 1977.
c) Using the Gordon formula (Eq. 13.21a), establish some benchmarks for measuring the influence of expected growth on the price of stocks. Assume earnings (next year) of $1 per share, a required *cost of equity capital* of 10%, and a dividend payout of 40%. What is the indicated price and price-earnings ratio if the expected growth rate per annum in dividends per share is (i) 9%, (ii) 5%, and (iii) zero?
d) Given the same assumptions for the DJIA and the three conglomerates as in (c), except that $k_e = 15\%$ for the three firms, what growth rates are implied by the price-earnings ratios you obtained for the DJIA and the three firms in 1962, 1968, and 1977? How do these compare with the historical 1962–68 growth rates measured in (a)?

REFERENCES

Conn, R. L., and J. F. Nielsen, "An Empirical Test of the Larson-Gonedes Exchange Ratio Determination Model," *Journal of Finance*, June 1977, 749–760.

Ellert, J. C., *Antitrust Enforcement and the Behavior of Stock Prices.* Doctoral dissertation, Graduate School of Business, University of Chicago, 1975.

————, "Mergers, Antitrust Law Enforcement, and Stockholder Returns," *Journal of Finance*, May 1976, 715–732.

FAMA, E. F., L. FISHER, M. JENSEN, and R. ROLL, "The Adjustment of Stock Prices to New Information," *International Economic Review*, February 1969, 1–21.

FAMA, E., and J. MACBETH, "Risk, Return and Equilibrium," *Journal of Political Economy*, May 1973, 607–636.

HALPERN, P. J., "Empirical Estimates of the Amount and Distribution of Gains to Companies in Mergers," *Journal of Business*, October 1973, 554–575.

HOGARTY, T., "The Profitability of Corporate Mergers," *Journal of Business*, July 1970, 317–327.

KELLY, E., "The Profitability of Growth Through Mergers," The Pennsylvania State University, University Park, 1967.

KROUSE, C. G., "A Test of Competition in the Capital Market: The Case of Mergers," manuscript of presentation to UCLA, AT & T Seminar, August 13, 1975.

LARSON, K. D., and N. J. GONEDES, "Business Combination: An Exchange Ratio Determination Model," *The Accounting Review*, October 1969, 720–728.

LEV, B., and G. MANDELKER, "The Microeconomic Consequences of Corporate Mergers," *Journal of Business*, January 1972, 85–104.

MANDELKER, G., "Risk and Return: The Case of Merging Firms," *Journal of Financial Economics*, 1974, 303–335.

WESTON, J. F., "Mergers and Acquisitions in Business Planning," *Revista Internazionale di Scienze Economiche e Commerciali*, April 1970, 309–320.

Chapter 19

International Finance: Exchange Rate Systems

*Like the traffic lights in a city, the international monetary system
is taken for granted until it begins to malfunction
and to disrupt people's daily lives.*

Robert Solomon, *The International Monetary System*, 1945–1976,
An Insider's View, New York, Harper & Row, 1977, p. 1

A. INTRODUCTION

From a general economic standpoint the main issues in international finance relate to the volume of trade, the adjustment processes for achieving international equilibrium, and the issue of whether there are segmented international markets. Our emphasis in this book will be on the implications of adjustment processes for corporate financial policy. These in turn have implications for the activities of firms, such as sales, purchases, and investment policy.

The nature of risks in an international financial setting takes on new dimensions. We shall focus on corporate financial policies to manage these risks. In addition to the pattern of cash inflows and cash outflows which the firm develops, we shall examine the changes in its balance sheet in terms of monetary versus nonmonetary net positions. We shall also examine the use of the forward market for dealing with foreign exchange fluctuations and analyze the use of money and capital markets for managing foreign exchange risks. Issues here are whether outlays to limit the risks of exchange rate fluctuations are worth the cost. These activities will also be examined for their influence on keeping the international financial markets performing as efficient markets.

Our presentation will emphasize some basic propositions in international finance which are the key to measuring returns and costs in international financial activities. These basic relations are best understood after background material on the adjustment processes in international finance have been developed first.

B. THE INTERNATIONAL FINANCIAL MECHANISM

The international financial markets as a part of a general system of financial intermediation perform the functions of increasing efficiency in the production and exchange of goods and services. Money and prices convey information about economic alternatives and guide the choices among the alternatives. International finance, like financial intermediation in general, provides for shifting patterns of investments and savings that increase productivity and provide opportunities for saving surplus units to postpone consumption and for saving deficit units to increase the output of real goods by utilizing the savings of (surplus) units willing to consume less now and more later.

1. The Economic Basis for International Transactions

In competitive markets, prices are a measure of opportunity costs. Opportunity costs indicate how much each good costs as a result of the firm's not having produced other goods. Two concepts have been stated as the rationale for international trade: one is absolute advantage; the other is comparative advantage. A country has an absolute advantage if it is able to produce a good at a lower cost than other countries can. Thus, if a product costs $10 to produce in country A and $8 to produce in country B, an opportunity for trade is created. Country A can obtain the product from country B for only $8 worth of its export products. To create the required exports, country A must cease to produce and consume other goods that would have been worth only $8. Hence importing products at money prices below the cost of making the goods at home yields real savings.

However, the fundamental basis for international trade is not *absolute cost advantages*, but the *principle of comparative advantage*. The law of comparative advantage states that trade will be mutually advantageous if one country is relatively more efficient in producing some products and other countries are relatively more efficient in producing other products. A classic illustration is the lawyer who is a better typist than his secretary, but hires her to type his materials because his comparative advantage is his knowledge of the law. Another illustration is that country A can produce product X for $10 and product Y for $5. Country B can produce product X for $6 and product Y for $2. The situation is shown below:

	Costs of producing	
	X	Y
Country A	$10	$5
Country B	$ 6	$2

Country B thus has an absolute advantage in the production of both X and Y, but has a comparative advantage in producing product Y.

Suppose each country has $100 to spend on production. If country B spends $100 on the production of Y, it will produce 50 units. If country A concentrates production on product X, it will produce 10 units of goods. Assume further that each country desires to split its wealth of $100 equally on the consumption of goods X and Y, $50 being spent on each. Country B could sell 25 units of Y to country A for 5 units of X. Hence the consumption pattern for each country would be as follows:

Country A	$5X$	$25Y$
Country B	$5X$	$25Y$

It can be readily proved that no other pattern of allocation of production in the two countries will yield equally high levels of consumption of X and Y in countries A and B.

We can now extend the example to consider different currencies and exchange rates. Let us postulate that opportunity costs in country A are reflected in prices of $3 for X and $1 for Y, while opportunity costs in country B result in prices of 12 marks for X and 6 marks for Y. The pattern is shown below:

	X	Y
Country A	$3	$1
Country B	M12	M6

At more than 6 marks per dollar, both goods X and Y would be cheaper in country B. Country B would export both X and Y and import neither. For example, at $M8 = 1, B could sell X in A for $1.50 and Y in A for $.75. On the other hand, a rate of less than 4 marks per dollar would make both goods cheaper in country A. Country A would export both and import neither. For example, at $M2 = 1, A could sell X in B for M6 and Y in B for M2. To achieve equilibrium between the two countries, the exchange rate would have to fall somewhere between 6 and 4 marks per dollar. Equilibrium would require that the exchange rate should be at the level at which each country's exports and imports are equal in total value measured in units of its own currency.

It can be seen from the example that the relative prices of X and Y are 3 to 1 in country A and 2 to 1 in country B. With a large number of products, the cheaper one country's currency is in relation to other currencies, the larger the range of that country's products that are underselling foreign products of the same type. As a result, the importing country will need greater amounts per unit of time of the exporting country's currency in order to buy the latter's relatively cheap goods. Differences in the patterns of relative prices result from differences among countries in resources, skills, and tastes, and in social and political aspects, which in turn lead to comparative advantages in different kinds of activities. As a consequence, there will be profit incentives for businessmen to engage in trade. These private benefits will, in turn, lead to social gains as the theory describes. Ideally, exchange rates will evolve to bring the trade between countries to levels on which the exports and imports of individual countries will be in balance in their own currency.

However, the ideal result is complicated by the existence of short- and long-term capital flows associated with borrowing and lending activities, shifts in the comparative rates of development of individual industries in different countries, differences in the domestic economic development programs among individual countries. What is required is some processes by which tendencies toward imbalances in international activities can be restored to relative equilibrium. We next examine the nature of these adjustment processes.

We propose to discuss the adjustment processes for international disequilibrium, using three broad types of mechanisms. First we assume a common currency and analyze the adjustment processes through changes in incomes, prices, production, and capital flows, demonstrating that an adjustment process is required even if exchange rates are not involved. Then we introduce exchange rates and examine the adjustment process required by two extreme exchange mechanisms: One is a gold standard with fixed exchange rates. The other postulates flexible exchange rates.

2. Adjustment Processes under a Common Currency

Let us first consider the situation of California vs. the rest of the United States and the world. Let us postulate that a balance of payments deficit develops for California either because the sales of California products such as fruits and vegetables decline, or because Californians shift their purchases from goods produced in California to goods produced out of state. Initially Californians are able to spend more than they currently earn by (a) drawing from their savings accounts or (b) increasing their debts outside the state. Because Californians are selling less, their incomes are down, and in addition, their holdings of cash or other financial assets have declined or their external debts have increased. If the imbalance is small, the income adjustment may be sufficient to bring about a new equilibrium. Because of reduced income Californians will reduce buying from each other and from outsiders; they will make vigorous efforts to sell to outsiders until a new equilibrium is achieved.

However, if the imbalance is large, another aspect of the adjustment process may lead to a decline in prices and costs of production. The prices and costs of goods consumed locally will fall in relation to international goods. Consumers will switch from imports to the consumption of local goods. Producers will seek to sell export goods for which they get relatively higher prices rather than local goods.

The adjustment process described involves a decline in money income as well as in wages and prices. In theory, if prices and wages were completely flexible, this decline in income and prices could take place without a reduction in employment and production. To the extent that prices and wages are sticky rather than flexible, the drop in money income is associated with a decline in employment and production as well.

The financial aspects of the adjustment process may also involve changes in the interest rates. An excess of imports over exports is equivalent to expenditure in excess of current income, implying a form of "investment." Thus the region may be regarded as increasing its investment activity and/or borrowing activity. This places upward pressures on interest rates in the deficit region. As a consequence, a financial adjustment may take place in which the deficit is cushioned by an increased flow of funds into the deficit region. Financial institutions in the region may sell investment securities from their portfolios on the national or international market in order to earn higher rates by making local loans. This process also involves a flow of outside capital into the region, and such flows of capital finance the deficit. To some degree they cushion the corrective process and may permit it to extend over a longer period of time, thus providing far less rapid and harsh adjustments of employment, production, wages, prices, and holdings of financial assets. Some correction through income and prices will be required, however, in order to restore international equilibrium.

In the description of the foregoing adjustment process, exchange rates did not enter into the discussion. However, since national currencies do differ, shifts in the exchange rates also perform a role in the adjustment process. We can see this in the adjustment processes under both fixed and flexible exchange rates.

3. Gold Standard and Fixed Exchange Rates

The mechanism governing the relationship of prices to the flow of gold was first formulated in the mid-eighteenth century. Country *A* runs an export balance surplus, while country *B* runs a deficit. Hence gold flows into *A* while it flows out of *B*. Domestic prices in *A* rise, the prices in *B* fall. Country *A* is an attractive market in which to increase sales from other countries, and *A*'s imports increase. Country *A*'s goods are more expensive in other countries, so its export sales decrease. Thus *A*'s export surplus will be reduced or reversed until equilibrium between relative price relationships of the countries is restored. The flow of gold operates through prices to function as an adjustment mechanism for international balances of trade and payments as well as to regulate the price-change relationships between countries.

In addition to price changes, income and employment effects may also enter into the adjustment process. If the surplus country was not functioning at full employment, the export surplus increases its income and employment. The export deficit decreases income and employment in the deficit country. Also, in the adjustment process, employment may decline in *A* and increase in *B*.

Under the gold standard, the exchange rates are said to remain "fixed" through this entire adjustment process, because of the inherent assumption that gold would flow to prevent exchange rates from moving beyond the "gold points." For example, let us suppose that the British pound contains four times as much gold as the U.S. dollar: the dollar contains .05 ounce of gold while the British pound contains .2 ounce of gold. A U.S. trade deficit vis-à-vis the United Kingdom would increase the demand for pounds to pay for the imports from the United Kingdom, and the dollar price of pounds would therefore rise, say to $4.10. We could take $1,000 to the U.S. Treasury and get 50 ounces of gold since $1 contains .05 ounce of gold. Next we could transport the 50 ounces of gold to the United Kingdom, where we would get £250 in exchange: 50 ÷ .2 = 250. With the rate of exchange of $4.10 to £1 less the cost of transporting the gold amounting to $.02 for insurance and interest loss, we would net $4.08 for each pound. Multiplying $4.08 times £250 yields $1,020, or a profit of $20. Thus at any rate of exchange above $4.02 or below $3.98, by the actions of the gold arbitrageurs, the rate of exchange would be checked from falling outside the "gold points."

To the extent that a gold standard with fixed exchange rates worked, it was because maintaining two-way convertibility between a nation's monetary unit and a fixed amount of gold was a policy goal which received great emphasis and high priority. So long as it was recognized that convertibility was a major policy goal, speculative capital movements were likely to be stabilizing rather than destabilizing. In other words, the general expectation that the convertibility of the currency would be maintained was so strong that when a gold standard currency did weaken almost to its gold export points, one could reasonably assume that it would not drop much lower and indeed would probably rise. Speculators would then take the position that a rise in the value of the currency was imminent, and this would, of course, strengthen the currency.

During the post World War II period the international monetary system was not a gold standard, but rather a gold exchange standard. In addition to gold, nations held claims on the currency of other countries. Most countries simply related their exchange rates to one of the "key" or "reserve" currencies, holding part of their official reserves in that currency. Dollars and sterling were key currencies immediately after the end of World War II. Thus the monetary authorities outside the United States had the assurance of the U.S. Treasury that the two-way convertibility between dollars and gold would be maintained.

Because the growing volume of international trade required an increase in the supply of international reserves, the initial balance of payments deficits of the United States during the 1950s performed the role of augmenting the supply of key currencies. The rate at which new gold was being produced was far too low to meet the rate of growth in demand for official reserves to support the growing volume of international trade. Problems developed with the gold exchange standard in the early 1970s, giving rise to a substantial shift to the use of flexible exchange rates. In the next section, we describe the nature of the adjustment process under flexible exchange rates. This provides a foundation for the discussion of the broader issues of achieving international equilibrium under current conditions in the international economy.

4. The Adjustment Process under Flexible Exchange Rates

Under a regime of flexible exchange rates no attempt is made to tie the value of a currency to gold or to any one foreign currency. The exchanges of currencies that take place in the international financial markets are based on the forces of demand

and supply. Exchange rates are likely to be roughly related to the purchasing powers over goods and services of the respective currencies.

To illustrate the operation of the adjustment process let us assume an initial relationship of 1 dollar to 4 deutschemarks: $1 = DM 4.

Let us now assume that the volume of imports in the United States exceeds its exports in relationship to countries whose currency is the deutschemark. The demand for deutschemarks relative to dollars increases. The value of the dollar falls. For purposes of illustration, let us assume $1 = DM 2.

At the new exchange rate the prices of our imports and exports in dollars rise. For example, suppose that the Volkswagen sold in the United States for $2,000 when the exchange rate was $1 to DM 4. A sale at $2,000 provided the German exporter with DM 8,000. At the new exchange rate the German exporter still seeks to receive DM 8,000. But at the new exchange rates he must now ask $4,000 for the VW.

Similarly, at the old exchange rate the price of wheat was $4 per bushel. To obtain this price we needed to get DM 16. Now at the new exchange rates, in order to receive $4 per bushel, we need get only DM 8. Thus the prices of imports in dollars rise substantially at the new exchange rates. Conversely, the prices of exports in the foreign currency fall. The dollar price of exports could be increased and still represent substantially lower prices in the foreign currency.

In the United States at the new exchange rates, import purchases would have to be made at higher prices and export sales could be made under more favorable conditions than before. Conversely, foreign countries faced with lower prices in deutschemarks for both their imports and exports would be motivated to increase their purchases from us and reduce sales to us.

An argument for the use of flexible exchange rates is that the relations between the prices of domestic and foreign goods adjust through exchange rates. The prices of internationally traded goods carry most of the adjustment process. It is argued that under the gold standard with fixed exchange rates an incorrect exchange rate is adjusted not by changing exchange rates but by adjusting all other things. Under flexible exchange rates, when exchange rates are out of line, the correction takes place in the exchange rates themselves. Since domestic wages and prices are relatively inflexible, they cannot, in fact, make the necessary adjustments. However, exchange rates do not have the same built-in institutional barriers to upward and downward flexibility and hence they are much more flexible tools of adjustment.

A possible technical defect in flexible exchange rates arises from the fact that the devaluation or depreciation of a currency will actually further aggravate the trade deficit of a country if the sum of the price elasticities of the goods traded is less than 1. Only if the sum of the price elasticities of the goods traded is greater than 1 will the trade balance of a deficit country improve as a result of the depreciation of its currency. However, it is argued that even when the sum of elasticities is less than 1 initially, the continued high volume of imports will force people to spend larger and larger amounts of home money and income on imported goods as the home-currency price of imports continues to rise. Since incomes and holdings of financial assets are limited, people in the home country could not continue to import virtually the same physical quantities of goods. The price elasticity of imported goods would therefore rise, the sum of the elasticities would become greater than 1, and depreciation of the home currency would produce a corrective adjustment.

The further argument can be made that the home country can avoid the constraints of limited money incomes and limited financial assets by increasing the money supply as well as the supply of near-monies. But if this occurs, then it is not the low price elasticities of demand but rather the inflationary monetary policies that prevent exchange rate movements from bringing the balance of payments into equilibrium.

C. THE SHIFT FROM FIXED TO FLEXIBLE EXCHANGE RATES

We have described the adjustment processes under three alternative types of mechanisms: common currency, fixed exchange rates, and flexible exchange rates. Beginning in the 18th century and continuing through the early 1970s, the world adhered at least nominally to a gold exchange standard with fixed exchange rates. But recurrent international crises disturbed equilibrium and periodic devaluations took place. With the development of the Bretton Woods institutions after World War II, the International Monetary Fund and the World Bank, there was hope for improved stability. However, these expectations were not realized.

Particularly after the serious recession of the early 1930s, governments placed increased emphasis on full-employment policies and consequently were unwilling to accept the adjustment processes consistent with the gold standard or related systems of fixed exchange rates, which call for shrinkage in the domestic money supplies and incomes of countries with external deficits. This shrinkage occurs through contraction in the reserves of member (of Federal Reserve System) banks which must make payments to foreigners in foreign currency when the home country imports more than it exports. The process is readily summarized by a series of journal entries that would take place. For an excess of imports into the United States from Japan the journal entries are as shown in Table 19.1.

On the assumption that credit balances are not expanded, the journal entries reflect the Japanese exporter's demand to be paid. The U.S. commercial bank obtains yen from the U.S. central bank (FED) by reducing its reserves with the Federal Reserve Bank (FED). The FED had purchased the yen by paying with gold certificates. The yen received by Mr. Han in Japan become primary deposits in a commercial bank in Japan. The reserves of the commercial banks in Japan increase and so do the holdings of gold certificates by the central bank of Japan.

The net result of the journal entries is a decrease in the deposits of the U.S. importer at his commercial bank accompanied by a reduction in the commercial bank's reserves with the FED. For the U.S. central bank, member bank deposits decrease as does its gold certificate account. The opposite net transactions take place in Japan.

Table 19.1

U.S. Commercial Bank	U.S. Central Bank (FED)
Dr. Yen	Dr. Yen
Cr. Reserves with FED (Central Bank)	Cr. Gold certificates
Dr. Deposits, Mr. Smith	Dr. Member bank deposits
Cr. Yen	Cr. Yen

Commercial Bank, Japan	Central Bank, Japan
Dr. Yen	Dr. Gold certificates
Cr. Deposits, Mr. Han	Cr. Yen
Dr. Reserves with Central Bank	Dr. Yen
Cr. Yen	Cr. Member bank deposits

For a normal volume of transactions, the exchange rate remains unchanged. However, there is a contraction in the effective money supply in the United States and an expansion in Japan. In utilizing its gold or other foreign-exchange reserves, the central bank is covering the country's balance of payments deficits. The shrinkage of domestic bank reserves would bring about a deflationary adjustment of the classic gold standard kind. The resulting multiple contraction in the domestic money supply would deflate incomes and prices, reduce spending on imports, and stimulate efforts to achieve exports.

However, to counteract the deflationary tendency, the governmental authorities of the deficit country may engage in offsetting transactions. The central bank in the deficit country could buy domestic securities to replenish the reserve positions of its commercial banks. It could also lower reserve requirements to strengthen the reserve positions of its commercial banks. Alternatively, in its domestic fiscal policy, the deficit country could run internal deficits to offset the influences of its external deficits.

The reverse process may take place in a country with a balance of payment surplus. It could offset the expansion of the domestic reserves of its commercial banks by selling securities in the open market. Alternatively, it could run substantial governmental surpluses.

Counteracting governmental policies can neutralize the adjustment processes under any exchange system. The practice of neutralizing the international adjustment process was particularly pronounced after World War II when greater emphasis was given to full employment policies in individual national economies. The unwillingness to accept the automatic adjustment processes of an international financial system was also accompanied by efforts to intervene against freedom of trade and the free flow of capital between nations. A desire to control the adjustment process has led to tariff increases, the use of import quotas, and restrictions on lending and investing abroad.

Unwillingness to accept the international adjustment process resulted in increasing flows of international reserves away from deficit countries. In the case of the United States, the early balance of payments deficits were welcomed. They had the positive benefit of mitigating the dollar shortage and of increasing the rate of growth in international foreign exchange reserves. However, as the gold account of the United States shrank and as its balance of payments deficits increased rather than diminished, speculators began to become increasingly confident that the foreign exchange value of the dollar would not be maintained. Speculative sales of the dollar in favor of stronger currencies such as the German mark or Swiss franc further aggravated the drain on U.S. foreign exchange reserves. Finally these pressures built up to such a degree that the United States recognized the inevitable and in August 1971 suspended gold convertibility: *de facto* the dollar began to float in terms of its value in relation to other major currencies.

A new element was added to the international economic scene in 1974 when the Organization of Petroleum Exporting Countries (OPEC) quadrupled the price of oil. This step placed burdens on all oil-import nations. The United States' response was unwillingness to permit the domestic price of oil and petroleum products to reflect the new world price levels of oil as set by the OPEC cartel. By imposing price controls on oil and petroleum products in the United States, the government discouraged domestic exploration and production while effectively subsidizing domestic consumption. As a result, the domestic consumption of oil in the United States was not greatly affected, and oil imports as a percentage of the total U.S. oil consumption increased in the years following 1974. Thus in 1977, for example, the United States imports of oil reached $46 billion, contributing importantly to the 1977 balance of trade deficit of approximately $27 billion. Under a regime of floating currencies, the value of the dollar in relation to the German mark, the Swiss franc, and the Japanese yen declined substantially.

Among the U.S. government policies attempting to deal with the increased price of oil was a shift in emphasis from the use of oil to that of coal. However, new problems arose when a prolonged strike of the coal miners' unions in 1978 forced the United States to reevaluate the desired shift to coal and to continue to rely on foreign oil imports, resulting in even larger oil purchases and trade deficits in 1978. In early 1978, the United States sought to offset speculative effects on the declining value of the dollar by support operations. These support operations were facilitated by substantial swap agreements with the central banks of countries with strong currencies. However, without corrective changes in the U.S. energy policy, support operations are insufficient to counter the strong expectations that continued U.S. trade deficits will result in a further weakening of the foreign exchange value of the dollar.

The previous analysis has made use of a balance of payments analysis in appraising the need for international adjustment processes, including the devaluation or depreciation of the dollar. We next consider in somewhat more detail the role of a balance of payments analysis in defining the kinds of policies and adjustments that may have to be made in corporate financial policy in order to deal with changes in the international financial environment.

D. BALANCE OF PAYMENTS ANALYSIS

The balance of payments of a nation is a double-entry accounting statement of its transactions with the rest of the world during a specified time period, usually one quarter or one year. Inflows are recorded as a plus. (Sometimes the words "receipts" and "credits" are used but the terms "plus" and "minus" are preferred as being more neutral in their implications.) Outflows are a minus. (Sometimes called "debits" or "payments" but again "minus" is preferred.)

The basic entries in the balance of payments statement can be summarized into four categories of items as shown in Table 19.2. This summary indicates how the adjustment process can be complicated by a number of relationships going in different directions. Thus, if a given country runs a deficit by having an excess of imports over exports, instead of settling the balance by payments in the foreign currency, a number of other offsets may take place. As shown in Table 19.2, the offsets can take the form of increasing liabilities to foreigners, decreasing claims on foreigners, liquidating assets, or decreasing other foreign investments. Consequently, there will be a lag in the pressures that would result if payments in foreign currencies had to be made immediately. This lag will postpone the contraction in the money supply or incomes of the deficit country.

Table 19.2 Effects on the balance of payments

Plus	Minus
Exports	Imports
Increase liabilities to foreigners	Decrease liabilities to foreigners
Decrease claims on foreigners	Increase claims on foreigners
Decrease investments; sell assets	Increase investments; buy assets

Similarly, a country that is increasing its investments abroad will improve its investment position, but it will be creating minus entries in its current balance of payments statement. The long-run outlook for a country which is making substantial foreign investments, however, may be favorable as a result of the future income that may be generated from those investments.

It is for the purpose of separating such influences that it is useful to analyze balance of payment statements. Until May 1976, the U.S. Department of Commerce followed the format for the balance of payment statement shown in Table 19.3.

In the traditional balance of payments statement, line 11, the balance on goods and services, is considered significant as an indicator of the basic trade position of the United States. However, some people argue for greater emphasis on line 15, the balance on current account, in the belief that U.S. government grants are determined by diplomatic and military considerations which are not necessarily responsive to international economic conditions.

Still others suggest emphasis on line 26, the balance on current account and long-term capital, referring to it as the "basic balance." This balance is basic in the

Table 19.3 Illustrative U.S. balance of payments

1.	Merchandise balance
2.	Exports
3.	Imports
4.	Military transactions
5.	Transportation and travel
6.	Investment income, net
9.	Other services, net
11.	Balance on goods and services
12.	Remittances
13.	Balance on goods, services, and remittances
14.	U.S. government grants
15.	Balance on current account
16.	Long-term private investment
26.	Balance on current account and long-term capital (basic balance)
	Nonliquid items
28.	Claims
30.	Liabilities
33.	Net liquidity balance
	Liquid items
35.	Claims
38.	Liabilities
42.	Official reserve transactions balance
43.	Liquid liabilities to official agencies
46.	U.S. reserve assets

sense that it excludes the influence of more volatile items such as short-term capital movements. It places trade transactions and long-term capital movements "above the line." Short-term capital movements are placed "below the line" on the theory that they are accommodating or compensating transactions which have no real impact on the reserve position of the nation. However, short-term capital movements may represent transactions initiated because of expectations of changes in relative interest rates or foreign exchange rates. Thus, they may not represent simple accommodating entries. Furthermore, with more flexible exchange rates, long-term private capital movements became less important as adjustment flows to maintain fixed exchange rates; instead they are more responsive to prospects for returns from investments in different countries.

Line 33, the net liquidity balance, is a broad indicator of the magnitude of changes in liquidity claims or accommodations required to maintain fixed exchange rates. The net liquidity balance measures the amount of required private lending by the United States (if the balance is positive) or the required private lending by foreigners (if the balance is negative) before changes in foreign exchange reserves or official balances become necessary.

Finally, line 42, official reserve transactions balances, measures what type and how much official action must be taken to accommodate or settle the effects of all other transactions. The use of this balance reflects the view that the key demarcation line in international transactions is between those of the official agencies and all other transactors.

Under flexible exchange rates, greater emphasis is placed on the fundamental transactions which determine the probable direction of changes in the foreign exchange value of the dollar. These include: balance on merchandise trade; balance on goods and services; balance on goods, services, and remittances; and current account balance. These balances successively indicate the effect of the basic transactions and of government loan and grant policies on the supply and demand for the currency of a country and, therefore, its probable exchange-rate movements. The short- or long-term private capital flows are not reflected since the prospects which give rise to their movements change within relatively short periods and hence do not have any fundamental, continuing effects on exchange rates.

The significance of alternative measures of "the balance of payments" depends on the circumstances of an individual country and the pattern of international economic developments taking place. To determine all contributing factors, one must analyze as many components of information as possible, including the more general economic developments taking place in individual countries. The balance of payments is one among a number of information sources that may be analyzed within a more general economic framework to develop judgments about adjustment processes taking place which will have implications for changes in foreign exchange rates as well. It is this kind of analysis which is required for formulating corporate financial policies of firms substantially affected by changes in foreign exchange rates. In Chapter 20, we analyze some of the fundamental relationships which reflect the broad economic adjustment forces reflected in balance of payments statements.

E. SUMMARY

International financial markets direct savings flows into countries which can best employ the funds. A country is said to have an absolute advantage if it is able to produce a good at a lower cost than other countries are. The law of comparative advantage states that trade will be mutually advantageous since different countries have different relative efficiencies in producing different goods. A comparative advantage means that even though one country could produce some good more efficiently in absolute terms, it has other opportunities which are so superior that it is preferable for some other country—less efficient and with lower opportunity cost—to produce the good.

The exchange rate between countries will tend to be the rate that equates import and export values in the long run, considering the comparative production advantages of each country. Shifts in comparative advantages over time cause capital to flow into and out of countries. Coupled with this is short-run disequilibrium in the balance of trade, which triggers an adjustment process. If countries (or states) are linked by a common currency, changes in comparative advantage will produce income shifts toward the country which has increased its comparative advantage. If the shift is large, it will result in declining prices and production costs for the country that has lost comparative advantage. The decline in prices will restore the trade balance but with relative incomes changed. A country that imports more than it exports is, in effect, borrowing on future production. This increased borrowing drives up the interest rate in the country with the trade deficit.

With a gold standard or fixed exchange rates, countries with surplus exports receive gold in exchange. Domestic prices in the country receiving gold rise, and this price increase in turn stimulates imports to restore the trade balance. Income and employment may also be affected by the adjustment process. Convertibility of currencies to gold at fixed rates forces exchange rates to be fixed. With fixed exchange rates, disequilibrium forces all adjustments to be on prices of individual goods or capital flows.

Floating exchange rates were introduced to allow currency value adjustments based on the relative price changes of each country. The primary advantage is that the exchange rate is a market rate and is more flexible than wages and prices in general. One problem with flexible exchange rates is that if the price elasticity of traded goods is less than 1, devaluation may make a country with a trade deficit even worse off. Ultimately, however, income adjustments would restore the trade balance.

When a trade surplus or deficit occurs, the settlement with the foreign country directly affects the domestic money supply: a trade deficit will reduce the money supply. Changes in money supply may cause domestic inflation or deflation. However, the government is able to protect domestic prices from the impact of money supply changes by making offsetting adjustments to the actual money supply.

Various countries have come up with numerous programs to avoid or retard the automatic exchange rate adjustment processes. These include tariffs, duties, quotas, and domestic price controls. Typically the impact is to force the adjustment into another direction, such as changes in real output. An example is the United States' response to the OPEC oil price increase, which ultimately has led to large balance of trade deficits.

In balance of payments accounting, inflows are recorded as pluses and outflows as minuses. A trade imbalance may trigger a number of offsetting transactions. The numerous subtotals of the balance of payments accounts provide much information about the short- and long-run developments for the economy of any country. Analysis of balance of payments trends can be useful for formulating corporate financial policy in managing exposure to exchange rate fluctuations and in the use of the international financial markets.

PROBLEM SET

19.1 You are given the prices of products in two countries as shown below:

	Product	
	X	Y
Country *A*	$3	$1
Country *B*	M12	M6

At an exchange rate of 5 marks per dollar, describe the pattern of exports and imports between countries *A* and *B*.

19.2 Country *A* and country *B* are each on a full gold standard with fixed exchange rates. Country *A* runs an export balance surplus while country *B* runs an export balance deficit. Describe the adjustment process that will restore balance to the flow of trade between the two countries.

19.3 Country *A* and country *B* are on the gold standard. The currency of country *A* contains .1 ounce of gold while the currency of country *B* contains .025 ounce of gold. What will be the par exchange rate between the two currencies?

19.4 Consider two countries *C* and *D* operating in a world with completely flexible exchange rates. Country *C* runs a substantial export surplus to country *D*, which experiences a substantial trade deficit. Assuming no initial offsetting capital flows, explain the adjustment process to bring the trade between the two countries into balance.

19.5 Keep in mind Table 19.4 listing the effects of individual transactions on the balance of payments.

Table 19.4 Effects on the balance of payments, country *A*

Plus (P)	Minus (M)
1. Exports	1. Imports
2. Increase liabilities to foreigners	2. Decrease liabilities to foreigners
3. Decrease claims on foreigners	3. Increase claims on foreigners
4. Decrease investments; sell assets	4. Increase investments; buy assets

Indicate the plus entry and the minus entry for the following transactions. For example, the country exports goods in the amount of $1000 paid for by the importer by a check on a foreign bank. The entry would be:

$$P1 \quad \$1000 \qquad M3 \quad \$1000$$

a) Country *A* exports $10,000 of goods to country *I* paid for by the importer by a check on his account with a bank in country *A*.

b) Country *A* imports $5000 worth of merchandise paid for by a check on a bank in country *A*.

c) Direct investment income of $2000 was received by a firm in country *A* from a foreign subsidiary which paid by drawing a check on a bank in its own country *F*.

d) A multinational firm domiciled in country A made an investment of $1 million on a direct basis to establish a foreign subsidiary in country G. Payment was made by drawing on its bank account in country A.

e) A citizen of country A made a gift of $3000 to a friend in a foreign country who deposited the check drawn on a bank in country A in his own bank in country M.

f) A citizen in country A bought an airline ticket to Europe which he purchased from Lufthansa Airlines by a check drawn on a bank in country A.

Appendix A to Chapter 19

Interactions of National Income, the Money Supply, and the Balance of Payments

I. Some fundamental economic relationships are:

A. *The quantity equation.*

$$MV = PQ,$$

where

M = quantity of money,
V = its velocity or turnover,
P = price level,
Q = total quantity of goods transacted.

B. *The national income equations.*

$$Y = C + I + G + X, \qquad \text{income creation,}$$

$$Y = C + S + T + M, \qquad \text{income disposal,}$$

$$Y = PQ, \qquad\qquad\qquad \text{definition,}$$

where

Y = gross national product,
C = consumption,
S = savings,
I = investment,
T = tax revenues,
G = government spending,
X = exports,
M = imports.

C. Both the quantity or monetarist approach and the national income or effective demand approach provide useful information on both domestic and international economic and financial developments. For some issues one framework may be used; for different issues the other framework may provide understanding more directly.

D. In either the quantity theory or national income equations framework, an increase in exports (X) from country A into country B (more imports M in country B) results in greater income in country A. If both countries were at full employment equilibrium before this shift, prices would rise in A and fall in B.

E. Table A19.1 illustrates how the income and price adjustment process might work using the national income equations.

Table A19.1 Exports and imports in the National Income Accounts in country A

	Income generated					Income disposal				
	C	I	G	X	Y	C	S	T	M	Y
Situation 1	750	100	100	50	1000	750	100	100	50	1000
Initial change				+20						
Further changes	+25					+25	+7	+9	+4	
Situation 2	775	100	100	70	1045	775	107	109	54	1045

Basic macroeconomic relations that apply:

$D = Y - T,$ D = disposable personal income,

$\Delta D = \Delta Y - \Delta T,$

$c = \dfrac{\Delta C}{\Delta D},$ c = marginal propensity to consume out of disposable income,

$s = \dfrac{\Delta S}{\Delta D},$ s = marginal propensity to save,

$m = \dfrac{\Delta M}{\Delta D},$ m = marginal propensity to import,

$r = \dfrac{\Delta T}{\Delta Y},$ r = marginal tax rate,

$\Delta Y = \dfrac{\Delta X}{1 - c + cr},$ $k = \dfrac{\Delta Y}{\Delta X} = \dfrac{1}{1 - c + cr}$ = income multiplier.

Assume: $c = .7, s = .2, m = .1, r = .2$. Then as a result of the increase in exports by 20, the new equilibrium, Y, is 1045, an increase of 45. This can be shown by the ΔY relation:

$$\Delta Y = \frac{\Delta X}{1 - c + cr} = \frac{20}{1 - .7 + (.7)(.2)} = \frac{20}{1 - .7 + .14} = \frac{20}{.44} = 45.5.$$

We can also quantify the other relations.

$$\Delta D = \Delta Y - \Delta T \cdot \Delta T = r \, \Delta Y = .2(45) = 9.$$

$$\Delta D = 45 - 9 = 36.$$

$$\Delta C = c \, \Delta D = .7(36) = 25.2 \simeq 25.$$

$$\Delta S = s \, \Delta D = .2(36) = 7.2 \simeq 7.$$

$$\Delta M = m \, \Delta D = .1(36) = 3.6 \simeq 4.$$

Appendix B to Chapter 19

A Formal Analysis of
the Effects of Devaluation

For the purpose of numerical illustration assume these facts. The value of the U.S. dollar declines from $1 = DM4 to $1 = DM3. The average price of goods exported to Germany from the United States is $50 or DM200 before the decline in value of the dollar. The average price of goods sold by Germany as imports into the United States is DM24 or $6 before the devaluation.

Case 1 The sum of elasticities is greater than 1. [*Note:* Symbols used: P = price, Q = quantity.]

U.S. IMPORTS (Fig. B19.1)

Before devaluation:
Demand for U.S. imports $Q = 400 - 20P$. Constant supply price = $6, which represents $DM\frac{24}{4} = \$6$. Substitute $6 into the demand equation to obtain $Q = 400 - 120 = 280$.

After devaluation:
Have the same demand curve, but the price is now $DM\frac{24}{3} = \$8$. When $8 is substituted into the demand equation, $Q = 400 - 160 = 240$ is obtained, that is, a decrease of U.S. imports from 280 to 240.

U.S. EXPORTS (Fig. B19.2)

Before devaluation:
Demand for U.S. exports $Q = 85 - 1.2P$. Constant supply price = $50 received by U.S. exporter. Substitute $50 into the demand equation to obtain $Q = 85 - 60 = 25$.

After devaluation:
The supply price remains the same, but the demand for exports reflects the reduced price in DM that would be paid by the German importer. The new DM value of the dollar is $\frac{3}{4}$ of the previous value. Hence, the slope of the new demand curve is

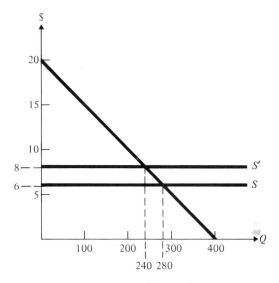

Fig. B19.1 United States imports

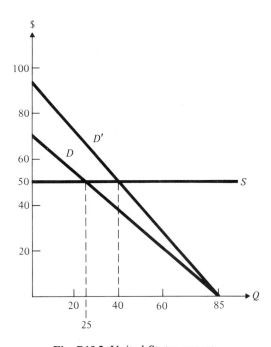

Fig. B19.2 United States exports

Table B19.1

	U.S. imports (M)			U.S. exports (X)			Balance of trade (X − M)
	P	Q	Value	P	Q	Value	
Before devaluation	$6	× 280 =	1680	$50	× 25 =	1250	− 430
After devaluation	$8	× 240 =	1920	$50	× 40 =	2000	+ 80

Sum of elasticities $\dfrac{.43 + .67}{2} + \dfrac{2.4 + 1.13}{2} = .55 + 1.76 = 2.31$, which is greater than 1.

$(\frac{3}{4})(1.2) = .9$. The new demand curve is $Q = 85 - .9P$. Substitute the $50 into the demand equation $Q = 85 - 45 = 40$, resulting in an increase of U.S. exports from 25 to 40. We summarize the results in Table B19.1.

Comments: This is the situation in which the sum of the price elasticities of demand for the product is greater than 1, as shown above. As a consequence, the trade balance of the United States, which was negative on these products, now becomes positive after devaluation. It moves from −430 to a +80.

Case 2 The sum of elasticities is less than 1.

U.S. IMPORTS (same as Case 1, Fig. B19.1) and U.S. EXPORTS (see Fig. B19.3).
Before devaluation:
Demand for U.S. exports $Q = 35 - .2P$. Constant supply price = $50 received by U.S. exporter. Substitute $50 into the demand equation to obtain $Q = 35 - 10 = 25$.
After devaluation:
The supply price remains the same, but the demand for exports reflects the price in DM that would be paid by the German importer. The new DM value of the dollar is 3 which is $\frac{3}{4}$ the previous value. Hence, the slope of the new demand curve is $(\frac{3}{4}) \times (.20) = .15$. The new demand curve is $Q = 35 - .15P$. Substitute the $50 into the demand equation $Q = 35 - 7.5 = 27.5$. We summarize the results in Table B19.2.

Table B19.2

	U.S. imports (M)			U.S. exports (X)			Balance of trade (X − M)
	P	Q	Value	P	Q	Value	
Before devaluation	$6	× 280 =	1680	$50	× 25 =	1250	− 430
After devaluation	$8	× 240 =	1920	$50	× 27.5 =	1375	− 545

Sum of elasticities $\dfrac{.43 + .67}{2} + \dfrac{.4 + .27}{2} = .55 + .33 = .88$, which is less than 1.

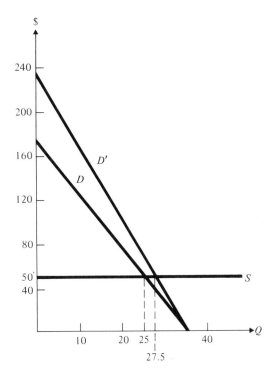

Fig. B19.3 United States exports

Comments: Thus, in the situation where the sum of the price elasticities of demand is less than 1, the negative trade balance of the United States is aggravated. It is not directly predictable what the effects of devaluation will be on the trade balance of a country.

However, the effect on prices in the devaluing country is more predictable. The dollar price of products imported into the United States becomes higher because of the lower value of the dollar. While initially the nominal dollar price of foreign exports may remain unchanged, the price has actually decreased when expressed in DM. Hence, given the more favorable demand conditions in the foreign country at the lower value of the dollar, an increase in the dollar price charged by the U.S. exporter may still represent a lower price when expressed in DMs. These relationships suggest that devaluation has further inflationary effects in the country which devalues. Recall also that the basic cause of devaluation may be associated with inflation in costs and prices in the devaluing country.

REFERENCES

ALIBER, R. Z., *The International Money Game*, 2nd ed. Basic Books, New York, 1976.

CAVES, R. E., and R. W. JONES, *World Trade and Payments: An Introduction*. Little, Brown, Boston, 1973.

KINDLEBERGER, C. P., *International Economics*, 4th ed. Richard D. Irwin, Homewood, Ill, 1968.

KREININ, M. E., *International Economics: A Policy Approach*, 2nd ed. Harcourt Brace Jovanovich, New York, 1975.

ROLFE, S. E., and J. L. BURTLE, *The Great Wheel: The World Monetary System.* Quadrangle/The New York Times Book Company, New York, 1973.

SOLNIK, B. H., *European Capital Markets.* Lexington Books, Lexington, Mass, 1973.

SOLOMON, R., *The International Monetary System, 1945–1976, An Insider's View.* New York, Harper & Row, 1977.

YEAGER, L. B., *International Monetary Mechanism.* Holt, Rinehart and Winston, New York, 1968.

Chapter 20

International Business Finance: Concepts and Applications

The exchanges between countries are at par only, whilst they have precisely that quantity of currency which in the actual situation of things, they should have to carry on the circulation of their commodities.

David Ricardo, *Principles of Political Economy and Taxation*, Gonner Edition, London, G. Bell and Sons, Ltd., 1927, pp. 213–214.

As a foundation for some business applications we first summarize the fundamental exchange rate relationships.

A. FUNDAMENTAL EXCHANGE RATE RELATIONSHIPS

We plan to treat five basic relationships:

1) Consistent foreign exchange rates
2) The Fisher effect
3) The interest rate parity theorem
4) The purchasing power parity theorem
5) The measurement of real gains or losses

As general background for discussing each of these five relationships, we briefly present some institutional material. International business transactions are conducted in many different currencies. However, a U.S. exporter selling to a foreigner expects to be paid in dollars. Conversely, a foreign importer buying from an American exporter may prefer to pay in his own currency. The existence of the foreign

exchange markets allows buyers and sellers to deal in the currencies of their preference. The foreign exchange markets consist of individual brokers, the large international money banks, and many commercial banks which facilitate transactions on
behalf of their customers. Payments may be made in one currency by an importer
and received in another by the exporter.

The foreign exchange rate represents the conversion relationship between currencies and depends on demand and supply relationships between the two currencies.
The exchange rate is the price of one currency in terms of another. Exchange rates
may be expressed in dollars per foreign unit or in foreign currency units per dollar.
An exchange rate of $.50 to FC 1 shows the value of 1 foreign currency unit in terms
of the dollar. We shall use E_0 to indicate the spot rate, E_f to indicate the forward rate
at the present time, and E_1 to indicate the actual future spot rate corresponding to
E_f. An exchange rate of FC 2 to $1 shows the value of the dollar in terms of the
number of foreign currency units it will purchase. We will use the symbol X with
corresponding subscripts to refer to the exchange rate expressed as the number of
foreign currency units per dollar. With this as a background we shall discuss each of
the fundamental relationships.

1.   Consistent Foreign Exchange Rates

Equilibrating transactions take place when exchange rates are not in proper relationships with one another. We illustrate this situation by some examples with (unrealis-
tically) rounded numbers to make the arithmetic of the calculations simple. The
analysis will point in the right direction if the reader remembers the general maxim
that arbitrageurs will seek to "sell high and to buy low." First we discuss the consistency of spot rates. Let us suppose the dollar value of the pound sterling is $2 in New
York City and $1.90 in London. The following adjustment actions would take place:
In New York City, we sell £190 for $380. We sell the pounds in New York because
this is where the pound value is high. In London, we sell $380 for £200. In London
the dollar value is high in relation to the pound. Thus £190 sold in New York City for
$380 can be used to buy £200 in London at a gain of £10. The sale of pounds in New
York causes the value of the pound to decline, and the purchase of pounds in London
causes their value to rise until no further arbitrage opportunities are left. Assuming
minimal transportation costs, we postulate that the same foreign exchange prices
obtain in all locations.

The relationship between the currencies of two individual localities can be generalized across all countries and is referred to as the *consistent cross rate*. It works in
the following fashion: Assume that the equilibrium relation between the dollar and
the pound is $2 to £1 and that that between the dollar and the franc is $.25 to fr. 1.
Now, suppose that in New York City, £.10 = fr. 1. The following adjustment process
will take place: We sell $200 for £100 and use these to obtain fr. 1000, which in turn
will buy $250. We thus make a profit of $50 over our initial $200. In general, then, we
sell dollars for pounds and pounds for francs since the pound is overvalued with
respect to the dollar-to-pound and dollar-to-franc relationships. The dollar will fall
in relation to the pound and the pound will fall in relation to the franc until consis-

tent cross rates are reached. If the relation were fr. 1 = £.125, the cross rates would be consistent. We check using the following relation:

$$\$1 = £.5, \qquad £1 = \text{fr. } 8, \qquad \text{fr. } 1 = \$.25.$$

The product of the right-hand sides of all three relationships must equal 1. *Check:* .5 × 8 × .25 = 1. We have thus established consistency between foreign exchange rates.

2. The Fisher Effect

The Fisher effect holds for the relationship between interest rates and the anticipated rate of inflation. While it can also be regarded as a purely domestic economic relationship, it is also used to develop some of the international relationships we shall present later. The Fisher effect states that nominal interest rates rise to reflect the anticipated rate of inflation. The Fisher effect can be stated in a number of forms, as shown below:

$$\frac{P_0}{P_1} = \frac{1+r}{1+R_n}, \tag{20.1a}$$

$$1 + r = (1 + R_n)\frac{P_0}{P_1}, \tag{20.1b}$$

$$r = \left[(1 + R_n)\frac{P_0}{P_1}\right] - 1, \tag{20.1c}$$

$$R_n = \left[(1 + r)\left(\frac{P_1}{P_0}\right)\right] - 1, \tag{20.1d}$$

where

P_0 = initial price level,
P_1 = subsequent price level,
P_1/P_0 = rate of inflation,
P_0/P_1 = relative purchasing power of the currency unit,
r = real rate of interest,
R_n = nominal rate of interest.

While the Fisher effect can be stated in a number of forms, its importance can be conveyed by a simple numerical example. Over a given period of time, if the price index is expected to rise 10% and the real rate of interest is 7%, then the current nominal rate of interest is

$$R_n = [(1.07)(1.10)] - 1 = 17.7\%.$$

Similarly, if the nominal rate of interest is 12% and the price index is expected to rise 10% over a given time period, the current real rate of interest is

$$r = [1.12(\tfrac{100}{110})] - 1 = 1.018 - 1 = .018 = 1.8\%.$$

3. The Interest Rate Parity Theorem (IRPT)

The interest rate parity theorem is an extension of the Fisher effect to international markets. It holds that the ratio of the forward and spot exchange rates will equal the ratio of foreign and domestic gross interest rates. The formal statement of the IRPT may be expressed as follows:

$$\frac{X_f}{X_0} = \frac{1 + R_{f0}}{1 + R_{d0}} = \frac{E_0}{E_f}, \qquad (20.2)$$

where

X_f = current forward exchange rate expressed as FC units per \$1,
E_f = current forward exchange rate expressed as dollars per FC 1,
X_0 = current spot exchange rate expressed as FC units per \$1,
E_0 = current spot exchange rate expressed as dollars per FC 1,
R_{f0} = current foreign interest rate,
R_{d0} = current domestic interest rate.

Thus, if the foreign interest rate is 15% while the domestic interest rate is 10% and the spot exchange rate is $X_0 = 10$, the predicted current forward exchange rate will be

$$X_f = \frac{1 + R_{f0}}{1 + R_{d0}} (X_0)$$

$$= \frac{1.15}{1.10} (10) = 10.45;$$

that is, 10.45 units of foreign currency equal \$1. Thus, viewed on an annual basis, the foreign forward rate is seen to be at a discount of 4.5%. If we assume the time period of a transaction to be 90 days, we must rework the problem accordingly. The first step is to prorate the interest rates on a quarterly basis: Thus for 90 days,

$$X_f = \frac{1.0375}{1.025} (10)$$

$$= 10.122;$$

that is, the 90-day forward rate is 10.122, and it follows that on the quarterly basis the discount on the 90-day forward rate is 1.22%.

Alternatively, we can formulate the example to determine the effect on interest rates of expected changes in future foreign exchange rates. There is a dynamic relationship here that needs to be recognized. If the foreign exchange rate is expected to rise over a period of time, relative interest rates will reflect the rate of change in the expected foreign exchange rates, as illustrated in Fig. 20.1.

Figure 20.1 shows that as the value of the foreign currency falls (the exchange rate expressed in the number of foreign currency units per dollar rises), the ratio of foreign interest rates to domestic interest rates will rise. At the inflection point of the

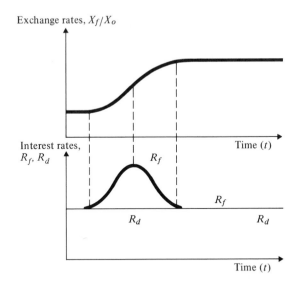

Fig. 20.1 Illustration of the interest rate parity theorem

rise in the expected number of foreign currency units per dollar, the ratio of foreign interest rates to domestic interest rates will peak. When the expected ratio of the foreign currency to the domestic currency levels off, then the former ratio of gross foreign interest rates to gross domestic interest rates will be reestablished.

We could also use the **IRPT** to express our results in terms of the interest rate parities required for given relationships between spot and future exchange rates. The transactions that result in interest rate parity are referred to as *covered interest arbitrage*. First, an arbitrage outflow situation will be described. The basic assumptions are as follows:

U.S. interest rate 5%,

German interest rate 7%,

Spot exchange rate $1 = DM 4,

Forward exchange rate discount 1% per annum.

The following arbitrage transaction will take place. In New York, we borrow $100,000 for 90 days (one quarter) at 5%. The loan repayment at the end of 90 days is

$$\$100{,}000[1 + (5\% \times \tfrac{1}{4})] = \$101{,}250.$$

At the spot exchange rate, we convert the $100,000 loan into DM 400,000. In Germany, we invest the DM 400,000 for 90 days at 7% and receive at the end of 90 days

$$DM\ 400{,}000[1 + (7\% \times \tfrac{1}{4})] = DM\ 407{,}000.$$

A covering transaction is also made. To insure against adverse changes in the spot rate during the 90-day investment period, we sell the investment proceeds forward. Since the forward exchange rate discount is 1%, then

$$4[1 + (1\% \times \tfrac{1}{4})] = DM\ 4.01$$

is required in exchange for $1 in 90 days (forward). We sell the investment proceeds forward, i.e., we contract to receive DM $407,000 \div 4.01 = \$101,496$. The result of the two transactions is shown below:

$$\text{Arbitrage profits} = \text{investment receipts} - \text{loan payments}$$

$$= \$101,496 - 101,250$$

$$= \$246.$$

The arbitrage transaction increases the *demand* for currency in New York and the *supply* of funds in Germany, which in turn raises the interest rate in New York and lowers it in Germany, thus narrowing the differential. The covering transaction increases the supply of German forward exchange while the arbitrage investment action increases the demand for spot funds. Both forces tend to increase the forward exchange discount. The interest rate differential decreases and the forward rate discount increases until both are equalized.

An arbitrage inflow takes place when the forward exchange rate discount exceeds the interest rate differential. The basic facts are now:

U.S. interest rate 5%,

German interest rate 6%,

Spot exchange rate DM 4 = $1,

Forward exchange rate discount 2% per annum.

The arbitrage transaction involves borrowing in the foreign country. In Germany, we borrow DM 400,000 for 90 days at 6%. The loan repayment at the end of 90 days is

$$DM\ 400,000[1 + (6\% \times \tfrac{1}{4})] = DM\ 406,000.$$

At the spot exchange rate, we convert the DM 400,000 loan into $100,000. In New York, we invest the $100,000 for 90 days at 5% and receive at the end of 90 days

$$\$100,000[1 + (5\% \times \tfrac{1}{4})] = \$101,250.$$

Again, we would make a covering transaction. To insure coverage for the loan repayment, we buy DM 406,000 forward. At a 2% forward exchange rate discount, it costs DM $4[1 + (2\% \times \tfrac{1}{4})] = DM\ 4.02$ to buy $1 forward. Thus, repayment of DM 400,000 requires

$$DM\ 406,000 \div 4.02 = \$100,995.$$

Thus we have

$$\text{Arbitrage profits} = \text{investment receipts} - \text{loan repayments}$$
$$= \$101{,}250 - \$100{,}995$$
$$= \$255.$$

The arbitrage transaction increases the *demand* for deutschemarks and increases the supply of dollars. The U.S. interest rate decreases and the German rate rises; thus the differential increases. Covering transactions increase the spot supply of deutschemarks, thus decreasing the premium on forward deutschemarks. The interest rate differential and the forward exchange rate discount decrease until both rates are equalized.

As a result of the covered interest arbitrage transactions of the types described, the relationships expressed by the IRPT do indeed hold. They determine the home-currency cost that will be incurred when a purchase or sale is made involving a future payment or receipt. We discuss these purchases and sales in a later section in which we present some of their corporate finance implications.

4. The Purchasing Power Parity Theorem (PPPT)

The purchasing power parity doctrine states that people will value currencies for what they will buy. If an American dollar buys the same basket of goods and services as five units of a foreign currency, we have an exchange rate of five foreign currency units to the dollar or 20 cents per foreign currency unit. An attempt to compare price indexes to computed purchasing power parity assumes that it is possible to compile comparable baskets of goods in different countries. As a practical matter, the parity rate is, in general, estimated from changes in the purchasing power of two currencies with reference to some past base period when the exchange rate was theoretically in equilibrium. Hence, in using the PPPT our emphasis is on formulating it as a statement that *changes* in exchange rates reflect *changes* in the relative prices between two countries. In formal terms, the PPPT may be stated as follows:

$$CX = \frac{X_1}{X_0} = \frac{P_{f1}/P_{f0}}{P_{d1}/P_{d0}} = RPC \tag{20.3}$$

where

$$\frac{X_1}{X_0} = \frac{E_0}{E_1},$$

$X_0 = $ LCs per dollar now,

$X_1 = $ LCs per dollar one period later,

$$E_0 = \frac{1}{X_0} = \text{dollars per LC now}$$

$$E_1 = \frac{1}{X_1} = \text{dollars per LC one period later,}$$

$$CX = \frac{X_1}{X_0} = \text{change in exchange rate,}$$

$$RPC = \frac{P_{f1}/P_{f0}}{P_{d1}/P_{d0}} = \text{change in relative prices,}$$

P_{f0} = initial price level in the foreign country,

P_{f1} = foreign country price level one period later,

P_{d0} = initial domestic price level,

P_{d1} = domestic price level one period later.

The nature of the relationships can vary. Some of the alternatives are suggested in Fig. 20.2. Line *a* implies that both the average and marginal relations are one to one. Line *b* implies that the marginal relation is one to one, but the average relation is not. Line *c* implies a relationship, but not a one-to-one relationship.

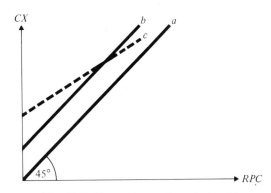

Fig. 20.2 Alternative parity relationships

A few numerical examples will illustrate some of the implications of the purchasing power parity doctrine. Let us assume that for a given period, foreign price levels have risen by 32% while domestic price levels have risen by 20%. If the initial exchange rate is FC 10 to $1, the subsequent new exchange rate will be

$$\frac{1.32}{1.20} = \frac{X_1}{10}, \qquad X_1 = 1.1(10) = 11.$$

It will now take 10% more foreign currency units to equal $1, because the relative inflation rate has been higher in the foreign country. Alternatively, with an exchange rate of FC 10 to $1, let us assume that foreign prices have risen by 17% while domestic prices have risen by 30%. The expected new exchange rate would be

$$\frac{1.17}{1.30} = \frac{X_1}{10}, \qquad X_1 = .9(10) = 9.$$

In the present instance, the number of foreign currency units needed to buy $1 would drop by 10%. Thus the value of the foreign currency has increased by 10% due to the differential rates of inflation in domestic prices vs. foreign prices.

Empirical studies indicate that while the purchasing power parity relationship does not hold perfectly, it does indicate a strong tendency. More fundamentally, the doctrine predicts that an equilibrium rate between two currencies will reflect market forces and that random deviations from the central tendency will tend to be self-correcting; that is, it suggests the existence of some strong equilibrating forces. Furthermore, it argues that the relations between exchange rates will not be hapha-zard but will reflect underlying economic conditions and changes in these conditions. The relationships are not precise because of a number of factors. These include:

1) Differences in incomes or other endowments between the two countries.

2) Changes in government policies.

3) Transportation costs.

4) Lags in market responses.

5) Differences between the two countries in the price ratios of internationally traded goods to domestically traded goods.

6) The addition of a risk premium influence.

Thus while the interest rate parity relationship is not a perfect predictor and discrepancies may be observed between calculated parities and exchange rates, the parity relationship reflects equilibrating forces. In addition, it provides a basis for predicting exchange rate movements if relevant price indexes are used for the coun-tries being compared.

5. Measurement of Real Gains or Losses

The real gain or loss from holding foreign currency units or net assets denominated in foreign currency units can be calculated by utilizing a number of the relationships set forth thus far. We begin with the end-of-period value of a foreign investment expressed in foreign currency. This is

$$1) \qquad\qquad F_0(1 + R_{f0}),$$

where F_0 is the value of the foreign investment expressed in foreign currency. If we multiply this expression by the value of a foreign currency unit expressed in dollars and also by the ratio of domestic prices to obtain real values in dollars, we have

$$2) \qquad\qquad E_1(P_0/P_1)[F_0(1 + R_{f0})].$$

The initial investment in dollars is

$$3) \qquad\qquad E_0 F_0.$$

Hence the real rate of domestic interest is equal to

$$4) \qquad\qquad E_0 F_0(1 + r_d).$$

The real return over the real rate of domestic interest is

5) $$1 + r_1 = \frac{E_1(P_0/P_1)[F_0(1 + R_{f0})]}{E_0 F_0(1 + r_d)}.$$

We may next make use of the Fisher relation in the form

6) $$1 + r_d = (1 + R_{d0})(P_0/P_1).$$

We then substitute the right-hand side of the above expression for $(1 + r_d)$ in Eq. (5) and obtain Eq. (7a). The F_0's cancel, and

7a) $$1 + r_1 = \frac{(E_1/E_0)(P_0/P_1)(1 + R_{f0})}{(1 + R_{d0})(P_0/P_1)}.$$

The price ratios cancel to give us Eq. (7b):

7b) $$1 + r_1 = \frac{(E_1/E_0)(1 + R_{f0})}{1 + R_{d0}}.$$

The interest rate parity relationship is written as Eq. (8):

8) $$\frac{E_0}{E_f} = \frac{1 + R_{f0}}{1 + R_{d0}}.$$

The right-hand side of the equation is substituted in Eq. (7b) yielding Eq. (9).

9) $$1 + r_1 = \frac{E_1}{E_0}\frac{E_0}{E_f}.$$

Next we cancel the E_0 and solve for r_1:

$$r_1 = (E_1/E_f) - 1. \tag{20.4}$$

Thus the real return (gain or loss) from a long or short position in a foreign currency or net assets denominated in foreign currency units can be determined by a relatively simple expression. It is the ratio of the actual value of the foreign currency's future spot rate in relation to the expected value of its future spot rate reflected in its current forward rate.[1] We can illustrate the measurement of real gains or losses by a number of simple examples. First let us assume that we are long in foreign currency units and that the relative devaluation of the foreign currency units is more than anticipated in the current spot rate (E_f):

$$E_1 = \$.20, \qquad E_f = \$.25.$$

---

[1] The insight that the real return on an investment in foreign currency over the real domestic rate of interest can be calculated from the divergence between the anticipated and actual future spot rates of exchange is presented in A. Farber, R. Roll, and B. Solnik, "An Empirical Study of Risk over Fixed and Flexible Exchange," *Journal of Monetary Economics*, Supplementary Series, 1977, 235–265.

The real gain or loss can therefore be calculated as follows:

$$r_1 = E_1/E_f = (.20/.25) - 1 = -20\%.$$

Thus, if we are long in foreign currency units and the forward value of the foreign currency unit was $.25 but its actual spot value at the end of the period is $.20, there has been a loss of 20%. On the other hand, if the spot rate one period later is $.30, we can calculate the real gain as follows:

$$r_1 = (.30/.25) - 1 = +20\%.$$

If we have a short position in the foreign currency units, the signs of the above calculations will be reversed. Thus we have a powerful but simple measurement of gains or losses from long or short positions in foreign currency units or in assets denominated in foreign currency units.

An issue raised with regard to the effect of the shift from fixed exchange rates to flexible exchange rates concerns the possibility of an increase in uncertainty under flexible exchange rates which in turn could dampen the rate of growth in international trade. But if hedging can be used to limit risks from exchange rate fluctuations, increased fluctuations will be no problem unless the foreign exchange premium is increased. Furthermore, if there were an increase in uncertainty and if it were accompanied by an increase in expected returns, the reward-risk ratio could remain unchanged. The simple expression for measuring real gains or losses could thus be used to measure, on a historical empirical basis, the extent to which net returns from unhedged positions were increased or decreased. Rational investors may choose portfolios of foreign-denominated assets and thus be able to use diversification to eliminate unsystematic or independent random variations in exchange rates. The forward exchange premiums would then reflect portfolio risks rather than the risks of individual positions in individual currencies.

A similar model was formulated by Grauer, Litzenberger, and Stehle [1976]. Their model can be expressed as follows:

$$X_{f0} = E_1(X_1) + L_1 \tag{20.5}$$

where

X_{f0} = the current forward exchange rate,
X_1 = the future spot exchange rate,
E_1 = the expected value operator at time 1,
L_1 = the premium or discount resulting from systematic risk.

Now we can employ our measure of the real return (gain or loss) from a long or short position in a foreign currency or net assets denominated in foreign currency units, as a measure of the premium or discount in the relationship between the current forward rate and the future spot rate. We repeat Eq. (20.4) expressed in dollars per foreign currency unit or foreign currency units per dollar:

$$r_1 = (E_1/E_f) - 1 = (X_f/X_1) - 1. \tag{20.4}$$

In terms of our previous examples, if we are long in foreign currency units and the current forward value of the foreign currency unit *was* $.25 but its actual spot value at the end of the period *is* $.20, the future spot rate is at a discount from the current forward rate. This implies that the purchasing power uncertainty reflected in exchange rates is negatively correlated with world wealth so that the risk premium represents a reduction rather than an addition to the real rate of return. Conversely, if the future spot rate is higher than the current forward rate, we obtain a real gain.

If we are in a short position in the foreign currency units, the determination of premiums or discounts will be reversed.

B. EMPIRICAL TESTS OF EXCHANGE MARKET RELATIONSHIPS

The foregoing analysis of the relationship between the current forward rate and the future spot rate yields an analytical framework. If the real systematic risk of purchasing power fluctuations and therefore exchange rate fluctuations is positively correlated with real world wealth or real gross world product, the result will be a premium. If the covariance relationship is negative, the result will be a discount.

Some argue that the premium must be paid in order to induce speculators to bear the risk of holding a position in forward exchange contracts. But this argument fails to recognize that a number of other possibilities exist. As we shall demonstrate in connection with the policies of individual firms, under some circumstances the firm will take a long position in forward contracts, while under other conditions it will take a short position. If forward contracts are used for hedging and the long position and short position requirements exactly offset each other, there will be neither a premium nor a discount. The emergence of a premium or discount under this reasoning would reflect the supply and demand for long vs. short positions in forward exchange contracts.

Cornell [1977] tested for exchange market efficiency by measuring the mean forecast error that occurs when the current forward rate is used as a predictor of the future spot rate. His results found that for none of the seven currencies tested for the period of April 1973 through January 1977 was there any evidence of a liquidity premium or discount.

Robichek and Eaker [1978] made a similar analysis. They measured the premium or discount in relation to the excess return on the world market in concept (although in fact they used the dividend adjusted yield on the Standard & Poor 500 as a proxy). They found a positive risk premium that is statistically significant for five of the nine countries tested over the period from June 1973 to June 1976. However, the percentage of variation explained by their regression is quite low [Giddy, 1978, p. 1031].

C. INTERNATIONAL ASSET PRICING. ALTERNATIVE VIEWS

The earlier papers by Grubel [1968] and Levy and Sarnat [1970] argued that there would be gains from internationally diversified portfolios. They further held that optimal portfolios should be different for investors of different countries because of exchange risks.

Recent papers have differed from these conclusions and raise issues with regard to the proper economic definition of exchange risk [Solnik, 1974; Grauer, Litzenberger, and Stehle, 1976; Solnik, 1977; and Stehle, 1977].

In choosing between these two different points of view we must consider a couple of points: (1) the use of the mean-variance asset pricing model, and (2) the nature of exchange risks and the effect of different types of exchange risk. Since the two differing views on international asset pricing must lean heavily on empirical analysis, the nature of the theoretical model used affects the interpretation of the empirical results.

1. The Use of the Mean-Variance Asset Pricing Model

Solnik relies heavily on the 1977 paper by Roll on "Limitations of Empirical Tests of the Mean Variance (MV) Asset Pricing Model (CAPM)." In a mean-variance framework, if an investor can lend and borrow in his own currency (riskless asset), he can achieve the level of risk desired by combining the risk-free asset with the specific risky portfolio (separation property). Assuming market perfection and homogeneous expectations, we find, as shown earlier, that this risky portfolio is the same for everyone and hence is the market portfolio. Solnik argues that Fama [1976] and Roll [1976] stress that this conclusion is the only real economic content of the model. If no risk-free asset exists, the economic conclusion is that the market portfolio is efficient [Black, 1974].

2. International Pricing with No Exchange Risks

We now consider the issue of international pricing as though there were no exchange risk. In theory, in a perfect mean-variance international capital market the (value-weighted) world market portfolio ought to be the optimal risky portfolio. But to test this theory, one must formulate what the data would look like if the markets were segmented instead of integrated. There is general agreement that the covariances between national stock markets are very small but slightly positive. Thus, if expected excess returns are positive and covariances low, an international mean-variance analysis produces optimal portfolios well diversified internationally to reduce risk. But this will also be true technically even if markets are totally and physically segmented. It is difficult to differentiate *ex ante* and even more difficult *ex post*. One approach to test for segmentation is to specify the type of imperfection which might create it and study its specific impact on portfolio optimality and asset pricing [Black 1974]. But the mean-variance framework is considered to be inefficient in discriminating between the hypotheses of integration vs. segmentation.

3. The Influence of Exchange Risks

Grauer, Litzenberger, and Stehle [1976] studied the influence of exchange risks from uncertain monetary inflation. Solnik [1974, 1977] analyzed the influence of exchange risks resulting from differences in consumption tastes among countries. Each will be considered in turn.

Grauer, *et al.* analyzed exchange risks resulting from monetary uncertainty. In their model all individuals consume the same good or basket independent of wealth and differ only in their propensity to lend or borrow. International trade is free and costless so that purchasing power parity always obtains. Fluctuations in exchange rates are caused by pure money inflation, while the prices of real goods are equal throughout the world. When an asset is really risk free, money inflation (exchange risk) has no influence on equilibrium consumption and investment decisions. The world market portfolio is optimal, and the traditional CAPM results obtain where returns are measured in real terms. In this model, nominal riskless bill pricing is influenced by exchange risk, resulting in a theoretical price for forward exchange.

Given homogeneous tastes and expectations, the separation property applies both *ex ante* and *ex post*. The test of the theory is whether the world market portfolio is tangent or efficient. To perform such a test, an appropriate inflation index must be subtracted from nominal returns. If inflation is not correlated with stock market returns, it will not affect the composition of the efficient frontier. But if there is some correlation between the rate of inflation and stock market returns, the optimal stock portfolio will be sensitive to the inflation index used in the empirical test. The theoretical results of Grauer *et al.* follow from their model, but the relevance to the real world faces difficult empirical measurement problems.

In his analysis, Solnik [1974, 1977] assumes differences in tastes within a free and perfect international capital market. Pure (neutral) money inflation is ruled out. In his earlier paper, Solnik assumed strict consumption taste separation; subsequently he hypothesizes that every country consumes the same commodities but in different proportions (different baskets). He considers a country to be defined by its tastes and therefore its consumption good or basket. Perfect trade markets are assumed with identical real prices for each commodity across the world. The purchasing power of each currency in terms of the domestic consumption good is certain. Exchange rates will fluctuate randomly with the relative values of the different national consumption baskets.

Solnik finds that a single risky portfolio will be optimal for everyone. This portfolio will be made up of the world market portfolio plus a mix of national bills which are pure exchange risk assets. He holds that the stock market portfolio is not necessarily globally optimal or efficient. It is simply the best stock portfolio that could be chosen to be included in the total portfolio of stocks and bills. The stock market portfolio could be inefficient if the subset of stocks is considered alone, excluding the other (exchange risk) assets. The weights of the various national bills in the optimal portfolio depend on net foreign investment positions and the relative risk aversion of people in different countries.

Solnik presents evidence to counter the earlier empirical work that optimal portfolios should be different for investors of different countries because of exchange risk. He argues that even on theoretical grounds a properly specified mean-variance model will always lead to an identical stock portfolio for everyone. He presents data under both continuously compounding and noncompounded rates of return on optimal portfolio composition for investors of different countries. The portfolios represent combinations of stocks from different countries and foreign bills. His data indicate that the *ex post* optimal stock portfolio is almost identical for investors from each country. He concludes that when the mean-variance framework is used on *ex post* data, the separation property will hold internationally even if all the data come from tables of random numbers and no one holds foreign stock. He also argues that exchange risks, real or monetary, cannot justify capital flows. He acknowledges that if some specific market imperfections are incorporated in the mean-variance analysis, the results could be different as a result of these imperfections, but not as a result of exchange risk.

Dumas [1977] has commented that while Solnik argues that real exchange risk is irrelevant for portfolio choice, other evidence suggests that real exchange risk is of negligible magnitude. He refers to a study by Kravis and others [1975], showing that the national consumption budgets of five developed countries are similar in composition. He also refers to tests of the purchasing power parity doctrine. While both the Grauer *et al.* and Solnik models are compatible with international parity of the prices of individual commodities, only Solnik's model can handle a disparity of purchasing power indexes. Dumas summarizes a test of purchasing power parity by Hodgson and Phelps [1975] which holds that deviations from purchasing power parity are relatively short-term phenomena. Hence it may not be necessary to consider them in a theory of asset pricing.

In this connection, Dumas [1977] observes that exchange rates represent relative prices and hence are likely to affect the value of a firm's outputs, thereby influencing the returns on nominal securities. This makes it doubtful whether it is appropriate to assume stochastic independence between nominal securities returns and exchange rates.

Clearly the literature on optimal international diversified portfolios is not in a settled state. While articles published in the late 1960s argue that optimal portfolios should be different for investors of different countries, later models and empirical tests are consistent with identical portfolios for investors in different countries. The later theories and data are consistent with the extension of portfolio separation into the international market. In this connection, Fama and Farber [1977] argue that in a world in which nominal bonds are freely traded across countries, uncertainty about future exchange rates has no relevance for investors' decisions on how portfolios should be allocated to national and international investments.

D. LIMITING EXPOSURE TO FOREIGN EXCHANGE RISKS

The exposure of a business firm to foreign exchange risks is defined by the pattern of its cash flow and assets stock positions which in turn depend upon the pattern of flow of future receipts and payments and the pattern of the firm's net monetary position. Monetary assets are those assets denominated in a fixed number of units of money such as cash, marketable securities, accounts receivable, tax refunds receivable, notes receivable, and prepaid insurance. Monetary liabilities are those liabilities expressed in fixed monetary terms, such as accounts payable, notes payable, tax liability reserves, bonds and preferred stock.

The effects of a net monetary position exposure can be formulated as follows:

$$C_p = [(MA - ML)/X_0 - (MA - ML)/X_1](1 - t_{U.S.})$$
$$= (E_0 - E_1)(MA - ML)(1 - t_{U.S.})$$
$$= (E_0 - E_1)(NMP)(1 - t_{U.S.}),$$

where

C_p = cost of net monetary position (NMP) due to exchange-rate changes,
MA = monetary assets,
ML = monetary liabilities,
X_0 = exchange rate at the beginning = $1/E_0$,
X_1 = exchange rate a period later = $1/E_1$,
$t_{U.S.}$ = tax rate in the United States.

The effects of a decline in foreign currency value are:

a) Net monetary debtor gains.
b) Net monetary creditor loses.

Let us assume that

$$MA = FC\ 200,000; \qquad X_0 = 4, \qquad t_{U.S.} = .5;$$
$$ML = FC\ 100,000; \qquad X_1 = 5.$$

We calculate the net monetary position to which the effect of the exchange rate shift is applied.

1) $NMP = MA - ML = 200,000 - 100,000 = 100,000;$

$$C_p = NMP(E_0 - E_1)(1 - t_{U.S.}) = 100,000(.25 - .20)(.5)$$
$$= \$5,000(.5) = \$2,500.$$

Our calculations show a decrease in the dollar value of our asset position; that is, a loss of $2,500.

We now let $ML = FC\ 300,000$. Then

2) $NMP = MA - ML = 200,000 - 300,000 = -100,000;$

$$C_p = NMP(E_0 - E_1)(1 - t_{U.S.}) = -100,000(.25 - .20)(.5)$$
$$= -\$2,500.$$

The net amount owed is decreased by $2,500, representing a gain.

The effects of an increase in FC value are:

a) Net monetary debtor loses.
b) Net monetary creditor gains.

1)   MA = FC 10 million, $X_0 = 5$,

   ML = FC 8 million, $X_1 = 4$,

   NMP = 10,000,000 − 8,000,000 = 2,000,000,

   $C_p = $ NMP$(E_0 - E_1) = 2,000,000(.20 - .25) = -\$100,000.$

The cost is a negative $100,000, representing a gain in the value of the net monetary position with revaluation upward in the FC currency.

2) Let MA = FC 6 million. Then

   NMP = 6,000,000 − 8,000,000 = −2,000,000,

   $C_p = $ NMP$(E_0 - E_1) = -2,000,000(.20 - .25) = +\$100,000.$

Both terms are negative, so their product is positive, indicating that revaluation upward results in a positive cost (or a *loss*) to a firm in a negative net monetary position (monetary liabilities exceed monetary assets). The FC values of its net obligations have increased.

The impact of an exposed position is similar if the exposure results from an excess of receipts over payments due to be paid in the foreign currency. A firm in this situation faces several combinations of patterns. We illustrate some of the alternatives:

1) The firm is exposed to a decline in the value of foreign currencies. Then:
    a) Expected future receipts exceed expected future payments.
    b) The net monetary position is positive—monetary assets exceed monetary liabilities.

A firm in such a position will lose from a devaluation (or decrease in value or depreciation in the value) of foreign currencies.

2) The firm is exposed to an increase in the value of foreign currencies. Then:
    a) Expected future payments exceed expected future receipts.
    b) The net monetary position is negative.

A firm in such a position is concerned about upward revaluation of foreign currencies.

We can state as a general proposition that unless the payments and receipts in relation to the future net monetary position of the firm exactly balance, the firm is exposed to a decline or increase in the value of foreign currencies. Ordinarily, the normal pattern of operations will put the firm in an exposed position which it can limit only by taking certain steps, all of which involve a cost. One strategy may be to rearrange the pattern of payments and the pattern of holdings of monetary assets and liabilities in foreign currencies to achieve perfect balance so that the net exposure is zero. But a change in the pattern of the flow of receipts and payments and holdings of monetary assets and liabilities represent departures from the normal pattern of the firm's operations under our initial postulates, and such artificial changes from the firm's normal pattern will involve costs. To determine whether such a pattern of behavior is better than alternative methods of limiting exposure requires that management calculate the costs of altering the patterns of cash flows and net monetary position. This clearly is a rather complex undertaking for an individual firm but is nonetheless necessary if the firm is to make a rational choice among alternatives.

The next broad strategic analysis of alternatives that a firm may make is to gather and evaluate information about expected future rates of exchange. The development of an information bank providing data which permit the formulation of expected future exchange rates involves costs. The firm could purchase a forecasting service instead of developing its own information, but this also requires costs as well as outlays and efforts to appraise the service's qualifications and reliability.

In one perspective, if the foreign exchange markets are efficient and the interest rate parity relationship always holds, then the future expected exchange rates will be reflected in the current forward rate of exchange. However, given the dynamic changes that take place in the world economic environment, it is likely that future spot rates will be different from the levels forecast for them by the current forward rates. In theory, random changes in the relationship could be eliminated by forming portfolios so that the relationships would be subject only to systematic changes. The true minimum cost of protection against foreign exchange risk exposure would then be measured by the covariance of the performance of existing portfolios with changes in a world (market) portfolio. Transaction costs occur in the formation of such portfolios.

The behavior of firms will inherently involve a comparison of three alternatives. One is to develop information about and formulate expectations of the relation between expected future exchange rates and the current forward rate. A second alternative is to seek to hedge by using the forward market. A third alternative is to hedge by utilizing the money and capital markets. A continuous comparison of these three alternatives will lead to arbitrage operations by the firms which will tend to produce efficiency in the foreign exchange markets. We next discuss a format for calculating the net receipts or costs of utilizing the three alternative approaches.

Initially we assume that it would be very expensive for the firm to rearrange the pattern of receipts and payments along with its position in monetary assets and monetary liabilities to achieve zero exposure. Let us then first consider the firm which, on balance, expects future receipts to exceed future payments and/or has a net monetary position that is positive. The risk exposure faced by the firm is a decline in the value of the foreign currency. Hence the firm fears depreciation in the value of the foreign currency and will take action to deal with this possibility. We now set forth the framework for analyzing the cost of the three alternative protective policies the firm may follow.

Let us initially assume that the current spot price of the foreign currency expressed in dollars is $\$.30 = E_0$. The exposure is FC 100,000. The forward rate, E_f, is equal to $\$.25$. The action taken by the firm depends upon its expectation of the future spot rate and the degree of confidence in that expectation. If the firm judges that the future spot rate will be $\$.23$ and does not hedge, it will incur a loss of $\$7,000$. However, if the firm expects the future spot rate to be $\$.27$, it will expect to incur a loss of only $\$3,000$. The current forward rate is the market's best judgment of what the future spot rate will be. If E_1 will actually be $\$.25$, it is a matter of indifference whether the firm hedges its long position in foreign currency or whether it does not purchase protection. There is an important consideration, however. If the firm enters into the forward market, it knows the cost of its foreign exchange risk exposure. This cost can be taken into account in the supply price of the goods and services sold. Therefore obtaining protection against the foreign exchange risk exposure limits the expected loss and removes uncertainty due to fluctuations between the current forward rate and the actual future spot rate.

The firm seeking protection against the foreign exchange risk exposure may employ two alternative methods.[2] One is the use of the forward market. The other is the use of the money and capital markets. If the interest rate parity relationship holds, it is a matter of indifference as to which of these two methods is employed. However, because temporary differences may develop, it is the arbitrage behavior, seeking to benefit from these divergences, that brings the markets back to interest rate parity. Let us suppose that interest rates in the foreign market are 32% while interest rates in the domestic market are 10%. Then the expected ratio between the current spot rate and the current forward rate is 1.2. If the current spot rate is .3, the equilibrium forward rate is .25 $(1.32/1.10 = .30/E_f)$.

If parity obtains, the cost of hedging in the forward market or of borrowing from foreign currency and investing in the United States is the same. For example, if the amount of foreign currency involved is 100,000 FC units, then the cost of hedging in the foreign market, C_f, is

$$C_f = (E_0 - E_f)F_0$$
$$= (.30 - .25)100,000$$
$$= \$5,000.$$

In the money and capital markets the situation is different from the covered interest arbitrage operation because an exposure of FC 100,000 already exists. If FC 100,000 is borrowed in the foreign country to neutralize the foreign exchange risk exposure, the principal is covered by the future net receipts or net monetary assets

---

[2] To simplify the discussion, we omit consideration of taxes here.

position of the firm. Hence the cost of using the money and capital markets by borrowing foreign currency and investing in the United States is

$$C_{bf} = \text{Cost of borrowing in foreign country}$$
$$= \bar{E}_1 F_0 R_f - E_0 F_0 R_{U.S.} = (\bar{E}_1 R_f - E_0 R_{U.S.})F_0$$
$$= [.32\bar{E}_1 - .30(.10)]100{,}000.$$

Now the cost of borrowing foreign currency depends upon what the future spot rate will be, because interest on the foreign borrowing must be paid at the future spot rate. The firm can remove this uncertainty by buying the foreign currency in the amount of the required interest to be paid at the current forward rate. The cost of borrowing foreign now becomes

$$C_{bf} = \text{FC } 32{,}000 E_f - \$3{,}000.$$

Next, we evaluate at the current forward rate:

$$C_{bf} = 32{,}000(.25) - \$3{,}000 = \$8{,}000 - \$3{,}000$$
$$= \$5{,}000.$$

The cost of borrowing foreign will now be $5,000, which is exactly the same as in the hedged case in which the foreign currency was sold in the forward exchange market. It should be emphasized that borrowing in the foreign market produces an interest obligation which will become due in the future. Hence to protect against this exposure, the action is to *buy* the foreign currency in the amount of the interest obligation in the forward market rather than *sell* it as in the hedging operation in the forward market. Because this strategy requires having foreign currency on hand in the future to pay the foreign interest, the effects on the position of the firm will be reversed if the firm does not cover its future interest payments to be made in foreign currency but permits matters to depend upon the future spot foreign exchange rate. For example, if the future spot foreign exchange rate is higher than the current forward rate, the cost of borrowing foreign will also be higher:

$$C_{bf} = (\bar{E}_1 R_f - E_0 R_{U.S.})100{,}000$$
$$= [.27(.32) - .30(.10)]100{,}000$$
$$= (.0864 - .03)100{,}000 = .0564(100{,}000)$$
$$= \$5{,}640.$$

With the future expected spot rate being $.27 rather than $.25, costs of borrowing foreign are in excess of $5,000. However, if the future spot rate falls below the current forward rate, the cost of borrowing foreign will be less than $5,000. Hence, if the firm does not immediately cover its future interest payments to be made in foreign currency, it continues to be exposed to risk.

We next consider the position of the firm which is in a negative net monetary position or which will be required, at some time in the future, to make net payments in excess of future receipts. The situation is the reverse of the firm in a positive monetary position. Instead of facing the risk of devaluation of FC units, the firm faces the risk of appreciation in the value of FC units. Hence its protective action in the forward market is to buy the FC units. If it does not obtain this protection, it will face an uncertain cost if the future spot rate is higher than the current forward rate. If it uses the money and capital markets, it will borrow in the United States and invest in the FC units in which it will have to make future payments.

This analysis demonstrates that if a firm is in an exposed foreign exchange position, it will incur some costs to obtain protection against that exposed position. Even rearranging the firm's pattern of payments and receipts or monetary assets and liabilities will represent a departure from normal operations and therefore involve some costs. If the firm uses the forward market or borrows, it incurs some costs, but it will know the exact amount of these costs. If the firm does not take action to fix the exact amount of these costs then, in compliance with current FASB 8 reporting regulations, it must report its gains or losses on its foreign exchange exposure whenever it issues financial statements. If the firm has not taken protective actions with regard to its foreign exchange exposure, its earnings may be subject to wide swings. However, if a firm has taken protective actions, FASB regulations simply provide for the systematic amortization over appropriate time periods of the costs incurred in achieving the hedged position. Apparently some confusion has arisen on this point because the FASB requires reports only on the hedged position without adding in the exposed net assets or net liability position of the firm which is being protected. The principles involved may be illustrated by the following case example.

Globalcorp, which is based in the United States, has a subsidiary in country X with a net monetary position of FC 300,000. High inflation in country X is putting devaluation pressure on the foreign currency vis-à-vis the dollar and Globalcorp sells a 90-day forward contract of FC 300,000 on November 1, 1975, at the forward rate of FC 1 = \$.09. Globalcorp's fiscal year corresponds to the calendar year. Five alternative possible foreign exchange rate patterns are illustrated in Table 20.1. We can determine the exchange gain or loss at year end and on January 31, 1976, under each set of assumptions of exchange-rate values.

The premium (discount) to be amortized over the life of the contract is

$$\text{Premium (discount)} = F_0(E_f - E_0) = 300{,}000(.09 - .11) = (\$6{,}000).$$

The gain or loss recognized at year end includes the amortized portion of the discount and the change in dollar value from the change in spot rates.

We can describe the net gains or losses at each reporting point. At 12/31/75, the amortized amount of the forward contract discount of \$4,000 is added to the gain or loss due to the change in the spot foreign exchange rates between 11/1/75 and 12/31/75. On 1/31/76, when the forward contract expires, the net gain or loss will be

Table 20.1

	Assumptions				
	A	B	C	D	E
November 1, 1975					
Spot rate	$E_0 = LC1 = \$.11$	\$.11	\$.11	\$.11	\$.11
90-day forward rate	$E_f = LC1 = .09$	.09	.09	.09	.09
December 31, 1975					
Spot rate	$E_1 = LC1 = .10$	.11	.10	.12	.05
January 31, 1976					
Spot rate	$E_2 = LC1 = .09$	.15	.05	.10	.11

the remainder of the forward contract discount, a gain of $2,000 plus or minus the gain or loss on the change in the spot foreign exchange rates between 12/31/75 and 1/31/76. Overall, the gain or loss recorded will be a gain of $6,000 plus or minus the gain or loss on the changes in the spot foreign exchange rates between 11/1/75 and 1/31/76.

The results presented in Table 20.2 list only the gain or loss from the use of the forward contract to hedge the exposed position. The gain or loss on the net monetary position (from translation of the financial statements) is equal to $F_0(E_2 - E_0)$, which when added to column 8 yields the net final gain (loss) of ($6,000). This is shown in Table 20.3.

In Table 20.3, the amortized net gain or loss from the use of the hedging operation is recorded at each reporting date. Since the term of the hedge is three months and two months have expired by the end of the year, two-thirds of the cost of establishing the hedge is charged to operations as of the end of the year. The remaining one-third is charged to operations at the end of the remaining third month. Table

Table 20.2 FASB reporting requirement on a hedging contract

(1)	(2)	(3)	(4)	(5)	(6)	(7)	(8)
Assumptions	Amortized portion of forward contract premium (discount) $(2/3) F_0(E_f - E_0)$	Gain (loss) on 12/31/75 $F_0(E_0 - E_1)$	Total gain (loss) on 12/31/75 (2) + (3)	Remainder of forward contract premium (discount) $(1/3) F_0(E_f - E_0)$	Gain (loss) 1/31/76 $F_0(E_1 - E_2)$	Total gain (loss) on 1/31/76 (5) + (6)	Overall gain (loss) 11/1/75– 1/31/76 (4) + (7)
A	($4,000)	$3,000	($1,000)	($2,000)	$3,000	$1,000	$0
B	(4,000)	0	(4,000)	(2,000)	(12,000)	(14,000)	(18,000)
C	(4,000)	3,000	(1,000)	(2,000)	15,000	13,000	12,000
D	(4,000)	(3,000)	(7,000)	(2,000)	6,000	4,000	(3,000)
E	(4,000)	18,000	14,000	(2,000)	(18,000)	(20,000)	(6,000)

Table 20.3 Overall gain or (loss) from hedging an exposed position

	12/31/75			1/31/76			Overall gain or (loss) from hedging and translation 11/1/75– 1/31/76
	Gain or (loss) on hedging contract	Translation gain or (loss)	Net gain or (loss)	Gain or (loss) on hedging contract	Translation gain or (loss)	Net gain or (loss)	
A	($ 1,000)	($ 3,000)	($4,000)	$ 1,000	($ 3,000)	($2,000)	($6,000)
B	(4,000)	0	(4,000)	(14,000)	(12,000)	($2,000)	(6,000)
C	(1,000)	(3,000)	($4,000)	13,000	(15,000)	($2,000)	(6,000)
D	(7,000)	3,000	(4,000)	4,000	(6,000)	(2,000)	(6,000)
E	14,000	(18,000)	(4,000)	(20,000)	(18,000)	(2,000)	(6,000)

20.3 underscores the principle that the use of the hedge fixes the net final cost of the exposed position to the discount between the current spot rate and the current forward rate.

Numerous complaints have been made that paragraph 25 of FASB 8 introduces unreal fluctuations into income statement results. These comments fail to take into consideration the gains or losses from translation of the financial statements. When combined with gains or losses on the forward contract, the net results are as shown in Table 20.3 and represent the amortization of the cost of hedging. However, if hedging is not used by the firm, gains or losses at each interim period simply record the reality to that point. Future changes could go in either direction.

E. SUMMARY

Foreign exchange markets enable buyers and sellers in different countries to deal in their own currencies. The foreign exchange rate is the price of one currency in terms of another and depends on the supply and demand relationships between the two currencies. There are strong forces linking spot, forward, future spot, and interest rates between countries. Arbitrage opportunities insure these relationships against breakdowns. The consistency of cross rates means that given any three countries, any one exchange rate will be determined by the other two exchange rates. If the relationship breaks down, an arbitrage opportunity will exist.

The Fisher effect holds that the nominal rate of interest is determined by the real rate of interest and the rate of inflation. The rate of inflation is also equal to the ratio of the expected future spot price to the current price. The current forward price is an estimate of what the future spot price will be.

The IRPT incorporates the Fisher effect by recognizing that between any two currencies the forward exchange rate should be the same as the spot exchange rate except for the anticipated effect of different rates of inflation. Since anticipated inflation rates are incorporated in the nominal interest rates of each country, there is a potential arbitrage possibility between current and forward exchange rates based on the relative interest rates of the countries. The process is known as covered interest arbitrage.

The purchasing power parity doctrine states that the change in exchange rates between countries depends on the relative changes in their prices for the same period. Thus, the relative values of the currencies depend on what they will buy.

The real return from holding an investment denominated in a foreign currency (over and above the domestic real return) is a simple relationship of the future spot to the forward exchange rate. This relationship directs the international flow of investible funds. The opportunity to make foreign investments broadens opportunities for portfolio diversification.

The CAPM can be used to express the uncertainty about spot and future exchange rates. If the covariance of purchasing power with the value of the market portfolio is positive, the expected rate of return on a bond with a certain nominal return will exceed the real risk-free rate of return, because of the purchasing power risk of the investment. The CAPM can be used to develop an expression for the forward exchange rate under uncertainty, and shows that the premium or discount on the forward rate as a predictor of the future spot rate depends on the relative purchasing power of the two currencies. If the current forward rate exceeds the future spot rate, a positive correlation of purchasing power risk with world wealth is implied, and conversely.

A number of studies of international capital markets have been undertaken to test whether international markets are segmented and to test for efficiency of the foreign exchange markets.

A firm is exposed to foreign exchange rate risks whenever monetary assets and liabilities are not in balance. The degree of exposure depends on the covariance of exchange rate movements in different countries where the company has monetary imbalance. Firms may limit risk exposures by hedging in the forward market or in the capital markets. The firm must consider the cost of each of these steps relative to the exposure risk.

Firms that have exposed net monetary positions are required by FASB 8 to report exchange rate gains and losses as incurred. Firms that have taken protective action are allowed to amortize gains and losses from exchange rate changes over the life of their hedged positions.

PROBLEM SET

20.1 In January 1977 (when DM 3 = $1) it was expected that by the end of 1977 the price level in the U.S. would have risen by 10% and in West Germany by 5%. The real rate of interest in both countries is 4%.

a) Use the PPPT to project the expected DMs per $1 at the end of 1977 (the expected future spot rate of DMs per $1).

b) Use the Fisher relation to estimate the nominal interest rates in each country which make it possible for investments in each country to earn their real rate of interest.
c) Use the IRPT to estimate the current one-year forward rate of DMs per $1.
d) Compare your estimate of the current forward rate in (c) with your estimate of the expected future spot rate in (a).
e) Prove analytically that the Fisher effect and the IRPT guarantee consistency with the PPPT relation when real interest rates in the different countries are equal. (Assume that all the fundamental relations hold.)

20.2 An American manufacturing company has imported industrial machinery at a price of DM 4.6 million. The machinery will be delivered and paid for in six months. For planning purposes, the American company wants to establish what the payment (in dollars) will be in six months. It decides to use the forward market to accomplish its objective. The company contacts its New York bank which provides the quotations given in Table 20.4. The bank states that it will charge a commission of $\frac{1}{4}\%$ on any transaction.

a) Does the American company enter the forward market to go long or short of forward DM?
b) What is the number of DM/$? What is the dollar value of the deutschemark?
c) What is the equilibrium forward rate for the deutschemark expressed as DM/$?
d) Does the commission increase or decrease the number of DM/$ in the transaction?
e) What price in dollars can the American company establish by using the forward market in deutschemarks?

Table 20.4

	DM	Swiss franc	$
Six-month Eurocurrency rates (% p.a.) denominated in the following currencies	8	7	9
Spot exchange rates (currency/Swiss franc)	1.1648		.56

20.3 A West German company buys industrial machinery from a U.S. company at a price of $10 million. The machinery will be delivered and paid for in six months. The German company seeks to establish its cost in deutschemarks. It decides to use the forward market to accomplish its objective. The company contacts its Bonn bank which provides the quotations listed in Table 20.5. The bank states that it will charge a commission of $\frac{1}{4}\%$ on any transaction.

a) Does the German company enter the forward market to go long or short of forward dollars?
b) What is the number of DM/$? What is the dollar value of the deutschemark?
c) What is the equilibrium forward rate for the deutschemark expressed as $/DM?
d) Does the commission increase or decrease the dollar value of the deutschemark?
e) What price in deutschemarks can the German company establish by using the forward market in dollars?

Table 20.5

	DM	£	$
Six-month Eurocurrency rates (% p.a.) denominated in the following currencies	8	9.5	9
Spot exchange rates (currency/U.K. £)	3.878		$1.90

20.4 Globalcorp makes a sale of goods to a foreign firm and will receive LC 380,000 three months later. Globalcorp has incurred costs in dollars and wishes to make definite the amount of dollars it will receive in three months. It plans to approach a foreign bank to borrow an amount of local currency such that the principal plus interest will equal the amount Global-corp expects to receive. The interest rate it must pay on its loan is 28%. With the borrowed funds, Globalcorp purchases dollars at the current spot rate which are invested in the United States at an interest rate of 8%. When Globalcorp receives the LC 380,000 at the end of three months, it uses the funds to liquidate the loan at the foreign bank. The effective tax rate in both countries is 40%.

a) What is the net amount that Globalcorp will receive if the current spot rate is LC 1.90 to the dollar?

b) How much less is this than the amount Globalcorp would have received if the remittance had been made immediately instead of three months later?

c) At what forward rate of exchange would the amount received by Globalcorp have been the same as that it would have obtained using the capital markets? Would Globalcorp have sold the LC forward short or long to hedge its position?

d) If a speculator took the opposite position from Globalcorp in the forward market for LC, would the speculator sell long or short? If the speculator received a risk premium for holding this position, would this place the current forward rate in LC above or below the expected future spot rate in LC per dollar?

20.5 Transcorp has made a purchase of goods from a foreign firm which will require the payment of LC 380,000 six months later. Transcorp wishes to make definite the amount of dollars it will need to pay the LC 380,000 on the due date. The foreign firm is domiciled in a country whose currency has been rising in relation to the dollar in recent years. The tax rate in both countries is 40%. Transcorp plans to borrow an amount in dollars from a U.S. bank to immediately exchange into LC's to buy securities in the foreign country which, with interest, will equal LC 380,000 six months later. The interest rate that will be paid in the United States is 12%, the interest rate that will be earned on the foreign securities is 8%. When at the end of six months, Transcorp is required to make the payment in LC, it will use the funds from the maturing foreign securities in LC to meet its obligation in LC. At the same time it will pay off the loan plus interest in the United States in dollars.

a) What is the net amount that Transcorp pays to meet the obligation of LC 380,000 in six months if the current spot rate is LC 2.00 to the dollar?

b) How much more is this than the amount Transcorp would have paid if payment had been made immediately instead of six months later?

c) At what forward rate of exchange would the amount paid by Transcorp have been the same as that it would have paid using the capital markets? Would Transcorp have taken the long position in the forward LC or have sold the LC forward short to hedge its position?

d) If a speculator took the opposite position from Transcorp in the forward market for LCs, would the speculator be long or short? If the speculator received a risk premium for holding this position, would this place the current forward rate in LC above or below the expected future spot rate in LC per dollar?

Appendix A to Chapter 20

Measuring the Percentage of Devaluation or Revaluation

Assume that the French franc has been devalued from 3 per U.S. dollar to 4 per U.S. dollar. This can be expressed as the percentage change in the number of French francs required to purchase 1 U.S. dollar $(=D_{\text{fd}})$. For example, when $X_0 = 3$ and $X_1 = 4$, then

$$\% \text{ change} = (X_1 - X_0)/X_0 = (4 - 3)/3 = \tfrac{1}{3}, \quad \text{or} \quad 33\tfrac{1}{3}\% = D_{\text{fd}}.$$

There has been an increase of $33\tfrac{1}{3}\%$ in the number of French francs required to equal 1 U.S. dollar.

To show the percentage change in the dollar value of the franc $(=D_{\text{df}})$, we use

$$E_0 = \frac{1}{X_0} = \frac{1}{3} \quad \text{and} \quad E_1 = \frac{1}{X_1} = \frac{1}{4}.$$

The percentage change is given by

$$\% \text{ change} = \frac{E_0 - E_1}{E_0} = \frac{(1/X_0) - (1/X_1)}{1/X_0}$$

$$= \left(\frac{1}{3} - \frac{1}{4}\right) \Big/ \left(\frac{1}{3}\right) = \frac{(4-3)/12}{1/3} = \frac{1}{4} = 25\% = D_{\text{df}}.$$

There has been a 25% decrease in the value of the franc in terms of the U.S. dollar.

Summary of exchange-rate relationships

D_{fd} is the change in value in terms of LC/\$.

D_{df} is the change in value in terms of \$/LC.

$$D_{\text{fd}} = \frac{X_1 - X_0}{X_0} = \frac{(1/E_1) - (1/E_0)}{1/E_0} = \frac{E_0}{E_1} - 1 = \frac{E_0 - E_1}{E_1},$$

$$D_{\text{df}} = \frac{E_0 - E_1}{E_0} = \frac{(1/X_0) - (1/X_1)}{1/X_0} = \frac{X_0}{X_0} - \frac{X_0}{X_1} = \frac{X_1 - X_0}{X_1}.$$

Appendix B to Chapter 20

Derivation of the Interest Rate Parity Theorem (IRPT)

Equilibrium among the current exchange rate, the forward exchange rate, the domestic interest rate, and the foreign interest rate is achieved through covered interest arbitrage. Assume the forward contract is for n days and that R_{f0} and R_{d0} are annual rates. A sequence of seven transactions takes place when the interest rate differential in X exceeds the forward exchange discount on the currency of X (Fig. B20.1).

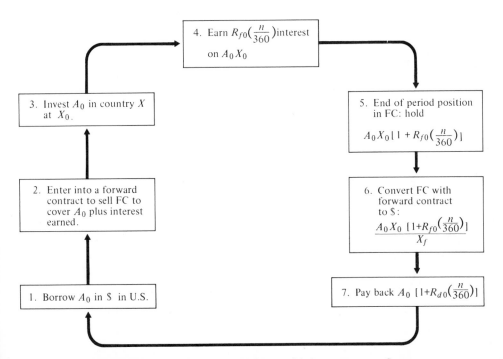

Fig. B20.1 Covered interest arbitrage with investment outflows

Equilibrium occurs when the principal + interest earned in country X equals the principal + interest paid in the United States, or when

$$\frac{A_0 X_0[1 + R_{fo}(n/360)]}{X_f} = A_0\left[1 + R_{do}\left(\frac{n}{360}\right)\right], \qquad \text{or} \qquad \frac{X_f}{X_0} = \frac{1 + (n/360)R_{fo}}{1 + (n/360)R_{do}}.$$

Alternatively, we would obtain the same equilibrium requirement if the interest rate differential in X were less than the forward exchange discount in the currency of X, by borrowing in the foreign country and buying FC to cover the amount borrowed plus interest owed (see Fig. B20.2).

Equilibrium occurs when the principal plus interest earned in the United States equals the principal plus interest paid in country X, or when

$$\left|\frac{F_0}{X_0}\left[1 + R_{do}\left(\frac{n}{360}\right)\right]\right|X_f = F_0\left[1 + R_{fo}\left(\frac{n}{360}\right)\right] \qquad \text{or} \qquad \frac{X_f}{X_0} = \frac{1 + R_{fo}(n/360)}{1 + R_{do}(n/360)}.$$

If the interest differentials are positive in the foreign country, the forward rate on the foreign currency will be negative. If negative, the forward rate on the foreign currency will be positive, as shown in Fig. B20.3.

The pair of relations followed by IF indicate foreign investment in the covered interest arbitrage operation. The pair of relations followed by IH leads to investment in the United States in the covered interest arbitrage operation.

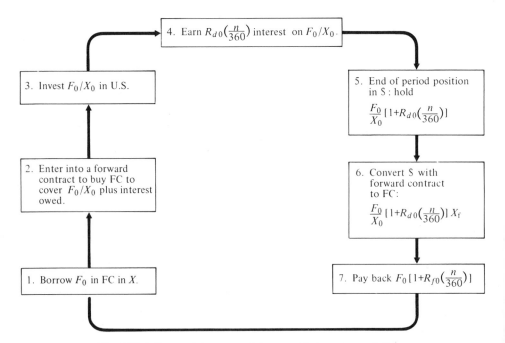

Fig. B20.2 Covered interest arbitrage with investment inflows

Interest rate differential
(Foreign currency less U.S. $)

		Plus	Minus
Forward market rates (in foreign currency units, X_f)	Discount	-1%, $+2\%$ IF -2%, $+1\%$ IH	
	Premium		$+1\%$, -2% IH $+2\%$, -1% IF

Fig. B20.3 Covered interest arbitrage.

As we have demonstrated, whether or not the covered interest arbitrage operation results in investment in a foreign country in preference to investment in the United States, the resulting equilibrium interest and forward exchange parity relationship is the same.

REFERENCES

ADLER, M., "The Cost of Capital and Valuation of a Two-Country Firm," *Journal of Finance*, March 1974, 119–132.

———, and B. DUMAS, "Optimal International Acquisitions," *Journal of Finance*, March 1975, 1–20.

BLACK, F., "International Capital Market Equilibrium with Investment Barriers," *Journal of Financial Economics*, December 1974, 337–352.

COHN, R. A., and J. J. PRINGLE, "Imperfections in International Financial Markets: Implications for Risk Premia and the Cost of Capital to Firms," *Journal of Finance*, March 1973, 59–66.

CORNELL, B., "Spot Rates, Forward Rates, and Exchange Market Efficiency," *Journal of Financial Economics*, August 1977, 55–65.

DUMAS, B., "Discussion," *The Journal of Finance*, May 1977, 512–515.

FAMA, E. F., *Foundations of Finance*, New York, Basic Books, 1976.

FAMA, E. F., and A. FARBER, "Money, Bonds and Foreign Exchange," October 1977, manuscript.

GIDDY, I. H., "Discussion," *The Journal of Finance*, June 1978, 1030–1031.

GRAUER, F. L. A., R. H. LITZENBERGER, and R. E. STEHLE, "Sharing Rules and Equilibrium in an International Capital Market Under Uncertainty," *Journal of Financial Economics*, June 1976, 233–256.

GRUBEL, H. G., "Internationally Diversified Portfolios: Welfare Gains and Capital Flows," *American Economic Review*, December 1968, 1299–1314.

HODGSON, J. S., and P. PHELPS, "The Distributed Impact of Price-Level Variation on Floating Exchange Rates," *Review of Economics and Statistics*, February 1975, 58–64.

KRAVIS, I. B., et al., *A System of International Comparisons of Gross Product and Purchasing Power*, Baltimore, Johns Hopkins University Press, 1975.

LEE, C., "A Stock Adjustment Analysis of Capital Movements: The U.S. Canadian Case," *Journal of Political Economy*, July 1969, 512–523.

LEE, W. Y., and K. S. SACHDEVA, "The Role of the Multinational Firm in the Integration of Segmented Capital Markets," *The Journal of Finance*, May 1977, 479–492.

LESSARD, D. R., "International Portfolio Diversification: A Multivariate Analysis for a Group of Latin-American Countries," *Journal of Finance*, June 1973, 619–633.

LEVY, H., and M. SARNAT, "International Diversification of Investment Portfolios," *American Economic Review*, September 1970, 668–675.

———, and ———, "Devaluation Risk and the Portfolio Analysis of International Investment," in Elton and Gruber, Eds., *International Capital Markets*. North Holland, 1975, 177–206.

ROBICHEK, A. A., and M. R. EAKER, "Foreign Exchange Hedging and the Capital Asset Pricing Model," *The Journal of Finance*, June 1978, 1011–1018.

ROLL, R., "A Critique of the Asset Pricing Theory's Tests; Part 1: On Past and Potential Testability of the Theory," *Journal of Financial Economics*, March 1977, 129–176.

SOLNIK, B. H., "An Equilibrium Model of the International Capital Market," Research Paper No. 129, Graduate School of Business, Stanford University, 1972.

———, "International Pricing of Risk: An Empirical Investigation of the World Capital Market Structure," *Journal of Finance*, May 1974, 365–378.

———, "An Equilibrium Model of the International Capital Market," *Journal of Economic Theory*, August 1974, 500–524.

———, "Testing International Asset Pricing: Some Pessimistic Views," *The Journal of Finance*, May 1977, 503–512.

STEHLE, R., "An Empirical Test of the Alternative Hypotheses of National and International Pricing of Risky Assets," *The Journal of Finance*, May 1977, 493–502.

WALLINGFORD, B. A., "International Asset Pricing: A Comment," *Journal of Finance*, May 1974, 392–395.

WESTON, J. F., and B. W. SORGE, *International Managerial Finance*, Homewood, Ill., Irwin, 1972.

———, and ———, *Guide to International Financial Management*, New York, McGraw-Hill, 1977.

Appendix A

Discounting

A. INTRODUCTION

In any economy, capitalistic or socialistic, we find positive rates of interest. This reflects two underlying influences: the productivity of economic goods and time preference. Capital goods are goods used in the production of other goods and services. Some capital goods are specialized machinery and others are materials—such as iron, copper, or textiles—used in the production of machinery to produce other goods. More basically, our productive efforts may be used to produce goods that we consume immediately or to produce goods that will produce other goods and services for future use. One reason to use some of our productive efforts to have goods that will produce future goods is that the postponement of current consumption will enable us to have more wealth in the future than we would otherwise have. This is true whether we think of the use of actual goods or financial spending power used on current consumption vs. goods that will produce future goods. For example, we can consume grains now or plant them to harvest future crops that will represent larger quantities than the seeds with which we started. Because of the productivity of goods they have a time value. A bushel of seeds today will become several bushels of grain in the future. So productivity is one basis for the time value of money and positive rates of interest.

A second basis is time preference. Would we rather have the use of an automobile now or wait five years? Clearly, it is more advantageous to have the use of goods now than to wait for them.

B. THE TIME VALUE OF MONEY: DISCRETE COMPOUNDING

1. Compound Future Sums
Because of productivity and time preference, a positive rate of interest is a universal phenomenon. It is a necessary guide to present vs. future uses of goods and to the

allocation of goods among alternative uses when time is involved. Since a positive rate of interest is a general phenomenon, future sums will be greater than present values. For example, assume that if a company received funds immediately, it could earn a 10% return on those funds. We could then state the problem as follows: Let

P = principal, or beginning amount   = $1000

r = interest rate   = $10\% = .10$

n = number of years   = 5

S_n = the value at the end of the year n

We can readily derive the applicable compound interest formula. The amount received at the end of the first year is $P(1 + r)$. This is again compounded to determine the amount received at the end of the second year and so on.

	End of Year 1	End of Year 2	End of Year 3	...	End of Year n
Amount Received	$P(1+r)$	$P(1+r)(1+r)$	$P(1+r)(1+r)(1+r)$		
	$P(1+r)$	$P(1+r)^2$	$P(1+r)^3$	...	$P(1+r)^n$

The result is the compound interest formula. In general terms it may be stated as follows:

$$S_n = P(1 + r)^n. \tag{A.1}$$

We now have all the information needed to compute the value at the end of the fifth year, using a compound interest table* (Table A.1):

$$S_5 = \$1000(1.10)^5.$$

We then look in the compound interest table to find that at 10% a dollar over a five-year period grows to $1.6105. Since the amount we have is $1000, it is multiplied times the interest factor:

$$S_5 = \$1000(1.6105) = \$1610.5.$$

Therefore, if the firm can earn 10% with the money, it is more worthwhile for it to receive the $1000 today rather than at the end of the fifth year.

2.   Future Amounts and Their Present Values

A similar type of problem occurs when a company is offered an amount to be received in the future. It is desirable to compare that amount with the value of whatever amount could be received today. This requires the computation of the present value of the amount to be received in the future. The determination of present

---

* All tables mentioned in Appendix A are located at the end of Appendix A.

values involves the same formula except that it is solved for P, representing present value, instead of for S_n, which, in this situation, is known. By simple algebra the required formula would be:

$$P = \frac{S_n}{(1 + r)^n}.$$
(A.2)

Using our previous example, we determined S_n to be $1611. Since the appropriate interest rate is 10% and the number of years is five, this is what is required to determine P. This can be done by using our previous information and making a division. We would be dividing $1611 by 1.611 to obtain the result $1000. But we can also use a present value interest table (Table A.2), which is the reciprocal of a compound interest table. In this case the formula is:

$$P = S_n(1 + r)^{-n}.$$
(A.2a)

We can now insert the illustrative numbers:

$$P = \$1611(0.621)$$

$$= \$1000.$$

The results of compound interest and present value computations are just two different ways of looking at the same relationship.

3. Constant Payment Annuities

An annuity is a series of periodic payments made over a span of time. This is a frequently encountered type of compound interest situation. For example, a firm may sell some goods that will be paid for in installments. A basic question is, what is the present value of those installment payments? Or, the firm makes an investment from which it expects to receive a series of cash returns over a period of years. At an appropriate discount rate, what would the series of future income receipts be worth today? The firm needs this information in order to determine whether it is worthwhile to make the investment.

Some specific examples will further illustrate these ideas. The firm makes an investment. It is promised the payment of $1000 a year for 10 years with an interest rate of 10%. What is the present value of such a series of payments?

The basic formula involved is the present value of an annuity.

$$A_{n,r} = a \left[\frac{1 - (1 + r)^{-n}}{r} \right],$$
(A.3)

where

A = present value of an annuity,
a = amount of the periodic annuity payment,
r = interest factor,
n = number of annuity payments.

Equation (A.3) is derived by discounting the stream of payments, the first of which is made at the end of the first year. Mathematically, this is

$$A_{n,r} = \frac{a}{1+r} + \frac{a}{(1+r)^2} + \frac{a}{(1+r)^3} + \cdots + \frac{a}{(1+r)^n}$$

If we let $u = [1/(1+r)]$ this becomes

$$A_{n,r} = au + au^2 + au^3 + \cdots + au^n. \tag{A.4}$$

Multiplying Eq. (A.4) by u and subtracting the result from Eq. (A.4) yields

$$A_{n,r} - uA_{n,r} = au - au^{n+1},$$

$$A_{n,r} = \frac{au(1-u^n)}{1-u}.$$

Substituting back the value of u we have:

$$A_{n,r} = \frac{a\left(\dfrac{1}{1+r}\right)\left[1 - \dfrac{1}{(1+r)^n}\right]}{\left(1 - \dfrac{1}{1+r}\right)}$$

$$= \frac{a[1 - (1+r)^{-n}]}{(1+r)\left(\dfrac{1+r-1}{1+r}\right)}$$

$$= a\left[\frac{1-(1+r)^{-n}}{r}\right]. \tag{A.3}$$

Note that if the number of payments is infinite, then the present value of the annuity becomes

$$\operatorname*{Lim}_{n\to\infty} A_{n,r} = \frac{a}{r}, \tag{A.5}$$

since we know that when $r > 0$, then $\operatorname{Lim}_{n\to\infty}(1+r)^{-n} = 0$. An example of an annuity with an infinite number of constant payments is a *consol* bond. It pays a coupon at the end of each time period (usually a year) and never matures.

The expression in brackets in Eq. (A.3) is rather cumbersome. For convenience, then, instead of the cumbersome expression set out above, we shall use the symbol $P_{n,r}$, where $P_{n,r}$ = present value of an annuity factor for n years at r percent. Equation (A.3) above can, therefore, be rewritten as:

$$A_{n,r} = aP_{n,r}. \tag{A.3a}$$

Substituting actual numbers and using Table A.4 (the present value of an annuity interest table), we would have the following for 10 years at 10%:

$$\$6145 = \$1000(6.145).$$

In other words, applying an interest factor of 10% a series of payments of $1000 received for 10 years would be worth $6145 today. Hence, if the amount of investment we were required to make were $8000, for example, or any amount greater than $6145, we would be receiving a return of less than 10% on our investment. Conversely, if the investment necessary to earn annual payments of $1000 for 10 years at 10% were $5000 or any amount less than $6145, we would be earning a return greater than 10%.

A number of other questions can be answered using these same relationships. Suppose the decision facing the firm requires determining the rate of return on an investment. For example, suppose we would have $6145 to invest and that an investment opportunity promises an annual return of $1000 for 10 years. What is the indicated rate of return on our investment? Exactly the same relationship is involved, but we are now solving for the interest rate. We can, therefore, rewrite our equation as follows:

$$P_{10,10\%} = \frac{A_{10,10\%}}{a}.$$

We can now substitute the appropriate figures.

$$P_{10,10\%} = \frac{\$6145}{\$1000} = 6.145.$$

In Table A.4, which shows the present value of periodic payments received annually, we look across the row for year 10 until we find the interest rate that corresponds to the interest factor 6.145. This is 10%. We are earning a 10% return on our investment.

Let us consider another situation. Suppose that we are going to receive a return of $2000 per year for five years from an investment of $8200. What is the return on our investment? This is generally referred to as the internal rate of return on the investment, or it is also sometimes referred to as the DCF or discounted cash flow approach to valuing an investment.

We follow the same procedure as before.

$$P_{5,r} = \frac{\$8424}{\$2000}$$

$$= 4.212.$$

We look again in the present value of an annuity table (Table A.4) along the row for the year 5 to find the interest factor 4.212. We then look at the interest rate at the top of the column to find that it is 6%. Thus, the return on that investment is 6%. If our required rate of return was 10% we would not find this investment attractive. On the other hand, if the required return on our investment were only 5% we would consider the investment attractive.

These relationships can be used in still another way. Taking the facts of the preceding illustration we may ask the following question: Given an investment that yields $2000 per year for five years, at an appropriate discount factor (or cost of capital) of 6%, what is that investment worth today? What is the present value of a series of future income flows? For example, if a firm were to make a sale of goods on an open account with a down payment of $1000 plus yearly payments of $2000 for five years, what would the present value of all of the payments be at a 6% interest rate? From our previous calculations we know that the series of payments of $2000 for five years at a 6% interest rate are worth $8424 today. When we add the $1000 down payment to this figure we would have a total of $9424.

4. Compound Sum of an Annuity

We may need to know the future value or future sum to which a series of payments will accumulate. The reason may be to determine the amount of funds required to repay an obligation in the future. The sum of an annuity can be determined from the following basic relationship:*

$$S_{n,r} = a \left[\frac{(1 + r)^n - 1}{r} \right], \tag{A.6}$$

where

$S_{n,r} =$ the future sum to which an annuity will accumulate in n years at rate r,
$a =$ the amount of the annuity payment.

Suppose the firm were to receive annual payments of $1,000 a year for 10 years and is earning an interest rate of 10%. What will be the amount that the firm will have at the end of 10 years? We can solve this problem by consulting Table A.3. Utilizing our equation we would have:

$$S_{n,r} = \$1,000 \; (15.937)$$

$$= \$15,937$$

The 10 payments of $1,000 with interest would amount to $15,937 by the end of the fifth year. Thus, if we had to make a payment of $15,937 in 10 years, we would be able to do it by annual payments of $1,000 per year into a fund that earns interest at 10% per year.

---

* Note that the present value of an annuity can be obtained by discounting the expression back to the present:

$$A_{n,r} = a \left[\frac{(1 + r)^n - 1}{r(1 + r)^n} \right].$$

Now divide both terms in the numerator by $(1 + r)^n$. We have

$$A_{n,r} = a \left[\frac{1 - (1 + r)^{-n}}{r} \right].$$

This is now in the form of Eq. (A.3), the present value of an annuity.

5. Calculations for a Series of Unequal Receipts or Payments

In all of the previous illustrations we have assumed that the receipts flowing in or the payments to be made are of equal amounts. This simplifies the calculations. However, if unequal receipts or unequal payments are involved the principles are again the same, but the calculations must be somewhat extended. For example, suppose that the firm makes an investment from which it will receive the following amounts:

Year	Receipts	× Interest factor (15%)	= Present value
1	$100	.870	$ 87.00
2	200	.756	151.20
3	600	.658	394.80
4	300	.572	171.60

PV of the investment $= \$804.60$

Using the present value interest table (Table A.2) at an interest rate of 15%, we obtain the amounts indicated above. The interest factor is multiplied by the receipts to provide the amounts in the present value column. The amounts for each year are then summed to provide the present value of the investment, which in this example is $804.60. What we are doing in this example is illustrating how an annuity of unequal payments which could not be computed directly from the present value of an annuity table (Table A.4) can be handled by breaking the problem into a series of one-year payments received at successively later time periods.

6. Annuities With Growing Payments

Previously we had assumed that annuity payments were constant through time. Now we consider the case where the payments are assumed to be growing at a constant rate, g. This is a more realistic assumption if, for example, we are modeling the growing dividends paid out by a firm. Let d_0 be the current dividend per share, and assume that it was paid just yesterday, so that it does not enter into the present value computations. The stream of growing dividends to be received starts with the first end-of-year dividend, $d_1 = d_0(1 + g)$. The dividend at the end of the second year is $d_2 = d_0(1 + g)^2$. The stream of payments is assumed to grow at a constant rate for n years, therefore its present value, PV, is

$$PV = \frac{d_1}{1 + r} + \frac{d_2}{(1 + r)^2} + \frac{d_3}{(1 + r)^3} + \cdots + \frac{d_n}{(1 + r)^n}$$

$$= \frac{d_0(1 + g)}{1 + r} + \frac{d_0(1 + g)^2}{(1 + r)^2} + \frac{d_0(1 + g)^3}{(1 + r)^3} + \cdots + \frac{d_0(1 + g)^n}{(1 + r)^n}$$

If we let $u = (1 + g)/(1 + r)$ this can be rewritten as

$$PV = d_0 u + d_0 u^2 + d_0 u^3 + \cdots + d_0 u^n$$

$$= u d_0(1 + u + u^2 + \cdots + u^{n-1}). \qquad (A.7)$$

By multiplying Eq. (A.7) by u and subtracting the result from Eq. (A.7), we obtain

$$\text{PV} - u\text{PV} = ud_0(1 - u^n),$$

and solving for the present value of the growing annuity, we have

$$\text{PV} = \frac{ud_0(1 - u^n)}{1 - u}.$$

Substituting back the value of u gives us

$$\text{PV} = \frac{\left(\dfrac{1 + g}{1 + r}\right)d_0\left[1 - \left(\dfrac{1 + g}{1 + r}\right)^n\right]}{1 - \left(\dfrac{1 + g}{1 + r}\right)}$$

By rearranging terms and recalling that $d_0(1 + g) = d_1$, we obtain

$$\text{PV} = \frac{d_1\left[1 - \left(\dfrac{1 + g}{1 + r}\right)^n\right]}{r - g}. \tag{A.8}$$

Equation (A.8) is the present value of n annuity payments which start at a level of d_0 and grow at a constant rate, g.

Note that if the number of payments is infinite, we can obtain a finite present value if we assume that the growth rate in dividends, g, is less than the time value of money, r. If $g < r$, then the second term in the numerator of Eq. (A.8) goes to zero in the limit as n approaches infinity

$$\lim_{n \to \infty} \left(\frac{1 + g}{1 + r}\right)^n = 0, \qquad \text{iff} \quad g < r.$$

Therefore, the present value of an infinite number of growing dividends is

$$\lim_{n \to \infty} \text{PV} = \frac{d_1}{r - g}. \tag{A.9}$$

Equation (A.9) is used frequently in the text, where it is called the *Gordon growth model*. It provides us with an estimate of the present value of a share of common stock where the stream of dividends received from it are assumed to grow at a constant rate which is assumed to be less than the discount rate (which in this case would be the cost of equity capital, k_e).

7. The Value Additivity Principle and the NPV Criterion

It is worth emphasizing that in calculating present value (PV) relationships we have been drawing on the value additivity principle. As the example from section B.5 illustrates, the present value of amounts $(A + B + C + D)$ is equal to the present value of A plus the present value of B plus the present value of C plus the present value of D. In this earlier example, we had four cash flows ($F_1 + F_2 + F_3 + F_4$). They came in different time periods. We can obtain the present value of cash flows that occur in different years by applying the appropriate discount factor and adding.

$$PV = \frac{F_1}{(1+r)} + \frac{F_2}{(1+r)^2} + \frac{F_3}{(1+r)^3} + \frac{F_4}{(1+r)^4}. \tag{A.10}$$

Using the actual numbers, we have:

$$PV = \frac{\$100}{(1.15)} + \frac{\$200}{(1.15)^2} + \frac{\$600}{(1.15)^3} + \frac{\$300}{(1.15)^4}.$$

This can also be written as:

$$PV = \$100(.870) + \$200(.756) + \$600(.658) + \$300(.572) = \$804.60.$$

In general, the present value calculations follow the principle of value additivity for any number of cash flows, simply involving addition of the individual flows. We can write:

$$PV = \frac{F_1}{(1+r_1)} + \frac{F_2}{(1+r_2)^2} + \cdots + \frac{F_n}{(1+r_n)^n}. \tag{A.11}$$

The value additivity relationship enables all types of computational operations to be performed. This makes possible the development of valuation relationships for a wide variety of cash flow patterns, as will be developed in the subsequent materials.

Another general principle that flows from the preceding compound interest relationships is the net present value criterion. The net present value (NPV) is obtained by calculating the discounted value of the cash returns and subtracting the discounted value of the investments (or cash outflows) required to produce the positive cash flows. If a single investment is made, we add a single negative term to the present value calculations set forth above.

$$NPV = -I_0 + \frac{F_1}{(1+r)} + \frac{F_2}{(1+r)^2} + \cdots + \frac{F_n}{(1+r)^n}. \tag{A.12}$$

If investments over a period of years are required to produce the cash flows, their values are accumulated to the present:

$$NPV = -I_{-2}(1+r)^2 - I_{-1}(1+r) - I_0 + \frac{F_1}{(1+r)} + \frac{F_2}{(1+r)^2} + \cdots + \frac{F_n}{(1+r)^n}. \tag{A.13}$$

The net present value represents the addition to value created by an investment project. The applicable discount factor is the rate of interest or cost of capital appropriate to the characteristics of a project. Hence the NPV criterion is a general rule for allocating resources. By following the NPV rule, the financial markets produce the maximum amount of additions to the value for the economy. Individual investors can then buy and sell in the financial markets to obtain the use of funds for consumption in early years or to postpone consumption to later years. Nor do managers of individual firms need to consult the preferences of their shareholders or owners to determine whether they prefer investments that come to fruition in early years or later years. By following the NPV criterion, the maximum amount of additions to wealth will be achieved. The financial markets provide opportunities to the individual investors to arrange their consumption over time in years that they prefer. The NPV rule leads to the fundamental principles of valuation for flows of different kinds and different time patterns.

8.   Compounding Periods Within One Year

In the illustrations set forth thus far the examples have been for returns that were received once a year or annually. If the interest rates are calculated for periods of time within one year a simple relationship can be followed, utilizing the principles already set forth. For compounding within one year, we simply divide the interest rate by the number of compoundings within a year and multiply the annual periods by the same factor. For example, in our first equation for compound interest we had the following:

$$S_n = P(1 + r)^n.$$

This was for annual compounding. For semiannual compounding we would follow the rule just set forth. The equation would become:

$$S_n = P\left(1 + \frac{r}{m}\right)^{nm}, \tag{A.14}$$

where m = the number of compoundings during a year.

We may apply this in a numerical illustration. Suppose the initial question is, "To how much would \$1000 at a 6% interest rate accumulate over a five-year period?" The answer is \$1338. Now we apply semiannual compounding. The equation would appear as follows:

$$S_{5/2} = \$1000\left(1 + \frac{.06}{2}\right)^{5(2)}.$$

Thus the new expression is equivalent to compounding the \$1000 at 3% for 10 periods. The compound interest table (Table A.1) for 10 years shows that the interest factor would be 1.344. Our equation would, therefore, read:

$$S_{5/2} = \$1000(1 + .03)^{10},$$

$$= \$1344.$$

It will be noted that with semiannual compounding the future sum amounts to \$1344 as compared with the \$1338 we had before. Frequent compounding provides compound interest paid on compound interest, so the amount is higher. Thus we would expect that daily compounding, as some financial institutions advertise, or continuous compounding, as is employed under some assumptions, would give somewhat larger amounts than annual or semiannual compounding. But the basic ideas are unchanged.

The same logic is equally applicable to all of the categories of relationships we have described. For example, suppose a problem on the present value of an annuity was stated as the payment of $1000 a year for 10 years with an interest rate of 10% compounded annually. If the compounding is semiannual we would employ an interest rate of 5% and apply the compounding to a period of 20 years. When we compound semiannually we also have to divide the annual payment by the number of times the compounding takes place within the year. We would have the following expression:

$$A_{nm,r/m} = \$500(P_{nm,r/m})$$

$$= \$500[P_{10(2),10\%/2}]$$

$$= \$500(P_{20,5\%})$$

$$= \$500(12.462)$$

$$= \$6231.$$

It will be noted that with annual compounding the present value of the annuities was $6145. With semiannual compounding the present value is $6231. With more frequent compounding the resulting amounts will be somewhat higher because interest is compounded on interest.

C. THE TIME VALUE OF MONEY: CONTINUOUS COMPOUNDING

1. Compound Sums and Present Values

Continuous compounding simply extends the ideas involved in compounding periods within one year. Let us restate Eq. (A.14) in somewhat more general symbols:

$$V_t = P_0 \left(1 + \frac{k}{q}\right)^{qt}. \tag{A.14a}$$

Since we can multiply qt by k/k, we can set $qt = (q/k)(kt)$ and rewrite Eq. (A.14a) as

$$V_t = P_0 \left[\left(1 + \frac{k}{q}\right)^{(q/k)}\right]^{(kt)}. \tag{A.15}$$

Define $m = q/k$ and rewrite Eq. (A.15) as

$$V_t = P_0 \left[\left(1 + \frac{1}{m}\right)^{m}\right]^{kt}. \tag{A.15a}$$

As the number of compounding periods, q, increases, k also increases; this causes the term in brackets in Eq. (A.15a) to increase. At the limit, when q and m approach infinity (and compounding is instantaneous, or continuous), the term in brackets approaches the value 2.718 .... The value e is defined as this limiting case:

$$e = \lim_{m \to \infty} \left(1 + \frac{1}{m}\right)^m = 2.718 \ldots.$$

We may substitute e for the bracketed term.

$$V_t = P_0 e^{kt}. \tag{A.16}$$

Equation (A.16) is the expression for the case of continuous compounding (or continuous growth).

It is convenient to use natural logarithms to evaluate the formula for continuous compounding. We can rewrite Eq. (A.16) to express it as the relationship for $1 of initial principal. We obtain Eq. (A.17).

$$V_t = e^{kt}. \tag{A.17}$$

Next express Eq. (A.17) in log form, letting ln denote log to the base e.

$$\ln V_t = kt \ln e. \tag{A.18}$$

Since e is the base of the system of natural logarithms, $\ln e$ is equal to 1. Hence to use the table of natural logs, we have Eq. (A.19).

$$\ln V_t = kt. \tag{A.19}$$

For example, suppose our problem is to determine the future value of $1000 compounded continuously at 10% for eight years. Then $t = 8$ and $k = .10$, so $kt = .80$. We find .8 in the body of Table A.5 to be between .79751 and .80200. The first number corresponds to an interest factor of 2.22. We can then interpolate up to the .80000. This is the ratio .00249/.00449 which equals .555. Hence the interest factor is 2.22555. So the $1000 would compound to $2225.55 in eight years at 10%. This compares with $2144.00 with compounding on an annual basis.

Equation (A.16) can be transformed into Eq. (A.20) and used to determine present values under continuous compounding. Using k as the discount rate, we obtain

$$PV = \frac{V_t}{e^{kt}} = V_t e^{-kt}. \tag{A.20}$$

Thus, if $2225 is due in five years and if the appropriate continuous discount rate k is 10%, the present value of this future payment is

$$PV = \frac{\$2225}{2.225} = \$1000.$$

2.   Constant Payment Annuities

If we assume that an asset pays a constant amount per unit time then we can write that the payment at any point in time, a_t, is a constant, a_0.

$$a_t = a_0. \tag{A.21}$$

Using basic integral calculus (discussed in appendix D), we can express the present value of a constant payment stream as the discounted value of the payment function given in Eq. (A.21)

$$PV = \int_0^n a_t e^{-kt}\, dt. \tag{A.22}$$

Note that we have employed Eq. (A.20) to discount each payment. The stream of payments is assumed to start immediately $(t = 0)$ and continue for n time periods. Hence the limits of integration in Eq. (A.22) are zero to n. Following the applicable rules of integral calculus to evaluate the definite integral, we obtain

$$PV = a_0 \int_0^n e^{-kt}\, dt$$

$$= a_0 \left[\frac{-e^{-kt}}{k}\right]\Big|_0^n$$

$$= a_0 \left[\frac{-e^{-kn}}{k} - \frac{-e^0}{k}\right]$$

$$= a_0 \left[\frac{1 - e^{-kn}}{k}\right]. \tag{A.23}$$

Equation (A.23) is the continuous time analogue to Eq. (A.3) which was the discrete time version of the present value of an annuity of constant payments. Note that the continuous discount factor e^{-kn} in Eq. (A.23) is roughly equivalent to the discrete discount factor $(1 + r)^{-n}$ in Eq. (A.3).

If we want the present value of an infinite stream of constant, continuously compounded payments we take the limit of Eq. (A.23) as n becomes infinite.

$$\lim_{n \to \infty} PV = \frac{a_0}{k}. \tag{A.24}$$

Equation (A.24) is exactly equal to Eq. (A.5).

3.   Annuities with Growing Payments

For a stream of growing payments we can see from Eq. (A.17) that the payment function is

$$a_t = a_0 e^{gt}. \tag{A.25}$$

The present value of such a stream is

$$PV = \int_0^n a_t e^{-kt} \, dt$$

$$= a_0 \int_0^n e^{gt} e^{-kt} \, dt.$$

Combining terms, we have

$$PV = a_0 \int_0^n e^{-(k-g)t} \, dt.$$

Using the rules of integral calculus, the solution to this integral is

$$PV = a_0 \left[\frac{-e^{-(k-g)t}}{k-g} \right]\Big|_0^n$$

$$= a_0 \left[\frac{-e^{-(k-g)n}}{k-g} - \left(\frac{-e^0}{k-g} \right) \right]$$

$$= a_0 \left[\frac{1 - e^{-(k-g)n}}{k-g} \right]. \tag{A.26}$$

Equation (A.26) is analogous to Eq. (A.9), the discrete compounding version of the present value of an annuity of growing payments which lasts for n years.

As before, the present value of an infinite stream of payments is obtained by taking the limit of Eq. (A.26) as n approaches infinity.

$$\operatorname*{Lim}_{n \to \infty} PV = \frac{a_0}{k-g}, \qquad \text{iff} \quad g < k. \tag{A.27}$$

D. SUMMARY

Consumption is allocated over time by "the" interest rate. Positive rates of interest induce people to postpone consumption and save part of their income. The pool of savings at any given time is used for investments which yield output in the form of goods that may be consumed at future dates.

The combined preferences of all members of society and the society's technology combine to determine the pattern of interest rates that will allocate consumption over time optimally. The structure of interest rates guides individuals into making investment decisions that are most desired by the society as a whole.

Present value or future value calculations at appropriately chosen interest rates, given the riskiness of the project, will tell an investor whether the future receipts are sufficient to justify the current investment. Since the pattern of interest rates is determined by the behavior of all members of society, a positive present value means not only that the project will yield a profit to the investor, but also that no member of the society has a superior use for the resources being invested. If many other investment opportunities were to appear that were superior to the one in question, the interest rate appropriate for the present value calculation would rise, and the present value of the project might then appear to be negative.

In order to evaluate projects with cash flows distributed over time it is necessary to express all flows in terms of their value at one specific point in time. Expressing them in terms of value today is discounting to net present value; expressing them at their value on some future date is compounding to future value. There is conceptually no difference between the two approaches.

Interest rates are traditionally expressed per annum, but cash flows may occur at discrete periods during the year, or may even be continuous. Again there is no conceptual difference between discrete and continuous formulations. However, the continuous form expressions are often more convenient for complex valuation problems. For example, some models of option pricing assume that stock price behavior is continuous, and consequently most option valuation expressions are in continuous form.

Table A.1 Compound sum of $1 $S_n = P(1 + r)^n$

Year	1%	2%	3%	4%	5%	6%	7%	8%	9%	10%	11%	12%	13%	14%	15%	16%
1	1.010	1.020	1.030	1.040	1.050	1.060	1.070	1.080	1.090	1.100	1.110	1.120	1.130	1.140	1.150	1.160
2	1.020	1.040	1.061	1.082	1.102	1.124	1.145	1.166	1.188	1.210	1.232	1.254	1.277	1.300	1.322	1.346
3	1.030	1.061	1.093	1.125	1.158	1.191	1.225	1.260	1.295	1.331	1.368	1.405	1.443	1.482	1.521	1.561
4	1.041	1.082	1.126	1.170	1.216	1.262	1.311	1.360	1.412	1.464	1.518	1.574	1.631	1.689	1.749	1.811
5	1.051	1.104	1.159	1.217	1.276	1.338	1.403	1.469	1.539	1.611	1.685	1.762	1.842	1.925	2.011	2.100
6	1.062	1.126	1.194	1.265	1.340	1.419	1.501	1.587	1.677	1.772	1.870	1.974	2.082	2.195	2.313	2.436
7	1.072	1.149	1.230	1.316	1.407	1.504	1.606	1.714	1.828	1.949	2.076	2.211	2.353	2.502	2.660	2.826
8	1.083	1.172	1.267	1.369	1.477	1.594	1.718	1.851	1.993	2.144	2.305	2.476	2.658	2.853	3.059	3.278
9	1.094	1.195	1.305	1.423	1.551	1.689	1.838	1.999	2.172	2.358	2.558	2.773	3.004	3.252	3.518	3.803
10	1.105	1.219	1.344	1.480	1.629	1.791	1.967	2.159	2.367	2.594	2.839	3.106	3.395	3.707	4.046	4.411
11	1.116	1.243	1.384	1.539	1.710	1.898	2.105	2.332	2.580	2.853	3.152	3.479	3.836	4.226	4.652	5.117
12	1.127	1.268	1.426	1.601	1.796	2.012	2.252	2.518	2.813	3.138	3.499	3.896	4.335	4.818	5.350	5.936
13	1.138	1.294	1.469	1.665	1.886	2.133	2.410	2.720	3.066	3.452	3.883	4.363	4.898	5.492	6.153	6.886
14	1.149	1.319	1.513	1.732	1.980	2.261	2.579	2.937	3.342	3.797	4.310	4.887	5.535	6.261	7.076	7.988
15	1.161	1.346	1.558	1.801	2.079	2.397	2.759	3.172	3.642	4.177	4.785	5.474	6.254	7.138	8.137	9.266
16	1.173	1.373	1.605	1.873	2.183	2.540	2.952	3.426	3.970	4.595	5.311	6.130	7.067	8.137	9.358	10.748
17	1.184	1.400	1.653	1.948	2.292	2.693	3.159	3.700	4.328	5.054	5.895	6.866	7.986	9.276	10.761	12.468
18	1.196	1.428	1.702	2.026	2.407	2.854	3.380	3.996	4.717	5.560	6.544	7.690	9.024	10.575	12.375	14.463
19	1.208	1.457	1.754	2.107	2.527	3.026	3.617	4.316	5.142	6.116	7.263	8.613	10.197	12.056	14.232	16.777
20	1.220	1.486	1.806	2.191	2.653	3.207	3.870	4.661	5.604	6.728	8.062	9.646	11.523	13.743	16.367	19.461

Source: Adapted from Jerome Bracken and Charles J. Christenson, *Tables for Use in Analyzing Business Decisions* (Homewood, Ill.: Richard D. Irwin, Inc., 1965).

Table A.2 Present value of $1 $P = S_n(1 + r)^{-n}$

Years Hence	1%	2%	4%	6%	8%	10%	12%	14%	15%	16%	18%	20%	22%	24%	25%	26%	28%	30%	35%	40%	45%	50%
1	0.990	0.980	0.962	0.943	0.926	0.909	0.893	0.877	0.870	0.862	0.847	0.833	0.820	0.806	0.800	0.794	0.781	0.769	0.741	0.714	0.690	0.667
2	0.980	0.961	0.925	0.890	0.857	0.826	0.797	0.769	0.756	0.743	0.718	0.694	0.672	0.650	0.640	0.630	0.610	0.592	0.549	0.510	0.476	0.444
3	0.971	0.942	0.889	0.840	0.794	0.751	0.712	0.675	0.658	0.641	0.609	0.579	0.551	0.524	0.512	0.500	0.477	0.455	0.406	0.364	0.328	0.296
4	0.961	0.924	0.855	0.792	0.735	0.683	0.636	0.592	0.572	0.552	0.516	0.482	0.451	0.423	0.410	0.397	0.373	0.350	0.301	0.260	0.226	0.198
5	0.951	0.906	0.822	0.747	0.681	0.621	0.567	0.519	0.497	0.476	0.437	0.402	0.370	0.341	0.328	0.315	0.291	0.269	0.223	0.186	0.156	0.132
6	0.942	0.888	0.790	0.705	0.630	0.564	0.507	0.456	0.432	0.410	0.370	0.335	0.303	0.275	0.262	0.250	0.227	0.207	0.165	0.133	0.108	0.088
7	0.933	0.871	0.760	0.665	0.583	0.513	0.452	0.400	0.376	0.354	0.314	0.279	0.249	0.222	0.210	0.198	0.178	0.159	0.122	0.095	0.074	0.059
8	0.923	0.853	0.731	0.627	0.540	0.467	0.404	0.351	0.327	0.305	0.266	0.233	0.204	0.179	0.168	0.157	0.139	0.123	0.091	0.068	0.051	0.039
9	0.914	0.837	0.703	0.592	0.500	0.424	0.361	0.308	0.284	0.263	0.225	0.194	0.167	0.144	0.134	0.125	0.108	0.094	0.067	0.048	0.035	0.026
10	0.905	0.820	0.676	0.558	0.463	0.386	0.322	0.270	0.247	0.227	0.191	0.162	0.137	0.116	0.107	0.099	0.085	0.073	0.050	0.035	0.024	0.017
11	0.896	0.804	0.650	0.527	0.429	0.350	0.287	0.237	0.215	0.195	0.162	0.135	0.112	0.094	0.086	0.079	0.066	0.056	0.037	0.025	0.017	0.012
12	0.887	0.788	0.625	0.497	0.397	0.319	0.257	0.208	0.187	0.168	0.137	0.112	0.092	0.076	0.069	0.062	0.052	0.043	0.027	0.018	0.012	0.008
13	0.879	0.773	0.601	0.469	0.368	0.290	0.229	0.182	0.163	0.145	0.116	0.093	0.075	0.061	0.055	0.050	0.040	0.033	0.020	0.013	0.008	0.005
14	0.870	0.758	0.577	0.442	0.340	0.263	0.205	0.160	0.141	0.125	0.099	0.078	0.062	0.049	0.044	0.039	0.032	0.025	0.015	0.009	0.006	0.003
15	0.861	0.743	0.555	0.417	0.315	0.239	0.183	0.140	0.123	0.108	0.084	0.065	0.051	0.040	0.035	0.031	0.025	0.020	0.011	0.006	0.004	0.002
16	0.853	0.728	0.534	0.394	0.292	0.218	0.163	0.123	0.107	0.093	0.071	0.054	0.042	0.032	0.028	0.025	0.019	0.015	0.008	0.005	0.003	0.002
17	0.844	0.714	0.513	0.371	0.270	0.198	0.146	0.108	0.093	0.080	0.060	0.045	0.034	0.026	0.023	0.020	0.015	0.012	0.006	0.003	0.002	0.001
18	0.836	0.700	0.494	0.350	0.250	0.180	0.130	0.095	0.081	0.069	0.051	0.038	0.028	0.021	0.018	0.016	0.012	0.009	0.005	0.002	0.001	0.001
19	0.828	0.686	0.475	0.331	0.232	0.164	0.116	0.083	0.070	0.060	0.043	0.031	0.023	0.017	0.014	0.012	0.009	0.007	0.003	0.002	0.001	
20	0.820	0.673	0.456	0.312	0.215	0.149	0.104	0.073	0.061	0.051	0.037	0.026	0.019	0.014	0.012	0.010	0.007	0.005	0.002	0.001	0.001	
21	0.811	0.660	0.439	0.294	0.199	0.135	0.093	0.064	0.053	0.044	0.031	0.022	0.015	0.011	0.009	0.008	0.006	0.004	0.002	0.001		
22	0.803	0.647	0.422	0.278	0.184	0.123	0.083	0.056	0.046	0.038	0.026	0.018	0.013	0.009	0.007	0.006	0.004	0.003	0.001	0.001		
23	0.795	0.634	0.406	0.262	0.170	0.112	0.074	0.049	0.040	0.033	0.022	0.015	0.010	0.007	0.006	0.005	0.003	0.002	0.001			
24	0.788	0.622	0.390	0.247	0.158	0.102	0.066	0.043	0.035	0.028	0.019	0.013	0.008	0.006	0.005	0.004	0.003	0.002	0.001			
25	0.780	0.610	0.375	0.233	0.146	0.092	0.059	0.038	0.030	0.024	0.016	0.010	0.007	0.005	0.004	0.003	0.002	0.001	0.001			
26	0.772	0.598	0.361	0.220	0.135	0.084	0.053	0.033	0.026	0.021	0.014	0.009	0.006	0.004	0.003	0.002	0.002	0.001				
27	0.764	0.586	0.347	0.207	0.125	0.076	0.047	0.029	0.023	0.018	0.011	0.007	0.005	0.003	0.002	0.002	0.001	0.001				
28	0.757	0.574	0.333	0.196	0.116	0.069	0.042	0.026	0.020	0.016	0.010	0.006	0.004	0.002	0.002	0.001	0.001	0.001				
29	0.749	0.563	0.321	0.185	0.107	0.063	0.037	0.022	0.017	0.014	0.008	0.005	0.003	0.002	0.002	0.001	0.001	0.001				
30	0.742	0.552	0.308	0.174	0.099	0.057	0.033	0.020	0.015	0.012	0.007	0.004	0.003	0.002	0.001	0.001	0.001	0.001				
40	0.672	0.453	0.208	0.097	0.046	0.022	0.011	0.005	0.004	0.003	0.001	0.001										
50	0.608	0.372	0.141	0.054	0.021	0.009	0.003	0.001	0.001	0.001												

Source: Adapted from Jerome Bracken and Charles J. Christenson, *Tables for Use in Analyzing Business Decisions* (Homewood, Ill.: Richard D. Irwin, Inc., 1965).

Table A.3 Sum of an annuity for $1 for n years

$$S_{\overline{n}|r} = \$1\left[\frac{(1+r)^n - 1}{r}\right] = \$1 C_{n,r}$$

Year	1%	2%	3%	4%	5%	6%	7%	8%	9%	10%	11%	12%	13%	14%	15%	16%
1......	1.000	1.000	1.000	1.000	1.000	1.000	1.000	1.000	1.000	1.000	1.000	1.000	1.000	1.000	1.000	1.000
2......	2.010	2.020	2.030	2.040	2.050	2.060	2.070	2.080	2.090	2.100	2.110	2.120	2.130	2.140	2.150	2.160
3......	3.030	3.060	3.091	3.122	3.152	3.184	3.215	3.246	3.278	3.310	3.342	3.374	3.407	3.440	3.473	3.506
4......	4.060	4.122	4.184	4.246	4.310	4.375	4.440	4.506	4.573	4.641	4.710	4.779	4.850	4.921	4.993	5.066
5......	5.101	5.204	5.309	5.416	5.526	5.637	5.751	5.867	5.985	6.105	6.228	6.353	6.480	6.610	6.742	6.877
6......	6.152	6.308	6.468	6.633	6.802	6.975	7.153	7.336	7.523	7.716	7.913	8.115	8.323	8.536	8.754	8.977
7......	7.214	7.434	7.662	7.898	8.142	8.394	8.654	8.923	9.200	9.487	9.783	10.089	10.405	10.730	11.067	11.414
8......	8.286	8.583	8.892	9.214	9.549	9.897	10.260	10.637	11.028	11.436	11.859	12.300	12.757	13.233	13.727	14.240
9......	9.369	9.755	10.159	10.583	11.027	11.491	11.978	12.488	13.021	13.579	14.164	14.776	15.416	16.085	16.786	17.518
10......	10.462	10.950	11.464	12.006	12.578	13.181	13.816	14.487	15.193	15.937	16.722	17.549	18.420	19.337	20.304	21.321
11......	11.567	12.169	12.808	13.486	14.207	14.972	15.784	16.645	17.560	18.531	19.561	20.655	21.814	23.044	24.349	25.733
12......	12.683	13.412	14.192	15.026	15.917	16.870	17.888	18.977	20.141	21.384	22.713	24.133	25.650	27.271	29.002	30.850
13......	13.809	14.680	15.618	16.627	17.713	18.882	20.141	21.495	22.953	24.523	26.212	28.029	29.985	32.089	34.352	36.786
14......	14.947	15.974	17.086	18.292	19.599	21.051	22.550	24.215	26.019	27.975	30.095	32.393	34.883	37.581	40.505	43.672
15......	16.097	17.293	18.599	20.024	21.579	23.276	25.129	27.152	29.361	31.772	34.405	37.280	40.417	43.842	47.580	51.659

Source: Adapted from Jerome Bracken and Charles J. Christenson, *Tables for Use in Analyzing Business Decisions* (Homewood, Ill.: Richard D. Irwin, Inc., 1965).

Table A.4 Present value of $1 received annually

$$A_{\overline{n}|r} = \$1\left[\frac{1-(1+r)^{-n}}{r}\right] = \$1 P_{n,r}$$

Years (n)	1%	2%	4%	6%	8%	10%	12%	14%	15%	16%	18%	20%	22%	24%	25%	26%	28%	30%	35%	40%	45%	50%
1	0.990	0.980	0.962	0.943	0.926	0.909	0.893	0.877	0.870	0.862	0.847	0.833	0.820	0.806	0.800	0.794	0.781	0.769	0.741	0.714	0.690	0.667
2	1.970	1.942	1.886	1.833	1.783	1.736	1.690	1.647	1.626	1.605	1.566	1.528	1.492	1.457	1.440	1.424	1.392	1.361	1.289	1.224	1.165	1.111
3	2.941	2.884	2.775	2.673	2.577	2.487	2.402	2.322	2.283	2.246	2.174	2.106	2.042	1.981	1.952	1.923	1.868	1.816	1.696	1.589	1.493	1.407
4	3.902	3.808	3.630	3.465	3.312	3.170	3.037	2.914	2.855	2.798	2.690	2.589	2.494	2.404	2.362	2.320	2.241	2.166	1.997	1.849	1.720	1.605
5	4.853	4.713	4.452	4.212	3.993	3.791	3.605	3.433	3.352	3.274	3.127	2.991	2.864	2.745	2.689	2.635	2.532	2.436	2.220	2.035	1.876	1.737
6	5.795	5.601	5.242	4.917	4.623	4.355	4.111	3.889	3.784	3.685	3.498	3.326	3.167	3.020	2.951	2.885	2.759	2.643	2.385	2.168	1.983	1.824
7	6.728	6.472	6.002	5.582	5.206	4.868	4.564	4.288	4.160	4.039	3.812	3.605	3.416	3.242	3.161	3.083	2.937	2.802	2.508	2.263	2.057	1.883
8	7.652	7.325	6.733	6.210	5.747	5.335	4.968	4.639	4.487	4.344	4.078	3.837	3.619	3.421	3.329	3.241	3.076	2.925	2.598	2.331	2.108	1.922
9	8.566	8.162	7.435	6.802	6.247	5.759	5.328	4.946	4.772	4.607	4.303	4.031	3.786	3.566	3.463	3.366	3.184	3.019	2.665	2.379	2.144	1.948
10	9.471	8.983	8.111	7.360	6.710	6.145	5.650	5.216	5.019	4.833	4.494	4.192	3.923	3.682	3.571	3.465	3.269	3.092	2.715	2.414	2.168	1.965
11	10.368	9.787	8.760	7.887	7.139	6.495	5.937	5.453	5.234	5.029	4.656	4.327	4.035	3.776	3.656	3.544	3.335	3.147	2.752	2.438	2.185	1.977
12	11.255	10.575	9.385	8.384	7.536	6.814	6.194	5.660	5.421	5.197	4.793	4.439	4.127	3.851	3.725	3.606	3.387	3.190	2.779	2.456	2.196	1.985
13	12.134	11.343	9.986	8.853	7.904	7.103	6.424	5.842	5.583	5.342	4.910	4.533	4.203	3.912	3.780	3.656	3.427	3.223	2.799	2.468	2.204	1.990
14	13.004	12.106	10.563	9.295	8.244	7.367	6.628	6.002	5.724	5.468	5.008	4.611	4.265	3.962	3.824	3.695	3.459	3.249	2.814	2.477	2.210	1.993
15	13.865	12.849	11.118	9.712	8.559	7.606	6.811	6.142	5.847	5.575	5.092	4.675	4.315	4.001	3.859	3.726	3.483	3.268	2.825	2.484	2.214	1.995
16	14.718	13.578	11.652	10.106	8.851	7.824	6.974	6.265	5.954	5.669	5.162	4.730	4.357	4.033	3.887	3.751	3.503	3.283	2.834	2.489	2.216	1.997
17	15.562	14.292	12.166	10.477	9.122	8.022	7.120	6.373	6.047	5.749	5.222	4.775	4.391	4.059	3.910	3.771	3.518	3.295	2.840	2.492	2.218	1.998
18	16.398	14.992	12.659	10.828	9.372	8.201	7.250	6.467	6.128	5.818	5.273	4.812	4.419	4.080	3.928	3.786	3.529	3.304	2.844	2.494	2.219	1.999
19	17.226	15.678	13.134	11.158	9.604	8.365	7.366	6.550	6.198	5.877	5.316	4.844	4.442	4.097	3.942	3.799	3.539	3.311	2.848	2.496	2.220	1.999
20	18.046	16.351	13.590	11.470	9.818	8.514	7.469	6.623	6.259	5.929	5.353	4.870	4.460	4.110	3.954	3.808	3.546	3.316	2.850	2.497	2.221	1.999
21	18.857	17.011	14.029	11.764	10.017	8.649	7.562	6.687	6.312	5.973	5.384	4.891	4.476	4.121	3.963	3.816	3.551	3.320	2.852	2.498	2.221	2.000
22	19.660	17.658	14.451	12.042	10.201	8.772	7.645	6.743	6.359	6.011	5.410	4.909	4.488	4.130	3.970	3.822	3.556	3.323	2.853	2.498	2.222	2.000
23	20.456	18.292	14.857	12.303	10.371	8.883	7.718	6.792	6.399	6.044	5.432	4.925	4.499	4.137	3.976	3.827	3.559	3.325	2.854	2.499	2.222	2.000
24	21.243	18.914	15.247	12.550	10.529	8.985	7.784	6.835	6.434	6.073	5.451	4.937	4.507	4.143	3.981	3.831	3.562	3.327	2.855	2.499	2.222	2.000
25	22.023	19.523	15.622	12.783	10.675	9.077	7.843	6.873	6.464	6.097	5.467	4.948	4.514	4.147	3.985	3.834	3.564	3.329	2.856	2.499	2.222	2.000
26	22.795	20.121	15.983	13.003	10.810	9.161	7.896	6.906	6.491	6.118	5.480	4.956	4.520	4.151	3.988	3.837	3.566	3.330	2.856	2.500	2.222	2.000
27	23.560	20.707	16.330	13.211	10.935	9.237	7.943	6.935	6.514	6.136	5.492	4.964	4.524	4.154	3.990	3.839	3.567	3.331	2.856	2.500	2.222	2.000
28	24.316	21.281	16.663	13.406	11.051	9.307	7.984	6.961	6.534	6.152	5.502	4.970	4.528	4.157	3.992	3.840	3.568	3.331	2.857	2.500	2.222	2.000
29	25.066	21.844	16.984	13.591	11.158	9.370	8.022	6.983	6.551	6.166	5.510	4.975	4.531	4.159	3.994	3.841	3.569	3.332	2.857	2.500	2.222	2.000
30	25.808	22.396	17.292	13.765	11.258	9.427	8.055	7.003	6.566	6.177	5.517	4.979	4.534	4.160	3.995	3.842	3.569	3.332	2.857	2.500	2.222	2.000
40	32.835	27.355	19.793	15.046	11.925	9.779	8.244	7.105	6.642	6.234	5.548	4.997	4.544	4.166	3.999	3.846	3.571	3.333	2.857	2.500	2.222	2.000
50	39.196	31.424	21.482	15.762	12.234	9.915	8.304	7.133	6.661	6.246	5.554	4.999	4.545	4.167	4.000	3.846	3.571	3.333	2.857	2.500	2.222	2.000

Source: Adapted from Jerome Bracken and Charles J. Christenson, *Tables for Use in Analyzing Business Decisions* (Homewood, Ill.: Richard D. Irwin, Inc., 1965).

Table A.5 Natural logarithms of numbers between 1.0 and 4.99

N	0	1	2	3	4	5	6	7	8	9
1.0	0.00000	.00995	.01980	.02956	.03922	.04879	.05827	.06766	.07696	.08618
.1	.09531	.10436	.11333	.12222	.13103	.13976	.14842	.15700	.16551	.17395
.2	.18232	.19062	.19885	.20701	.21511	.22314	.23111	.23902	.24686	.25464
.3	.26236	.27003	.27763	.28518	.29267	.30010	.30748	.31481	.32208	.32930
.4	.33647	.34359	.35066	.35767	.36464	.37156	.37844	.38526	.39204	.39878
.5	.40547	.41211	.41871	.42527	.43178	.43825	.44469	.45108	.45742	.46373
.6	.47000	.47623	.48243	.48858	.49470	.50078	.50682	.51282	.51879	.52473
.7	.53063	.53649	.54232	.54812	.55389	.55962	.56531	.57098	.57661	.58222
.8	.58779	.59333	.59884	.60432	.60977	.61519	.62058	.62594	.63127	.63658
.9	.64185	.64710	.65233	.65752	.66269	.66783	.67294	.67803	.68310	.68813
2.0	0.69315	.69813	.70310	.70804	.71295	.71784	.72271	.72755	.73237	.73716
.1	.74194	.74669	.75142	.75612	.76081	.76547	.77011	.77473	.77932	.78390
.2	.78846	.79299	.79751	.80200	.80648	.81093	.81536	.81978	.82418	.82855
.3	.83291	.83725	.84157	.84587	.85015	.85442	.85866	.86289	.86710	.87129
.4	.87547	.87963	.88377	.88789	.89200	.89609	.90016	.90422	.90826	.91228
.5	.91629	.92028	.92426	.92822	.93216	.93609	.94001	.94391	.94779	.95166
.6	.95551	.95935	.96317	.96698	.97078	.97456	.97833	.98208	.98582	.98954
.7	.99325	.99695	.00063[a]	.00430[a]	.00796[a]	.01160[a]	.01523[a]	.01885[a]	.02245[a]	.02604[a]
.8	1.02962	.03318	.03674	.04028	.04380	.04732	.05082	.05431	.05779	.06126
.9	.06471	.06815	.07158	.07500	.07841	.08181	.08519	.08856	.09192	.09527
3.0	1.09861	.10194	.10526	.10856	.11186	.11514	.11841	.12168	.12493	.12817
.1	.13140	.13462	.13783	.14103	.14422	.14740	.15057	.15373	.15688	.16002
.2	.16315	.16627	.16938	.17248	.17557	.17865	.18173	.18479	.18784	.19089
.3	.19392	.19695	.19996	.20297	.20597	.20896	.21194	.21491	.21788	.22083
.4	.22378	.22671	.22964	.23256	.23547	.23837	.24127	.24415	.24703	.24990
.5	.25276	.25562	.25846	.26130	.26413	.26695	.26976	.27257	.27536	.27815
.6	.28093	.28371	.28647	.28923	.29198	.29473	.29746	.30019	.30291	.30563
.7	.30833	.31103	.31372	.31641	.31909	.32176	.32442	.32708	.32972	.33237
.8	.33500	.33763	.34025	.34286	.34547	.34807	.35067	.35325	.35584	.35841
.9	.36098	.36354	.36609	.36864	.37118	.37372	.37624	.37877	.38128	.38379
4.0	1.38629	.38879	.39128	.39377	.39624	.39872	.40118	.40364	.40610	.40854
.1	.41099	.41342	.41585	.41828	.42070	.42311	.42552	.42792	.43031	.43270
.2	.43508	.43746	.43984	.44220	.44456	.44692	.44927	.45161	.45395	.45629
.3	.45862	.46094	.46326	.46557	.46787	.47018	.47247	.47476	.47705	.47933
.4	.48160	.48387	.48614	.48840	.49065	.49290	.49515	.49739	.49962	.50185
.5	.50408	.50630	.50851	.51072	.51293	.51513	.51732	.51951	.52170	.52388
.6	.52606	.52823	.53039	.53256	.53471	.53687	.53902	.54116	.54330	.54543
.7	.54756	.54969	.55181	.55393	.55604	.55814	.56025	.56235	.56444	.56653
.8	.56862	.57070	.57277	.57485	.57691	.57898	.58104	.58309	.58515	.58719
.9	.58924	.59127	.59331	.59534	.59737	.59939	.60141	.60342	.60543	.60744

[a]Add 1.0 to indicated figure.

Appendix B

Matrix Algebra

A. MATRICES AND VECTORS

A matrix is a rectangular array of numbers. The following are examples of matrices:

$$\underset{(3 \times 2)}{A} = \begin{pmatrix} 1 & 2 \\ 0 & 1 \\ -1 & 4 \end{pmatrix}, \qquad \underset{(3 \times 4)}{B} = \begin{pmatrix} 2 & 3 & 1.5 & 0 \\ -1 & 4 & -1 & -1 \\ 3 & 1.1 & 2 & -5 \end{pmatrix},$$

$$\underset{(2 \times 2)}{C} = \begin{pmatrix} 2 & 1 \\ 1 & -2 \end{pmatrix}.$$

The matrix A is a 3×2 matrix because it has three rows and two columns. The matrix B is a 3×4 matrix because it has three rows and four columns. The matrix C is a 2×2 square matrix because it has two rows and two columns.

Each number in a matrix is called an element. The element on the ith row and jth column of the matrix A is designated by a_{ij}. For example, in the matrix A above, $a_{11} = 1$, $a_{12} = 2$, $a_{21} = 0$ and so on. Similarly, in the matrix B, $b_{12} = 3$, $b_{32} = 1.1$.

We say that two $m \times n$ matrices are equal if all their corresponding elements are identical. In other words, if both R and S are $m \times n$ matrices, then $R = S$ if and only if $r_{ij} = s_{ij}$ for all $i = 1, 2, \ldots, m$ and $j = 1, 2, \ldots, n$. For example,

$$\begin{pmatrix} 1 & 2 \\ -1 & 1 \end{pmatrix} = \begin{pmatrix} 1 & 2 \\ -1 & 1 \end{pmatrix} \quad \text{but} \quad \begin{pmatrix} 1 & 1 \\ 0 & 1 \end{pmatrix} \neq \begin{pmatrix} 1 & 0 \\ 1 & 1 \end{pmatrix}.$$

Vectors are matrices with only one row or one column. A $1 \times m$ matrix is called a row vector and a $m \times 1$ matrix is called a column vector. For example,

$$\underset{(1 \times 3)}{a} = (1 \quad -1 \quad 1), \qquad \underset{(1 \times 4)}{b} = (1 \quad 2 \quad 0 \quad 1)$$

are row vectors and

$$c \atop (2 \times 1) = \begin{pmatrix} 1 \\ -1 \end{pmatrix}, \qquad d \atop (3 \times 1) = \begin{pmatrix} 1 \\ 3 \\ 2 \end{pmatrix}$$

are column vectors. Each number in a vector is called a component of that vector. The ith component of the vector a is designated by a_i. So, $a_1 = 1, a_2 = -1, a_3 = 1$ in the vector a above.

Two $1 \times n$ row vectors or two $m \times 1$ column vectors are equal if all the corresponding components are the same. For example,

$$\begin{pmatrix} 1 \\ 2 \end{pmatrix} = \begin{pmatrix} 1 \\ 2 \end{pmatrix}, \qquad (3 \quad 1 \quad 2) = (3 \quad 1 \quad 2),$$

but

$$\begin{pmatrix} 1 \\ 2 \end{pmatrix} \neq (1 \quad 2), \qquad \begin{pmatrix} 1 \\ 2 \end{pmatrix} \neq \begin{pmatrix} 2 \\ 1 \end{pmatrix}, \qquad \begin{pmatrix} 1 \\ 2 \end{pmatrix} \neq \begin{pmatrix} 1 \\ 2 \\ 3 \end{pmatrix}.$$

B. THE OPERATIONS OF MATRICES

Addition and subtraction of two matrices A and B can be performed if A and B have the same dimension—that is, if the number of rows and the number of columns are the same. Addition and subtraction is carried out on each corresponding pair of elements. If $A + B = C$, then $a_{ij} + b_{ij} = c_{ij}$. For example,

$$\begin{pmatrix} 1 & 2 \\ 3 & 4 \end{pmatrix} + \begin{pmatrix} -1 & 1 \\ 2 & -1 \end{pmatrix} = \begin{pmatrix} 1-1 & 2+1 \\ 3+2 & 4-1 \end{pmatrix} = \begin{pmatrix} 0 & 3 \\ 5 & 3 \end{pmatrix},$$

$$\begin{pmatrix} 1 & 2 \\ 3 & 4 \end{pmatrix} - \begin{pmatrix} -1 & 1 \\ 2 & -1 \end{pmatrix} = \begin{pmatrix} 1-(-1) & 2-1 \\ 3-2 & 4-(-1) \end{pmatrix} = \begin{pmatrix} 2 & 1 \\ 1 & 5 \end{pmatrix},$$

$$\begin{pmatrix} 1 \\ 2 \end{pmatrix} - \begin{pmatrix} 1 \\ 1 \end{pmatrix} = \begin{pmatrix} 0 \\ 1 \end{pmatrix}, \qquad \begin{pmatrix} 1 \\ 2 \end{pmatrix} + \begin{pmatrix} 1 \\ 1 \end{pmatrix} = \begin{pmatrix} 2 \\ 3 \end{pmatrix}.$$

If we multiply a matrix A by a scalar, the resultant matrix is obtained by multiplying each element of A by that scalar. So if

$$A = \begin{pmatrix} 1 & 2 & 3 \\ -1 & 1 & 2 \end{pmatrix},$$

then

$$2A = \begin{pmatrix} 2 & 4 & 6 \\ -2 & 2 & 4 \end{pmatrix}, \qquad -3A = \begin{pmatrix} -3 & -6 & -9 \\ 3 & -3 & -6 \end{pmatrix}.$$

We can also multiply two matrices together provided that the number of columns in the first matrix is equal to the number of rows in the second matrix. In order to form the product AB of the two matrices A and B, the number of columns of A must be equal to the number of rows of B. If we designate the result of the matrix multiplication AB by C, then C is again a matrix and C has the same number of rows as A and the same number of columns as B. To summarize: if A is an $m \times n$ matrix and B a $p \times q$ matrix, then the product AB can be formed only if $n = p$; further, if $C = AB$, then C is an $m \times q$ matrix.

To complete our definition of matrix multiplication, we have to describe how the elements of C are obtained. The following rule specifies c_{ij}, the element in the ith row and jth column of the resultant matrix C, in terms of elements in A and B:

$$c_{ij} = a_{i1}b_{1j} + a_{i2}b_{2j} + \cdots + a_{in}b_{nj} = \sum_{k=1}^{n} a_{ik}b_{kj}, \tag{B.1}$$

where n = number of columns of A = number of rows of B.

Equation (B.1) tells us that c_{ij} is a sum of products. Each product consists of an element from the ith row of A and an element from the jth row of B. We multiply the first element in the ith row of A with the first element in the jth column of B, the second element in the ith row of A with the second element in the jth column of B—and so on until the last element in the ith row of A is multiplied with the last element in the jth column of B—and then sum all the products. Another way to look at this is: to obtain c_{ij}, we "multiply" the ith row of A with the jth column of B.

An example further clarifies Eq. (B.1). Consider $C = AB$, where

$$A = \begin{pmatrix} 1 & 2 & 3 \\ 1 & 0 & 1 \end{pmatrix} \qquad B = \begin{pmatrix} -1 & 3 & 0 & 0 \\ 2 & 1 & 1 & 0 \\ 1 & 0 & 0 & 1 \end{pmatrix}.$$

Since A is 2×3 and B is 3×4, the product AB can be formed and C would be 2×4. According to Eq. (B.1),

$$c_{11} = a_{11}b_{11} + a_{12}b_{21} + a_{13}b_{31} = 1 \times (-1) + 2 \times 2 + 3 \times 1 = 6,$$

$$c_{12} = a_{11}b_{12} + a_{12}b_{22} + a_{13}b_{32} = 1 \times 3 + 2 \times 1 + 3 \times 0 = 5,$$

and so on. The result $AB = C$ is

$$\begin{pmatrix} \boxed{1 \quad 2 \quad 3} \\ 1 \quad 0 \quad 1 \end{pmatrix} \begin{pmatrix} -1 & \boxed{3} & 0 & 0 \\ 2 & \boxed{1} & 1 & 0 \\ 1 & \boxed{0} & 0 & 1 \end{pmatrix} = \begin{pmatrix} 6 & \boxed{5} & 2 & 3 \\ 0 & 3 & 0 & 1 \end{pmatrix}$$

We should emphasize at this point that the product BA may not be defined even though AB is. We can take the above as an example. A is $2 \times \underline{3}$ and B is $\underline{3} \times 4$, so AB is defined, but BA is not, since $4 \neq 2$. In the event that BA is also defined, $BA \neq AB$ in general. For example, let

$$A = \begin{pmatrix} 1 & 1 \\ 0 & 1 \end{pmatrix}, \quad B = \begin{pmatrix} 1 & 0 \\ 1 & 1 \end{pmatrix},$$

then

$$AB = \begin{pmatrix} 2 & 1 \\ 1 & 1 \end{pmatrix} \quad \text{but} \quad BA = \begin{pmatrix} 1 & 1 \\ 1 & 2 \end{pmatrix}.$$

C. LINEAR EQUATIONS IN MATRIX FORM

A system of linear equations can be expressed in matrix form. First, let us consider one simple linear equation, say $X_1 - 2X_2 + 2X_3 = 4$. Using matrix multiplication, the equation can be expressed as

$$(1 \quad -2 \quad 2) \begin{pmatrix} X_1 \\ X_2 \\ X_3 \end{pmatrix} = (1X_1 + (-2)X_2 + 2X_3) = 4.$$

Suppose we now have the following system of three equations:

$$\begin{aligned} X_1 \quad -2X_2 \quad +2X_3 &= 4, \\ X_1 \quad + X_2 \quad + X_3 &= 5, \\ -X_1 \quad +5X_2 \quad -3X_3 &= 1, \end{aligned}$$

using matrix multiplication, this is equivalent to

$$\underset{3 \times 3}{\begin{pmatrix} 1 & -2 & 2 \\ 1 & 1 & 1 \\ -1 & 5 & -3 \end{pmatrix}} \underset{3 \times 1}{\begin{pmatrix} X_1 \\ X_2 \\ X_3 \end{pmatrix}} = \begin{pmatrix} 1 \cdot X_1 - 2 \cdot X_2 + 2 \cdot X_3 \\ 1 \cdot X_1 + 1 \cdot X_2 + 1 \cdot X_3 \\ -1 \cdot X_1 + 5 \cdot X_2 - 3 \cdot X_3 \end{pmatrix} = \underset{3 \times 1}{\begin{pmatrix} 4 \\ 5 \\ 1 \end{pmatrix}}.$$

And because of the equality definition of vectors, we must equate $(1 \cdot X_1 - 2 \cdot X_2 - 2 \cdot X_3)$ to 4 and $(1 \cdot X_1 + 1 \cdot X_2 + 1 \cdot X_3)$ to 5 and $(-1 \cdot X_1 + 5 \cdot X_2 - 3 \cdot X_3)$ to 1, which shows that the matrix formulation

$$\begin{pmatrix} 1 & -2 & 2 \\ 1 & 1 & 1 \\ -1 & 5 & -3 \end{pmatrix} \begin{pmatrix} X_1 \\ X_2 \\ X_3 \end{pmatrix} = \begin{pmatrix} 4 \\ 5 \\ 1 \end{pmatrix} \tag{B.2}$$

is equivalent to the system of linear equations. In general, Eq. (B.2) is written as $Ax = b$, where

$$A = \begin{pmatrix} 1 & -2 & 2 \\ 1 & 1 & 1 \\ -1 & 5 & -3 \end{pmatrix}, \quad x = \begin{pmatrix} X_1 \\ X_2 \\ X_3 \end{pmatrix}, \quad b = \begin{pmatrix} 4 \\ 5 \\ 1 \end{pmatrix}.$$

A is called the coefficient matrix, x is the vector of unknowns, and b is the vector of constants. Finding the solution to a system of linear equations is equivalent to solving for the unknown vector x in the matrix equation $Ax = b$. We will come back to solving $Ax = b$ in a later section.

D. SPECIAL MATRICES

There are several types of matrices that possess useful properties. Here we list some of the more important ones.

The zero (or null) matrix is a matrix with all elements (or components) being zero. For example,

$$\begin{pmatrix} 0 & 0 \\ 0 & 0 \end{pmatrix}, \qquad \begin{pmatrix} 0 & 0 & 0 & 0 \\ 0 & 0 & 0 & 0 \\ 0 & 0 & 0 & 0 \end{pmatrix}$$

are null matrices of dimensions 2×2 and 3×4. The zero matrix $\mathbf{0}$ possesses the property that

$$A + \mathbf{0} = \mathbf{0} + A = A$$

for any matrix A of the same dimension.

A diagonal matrix is a square matrix whose elements are all zeros except on the *main diagonal*, that is, D is a diagonal matrix if $d_{ij} = 0$ for $i \neq j$. For example,

$$\begin{pmatrix} 1 & 0 \\ 0 & 2 \end{pmatrix}, \qquad \begin{pmatrix} 1 & 0 & 0 \\ 0 & 3 & 0 \\ 0 & 0 & 4 \end{pmatrix}$$

are diagonal matrices. The elements $d_{11}, d_{22}, \ldots, d_{nn}$ are called elements on the main diagonal. Note that all diagonal matrices are square by definition.

The identity matrix, I, is a diagonal matrix which has ones on the main diagonal and zeros everywhere else. For example,

$$\begin{pmatrix} 1 & 0 \\ 0 & 1 \end{pmatrix}, \qquad \begin{pmatrix} 1 & 0 & 0 \\ 0 & 1 & 0 \\ 0 & 0 & 1 \end{pmatrix}, \qquad \begin{pmatrix} 1 & 0 & 0 & 0 \\ 0 & 1 & 0 & 0 \\ 0 & 0 & 1 & 0 \\ 0 & 0 & 0 & 1 \end{pmatrix}$$

are identity matrices of dimensions 2×2, 3×3, 4×4. The identity matrix has the useful property that

$$AI = A, \qquad IB = B$$

for all matrices A and B provided the matrix multiplication is defined; that is, A and B must be of appropriate dimensions.

E. MATRIX INVERSION DEFINED

Now, given a square matrix A, there may exist a matrix B, such that

$$AB = BA = I.$$

If such matrix B exists, then A is said to be nonsingular and the matrix B is called the multiplicative *inverse* of A. We usually write B as A^{-1} to denote inverse. A^{-1} plays a very significant role in solving the matrix equation $Ax = b$. If A^{-1} is known, we can premultiply both sides of the matrix equation by A^{-1} to get

$$A^{-1}Ax = A^{-1}b,$$

Since $A^{-1}A = I$, the equation becomes

$$Ix = A^{-1}b.$$

But $Ix = x$ where x is an $(m \times 1)$ matrix, therefore

$$x = A^{-1}b.$$

The system can now be solved for the unknown vector, x, by carrying out the matrix multiplication, $A^{-1}b$.

F. MATRIX TRANSPOSITION

Before we describe how to compute A^{-1}, first we must define the transpose of a matrix. For a given matrix A, the transpose of A, denoted by A', is obtained from A by writing the columns of A as rows of A'. Formally, we have $a'_{ij} = a_{ji}$. For example, if

$$A = \begin{pmatrix} 1 & 2 & 3 \\ 3 & 2 & 1 \\ 4 & 3 & 2 \end{pmatrix}, \qquad \text{then} \qquad A' = \begin{pmatrix} 1 & 3 & 4 \\ 2 & 2 & 3 \\ 3 & 1 & 2 \end{pmatrix}.$$

Finally, if $A = A'$, then we say that A is a symmetric matrix. For example,

$$A = \begin{pmatrix} 1 & -1 & 4 \\ -1 & 2 & 5 \\ 4 & 5 & 3 \end{pmatrix}$$

is a symmetric matrix. Notice the entries of A are symmetric across the main diagonal, hence all diagonal matrices are symmetric.

The class of symmetric matrices is very important and arises very often in many real life problems. The covariance matrix in portfolio theory is a symmetric matrix. Furthermore, algebraic systems involving symmetric matrices are in general easier to solve.

G. DETERMINANTS

Given $x = A^{-1}b$, and A, the first step in finding A^{-1} is to first determine if A is nonsingular. To do that, we make use of the determinant function which is defined for all square matrices.

The determinant of a square matrix A, denoted by $|A|$, is a unique number associated with that matrix. For a 2×2 matrix

$$A = \begin{pmatrix} a_{11} & a_{12} \\ a_{21} & a_{22} \end{pmatrix}, \qquad |A| = a_{11}a_{22} - a_{12}a_{21}.$$

For example,

$$\begin{vmatrix} 2 & 1 \\ 3 & 4 \end{vmatrix} = (2 \times 4) - (1 \times 3) = 8 - 3 = 5.$$

So, the determinant of the matrix is 5.

The definition of a determinant of a 3×3 or higher order square matrix involves the notion of minors and cofactors of elements of the matrix. The minor of a_{ij}, denoted by $|M_{ij}|$, is the determinant of the *submatrix* of A obtained by deleting the ith row and jth column of A. Suppose

$$A = \begin{pmatrix} a_{11} & a_{12} & a_{13} \\ a_{21} & a_{22} & a_{23} \\ a_{31} & a_{32} & a_{33} \end{pmatrix},$$

then

$$|M_{11}| = \begin{vmatrix} a_{11} & a_{12} & a_{13} \\ a_{21} & a_{22} & a_{23} \\ a_{31} & a_{32} & a_{33} \end{vmatrix} = \begin{vmatrix} a_{22} & a_{23} \\ a_{32} & a_{33} \end{vmatrix} = a_{22}a_{33} - a_{23}a_{32},$$

$$|M_{21}| = \begin{vmatrix} a_{11} & a_{12} & a_{13} \\ a_{21} & a_{22} & a_{23} \\ a_{31} & a_{32} & a_{33} \end{vmatrix} = \begin{vmatrix} a_{12} & a_{13} \\ a_{32} & a_{33} \end{vmatrix} = a_{12}a_{33} - a_{13}a_{32},$$

and so on. The cofactor of a_{ij}, denoted by $|C_{ij}|$, is equal to $(-1)^{i+j}|M_{ij}|$. That is why sometimes cofactors are called signed minors. Whenever $i + j$ is even, $|C_{ij}| = |M_{ij}|$ and whenever $i + j$ is odd, $|C_{ij}| = -|M_{ij}|$. Take the 3×3 matrix, A,

$$A = \begin{pmatrix} 1 & 2 & 1 \\ 3 & 0 & 4 \\ 0 & 1 & 5 \end{pmatrix}, \qquad \text{then} \qquad |M_{11}| = \begin{vmatrix} 0 & 4 \\ 1 & 5 \end{vmatrix} = -4,$$

$$|M_{12}| = \begin{vmatrix} 3 & 4 \\ 0 & 5 \end{vmatrix} = 15, \qquad |M_{13}| = \begin{vmatrix} 3 & 0 \\ 0 & 1 \end{vmatrix} = 3.$$

The reader may check that $|M_{21}| = 9$, $|M_{22}| = 5$, $|M_{23}| = 1$, $|M_{31}| = 8$, $|M_{32}| = 1$, $|M_{33}| = -6$. Hence, $|C_{11}| = -4$, $|C_{12}| = -15$, $|C_{13}| = 3$, $|C_{21}| = -9$, $|C_{22}| = 5$, $|C_{23}| = -1$, $|C_{31}| = 8$, $|C_{32}| = -1$, $|C_{33}| = -6$.

The determinant of a general $n \times n$ matrix can now be defined in terms of minors, which are themselves determinants of $(n-1) \times (n-1)$ matrices. The rule is

$$|A| = a_{i1}(-1)^{i+1}|M_{i1}| + a_{i2}(-1)^{i+2}|M_{i2}| + \cdots + a_{in}(-1)^{i+n}|M_{in}| \qquad \text{(B.3a)}$$

$$= \sum_{j=1}^{n} a_{ij}(-1)^{i+j}|M_{ij}|.$$

The operation described is known as finding the determinant by expansion by the ith row of A. It is possible to expand by any row or column in A to find $|A|$, hence, expanding by the jth column, we have

$$|A| = a_{1j}(-1)^{1+j}|M_{ij}| + a_{2j}(-1)^{j+2}|M_{2j}| + \cdots + a_{nj}(-1)^{n+j}|M_{nj}| \qquad \text{(B.3b)}$$

$$= \sum_{i=1}^{n} a_{ij}(-1)^{i+j}|M_{ij}|.$$

Although Eq. (B.3a) and Eq. (B.3b) may look rather complicated at first glance, they are in fact quite simple. Each term of the sum in Eq. (B.3a) simply consists of an element in the ith row and its cofactor (signed minor). An example will clarify this further: Let

$$A = \begin{pmatrix} 1 & 2 & 1 \\ 3 & 0 & 4 \\ 0 & 1 & 5 \end{pmatrix}.$$

From Eq. (B.3a), taking $i = 1$, and expanding by the ith row,

$$|A| = a_{11}(-1)^{1+1}|M_{11}| + a_{12}(-1)^{1+2}|M_{12}| + a_{13}(-1)^{1+3}|M_{13}|$$

$$= 1 \cdot (-1)^2 \cdot \begin{vmatrix} 0 & 4 \\ 1 & 5 \end{vmatrix} + 2(-1)^3 \begin{vmatrix} 3 & 4 \\ 0 & 5 \end{vmatrix} + 1 \cdot (-1)^4 \begin{vmatrix} 3 & 0 \\ 0 & 1 \end{vmatrix}$$

$$= -4 + (-30) + 3 = -31.$$

In the above example $|A|$ was evaluated through expansion by the 1st row. According to Eq. (B.3b), we can also evaluate $|A|$ through expansion by the jth column. Let us take $j = 2$,

$$|A| = a_{12}(-1)^{1+2}|M_{12}| + a_{22}(-1)^{2+2}|M_{22}| + a_{32}(-1)^{3+2}|M_{32}|$$

$$= 2(-1)^3 \begin{vmatrix} 3 & 4 \\ 0 & 5 \end{vmatrix} + 0 \cdot (-1)^4 \begin{vmatrix} 1 & 1 \\ 0 & 5 \end{vmatrix} + 1(-1)^5 \begin{vmatrix} 1 & 1 \\ 3 & 4 \end{vmatrix}$$

$$= -30 + 0 + (-1) = -31,$$

which agrees with our previous result.

A key observation regarding the definition of the determinant of an $n \times n$ matrix is that we can express it in terms of determinants of $(n-1) \times (n-1)$ matrices (the minors). As in the above example, we reduce the determinant of a 3×3 matrix into sum of terms involving determinants of 2×2 matrices. Since we know how to evaluate 2×2 determinants, the problem is solved. Now to evaluate a 4×4 determinant, we must first use Eq. (B.3a) or Eq. (B.3b) to reduce it in terms of 3×3 determinants, then use Eq. (B.3a) or Eq. (B.3b) again to reduce each 3×3 determinant to sum of 2×2 determinants and then evaluate. So the reduction goes on, and we can now evaluate determinants of any size.

A well known theorem in matrix algebra states that a square matrix A is nonsingular if and only if $|A| \neq 0$. So the matrix in the previous example has a multiplicative inverse because $|A| = -31 \neq 0$.

H. THE INVERSE OF A SQUARE MATRIX

Given a nonsingular square matrix A, construct a new matrix B of the same dimension with $b_{ij} = |C_{ij}|$, the cofactor of a_{ij}. Then transpose B and call the resultant matrix the adjoint of A, "adj A." That is, adj $A = B'$. It can be shown that

$$(\text{adj } A)(A) = |A| \cdot I.$$

Since the nonsingularity of A implies $|A| \neq 0$, we can divide both sides by the scalar $|A|$:

$$\frac{1}{|A|}(\text{adj } A)(A) = I,$$

since $A^{-1}A = I$, it is immediately evident that $(1/|A|)(\text{adj } A) = A^{-1}$.

As an example take the 3×3 matrix A from the previous section. We have already computed the determinant as well as all the cofactors, so

$$B = \begin{pmatrix} C_{11} & C_{12} & C_{13} \\ C_{21} & C_{22} & C_{23} \\ C_{31} & C_{32} & C_{33} \end{pmatrix} = \begin{pmatrix} -4 & -15 & 3 \\ -9 & 5 & -1 \\ 8 & -1 & -6 \end{pmatrix},$$

$$\text{adj } A = B' = \begin{pmatrix} -4 & -9 & 8 \\ -15 & 5 & -1 \\ 3 & -1 & -6 \end{pmatrix}.$$

Since $|A| = -31$, the inverse of A is simply

$$A^{-1} = \frac{1}{|A|}\text{adj } A = \begin{vmatrix} \dfrac{4}{31} & \dfrac{9}{31} & \dfrac{-8}{31} \\[2mm] \dfrac{15}{31} & \dfrac{-5}{31} & \dfrac{1}{31} \\[2mm] \dfrac{-3}{31} & \dfrac{1}{31} & \dfrac{6}{31} \end{vmatrix}.$$

The curious reader may verify that $A^{-1}A = I = AA^{-1}$, or

$$
\begin{pmatrix} \dfrac{4}{31} & \dfrac{9}{31} & \dfrac{-8}{31} \\[2mm] \dfrac{15}{31} & \dfrac{-5}{31} & \dfrac{1}{31} \\[2mm] \dfrac{-3}{31} & \dfrac{1}{31} & \dfrac{6}{31} \end{pmatrix}
\begin{pmatrix} 1 & 2 & 1 \\ 3 & 0 & 4 \\ 0 & 1 & 5 \end{pmatrix}
= \begin{pmatrix} 1 & 0 & 0 \\ 0 & 1 & 0 \\ 0 & 0 & 1 \end{pmatrix}
= \begin{pmatrix} 1 & 2 & 1 \\ 3 & 0 & 4 \\ 0 & 1 & 5 \end{pmatrix}
\begin{pmatrix} \dfrac{4}{31} & \dfrac{9}{31} & \dfrac{-8}{31} \\[2mm] \dfrac{15}{31} & \dfrac{-5}{31} & \dfrac{1}{31} \\[2mm] \dfrac{-3}{31} & \dfrac{1}{31} & \dfrac{6}{31} \end{pmatrix}.
$$

I. SOLVING LINEAR EQUATION SYSTEMS

Now suppose we have a system of linear equations:

$$
\begin{aligned}
X_1 + 2X_2 + X_3 &= 1 \\
3X_1 \qquad\ + 4X_3 &= -1 \\
X_2 + 5X_3 &= 2
\end{aligned}
$$

The matrix formulation would look like $Ax = b$, or

$$
\begin{pmatrix} 1 & 2 & 1 \\ 3 & 0 & 4 \\ 0 & 1 & 5 \end{pmatrix}
\begin{pmatrix} X_1 \\ X_2 \\ X_3 \end{pmatrix}
= \begin{pmatrix} 1 \\ -1 \\ 2 \end{pmatrix}.
$$

We know what A^{-1} is, and we know that the solution of the system is $x = A^{-1}b$, therefore

$$
\begin{pmatrix} X_1 \\ X_2 \\ X_3 \end{pmatrix}
= \underbrace{\begin{pmatrix} \dfrac{4}{31} & \dfrac{9}{31} & \dfrac{-8}{31} \\[2mm] \dfrac{15}{31} & \dfrac{-5}{31} & \dfrac{1}{31} \\[2mm] \dfrac{-3}{31} & \dfrac{1}{31} & \dfrac{6}{31} \end{pmatrix}}_{3 \times 3}
\underbrace{\begin{pmatrix} 1 \\ -1 \\ 2 \end{pmatrix}}_{3 \times 1}
= \underbrace{\begin{pmatrix} \dfrac{-21}{31} \\[2mm] \dfrac{22}{31} \\[2mm] \dfrac{8}{31} \end{pmatrix}}_{3 \times 1},
$$

or

$$
X_1 = \dfrac{-21}{31}, \qquad X_2 = \dfrac{22}{31}, \qquad X_3 = \dfrac{8}{31}.
$$

As a check on the solution, we can insert the values into the original equation system.

$$\frac{-21}{31} + \frac{44}{31} + \frac{8}{31} = 1$$

$$\frac{-63}{31} + 0 + \frac{32}{31} = -1$$

$$0 + \frac{22}{31} + \frac{40}{31} = 2 .$$

J. CRAMER'S RULE

A direct but not obvious corollary to our derivation of A^{-1} is Cramer's rule for the solution of a linear equation. The rule states that

$$X_i = \frac{|\hat{A}_i|}{|A|}$$

where $\hat{A}_i$ is the matrix obtained from A by replacing the ith column with the *constant vector*. Using the same example and applying Cramer's rule, we first substitute the constant vector for the first column in the numerator and then expand by the first row. Recall that the sign changes are the result of converting minors to cofactors.

$$X_1 = \frac{\begin{vmatrix} 1 & 2 & 1 \\ -1 & 0 & 4 \\ 2 & 1 & 5 \end{vmatrix}}{|A|} = \frac{1 \cdot \begin{vmatrix} 0 & 4 \\ 1 & 5 \end{vmatrix} - 2 \begin{vmatrix} -1 & 4 \\ 2 & 5 \end{vmatrix} + \begin{vmatrix} -1 & 0 \\ 2 & 1 \end{vmatrix}}{-31}$$

$$= \frac{-4 + 26 - 1}{-31} = -\frac{21}{31} .$$

Next we replace the second column of the original numerator by the constant vector, and again expand by the first row

$$X_2 = \frac{\begin{vmatrix} 1 & 1 & 1 \\ 3 & -1 & 4 \\ 0 & 2 & 5 \end{vmatrix}}{-31} = \frac{1 \cdot \begin{vmatrix} -1 & 4 \\ 2 & 5 \end{vmatrix} - 1 \begin{vmatrix} 3 & 4 \\ 0 & 5 \end{vmatrix} + 1 \cdot \begin{vmatrix} 3 & -1 \\ 0 & 2 \end{vmatrix}}{-31}$$

$$= \frac{-13 - 15 + 6}{-31} = \frac{22}{31} ,$$

and again for the third column,

$$X_3 = \frac{\begin{vmatrix} 1 & 2 & 1 \\ 3 & 0 & -1 \\ 0 & 1 & 2 \end{vmatrix}}{-31} = \frac{1 \cdot \begin{vmatrix} 0 & -1 \\ 1 & 2 \end{vmatrix} - 2 \begin{vmatrix} 3 & -1 \\ 0 & 2 \end{vmatrix} + 1 \cdot \begin{vmatrix} 3 & 0 \\ 0 & 1 \end{vmatrix}}{-31}$$

$$= \frac{1 - 12 + 3}{-31} = \frac{8}{31}.$$

This agrees with the previous result. All the determinants above were evaluated by expanding by the first row.

K. APPLICATIONS

In this section we present two applications of matrix algebra in the theory of finance.

1. Minimum Variance Portfolio

Suppose we are considering investing in three securities: X_1, X_2, and X_3, and we want to form the portfolio that minimizes the variance of return. Let σ_1^2, σ_2^2, σ_3^2 be individual variances of return, and x_1, x_2, x_3 be weights of investment in the portfolio of securities X_1, X_2, X_3 respectively. So $x_1 + x_2 + x_3 = 1$. Furthermore, let $\sigma_{12} = \sigma_{21}$ be the covariance of return between X_1 and X_2, $\sigma_{13} = \sigma_{31}$ the covariance of return between X_1 and X_3, $\sigma_{23} = \sigma_{32}$ the covariance of return between X_2 and X_3. Constructing the covariance matrix A we wish to solve for the weight vector X that will minimize the variance. Let

$$\underset{(3 \times 3)}{A} = \begin{pmatrix} \sigma_1^2 & \sigma_{12} & \sigma_{13} \\ \sigma_{21} & \sigma_2^2 & \sigma_{23} \\ \sigma_{31} & \sigma_{32} & \sigma_3^2 \end{pmatrix}, \qquad \underset{(3 \times 1)}{X} = \begin{pmatrix} x_1 \\ x_2 \\ x_3 \end{pmatrix}.$$

The variance of the portfolio with x_1 of X_1, x_2 of X_2, x_3 of X_3 can be expressed in matrix form as $\sigma_p^2 = X'AX$. To minimize the variance of the portfolio is equivalent to minimizing σ_p^2 subject to the weight constraint $x_1 + x_2 + x_3 = 1$. This constrained optimization problem can be solved by the method of the LaGrange multiplier.[1] Let

$$g(x_1, x_2, x_3, \lambda') = \sigma_p^2 + \lambda'(1 - x_1 - x_2 - x_3)$$
$$= X'AX + \lambda'(1 - x_1 - x_2 - x_3),$$

where $X'AX$ is the variance-covariance matrix of the portfolio and $(1 - x_1 - x_2 - x_3)$ is the implicit expression of the constraint which requires that the sum of the weights equal one. Then the first order conditions for an extremum are attained

---

[1] Readers unfamiliar with the method of solving constrained optimization problems using Lagrange multipliers should consult Appendix D.

by setting all of the partial derivatives of g equal to zero:

$$\frac{\partial g}{\partial x_1} = 0 \tag{B.4a}$$

$$\frac{\partial g}{\partial x_2} = 0 \tag{B.4b}$$

$$\frac{\partial g}{\partial x_3} = 0 \tag{B.4c}$$

$$\frac{\partial g}{\partial \lambda'} = 0 \tag{B.4d}$$

The Eqs. (B.4a), (B.4b), and (B.4c) in matrix notation can be expressed as:

$$AX = \lambda e \quad \text{where} \quad e = \begin{pmatrix} 1 \\ 1 \\ 1 \end{pmatrix} \quad \text{and} \quad \lambda = \lambda'/2, \tag{B.5}$$

and (B.4d) is simply the reiteration of the constraint $x_1 + x_2 + x_3 = 1$. The solution to the matrix Eq. (B.5) will give us the answer in terms of λ, and the constraint condition will give us the value of λ, hence the complete solution.

As a numerical example, take

$$A = \begin{pmatrix} 2 & -1 & 0 \\ -1 & 2 & -1 \\ 0 & -1 & 2 \end{pmatrix}$$

as the covariance matrix for securities X_1, X_2, X_3. Then (B.5) becomes

$$\begin{pmatrix} 2 & -1 & 0 \\ -1 & 2 & -1 \\ 0 & -1 & 2 \end{pmatrix} \begin{pmatrix} X_1 \\ X_2 \\ X_3 \end{pmatrix} = \lambda \begin{pmatrix} 1 \\ 1 \\ 1 \end{pmatrix} = \begin{pmatrix} \lambda \\ \lambda \\ \lambda \end{pmatrix}.$$

Using Cramer's rule, substituting the λ vector for the first column, and expanding both numerator and denominator by the first column, we have

$$X_1 = \frac{\lambda \begin{vmatrix} 2 & -1 \\ -1 & 2 \end{vmatrix} - \lambda \begin{vmatrix} -1 & 0 \\ -1 & 2 \end{vmatrix} + \lambda \begin{vmatrix} -1 & 0 \\ 2 & -1 \end{vmatrix}}{2 \begin{vmatrix} 2 & -1 \\ -1 & 2 \end{vmatrix} + 1 \begin{vmatrix} -1 & 0 \\ -1 & 2 \end{vmatrix} + 0} = \frac{3\lambda + 2\lambda + \lambda}{6 - 2} = \frac{6\lambda}{4} = \frac{3}{2}\lambda.$$

Then substituting the vector λ in column 2 and expanding by column 1,

$$X_2 = \frac{2 \begin{vmatrix} \lambda & -1 \\ \lambda & 2 \end{vmatrix} + 1 \begin{vmatrix} \lambda & 0 \\ \lambda & 2 \end{vmatrix} + 0}{4} = \frac{6\lambda + 2\lambda}{4} = \frac{8\lambda}{4} = 2\lambda,$$

and finally substituting the vector λ in column 3,

$$X_3 = \frac{2\begin{vmatrix} 2 & \lambda \\ -1 & \lambda \end{vmatrix} + 1\begin{vmatrix} -1 & \lambda \\ -1 & \lambda \end{vmatrix} + 0}{4} = \frac{6\lambda + 0}{4} = \frac{6\lambda}{4} = \frac{3}{2}\lambda.$$

Since $1 = x_1 + x_2 + x_3 = \frac{3}{2}\lambda + 2\lambda + \frac{3}{2}\lambda = 5\lambda$, we have $\lambda = \frac{1}{5}$. Hence $x_1 = \frac{3}{10}$, $x_2 = \frac{2}{5}$, $x_3 = \frac{3}{10}$. In other words, if you have \$1,000 to invest, you should put \$300 in X_1, \$400 in X_2 and \$300 in X_3 to form the minimum variance portfolio. Note that we have not actually established that this is the minimum variance portfolio. We have merely determined an extreme point which may be either a maximum or a minimum. To guarantee that this is the minimum variance portfolio we would need to examine the second order conditions. (For a discussion, see Appendix D.)

2. Linear Regression

Very often, when we consider a security, we like to know how its return varies as the market fluctuates. Suppose we have the data in Table B.1:

Table B.1

	Return (in %)					
Security A	9	9.5	10.5	10.5	11	12
Market	8	9	10	11	12	13
STATE	1	2	3	4	5	6

Can we discern any pattern or simple relation between the return on security A and the market? First, we put the data on a graph:

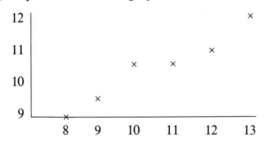

We can see that an approximately linear pattern exists. The following question naturally arises: What is the equation of the straight line that "best" fits the data points? In mathematical terms, this is equivalent to finding the values of two constants a and b such that whenever the return on the market is given, then the expression $[a + b \times (\text{return on market})]$ will give the "best overall" predictive value of the return on security A. In symbols, let X_i, $i = 1, 2, 3, 4, 5, 6$, be the returns on the market given the various states of the world, let Y_i be the returns on security A, and let $\hat{Y}_i = a + bX_i$, the predicted return on security A using the best fitting straight line. We call $e_i = Y_i - \hat{Y}_i$, which is the difference between the observed value and the predicted value of return on security A, the error term. These error terms can be positive or negative. To find the best fitting straight line is equivalent to minimizing the magnitude of the error terms in a certain sense. The technique of minimizing the sum of the square of the error terms is called linear regression. In our example above with six different states, we have six error terms. Let

$$g(a, b) = \sum_{i=1}^{6} e_i^2 = \sum_{i=1}^{6} (Y_i - \hat{Y}_i)^2 = \sum_{i=1}^{6} (Y_i - a - bX_i)^2$$

be the sum of the squares of the error terms. The first order conditions for minimizing $g(a, b)$ are:

$$\frac{\partial g}{\partial a} = 0 \tag{B.6a}$$

$$\frac{\partial g}{\partial b} = 0 \tag{B.6b}$$

Equations (B.6a) and (B.6b) written in matrix form turn out to be:

$$\begin{pmatrix} 1 & 1 & 1 & 1 & 1 & 1 \\ X_1 & X_2 & X_3 & X_4 & X_5 & X_6 \end{pmatrix} \begin{pmatrix} 1 & X_1 \\ 1 & X_2 \\ 1 & X_3 \\ 1 & X_4 \\ 1 & X_5 \\ 1 & X_6 \end{pmatrix} \begin{pmatrix} a \\ b \end{pmatrix} = \begin{pmatrix} 1 & 1 & 1 & 1 & 1 & 1 \\ X_1 & X_2 & X_3 & X_4 & X_5 & X_6 \end{pmatrix} \begin{pmatrix} Y_1 \\ Y_2 \\ Y_3 \\ Y_4 \\ Y_5 \\ Y_6 \end{pmatrix}$$

Performing matrix multiplication, explained above, we get:

$$\begin{pmatrix} 6 & \sum_{i=1}^{6} X_i \\ \sum_{i=1}^{6} X_i & \sum_{i=1}^{6} X_i^2 \end{pmatrix} \begin{pmatrix} a \\ b \end{pmatrix} = \begin{pmatrix} \sum_{i=1}^{6} Y_i \\ \sum_{i=1}^{6} X_i Y_i \end{pmatrix},$$

This is equivalent to two equations and two unknowns (a and b). As a numerical example, let us take the data from Table B.1:

$$\sum_{i=1}^{6} X_i = 8 + 9 + 10 + 11 + 12 + 13 = 63,$$

$$\sum_{i=1}^{6} X_i^2 = 8^2 + 9^2 + 10^2 + 11^2 + 12^2 + 13^2 = 679,$$

$$\sum_{i=1}^{6} Y_i = 9 + 9.5 + 10.5 + 10.5 + 11 + 12 = 62.5,$$

$$\sum_{i=1}^{6} X_i Y_i = 8 \times 9 + 9 \times 9.5 + 10 \times 10.5 + 11 \times 10.5 + 12 \times 11 + 13 \times 12 = 666,$$

so

$$\begin{pmatrix} 6 & 63 \\ 63 & 679 \end{pmatrix} \begin{pmatrix} a \\ b \end{pmatrix} = \begin{pmatrix} 62.5 \\ 666 \end{pmatrix}.$$

By Cramer's rule, we have

$$a = \frac{\begin{vmatrix} 62.5 & 63 \\ 666 & 679 \end{vmatrix}}{\begin{vmatrix} 6 & 63 \\ 63 & 679 \end{vmatrix}} = \frac{479.5}{105} = 4.57$$

$$b = \frac{\begin{vmatrix} 6 & 62.5 \\ 63 & 666 \end{vmatrix}}{\begin{vmatrix} 6 & 63 \\ 63 & 679 \end{vmatrix}} = \frac{58.5}{105} = 0.56.$$

Therefore, the equation of the best fitting straight line is $Y = 4.57 + 0.56X$. Note that b is the slope of the straight line. Both the sign and the magnitude of b contain important information. If b is positive, we would expect that the return on security A moves with the market, while a negative b implies that returns on security A and the market generally move in opposite directions. The magnitude of b measures the degree of volatility of security A. The larger the magnitude of b, the more volatile the return on security A.

Appendix C

An Introduction to Multiple Regression

Business students are frequently confronted with journal articles that are riddled with econometrics. On the other hand, econometrics courses assume prior knowledge of matrix algebra and calculus and therefore present a formidable barrier to the curious. This appendix is written to provide an overview of multiple regression techniques which assumes only the rudimentary knowledge of calculus and matrix algebra provided in the other appendices. While not a substitute for a good econometrics course, this appendix enables the reader to understand and interpret the computer output from a typical multiple regression software package, and to have an introductory level of understanding of some of the typical errors made in econometric studies.

A. ORDINARY LEAST SQUARES LINEAR ESTIMATION

If we are trying to explain the distribution of sales revenue for the XYZ Company given a forecast of gross national product, we might choose a linear model like

$$\tilde{Y}_t = a + bX_t + \tilde{\epsilon}_t, \tag{C.1}$$

where

$\tilde{Y}_t =$ sales revenue in year t,
$X_t =$ forecast of gross national product for year t,
$\tilde{\epsilon}_t =$ error term (the difference between actual sales revenue and that predicted by the model).

Linear relationships have the virtue that they are simple and robust. Many natural phenomena are not linearly related, but linear approximations usually work very well within a limited range.

The object is to find the set of weights (a and b) in Eq. (C.1) which provide the best unbiased estimate of revenue given GNP. If GNP has any explanatory power

the conditional distribution of revenues, $\tilde{Y}_t | X_t$, will be different from their uncondi-
tional distribution. This is illustrated in Fig. C.1. The mean and standard deviation of
the unconditional distribution of Y_t are \$196.9 and \$60.1. The unconditional probability distribution of revenues is plotted along the y-axis. The conditional distribution
of $Y_t | X_t$ is the distribution of error terms, ϵ_t. For example, given that $X_t = \$1.26$ (its
mean) then the estimated revenue is \$196.9 (its mean) and the standard deviation of
the estimate is \$33.73. Notice that the conditional distribution has lower variance
than the unconditional distribution. This is because knowledge of predicted GNP
allows us to refine our estimate of sales revenue.

In order to obtain the best linear model to predict Y_t given X_t, we want to find
the equation which minimizes the squared error terms. The error term is the difference between the actual revenue and the revenue predicted by the linear model. If we
minimize the squared error terms, we are, in effect, minimizing the variance of the
conditional distribution. To see how this is accomplished rewrite Eq. (C.1) as
follows:

$$\epsilon_t = Y_t - a - bX_t$$

The variance of the error terms is:[1]

$$\sigma_\epsilon^2 = E[(Y_t - a - bX_t) - (\bar{Y}_t - a - b\bar{X}_t)]^2, \tag{C.2}$$

$$\sigma_\epsilon^2 = E[(Y_t - \bar{Y}_t) - b(X_t - \bar{X}_t)]^2,$$

$$\sigma_\epsilon^2 = \sigma_Y^2 - 2b \, \text{COV}(Y, X) + b^2 \sigma_X^2.$$

We want to choose the slope, b, and the intercept, a, which minimize the squared
error terms. To do this, take the derivative of σ_ϵ^2 with respect to b and set the result
equal to zero:

$$\frac{\delta \sigma_\epsilon^2}{\delta b} = -2 \, \text{COV}(Y, X) + 2b\sigma_X^2 = 0.$$

Solving for $\hat{b}$, the estimated slope term, we have

$$\hat{b} = \frac{\text{COV}(Y, X)}{\sigma_X^2}. \tag{C.3}$$

The intercept is determined by the fact that the line must pass through the mean
values for both $\bar{Y}$ and $\bar{X}$. At that point, we have

$$\bar{Y} = \hat{a} + \hat{b}\bar{X}.$$

Therefore, solving for $\hat{a}$, we have

$$\hat{a} = \bar{Y} - \hat{b}\bar{X}. \tag{C.4}$$

The estimated slope and intercept terms are computed in Table C.1.

---

[1] This result follows from the properties of random variables discussed in Chapter 6.

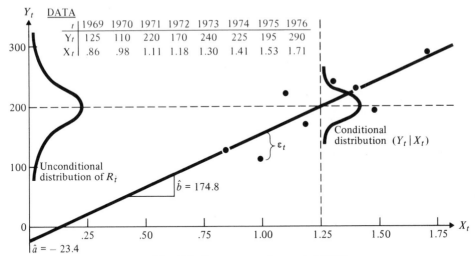

Fig. C.1 Revenues vs forecasted GNP

Having obtained estimates of the slope and intercept which minimize the squared error terms we now have the following linear equation

$$\hat{Y}_t = -23.42 + 174.84 X_t.$$

It can be used to predict sales revenue when given a forecast of GNP. The difference between predicted revenue and actual revenue in any given year is the error of estimate, often called the residual.

$$\epsilon_t = Y_t - \hat{Y}_t.$$

Note that in Table C.1 the average error term $\bar{\epsilon}_t$ (except for rounding error in the calculations) is zero. This implies that the linear estimate is unbiased. In other words, on average, there is no error of estimate.

In linear regression, the residual errors indicate the extent of movement in the dependent variable (the variable on the left-hand side of the regression equation) which is not explained by the independent variable(s)—(the variable(s) on the right-hand side). If the residuals are small relative to the total movement in the dependent variable, then it follows that a major part of the movement has been explained. We define the summary statistic known as the squared multiple correlation coefficient, r^2, as the percentage of the total variation in the dependent variable which is explained by the regression equation. The square of the correlation coefficient is

$$r^2 = \frac{\text{variation explained by the regression equation}}{\text{total variation of the dependent variable}}$$

$$= \frac{\sum (Y - \bar{Y})^2 - \sum (\epsilon - \bar{\epsilon})^2}{\sum (Y - \bar{Y})^2}.$$

Table C.1 Simple regression computations

t	Y	$Y - \bar{Y}$	$(Y - \bar{Y})^2$	X	$X - \bar{X}$	$(X - \bar{X})^2$	$(Y - \bar{Y})(X - \bar{X})$	$\epsilon = \hat{Y} - Y$	ϵ^2
1969	125	−71.875	5,166.01	.86	−.40	.1600	28.750	−1.94	3.7636
1970	110	−86.875	7,547.27	.98	−.28	.0784	24.325	−37.92	1437.9264
1971	220	23.125	534.76	1.11	−.15	.0225	−3.469	49.35	2435.4225
1972	170	−26.875	722.27	1.18	−.08	.0064	2.150	−12.89	166.1521
1973	240	43.125	1,859.76	1.30	.04	.0016	1.725	36.13	1305.3769
1974	225	28.125	791.02	1.41	.15	.0225	4.219	1.90	3.6100
1975	195	−1.875	3.52	1.53	.27	.0729	−.506	−49.09	2409.8281
1976	290	93.125	8,672.27	1.71	.45	.2025	41.906	14.44	208.5136
Sum	1575		25,296.89	10.08		.5668	99.100	−.02≈0	7970.5932

$$\bar{Y} = \frac{\sum Y}{N} = \frac{1575}{8} = 196.875$$

$$\sigma_Y^2 = \frac{\sum (Y - \bar{Y})^2}{N - 1} = \frac{25,296.89}{7} = 3613.84$$

$$\sigma_Y = \sqrt{\sigma_Y^2} = \sqrt{3613.84} = 60.12$$

$$\text{COV}(Y, X) = \frac{\sum (X - \bar{X})(X - \bar{Y})}{N - 1} = \frac{99.10}{7} = 14.16$$

$$\bar{X} = \frac{\sum X}{N} = \frac{10.08}{8} = 1.26$$

$$\sigma_X^2 = \frac{\sum (X - \bar{X})^2}{N - 1} = \frac{.5668}{7} = .0809714$$

$$\sigma_X = \sqrt{\sigma_X^2} = .2846$$

$$\hat{b} = \frac{\text{COV}(Y, X)}{\sigma_X^2} = \frac{14.16}{.0809714} = 174.88$$

$$\hat{a} = \bar{X} - \hat{b}\bar{X} = 196.876 - 174.84(1.26) = 23.42$$

Symbol Definitions:

$\bar{Y}, \bar{X}$ = The means of revenue and GNP respectively

N = The number of observations in the sample

σ_Y^2, σ_X^2 = The variances of revenue and GNP respectively

$\text{COV}(Y, X)$ = The covariance between revenue and GNP

$\hat{a}, \hat{b}$ = The intercept and slope estimates

ϵ = The error term

Note that $\sum (Y - \bar{Y})^2$ is the variance of the dependent variable, σ_Y^2, in our example. Note also that $\sum (\epsilon - \bar{\epsilon})^2$ is the variance of the residuals. Furthermore, the average error term, $\bar{\epsilon}$, is always zero, therefore, we can rewrite the squared correlation coefficient as[2]

$$r^2 = \frac{\sum (Y - \bar{Y})^2 - \sum \epsilon^2}{\sum (Y - \bar{Y})^2}. \tag{C.5}$$

Using the numbers from Table C.1,

$$r^2 = \frac{25{,}296.89 - 7970.5932}{25{,}296.89} = .6849.$$

This means that about 68.5% of the variance in the dependent variable, sales revenue, is explained by the independent variable, GNP. If all of the variance were explained, then the sum of the squared residuals, $\sum e^2$, would be zero and we would have $r^2 = 1$. At the opposite extreme the equation would not reduce the variance of the dependent variable at all, in which case we would have $r^2 = 0$.

B. SIMPLE HYPOTHESIS TESTING OF THE LINEAR REGRESSION ESTIMATES

Now that we know how to estimate the slope and the intercept, the next logical question is whether or not we can reject the null hypothesis that they are equal to

---

[2] An important relationship, which is used in Chapter 6, is that

$$r = \frac{\mathrm{COV}(Y, X)}{\sigma_Y \sigma_X}.$$

Proof follows from the definition of r^2, of σ_ϵ^2, and of b. First, rewrite r^2 and solve for r

$$r^2 = \frac{\sigma_Y^2 - \sigma_\epsilon^2}{\sigma_Y^2},$$

$$r = \sqrt{\left(\frac{\sigma_Y - \sigma_\epsilon}{\sigma_Y}\right)\left(\frac{\sigma_Y + \sigma_\epsilon}{\sigma_Y}\right)}.$$

From Eq. (C.2), we have

$$\sigma_\epsilon^2 = \sigma_y^2 - 2b\,\mathrm{COV}(Y, X) + b^2\sigma_x^2 = (\sigma_y - b\sigma_x)^2.$$

Substituting this into the positive root for r,

$$r = \frac{\sigma_y - \sigma_y - b\sigma_x}{\sigma_y} = \frac{b\sigma_x}{\sigma_y}.$$

Then we substitute Eq. (C.3), the definition of b, into the above formula

$$r = \frac{\mathrm{COV}(Y, X)\sigma_x}{\sigma_x^2\sigma_y} = \frac{\mathrm{COV}(Y, X)}{\sigma_x\sigma_y} \qquad \text{QED.}$$

zero. In order to do this we can calculate t-statistics in order to test the significance of the slope and intercept terms.

The t-statistics are defined as the estimates of the intercept, $\hat{a}$, or the slope, $\hat{b}$, divided by their respective standard errors of estimate[3]

$$t_a = \frac{\hat{a}}{se(\hat{a})}, \qquad t_b = \frac{\hat{b}}{se(\hat{b})}. \tag{C.6}$$

We shall assume that the independent variable, X, can be treated as a constant in repeated samplings. In fact, this is where regression analysis derives its name. We say that Y is regressed on X. We also assume that the error terms are generated by random selection from a stationary statistical distribution with a mean of zero and a constant variance, σ_ϵ^2. Also, the error terms in successive samplings are independent. This specification of the error-generating process may be stated as

$$E(\epsilon) = 0 \tag{C.7}$$

$$\text{VAR}(\epsilon) = E[\epsilon - E(\epsilon)]^2 = E(\epsilon)^2 = \sigma_\epsilon^2 \tag{C.8}$$

$$\text{COV}(\epsilon_t, \epsilon_{t-1}) = 0. \tag{C.9}$$

In order to determine the standard error of estimate for $\hat{b}$, recall the definition given in Eq. (C.3).

$$\hat{b} = \frac{\text{COV}(Y, X)}{\sigma_x^2}. \tag{C.3}$$

We also know the observed values of Y are

$$Y = a + bX + \epsilon$$

Rewriting Eq. (C.3), using the definitions of $\text{COV}(Y, X)$ and σ_X^2, we have

$$b = \frac{\sum [(X - \bar{X})(Y - \bar{Y})]}{\sum [(X - \bar{X})(X - \bar{X})]}.$$

Substituting in Y yields

$$\hat{b} = \frac{\sum [(X - \bar{X})(a + bX + \epsilon - \bar{a} - \bar{b}X)]}{\sum [(X - \bar{X})(X - \bar{X})]}$$

$$= \frac{\sum [(X - \bar{X})(Y - \bar{Y}) + (X - \bar{X})\epsilon]}{\sum [(X - \bar{X})(X - \bar{X})]}$$

$$= \frac{\sum [(X - \bar{X})(Y - \bar{Y})]}{\sum [(X - \bar{X})(X - \bar{X})]} + \frac{\sum [(X - \bar{X})\epsilon]}{\sum [(X - \bar{X})(X - \bar{X})]}$$

$$= b + \frac{\sum [(X - \bar{X})\epsilon]}{\sum [(X - \bar{X})^2]}. \tag{C.10}$$

---

[3] A good reference to the t-distribution is Hoel [1954], pp. 274–283.

Equation (C.10) tells us that the estimated slope, $\hat{b}$, is equal to the true slope, b, plus a term which depends on the variance of X (in the denominator) and the error terms (in the numerator). The expected value of $\hat{b}$ is

$$E(\hat{b}) = b, \quad \text{since} \quad E(\epsilon) = 0. \tag{C.11}$$

Note that the expected value of the slope is equal to the true slope. Therefore we can say that the slope estimate is unbiased. The variance of b is

$$VAR(\hat{b}) = E[\hat{b} - E(\hat{b})]^2$$

$$= E\left[\hat{b} + \frac{\sum [(X_i - \bar{X})\epsilon_i]}{\sum (X_i - \bar{X})^2} - \hat{b}\right]^2$$

$$= E\left[\frac{\sum [(X_i - \bar{X})\epsilon_i]}{\sum (X_i - \bar{X})^2}\right]^2,$$

and since X is assumed to be a constant, we have

$$VAR(\hat{b}) = \left[\frac{1}{\sum (X_i - \bar{X})^2}\right]^2 E[\sum (X_i - \bar{X})\epsilon_i]^2.$$

Expanding the second term yields

$$E[\sum (X_i - \bar{X})\epsilon_i]^2 = E[(X_1 - \bar{X})^2\epsilon_1^2 + (X_2 - \bar{X})^2\epsilon_2^2 + \cdots$$

$$+ 2(X_1 - \bar{X})(X_2 - \bar{X})\epsilon_1\epsilon_2 + \cdots]$$

$$= (X_1 - \bar{X})^2 E(\epsilon_1^2) + (X_2 - \bar{X})^2 E(\epsilon_2^2) + \cdots$$

$$+ 2(X_1 - \bar{X})(X_2 - \bar{X})E(\epsilon_1\epsilon_2) + \cdots.$$

Using Eqs. (C.8) and (C.9), the above result can be reduced to

$$E[\sum (X_i - \bar{X})\epsilon_i]^2 = [\sum (X_i - \bar{X})^2]\sigma_\epsilon^2.$$

This means that the variance of the estimate of b can be written as

$$VAR(\hat{b}) = \frac{\sum (X - \bar{X})^2}{[\sum (X - \bar{X})^2]^2}\sigma_\epsilon^2$$

$$= \frac{\sigma_\epsilon^2}{\sum (X - \bar{X})^2}. \tag{C.12}$$

We now have the result that the slope estimate, $\hat{b}$, is distributed normally with a mean of b and a variance of $\sigma_\epsilon^2/\sigma_X^2$. The variance of the estimate of $\hat{b}$ provides a measure of the precision of the estimate. The larger the variance of the estimate, the more widespread the distribution and the smaller the precision of the estimate.

A similar derivation would show that the intercept estimate, $\hat{a}$, is also normally distributed with a mean of

$$E(\hat{a}) = a \tag{C.13}$$

and a variance of

$$\text{VAR}(\hat{a}) = \frac{(\sum X^2)\sigma_\epsilon^2}{N\sigma_X^2}, \qquad se(\hat{a}) = \sqrt{\text{VAR}(\hat{a})}, \tag{C.14}$$

where N is the number of observations in the sample.

Using Eqs. (C.12) and (C.14) for the sample problem of Table C.1, and given that the t-statistics defined in Eq. (C.6) have $N - m$ degrees of freedom (where $N = 8 =$ the number of observations and $m = 2 =$ the number of independent variables including the constant term), we can compute the appropriate significance tests for the slope and intercept. The standard error for the slope term is

$$se(\hat{b}) = \sqrt{\frac{\sigma_\epsilon^2}{(X - X)^2}} = \sqrt{\frac{7970.5932/(8 - 2)}{.5668}} = 48.41$$

and the t-statistic for b is

$$t(\hat{b}) = \frac{\hat{b}}{se(\hat{b})} = \frac{174.84}{48.41} = 3.61.$$

We refer to the table of t-statistics (Table C.2) for $8 - 2 = 6$ degrees of freedom and a 95% confidence interval (in a two-tail t-test). That table shows that the t-statistic must be greater than 2.477 in order to reject the null hypothesis that the slope coefficient is not significantly different from zero. It is. Therefore, we can say that predicted GNP, the independent variable, is a significant explanatory variable for sales revenue given our sample data.

Next, compute the t-test to determine whether or not the intercept estimate, $\hat{a}$, is significantly different from zero. The standard error of $\hat{a}$ is

$$se(\hat{a}) = \frac{(\sum X^2)\sigma_\epsilon^2}{N \sum (X - \bar{X})^2}$$

$$= \frac{(13.2676)(7970.5932/6)}{8(.5668)} = 65.35$$

and the t-statistic is

$$t(\hat{a}) = \frac{\hat{a}}{se(\hat{a})} = \frac{-23.42}{62.35} = -.375.$$

The t-statistic for $\hat{a}$ is less than 2.447, the required level for significance. Therefore, we cannot conclude that the intercept term is significantly different from zero.

Summarizing, up to this point we can write the results of the regression analysis as follows:

$$Y_t = -23.42 + 174.84X_t, \qquad R^2 = .6849$$

$$(-.38) \qquad (3.61) \qquad df = 6$$

The numbers in parentheses are the appropriate t-statistics, and df designates the degrees of freedom.

Table C.2 Student's t distribution

Degrees of Freedom	Probability of a Value Greater in Value than the Table Entry					
	0.005	0.01	0.025	0.05	0.1	0.15
1	63.657	31.821	12.706	6.314	3.078	1.963
2	9.925	6.965	4.303	2.920	1.886	1.386
3	5.841	4.541	3.182	2.353	1.638	1.250
4	4.604	3.747	2.776	2.132	1.533	1.190
5	4.032	3.365	2.571	2.015	1.476	1.156
6	3.707	3.143	2.447	1.943	1.440	1.134
7	3.499	2.998	2.365	1.895	1.415	1.119
8	3.355	2.896	2.306	1.860	1.397	1.108
9	3.250	2.821	2.262	1.833	1.383	1.100
10	3.169	2.764	2.228	1.812	1.372	1.093
11	3.106	2.718	2.201	1.796	1.363	1.088
12	3.055	2.681	2.179	1.782	1.356	1.083
13	3.012	2.650	2.160	1.771	1.350	1.079
14	2.977	2.624	2.145	1.761	1.345	1.076
15	2.947	2.602	2.131	1.753	1.341	1.074
16	2.921	2.583	2.120	1.746	1.337	1.071
17	2.898	2.567	2.110	1.740	1.333	1.069
18	2.878	2.552	2.101	1.734	1.330	1.067
19	2.861	2.539	2.093	1.729	1.328	1.066
20	2.845	2.528	2.086	1.725	1.325	1.064
21	2.831	2.518	2.080	1.721	1.323	1.063
22	2.819	2.508	2.074	1.717	1.321	1.061
23	2.807	2.500	2.069	1.714	1.319	1.060
24	2.797	2.492	2.064	1.711	1.318	1.059
25	2.787	2.485	2.060	1.708	1.316	1.058
26	2.779	2.479	2.056	1.706	1.315	1.058
27	2.771	2.473	2.052	1.703	1.314	1.057
28	2.763	2.467	2.048	1.701	1.313	1.056
29	2.756	2.462	2.045	1.699	1.311	1.055
30	2.750	2.457	2.042	1.697	1.310	1.055
∞	2.576	2.326	1.960	1.645	1.282	1.036

Source: Reprinted from Table IV in Sir Ronald A. Fisher, *Statistical Methods for Research Workers*, 13th edition, Oliver & Boyd Ltd., Edinburgh, 1963, with the permission of the publisher and the late Sir Ronald Fisher's Literary Executor.

C. BIAS AND EFFICIENCY

1. The Mean Square Error Criterion

The researcher is always interested in the bias and efficiency of the estimated regression equations. Unbiased estimates have the property that on average the sample statistic equals the true value of the underlying population parameter. The most efficient estimate is the one with the lowest possible variance of estimation. Frequently there is a tradeoff between bias and efficiency. One rule which weighs both of these aspects is the concept of "quadratic loss." The expected value of the distribution of quadratic loss is called the mean square error. It may be formally defined as

$$\text{MSE}(\hat{\theta}) = E(\hat{\theta} - \theta)^2, \tag{C.15}$$

where θ is the population parameter and $\hat{\theta}$ is the estimate of that parameter.

The mean square error can be expressed in terms of the variance and the bias of the estimate by first adding then subtracting $E(\hat{\theta})$ in Eq. (C.15). The result is

$$\text{MSE}(\hat{\theta}) = E[\hat{\theta} - E(\hat{\theta}) + E(\hat{\theta}) - \theta]^2$$
$$= E[\hat{\theta} - E(\hat{\theta})]^2 + [E(\hat{\theta}) - \theta]^2$$

because the cross-product term has a zero expected value. Therefore, the mean square error can be written as

$$\text{MSE}(\hat{\theta}) = \text{Variance } (\hat{\theta}) + [\text{bias } (\hat{\theta})]^2. \tag{C.16}$$

Minimizing the MSE imposes an arbitrary judgment as to the relative importance of bias and variance. If it is thought that minimizing bias is of paramount importance then the MSE may be inappropriate.

2. Sources of Bias

a. Left-out variables   One of the most frequently encountered problems of regression analysis is that the empirical model is not founded on a sound theoretical footing. When this happens we say that the model is misspecified. If an important explanatory variable is left out of the regression equation, then the estimates of the coefficients for the variables included in the equations can be biased. This was one of the empirical difficulties in the early attempt to test for relationships between capital structure and value (see Chapter 11). The empirical work was done before a theoretical model of value had been derived. Therefore, relevant variables were often left out and the empirical results were biased.

Suppose that the true theoretical relationship is

$$Y_t = a + b_1 X_{1t} + b_2 X_{2t} + \epsilon_t, \tag{C.17}$$

but that the researcher mistakenly estimates the following regression equation

$$Y_t = a + \tilde{b}_1 X_{1t} + U_t. \tag{C.18}$$

From Eq. (C.3) the ordinary least squares estimate of $\tilde{b}_1$ is

$$\tilde{b}_1 = \frac{\sum (X_1 - \bar{X}_1)(Y - \bar{Y})}{\sum (X_1 - \bar{X}_1)(X_1 - \bar{X}_1)}. \tag{C.19}$$

By substituting the true relation (Eq. C.17) for Y into Eq. (C.19), we obtain

$$\tilde{b}_1 = \frac{\sum (X_1 - \bar{X}_1)(a + b_1 X_1 + b_2 X_2 + \epsilon - a - b_1 \bar{X}_1 - b_2 \bar{X}_2)}{\sum (X_1 - \bar{X}_1)(X_1 - \bar{X}_1)}$$

$$= \frac{\sum (X_1 - \bar{X}_1)(a + b_1 X_1 - a - b_1 \bar{X}_1)}{\sum (X_1 - \bar{X}_1)^2}$$

$$+ \frac{\sum (X_1 - \bar{X}_1)(b_2 X_2 - b_2 \bar{X}_2)}{\sum (X_1 - \bar{X}_1)^2} + \frac{\sum (X_1 - \bar{X}_1)\epsilon}{\sum (X_1 - \bar{X}_1)^2},$$

and because the error terms are assumed to follow Eqs. (C.7), (C.8), and (C.9), we have

$$\tilde{b}_1 = b_1 + b_2 \frac{\sum (X_1 - \bar{X}_1)(X_2 - \bar{X}_2)}{\sum (X_1 - \bar{X}_1)^2}. \tag{C.20}$$

Equation (C.20) shows that when a relevant variable is left out of the equation, specification the slope estimate, $\tilde{b}$, is biased. The direction of the bias depends on the sign of b_2 (the relationship between Y and X_2) and on $\sum (X_1 - \bar{X}_1)(X_2 - \bar{X}_2)$, (the relationship between the independent variables, X_1 and X_2). If X_1, X_2, and Y are all positively related, then b will be biased upward. In general, the only way to eliminate misspecification bias is to be sure that the empirical test is appropriately founded on sound theory, rather than going on an ad hoc "fishing trip".

b. Errors in variables There is almost always some measurement error involved when taking sample statistics. The degree of accuracy in estimating both independent and dependent variables can vary considerably, and unfortunately this problem also results in bias. For example, in Chapter 14, Friend and Puckett showed that measurement error is important when trying to estimate the relative effect of dividends and retained earnings on the price of common stock. The estimated equation was

$$P_{it} = a + bD_{it} + cR_{it} + \epsilon_{it},$$

where

P_{it} = the price per share,
D_{it} = the aggregate dividends paid out,
R_{it} = the retained earnings of the firm,
ϵ_{it} = the error term.

Dividends can be measured without any error whatsoever, but retained earnings (the difference between accounting earnings and dividends paid) is only an estimate of true economic retained earnings on which value is based. Thus, retained earnings possesses a great deal of measurement error. Consequently, the estimate of the effect of retained earnings on the price per share was biased downward. This led earlier researchers to incorrectly conclude that dividends had a greater effect on price per share than retained earnings.

To demonstrate the effect of measurement error, suppose that both the independent and dependent variables have sampling error. This may be written as

$$X = x + w \tag{C.21}$$

$$Y = y + v, \tag{C.22}$$

where X and Y indicate the observations, x and y are the true values, and w and v are the measurement errors. Suppose, further, that the true variables have the following relationship:

$$y = a + bx. \tag{C.23}$$

We would like to have unbiased estimates of a and b.

Substituting Eqs. (C.21) and (C.22) into Eq. (C.23) gives

$$Y = a + bX + z,$$

where

$$z = v - bw.$$

From Eq. (C.3), the estimate of b is

$$\hat{b} = \frac{\sum (X - \bar{X})(Y - \bar{Y})}{\sum (X - \bar{X})(X - \bar{X})}$$

$$= \frac{\sum (x + w - \bar{x} - \bar{w})(y + v - \bar{y} - \bar{v})}{\sum (x + w - \bar{x} - \bar{w})^2}$$

$$= \frac{\sum (x - \bar{x})(y - \bar{y}) + \sum (x - \bar{x})(v - \bar{v}) + \sum (y - \bar{y})(w - \bar{w}) + \sum (w - \bar{w})(v - \bar{v})}{\sum (x - \bar{x})^2 + 2 \sum (x - \bar{x})(w - \bar{w}) + \sum (w - \bar{w})^2}.$$

Given that the measurement errors, w and v, are distributed independently of each other and of the true parameters, then the last three terms in the numerator and the middle term in the denominator vanish as the sample size becomes large. Therefore, the limiting value of b is

$$\text{plim } \hat{b} = \frac{\sum (x - \bar{x})(y - \bar{y})}{\sum (x - \bar{x})^2 + \sum (w - \bar{w})^2}.$$

Dividing numerator and denominator by $\sum (x - \bar{x})^2$, we have,

$$\hat{b} = \frac{b}{(1 + [\sum (w - \bar{w})^2 / \sum (x - \bar{x})^2])}. \tag{C.24}$$

Equation (C.24) shows that even if the errors of measurement are assumed to be mutually independent, independent of the true values, and have constant variance, the estimate, b, will be biased downward. The greater the measurement error, the greater the downward bias.

There are two generally accepted techniques for overcoming the problem of errors in variables: (1) grouping and (2) instrumental variables. Grouping procedures can reduce measurement error because when grouped the errors of individual observations tend to be canceled out by their mutual independence. Hence there is less measurement error in a group average than there would be if sample data were not grouped. An instrumental variable is one which is highly correlated with the independent variable but which is independent of the errors w and v (in Eqs. C.21 and C.22). This was the technique employed by Friend and Puckett in testing dividend policy. Instead of using the accounting measure of earnings, they used normalized earnings (a time series estimate of predicted earnings) to eliminate most of the measurement error bias.

3. Loss of Efficiency

a. Multicollinearity   When two or more independent variables are highly correlated, it frequently becomes difficult to distinguish their separate effects on the dependent variable. In fact, if they are perfectly correlated it is impossible to distinguish. For example, consider the following equation:

$$S_t = a + b_1 R_t + b_2 L_t + b_3 O_t + \epsilon_t.$$

Where S_t is the sales revenue of a ski shop, R_t and L_t are the sales of left and right downhill skis and O_t is the sales of other items. The estimated coefficient b_1 is supposed to measure the impact of the sale of the right skis, holding all other variables constant. Of course this is nonsense, since right and left skis are sold simultaneously.

The usual multicollinearity problem occurs when two independent variables are highly, but not perfectly, correlated. And usually the effect is to reduce the efficiency of estimates of b_1 and b_2 by increasing the standard error of estimate. The best remedy for the problem is larger sample sizes.

b. Serial correlation   One of the important assumptions for linear regression, Eq. (C.9), is that samplings are drawn *independently* from the same multivariate distribution. In other words, successive error terms should be independent. If this is not the case, we still obtain unbiased estimates of the slope and intercept terms, but there is a loss of efficiency because the sampling variances of these estimates may be unduly large. Consider the following two variable cases. Suppose that

$$Y_t = a + bX_t + \epsilon_t,$$

but that the error term follows a first order autoregressive scheme such as

$$\epsilon_t = K\epsilon_{t-1} + U_t$$

where $|K| < 1$ and U_t satisfies the assumptions

$$E(U_t) = 0,$$

$$E(U_t, U_{t-N}) = \begin{cases} \sigma_U^2 & \text{if } N = 0 \\ 0 & \text{if } N \neq 0 \end{cases}.$$

In general the tth error term can be written as

$$\epsilon_t = K\epsilon_{t-1} + U_t$$

$$= K(K\epsilon_{t-2} + U_{t-1}) + U_t$$

$$= U_t + KU_{t-1} + K^2 U_{t-2} + \cdots + K^n U_{t-n}$$

$$= \sum_{\tau=0}^{\infty} K^\tau U_{t-\tau},$$

$$E(\epsilon_t) = 0 \qquad \text{since } E(U_t) = 0 \text{ for all } t.$$

The expected value of the squared error terms is

$$E(\epsilon_t^2) = E(U_t^2) + K^2 E(U_{t-1}^2) + K^4 E(U_{t-2}^2) + \cdots,$$

since the error terms, U_t, are serially independent. Consequently,

$$E(\epsilon_t^2) = (1 + K^2 + K^4 + \cdots)\sigma_U^2.$$

This is a geometric series which reduces to

$$E(\epsilon_t^2) = \sigma_\epsilon^2 = \frac{\sigma_U^2}{1 - K^2}. \tag{C.25}$$

Equation (C.25) shows that the closer the relationship between ϵ_t and ϵ_{t-1}, the closer K is to unity and the greater will be the estimated error term and the loss of efficiency.

We can test for serial correlation by using the Durbin-Watson d statistic. If ϵ_t are the residuals from a fitted least squares equation, then d is defined as

$$d = \frac{\sum_{t=2}^{n} (\epsilon_t - \epsilon_{t-1})^2}{\sum_{t=1}^{n} \epsilon_t^2}.$$

Durbin and Watson have tabulated upper and lower bounds d_l and d_u for various numbers of observations, n, and numbers of independent variables, K.

When the error terms are serially independent, the d statistic has a theoretical distribution with a mean of 2, but sampling fluctuations may lead to a different estimate even when the errors are not autocorrelated. Table C.3 provides critical values for the d-statistic. If the computed d is smaller than the lower critical value, d_l, or above the critical value $(4 - d_l)$, then the null hypothesis of serial independence is

Table C.3 Critical values for the Durbin-Watson test: 5% significance points of d_1 and d_u in two-tailed tests

n	$k' = 1$		$k' = 2$		$k' = 3$		$k' = 4$		$k' = 5$	
	d_l	d_u	d_l	d_u	d_l	d_u	d_l	d_u	d_l	d_u
15	0.95	1.23	0.83	1.40	0.71	1.61	0.59	1.84	0.48	2.09
16	0.98	1.24	0.86	1.40	0.75	1.59	0.64	1.80	0.53	2.03
17	1.01	1.25	0.90	1.40	0.79	1.58	0.68	1.77	0.57	1.98
18	1.03	1.26	0.93	1.40	0.82	1.56	0.72	1.74	0.62	1.93
19	1.06	1.28	0.96	1.41	0.86	1.55	0.76	1.72	0.66	1.90
20	1.08	1.28	0.99	1.41	0.89	1.55	0.79	1.70	0.70	1.87
21	1.10	1.30	1.01	1.41	0.92	1.54	0.83	1.69	0.73	1.84
22	1.12	1.31	1.04	1.42	0.95	1.54	0.86	1.68	0.77	1.82
23	1.14	1.32	1.06	1.42	0.97	1.54	0.89	1.67	0.80	1.80
24	1.16	1.33	1.08	1.43	1.00	1.54	0.91	1.66	0.83	1.79
25	1.18	1.34	1.10	1.43	1.02	1.54	0.94	1.65	0.86	1.77
26	1.19	1.35	1.12	1.44	1.04	1.54	0.96	1.65	0.88	1.76
27	1.21	1.36	1.13	1.44	1.06	1.54	0.99	1.64	0.91	1.75
28	1.22	1.37	1.15	1.45	1.08	1.54	1.01	1.64	0.93	1.74
29	1.24	1.38	1.17	1.45	1.10	1.54	1.03	1.63	0.96	1.73
30	1.25	1.38	1.18	1.46	1.12	1.54	1.05	1.63	0.98	1.73
31	1.26	1.39	1.20	1.47	1.13	1.55	1.07	1.63	1.00	1.72
32	1.27	1.40	1.21	1.47	1.15	1.55	1.08	1.63	1.02	1.71
33	1.28	1.41	1.22	1.48	1.16	1.55	1.10	1.63	1.04	1.71
34	1.29	1.41	1.24	1.48	1.17	1.55	1.12	1.63	1.06	1.70
35	1.30	1.42	1.25	1.48	1.19	1.55	1.13	1.63	1.07	1.70
36	1.31	1.43	1.26	1.49	1.20	1.56	1.15	1.63	1.09	1.70
37	1.32	1.43	1.27	1.49	1.21	1.56	1.16	1.62	1.10	1.70
38	1.33	1.44	1.28	1.50	1.23	1.56	1.17	1.62	1.12	1.70
39	1.34	1.44	1.29	1.50	1.24	1.56	1.19	1.63	1.13	1.69
40	1.35	1.45	1.30	1.51	1.25	1.57	1.20	1.63	1.15	1.69
45	1.39	1.48	1.34	1.53	1.30	1.58	1.25	1.63	1.21	1.69
50	1.42	1.50	1.38	1.54	1.34	1.59	1.30	1.64	1.26	1.69
55	1.45	1.52	1.41	1.56	1.37	1.60	1.33	1.64	1.30	1.69
60	1.47	1.54	1.44	1.57	1.40	1.61	1.37	1.65	1.33	1.69
65	1.49	1.55	1.46	1.59	1.43	1.62	1.40	1.66	1.36	1.69
70	1.51	1.57	1.48	1.60	1.45	1.63	1.42	1.66	1.39	1.70
75	1.53	1.58	1.50	1.61	1.47	1.64	1.45	1.67	1.42	1.70
80	1.54	1.59	1.52	1.62	1.49	1.65	1.47	1.67	1.44	1.70
85	1.56	1.60	1.53	1.63	1.51	1.65	1.49	1.68	1.46	1.71
90	1.57	1.61	1.55	1.64	1.53	1.66	1.50	1.69	1.48	1.71
95	1.58	1.62	1.56	1.65	1.54	1.67	1.52	1.69	1.50	1.71
100	1.59	1.63	1.57	1.65	1.55	1.67	1.53	1.70	1.51	1.72

SOURCE: J. Durbin and G. S. Watson, "Testing for Serial Correlation in Least Squares Regression." *Biometrika*, vol. 38 (1951), pp. 159–177. Reprinted with the permission of the authors and the Trustees of Biometrika.

rejected. When the statistic is larger than d_u but smaller than $(4 - d_u)$, then the null hypothesis is accepted. When neither of these two cases is true, then the test is inconclusive.

For the set of sample data in Table C.1, the estimated d statistic is computed below:

t	ϵ_t	$\epsilon_t - \epsilon_{t-1}$	ϵ_t^2	$(\epsilon_t - \epsilon_{t-1})^2$
1976	14.44	63.53	208.5136	4036.0609
1975	−49.09	50.99	2409.8281	2599.9801
1974	1.90	−34.23	3.6100	1171.6929
1973	36.13	49.02	1305.3769	2402.9604
1972	−12.89	62.24	166.1521	3873.8176
1971	49.35	87.27	2435.4225	7616.0529
1970	−37.92	35.98	1437.9264	1294.5604
1969	−1.94	—	3.7636	—
Sum			7970.5932	22995.122

$$d = \frac{22{,}995.122}{7{,}970.5932} = 2.88.$$

From Table C.3 the critical values for the Durbin-Watson test are $d_l = .95$ and $d_u = 1.23$. Since our computed value is neither below $d_l = .95$ nor above the critical value of $(4 - d_l) = 3.05$, the null hypothesis of serial independence cannot be rejected. However, because $d = 2.88$ is greater than $d_u = 1.23$ but not smaller than $(4 - d_u) = 2.77$, we cannot accept the null hypothesis. Because serial correlation cannot be either accepted nor rejected, the test is inconclusive in this case.

D. SUMMARY

This has been an extremely brief overview of linear regression analysis. We have shown how to estimate the slope, the intercept, the standard errors of each, their t-statistics, and the correlation coefficient for a two variable case. Multivariate estimates of the same variables in a multiple regression equation have the same interpretations and are provided by many different computer software packages. The summary statistics for the example problem of Table C.1 would appear in a computer printout in something like the following form:

$$Y_t = -23.42 + 174.84X_t \qquad R^2 = .6849 \qquad d = 2.88.$$
$$(-.38) \quad (3.61) \qquad\qquad df = 6$$

We can infer that sales revenue is significantly related to predicted GNP, with an intercept term insignificantly different from zero and a significant slope term. Because the Durbin-Watson test is inconclusive we cannot be sure whether or not serial correlation has reduced the efficiency of our estimates. Furthermore, additional testing would be necessary to determine whether or not left-out variables have caused a biased estimate of b_1.

The mean square error criterion is one way of trading off bias and loss of efficiency. It may be desirable, for example, to accept a small bias in order to gain much greater efficiency. Although we have not discussed all of the causes of bias or inefficiency, a few of the more important ones were covered. The interested reader should refer to an econometrics text for a more rigorous and detailed presentation.

REFERENCES

CHRIST, C. G., *Econometric Models and Methods*, Wiley, New York, 1966.

DHRYMES, P. J., *Econometrics: Statistical Foundations and Applications*, New York, Harper and Row, 1970.

GOLDBERGER, A. S., *Econometric Theory*, Wiley, New York, 1964.

HOEL, P. G., *Introduction to Mathematical Statistics*, 3rd ed., Wiley, New York, 1954.

JOHNSTON, J., *Econometric Methods*, McGraw-Hill, New York, 1963.

RAO, P., and L. MILLER, *Applied Econometrics*, Wadsworth, Belmont, Calif., 1971.

WONNACOTT, R. J., and T. H. WONNACOTT, *Econometrics*, Wiley, New York, 1970.

Appendix D

Calculus and Optimization

Optimizing or maximizing are concepts basic to finance theory as well as to economics. In this brief review, we shall summarize the main concepts drawn on in the text. These include:

- A. Functions
- B. Differential Calculus
- C. Optimization
- D. Series
- E. Integral Calculus

A. FUNCTIONS

A fundamental notion used in finance is the concept of a function. There are three ways to express functions: as (1) mathematical equations, (2) graphs, and (3) tables.

Example: Suppose a variable Y is related to a variable X by the following mathematical equation:

$$Y = 2X^2 - 3X + 6.$$

A shorthand way of expressing this relationship is to write $Y = f(X)$, which is read "Y is a function of the variable X" and where Y is the range and X is the domain of the function. X is also called the independent variable and Y the dependent variable, since Y's value $[f(X)]$ is *posited* to depend on X's value.

   We can also express the function in a tabular and graphical manner. Thus the equation enables us to construct a range of Y values for a given table of X values. The data in the table can then be plotted in a graph as in Fig. D.1.

> *Definition:*   The *dimension* of a function is determined by the number of independent variables in the domain of the function.

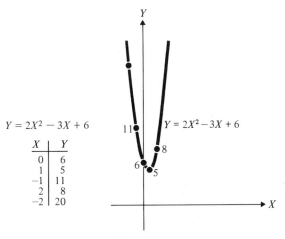

Figure D.1

Example: $Y = f(X, Z)$ is a two-dimensional function

$Y = f(X_1, X_2, \ldots, X_n)$ is an *n*-dimensional function.

Example: From basic capital budgeting concepts (see Chapter 2), we know that the net present value (NPV) of an investment project is equal to

$$\text{NPV} = \sum_{t=1}^{N} \frac{\text{NCF}_t}{(1 + k)^t} - I_0,$$

where

$\text{NCF}_t =$ net cash flow in time period t,
$I_0 =$ the project's initial cash outlay,
$k =$ the firm's cost of capital,
$N =$ the number of years in the project.

We can express this relationship functionally as:

$$\text{NPV} = f(\text{NCF}_t, I_0, k, N) \qquad t = 1, \ldots, N.$$

Given values for the right-hand side independent variables we can determine the left-hand dependent variable, NPV. The functional relationship tells us that for every X which is in the domain of the function, a unique value of Y can be determined.

1. Inverse Functions
How about going the other way? Given Y, can we determine X? Yes, we can.

Definition: The function that expresses the variable X in terms of the variable Y is called the *inverse function* and is denoted $X = f^{-1}(Y)$.

Example: $Y = f(X) = 2X - 5$

solving for X in terms of Y

$$X = \frac{Y+5}{2} = 2.5 + .5Y = f^{-1}(Y).$$

The inverse relationship can be seen more clearly if we graph the two functions (Fig. D.2). The inverse function, however, does not exist for all functions. But the inverse of a function always exists when we are dealing with one-to-one functions.

2. Linear Functions

An important type of function consists of *linear functions* of the form:

$$Y = a_1 X_1 + a_2 X_2 + \cdots + a_n X_n.$$

These functions are used in regression and in the CAPM. In two dimensions a linear function is a straight line, usually written as $Y = a + bX$ where a is the intercept on the Y axis and b is the *slope* of the line:

$$\text{slope} = \frac{Y_1 - Y_2}{X_1 - X_2} = \frac{\Delta Y}{\Delta X}$$

$$= \frac{\text{change in } Y}{\text{change in } X} = \frac{\text{rise}}{\text{run}}.$$

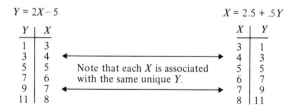

$Y = 2X-5$				$X = 2.5 + .5Y$

Y	X		X	Y
1	3		3	1
3	4	Note that each X is associated	4	3
5	5	with the same unique Y.	5	5
7	6		6	7
9	7		7	9
11	8		8	11

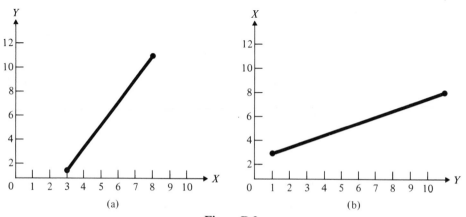

(a)   (b)

Figure D.2

The CAPM is of the form $Y = a + bX$ where $E(R_j) = R_f + \lambda\beta_j$. This equation plots like the relationship in Fig. D.3a, as we see in Fig. D.3b.

The slope of the security market line in Fig. D.3b is $[E(R_m) - R_f]$, which is the market risk premium, λ.

The slope of a function is an important concept: it tells us the change in Y from a per unit change in X. The various types of slopes are pictured in Fig. D.4.

Example: Straightline depreciation is a simple linear function.

$$\text{BV} = c - \left(\frac{c}{N}\right)X,$$

where

BV = book value of the asset,
 c = original cost of the asset,
 N = estimated economic life of the asset,
 X = number of years that have elapsed,

so that the book value after two years is $\text{BV} = c - (c/N)2$.

3. Exponential Functions

As their names suggest, exponential functions are those in which the independent variable X appears as an exponent. They are useful for describing growth and compound interest. More formally:

Definition: The equation $Y = ma^X$ (a always > 0) is called an exponential function, and a is called the base.

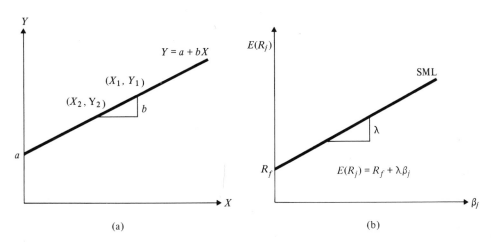

(a)   (b)

Figure D.3

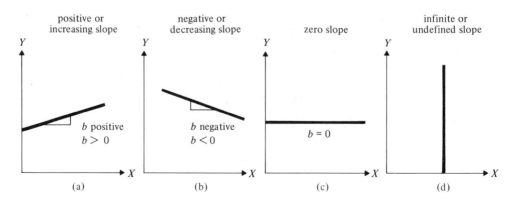

Figure D.4

Some properties of the exponential function are:

1. If $m > 0$, $a > 0$, then the function lies above the X axis.
2. If $m < 0$, $a > 0$, then the function lies below the X axis.
3. If $a > 1$, $m > 0$, then the curve rises to the right.
4. If $a < 1$, $m > 0$, then the curve rises to the left.

Example: An example of 3 and 4 above appears in Fig. D.5.

Example: Compound interest can be shown to be an exponential function. If you invest Z dollars in a bank that pays $r\%$ compound annual interest, then:

$Y_1 = Z + Zr = Z(1 + r) =$ amount your money will grow at the end of the first year,

$Y_2 = Z(1 + r) + [Z(1 + r)]r = Z(1 + r)(1 + r)$

$\quad = Z(1 + r)^2 =$ amount your money will grow at the end of the second year,

$$\vdots$$

$Y_n = Z(1 + r)^n =$ amount at the end of n years.

This last expression is simply an exponential function

$$Y_n = Z(1 + r)^n$$

$Y = ma^X$, where the base is $(1 + r)$ and only n can vary.

Note that money grows exponentially (as in Fig. D.6a) when it is paid compound interest.

Example: Both compound value interest factors (CVIF) and present value interest

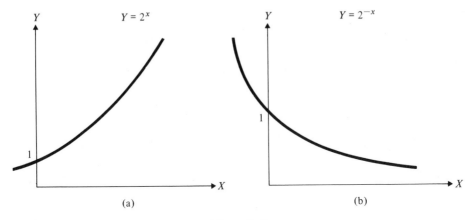

Figure D.5

factors (PVIF) are exponential functions. Consider the case of compounding and discounting $10 for five periods when the appropriate interest rate is 10%.

Compound sum	Present value
$Y = ma^X$	$Y = ma^{-X}$
$S = m(1 + r)^n$	$P = m(1 + r)^{-n}$
$a = (1 + r) > 1$	$a = (1 + r) > 1$
$n = 1, 2, \ldots, N$	$n = 1, 2, \ldots, N$
For $r = 10\%$	For $r = 10\%$
$m = \$10$	$m = \$10$
$n = 1, 2, \ldots, 5$	$n = 1, 2, \ldots, 5$
$S = 10 \cdot (1 + r)^n =$ compound value of $10 at the end of the nth period	$P = 10 \cdot (1 + r)^{-n} =$ present value of $10 at the end of the nth period

4. Logarithmic Functions

Definition: If $N = b^r$, where both $n > 0$, $b > 0$, then we define $r \equiv \log_b N$, which is read "r is the log to the base b of N."

In other words, $\log_b N$ is the number to which b has to be raised exponentially in order to equal N. So a log is simply an exponent.

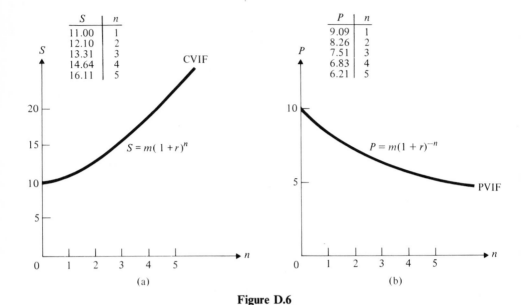

Figure D.6

Examples:

$$100 = 10^2$$

$$\text{so } \log_{10} 100 = 2$$

$$\tfrac{1}{2} = 2^{-1}$$

$$\text{so } \log_2 \tfrac{1}{2} = -1.$$

The two most widely used bases for logarithms are base 10 and base e, where e is an irrational number equal to 2.7182818 ....

Definition: The logarithm to the base 10 of N is called the "common logarithm of N." It is usually designated log N.

Definition: The logarithm to the base e of N is called the "*natural logarithm of N*." To differentiate it from the common log, the natural log is usually designated ln N.

Definition: The function $Y = \log_b X$ is called a *logarithmic function.*

Since by definition $Y = \log_b X$ if and only if $X = b^Y$, we see that the exponential and logarithmic functions are inverse functions of each other:

$$X = 10^Y \Leftrightarrow Y = \log_{10} X$$

$$X = e^Y \Leftrightarrow Y = \ln X.$$

The logarithmic function $Y = \ln X$ is graphed in Fig. D.7.

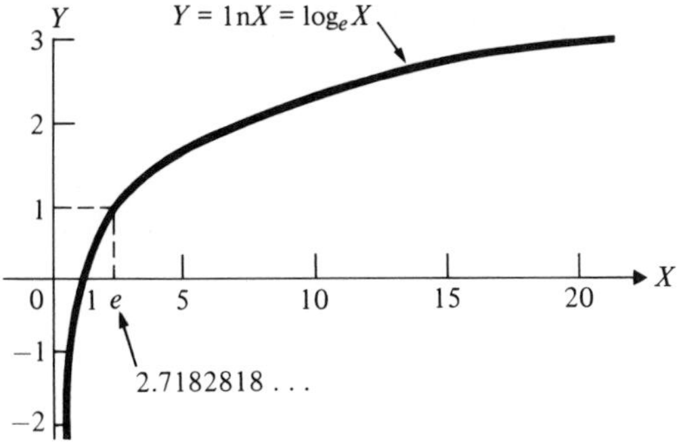

$Y = \ln X = \log_e X$

$Y = \ln X$	
X	Y
0.14	−2.0
0.37	−1.0
1.00	0
e≅2.72	1.0
7.39	2.0
20.10	3.0

2.7182818 . . .

Figure D.7

Some properties of the logarithmic function $Y = \log_b X$ are as follows:

1. The function equals zero when $X = 1$.
2. The function is an increasing function (i.e., it rises to the right) for all $b > 1$.
3. The function is a decreasing function (i.e., it falls to the right) for $0 < b < 1$. See Fig. D.8.
4. The function is negative when $0 < X < 1$ and $b > 1$.
5. The function is positive when $1 < X < \infty$.
6. The function is not defined when X is negative.

Example:

$$X = 2^{-Y} = \frac{1}{2^Y} = \left(\frac{1}{2}\right)^Y$$

so $Y = \log_{1/2} X$.

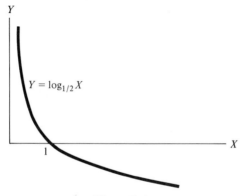

$Y = \log_{1/2} X$

Figure D.8

Since logarithms are simply exponents, the rules of logs simply mirror the rules of exponents:

Exponents	Logarithms
$a^m \cdot a^n = a^{m+n}$	$\log_a (XY) = \log_a X + \log_a Y$
$\dfrac{a^m}{a^n} = a^{m-n}$ if $m > n$	$\log_a \dfrac{X}{Y} = \log_a X - \log_a Y$
$(a^m)^n = a^{mn}$	$\log_a (X^n) = n \log_a X$

B. DIFFERENTIAL CALCULUS

1. Limits

The central idea in calculus is the concept of the limit of a function. Often we want to know how the values of a function, $f(X)$, behave as the independent variable X approaches some particular point, a. If as $X \to a$ (read "X approaches a"), $f(X)$ approaches some number L, then we say that *the limit* of $f(X)$ as X approaches a is L. This is written more compactly as

$$\lim_{X \to a} f(X) = L.$$

Intuitively, the existence of a limit L means that the function $f(X)$ will take on a value as close to L as one may desire, given that the independent variable takes a value that is sufficiently close to a.

Example: Many times we are interested in just what happens to a function as X increases without bound, that is when $X \to \infty$ (read "X approaches infinity"). For instance, what is lim. as $x \to \infty$ of $[(X + 1)/X]$? The way to evaluate this limit is to observe the behavior of $f(X)$ as X gets larger and larger. From the table and the graph in Fig. D.9 we see that $f(X)$ approaches 1 as $X \to \infty$, so we can write lim. as $x \to \infty$ of $[(X + 1)/X] = 1$.

Intuitively, as X gets very, very large, the fact that the numerator is greater by one than the denominator doesn't matter "much," so we have $X/X = 1$.

Example: As we will see next, we are often interested in what happens to $f(X)$ as X gets very, very small—that is, when $X \to 0$. For instance, what is the lim. as $x \to 0$ of $(3X/X^2)$? Again, to evaluate this limit we see what happens to $f(X)$ as $X \to 0$ (Fig. D.10).

Example: Generally we assume that compounding and discounting occur discretely in annual periods. If the compounding is more than once a year the compound value interest factor is changed from $(1 + r)^n$ to $[(1 + r/m)]^{nm}$, where m is the number of

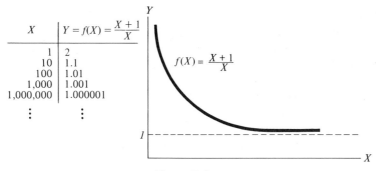

X	$Y = f(X) = \dfrac{X+1}{X}$
1	2
10	1.1
100	1.01
1,000	1.001
1,000,000	1.000001
$\vdots$	$\vdots$

Figure D.9

times per year compounding occurs. We can now see with limits what is the relationship between the continuous compounding rate and the discrete compounding rate. Continuous compounding means

$$\lim_{m \to \infty} \left[\left(1 + \frac{r}{m}\right)^{nm} \right] = e^{rn} \qquad \text{by definition of } e.$$

If r_c = the continuous compounding rate and r_d = the discrete compounding rate, then $e^{r_c n} = (1 + r_d)^n$. Taking natural logs:

$$\ln \left[e^{r_c n} \right] = \ln (1 + r_d)^n,$$

$$r_c n \ln e = n \ln (1 + r_d),$$

$$r_c n = n \ln (1 + r_d) \qquad \text{since } \ln e \equiv 1,$$

$$r_c = \ln (1 + r_d).$$

So 5.25% continuously compounded is equal to 5.39% compounded annually. That is, if $r_c = 5.25\%$, then using $\ln (1 + r_d) = 5.25\%$, r_d must be 5.39%.

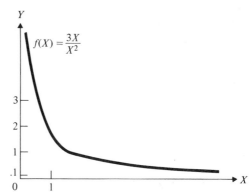

X	$Y = f(X) = \dfrac{3X}{X^2}$
1	3
.05	60
.01	300
.001	3,000
.0001	30,000
$\vdots$	$\vdots$

So we see that $\displaystyle \lim_{X \to 0} \frac{3X}{X^2} = \infty$

Figure D.10

2. Derivatives

The rate of change of a function (the change in Y from a per unit change in X) is an important concept in mathematics. It is referred to as the *derivative* of Y with respect to X. In finance and economics the rate of change is called "marginal." For example, the marginal cost of capital (MCC) is the rate of change of the total cost of capital per change in new capital raised. Analytically, the marginal quantities are simply the *slopes* of the total quantities.

The derivative is usually denoted as dY/dX, or $f'(X)$. The advantage of the $f'(X)$ notation is that it reminds us that *the derivative is itself a function*: the value of the derivative depends on where it is evaluated. Fortunately there are special rules of differentiation that can be used to guide calculations.

3. Rules of Differentiation

1. $f(X) = c$ (c is a constant), $f'(X) = 0$. This rule states that the slope of a horizontal line is zero, since by definition Y does not change when X changes.
2. $f(X) = X^n$, $f'(X) = nX^{n-1}$. In order to differentiate X^n, reduce the exponent by one and multiply by n.
3. $f(X) = g(X) \cdot h(X)$, $f'(X) = g'(X) \cdot h(X) + h'(X) \cdot g(X)$. The derivative of $g(X) \cdot h(X)$ equals $h(X)$ times the derivative of $g(X)$ plus $g(X)$ times the derivative of $h(X)$.
4. $f(X) = g(X)/h(X)$, $[h(X) \neq 0]$, $f'(X) = [g'(X)h(X) - g(X)h'(X)]/[h(X)]^2$.
5. $f(X) = c \cdot g(X)$, $[c$ constant$]$, $f'(X) = c \cdot g'(X)$.
6. $f(X) = g(X) + h(X)$, $f'(X) = g'(X) + h'(X)$.
7. $f(X) = \ln X$, $f'(X) = 1/X$.
8. $f(X) = e^{g(X)}$, $f'(X) = g'(X)e^{g(X)}$.
9. $f(X) = X$, $f'(X) = 1$.
10. $f(X) = a^X$, $f'(X) = a^X \cdot \ln a$.
11. $f(X) = \log_b X$, $f'(X) = 1/(X \ln b)$.
12. $f(X) = \log [g(X)]$, $f'(X) = g'(X)/g(X)$.

Examples

1) $Y = 6X^3 - 3X^2 + 4X + 7$,

$$\frac{dY}{dX} = 6 \cdot \frac{d}{dX} (X^3) - 3 \cdot \frac{d}{dX} (X^2) + 4 \cdot \frac{d}{dX} (X) + \frac{d}{dX} (7)$$

$$= 6(3X^2) - 3(2X) + 4(1) + 0$$

$$= 18X^2 - 6X + 4.$$

2) $Y = X^2(X + 3)$

$$\frac{dY}{dX} = \left[\frac{d}{dX} (X^2) \right] (X + 3) + \left[\frac{d}{dX} (X + 3) \right] X^2$$

$$= 2X(X + 3) + (1)X^2 = 3X^2 + 3X$$

3) $Y = X^{-4}$,

$$\frac{dY}{dX} = -4X^{-5} = \frac{-4}{X^5}.$$

4) $Y = \frac{(2X^2 + 6)}{X^3}$

$$\frac{dY}{dX} = \frac{3X^2(2X + 6) - X^3 4X}{(X^3)^2} = \frac{2X^4 + 18X^2}{X^6}$$

5) $Y = \frac{2}{\sqrt{X}} = 2X^{-1/2}$,

$$\frac{dY}{dX} = 2 \cdot -\frac{1}{2} \cdot X^{-3/2} = -X^{-3/2} = \frac{-1}{X^{3/2}} = \frac{-1}{\sqrt{X^3}}$$

4. Chain Rule

An extremely useful and powerful tool in differential calculus is the chain rule, or the function of a function rule. Suppose Y is a function of a variable Z:

$$Y = f(Z),$$

but Z is in turn a function of another variable X:

$$Z = g(X)$$

Because Y depends on Z, and Z in turn depends on X, Y is also a function of X. We can express this fact by writing Y as a composite function (i.e., a function of a function) of X: $Y = f[g(X)]$.

In order to determine the change in Y from a change in X, the chain rule says:

$$\boxed{\frac{dY}{dX} = \frac{dY}{dZ} \frac{dZ}{dX} = f'(Z) \cdot g'(X)} \qquad \text{Chain Rule}$$

Intuitively the chain rule says, "Take the derivative of the outside (function) and multiply it by the derivative of the inside (function)." The reason behind the name "chain" rule is that there is a chain reaction relationship between X, Z and Y:

$$\Delta X \xrightarrow{\text{via } g} \Delta Z \xrightarrow{\text{via } f} \Delta Y.$$

In words, a change in X has an ultimate impact on Y by causing a change in Z via function g, and this change in Z will in turn cause a change in Y by function f.

There is a temptation to look at the chain rule by canceling the intermediate dZ term:

$$\frac{dY}{dX} = \frac{dY}{dZ} \cdot \frac{dZ}{dX} = \frac{dY}{dX}.$$

This is incorrect! It is no more valid than canceling the 3s in:

$$3 = \frac{39}{13} \neq \frac{9}{1} \neq 9.$$

The usefulness of the chain rule can best be seen by considering some examples in which it is used.

Examples:

1) Suppose we wanted to differentiate

$$Y = (3 + 6X^2)^{10}.$$

We could, by a considerable amount of work, expand $(3 + 6X^2)^{10}$ and differentiate term by term. Instead we can use the chain rule. Note that if we wanted to simply differentiate $Z = (3 + 6X^2)$ that would pose no problem:

$$\frac{dZ}{dX} = \frac{d}{dX}(3) + \frac{d(6X^2)}{dX}$$

$$= 0 + 12X,$$

$$\frac{dZ}{dX} = 12X.$$

Likewise, if we let

$$Y = (Z)^{10},$$

then we can differentiate easily

$$\frac{dY}{dZ} = \frac{d(Z)^{10}}{dZ} = 10Z^{10-1} = 10 \cdot Z^9.$$

The chain rule says to simply multiply these two results together to get dY/dX:

$$\frac{dY}{dX} = \frac{dY}{dZ} \cdot \frac{dZ}{dX}$$

$$= [10 \cdot Z^9]12X$$

$$= [10 \cdot (3 + 6X^2)^9]12X$$

$$= 120X(3 + 6X^2)^9.$$

Intuitively, the chain rule says to take the derivative of the function outside the parentheses—in this case, $10 \cdot (\ )^9$—and multiply it by the derivative of what is inside the parentheses—that is, $12X$. So what seemed to be at first a rather forbidding problem turns out to be very easy to solve. Two examples are given below:

$$\frac{d}{dX} (\sqrt[3]{5X + 7}) = \frac{d}{dX} (5X + 7)^{1/3}$$

$$= \tfrac{1}{3}(5X + 7)^{-2/3} \cdot 5$$

$$= \frac{5}{3} \frac{1}{(\sqrt[3]{5X + 7})^2}$$

$$= \frac{5}{3(5X + 7)^{2/3}} \cdot$$

$$\frac{d}{dX} (e^{3X-4}) = e^{3X-4} \cdot 3$$

$$= 3e^{3X-4}.$$

5. Higher-Order Derivatives

In our development of derivatives we have emphasized that the derivative of a function is also a function. That is, the value of the derivative depends on the Point X at which it is being evaluated. Like $f(X), f'(X)$ is also a function of X.

Example: Consider the function

$$f(X) = -10X^2 + 2{,}400X - 8{,}500, \qquad \text{then}$$

$$f'(X) = -20X + 2{,}400.$$

The value of this derivative depends on the point at which it is being evaluated:

$$f'(120) = -20(120) + 2{,}400 = 0,$$

$$f'(60) = -20(60) + 2{,}400 = 1{,}200.$$

Because it is also a function of X, we can take the derivative of $f'(X)$. This new function, $f''(X)$, is called the *second derivative* of the original function, $f(X)$. The *third derivative* is the derivative of the second derivative and is written $f'''(X)$. In principle we can go on forever and form derivatives of as high order as we like. Notationally these higher-order derivatives are symbolized in the same manner as the second derivative

$$f'''(X), f^{(4)}(X), f^{(5)}(X), \dots, f^{(n)}(X)$$

$$\frac{d^3 Y}{dX^3}, \frac{d^4 Y}{dX^4}, \frac{d^5 Y}{dX^5}, \dots, \frac{d^n Y}{dX^n} \cdot$$

Example:

$$Y = f(X) = X^3 - 7X^2 + 6X - 5,$$
$$f'(X) = 3X^2 - 14X + 6,$$
$$f''(X) = 6X - 14,$$
$$f'''(X) = 6,$$
$$f^{(4)}(X) = 0,$$
$$f^{(5)}(X) = 0,$$
$$\vdots$$
$$f^{(n)}(X) = 0.$$

As we shall see, higher-order derivatives play an important role in Taylor and MacLaurin series (see Section D of this appendix). The most important of the higher-order derivatives is the second derivative. Understanding the meaning of the second derivative is crucial. We know that the first derivative of a function, $f'(X)$, is the slope of a function or the rate of change of Y as a result of a change in X. The second derivative, $f''(X)$, is the rate of change of the slope of $f(X)$; that is, it is the rate of change of the rate of change of the original function, $f(X)$. Table D.1 and Fig. D.11 show various combinations of signs for $f'(X)$ and $f''(X)$ and the implied shape of the graph of $f(X)$.

Table D.1

	$f'(X)$	$f''(X)$	$f(X)$ is
a)	>0	>0	Increasing at an increasing rate
b)	>0	<0	Increasing at a decreasing rate
c)	<0	<0	Decreasing at an increasing rate
d)	<0	>0	Decreasing at a decreasing rate

Example: In developing the theory of investor choice under uncertainty, cardinal utility functions $[U(W)]$ are used. These utility functions should have the following property: $U'(W) > 0$, $U''(W) < 0$. That is, they should look like Fig. D.11b. Check to see if and when the following four functions have this property.

1) $U(W) = aw - bw^2$ (quadratic utility function),

$U'(W) = a - 2bw > 0$ when $a > 2bw$,

$U''(W) = -2b < 0$ when $b > 0$.

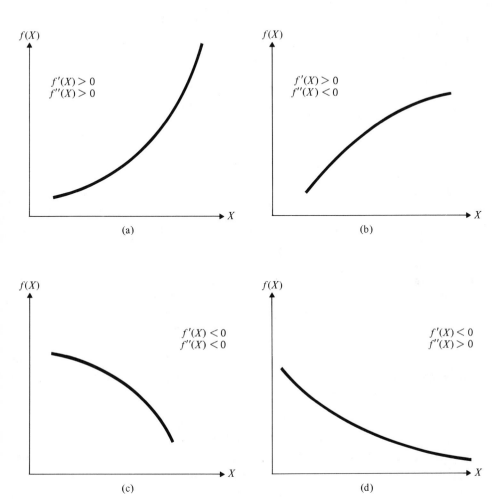

Figure D.11

2) $U(W) = \ln W$ (logarithmic utility function),

$U'(W) = \dfrac{1}{W} > 0$ W always > 0 by definition of log function.

$U''(W) = \dfrac{-1}{W^2} < 0$

3) $U(W) = -e^{-aW}$ (exponential utility function),

$U'(W) = -(-a)e^{-aW} = ae^{-aW} > 0$ if $a > 0$,

$U''(W) = -a^2 e^{-aW} < 0.$

4) $U(W) = W^a$ (power utility function),

$U'(W) = aW^{a-1} > 0,$

$U''(W) = a(a-1)W^{a-2} < 0$ when $a < 1.$

Example: Given the following linear demand function

$$p = 100 - 10q,$$

where

$p =$ price per unit sold (i.e., average revenue)
$q =$ quantity sold
(note that p is the dependent variable here).

We can obtain the total revenue function by multiplying through by q:

$$\text{TR} \equiv pq = 100q - 10q^2, \qquad \text{which is a quadratic equation.}$$

The first derivative of total revenue tells us how total revenue responds to changes in the quantity sold. Economists call this function the marginal revenue:

$$\text{MR} \equiv \frac{d(\text{TR})}{dq} = 100 - 20q.$$

If we want to know by how much marginal revenue itself varies when quantity sold varies, we compute the slope of the marginal revenue. This is the second derivative of the total revenue function:

$$\frac{d(\text{MR})}{dq} = \frac{d^2(\text{TR})}{dq^2} = -20.$$

So marginal revenue declines at a constant rate of -20 per unit increase in quantity sold. Graphically the relationship between total, average, and marginal revenue is shown in Fig. D.12.

> *Definition:* An important class of functions are those functions whose first derivative is positive for all values of the independent variable. Such functions are called *monotonically increasing* functions. Likewise, functions whose first derivative is negative for all values of the independent variable are *monotonically decreasing.*

6. Differentials

Let $Y = f(X)$, then the differential, dY, is defined as

$$dY = f'(X)\, dX.$$

If we regard $dX \equiv \Delta X$, a small increment in the independent variable X, then we can see that dY is an approximation to ΔY induced by ΔX because $f'(X) = \lim$. as $\Delta X \to 0$ of $(\Delta Y/\Delta X).$

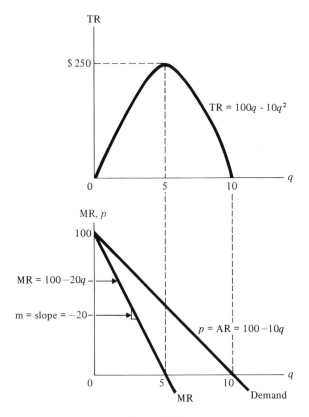

Figure D.12

Example: Let $Y = 2X^2 + X + 2$, then $dY = (4X + 1)\, dX$. The concept of differentials is very useful when we consider integration later in Section E.

7. Partial Differentiation

So far we have only considered differentiation of functions of one independent variable. In practice, functions of two or more independent variables do arise quite frequently. Since each independent variable influences the function differently, when we consider the instantaneous rate of change of the function, we have to isolate the effect of each of the independent variables. Let $W = f(X, Y, Z)$. When we consider how W changes as X changes, we want to hold the variable Y and Z constant. This gives rise to the concept of partial differentiation. Note that only the variable X is changing, while both Y and Z remain constant. The rules for partial differentiation and ordinary differentiation are exactly the same except that when we are taking partial derivative of one independent variable, we regard *all other independent variables as constants.*

Examples:

1) $W = XY + YZ + XZ$,

$$\frac{\partial W}{\partial X} = Y + 0 + Z = Y + Z,$$

$$\frac{\partial W}{\partial Y} = X + Z + 0 = X + Z,$$

$$\frac{\partial W}{\partial Z} = 0 + Y + X = Y + X.$$

2) $W = X^2 Y Z^3 + e^X + \ln YZ$,

$$\frac{\partial W}{\partial X} = 2XYZ^3 + e^X,$$

$$\frac{\partial W}{\partial Y} = X^2 Z^3 + \frac{1}{YZ} \cdot Z = X^2 Z^3 + \frac{1}{Y},$$

$$\frac{\partial W}{\partial Z} = 3X^2 YZ^2 + \frac{1}{YZ} \cdot Y = 3X^2 YZ^2 + \frac{1}{Z}.$$

C. OPTIMIZATION

A company seeks to maximize its profit. A production unit seeks to minimize its cost for a given level of output. An individual investor seeks to maximize his utility when choosing among investment alternatives. Indeed, we are all engaged in big and small optimization problems every day at work or at leisure. If we have a mathematical objective function, then we can solve our optimization problem using calculus. The procedure is divided into two steps:

1. Locate all *relative* maxima and minima of the objective function.
2. Compare the function value at the relative maxima and minima and at the boundary points (to be explained later) to pick the highest (lowest) value to be the *global* maximum (minimum).

To accomplish step 1, let us first consider the graph of a function $f(X)$ that appears in Fig. D.13. At the point $X = a$, the function $f(X)$ is said to have a relative maximum because $f(a) > f(Z)$ for all Z sufficiently close to a. Similarly, $f(X)$ has a relative maximum at $X = c$ and $f(X)$ has relative minima at $X = b$ and $X = d$. One common characteristic those four points share is the slope of $f(X)$ at those points. If we draw tangent lines to $f(X)$ at $x = a, b, c, d$, then all the tangent lines must be

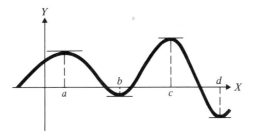

Figure D.13

perfectly horizontal. In other words, the slopes $f'(a) = f'(b) = f'(c) = f'(d) = 0$. Thus we have the following theorem:

Theorem: If $f(X)$ has a relative maximum or minimum at $X = a$, then $f'(a) = 0$.

Note that the theorem does *not* say that if $f'(a) = 0$, then $X = a$ is a relative maximum or minimum. It says that if $f'(a) = 0$, then $X = a$ is a *candidate* for relative maximum or minimum. There exist points for which the derivative of $f(X)$ is zero, but the points are neither relative maxima nor minima. Nevertheless, to locate all relative maxima and minima, we differentiate $f(X)$, set the result to zero and solve for X. That is, find all the solutions to the equation

$$f'(X) = 0.$$

The above equation is called the first order condition. The solutions are candidates for relative maxima and minima. To determine which of these solutions are indeed relative maxima or minima, we need the so-called second order conditions. Consider the relative maximum shown in Fig. D.14a. The slope, $f'(X)$, is zero at the top, positive to the left of the top and negative to the right of the top. Therefore, as X increases from left to right, the slope, $f'(X)$, is decreasing from positive to zero to negative. We know from the previous section that if $f'(X)$ is decreasing, then the derivative of $f'(X)$, $f''(X)$, is *negative*. The condition $f''(X) < 0$ is called the second order condition for relative maxima. Similar reasoning would indicate that at a relative minimum, $f''(X) > 0$. We can now summarize step one: Find all the X such that $f'(X) = 0$; then for each of those x, if $f''(X) > 0$, it is a relative minimum, if

(a)   (b)

Figure D.14

$f''(X) < 0$, it is a relative maximum, if $f''(X) = 0$, we cannot tell (and have to use more sophisticated techniques).

Step two requires us to compare function value at the relative maxima and minima and the boundary points to determine the global optimum. Boundary points exist because we generally wish to optimize $f(X)$ in some interval, say $a \leq x \leq b$, then a and b are boundary points. Sometimes, the global maximum or minimum occurs at the boundary (see Fig. D.15). That is why we want to evaluate $f(X)$ at the boundary.

Example: A monopolist faces a downward sloping demand curve given by $p(X) = 100 - 2X$, where X is the quantity and $p(X)$ is the price at that quantity. Suppose the fixed cost of production is 10 and variable cost is constant at 8 per unit. How many units should the monopolist produce to maximize profit?

$$\text{Profit} = \text{total revenue} - \text{total cost}$$

$$= \text{price} \times \text{quantity} - (\text{total variable cost} + \text{fixed cost}),$$

$$\pi(X) = (100 - 2X)X - (8X + 10)$$

$$= 100X - 2X^2 - 8X - 10$$

$$= 92X - 2X^2 - 10,$$

$$\pi'(X) = 92 - 4X = 0 \text{ (1st-order condition)},$$

so

$$92 = 4X \text{ or } X = 23,$$

$$\pi''(X) = -4,$$

hence

$$\pi''(23) < 0 \text{ (2nd-order condition)}.$$

Therefore, $X = 23$ is a relative maximum. Implicit in this problem is the boundary $X \geq 0$. So, $X = 0$ is a boundary. Obviously $\pi(0) = 0$ because this is the decision of not getting into the business at all. $\pi(23) = 92 \times 23 - 2 \times (23)^2 - 10 = 1048 > \pi(0)$.

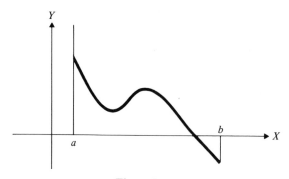

Figure D.15

The solution to this problem is therefore $X = 23$. The monopolist should produce 23 units. If we change the original problem by making the fixed cost 1060 instead of 10, then $X = 23$ is still the only relative maximum. But now $\pi(23) = -2 < \pi(0)$. So the monopolist is better off not getting into the business at all. Here the optimum point occurs at the boundary.

If our objective function has two independent variables, then we have to resort to partial derivatives. Suppose $Z = f(X, Y)$, let

$$f_x = \frac{\partial Z}{\partial X}, f_y = \frac{\partial Z}{\partial Y}, f_{xx} = \frac{\partial}{\partial X}\left(\frac{\partial Z}{\partial X}\right)$$

(taking partial derivative twice with respect to X),

$$f_{yy} = \frac{\partial}{\partial Y}\left(\frac{\partial Z}{\partial Y}\right), f_{xy} = f_{yx} = \frac{\partial}{\partial X}\left(\frac{\partial Z}{\partial Y}\right)$$

(taking partial derivative twice, first with respect to Y, then with respect to X). The conditions for relative maxima and minima are:

$$\left.\begin{array}{l} f_x = 0 \\ f_y = 0 \end{array}\right\} \quad \text{(1st-order conditions).}$$

In addition, if $f_{xx} f_{yy} > f_{xy}^2$, then the point is either a relative maximum or minimum. To distinguish relative maximum and minimum, we have

$$\left.\begin{array}{ll} f_{xx}, f_{yy} < 0 & \text{maximum} \\ f_{xx}, f_{yy} > 0 & \text{minimum} \end{array}\right\} \quad \text{(2nd-order conditions).}$$

An example of using partial derivatives to find the optimum point is given in the application section of Appendix B.

1. Constrained Optimization

Very often, a business entity operates under certain constraints. They may be budgetary, technological or physical constraints. To solve this constrained optimization problem, we can use the method of Lagrange multipliers if the constraints are given as equations. For example, the production function of a firm may be $f(X, Y) = 2XY$, where X represents units of labor and Y represents units of capital. The budgetary constraint may look like

$$g(X, Y) = 100 - 2X - 10Y = 0,$$

where 100 represents the maximum amount of money to be spent on this production and 2 and 10 represent unit costs of labor and capital respectively. To use the method of Lagrange multipliers, we first construct a new function of three independent variables:

$$L(X, Y, \lambda) = f(X, Y) + \lambda g(X, Y)$$

$$= 2XY + \lambda(100 - 2X - 10Y),$$

where λ is a new variable which is called the Lagrange multiplier. The constrained optimum will appear as a solution to the first order condition:

$$\frac{\partial L}{\partial X} = L_x = 0$$

$$\frac{\partial L}{\partial Y} = L_y = 0 \quad \text{(1st-order conditions)}.$$

$$\frac{\partial L}{\partial \lambda} = L_\lambda = 0$$

Let

$$H = \begin{pmatrix} 0 & g_x & g_y \\ g_x & L_{xx} & L_{xy} \\ g_y & L_{yx} & L_{yy} \end{pmatrix} \text{ and } |H| = \text{determinant of } H \text{ (defined in Appendix B)},$$

then

$$\begin{matrix} |H| < 0 & \text{relative minimum} \\ |H| > 0 & \text{relative maximum} \end{matrix} \quad \text{(2nd-order conditions)}.$$

Example: Take the production function and the budgetary constraint above and find the optimal combination of labor and capital.

$$L(X, Y, \lambda) = 2XY + \lambda(100 - 2X - 10Y)$$

$$L_x = 2Y - 2\lambda = 0$$

$$L_y = 2X - 10\lambda = 0 \quad \text{(1st-order conditions)}.$$

$$L_\lambda = 100 - 2X - 10Y = 0$$

Solving these equations simultaneously gives us $X = 25$, $Y = 5$, $\lambda = 5$. (For a discussion of methods of solving system of linear equations, see Appendix B.) Therefore, under the budgetary constraint, the maximum output level is $f(25, 5) = 2 \times 25 \times 5 = 250$ when we employ 25 units of labor and 5 units of capital. We know that this must be the maximum point before computing the second order condition because a relative maximum is the only sensible solution. The interested reader may check that

$$|H| = \begin{vmatrix} 0 & -2 & -10 \\ -2 & 0 & 2 \\ -10 & 2 & 0 \end{vmatrix} = 80 > 0.$$

Another example of using the method of Lagrange multiplier can be found in the application section of Appendix B regarding the minimum variance portfolio.

The Meaning of λ

The solution of λ also has a meaning. The magnitude of λ measures how much the optimum changes as we relax the constraint. In the above example, the solution of λ

is 5. That means if we relax the budgetary constraint one unit from 100 to 101, the optimal level of output would increase approximately 5 units to 255.

If the solution to λ is equal to zero, then the constraint is not binding. That means the constrained optimum is equal to the unconstrained optimum.

D. TAYLOR AND MACLAURIN SERIES

The Taylor and MacLaurin series are widely used in economics and finance. Their most important use is to help evaluate the value of a function around a certain point. Suppose we are interested in evaluating the function $Y = f(X)$ around a point a in its domain. Then we can make use of Taylor's theorem:

Taylor's Theorem. In the one-dimensional case we can evaluate the function $Y = f(X)$ around the point a in terms of its derivatives as follows:

$$f(X) = f(a) + f'(a)(X - a) + \frac{f''(a)(X - a)^2}{2!}$$

$$+ \frac{f'''(a)(X - a)^3}{3!} + \cdots + \frac{f^{(n)}(a)(X - a)^n}{n!}.$$

Alternatively, if we let $h = (X - a)$, then the Taylor series is:

$$f(a + h) = f(a) + f'(a)h + \frac{f''(a)h^2}{2!}$$

$$+ \frac{f'''(a)h^3}{3!} + \cdots + \frac{f^{(n)}(a)h^n}{n!}, \qquad \text{[Pratt (1964) uses this.]}$$

where $f(a) =$ value of the function at point a. This is called a *Taylor series.*

Definition: If we evaluate the function around zero (i.e., if $a = 0$ above) then we have what is called a *MacLaurin series:*

$$f(X) = f(0) + f'(0) \cdot X + \frac{f''(0)}{2!} \cdot X^2 + \frac{f'''(0)}{3!} \cdot X^3 + \cdots + \frac{f^{(n)}(0)}{n!} \cdot X^n.$$

Definition: The symbol $n!$ [read "n *factorial*"] represents the product of all positive integers from 1 to n (or vice versa). That is:

$$n! = n \cdot (n - 1) \cdot (n - 2) \cdot (n - 3) \cdot (n - 4) \cdots 4 \cdot 3 \cdot 2 \cdot 1.$$

Examples:

$$5! = 5 \cdot 4 \cdot 3 \cdot 2 \cdot 1 = 1 \cdot 2 \cdot 3 \cdot 4 \cdot 5 = 120,$$

$$10! = 10 \cdot 9 \cdot 8 \cdot 7 \cdot 6 \cdot 5 \cdot 4 \cdot 3 \cdot 2 \cdot 1 = 3,628,800,$$

$$(n - r)! = (n - r) \cdot (n - r - 1) \cdot (n - r - 2) \cdot (n - r - 3) \cdots 4 \cdot 3 \cdot 2 \cdot 1.$$

By definition $1! = 0! = 1$.

Intuitively, what the Taylor series is trying to do is to approximate the function $f(X)$ with the following polynomial:

1) $f(X) \approx T_0 + T_1(X - a) + T_2(X - a)^2 + T_3(X - a)^3 + \cdots$. The problem is to find the values of the coefficients (the Ts) of this polynomial. To find them, take the higher order derivatives of (1):

2) $f'(X) = T_1 + T_2 \cdot 2(X - a) + T_3 \cdot 3(X - a)^2 + T_4 \cdot 4(X - a)^3 + \cdots$

3) $f''(X) = 2T_2 + T_3 \cdot 2 \cdot 3(X - a) + T_4 \cdot 4 \cdot 3(X - a)^2 + \cdots$

4) $f'''(X) = 2 \cdot 3T_3 + T_4 \cdot 4 \cdot 3(X - a) + T_5 \cdot 5 \cdot 4 \cdot 3(X - a)^2 + \cdots$

$\vdots \qquad \vdots$

If we evaluate (1) through (4) at $X = a$, then $(X - a) = 0$, so all terms involving $(X - a)$ will vanish:

1') $f(X) = T_0$

2') $f'(X) = T_1$

3') $f''(X) = 2 \cdot T_2$

4') $f'''(X) = 2 \cdot 3T_3$

$\left. \right\}$ Solving for the Ts

$\left(\begin{array}{l} T_0 = f(X) \\[4pt] T_1 = f'(X) \\[4pt] T_2 = \dfrac{f''(X)}{2} = \dfrac{f''(X)}{2 \cdot 1} = \dfrac{f''(X)}{2!} \\[8pt] T_3 = \dfrac{f'''(X)}{3 \cdot 2} = \dfrac{f'''(X)}{3 \cdot 2 \cdot 1} = \dfrac{f'''(X)}{3!} \end{array}\right.$

$\vdots \qquad \vdots \qquad \vdots \qquad \vdots$

Plugging these values of the Ts into (1) results in the Taylor series we stated earlier. The usefulness of Taylor series can best be seen with the help of a numerical example.

Example: Expand the function $f(X) = 1/X$ around 1, for $n = 0, 1, 2, 3$. Computing the derivatives:

$$f(X) = \frac{1}{X} \quad \text{so} \quad f(1) = \frac{1}{1} = 1,$$

$$f'(X) = \frac{-1}{X^2} \quad \text{so} \quad f'(1) = \frac{-1}{(1)^2} = -1,$$

$$f''(X) = \frac{2}{X^3} \quad \text{so} \quad f''(1) = \frac{2}{(1)^3} = 2,$$

$$f'''(X) = \frac{-6}{X^4} \quad \text{so} \quad f'''(1) = \frac{-6}{(1)^4} = -6.$$

a) The Taylor series approximation when $n = 0$ is:

$T_0(X) = f(a)$,   since $a = 1$ (we're expanding around 1)

$T_0(X) = f(1) = 1$.

b) The Taylor approximation when $n = 1$ is:

$$T_1(X) = f(a) + f'(a)(X - a)$$
$$= f(1) + (-1)(X - 1)$$
$$= 1 - (X - 1).$$

c) The approximation when $n = 2$ is:

$$T_2(X) = f(a) + f'(a)(X - a) + \frac{f''(a)}{2!}(X - a)^2$$

$$= f(1) + (-1)(X - 1) + \frac{2}{2 \cdot 1}(X - 1)^2$$

$$= 1 - (X - 1) + (X - 1)^2.$$

d) The approximation when $n = 3$ is:

$$T_3(X) = f(a) + f'(a)(X - a) + \frac{f''(a)}{2!}(X - a)^2 + \frac{f'''(a)}{3!}(X - a)^3$$

$$= 1 - (X - 1) + (X - 1)^2 + \frac{-6}{3 \cdot 2 \cdot 1}(X - 1)^3$$

$$= 1 - (X - 1) + (X - 1)^2 - (X - 1)^3.$$

Expanding and rearranging the polynomials:

$T_0(X) = 1$ (constant),

$T_1(X) = 1 - (X - 1) = -X + 2$ (straight line),

$T_2(X) = 1 - (X - 1) + (X - 1)^2 = X^2 - 3X + 3$ (parabola),

$T_3(X) = 1 - (X + 1) + (X - 1)^2 - (X - 1)^3 = -X^3 + 4X^2 - 6X + 4$ (cubic).

Figure D.16 graphs the function $f(X) = 1/X$ and each of the approximating polynomials:

$$\frac{dT_2(X)}{dX} = 2X - 3 = 0, \qquad X = 1.5 = \text{min},$$

$$\frac{dT_3(X)}{dX} = -3X^2 + 8X - 6 = 0$$

$$(-3X + 2)(X - 3) \qquad \text{inflection point} > 1.$$

From the graph we see that each successive Taylor series does a better job of approximating $f(X) = 1/X$ in the vicinity of 1; see Fig. D.17.

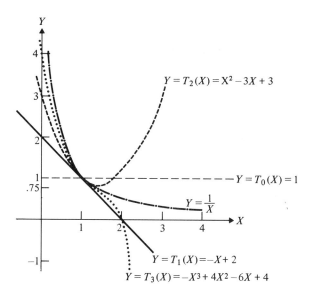

$Y = T_2(X) = X^2 - 3X + 3$

$Y = T_0(X) = 1$

$Y = \dfrac{1}{X}$

$Y = T_1(X) = -X + 2$

$Y = T_3(X) = -X^3 + 4X^2 - 6X + 4$

Figure D.16

Example: Pratt (1964) uses Taylor series to derive a measure of absolute relative risk aversion. Let

X = amount of wealth,

U = acceptable utility function,

π = risk premium, π is a function of $\pi(X, \tilde{Z})$,

$\tilde{Z}$ = a gamble (and a random variable),

$\tilde{Z} \sim E(\tilde{Z}) - \pi(X, \tilde{Z})$.

1) $E\{U(X + \tilde{Z})\} = U[X + E(\tilde{Z}) - \pi(X, \tilde{Z})]$
   by choosing an actuarially neutral risk $E(\tilde{Z}) = 0$. So
1') $E\{U(X + \tilde{Z})\} = U[X - \pi(X, \tilde{Z})]$.

Expand the right-hand side of (1') using Taylor series:

$$U(X - \pi) = U(X) + \pi \cdot U'(X) - \frac{\pi^2}{2!} U''(X) - \cdots$$

Pratt assumes second order and higher terms are insignificant.

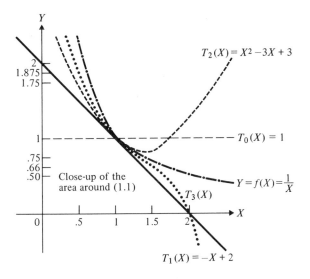

$T_2(X)$			$T_3(X)$			$f(X)$	
X^2-3X+3			$-X^3+4X^2-6X+4$			$Y=\dfrac{1}{X}$	
X	Y		X	Y		X	Y
0	3		0	4		0	∞
1	1		2	0		1	1
1.5	.75	$-$min	1	1		1.5	.666
.5	1.75		.5	1.875		2	.500
						.5	2

Figure 2.17

Expand the left-hand side of (1') using Taylor series:

$$E\{U(X)+\tilde{Z}\} = E\{U(X)+\tilde{Z}U'(X)+\frac{\tilde{Z}^2}{2!}\,U''(X)+\cdots$$

$$\approx 0$$

$$= E\{U(X)\} + E\{\tilde{Z}\}U'(X) + \frac{E(\tilde{Z}^2)}{2!}\,U''(X).$$

But:

$$E\{U(X)\} = U(X) \qquad \text{not a random variable,}$$

$$E\{\tilde{Z}\} = 0,$$

$$E\{\tilde{Z}^2\} = \sigma^2 \qquad \text{since} \quad \sigma_Z^2 = \sum p_i[Z_i - E(Z_i)]^2 = \sum p_i Z_i^2 = E(Z_i^2).$$

$$0$$

So

$$E\{U(X) + \tilde{Z}\} = U(X) + 0 + \frac{\sigma_{\tilde{Z}}^2}{2} U''(X).$$

Putting the left-hand and right-hand sides together:

$$U(X) + \frac{\sigma_{\tilde{Z}}^2}{2} U''(X) = U(X) - \pi U'(X).$$

Solving for π, the risk premium:

$$\pi = \tfrac{1}{2}\sigma_{\tilde{Z}}^2 \left[-\frac{U''(X)}{U'(X)} \right] \qquad \text{a function of } \tilde{Z} \text{ and } X$$

always positive   a measure of absolute
by definition of   risk aversion
variance

E. INTEGRAL CALCULUS

1. Indefinite Integrals
Integration is the reverse process to differentiation. Given a function $f(X)$, the indefinite integral of $f(X)$, denoted by $\int f(X)\, dX$, is a function whose derivative is $f(X)$. In other words,

$$\int f(X)\, dX = F(X) \quad \text{if and only if} \quad F'(X) = f(X).$$

A peculiar feature regarding indefinite integral of $f(X)$ is that it is not unique. Observe the following fact: if $F'(X) = f(X)$, so is $[F(X) + C]' = F'(X) + 0 = f(X)$ where C is an arbitrary constant. Therefore, both $F(X)$ and $F(X) + C$ can be an indefinite integral of $f(X)$. So, in general, we write

$$\int f(X)\, dX = F(X) + C$$

to indicate that an arbitrary constant may be added to the answer.

As in differentiation, we have rules of integration which correspond very closely with those of differentiation.

2. Rules of Integration

1. $\displaystyle \int X^n\, dX = \frac{1}{n+1} X^{n+1} + C. \qquad (n \neq -1)$

2. $\displaystyle \int \frac{1}{X}\, dX = \ln X + C. \qquad (X > 0)$

3. $\displaystyle \int e^X\, dX = e^X + C.$

4. $\int c \cdot g(X) \, dX = c \cdot \int g(X) \, dX.$ $(c = \text{constant})$

5. $\int [g(X) + h(X)] \, dX = \int g(X) \, dX + \int h(X) \, dX.$

6. $\int a^X \, dX = \dfrac{1}{\ln a} a^X + C.$

7. Method of substitution (counterpart of chain rule in differentiation)

$$\int g(u) \frac{du}{dX} \, dX = \int g(u) \, du.$$

Example: $\int e^{2X} \, dX$. To compute this integral, we first substitute $u = 2X$, then $du = 2 \cdot dX$ (recall $du = (du/dX) \cdot dX$, the differential), therefore $dX = (du/2)$. Hence $\int e^{2X} \, dX = \int e^u (du/2)$, by substituting u for $2X$ and $(du/2)$ for dX. But $\int e^u (du/2) = \frac{1}{2} \int e^u \, du$ (by rule 4) $= \frac{1}{2} e^u + C$ (by rule 3) $= \frac{1}{2} e^{2X} + C$ (by substituting back $2X$ for u). This example shows the essence of the method of substitution. When it is not obvious how to integrate directly, we substitute u for part of the expression, write everything in terms of u and du, and hopefully we come up with an expression in u that is easier to integrate (see also examples below).

Examples:

1) $\displaystyle \int 2X^2 + 3X + 1 \, dX = 2 \int X^2 \, dX + 3 \int X \, dX + \int 1 \, dX$

$$= 2 \cdot \frac{X^3}{3} + 3 \frac{X^2}{2} + X + C$$

$$= \tfrac{2}{3} X^3 + \tfrac{3}{2} X^2 + X + C.$$

2) $\displaystyle \int \frac{2X + 1}{X^2 + X} \, dX.$ Here we have to use the method of substitution again.

Let $u = X^2 + X$, then $du = (2X + 1) \, dX$,

$$\int \frac{2X + 1}{X^2 + X} \, dX = \int \frac{1}{u} \, du = \ln u + C = \ln (X^2 + X) + C.$$

3) $\displaystyle \int X\sqrt{X^2 + 1} \, dX.$ Let $u = X^2 + 1$, then $du = 2X \, dX$ or $dX = (du/2X)$.

$$\int X\sqrt{X^2 + 1} \, dX = \int X\sqrt{u} \, \frac{du}{2X} = \int \tfrac{1}{2}\sqrt{u} \, du$$

$$= \tfrac{1}{2} \int u^{1/2} \, du = \tfrac{1}{2} \cdot \frac{1}{3/2} u^{3/2} + C$$

$$= \tfrac{1}{3}(X^2 + 1)^{3/2} + C.$$

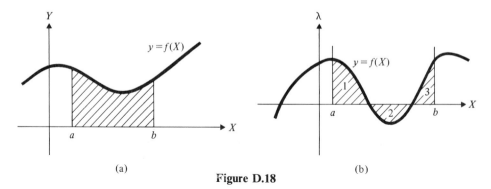

Figure D.18

3. Definite Integrals

A typical definite integral looks like $\int_a^b f(X)\, dX$ (read "integral of $f(X)$ from a to b"). Here, $f(X)$ is called the integrand, a is called the lower limit, and b is called the upper limit of integration. The main difference between an indefinite and a definite integral is that the result of indefinite integration is a function, while the result of definite integration is a number. The meaning of that number is as follows:

Let $\int_a^b f(X)\, dX = A$. If $f(X) \geq 0$, then A is simply the area under the curve $Y = f(X)$ from a to b, shown in Fig. D.18a. That area is equal to $\int_a^b f(X)\, dX$. Suppose now $f(X)$ is both positive and negative in the range of $a \leq X \leq b$, then A, the result of $\int_a^b f(X)\, dX$, is the *signed* area "under" $f(X)$ from a to b. By "signed area," we mean that the area above the X-axis is assigned a positive sign and the area below the X-axis is assigned a negative sign. Then A is the sum of all the positive and negative area (see Fig. D.18b). If the curve of $f(X)$ is the one in Fig. D.18b, then $\int_a^b f(X)\, dX = A =$ area 1 − area 2 + area 3.

The link between the definite integral and the indefinite integral is given by the next theorem, which is called the Fundamental Theorem of Calculus.

Theorem: Let $F(X)$ be an indefinite integral of $f(X)$, then

$$\int_a^b f(X)\, dX = F(b) - F(a).$$

The theorem shows us a way to evaluate the definite integral. We need only to find the indefinite integral of the integrand and then substitute the upper and lower limits and find the difference. Although the indefinite integral of a function is not unique, the theorem says that any one will do, as long as it is the same one in which you substitute the upper and lower limits.

Examples:

1) $\displaystyle \int_1^2 (X + 2)\, dX = \left(\frac{X^2}{2} + 2X\right)\Bigg|_1^2 = \left[\frac{2^2}{2} + 2(2)\right] - \left[\frac{1^2}{2} + 2\cdot 1\right]$

$$= (2 + 4) - (\tfrac{1}{2} + 2) = 3\tfrac{1}{2},$$

2) $\displaystyle \int_0^1 e^X\, dX = e^X\Bigg|_0^1 = [e^1] - [e^0] = e - 1.$

Properties of Definite Integrals

1. $\int_a^a f(X)\, dX = 0.$

2. $\int_a^b f(X)\, dX = -\int_b^a f(X)\, dX.$

3. If $a < c < b$, then $\int_a^b f(X)\, dX = \int_a^c f(X)\, dX + \int_c^b f(X)\, dX.$

4. $\int_a^b cf(X)\, dX = c \int_a^b f(X)\, dX.$

5. $\int_a^b [f(X) + g(X)]\, dX = \int_a^b f(X)\, dX + \int_a^b g(X)\, dX.$

4. Applications

Example 1: Let the fixed cost of production be 100 and marginal cost be $10/\sqrt{x}$ per unit. What is the total cost function for producing q units?

$$\text{Total cost} = \text{fixed cost} + \text{total variable cost}$$

$$= 100 + \int_0^q 10/\sqrt{x}\, dX$$

$$= 100 + \int_0^q 10 X^{-1/2}\, dX$$

$$= 100 + 10\, \frac{1}{1/2} \cdot X^{1/2} \Big|_0^q$$

$$= 100 + [20\sqrt{q}] - [20\sqrt{0}]$$

$$= 100 + 20\sqrt{q}.$$

Example 2: Suppose an income stream of 10,000/yr. is coming in continuously for the next 10 years. How much is it worth today if the discount rate is 5%?

$$\text{Present value} = \int_0^{10} 10{,}000 e^{-.05t}\, dt$$

$$= 10{,}000 \times \frac{-1}{.05} e^{-.05t} \Big|_0^{10}$$

$$= 10{,}000 \times \left(-\frac{1}{.05}\right) [e^{-.05 \times 10} - e^{-.05 \times 0}]$$

$$= -200{,}000[0.6065 - 1]$$

$$= 78{,}693.87.$$

Note that the formula for the present value of continuous discounting of a continuous flow is $\int_0^T (CF)e^{-rt}\, dt$, where CF = cash flow per time unit, T = time where cash flow ends, and r = discount rate.

5. Improper Integrals

Sometimes the limits of integration may be $-\infty$ or $+\infty$. Such a definite integral is called an improper integral. To evaluate an improper integral, we do not substitute $-\infty$ or $+\infty$ into the indefinite integral, but rather we substitute a variable b in place of $+\infty$ (or $-\infty$) and let $b \to \infty$ (or $-\infty$). In other words:

$$\int_a^{\infty} f(X)\, dX = \lim_{b \to \infty} \int_a^b f(X)\, dX,$$

$$\int_{-\infty}^a f(X)\, dX = \lim_{b \to -\infty} \int_b^a f(X)\, dX,$$

$$\int_{-\infty}^{\infty} f(X)\, dX = \lim_{\substack{a \to -\infty \\ b \to +\infty}} \int_b^a f(X)\, dX.$$

Example: Suppose the income stream in the previous example is perpetual, then the present value would be

$$PV = \int_0^{\infty} 10{,}000e^{-.05t}\, dt$$

$$PV = \lim_{b \to \infty} \int_0^b 10{,}000e^{-.05}\, dt$$

$$= \lim_{b \to \infty} 10{,}000 \left(-\frac{1}{.05}\right)[e^{-.05b} - e^{-.05 \times 0}]$$

$$= 10{,}000 \times (-20)[0 - 1], \quad \text{since } e^{-.05b} \to 0 \text{ as } b \to \infty.$$

$$PV = \$200{,}000.$$

Note that for a perpetual stream, we also have

$$PV = \frac{CF}{i} = \frac{10{,}000}{.05} = \$200{,}000 \qquad \text{where CF is the cost flow.}$$

This gives the same result as the integral calculus method.

REFERENCE

Pratt, J. W., "Risk Aversion in the Small and in the Large," *Econometrica*, January/April 1964, 122–136.

Author Index

Subject Index

611